BOOKS
rule 15

DEBORAH L.

CHARLES DI(

Penguin Bo(

21 CHARLES

PRACTICE AN

MW01014878

pamphlets
rule 15

WOMEN'S BUR... .... OF LABOR, LEAFLET NO. 55,
A WORKING WOMAN'S GUIDE TO HER JOB RIGHTS (1978).

works in
collection
rule 15.5

Kay Deaux & Brenda Major, *A Social-Psychological Model of
Gender, in* THEORETICAL PERSPECTIVES ON SEXUAL DIFFERENCE 89,
89 (Deborah L. Rhode ed., 1990).

OLIVER WENDELL HOLMES, *Law in Science and Science in Law,
in* COLLECTED LEGAL PAPERS 210, 210 (1920).

John Adams, Argument and Report, *in* 2 LEGAL PAPERS OF JOHN
ADAMS 285, 322–35 (L. Kinvin Wroth & Hiller B. Zobel eds., 1965).

PERIODICAL MATERIALS rule 16

consecutively
paginated
journals
rule 16.4

David Rudovsky, *Police Abuse: Can the Violence Be Contained?,*
27 HARV. C.R.-C.L. L. REV. 465, 500 (1992).

Thomas R. McCoy & Barry Friedman, *Conditional Spending:
Federalism's Trojan Horse,* 1988 SUP. CT. REV. 85, 100.

nonconsecutively
paginated journals
rule 16.5

Barbara Ward, *Progress for a Small Planet,* HARV. BUS. REV.,
Sept.–Oct. 1979, at 89, 90.

student-
written work
rule 16.7.1

Ellen London, Comment, *A Critique of the Strict Liability Standard
for Determining Child Support in Cases of Male Victims of Sexual
Assault and Statutory Rape,* 152 U. PA. L. REV. 1957, 1959–63 (2004).

Note, *The Death of a Lawyer,* 56 COLUM. L. REV. 606 (1956).

book review
rule 16.7.2

Bruce Ackerman, *Robert Bork's Grand Inquisition,* 99 YALE L.J.
1419, 1422–25 (1990) (book review).

newspaper
rule 16.6

Andrew Rosenthal, *White House Tutors Kremlin in How a
Presidency Works,* N.Y. TIMES, June 15, 1990, at A1.

Cop Shoots Tire, Halts Stolen Car, S.F. CHRON., Oct. 10, 1975, at 43.

INTERVIEWS
rule 17.2.5

Telephone Interview with Michael Leiter, President, Harvard Law
Review (Oct. 22, 1999).

FORTHCOMING
PUBLICATIONS
rule 17.3

Sarah Greenberger, Comment, *Enforceable Rights, No Child Left
Behind, and Political Patriotism: A Case for Open-Minded Section
1983 Jurisprudence,* 153 U. PA. L. REV. (forthcoming Jan. 2005).

THE
INTERNET
rule 18.2

Eric Posner, *More on Section 7 of the Torture Convention,* THE
VOLOKH CONSPIRACY (Jan. 29, 2009, 10:04 AM), http://www.
volokh.com/posts/123324158.shtml.

TREATIES
rule 21.4

Treaty of Friendship, Commerce and Navigation, U.S.-Japan, art. X,
Apr. 2, 1953, 4 U.S.T. 2063.

UNITED
NATIONS
OFFICIAL RECORDS
rule 21.7.1

U.N. GAOR, 56th Sess., 1st plen. mtg. at 3, U.N. Doc A/56/PV,1
(Sept. 12, 2001).

28 U.S.C.A § 2241 (C)(1) (West 2011),
Title   US code Ann   Section Pin

<u>Walker v. Smith</u>, 120 P.3d 56, 58 (Ariz. Ct. App. 200
   Case   Volume Pacific start
                      reporter Pin AZ ct of appeal)

☆ Intervening - <u>Walker</u>, 120 P.3d at 60.

☆ No Intervening- <u>Id.</u>
   Same page

☆ No Intervening - <u>Id.</u> at 65.
   Diff page

Ariz. Rev. Stat. Ann. § 12-2604 (2012)
  AZ Rev annotated   title section year

☆ one intervening - § 12-2604.

Published and Distributed by
The Harvard Law Review Association
Gannett House
1511 Massachusetts Avenue
Cambridge, Massachusetts 02138
U.S.A.

Page 87 Cases

First Printing 2010
Second Printing 2010
Third Printing 2010
Fourth Printing 2011
Fifth Printing 2011
Sixth Printing 2012
Seventh Printing 2013
Printings are updated as appropriate.

<u>Id.</u> (exact Same Source)
          underline Period
<u>Id.</u> at 617. (Different Page)

Coordinating Editor:
Mary Miles Prince, Associate Director
Vanderbilt University Law School Library
With special editorial assistance on the citations of foreign
jurisdictions from the Directorate of Legal Research of the
Law Library of Congress.
Designed by Dynamic Diagrams
ISBN 9780615361161

IF Intervening <u>can't</u> use ID

<u>Love</u>, 897 P.2d at 628.

IF case name used in preceding
sentence. 897 P.2d at 628.

THE
BLUEBOOK®

A Uniform System of Citation®
Nineteenth Edition

www.legalbluebook.com

Compiled by the editors of
the Columbia Law Review,
the Harvard Law Review,
the University of Pennsylvania Law Review,
and The Yale Law Journal.

BLUEBOOK
Online free trial

Go to www.legalbluebook.com and enter the
access key below in the KEY REDEMPTION section
of the page for a free trial to the Bluebook Online.

BLUEBOOK ONLINE ACCESS KEY:

e070c184-841d-4d26-a2d0-f7d379112208

rule**book**™

✦

THE BLUEBOOK®

The Bluebook® is now available on iPad®,
iPhone® and iPod touch® via the
rule**book**™ app.

Reference The Bluebook® and your court
rules in a clear, easy-to-use digital format.

(Custom versions of the rulebook™ app are available on an
enterprise basis for law firms and other organizations.)

Preface to the Nineteenth Edition

The current edition of *The Bluebook* retains the same basic approach to legal citation established by its predecessors. The layout of *The Bluebook* has been updated to make the information easier to access. Some citation forms have been expanded, elaborated upon, or modified from previous editions to reflect the ever-expanding range of authorities used in legal writing and to respond to suggestions from the legal community. Here are some of the more noteworthy changes:

The Bluepages, introduced in the Eighteenth Edition, have been considerably overhauled for the Nineteenth Edition. In addition to general expansion and clarification, the Bluepages now include detailed information for citation to Electronic Case Files (ECF) documents. Bluepages table BT2 has also been updated and expanded to include more local citation rules. Please note that these rules, which many state and federal courts promulgate, take precedence over *Bluebook* rules in documents submitted to those courts. When preparing court documents, always check the most recent version of the court's local citation rules.

In addition to edits for clarity, concision, and consistency, the Nineteenth Edition contains the following significant changes: Rule 1.5(b) now provides comprehensive guidance on the order of multiple parentheticals in a single citation. Rule 10.4(b) now allows omission of the jurisdiction *and* court abbreviation of state courts if unambiguously conveyed by the reporter title. Rule 10.6.1(c) now provides guidance on citation to seriatim opinions of the early Supreme Court. Rule 10.8.3 now provides details for citations to audio recordings of court proceedings. Rule 13.4(d) now establishes specific citation formats for Congressional Research Services and Government Accountability Office reports. Rule 14 has been considerably revised to improve citation to administrative agency materials. The rule itself, however, is now shorter as many details on citation to specific agencies have been moved to table T1.2. Rule 16.6 now includes provisions for citation to wire services.

Rule 18 has changed considerably, primarily to allow increased citation to Internet sources. Specific changes include: Rule 18.2.1(a) now provides guidance allowing citation to authenticated and official Internet sources as well as exact digital scans of print sources as if they were the original print source. These changes in rule 18 allowing citation to official, authenticated, or exact Internet copies of cited materials are also reflected in rules 10, 12, 15, 16, and 17. Guidance for citation to webpage titles of main pages and subheadings has been expanded in rule 18.2.2(b). Rule 18.2.2(a) now states that when no author of an Internet source is clearly announced, the author information should be omitted from the citation, unless there is a clear institutional owner of the domain. Additionally, institutional authors of Internet sources should be abbreviated according to rule 15.1(d). Rule 18.2.2(c) now states that citations to Internet sources should be dated as they appear on the Internet site, using only dates that refer clearly to the material cited. When material is undated, the date of the author's last visit to the website should be placed in a parenthetical after the URL. Rule 18.2.2(c) now also states that for blogs and other frequently updated websites, citations should include timestamps whenever possible. Rule 18.2.2(h) still encourages the archiving of Internet sources, but does not require the citation to indicate the location of an archival copy. Rules 18.6 and 18.7 now allow for the use of timestamps in citations to audio and video recordings. Rule 18.7.3 now provides citation guidance for podcasts and online recordings. Professor James Grimmelmann provided vital advice and assistance in revising rule 18.

Rule 20 has been expanded to provide clearer guidance and more comprehensive examples. William B. McCloy aided in the revision to Rule 20. Rule 21 has been updated and now includes improved citations to United Nations materials. Rule 21 also specifies the citation format for the International Criminal Court. The American Society of International Law assisted in the revision to rule 21, as well as tables T3 through T5. Maria Smolka-Day also provided assistance with the revisions to rule 21, and Patricio Nazareno aided in revising citations to the Inter-American Court of Human Rights.

All of the tables have been revised and updated. Table T1 has been subdivided into four sections: T1.1 (Federal Judicial and Legislative Materials), T1.2 (Federal Administrative and Executive Materials), T1.3 (States and the District of Columbia), and T1.4 (Other United States Jurisdictions). Table T1.2 represents a significant expansion in the coverage of administrative agency materials. Many federal agencies and the Board and Staff of the *Administrative Law Review* provided vital assistance in revising and expanding table T1.2. The following were instrumental in constructing citation formats related to government contracts in table T1.2: Philip Green, Jason Daniel Morgan, and Richard Lieberman, all of the George Washington University Law School. Table T2 has incorporated significant organizational and substantive improvements for each existing country, and seven new countries have been added: Belgium, Chile, Colombia, Egypt, Iraq, Pakistan, and South Korea. The compilers are indebted to the following experts in foreign legal citation for their help in enhancing table T2: Francisco A. Avalos, Annette L. Demers, Christoph Malliet, William B. McCloy, Michael Newton, Yukino Nakashima, and E. Dana Neacsu.

The compilers wish to thank our Coordinating Editor Mary Miles Prince for working with us in revising, clarifying, updating, and improving *The Bluebook*. The compilers would also like to acknowledge outside commentators who contributed their expertise to the Nineteenth Edition of *The Bluebook*. The following provided invaluable assistance in planning and revising this edition: Hongxia Liu, Kersi Shroff, and Andrew Weber. The compilers are grateful to the law journal editors, law librarians, and practitioners who responded to our call for suggestions with helpful advice and comments.

Finally, the compilers request that any errors or omissions be reported and that suggestions for revisions be sent to the Harvard Law Review, Gannett House, 1511 Massachusetts Ave., Cambridge, Massachusetts 02138.

Acknowledgements

The Bluebook: A Uniform System of Citation is compiled by the editors of the *Columbia Law Review*, the *Harvard Law Review*, the *University of Pennsylvania Law Review*, and *The Yale Law Journal*. *The Bluebook* is published and distributed by the Harvard Law Review Association. The Coordinating Editor of *The Bluebook* is Mary Miles Prince, Associate Director, Vanderbilt University Law School Library, with special editorial assistance on the citations of foreign jurisdictions from the Directorate of Legal Research of the Law Library of Congress.

Contents

Preface VII
Introduction 1
    Structure of *The Bluebook* 1
    General Principles of Citation 1
    Getting Started 2

The Bluepages: An Introduction to Basic Legal Citation

    Introduction 3
B1 Typeface Conventions. 3
B2 Citation Sentences and Clauses 4
B3 Introductory Signals 5
B4 Sources and Authorities: Cases 7
B5 Sources and Authorities: Statutes, Rules, and Regulations 15
B6 Sources and Authorities: Constitutions 19
B7 Sources and Authorities: Court and Litigation Documents 19
B8 Sources and Authorities: Books and Other Nonperiodic Materials . . . 23
B9 Sources and Authorities: Journal, Magazine, and Newspaper Articles . 24
B10 Sources and Authorities: The Internet 25
B11 Explanatory Parentheticals 26
B12 Quotations 27

The Bluepages Tables

BT1 Court Documents 28
BT2 Jurisdiction-Specific Citation Rules and Style Guides 30
    BT2.1 Federal Courts 30
    BT2.2 State Courts 40
    BT2.3 Territories 51

Rules

Rule 1 Structure and Use of Citations 53
    1.1 Citation Sentences and Clauses in Law Reviews 53
    1.2 Introductory Signals 54
    1.3 Order of Signals 56
    1.4 Order of Authorities Within Each Signal 56
    1.5 Parenthetical Information 59
    1.6 Related Authority 61

Rule 2 Typefaces for Law Reviews 62
    2.1 Typeface Conventions for Citations 62
    2.2 Typeface Conventions for Textual Material 64

Rule 3 Subdivisions 66
    3.1 Volumes, Parts, and Supplements 66
    3.2 Pages, Footnotes, Endnotes, and Graphical Materials 67
    3.3 Sections and Paragraphs 69
    3.4 Appended Material 70
    3.5 Internal Cross-References 71

Rule 4 Short Citation Forms **72**
   4.1 "*Id.*" 72
   4.2 "*Supra*" and "Hereinafter" 74

Rule 5 Quotations **76**
   5.1 Formatting of Quotations 76
   5.2 Alterations and Quotations Within Quotations 77
   5.3 Omissions 78

Rule 6 Abbreviations, Numerals, and Symbols **80**
   6.1 Abbreviations 80
   6.2 Numerals and Symbols 81

Rule 7 Italicization for Style and in Unique Circumstances **83**

Rule 8 Capitalization **84**

Rule 9 Titles of Judges, Officials, and Terms of Court **87**

Rule 10 Cases **87**
   10.1 Basic Citation Forms 88
   10.2 Case Names 89
      10.2.1 General Rules for Case Names 89
      10.2.2 Additional Rules for Case Names in Citations 94
   10.3 Reporters and Other Sources 95
      10.3.1 Parallel Citations and Which Source(s) to Cite 95
      10.3.2 Reporters 96
      10.3.3 Public Domain Format 96
   10.4 Court and Jurisdiction 97
   10.5 Date or Year 99
   10.6 Parenthetical Information Regarding Cases 100
      10.6.1 Weight of Authority 100
      10.6.2 Quoting/Citing Parentheticals in Case Citations 100
      10.6.3 Order of Parentheticals 101
   10.7 Prior and Subsequent History 101
      10.7.1 Explanatory Phrases and Weight of Authority 102
      10.7.2 Different Case Name on Appeal 103
   10.8 Special Citation Forms 104
      10.8.1 Pending and Unreported Cases 104
      10.8.2 Fifth Circuit Split 105
      10.8.3 Briefs, Court Filings, and Transcripts 106
      10.8.4 Court Administrative Orders 107
   10.9 Short Forms for Cases 107

Rule 11 Constitutions **110**

Rule 12 Statutes **111**
   12.1 Basic Citation Forms 111
   12.2 Choosing the Proper Citation Form 112
      12.2.1 General Rule 112
      12.2.2 Exceptions 113
   12.3 Current Official and Unofficial Codes 114
      12.3.1 Additional Information 114
      12.3.2 Year of Code 115
   12.4 Session Laws 116
   12.5 Electronic Media and Online Sources 117

12.6 Other Secondary Sources 118
12.7 Invalidation, Repeal, Amendment, and Prior History 119
    12.7.1 Invalidation 119
    12.7.2 Repeal 119
    12.7.3 Amendment 119
    12.7.4 Prior History 119
12.8 Explanatory Parenthetical Phrases 120
12.9 Special Citation Forms 120
    12.9.1 Internal Revenue Code 120
    12.9.2 Ordinances 120
    12.9.3 Rules of Evidence and Procedure 121
    12.9.4 Uniform Acts 121
    12.9.5 Model Codes, Restatements, Standards, and
          Sentencing Guidelines 122
    12.9.6 ABA Code of Professional Responsibility and Opinions
          on Ethics 123
12.10 Short Forms for Statutes 124

Rule 13 Legislative Materials **126**
13.1 Basic Citation Forms 126
13.2 Bills and Resolutions 127
13.3 Hearings 128
13.4 Reports, Documents, and Committee Prints 129
13.5 Debates 130
13.6 Separately Bound Legislative Histories 131
13.7 Electronic Media and Online Sources .131
13.8 Short Forms for Legislative Materials .132

Rule 14 Administrative and Executive Materials **133**
14.1 Basic Citation Forms 133
14.2 Rules, Regulations, and Other Publications 133
14.3 Administrative Adjudications and Arbitrations 135
    14.3.1 Names 135
    14.3.2 Which Source(s) to Cite 136
    14.3.3 Issuing Agency 136
14.4 Short Forms for Regulations 136

Rule 15 Books, Reports, and Other Nonperiodic Materials **138**
15.1 Author 138
15.2 Editor or Translator 139
15.3 Title 140
15.4 Edition, Publisher, and Date 140
15.5 Shorter Works in Collection 142
    15.5.1 Works in Collection Generally 142
    15.5.2 Collected Documents 143
15.6 Prefaces, Forewords, Introductions, and Epilogues 143
15.7 Serial Number 143
15.8 Special Citation Forms 144
15.9 Electronic Media and Online Sources .145
15.10 Short Citation Forms 145
    15.10.1 Short Forms for Works in Collection 146

Rule 16 Periodical Materials **147**
16.1 Basic Citation Forms 147
16.2 Author 149
16.3 Title 149
16.4 Consecutively Paginated Journals .150
16.5 Nonconsecutively Paginated Journals and Magazines 150
16.6 Newspapers 151
16.7 Special Citation Forms 153
        16.7.1 Student-Written Law Review Materials 153
        16.7.2 Non-Student-Written Book Reviews 154
        16.7.3 Symposia, Colloquia, and Surveys 155
        16.7.4 Commentaries and Other Special Designations 155
        16.7.5 Multipart Articles 155
        16.7.6 Annotations 156
        16.7.7 Proceedings, Regular Publications by Institutes, and
                ABA Section Reports 156
        16.7.8 Newsletters and Other Noncommercially
                Distributed Periodicals 157
16.8 Electronic Media and Online Sources 157
16.9 Short Citation Forms 157

Rule 17 Unpublished and Forthcoming Sources **159**
17.1 Basic Citation Forms 159
17.2 Unpublished Materials 159
        17.2.1 Manuscripts 159
        17.2.2 Dissertations and Theses 160
        17.2.3 Letters, Memoranda, and Press Releases 160
        17.2.4 E-Mail Correspondence and Listserv Postings 160
        17.2.5 Interviews 161
        17.2.6 Speeches and Addresses 161
17.3 Forthcoming Publications 162
17.4 Working Papers 162
17.5 Electronic Media and Online Sources 162
17.6 Short Citation Forms 163

**Rule 18 The Internet, Electronic Media, and Other Nonprint
        Resources** **164**
18.1 Basic Citation Forms 164
18.2 The Internet 165
        18.2.1 General Internet Citation Principles 165
        18.2.2 Direct Citations to Internet Sources 166
        18.2.3 Parallel Citations to Internet Sources 169
18.3 Commercial Electronic Databases 171
        18.3.1 Cases 171
        18.3.2 Constitutions and Statutes .171
        18.3.3 Legislative, Administrative, and Executive Materials 172
        18.3.4 Books, Periodicals, and Other Secondary Materials 172
18.4 CD-ROM and Other Electronic Storage Media 173
18.5 Microform 173
        18.5.1 Microform Collections Reproducing Preexisting
                Materials 173
        18.5.2 Microform Collections Containing Original Materials 174

18.6 Films, Broadcasts, and Noncommercial Video Materials 174
18.7 Audio Recordings 174
    18.7.1 Commercial Recordings 174
    18.7.2 Noncommercial Recordings 175
    18.7.3 Podcasts and Recordings Available Online 175
18.8 Short Citation Forms 175

Rule 19 Services **177**
19.1 Citation Form for Services 177
19.2 Short Citation Forms 178

Rule 20 Foreign Materials **179**
20.1 Jurisdiction 179
20.2 Non-English-Language Documents 179
    20.2.1 Documents Appearing in More than One Language 179
    20.2.2 Titles and Names of Documents in Languages Other
           than English 179
    20.2.3 Abbreviations in Languages Other than English 180
    20.2.4 Languages That Do Not Use the Roman Alphabet 180
    20.2.5 Citations to Translations of Non-English-Language
           Documents 181
20.3 Cases 182
    20.3.1 Common Law Cases 182
    20.3.2 Civil Law and Other Non-Common-Law Cases 182
20.4 Constitutions 182
20.5 Statutes 183
    20.5.1 Statutes in Common Law Systems 183
    20.5.2 Statutes in Civil Law and Other Non-Common-Law
           Jurisdictions 183
20.6 Non-English-Language and Foreign Periodicals 183
20.7 Short Citation Forms 184

Rule 21 International Materials **185**
21.1 Basic Citation Forms 185
21.2 Non-English-Language Documents 187
21.3 Jurisdiction Not Evident from Context 187
21.4 Treaties and Other International Agreements 187
    21.4.1 Name of the Agreement 188
    21.4.2 Parties to the Agreement 188
    21.4.3 Subdivisions 189
    21.4.4 Date of Signing 189
    21.4.5 Treaty Sources 189
21.5 International Law Cases 191
    21.5.1 The International Court of Justice and the Permanent
           Court of International Justice (The World Court) 191
    21.5.2 European Union Courts 193
    21.5.3 European Court of Human Rights 194
    21.5.4 Inter-American Commission on Human Rights 195
    21.5.5 Inter-American Court of Human Rights 195
    21.5.6 International Tribunal for the Law of the Sea 196
    21.5.7 International Criminal Tribunals 197
    21.5.8 Other Multinational Courts 197

21.5.9 International Cases in National Courts 197
21.6 International Arbitrations and Claims Commissions 198
21.7 United Nations Sources 198
    21.7.1 Verbatim and Summary Records 199
    21.7.2 Resolutions and Decisions .199
    21.7.3 U.N. Reports 201
    21.7.4 Masthead Documents 202
    21.7.5 U.N. Press Releases and Memoranda 203
    21.7.6 Adjudicatory Bodies Established by the
            United Nations 203
    21.7.7 Sales Publications 203
    21.7.8 Yearbooks and Periodicals .204
    21.7.9 Regional Organization Documents 205
    21.7.10 U.N. Charter 205
    21.7.11 U.N. Internet Materials 205
21.8 League of Nations 205
21.9 European Union and European Community 205
21.10 Council of Europe 209
21.11 World Trade Organization 209
21.12 Other Intergovernmental Organizations 211
21.13 International Committee of the Red Cross and International
      Non-Governmental Organizations .212
21.14 Yearbooks 212
21.15 Digests 213
21.16 Short Citation Forms 213

Tables

Table T1 United States Jurisdictions 215
  T1.1 Federal Judicial and Legislative Materials 215
  T1.2 Federal Administrative and Executive Materials 218
  T1.3 States and the District of Columbia 228
      Alabama (AL) 228
      Alaska (AK) 229
      Arizona (AZ) 230
      Arkansas (AR) 230
      California (CA) 231
      Colorado (CO) 233
      Connecticut (CT) 234
      Delaware (DE) 235
      District of Columbia (DC) 236
      Florida (FL) 237
      Georgia (GA) 237
      Hawaii (HI) 238
      Idaho (ID) 239
      Illinois (IL) 239
      Indiana (IN) 240
      Iowa (IA) 241
      Kansas (KS) 241
      Kentucky (KY) 242

Louisiana (LA) 243
Maine (ME) 244
Maryland (MD) 245
Massachusetts (MA) 246
Michigan (MI) 247
Minnesota (MN) 248
Mississippi (MS) 248
Missouri (MO) 249
Montana (MT) 250
Nebraska (NE) 250
Nevada (NV) 251
New Hampshire (NH) 251
New Jersey (NJ) 252
New Mexico (NM) 253
New York (NY) 253
North Carolina (NC) 258
North Dakota (ND) 259
Ohio (OH) 259
Oklahoma (OK) 261
Oregon (OR) 262
Pennsylvania (PA) 262
Rhode Island (RI) 264
South Carolina (SC) 264
South Dakota (SD) 265
Tennessee (TN) 266
Texas (TX) 267
Utah (UT) 269
Vermont (VT) 270
Virginia (VA) 271
Washington (WA) 272
West Virginia (WV) 272
Wisconsin (WI) 273
Wyoming (WY) 273
T1.4 Other United States Jurisdictions .274
American Samoa 274
Canal Zone (CZ) 274
Guam (GU) 275
Navajo Nation 275
Northern Mariana Islands 275
Oklahoma Native Americans 276
Puerto Rico (PR) 276
Virgin Islands (VI) 277
Table T2 Foreign Jurisdictions 277
T2.1 Argentine Republic 277
T2.2 Australia 280
T2.2.1 Australian States and Territories 285
T2.3 Austria, Republic of 286
T2.3.1 Austrian Länder 290
T2.4 Belgium, Kingdom of 291

T2.5 Brazil, Federative Republic of 295
T2.6 Canada 298
T2.7 Catholic Church 305
T2.8 Chile, Republic of 306
T2.9 China, People's Republic of 308
T2.10 Colombia, Republic of 312
T2.11 Czech Republic 315
T2.12 Egypt, Arab Republic of 317
T2.13 France, Republic of 319
T2.14 Germany, Federal Republic of 323
        T2.14.1 German Länder 328
T2.15 Greece 329
T2.16 Hong Kong 331
T2.17 Hungary, Republic of 333
T2.18 India 335
T2.19 Iran, Islamic Republic of 338
T2.20 Iraq, Republic of 341
T2.21 Ireland (Éire), Republic of 342
T2.22 Israel 345
T2.23 Italy, Republic of 348
T2.24 Japan 350
T2.25 Kenya 357
T2.26 Lebanon, Republic of 358
T2.27 Mexico 360
T2.28 Netherlands, Kingdom of the 366
T2.29 New Zealand 369
T2.30 Nicaragua 373
T2.31 Nigeria 375
T2.32 Pakistan, Islamic Republic of 377
T2.33 Philippines 379
T2.34 Roman Law 381
T2.35 Russian Federation 382
T2.36 South Africa 387
T2.37 South Korea 391
T2.38 Spain 394
T2.39 Sweden 396
T2.40 Switzerland 399
        T2.40.1 Swiss Cantons 403
T2.41 Taiwan, Republic of China 404
T2.42 United Kingdom 406
        T2.42.1 England and Wales 413
        T2.42.2 Northern Ireland (and Ireland Until 1924) 418
        T2.42.3 Scotland 421
T2.43 Zambia, Republic of 424

Table T3 Intergovernmental Organizations 426
T3.1 United Nations 426
T3.2 League of Nations 426
T3.3 European Communities 426

T3.4	European Court and Commission of Human Rights	427
T3.5	Inter-American Commission on Human Rights	427
T3.6	Inter-American Court of Human Rights	427
T3.7	International Tribunal for the Law of the Sea	428
Table T4	**Treaty Sources**	**428**
T4.1	Official U.S. sources	428
T4.2	Intergovernmental treaty sources	429
T4.3	Unofficial treaty sources	429
Table T5	**Arbitral Reporters**	**429**
Table T6	**Case Names and Institutional Authors in Citations**	**430**
Table T7	**Court Names**	**432**
Table T8	**Explanatory Phrases**	**434**
Table T9	**Legislative Documents**	**435**
Table T10	**Geographical Terms**	**436**
T10.1	U.S. states, cities, and territories	436
T10.2	Australian states and Canadian provinces and territories	438
T10.3	Foreign countries and regions	438
Table T11	**Judges and Officials**	**443**
Table T12	**Months**	**444**
Table T13	**Periodicals**	**444**
Table T14	**Publishing Terms**	**468**
Table T15	**Services**	**468**
Table T16	**Subdivisions**	**472**

Index

Index	475

THE
BLUEBOOK®

A Uniform System of Citation®

Nineteenth Edition

Introduction

Welcome to *The Bluebook*, the definitive style guide for legal citation in the United States. For generations, law students, lawyers, scholars, judges, and other legal professionals have relied on *The Bluebook*'s unique system of citation. In a diverse and rapidly changing legal profession, *The Bluebook* continues to provide a systematic method by which members of the profession communicate important information about the sources and authorities upon which they rely in their work.

The Bluebook can often be intimidating for new users. This introduction is meant to assist you as you begin what will likely become a lifelong relationship with the *Bluebook* system of legal citation.

Structure of *The Bluebook*

The Bluebook contains three major parts. The first part is the Bluepages, a how-to guide for basic legal citation. Unlike the remainder of *The Bluebook*, which is designed in a style and at a level of complexity commensurate with the needs of the law journal publication process, the Bluepages provide easy-to-comprehend guidance for the everyday citation needs of first-year law students, summer associates, law clerks, practicing lawyers, and other legal professionals. The examples used throughout the Bluepages are printed using simple typeface conventions common in the legal profession.

The second part is the heart of the *Bluebook* system of citation: the rules of citation and style. This part is subdivided into two main sections. The first section, consisting of rules 1 through 9, establishes general standards of citation and style for use in all forms of legal writing. The second section, consisting of rules 10 through 21, presents rules for citation of specific kinds of authority such as cases, statutes, books, periodicals, and foreign and international materials. The examples used throughout this part are printed using typeface conventions standard in law journal footnotes.

The third part consists of a series of tables to be used in conjunction with the rules. The tables show, among other things, which authority to cite and how to abbreviate properly. Individual tables are referenced throughout the book. Finally, there is a comprehensive index.

General Principles of Citation

The central function of a legal citation is to allow the reader to efficiently locate the cited source. Thus, the citation forms in *The Bluebook* are designed to provide the information necessary to lead the reader directly to the specific items cited. Because of the ever-increasing range of authorities cited in legal writing, no system of citation can be complete. Therefore, when citing material of a type not explicitly discussed in this book, try to locate an analogous type of authority that is discussed and use that citation form as a model. Always be sure to provide sufficient information to allow the reader to find the cited material quickly and easily.

Getting Started

The Bluepages provide the best place to begin study of the *Bluebook* system of legal citation. Indeed, first-year legal writing professors may wish to rely on the Bluepages as a teaching aid. The Bluepages provide only an abbreviated introduction to the *Bluebook* system, however, and will not contain answers to more difficult citation questions. For this reason, the Bluepages contain references to related rules and tables found in other parts of the book.

INTRODUCTION

The Bluepages is a how-to guide created primarily for practitioners and law clerks to use when citing authority within non-academic legal documents. Keep the following in mind:

Local Rules. Many courts have their own rules of citation that differ in some respects from <u>The Bluebook</u>. Make sure you are familiar with and abide by any additional or different citation requirements of the court to which your document is being submitted. An index of jurisdiction-specific citation rules and style manuals is contained in **Bluepages table BT2**.

Typeface. The Bluepages keeps with the tradition of <u>underlining</u> certain text. So long as you are consistent, however, you may substitute *italic type* wherever <u>underlining</u> is used in the Bluepages. You will notice that the remainder of <u>The Bluebook</u> employs a more complex array of typeface conventions, including ordinary roman type, *italics*, and Large and Small Caps. The differences are explained in detail in **Bluepages B1**.

The Whitepages. Where the Bluepages or local court rules are silent regarding the citation of a particular document, the other rules in <u>The Bluebook</u>, commonly referred to as the "Whitepages," can be used to supplement the Bluepages. Keep in mind the typeface differences between academic documents and legal documents as explained in **Bluepages B1**.

The Elements of a Citation. Generally, a legal citation is composed of three principal elements: (1) a signal; (2) the source or authority; and (3) parenthetical information, if any. The Bluepages will explore each of these elements in detail.

Typeface Conventions   B1

For citations that appear in non-academic legal documents, the following, and <u>only</u> the following, are underscored (or italicized):

Case names, including procedural phrases introducing case names;

Titles of books and articles;

Titles of some legislative materials;

Introductory signals;

Explanatory phrases introducing subsequent case history;

Cross references, such as <u>id.</u> and <u>supra</u>; and

Words and phrases introducing related authority, such as "<u>quoted in</u>."

In addition, underscore (or italicize) the following words when they appear in the text, rather than a citation:

Titles of publications, such as the <u>New York Times</u>;

Words italicized in the original of a quotation; and

Any other word that would otherwise be italicized in the text, such as uncommon foreign words.

Differences between academic citations and the citation format described in the Bluepages:

	Academic Citation (the Whitepages)	Non-Academic Citation (the Bluepages)
Typeface: Italics	The following are *italicized*:	The following are either *italicized* or <u>underscored</u>:
	Introductory signals	Introductory signals
	Short form case names	Full and short case names
	Procedural and explanatory phrases in case citations	Procedural and explanatory phrases in case citations
	"*Id.*"	"<u>Id.</u>" or "*Id.*"
	Titles of articles in periodicals	Titles of books, articles, and essays
	Titles of congressional committee hearings	Titles of legislative materials
	Punctuation that falls within italicized material	Punctuation that falls within italicized or underscored material
	Introductory phrases for related authority	Introductory phrases for related authority
	Internal cross-references	Internal cross-references
Typeface: Caps	The following are in Large and Small Caps:	Large and Small Caps are never used
	Authors and titles of books, including institutional authors	
	Titles of periodicals	

B2 Citation Sentences and Clauses

In non-academic legal documents, citations appear within the text of the document as full sentences or as clauses within sentences directly after the propositions they support. As opposed to academic legal documents, which cite to authority using footnotes, footnotes should only be used in non-academic legal documents when permitted by local court rules.

A citation may be inserted into the text in one of two ways: as a stand-alone citation sentence or as a citation clause.

Like any other sentence, a **citation sentence** begins with a capital letter and ends with a period. One citation sentence will often contain numerous citations, each set off by a semicolon. Use citation sentences to cite sources and authorities that relate to the <u>entire</u> preceding sentence.

Citation clauses are set off from the text by commas and immediately follow the proposition to which they relate. Do not begin a citation clause with a capital letter, unless the clause begins directly with a source that would otherwise be capitalized. Do not end a citation clause with a period, unless it is the last clause in the sentence. Use citation clauses to cite sources and authorities that relate to <u>only part</u> of a sentence:

The ITC's findings of fact should not be overturned because they are supported by substantial evidence, defined by <u>Corning Glass Works</u> as "such relevant evidence as a reasonable mind might accept as adequate to support a conclusion," <u>Corning Glass Works v. U.S. Int'l Trade Comm'n</u>, 799 F.2d 1559, 1566 (Fed. Cir. 1986), which will not be reweighed by the Federal Circuit on appeal even if an alternative conclusion can be drawn, <u>Nutrinova Nutrition Specialties & Food Ingredients GmbH v. U.S. Int'l Trade Comm'n</u>, 224 F.3d 1356, 1359 (Fed. Cir. 2000); <u>see also</u> <u>Tandon Corp. v. U.S. Int'l Trade Comm'n</u>, 831 F.2d 1017, 1019 (Fed. Cir. 1987) (differentiating the "substantial" evidence from the "clearly erroneous" standard).

Introductory Signals

A **signal** sends a shorthand message to the reader about the relationship between the **proposition** stated and the source or authority cited in relation to that proposition. Mastering the use of signals is an important step toward learning to cite authorities effectively.

- **Bluepages Tip:** Signals are capitalized when used to begin a citation sentence but in lower case when used to begin a citation clause.

[no signal]

Use a citation without a signal for (1) an authority that directly states the proposition; (2) the source of a quotation; or (3) an authority referred to in the preceding text:

A law declaring that one group of citizens shall not be afforded equal opportunity to seek assistance from the government violates the Equal Protection Clause. <u>Romer v. Evans</u>, 517 U.S. 620, 633 (1996).

The Supreme Court has stated that the principle of equal access to government is "central" to "our constitutional tradition." <u>Romer v. Evans</u>, 517 U.S. 620, 633 (1996).

These divisions within the Court tend to surface most openly in cases, like <u>Romer</u>, in which the Court is asked to address a divisive social issue. <u>Romer v. Evans</u>, 517 U.S. 620 (1996).

<u>E.g.</u>,

Use <u>e.g.</u>, to introduce an authority that is one of multiple authorities (or multiple jurisdictions) directly stating the same proposition. Use <u>e.g.</u>, in combination with <u>see</u> to introduce an authority that is one of multiple authorities (or multiple jurisdictions) clearly supporting the same proposition:

Many states have established a statutory presumption in favor of equal division of marital property. <u>E.g.</u>, N.C. Gen. Stat. § 50-20(c) (2001); Wis. Stat. Ann. § 767.255(3) (West 2001).

> Federal courts have consistently held that statutory claims of employment discrimination can be subject to mandatory arbitration. <u>See, e.g.</u>, <u>Circuit City Stores, Inc. v. Adams</u>, 532 U.S. 105, 123 (2001) (holding that arbitration agreements can be enforced without contravening policies of federal employment discrimination law); <u>Desiderio v. Nat'l Ass'n of Sec. Dealers, Inc.</u>, 191 F.3d 198, 203 (2d Cir. 1999) (upholding arbitrability of Title VII claims).

- **Bluepages Tip:** The underline beneath the combined signal "<u>see, e.g.</u>," is continuous up to but not including the second comma.

B3.3   <u>See</u>

Use <u>see</u> to introduce an authority that clearly supports, but does not directly state, the proposition:

> The Sixth Amendment's guarantee of the right to assistance of counsel ensures that criminal defendants without legal training are not left to fend for themselves in our complex system of criminal justice. <u>See</u> <u>Powell v. Alabama</u>, 287 U.S. 45, 69 (1932) (arguing that, without guidance of counsel, a layperson charged with a crime "faces the danger of conviction because he does not know how to establish his innocence").

> The statutory standard for recusal of federal judges is broad, <u>see</u> 28 U.S.C. § 455(a) (2000) (requiring removal in any proceeding in which judge's impartiality "might reasonably be questioned"), and has been interpreted as going beyond what is required by the Due Process Clause, <u>see</u> <u>United States v. Couch</u>, 896 F.2d 78, 81 (5th Cir. 1990) (listing cases).

B3.4   Other Signals

Other frequently used signals include <u>see also</u>, <u>accord</u>, and <u>cf.</u> Refer to **rule 1.2** for more information on how to use these and other signals.

B3.5   Order of Signals

When more than one signal is used, the signals (together with the authorities they introduce) should appear in the order listed in **rule 1.2**. For more information about the ordering and grouping of signals within citation sentences, consult **rule 1.3**.

- **Bluepages Tip:** Authorities within each signal are separated by semicolons. If one authority is considerably more helpful or authoritative than the other authorities cited within a signal, it should precede the others. Otherwise, authorities are generally cited in this order:

  1. constitutions;
  2. federal statutes;
  3. state statutes;
  4. federal cases (in order of descending authority);

5. state cases (alphabetically by state and then in order of descending authority);

6. legislative materials;

7. executive and administrative materials;

8. court and litigation documents;

9. books and pamphlets;

10. journal articles; and

11. magazine and newspaper articles.

For further guidance on the order of authorities, see **rule 1.4**.

Sources and Authorities: Cases　　　　　　　　　　　**B4**

....

Full Citation　　　　　　　　　　　　　　　　　　　**B4.1**

A full case citation includes five basic components: (1) the name of the case; (2) the published source in which the case may be found; (3) a parenthetical indicating the court and year of decision; (4) other parenthetical information, if any; and (5) the subsequent history of the case, if any:

> Holland v. Donnelly, 216 F. Supp. 2d 227, 243 (S.D.N.Y. 2002) ("[W]here the state courts have rejected a constitutional claim, a habeas court may not grant relief simply because it believes constitutional error has been committed."), aff'd, 324 F.3d 99 (2d Cir. 2003).

> Green v. Georgia, 442 U.S. 95, 97 (1979) (per curiam) (holding that exclusion of relevant evidence at sentencing hearing constitutes denial of due process).

Case Name　　　　　　　　　　　　　　　　　　　　**B4.1.1**

The case name that appears at the beginning of published opinions typically includes too much information. **Rule 10.2** provides numerous rules to guide you in citing only what is necessary; the most important of these rules are introduced here.

(i) Omit all parties other than the first listed on each side of the "v.":

> Dow Jones & Co. v. Harrods, Ltd.

Not: Dow Jones & Company, Inc., Plaintiff, v. Harrods, Limited and Mohamed Al Fayed, Defendants

- **Bluepages Tip:** Underline the entire case name up to but not including the comma that follows the case name.

(ii) For names of individuals, use only the surname (family name), omitting given names and initials:

> Spiller v. Ware

Not: Martin D. Spiller v. Elliot A. Ware and Randle S. Scott

(iii) Omit words indicating multiple parties, such as "et al.," and alternative names:

> Acree v. Walker

Not: Clinton Acree, et al. v. Freddie Lawrence Walker, a/k/a Big Freddie

(iv) Some case names may include a **procedural phrase**. Abbreviate "on the relation of," "on behalf of," and similar expressions to "ex rel." Abbreviate "in the matter of," "petition of," and similar expressions to "In re." When adversary parties are named, omit all procedural phrases except "ex rel.":

> Dombroski ex rel. Dombroski v. Chi. Park Dist.

Not: Michael Dombroski, as Administrator of Estate of His Minor Child, Samuel Dombroski v. Chicago Park District, et al.

> Ex parte Zeidner

Not: Ex parte Richard Zeidner

> In re Fairfax

Not: In the Matter of J. Fairfax

(v) Always abbreviate any word listed in table T6, unless the citation appears in a textual sentence as explained in (vi) below. Abbreviate states, countries, and other geographical units as indicated in table T10 unless the geographical unit is a named party. Never abbreviate "United States" when it is a named party. Omit "The" as the first word of a party's name unless it is part of the name of the object of an in rem action. You may also abbreviate other words of eight letters or more if substantial space is saved and the result is unambiguous. Some entities with widely recognized initials, such as NAACP and FCC, may be abbreviated without periods:

> Miami Herald v. Univ. of Fla.

Not: The Miami Herald v. The University of Florida

> United States v. Haskell

Not: U.S. v. Erin Haskell, et al.

> Indus. Chems., Inc. v. City of Tuscaloosa

Not: Industrial Chemicals, Inc. v. The City of Tuscaloosa

> Laidlaw Corp. v. NLRB

Not: The Laidlaw Corporation v. National Labor Relations Board

For more guidance on abbreviation, see rule 10.2.

(vi) When referring to the full name of a case in a textual sentence, as opposed to in a citation, underline the case name, and only abbreviate widely known acronyms and these eight words: "&," "Ass'n," "Bros.," "Co.," "Corp.," "Inc.," "Ltd.," and "No." The first time you mention a case in the text, follow the case name with the remaining elements of a full citation, set off by commas:

> In Penn Central Transportation Co. v. City of New York, 366 N.E.2d 1271 (N.Y. 1977), the court applied a version of the diminution in value rule.

Not: In Penn Cent. Transp. Co. v. City of New York, 366 N.E.2d 1271 (N.Y. 1977), the court applied a version of the diminution in value rule.

In a subsequent reference to the case within the same general discussion, you may simply refer to one party's name (or a readily identifiable shorter version of one party's name) if the reference is unambiguous:

▶ The Supreme Court's recent takings jurisprudence has gradually moved away from the New York Court of Appeals's formulation in <u>Penn Central</u>.

Not: The Supreme Court's recent takings jurisprudence has gradually moved away from the New York Court of Appeals's formulation in <u>City of New York</u>.

Reporter and Pinpoint Citation   B4.1.2

A **reporter** is a series of books collecting the published cases within a given jurisdiction or set of jurisdictions. Typically, a case citation will tell the reader where the case can be found by listing: (1) the volume number of the reporter in which the case is published; (2) the abbreviated name of the reporter (listed by jurisdiction in table T1); and (3) the page on which the case report begins:

Citation	Reporter
<u>Meritor Sav. Bank v. Vinson</u>, 477 U.S. 57	Vol. 477, p. 57 of <u>United States Reports</u>
<u>Envtl. Def. Fund v. EPA</u>, 465 F.2d 528	Vol. 465, p. 528 of <u>Federal Reporter, Second Series</u>
<u>Hosier v. Evans</u>, 314 F. Supp. 316	Vol. 314, p. 316 of <u>Federal Supplement</u>
<u>Dean v. District of Columbia</u>, 653 A.2d 307	Vol. 653, p. 307 of <u>Atlantic Reporter, Second Series</u>
<u>Goodridge v. Dep't of Pub. Health</u>, 440 Mass. 309	Vol. 440, p. 309 of <u>Massachusetts Reports</u>

To point your reader to the specific page(s) that relate to the cited proposition, you must also include a **pinpoint citation**, often called a "**pincite**." Pincites are placed after the page on which the case report begins, separated by a comma and one space. Pincites are critical: they provide the only means by which you can direct the reader to the exact page that contains the information or quotation on which you are relying for support.

A pincite may consist of a **page range**, in which case you should indicate the first and last page of the range separated by one dash (e.g., 92–97). Where the page numbers consist of three or more digits, you should drop any repetitive digit(s) other than the final two digits (e.g., 102–06; 1020–30). To cite to **multiple pages that are not consecutive**, list each page, separated by a comma and one space (e.g., 103, 106, 132). If the material you wish to reference appears on more nonconsecutive pages than is convenient to list in one citation, you may use <u>passim</u> in lieu of a pincite. To cite a **footnote**, give the page on which the footnote appears, "n.," and the footnote number, with no space between "n." and the footnote number:

▶ <u>Baker v. Carr</u>, 369 U.S. 186, 195.

▶ <u>Shah v. Leonard</u>, 784 F.2d 1209, 1215–16.

▶ <u>Ells v. Anandaiah</u>, 769 F.2d 195, 196, 199 n.4.

- **Bluepages Tip:** Do not omit a pincite merely because it is the same as the first page of the case report. Without the pincite, the reader will have no way of knowing where the cited material is located. Instead, just repeat the page number:

  United States v. Baxter, 492 F.2d 150, 150.

For further guidance on pincites, see rule 3.2.

B4.1.3   Court and Year of Decision

In general, case citations should indicate parenthetically the deciding court followed by the year of decision (immediately following the page reference, separated by one space). However, when citing decisions of the United States Supreme Court or the highest court of any individual state, do not include the name of the deciding court. Table T1 lists the correct abbreviations for courts at various levels in all major U.S. jurisdictions.

Examples

(i) The United States Supreme Court: Cite to United States Reports (U.S.) if the opinion appears therein; otherwise cite to Supreme Court Reporter (S. Ct.):

  Meritor Sav. Bank v. Vinson, 477 U.S. 57, 60 (1986).

  Tennessee v. Lane, 124 S. Ct. 1978, 1980 (2004).

(ii) Federal Courts of Appeals: Cite to Federal Reporter (F., F.2d, F.3d) and indicate the name of the court parenthetically:

  Envtl. Def. Fund v. EPA, 465 F.2d 528, 533 (D.C. Cir. 1972).

  United States v. Jardine, 364 F.3d 1200, 1203 (10th Cir. 2004).

(iii) Federal District Courts: Cite to Federal Supplement (F. Supp., F. Supp. 2d) and indicate the name of the court parenthetically:

  W. St. Group LLC v. Epro, 564 F. Supp. 2d 84, 91 (D. Mass. 2008).

  Harris v. Roderick, 933 F. Supp. 977, 985 (D. Idaho 1996).

- **Bluepages Tip:** The correct abbreviation for each state is listed in **table T10**. You will notice that some state names are abbreviated with two capital letters (e.g., **N.Y.**), while others are abbreviated with one capital letter and several lower case letters (e.g., **Mich.**). This implicates The Bluebook's spacing rules (**rule 6.1(a)**). Do not include a space between adjacent single capital letters (e.g., **S.D.N.Y.**), but <u>do</u> include a space between a single capital letter and a longer abbreviation (e.g., "**D. Conn.**" for "District of Connecticut" and "**S.D. Cal.**" for "Southern District of California").

(iv) State High Courts: Cite to the regional reporter for the region in which the court sits, if the opinion appears therein; otherwise cite to the state's official reporter, as listed in table T1. Indicate the state parenthetically, unless it is unambiguously conveyed by the reporter title:

  People v. Armour, 590 N.W.2d 61 (Mich. 1999).

  Chaudhary v. Gen. Motors Corp., 649 P.2d 224 (Cal. 1982).

> Bates v. Tappan, 99 Mass. 376 (1868).

(v) Other State Courts: Cite to the regional reporter for the region in which the court sits, if the opinion appears therein; otherwise cite to the state's official reporter, as listed in table T1. Indicate parenthetically the state and court of decision, unless unambiguously conveyed by the reporter title. Do not indicate the department or district of intermediate state courts:

> Kaplan v. Ziff, 530 N.W.2d 807 (Minn. Ct. App. 1995).

> Rusk v. State, 406 A.2d 624 (Md. Ct. Spec. App. 1979), rev'd, 424 A.2d 720 (Md. 1981).

> Campbell v. Sellers-Morris Corp., 82 Cal. Rptr. 2d 202 (Ct. App. 1999).

Parallel Citation in State Court Documents

In documents submitted to state courts, all case citations should be to the reporters required by **local rules**. To find local rules for the court in which you are submitting a document, refer to **Bluepages table BT2**.

Local rules often require citation to both the official state reporter *and* the unofficial regional and/or state-specific reporter, one following the other. This is called **parallel citation**. Where a pincite is necessary, be sure to include one for each reporter citation. When the state or court is clear from the official reporter title, it should be omitted from the date parenthetical:

> Pledger v. Halvorson, 324 Ark. 302, 921 S.W.2d 576 (1996).

> Kenford Co. v. County of Erie, 73 N.Y.2d 312, 537 N.E.2d 176, 540 N.Y.S.2d 1 (1989).

Pending and Unreported Cases   B4.1.4

In practice, you will frequently need to cite a case or slip opinion that has not been or will not be assigned to a reporter for publication. For further guidance, see **rules 10.8.1 and 18.3.1**.

(i) LEXIS and Westlaw cases: Cite to the LEXIS or Westlaw electronic report of the case when one is available. Citations to these electronic databases are slightly more complex than the basic reporter citation form: <case name>, <case docket number>, <database identifier and electronic report number>, at *<star page number> (<court and full date parenthetical>).

The proper format is as follows:

> Albrecht v. Stranczek, No. 87 C 9535, 1991 U.S. Dist. LEXIS 5088, at *1, *3 (N.D. Ill. Apr. 15, 1991).

> Kvass Constr. Co. v. United States, No. 90-266C, 1991 WL 47632, at *2–3 (Cl. Ct. Apr. 8, 1991).

• **Bluepages Tip:** Different courts and publishers use different formats for case docket numbers (e.g., CIV-A, Civ. A., Civ., No., etc.). Cite to the case docket number exactly as it appears. If more than one docket number is assigned to a case, the lead-in language (e.g., CIV-A, Civ. A., Civ., No., etc.) may be omitted after the first reference:

> <u>PKFinans Int'l Corp. v. IBJ Schroder Leasing Corp.</u>, Nos. 93 Civ. 5375, 96 Civ. 1816 (SAS) (HBP), 1996 WL 525862 (S.D.N.Y. Sept. 17, 1996).

(ii) Slip opinions: When a case is unreported, but separately available as a slip opinion, give the docket number, the court, and the full date of the most recent major disposition of the case:

> <u>Groucho Marx Prods. v. Playboy Enters.</u>, No. 77 Civ. 1782 (S.D.N.Y. Dec. 30, 1977).

For further guidance on slip opinions, see **rule 10.8.1(b)**.

(iii) Opinions only available online, but not in an electronic database: Some cases, particularly ones that are pending, can only be accessed through a court's website. In this situation, the URL may be included for easier access:

> <u>Kaye v. Trump</u>, No. 5128, slip op. at 1 (N.Y. App. Div. Jan. 29, 2009), http://www.nycourts.gov/reporter/3dseries/2009/2009_00452.htm.

B4.1.5 Weight of Authority and Explanatory Parentheticals

To add information indicating the weight of the cited authority to a citation, insert an additional parenthetical with this information following the date parenthetical. Always indicate when you are citing a concurring or dissenting opinion:

> <u>Webb v. Baxter Healthcare Corp.</u>, 57 F.3d 1067 (4th Cir. 1995) (unpublished table decision).

> <u>Parker v. Randolph</u>, 442 U.S. 62, 84 (1979) (Stevens, J., dissenting).

> <u>Garcia v. San Antonio Metro. Transit Auth.</u>, 469 U.S. 528, 570 (1985) (5-4 decision) (Powell, J., dissenting).

> <u>Wersba v. Seiler</u>, 393 F.2d 937 (3d Cir. 1968) (per curiam).

An **explanatory parenthetical** may also be added to explain briefly the proposition for which the case stands:

> <u>Green v. Georgia</u>, 442 U.S. 95, 97 (1979) (per curiam) (holding that exclusion of relevant evidence at sentencing hearing constitutes denial of due process).

For further guidance on explanatory parentheticals, see **Bluepages B11** and **rule 10.7.1**.

B4.1.6 Prior or Subsequent History

A full citation should include the **prior** or **subsequent history** of the case, subject to several exceptions discussed in **rule 10.7**. Use one of the abbreviated explanatory phrases listed in **table T8** to introduce the prior or subsequent history. Commonly used explanatory phrases including "aff'd," "aff'g," "cert. denied" (subject to the two year limitation in **rule 10.7**), "cert. granted," "rev'd," and "rev'd on other grounds" should be included for every citation when available. The explanatory phrase is underlined or italicized:

> <u>Gucci Am., Inc. v. Gold Ctr. Jewelry</u>, 997 F. Supp. 399 (S.D.N.Y.), <u>rev'd</u>, 158 F.3d 631 (2d Cir. 1998).

> Cooper v. Dupnik, 924 F.2d 1520, 1530-31 (9th Cir. 1991) (holding that police officers' actions did not rise to level of due process violation), rev'd en banc, 963 F.2d 1220 (9th Cir. 1992).

> Cent. Ill. Pub. Serv. Co. v. Westervelt, 342 N.E.2d 463 (Ill. App. Ct. 1976), aff'd, 367 N.E.2d 661 (Ill. 1977).

- **Bluepages Tip:** Notice in the second example above that the explanatory parenthetical precedes the subsequent history. This is because in this instance the parenthetical relates to the Ninth Circuit panel decision, not the en banc reversal. Explanatory parenthetical information about a case should always immediately precede any subsequent history.

When the case has a different name in the subsequent history, provide the new case name, preceded by the underlined phrase "sub nom." ("under the name of"). There is no need to provide the new case name if the parties' names are merely reversed or if the subsequent history is simply a denial of certiorari or rehearing:

> Great W. United Corp. v. Kidwell, 577 F.2d 1256 (5th Cir. 1978), rev'd sub nom. Leroy v. Great W. United Corp., 443 U.S. 173 (1979).

....

Short Form Citation   B4.2

Once you have provided one full citation to an authority, you may use a "short form" in later citations to the same authority, so long as (1) it will be clear to the reader from the short form what is being referenced; (2) the earlier full citation falls in the same general discussion; and (3) the reader will have little trouble quickly locating the full citation. There are several acceptable short forms for case citations, illustrated below. The common feature of these forms is that they include "at" followed by a pincite.

The following are all acceptable short form citations to page 100 of Palsgraf v. Long Island Railroad Co., 162 N.E. 99 (N.Y. 1928) (Cardozo, J.), provided the three conditions listed above are fulfilled:

> Palsgraf, 162 N.E. at 100.

> 162 N.E. at 100.

> Id. at 100.

When using only one party name in a short form citation, use the name of the first party, unless that party is a geographical or governmental unit or other common litigant. You may also shorten a long party name, for example from First Nat'l Trust & Inv. Corp. to First Nat'l, so long as the reference remains unambiguous.

For cases in which a parallel citation is required, short citations take a slightly different form. Thus, Chalfin v. Specter, 426 Pa. 464, 465, 233 A.2d 562, 563 (1967), becomes one of the following short forms:

> Chalfin, 426 Pa. at 465, 233 A.2d at 563.

> 426 Pa. at 465, 233 A.2d at 563.

Id.

"<u>Id.</u>" is the short form used to refer to the immediately preceding authority. The main purpose of "<u>id.</u>" is to save space and reduce the amount of citation clutter in your writing. While these goals are important, especially when writing within strict page limits, remember that the overriding purpose of citation is to quickly and conveniently provide the reader with relevant information about the cited sources. To prevent "<u>id.</u>" from becoming a source of confusion, <u>The Bluebook</u> establishes a set of ground rules for its usage, the most significant of which are introduced here.

- **Bluepages Tip:** The "i" in "<u>id.</u>" is only capitalized when it begins a citation sentence. The underline always runs under the period.

(i) When used alone, "<u>id.</u>" refers to the identical pincite referenced in the immediately preceding citation:

> The Supreme Court has stated unequivocally that "apprehension by the use of deadly force is a seizure subject to the reasonableness requirement of the Fourth Amendment." <u>Tennessee v. Garner</u>, 471 U.S. 1, 7 (1985). By contrast, minimal police interference will not always constitute a "seizure" for Fourth Amendment purposes. <u>Id.</u>

(ii) To refer to a different page or footnote within the immediately preceding authority, add "at" and the new pincite:

> To determine whether a particular exercise of non-lethal police force was reasonable, courts engage in a balancing process that weighs the nature of the intrusion against the "governmental interests." <u>Id.</u> at 8.

(iii) "<u>Id.</u>" may only be used when the preceding citation cites to only <u>one</u> source:

> This process weighs the nature of the exertion of force against the governmental interests at stake. <u>See</u> <u>Heath</u>, 854 F.2d at 9. This is an "objective reasonableness" test. <u>Id.</u>

In the example above it is clear that "<u>id.</u>" refers to <u>Heath</u>. By contrast, the use of "<u>id.</u>" in the following example is improper because it is not clear to which authority "<u>id.</u>" refers:

> Not: To determine whether a particular exercise of non-lethal police force was reasonable, courts engage in a balancing process. <u>Tennessee v. Garner</u>, 471 U.S. 1, 8 (1985); <u>see also</u> <u>Heath v. Henning</u>, 854 F.2d 6, 8 (2d Cir. 1988). This process weighs the nature of the exertion of force against the governmental interests at stake. <u>See</u> <u>id.</u> at 9.

- **Bluepages Tip:** Sources identified in explanatory parentheticals, explanatory phrases, or prior/subsequent history are ignored for the purposes of this rule.

(iv) The "<u>id.</u>" form for cases requiring parallel citations is as follows:

> The Pennsylvania Supreme Court grappled with a similarly complicated issue in an election dispute in 1967. <u>See</u> <u>Chalfin v. Specter</u>, 426 Pa. 464, 477, 233 A.2d 562, 568 (1967). In <u>Chalfin</u>, the court was

forced to reach a decision under a severely rushed schedule. <u>See</u> <u>id.</u> at 468, 233 A.2d at 564.

(v) "<u>Id.</u>" can be used for various types of authorities—not only for cases. The sections below will provide illustrations of the correct usage of "<u>id.</u>" in citations to other types of authorities. For further guidance on the use of "<u>id.</u>," see **rule 4.1.**

Sources and Authorities: Statutes, Rules, and Regulations   B5

Full Citation   B5.1

Federal Statutes   B5.1.1

A full citation to a federal statute includes three basic elements: (1) the official name of the act; (2) the published source in which the act may be found; and (3) a parenthetical indicating either (i) the year the source was published (used for code citations); or (ii) the year the statute was passed (used for citations to session laws):

> Comprehensive Environmental Response, Compensation, and Liability Act, 42 U.S.C. §§ 9601–9675 (2006).

> Department of Transportation Act, Pub. L. No. 89-670, § 9, 80 Stat. 931, 944–47 (1966).

- **Bluepages Tip:** Nothing is underlined in a statute citation. "Section" is indicated by the "§" symbol, the plural of which is "§§." For further guidance concerning citation to individual sections and subsections, see **rule 3.3.**

Codes and Session Laws

Statutes may be cited to a current official or unofficial **code**, an official or privately published collection of **session laws**, or a **secondary source**. **Rule 12** provides a full explanation of these sources and how to decide which one to include in your citation.

Whenever possible, cite to the current official code for statutes currently in force. A **code** is a set of books containing all of the statutes in force in a given jurisdiction, organized by subject matter. The official code for federal statutes is the <u>United States Code</u>, which is abbreviated as "U.S.C." Codes are frequently divided into "titles," which are then further subdivided into "chapters" and "sections."

A statute citation to an official or unofficial code will tell the reader where the act can be found by listing: (1) the title number; (2) the abbreviated name of the code; (3) the section number(s) in which the act is codified; and (4) the year of the cited code edition (not the year the act was passed). Citations to an unofficial code, such as an "annotated code," must also include the name of the publisher in the date parenthetical:

> 35 U.S.C. § 271 (2006).

> 15 U.S.C.A. § 205 (West 2008).

- **Bluepages Tip:** The <u>United States Code</u> is only codified once every six years. Therefore, citations to the "**U.S.C.**" should be cited to the appropriate codifying year, such as 2000 or 2006. Exact copy pdf versions of the <u>United States Code</u> may be found at **http://uscode.house.gov/ download/downloadPDF.shtml**. Note that electronic databases like Westlaw or LEXIS generally refer to the most recent unofficial code, such as the "**U.S.C.A.**," and should be cited accordingly.

To cite to an individual provision of a statute, rather than to the entire act, include the original section number of the provision you wish to cite following the statute name. Note that the "original section number" as used in this context refers to a particular section of the act, not to the section of the code in which that provision has been codified. Thus, in the first example below, "§ 6" refers to section 6 of the APA, while "§ 555" refers to section 555 of Title V of the <u>United States Code</u>:

> Administrative Procedure Act § 6, 5 U.S.C. § 555 (2006).

> National Environmental Policy Act of 1969 § 102, 42 U.S.C. § 4332 (2006).

> Digital Millennium Copyright Act of 1998 § 103, 17 U.S.C.A. § 1201 (West 2008).

Cite to the **session laws** if the official or unofficial code is unavailable or insufficient, for example, when the statute does not yet appear in a code or when you need to refer to the historical fact of the statute's enactment. Session laws are a bound collection of all statutes enacted by a given legislature, arranged chronologically in the order they were passed. These session laws will later be "codified" and inserted into the official code, which is arranged by subject matter rather than by year of enactment.

The official compilation of federal session laws is the <u>Statutes at Large</u>, abbreviated as "Stat." A citation to <u>Statutes at Large</u> includes the following elements: (1) the official or popular name of the statute; (2) the public law number, abbreviated "Pub. L. No."; (3) the section number, if any; (4) the volume number, followed by "Stat." and the page number; and (5) the year the statute was passed. Session law citations may also include pincites to the particular provision of the act cited and to the particular page of the session laws on which that provision appears:

> Department of Transportation Act, Pub. L. No. 89-670, § 9, 80 Stat. 931, 944-47 (1966).

> Health Professions Education Extension Amendments of 1992, Pub. L. No. 102-408, 106 Stat. 1992.

- **Bluepages Tip:** Notice in the second example above that the year parenthetical is omitted because the name of the statute includes its year of enactment.

For guidance on how to indicate a statute's prior or subsequent history, see **rule 12.7**.

State Statutes

Cite state statutes, like federal statutes, to an official code whenever possible. Table T1.3 lists the official and unofficial statutory compilations of each state, with the preferred official code listed first. Although the citation form for individual state codes varies, as indicated in table T1.3, a full citation to most state codes includes the following elements: (1) the abbreviated name of the code, as listed in table T1.3; (2) the cited section number(s); and (3) the year of the cited code edition (not the year the act was passed). Citations to an unofficial state code must also include the name of the publisher in the date parenthetical:

> Fla. Stat. § 120.52 (2000).

> Cal. Fin. Code § 500 (West 2000).

> N.Y. Bus. Corp. Law § 717 (McKinney 2000).

For guidance on citing state session laws, see rule 12.4.

Rules of Evidence and Procedure; Restatements; Uniform Acts

> Fed. R. Civ. P. 12(b)(6).

> Fed. R. Evid. 410.

> Restatement (Second) of Contracts § 90 (1981).

> Restatement (Second) of Torts § 90 cmt. a (1965).

> U.C.C. § 2-202 (1977).

> U.S. Sentencing Guidelines Manual § 2D1.1(c) (2004).

For further guidance on citing these types of sources, see rule 12.9.

Administrative Rules and Regulations

> 7 C.F.R. § 319.76 (2000).

For further guidance on citing rules and regulations, see rule 14.2.

Federal Taxation Materials

Citation of federal tax materials is governed by special rules discussed in detail in rule 12.9.1 and table T1.2. In court documents and other legal memoranda that discuss only the current version of federal taxation laws, you may omit the year and publisher parenthetical from citations to the Internal Revenue Code ("I.R.C.") and Treasury regulations.

Internal Revenue Code

In citations to the Internal Revenue Code, "26 U.S.C." may be replaced with "I.R.C.":

> 26 U.S.C. § 61 (2006).

becomes: I.R.C. § 61 (2006).

Treasury Regulations

> Treas. Reg. § 1.72-16(a).

> Treas. Reg. § 1.72-16(a), Q&A (3)(a).

Treasury Determinations

When citing Treasury determinations in court documents and other legal memoranda, you may use the abbreviations contained in the introductory pages of the <u>Cumulative Bulletin</u>. Thus, General Counsel Memoranda may be cited "G.C.M." instead of "Gen. Couns. Mem." In addition, when citing Private Letter Rulings, you may use the abbreviation "P.L.R." instead of "Priv. Ltr. Rul." and you may omit the dashes from the ruling number:

> Rev. Rul. 83-137, 1983-2 C.B. 41.

> I.R.S. P.L.R. 8601012 (Sept. 30, 1985).

> I.R.S. G.C.M. 39,417 (Sept. 30, 1985).

• **Bluepages Tip:** Tax Court and Board of Tax Appeals decisions are cited as court decisions, not agency decisions. For further guidance, see **table T1.1**.

For guidance on citing materials from other administrative agencies, see **table T1.2**.

B5.1.6 Legislative Materials

A full citation to legislative material generally includes the following basic components, although not necessarily in the following order: (1) the title of the material; (2) the abbreviated name of the legislative body; (3) the number assigned to the material; (4) the number of the Congress and/or legislative session; and (5) the year of publication.

Unenacted Federal Bill

> Protection from Personal Intrusion Act, H.R. 2448, 105th Cong. § 2(a) (1997).

Federal Congressional Hearing

> <u>Toxic Substances Control Act: Hearings on S. 776 Before the Subcomm. on the Env't of the Senate Comm. on Commerce</u>, 94th Cong. 343 (1975).

Federal Congressional Report

> S. Rep. No. 89-910, at 4 (1965).

State Bills and Resolution

> H.D. 636, 1999 Leg., 413th Sess. (Md. 1999).

For further guidance on citing legislative materials, see **rule 13**.

B5.2 Short Form Citation

As with cases, the first mention of a statute, rule, regulation, or legislative material requires a full citation. Subsequent citations in the same general discussion may employ any short form that clearly identifies the source. **Rules 12.10, 13.8,** and **14.4** include tables illustrating various acceptable short forms for statutes, legislative materials, and regulations.

You may also use "<u>id.</u>" to refer to a statute or regulation codified within the same title as the statute or regulation cited in the immediately preceding citation:

Full Citation	<u>Id.</u> Citation for Identical Provision	<u>Id.</u> Citation for Different Provision Within Same Title
28 U.S.C. § 1331 (2006).	<u>Id.</u>	<u>Id.</u> § 1332(a)(1).
7 C.F.R. § 319.76 (2006).	<u>Id.</u>	<u>Id.</u> § 300.

Sources and Authorities: Constitutions   **B6**

> U.S. Const. amend. XIV, § 2.

> U.S. Const. art. I, § 9, cl. 2.

> N.M. Const. art. IV, § 7.

- **Bluepages Tip:** Do not use a short citation form (other than <u>id.</u>) for constitutions.

For further guidance on citing constitutions, see **rule 11.**

Sources and Authorities: Court and Litigation Documents   **B7**

Court and litigation documents carry different citation styles when a practitioner cites to a filing from the same case and when she cites to a filing from a different case. This rule focuses on citation to documents filed from the same case; for citation to court documents filed in a different case, consult **rule 10.8.3.**

Full Citation   **B7.1**

A full citation to a court or litigation document includes the following elements: (1) the name of the document, abbreviated when appropriate; (2) the pinpoint citation; and (3) the date of the document, if required. When appropriate, the citation should also include the Electronic Case Filing number found on PACER.

Abbreviation   **B7.1.1**

If it is clear to which court document you are referring, you should abbreviate references to the title of that document as suggested by the abbreviations listed in **Bluepages table BT1.** Where there is an official record, such as the Record on Appeal in appellate litigation, always abbreviate "Record" to "R." Remember the general rule, however, to never use an abbreviation when doing so would likely confuse your reader:

> Petitioner admits filing suit more than one year after knowledge of the facts underlying its claim, Pet'r's Br. 6, and further admits the applicability of a one-year statute of limitations, Pet'r's Br. 7.

▸ In Defendant's Memorandum of Points and Authorities in Support of Defendant's Motion for Summary Judgment, Defendant asserts that the dangerous conditions giving rise to the accident resulted from someone else's negligence, Def.'s Mem. Supp. Summ. J. 6, 9, implying that Defendant was, indeed, aware of the risk. Yet, in his Affidavit filed in support of the Motion, Defendant explicitly states that he had no knowledge of the rising water level. Def.'s Aff. ¶¶ 5–7; <u>see also</u> Jones Aff. Ex. A, at 2.

- **Bluepages Tip:** Citations to court and litigation documents can optionally be enclosed in parentheses:

  ▸ (Def.'s Resp. to Pl.'s Interrog. No. 3.)

B7.1.2 Pinpoint Citations

Pincites are particularly important when citing court documents. Give as precise a reference as practicable to the cited document, such as to the page and line on which the material appears in the cited deposition or trial transcript. Use commas only to avoid confusion; separate page and line references by a colon. Page references should not be preceded by "p.," but other subdivisions should be identified. You are generally not required to precede pincites with "at," although it is customary to use "at" in references to some sources such as the appellate record (e.g., R. at 5):

▸ Friedberg Aff. 6.

▸ Trial Tr. vol. 2, 31, June 19, 2004.

▸ Pet'r's Br. 6.

▸ Yee Dep. 15:21–16:4, July 27, 1982.

▸ Pls.' Am. Answer to Def.'s Countercl. 3–4.

▸ Rodriguez Decl. Ex. B, at 3.

▸ R. at 9.

B7.1.3 Date

Provide the date of the document at the conclusion of the citation in references to depositions, trial or hearing testimony, judgments and orders, and other documents when: (1) more than one such document bears the same title; (2) when the date of the document is significant to the discussion; or (3) as needed to avoid confusion:

▸ Plaintiff alleged that Defendant was driving at a rate far in excess of the posted speed limit. Compl. ¶ 7. However, her sworn testimony is to the effect that she never saw the Defendant before the accident and was thus unable to gauge his speed. Perryman Dep. 34:15–18, Aug. 7, 2002; Trial Tr. vol. 2, 51-52, Dec. 12, 2002.

▸ Mr. Duggan attests that Plaintiff's president cared not about the age of the inventory but only about its marketability. Duggan Aff. ¶ 5. In addition, Ms. Toms swears that Plaintiff's president had the authority to waive the condition concerning the age of the inventory, Toms Aff. ¶ 9, May 10, 2003, and that no other corporate official had such authority, Toms Aff. ¶ 2, June 2, 2003.

Electronic Case Filings (ECF)   B7.1.4

Court documents filed with the electronic case management system employed by PACER for federal cases (CM/ECF) are assigned document numbers. For easier access, add the ECF number for documents that have been filed electronically.

For ECF documents, include: (1) the name or abbreviation of the document (**Bluepages B7.1.1** and **Bluepages table BT1**); (2) the pinpoint citation (**Bluepages B7.1.2**); (3) the date of the document, if required (**Bluepages B7.1.3**); and (4) the document number assigned by the court (ECF No.), found on PACER:

> ▶ Rubio Dep. 5:30–12:10, June 7, 2008, ECF No. 16.

> ▶ Def.'s Mot. Summ. J. 2, ECF No. 15.

- **Bluepages Tip:** Documents filed on PACER are imprinted with an ECF header, placed either at the top or bottom of each page. These page numbers are sometimes different from the page numbers of the filed document; the pagination of the original document should be followed.

Short Form Citation   B7.2

Once a full citation is given, you should use a short form so long as: (1) it will be clear to the reader what is being referenced by the short form; (2) the earlier full citation falls in the same general discussion; and (3) the reader will have little trouble locating the full citation quickly:

First Reference	Succeeding Reference
Smith Dep. 27:4–28:2, Feb. 5, 2001.	Smith Dep. 30:4–18.
TRO Hr'g Tr. 21, Jan. 9, 2003.	TRO Hr'g Tr. 24, or Hr'g Tr. 24.
App. to Pet. Cert. 137–39, ECF No. 15	App. 137–39, ECF No. 15, or App. 137-39.

- **Bluepages Tip:** For court documents, <u>id.</u> should only be used if significant space will be saved.

> ▶ The liquid left on the floor by Defendant caused Plaintiff to lose her balance, slip, and fall. Leach Aff. 33–39. This fall led to numerous hospital visits costing well over $10,000. <u>Id.</u> at 52.

> But: The liquid left on the floor by Defendant caused Plaintiff to lose her balance, slip, and fall. R. at 5. This fall led to numerous hospital visits costing well over $10,000. R. at 12.

Capitalization in Textual Sentences   B7.3

Rule 8 provides the generally applicable rules on capitalization. In court documents and legal memoranda, the following exceptions to **rule 8** apply:

B7.3.1 Court

In addition to capitalizing "Court" when naming any court in full or when referring to the U.S. Supreme Court, also capitalize "Court" in a court document when referring to the court that will be receiving that document:

> This Court has already ruled on Defendant's Motion To Dismiss.

> But: The court in <u>Watkins</u> was attempting to distinguish earlier precedent pointing in the other direction.

B7.3.2 Party Designations

Only capitalize party designations such as "Plaintiff," "Defendant," "Appellant," and "Appellee" when referring to parties in the matter that is the subject of your document:

> Plaintiff denies Defendant's baseless allegations of misconduct.

> But: In <u>Smith</u>, the plaintiffs alleged that the defendant acted in bad faith.

B7.3.3 Titles of Court Documents

Capitalize the title of a court document only when: (1) the document has been filed in the matter that is the subject of your document; and (2) the reference is to the document's actual title or a shortened form thereof. Do not capitalize references to the generic name of a court document:

> In their Memorandum of Points and Authorities in Opposition to Defendant's Motion to Dismiss, Plaintiffs argue that Defendants are strictly liable for Plaintiff's injuries.

> The Court's Order of May 7, 2004, directed Plaintiffs to cease production immediately.

> But: There is no doubt that the initial temporary restraining order was within the bounds of the court's discretion.

- **Bluepages Tip:** Do not abbreviate the titles of court documents in textual sentences:

> For all the above reasons, Appellant's Petition for Rehearing ought to be granted.

> Not: For all of the above reasons, Appellant's Pet. Reh'g ought to be granted.

Sources and Authorities: Books and Other Nonperiodic Materials   B8

Full Citation   B8.1

Citations to books, treatises, pamphlets, and other nonperiodic materials should include the following elements: (1) the volume number (used only for multi-volume sets); (2) the full name(s) of the author(s) as it appears on the publication; (3) the title of the publication (underlined); (4) a pincite; and (5) a parenthetical indicating the year of publication, as well as the name of the editor, if any, and the edition, if more than one.

Two authors should appear separated by an ampersand ("&") in the order in which they are listed on the publication. If a work has more than two authors, either use the first author's name followed by "et al." or list all authors' names:

> 21 Charles Alan Wright & Arthur R. Miller, <u>Federal Practice and Procedure</u> § 1006 (3d ed. 1998).

> A. Leo Levin et al., <u>Dispute Resolution Devices in a Democratic Society</u> 77 (1985).

> <u>AIDS and the Law</u> 35 (Harlon L. Dalton et al. eds., 1987).

> Deborah L. Rhode, <u>Justice and Gender</u> 56 (1989).

> Richard H. Fallon, Jr., Daniel J. Meltzer & David L. Shapiro, <u>Hart and Wechsler's The Federal Courts and the Federal System</u> 685 (5th ed. 2003).

There are special citation forms for a few frequently cited works:

> <u>Black's Law Dictionary</u> 712 (9th ed. 2009).

> 17 Am. Jur. 2d <u>Contracts</u> § 74 (1964).

> 88 C.J.S. <u>Trial</u> § 192 (1955).

For further guidance on citing to books and other nonperiodic material, see **rule 15**.

Short Form Citation   B8.2

Use "<u>id.</u>" to refer to a book or other nonperiodical material cited in the immediately preceding citation. Otherwise, use "<u>supra</u>." The "<u>supra</u>" form consists of: (1) the author's last name; (2) "<u>supra</u>," underlined up to but not including the comma; and (3) a new pincite:

Full Cite	<u>Id.</u> Cite	<u>Supra</u> Cite
Deborah L. Rhode, <u>Justice and Gender</u> 56 (1989).	<u>Id.</u> at 60–61.	Rhode, <u>supra</u>, at 60–61.
A. Leo Levin et al., <u>Dispute Resolution Devices in a Democratic Society</u> 77 (1985).	See <u>id.</u> at 80.	<u>See</u> Levin et al., <u>supra</u>, at 80.
Fleming James, Jr. & Geoffrey C. Hazard, Jr., <u>Civil Procedure</u> § 2.35 (5th ed. 2001).	<u>Id.</u> § 1.7.	James & Hazard, <u>supra</u>, § 1.7.

- **Bluepages Tip:** For further guidance on short forms, see **rules 4**, **15.10**, **16.9**, **17.6**, and **18.8**. Since you will not be using footnote citations, simply omit any reference to "**note x**" in the <u>supra</u> examples provided in those rules.

B9 Sources and Authorities: Journal, Magazine, and Newspaper Articles

B9.1 Full Citation

A full citation to periodical material generally includes the following elements: (1) the full name(s) of the author(s); (2) the title of the article (underlined); (3) the abbreviated name of the publication; (4) a pincite; and (5) the date of publication. The basic citation form differs somewhat depending on the type of periodical cited. For further guidance, see **rule 16**.

B9.1.1 Consecutively Paginated Journals

Most law journals are paginated consecutively throughout an entire volume (i.e., individual "issues" or "books" within a given volume do not begin at page "1," but rather pick up where the previous issue left off). To cite material appearing in a consecutively paginated periodical, follow this format: <author(s)>, <title of work>, <volume number> <abbreviated periodical name> <first page of article>, <pincite> (<year of publication>).

> Kenneth R. Feinberg, <u>Mediation—A Preferred Method of Dispute Resolution</u>, 16 Pepp. L. Rev. 5, 14 (1989).

> Patricia J. Williams, <u>Alchemical Notes: Reconstructed Ideals from Deconstructed Rights</u>, 22 Harv. C.R.-C.L. L. Rev. 401, 407 (1987).

For appropriate abbreviations of periodical names, see **table T13**.

B9.1.2 Nonconsecutively Paginated Journals and Magazines

> Lynn Hirschberg, <u>The Misfit</u>, Vanity Fair, Apr. 1991, at 158.

B9.1.3 Student-Written Work

> Philip Mariani, Comment, <u>Assessing the Proper Relationship Between the Alien Tort Statute and the Torture Victim Protection Act</u>, 156 U. Pa. L. Rev. 1383, 1409 n.112 (2008).

> Note, <u>The Death of a Lawyer</u>, 56 Colum. L. Rev. 606 (1956).

B9.1.4 Newspaper Articles

> Andrew Rosenthal, White <u>House Tutors Kremlin in How a Presidency Works</u>, N.Y. Times, June 15, 1990, at A1.

> <u>Cop Shoots Tire, Halts Stolen Car</u>, S.F. Chron., Oct. 10, 1975, at 43.

Short Form Citation B9.2

Once a work in a periodical has been cited in full, use "<u>id.</u>" or "<u>supra</u>" in subsequent citations. Use "<u>id.</u>" to refer to periodical material cited in the immediately preceding citation. Otherwise, use the "<u>supra</u>" form introduced in **Bluepages B8.2.**

- **Bluepages Tip:** When your document includes citations to more than one source by the same author, include an abbreviated reference to the title of the cited source in any <u>supra</u> citation:

> Feinberg, <u>Mediation</u>, <u>supra</u>, at 15.

Sources and Authorities: The Internet **B10**

Full Citation B10.1

Direct Citations B10.1.1

A full, direct citation to an internet source includes the following: (1) the name of the author(s) (if applicable); (2) the title of the specific page of the website, such as a posting or comment (if applicable) (underlined); (3) the title of the main page of the website; (4) the date and time (omit the time when a source is not updated multiple times in a day, or if no time is listed); and (5) the URL. For further guidance on citing internet sources, see **rule 18.2**:

> Eric Posner, <u>More on Section 7 of the Torture Convention</u>, Volokh Conspiracy (Jan. 29, 2009, 10:04 AM), http://www.volokh.com/posts/1233241458.shtml.

> Ashby Jones, <u>Activists, Research Facilities Taking Disclosure Battles to the Courts</u>, Wall St. J. L. Blog (Feb. 26, 2009, 9:40 AM), http://blogs.wsj.com/law/2009/02/26/activists-research-facilities-taking-disclosure-battles-to-the-courts.

> Daily Kos (Jan. 19, 2009), http://www.dailykos.com/storyonly/2009/1/18/235223/489/683/685802.

- **Bluepages Tip:** If a source is available in both an HTML format and another format which preserves pagination and other attributes of printed work (such as a PDF file), the latter format should always be cited. A pincite should be provided for these sources when appropriate:

> John Roman, Michael Kane, Emily Turner & Beverly Frazier, <u>Instituting Lasting Reforms for Prisoner Reentry in Philadelphia</u>, Urban Inst., 8 (June 27, 2006), http://www.urban.org/UploadedPDF/411345_lastingreforms.pdf.

If there is no date associated with the specific matter of the citation, then the citation should list the date when the website was "last modified" or "last updated" after the URL. If these indicators are unavailable, use the date on which the site was "last visited":

> Yahoo! Home Page, http://www.yahoo.com (last visited Dec. 10, 2005).

B10.1.2   Parallel Citations

For traditional printed material, a parallel citation to an Internet source may be provided if it will increase access to the source. The material should be cited in the same way as the traditional material, with the URL introduced by the explanatory phrase "<u>available at</u>" appended to the end:

> <u>Am. Mining Cong. v. U.S. Army Corps of Eng'rs</u>, No. CIV. A. 93-1754 SSH (D.D.C. Jan. 23, 1997), <u>available at</u> http://www.wetlands.com/fed/tulloch1.htm.

B10.2   Short Form Citation

Once internet material has been cited in full, use <u>id.</u> or <u>supra</u> in subsequent citations per **rules 4** and **18.8(a)**:

> Posner, <u>supra</u>.

> Daily Kos, <u>supra</u>.

B11   Explanatory Parentheticals

Regardless of the type of authority you are citing, it is often helpful to include additional information to explain the relevance of the cited authority. Append this information parenthetically at the end of your citation but preceding any citation to subsequent history.

Explanatory parentheticals should take the form of a phrase that begins with a present participle, a quoted sentence, or a short statement that is appropriate in context. To save space, you may omit extraneous words such as "the" unless doing so would cause confusion. Do not begin with a capital letter or end with a period <u>unless</u> the parenthetical consists of a quotation that reads as a full sentence:

> <u>See</u> <u>Flanagan v. United States</u>, 465 U.S. 259, 264 (1989) (explaining that final judgment rule reduces potential for parties to "clog the courts" with time-consuming appeals).

> <u>Atl. Richfield Co. v. Fed. Energy Admin.</u>, 429 F. Supp. 1052, 1061-62 (N.D. Cal. 1976) ("Not every person aggrieved by administrative action is necessarily entitled to due process.").

> 5 U.S.C. § 553(b) (2000) (requiring agencies to publish notice of proposed rulemaking in the <u>Federal Register</u>).

> Such standards have been adopted to address a variety of environmental problems. <u>See, e.g.</u>, H.B. Jacobini, <u>The New International Sanitary Regulations</u>, 46 Am. J. Int'l L. 727, 727-28 (1952) (health-related water quality); Robert L. Meyer, <u>Travaux Preparatoires for the UNESCO World Heritage Convention</u>, 2 Earth L.J. 45, 45-81 (1976) (conservation of protected areas).

For further guidance on explanatory parentheticals, see **rule 1.5**.

Quotations   B12

Generally   B12.1

With the exception of block quotations, quotations should be enclosed in quotation marks but not otherwise set off from the rest of the text. Commas or periods should be placed inside the quotation marks, while all other punctuation should only be placed inside the quotation marks if part of the original text:

- **Bluepages Tip:** A quotation appearing within another quotation can either be parenthetically attributed to its original source or otherwise acknowledged by indicating that a citation has been omitted.

    "When, as here, the plaintiff is a public figure, he cannot recover unless he proves by clear and convincing evidence that the defendant published the defamatory statement with actual malice, i.e., with 'knowledge that it was false or with reckless disregard of whether it was false or not.'" Masson v. New Yorker Magazine, 501 U.S. 496, 510 (1991) (quoting N.Y. Times Co. v. Sullivan, 376 U.S. 254, 279-80 (1964)).

    "We refused to permit recovery for choice of language which, though perhaps reflecting a misconception, represented 'the sort of inaccuracy that is commonplace in the forum of robust debate to which the New York Times rule applies.'" Masson v. New Yorker Magazine, 501 U.S. 496, 519 (1991) (citation omitted).

For further guidance on other aspects of quotations, including omissions from and alterations of original quoted material, see **rule 5**.

Block Quotations   B12.2

Quotations of <u>fifty or more words</u> should be single spaced, indented left and right, justified, and without quotation marks. This is known as a **block quotation**. Quotation marks <u>within</u> a block quotation should appear as they do in the original. The citation following a block quotation should not be indented but should begin at the left margin on the line following the quotation, as shown in this example:

    [T]his presumptive privilege must be considered in light of our historic commitment to the rule of law. This is nowhere more profoundly manifest than in our view that "the twofold aim [of criminal justice] is that guilt shall not escape or innocence suffer." We have elected to employ an adversary system of criminal justice in which the parties contest all issues before a court of law. . . . To ensure that justice is done, it is imperative to the function of courts that compulsory process be available for the production of evidence needed either by the prosecution or by the defense.

United States v. Nixon, 418 U.S. 683, 708–09 (1974) (citation omitted). The Court then balanced this interest against the evils of forced disclosure. Id. at 710.

THE BLUEPAGES TABLES

BT1   Court Documents

This table provides suggested abbreviations for words commonly found in the titles of court documents. Use these abbreviations in citations to court documents according to Bluepages B7.1.1 and B7.2. This table also indicates certain words that should not be abbreviated. Unless otherwise indicated, plurals are formed by adding the letter "s."

Words of more than six letters not appearing in this table may also be abbreviated if the abbreviation selected is unambiguous.

Unless it would be confusing to the reader, omit all articles and prepositions from any abbreviated title. Other extraneous words may also be omitted so long as the cited document can be unambiguously identified without them.

Admission	Admis.
Affidavit	Aff.
Affirm	Affirm
Amended	Am.
Answer	Answer
Appeal	Appeal
Appellant	Appellant
Appellee	Appellee
Appendix	App. (except when citing to Joint Appendix)
Application	Appl.
Argument	Arg.
Attachment	Attach.
Attorney	Att'y
Brief	Br.
Certiorari	Cert.
Compel	Compel
Complaint	Compl.
Counterclaim	Countercl.
Court	Ct.
Cross-claim	Cross-cl.
Declaration	Decl.
Defendant ['s]	Def. ['s]
Defendants [']	Defs. [']
Demurrer	Dem.
Deny [ing]	Den.
Deposition	Dep.
Discovery	Disc.

Dismiss	Dismiss
Document	Doc.
Exhibit	Ex.
Grant	Grant
Hearing	Hr'g
Injunction	Inj.
Interrogatory	Interrog.
Joint Appendix	J.A.
Judgment	J.
Memorandum	Mem.
Minutes	Mins.
Motion	Mot.
Opinion	Op.
Opposition	Opp'n
Order	Order
Petition	Pet.
Petitioner ['s]	Pet'r ['s]
Petitioners [']	Pet'rs [']
Plaintiff ['s]	Pl. ['s]
Plaintiffs [']	Pls. [']
Points and Authorities	P. & A.
Preliminary	Prelim.
Produc [e, tion]	Produc.
Quash	Quash
Reconsideration	Recons.
Record	R.
Rehearing	Reh'g
Reply	Reply
Reporter	Rep.
Request	Req.
Respondent	Resp't
Response	Resp.
Stay	Stay
Subpoena	Subpoena
Summary	Summ.
Support	Supp.
Suppress	Suppress
Temporary Restraining Order	TRO
Testimony	Test.
Transcript	Tr.
Verified Statement	V.S.

BT2 Jurisdiction-Specific Citation Rules and Style Guides

This table references some helpful local court rules and a number of jurisdiction-specific manuals that provide guidance on local citation practices, which take precedence over <u>Bluebook</u> rules in documents submitted to those courts. The parenthetical information after each entry describes the type of citation located at the corresponding rule. For example, parentheticals beginning with the words "cite as" explain the exact citation that the rule requires in citing to that rule type. Furthermore, while some of the parentheticals give the exact citation format established by the jurisdiction, it is important to check the most recent version of the court's citation rules to ensure that they are relevant.

BT2.1 Federal Courts

United States Court of Appeals for the First Circuit
    1st Cir. R. 32.1.0 (citation of unpublished opinions)
    1st Cir. R. 32.2 (citation of State or Commonwealth courts and to unpublished law review articles)

Bankruptcy Appellate Panel for the First Circuit
    1st Cir. Bankr. App. Panel R. 8001-1 (cite as "1st Cir. BAP L.R.__")

United States Court of Appeals for the Second Circuit
    2d Cir. R. 32.1 (citation of summary orders)

United States Court of Appeals for the Third Circuit
    3d Cir. R. 1.2 (cite as "3rd Cir. LAR __.__ (1997)")
    3d Cir. R. 28.3(a) (citation of various types of legal authority)

United States Court of Appeals for the Fourth Circuit
    4th Cir. R. 32.1 (citation of unpublished 4th Cir. dispositions prior to Jan. 1, 2007)

United States Court of Appeals for the Fifth Circuit
    5th Cir. R. 28.7, 47.5.3-4 (citation of unpublished opinions)

United States Court of Appeals for the Sixth Circuit
    6th Cir. R. 28(f) (citation of unpublished opinions)

United States Court of Appeals for the Seventh Circuit
    7th Cir. R. 32.1(b), (d) (citation of orders)

United States Court of Appeals for the Eighth Circuit
    8th Cir. R. 32.1A (citation of unpublished opinions)

United States Court of Appeals for the Ninth Circuit
    9th Cir. R. 36-3 (citation of unpublished opinions and orders)

United States Court of Appeals for the Tenth Circuit
    10th Cir. R. 32.1 (citation of unpublished opinions)

United States Court of Appeals for the Eleventh Circuit
    11th Cir. R. 28-1(k) (required use of <u>Bluebook</u> or <u>ALWD Manual</u>; citation of cases)

United States Court of Appeals for the District of Columbia
    D.C. Cir. R. 28(b) (citation of various types of legal authority)
    D.C. Cir. R. 28(a)(1)(A) (citation of rulings under review)

- D.C. Cir. R. 32.1 (citation of published opinions and statutes; citation of unpublished dispositions)
- D.C. Cir. Handbook of Practice and Internal Procedures I.D (cite local rules as "D.C. Cir. Rule __")
- D.C. Cir. Handbook of Practice and Internal Procedures IX.A.8 (citation of various types of legal authority)

United States Court of Appeals for the Federal Circuit
- Foreword to Fed. Cir. Local Rules (cite as "Fed. Cir. R.")
- Fed. Cir. R. 28(e) (citation of cases)
- Fed. Cir. R. 32.1 (citation of nonprecedential opinions or orders)

United States District Court for the Middle District of Alabama
- M.D. Ala. Civ. R. 1.1 (a) (cite civil rules as "M.D. Ala. LR" and criminal rules as "M.D. Ala. LCrR")

United States Bankruptcy Court for the Middle District of Alabama
- Bankr. M.D. Ala. R. 1000-1 (cite as "LBR __, Bankr. M.D. Ala.")

United States District Court for the Southern District of Alabama
- S.D. Ala. R. 1.1(a) (cite as "SD ALA LR __")
- S.D. Ala. Loc. Adm. R. 1 (cite as "SD ALA LAR __")

United States District Court for the District of Alaska
- D. Alaska Civ. R. 85.1 (cite as "D.Ak. LR __")
- D. Alaska Crim. R. 61.1 (cite as "D.Ak.LCrR")
- D. Alaska Loc. Adm. R. (a)-1(c) (cite as "D.Ak. LAR __")
- D. Alaska Loc. Habeas Corpus R. 1.1(b) (cite as "D.Ak.HCR __")
- D. Alaska Loc. Mag. R. 1(a) (cite as "D.Ak.LMR __")

United States Bankruptcy Court for the District of Alaska
- Bankr. D. Alaska R. 1001-1(e) (cite as "AK LBR __")

United States District Court for the District of Arizona
- Foreword to D. Ariz. Loc. R. (cite civil rules as "LRCiv," criminal rules as "LRCrim," and bankruptcy rules as "LRBankr")

United States District Court for the Central District of California
- C.D. Cal. R. 11-3.9 (citation of various types of legal authority)
- C.D. Cal. Crim. R. 60-1 (cite as "L.Cr.R.")

United States Bankruptcy Court for the Central District of California
- Bankr. C.D. Cal. R. 1001-1(a) (cite as "LBR__")
- Bankr. C.D. Cal. R. 9013-2(c) (citation of various types of legal authority)

United States District Court for the Eastern District of California
- E.D. Cal. R. 5-133(i) (citation of various types of legal authority)
- E.D. Cal. R. 1-100(a) (cite as "L.R.")

United States Bankruptcy Court for the Eastern District of California
- Bankr. E.D. Cal. R. 1001-1(a) (cite as "LBR")

United States District Court for the Northern District of California
- N.D. Cal. Civ. R. 1-1 (cite as "Civil L.R. __")
- N.D. Cal. Civ. R. 3-4(d) (citation of various types of legal authority)

N.D. Cal. Civ. R. 3-4(e) (citation of uncertified opinions)

N.D. Cal. Crim. R. 1-1 (cite as "Crim. L.R. __")

N.D. Cal. Loc. Pat. R. 1-1 (cite as "Patent L.R. __")

United States Bankruptcy Court for the Northern District of California

Bankr. N.D. Cal. R. 1001-1(b) (cite as "B.L.R. __-__")

United States District Court for the Southern District of California

S.D. Cal. Civ. R. 1.1(a) (cite as "CivLR __")

S.D. Cal. Civ. R. 5.1(l) (citation of federal statutes and regulations)

S.D. Cal. Crim. R. 1.1(a) (cite as "CrimLR __")

United States District Court for the District of Colorado

D. Colo. Civ. R. 1.1(A) (cite as "D.C.COLO.LCivR __")

D. Colo. Civ. R. 7.1(D) (citation in motions)

D. Colo. Crim. R. 1.1(A) (cite as "D.C.COLO.LCrR __")

United States Bankruptcy Court for the District of Colorado

Bankr. D. Colo. R. 101 (cite rules as "L.B.R." and forms as "L.B.F.")

United States District Court for the District of Connecticut

D. Conn. Civ. R. 1(a) (cite as "D. Conn. L. Civ. R. __")

D. Conn. Crim. R. 1(a) (cite as "D. Conn. L. Cr. R. __")

United States Bankruptcy Court for the District of Connecticut

Bankr. D. Conn. R. 1001-1(a) (cite as "D. Conn. LBR __-__")

United States District Court for the District of Delaware

D. Del. R. 1.1(a) (cite as "D. Del. LR __")

D. Del. R. 7.1.3(a)(5) (required use of <u>Bluebook</u>)

D. Del. R. 7.1.3(a)(6) (citation of earlier-filed court papers)

D. Del. R. 7.1.3(a)(7) (citation of unpublished opinions)

United States Bankruptcy Court for the District of Delaware

Bankr. D. Del. R. 1001-1(a) (cite as "Del. Bankr. L.R. __")

Bankr. D. Del. R. 7007-2(a)(v) (required use of <u>Bluebook</u>; citation of cases)

Bankr. D. Del. R. 7007-2(a)(vi) (citation to earlier-filed papers)

Bankr. D. Del. R. 7007-2(a)(v) (citation of unreported opinions)

United States District Court for the Middle District of Florida

M.D. Fla. R. 7.01(b) (citation of supplemental rules, local rules, and local admiralty and maritime rules)

United States Bankruptcy Court for the Middle District of Florida

Bankr. M.D. Fla. R. 1001-1(e) (cite as "Local Rules")

United States District Court for the Northern District of Florida

N.D. Fla. R. 1.1(a) (cite as "N.D. Fla. Loc. R. __")

N.D. Fla. Adm. & Mar. R. A(2) (citation of supplemental rules, local rules, and local admiralty and maritime rules)

United States Bankruptcy Court for the Northern District of Florida

Bankr. N.D. Fla. R. 1001-1(A) (cite as "N.D. Fla. LBR __")

United States District Court for the Southern District of Florida
> S.D. Fla. R. 1.1(a) (cite as "S.D. Fla. L.R. __")
> S.D. Fla. Adm. & Mar. R. 1(b) (citation of supplemental rules and local admiralty and maritime rules)

United States District Court for the Northern District of Georgia
> N.D. Ga. R. 5.1(E) (citation of federal statutes and regulations)
> N.D. Ga. Civ. R. 1.1 (cite as "LR __, NDGa")
> N.D. Ga. Crim. R. 1.1(A) (cite as "LCrR __, NDGa")

United States Bankruptcy Court for the Northern District of Georgia
> Bankr. N.D. Ga. R. 1001-1 (cite as "BLR")

United States District Court for the District of Hawaii
> D. Haw. R. 1.1 (cite as "LR__," "CrimLR__," or "LBR__")
> Amended General Order Adopting Electronic Case Filing Procedures § 12 (D. Haw. Feb. 1, 2006) (citation using hyperlinks)

United States Bankruptcy Court for the District of Hawaii
> Bankr. D. Haw. R. 1001-1(b) (cite as "LBR __-__")

United States District Court for the District of Idaho
> D. Idaho R. 1.1(a) (cite as "Dist. Idaho Loc. Civ. R. __" or "Dist. Idaho Loc. Crim. R. __")

United States Bankruptcy Court for the District of Idaho
> Bankr. D. Idaho R. 1001.1(a) (cite as "LBR __")

United States District Court for the Central District of Illinois
> C.D. Ill. R. 1.1 (cite as "CDIL-LR __")

United States District Court for the Northern District of Illinois
> N.D. Ill. Crim. R. 1.1 (cite as "LCrR.__")

United States Bankruptcy Court for the Northern District of Illinois
> Bankr. N.D. Ill. R. 1001-2(A) (cite as "Local Bankruptcy Rules")

United States District Court for the Southern District of Illinois
> S.D. Ill. R. 1.1(a) (cite as "SDIL-LR __")

United States Bankruptcy Court for the Southern District of Illinois
> Bankr. S.D. Ill. R. 1001-1 (cite as "S.D. Ill. LBR __-__")

United States District Court for the Northern District of Indiana
> N.D. Ind. R. 1.1(a) (cite as "N.D. Ind. L.R. __")

United States Bankruptcy Court for the Northern District of Indiana
> Bankr. N.D. Ind. R. 1001-1(a) (cite as "N.D. Ind. L.B.R. B-__")

United States District Court for the Southern District of Indiana
> S.D. Ind. R. 1.1(a) (cite as "S.D.Ind.L.R. __")
> S.D. Ind. A.D.R. R. 1.1(a) (cite as "S.D.Ind. Local A.D.R. Rule __")

United States Bankruptcy Court for the Southern District of Indiana
> Bankr. S.D. Ind. R. 1001-1(c) (cite as "S.D.Ind. B-__")

United States District Courts for the Northern and Southern Districts of Iowa
> N.D. & S.D. Iowa Civ. R. 1(a) (cite as "LR __")

▸ N.D. & S.D. Iowa Civ. R. 10(e) (citation of statutes)
▸ N.D. & S.D. Iowa Crim. R. 1(a) (cite as "LCrR __")

United States Bankruptcy Court for the Northern District of Iowa
▸ Bankr. N.D. Iowa 9004-1(a) (cite as "Local Rule __" or "L.R. __")

United States District Court for the District of Kansas
▸ D. Kan. R. 1.1 (cite as "D. Kan. Rule __")
▸ D. Kan. R. 7.6(b) (citation of unpublished opinions)
▸ D. Kan. R. 83.1.2(a) (cite standing orders as "D. Kan. S.O. __")

United States Bankruptcy Court for the District of Kansas
▸ Bankr. D. Kan. R. 1001.1(b) (cite as "D. Kan. LBR __")
▸ Bankr. D. Kan. R. 9013.1(c) (citation of unpublished decisions)
▸ Bankr. D. Kan. R. 9029.2 (cite standing orders as "D. Kan. Bk. S.O. __")

United States District Courts for the Eastern and Western Districts of Kentucky
▸ Joint Ky. Loc. Civ. Prac. R. 85.1 (cite as "LR __")
▸ Joint Ky. Loc. Crim. Prac. R. 60.1 (cite as "LCrR __")

United States Bankruptcy Court for the Eastern District of Kentucky
▸ Bankr. E.D. Ky. R. 1001-1 (cite as "E.D. Ky. LBR __-__")

United States District Courts for the Eastern, Middle, and Western Districts of Louisiana
▸ Preamble to Unif. Loc. R. La. (cite Local Civil Rules as "LR __," Local Admiralty Rules as "LAR __," and Local Criminal Rules as "LCrR __")

United States Bankruptcy Court for the Eastern District of Louisiana
▸ Preamble to Bankr. E.D. La. R. (cite as "LBR __")

United States Bankruptcy Court for the Western District of Louisiana
▸ Table of Rules to Bankr. W.D. La. R. (cite as "W.D. La. LBR __")

United States Bankruptcy Court for the District of Maine
▸ Bankr. D. Me. R. 1001-1 (cite as "D. Me. LBR __-__")

United States District Court for the District of Maryland
▸ D. Md. Loc. Adm. R. (a)(2) (cite as " LAR__")

United States Bankruptcy Court for the District of Maryland
▸ D. Md. Admin. Order 07-02 (cite as "MD LOCAL BANKRUPTCY RULES")

United States District Court for the District of Massachusetts
▸ D. Mass. R. 1.1 (cite as "LR, D. Mass" or "LR")

United States District Court for the Eastern District of Michigan
▸ E.D. Mich. R. 1.1(a) (cite as "E.D.Mich. LR __" or "E.D.Mich. LCrR __")
▸ E.D. Mich. ECF R. 5(d) (use of hyperlinks)

United States Bankruptcy Court for the Eastern District of Michigan
▸ Bankr. E.D. Mich. R. 9029-1(b) (cite rules as "E.D. Mich. LBR___-__")
▸ Bankr. E.D. Mich. ECF R. 8(b) (use of hyperlinks)

United States District Court for the Western District of Michigan
▸ W.D. Mich. Civ. R. 1.2 (cite as "W.D.Mich. LCivR __")

W.D. Mich. Crim. R. 1.2 (cite as "W.D. Mich. LCrR __")

United States Bankruptcy Court for the Western District of Michigan
Bankr. W.D. Mich. R. 1001(b) (cite as "LBR __")

United States District Court for the District of Minnesota
D. Minn. R. 1.1(a) (cite as "D.Minn. LR __")

D. Minn. CM/ECF Civ. P. II(M)(4) (use of hyperlinks)

D. Minn. CM/ECF Crim. P. II(K)(4) (use of hyperlinks)

United States Bankruptcy Court for the District of Minnesota
Bankr. D. Minn. R. 9029-1(d) (cite rules as "Local Rule __" and forms as "Local Form __")

United States District Court for the Western District of Missouri
Preface to W.D. Mo. R. (cite as "Local Rule __" or "L.R. __")

United States District Court for the District of Montana
D. Mont. R. 1.1 (cite as "L. R. __")

D. Mont. R. 10.3(a) (required use of Bluebook or ALWD Manual; use of pinpoint citations)

D. Mont. R. 10.3(b) (citation of various types of legal authority)

D. Mont. R. 10.3(c) (use of hyperlinks)

United States Bankruptcy Court for the District of Montana
Bankr. D. Mont. R. 1001-1(a) (cite rules as "Mont. LBR __" and forms as "Mont. LBF __")

Bankr. D. Mont. R. 5005-3(a)(7) (required use of Bluebook or ALWD Manual)

United States District Court for the District of Nebraska
D. Neb. Gen. R. 1.1(a) (cite as "NEGenR __")

D. Neb. Civ. R. 10.1(a)(4) (use of hyperlinks)

D. Neb. Civ. R. 85.1 (cite as "NECivR __")

D. Neb. Crim. R. 49.2(a)(4) (use of hyperlinks)

D. Neb. Crim. R. 61.1 (cite as "NECrimR __")

United States Bankruptcy Court for the District of Nebraska
Bankr. D. Neb. R. 1001-1.A (cite as "Neb. R. Bankr. P. __" or "Local Rule __")

United States District Court for the District of Nevada
D. Nev. R. 7-3 (citation of various types of legal authority)

D. Nev. R. 12(5) (citation of cases)

D. Nev. Crim. R. 47-8 (citation of various types of legal authority)

United States District Court for the District of New Hampshire
D.N.H. R. 1.1(a) (cite as "LR __")

D.N.H. R. 5.3 (citation of cases)

D.N.H. Crim. R. 1.1(a) (cite as "LCrR __")

United States Bankruptcy Court for the District of New Hampshire
Preface to Bankr. D.N.H. R. (cite as "LBR")

Bankr. D.N.H. R. 1050-1 (citation of cases)

Bankr. D.N.H. R. 9029-2 (cite administrative orders as "AO")

United States District Court for the District of New Jersey
- D.N.J. Civ. R. 9.2(a)(2) (cite local admiralty and maritime rules as "LAMR __")
- D.N.J. Civ. R. 85.1 (cite as "L.Civ.R.")
- D.N.J. Crim. R. 60.1 (cite as "L.Cr.R.")

United States Bankruptcy Court for the District of New Jersey
- Bankr. D.N.J. R. 1001-1(a) (cite as "District of New Jersey Local Bankruptcy Rules, D.N.J. LBR __")

United States District Court for the District of New Mexico
- D.N.M. Civ. R. 1.1 (cite as "D.N.M.LR-Civ. __")
- D.N.M. Crim. R. 1.1 (cite as "D.N.M.LR-Cr. __")

United States Bankruptcy Court for the District of New Mexico
- Preface to Bankr. D.N.M. R. (cite as "NM LBR __")

United States Bankruptcy Court for the Eastern District of New York
- Bankr. E.D.N.Y. R. 1001-1(b)(ii) (cite as "E.D.N.Y. LBR __")

United States District Court for the Northern District of New York
- N.D.N.Y. R. 1.1 (cite as "L.R. __")
- N.D.N.Y. R. 7.1(a)(1) (citation of cases)
- N.D.N.Y. R. Crim. P. 1.1 (cite as "L. R. Cr. P. __")
- N.D.N.Y. Loc. Adm. & Mar. R. A(a)(3) (cite as "LAR")

United States Bankruptcy Court for the Northern District of New York
- Bankr. N.D.N.Y. R. 1001-1(a) (cite as "Local Bankruptcy Rule __-__" or "LBR __-__")

United States Bankruptcy Court for the Southern District of New York
- Bankr. S.D.N.Y. R. 1001-1(a) & cmt. (citation of local bankruptcy rules)

United States District Court for the Eastern District of North Carolina
- E.D.N.C. Civ. R. 1.1 (cite as "Local Civil Rule __, EDNC")
- E.D.N.C. Civ. R. 7.2(b)-(d) (citation of cases)
- E.D.N.C. Crim. R. 1.1 (cite as "Local Criminal Rule __, EDNC")
- E.D.N.C. Crim. R. 47.2(b)-(d) (citation of cases)
- E.D.N.C. Loc. Pat. R. 301.1 (cite as "Local Patent Rule __, EDNC")

United States Bankruptcy Court for the Eastern District of North Carolina
- Preface to Bankr. E.D.N.C. R. (cite as "E.D.N.C. LBR __")

United States District Court for the Middle District of North Carolina
- M.D.N.C. R. 7.2(b)-(d) (citation of cases)
- Preface to M.D.N.C. Civ. R. (cite as "LR __")
- Preface to M.D.N.C. Crim. R. (cite as "LCrR __")

United States District Court for the District of North Dakota
- Preface to D.N.D. R. (cite as "D.N.D. Gen. L. R. __," "D.N.D. Civ. L. R. __," or "D.N.D. Crim. L. R. __")

United States District Court for the Southern District of Ohio
- S.D. Ohio Civ. R. 1.1(a) (cite as "S. D. Ohio Civ. R. __")
- S.D. Ohio Civ. R. 7.2(b) (citation of various types of legal authority)

> S.D. Ohio Crim. R. 1.1(a) (cite as "S. D. Ohio Crim. R. __")

United States District Court for the Northern District of Ohio
> N.D. Ohio R. 1.1(b) (cite local rules as "Local Rules" or "LR" and Supplemental Local Rules for Certain Admiralty and Maritime Claims as "Local Supplemental Rule" or "LSuppR")
> N.D. Ohio Crim. R. 1.1(b) (cite as "LCrR")

United States Bankruptcy Court for the Northern District of Ohio
> Bankr. N.D. Ohio R. 1001-1(b) (cite as "Local Bankruptcy Rule(s)" or "LBR")

United States District Court for the Eastern District of Oklahoma
> E.D. Okla. Civ. R. 1.2(e) (cite as "LCvR __")
> E.D. Okla. Crim. R. 1.1(A) (cite as "LCrR __")

United States District Court for the Northern District of Oklahoma
> N.D. Okla. Civ. R. 1.2(e) (cite as "LCvR __")
> N.D. Okla. Crim. R. 1.1(A) (cite as "N.D. LCR __")

United States Bankruptcy Court for the Northern District of Oklahoma
> Bankr. N.D. Okla. R. 1001-1(B) (cite as "Bankr. N.D. Okla. LR __," "LR __," or "Local Rule __")

United States District Court for the Western District of Oklahoma
> W.D. Okla. Civ. R. 1.2(d) (cite as "LCvR __")
> W.D. Okla. Crim. R. 1.2(e) (cite as "LCrR __")

United States District Court for the District of Oregon
> D. Or. R. 1.3 ("LR __.__")
> D. Or. R. 100.8 (use of hyperlinks)

United States Bankruptcy Court for the Eastern District of Pennsylvania
> Bankr. E.D. Pa. R. 1001-1(b) (cite rules as "L.B.R." and forms as "L.B.F.")

United States Bankruptcy Court for the Middle District of Pennsylvania
> Bankr. M.D. Pa. R. 1001-1(b) (cite rules as "L.B.R." and forms as "L.B.F.")

United States Bankruptcy Court for the Western District of Pennsylvania
> Bankr. W.D. Pa. R. 1001-1 (cite as "Local Rules (LR)")

United States District Court for the District of Rhode Island
> D.R.I. R. 101 (cite as "Local Rules" or "DRI LR __")

United States Bankruptcy Court for the District of Rhode Island
> Bankr. D.R.I. R. 1001-1(a) (cite as "R.I. LBR" or "LBR")

United States District Court for the District of South Carolina
> D.S.C. Civ. R. 1.01 (cite as "Local Civil Rule __ DSC")
> D.S.C. Crim. R. 1.01 (cite as "Local Criminal Rule __ DSC")

United States Bankruptcy Court for the District of South Carolina
> Bankr. D.S.C. R. 1001-1(a) (cite as "SC LBR __")

United States District Court for the District of South Dakota
> D.S.D. R. 1.1(A) (cite as "D.S.D. CIV. LR __")

United States Bankruptcy Court for the District of South Dakota
> Bankr. D.S.D. R. 1001-1 (cite as "LBR __" or "D.S.D. LBR __")

United States District Court for the Eastern District of Tennessee
> E.D. Tenn. R. 1.1(a) (cite as "E.D.TN. LR __")
> E.D. Tenn. R. 7.4 (citation of various types of authority)

United States Bankruptcy Court for the Eastern District of Tennessee
> Bankr. E.D. Tenn. R. 1001-1(b) (cite as "E.D. Tenn. LBR __")

United States District Court for the Middle District of Tennessee
> M.D. Tenn. R. 7.01(e)(2)-(5) (citation of various types of legal authority)
> M.D. Tenn. Loc. R. Mag. P. 1(c) (cite as "L.R.M.J. __")

United States Bankruptcy Court for the Middle District of Tennessee
> Bankr. M.D. Tenn. R. 9029-1(b) (cite as "LBR __")

United States District Court for the Western District of Tennessee
> W.D. Tenn. Civ. R. 83.6 (citation of cases and statutes)

United States Bankruptcy Court for the Western District of Tennessee
> Bankr. W.D. Tenn. R. 2001-1(b) (citation of cases)
> Bankr. W.D. Tenn. R. 9029-1(b) (cite as "L.B.R. __")

United States District Court for the Eastern District of Texas
> E.D. Tex. Civ. R. 1(b) (cite as "Local Civil Rules")
> E.D. Tex. Crim. R. 1(b) (cite as "Local Criminal Rules")
> E.D. Tex. R. App. J. (a)(3) (cite local admiralty rules as "LAR __")

United States Bankruptcy Court for the Northern District of Texas
> Bankr. N.D. Tex. R. 1001.1 (cite as "N.D. TX L.B.R. __")

United States Bankruptcy Court for the Southern District of Texas
> Bankr. S.D. Tex. R. 1001(a) (cite as "BLR __")

United States District Court for the Western District of Texas
> W.D. Tex. Civ. R. 1(c) (cite as "Local Court Rules")

United States District Court for the District of Utah
> D. Utah Civ. R. 7-2 (citation of unpublished decisions)
> D. Utah, Local Rules of Practice Information, <u>available at</u> http://www.utd.uscourts.gov/documents/local_rules_info.html (cite local rules as "DUCiv R __-__" and criminal rules as "DUCrim R __-__")

United States Bankruptcy Court for the District of Utah
> Bankr. D. Utah R. 1001-1(a) (cite as "Bankr. D. Ut. LBR __" or "Local Rule __")
> Bankr. D. Utah R. 9013-1(d)(3) (citation of unpublished decisions)

United States District Court for the District of Vermont
> D. Vt. R. 1.1(a) (cite civil rules as "L.R. __" and criminal rules as "L.Cr.R. __")

United States Bankruptcy Court for the District of Vermont
> Bankr. D. Vt. R. 9029-1(a)(1) (cite as "Vt. LBR __")
> Bankr. D. Vt. R. 9029-1(a)(2) (cite supplement appendices as "Vt. LB Appendix __"; cite supplement forms as "Vt. LB Form __")

United States District Court for the Eastern District of Virginia
- E.D. Va. Loc. Adm. R. (a)(3) (cite as "LAR __")

United States District Court for the Eastern District of Washington
- E.D. Wash. R. Intro. (cite as "LR __" or "LMR __")
- E.D. Wash. R. 7.1(g) (citation of cases)

United States Bankruptcy Court for the Eastern District of Washington
- Bankr. E.D. Wash. R. 9013-1(d)(2) (citation of cases)

United States District Court for the Western District of Washington
- W.D. Wash. R. 1 (cite as "Local Rules, W.D.Wash.")
- W.D. Wash. Supp. Adm. R. 100 (cite as "Local Admiralty Rules")

United States District Court for the Northern District of West Virginia
- Preface to N.D. W. Va. R. (citation of local rules)

United States Bankruptcy Court for the Northern District of West Virginia
- Preface to Bankr. N.D. W. Va. R. (cite as "N.D.W.V. LBR __-__")

United States District Court for the District of Wyoming
- D. Wyo. Civ. R. 1.1(a) (cite as "U.S.D.C.L.R. __")
- D. Wyo. Crim. R. 1.1(a) (cite as "L.Cr.R. __")

United States Bankruptcy Court for the District of Wyoming
- Bankr. D. Wyo. R. 1001-1(A) (cite as "Wyoming LBR __-__")

United States District Court for the District of Guam
- D. Guam R. 1.1(a) (citation of various rules)
- D. Guam R. 4.1(b) (required use of Bluebook)

United States District Court for the Northern Mariana Islands
- D. N. Mar. I. Civ. R. 1.1(a) (cite as "LR __")
- D. N. Mar. I. Civ. R. 5.2(c) (citation form)
- Preface to D. N. Mar. I. Crim. R. (cite as "LCrR __")
- Preface to D. N. Mar. I. Bankr. R. (cite as "LBR __")
- Preface to D. N. Mar. I. Disc. R. (cite as "LDR __")
- Preface to D. N. Mar. I. Loc. Adm. R. (cite as "LAR __")

United States District Court for the District of Puerto Rico
- D.P.R. Civ. R. 1(e) (citation of local civil rules)
- D.P.R. Crim. R. 101(e) (citation of local criminal rules)

United States Bankruptcy Court for the District of Puerto Rico
- Bankr. D.P.R. R. 1001-1(a) (cite as "P.R. LBR" or "LBR")

United States District Court for the District of the Virgin Islands
- D.V.I. Civ. R. 1.1(a) (cite as "LRCi __")
- D.V.I. Civ. R. 5.4(m)(2) (use of hyperlinks)
- D.V.I. Crim. R. 1.1(a) (cite as "LRCr __")
- D.V.I. R. App. P. 1(a) (cite as "V.I. R. App. P." or "VIRAP")
- D.V.I. R. App. P. 22(i) (citation of cases)
- D.V.I. Bankr. R. 1001-1 (cite as "Local Bankruptcy Rules (LBR)")

United States Court of Appeals for the Armed Forces
- C.A.A.F. R. 37(c)(2) (required use of Bluebook)

United States Court of International Trade
> U.S. Ct. Int'l Trade R. 81 (citation of various types of legal authority)

United States Tax Court
> T.C. R. 23(f) (citation of cases)

United States Court of Appeals for Veterans Claims
> Vet. App. R. 30 (citation of nonprecedential and supplemental authority)
> Order re Citing Rules (Vet. App. Apr. 4, 1991) (cite as "U.S. Vet. App. R.")

BT2.2 State Courts

Alabama
> Ala. R. App. P. 28(a)(10) (required use of <u>Bluebook</u>, <u>ALWD Citation Manual</u>, or style and form used in opinions of Ala. Sup. Ct.)
> Ala. R. App. P. 53(d) (citation of "no opinion" affirmance orders)
> Ala. R. Evid. 1102 (cite as "Ala. R. Evid. __")

Alaska
> Alaska R. App. P. 214(d) (citation of unpublished decisions)
> Alaska Stat. § 01.05.011 (2008) (cite as "AS __")

Arizona
> Ariz. R. Civ. App. P. 13(a)(6) (citation of cases)
> Ariz. R. Civ. App. P. 28(c) (citation of memorandum decisions)
> Ariz. R. Sup. Ct. 111(c) (citation of memorandum decisions)
> Ariz. Rev. Stat. Ann. § 1-101 (2002) (cite as "A.R.S. __")

Arkansas
> Ark. R. Civ. P. 85 (cite as "ARCP")
> Ark. R. Evid. 1102 (cite as "A.R.E. Rule __")
> Ark. Sup. Ct. R. 4-2(a)(7) (citation of cases)
> Ark. Sup. Ct. R. 5-2(b) to (d) (citation of Ark. Sup. Ct. and Ark. Ct. App. published and unpublished opinions)
> Ark. Code Ann. § 1-2-113(c) (1987) (cite as "A.C.A. __")

California
> Cal. R. Ct. 1.200 (required use of either <u>California Style Manual</u> or <u>Bluebook</u>)
> Cal. R. Ct. 3.1113(c) (citation of cases)
> Larry D. Dershem, <u>California Legal Research Handbook</u> ch. 4-9 (2d ed. 2008)
> Edward W. Jessen, <u>California Style Manual</u> (4th ed. 2000)
> Hether C. Macfarlane & Suzanne E. Rowe, <u>California Legal Research</u> ch. 11 (2008)

Colorado
> Colo. R. Civ. P. 1(c) (cite as "C.R.C.P. __")
> Colo. App. R. 58 (cite as "C.A.R. __")
> Colo. R. Prob. P. 1(b) (cite as "C.R.P.P. __")
> Colo. R.P. Small Cl. Cts. 501(a) (cite as "C.R.C.P. __")

- Colo. R. Prof'l Conduct 9 (cite as "Colo. RPC")
- Colo. R. County Ct. Civ. P. 301(b) (cite as "C.R.C.P. __")

Connecticut
- Conn. R. App. P. § 67-11 (citation of cases)

Delaware
- Del. Sup. Ct. R. 14(g)(iii), 93(d)(ii) (citation of unreported opinions; required use of Bluebook for other authority)
- Del. Sup. Ct. Internal Operating P. X(8) (citation of Del. Sup. Ct. orders)
- Del. Ch. Ct. R. 171(g) (citation of cases)
- Del. Super. Ct. R. Civ. P. 107(d)(4) (citation of unreported opinions; required use of Bluebook)
- Del. Super. Ct. Crim. P. 60 (cite as "Super. Ct. Crim. R. __")
- Del. Ct. C.P. Civ. R. 107(c)(4) (citation of cases; required use of Bluebook)
- Del. Ct. C.P. Civ. R. 107(c)(5) (citation of unreported opinions and orders)
- Del. Fam. Ct. R. Civ. P. 7(b)(6) (citation of Del. cases; required use of Bluebook; citation of unreported and memorandum opinions)
- Del. Fam. Ct. R. Civ. P. 10(d) (citation of Del. cases; required use of Bluebook; citation of unreported and memorandum opinions)
- Del. Fam. Ct. R. Civ. P. 107(c)(5) (citation of Del. cases; required use of Bluebook)
- Del. Fam. Ct. R. Civ. P. 107(f) (citation of unreported and memorandum decisions)
- Del. Code Ann. tit. 1 § 101(b) (2001) (cite as "__ Del. C. __")

District of Columbia
- D.C. Ct. App. R. 28(h) (citation of administrative agency materials)
- D.C. Super. Ct. R. Civ. P. 12-I(e) (citation of cases from D.C. Cir.)
- D.C. Super. Ct. R. Crim. P. 47-I(b) (citation of cases from D.C. Cir.)
- D.C. Super. Ct. R. Crim. P. 60 (cite as "Superior Court Rules—Criminal" or "SCR—Criminal")
- D.C. Super. Ct. Dom. Rel. R. 7(b)(1)(A) (citation of cases from D.C. Cir.)
- D.C. Super. Ct. Fam. Div. R. Intro. N. (citation of Family Division rules)
- D.C. Super. Ct. Juv. P.R. 47, 47-I(b) (citation of cases from D.C. Cir.)
- D.C. Super. Ct. Land. & Ten. R. 13(a) (citation of cases from D.C. Cir.)
- D.C. Super. Ct. Negl. & Abuse R. 28(a) (citation of cases from D.C. Cir.)
- D.C. Super. Ct. Small Cl. R. 13(a) (citation of cases from D.C. Cir.)
- D.C. Super. Ct. Tax R. 9(b) (citation of cases from D.C. Cir.)
- D.C. Court of Appeals, Citation and Style Guide (2009), available at http://www.dcappeals.gov/dccourts/docs/RevisedCitationGuide2009.pdf
- Leah F. Chanin et al., Legal Research in the District of Columbia, Maryland and Virginia app. V (2d ed. 2000)

Florida
- Fla. R. App. P. 9.010 (cite as "Fla. R. App. P. __")

> Fla. R. App. P. 9.800 (citation of various types of legal authority; required use of <u>Bluebook</u> or <u>Florida Style Manual</u> for remainder)

> Fla. Small Cl. R. 7.010(a) (cite as "Fla. Sm. Cl. R. __")

> Fla. State Univ. Law Review, <u>Florida Style Manual</u>, 30 Fla. St. U. L. Rev. i (2003)

> Barbara J. Busharis & Suzanne E. Rowe, <u>Florida Legal Research: Sources, Process, and Analysis</u> ch. 10 (3d ed. 2007)

Georgia

> Ga. Ct. App. R. 24(d) (citation of cases)

> Ga. Code Ann. § 1-1-8(e) (2004) (cite as "O.C.G.A.")

> Leah F. Chanin & Suzanne L. Cassidy, <u>Guide to Georgia Legal Research and Legal History</u> app. V (1990)

> Nancy P. Johnson & Elizabeth G. Adelman, <u>Georgia Legal Research</u> app. A (2007)

Hawaii

> Haw. R. App. P. 1(c) (cite as "HRAP")

> Haw. R. App. P. 28(b)(1) (citation of cases)

> Haw. R. App. P. 35(c) (citation of dispositions)

> Haw. R. Evid. 100 (cite as "Rule __, Hawaii Rules of Evidence, Chapter 626, Hawaii Revised Statutes")

> Haw. R. Penal P. 60 (cite as "Hawai'i Rules of Penal Procedure")

> Haw. Fam. Ct. R. 85 (cite as "HFCR")

> Haw. R. Civ. P. 85 (cite as "Hawai'i Rules of Civil Procedure")

> Haw. Lawyers' Fund R. & Reg. 1 (cite as "LF")

Idaho

> Idaho R. Evid. 101(a) (cite as "I.R.E.")

> Idaho Crim. R. 2(b) (cite as "I.C.R.")

> Idaho App. R. 1 (cite as "I.A.R.")

> Idaho R. Civ. P. 87 (cite as "I.R.C.P.")

> Idaho Juv. R. 60 (cite as "The Idaho Juvenile Rules" or "I.J.R.")

> Idaho Sup. Ct. Internal Operating R. 15(e) (required use of <u>Bluebook</u>)

> Idaho Sup. Ct. Internal Operating R. 15(f) (citation of no unpublished Sup. Ct. opinions)

> Tenielle Fordyce-Ruff & Suzanne E. Rowe, <u>Idaho Legal Research</u> app. A (2008)

Illinois

> Ill. Sup. Ct. R. 6 (citation of various types of legal authority)

> Ill. 2d J. Cir. Ct. R. 18 (citation of cases)

> <u>Preface</u> to <u>Illinois Compiled Statutes Annotated</u> volumes (cite as "__ ILCS __")

Indiana

> Ind. R. App. P. 22 (citation of various types of legal authority)

> Ind. Small Cl. R. 1(B) (cite as "S.C. __")

> Ind. Code § 1-1-1-1 (2002) (cite as "IC")

Iowa

- Iowa R. App. P. 6.904(2) (citation of various types of legal authority)
- Iowa R. Evid. 5.1103 (cite as "Iowa R. Evid. __")
- John D. Edwards, <u>Iowa Legal Research Guide</u> 90-92 (2003)

Kansas

- Kan. Sup. Ct. R. 6.08 (citation of cases within briefs)
- Kan. R. Prof'l Conduct Prefatory R. (cite as "KRPC __")
- Title pages to <u>Kansas Statutes Annotated</u> volumes (cite as "K.S.A. __")
- Joseph A. Custer & Christopher L. Steadham, <u>Kansas Legal Research</u> app. A (2008)

Kentucky

- Ky. R. Civ. P. 1(1) (cite as "Civil Rules" or "CR")
- Ky. R. Civ. P. 76.12(4)(g) (citation of Ky. statutes and cases)
- Ky. R. Civ. P. 76.28(4)(c) (citation of unpublished decisions)
- Ky. R. Crim. P. 1.02(1) (cite as "Criminal Rules" or "RCr")
- Ky. R. Evid. 101 (cite as "KRE __")
- Ky. Sup. Ct. R. 1.000 (cite as "SCR")
- Kurt X. Metzmeier et al., <u>Kentucky Legal Research Manual</u> ch. 12 (3d ed. 2005)

Louisiana

- La. Code Civ. P. 2168 (citation of unpublished opinions)
- La. Code Crim. P. art. 1 (cite as "C.Cr.P.")
- La. Sup. Ct. Gen. Admin. R. Pt. G. § 8 (citation of La. cases; public domain citation)
- La. Ct. App. Unif. R. 2-12.4 (citation of cases)
- Win-Shin S. Chiang, <u>Louisiana Legal Research</u> app. M (2d ed. 1990) (commonly used abbreviations)

Maine

- Me. Admin. Order, No. SJC-216 (Aug. 20, 1996) (citation of Me. cases, memorandum decisions, and summary orders)
- <u>Preface</u> to <u>Maine Revised Statutes Annotated</u> volumes (cite as "M.R.S.A. __")
- Me. Law Review, <u>Uniform Maine Citations</u> (3d ed. 2003), <u>available at</u> http://mainelaw.maine.edu/academics/pdf/UMC3rdupdate2009.pdf

Maryland

- Md. R. 1-103 (cite as "Md. Rules" or "Rule __")
- Md. R. 1-104(b) (citation of unreported Ct. App. and Ct. Special App. opinions)
- Md. R. 6-103 (cite settlement of decedents' estates rules as "Md. Rules" or "Rule __")
- Md. R. 8-504(a)(1) (citation of Md. cases)
- Leah F. Chanin et al., <u>Legal Research in the District of Columbia, Maryland and Virginia</u> §§ 4.2-4.3 (2d ed. 2000)

Massachusetts

- Mass. R. App. P. 16(g) (citation of cases and Mass. statutes)

> Mass. Dist. & Mun. App. Div. R. 16(g) (citation of cases and Mass. statutes)

> Preface to Massachusetts General Laws Annotated volumes (citation of Massachusetts General Laws Annotated)

Michigan

> Mich. Ct. R. 1.101 (cite as "MCR __")

> Mich. Ct. R. 7.215(c)(1) (citation of unpublished Ct. App. opinions)

> Mich. R. Evid. 1102 (cite as "MRE")

> Mich. Prof'l Conduct R. 1.0(a) (cite as "MRPC __")

> Preface to Michigan Compiled Laws Annotated volumes (citation of Michigan Compiled Laws Annotated)

> Mich. Supreme Court, Michigan Uniform System of Citation (2006), available at http://coa.courts.mi.gov/rules/documents/9Michigan UniformSystemOfCitation.pdf

Minnesota

> Minn. R. Civ. P. 85 (cite as "Rules of Civil Procedure")

> Minn. R. Civ. App. P. 136.01(1)(b) (citation of unpublished and order opinions)

> Minn. R. Civ. App. P. 146 (cite as "Rules of Civil Appellate Procedure")

> Minn. Civ. Trialbook § 1 (cite as "Minn. Civ. Trialbook § __")

> Minn. Gen. R. Prac. 1.01 (cite as "Minn. Gen. R. Prac. __")

Mississippi

> Miss. R. Civ. P. 85 (cite as "M.R.C.P. __")

> Miss. R. App. P. 28(e) (citation of Miss. cases)

> Miss. R. App. P. 49 (cite as "M.R.A.P.")

> Miss. R. Evid. 1102 (cite as "M.R.E. __")

> Miss. Elec. & Photo. Cov. J.P.R. 1 (cite as "MREPC")

> Miss. Unif. Cir. & County Ct. R. 1.01 (cite as "URCCC __")

Missouri

> Mo. Sup. Ct. R. 1.01 (cite as "Rule __")

> Mo. Sup. Ct. R. 84.16(b) (citation of memorandum decisions and written orders)

Montana

> Mont. R. App. P. 1 (cite as "M. R. App. P.")

> Mont. Sup. Ct. Internal Operating R. § I.3(c) (Mar. 1, 2008) (noncitable opinions)

> Order In re: Opinion Forms and Citation Standards of the Supreme Court of Montana; and the Adoption of Public Domain and Neutral-Format Citation (Dec. 16, 1997)

> Order In the Matter of Amending Citation Standards for the Montana Supreme Court (Jan. 22, 2009)

> Preface to Mont. Code Ann. (2009) (cite as "MCA")

Nebraska

> Preface to Neb. Ct. R. (citation of various rules)

> Neb. Sup. Ct. R. § 2-109(C)(4)-(6) (citation of various types of legal authority)

- Neb. Unif. Dist. Ct. R. § 6-1505(C) (citation of Neb. cases and other authorities)
- Neb. Worker's Comp. R. 16(B)(4)-(6) (citation of various types of legal authority)
- <u>Preface</u> to <u>Reissue Revised Statutes of Nebraska</u> volumes (cite as "REISSUE REVISED STATUTES OF NEBRASKA, 2008" in full, or "R.R.S.2008" for abbreviation)

Nevada

- Nev. R. Civ. P. 85 (cite as "N.R.C.P.")
- Nev. R. App. P. 48 (cite as "N.R.A.P.")
- Nev. R. Admin. Docket § 14 (cite as "NRAD")
- Nev. Short Trial R. 35 (cite as "N.S.T.R.")
- Nev. Sup. Ct. R. 1 (cite as "S.C.R.")
- Nev. 1st J. Dist. Ct. R. 1.2 (cite as "F.J.D.C.R.")
- Nev. 2d J. Dist. Ct. R. 1.1 (cite rules 1-26 as "WDCR"; cite rules 27-57 as "WDFCR")
- Nev. 3d J. Dist. Ct. R. 1.B (cite as "T.J.D.C.R.")
- Nev. 4th J. Dist. Ct. R. 1.1 (cite as "4JDCR")
- Nev. 7th J. Dist. Ct. R. 1.1 (cite as "7JDCR")
- Nev. 8th J. Dist. Ct. R. 1.01 (cite as "EDCR")
- Nev. 9th J. Dist. Ct. R. 1(a) (cite as "N.J.D.C.R.")
- Nev. Justice Ct. R. Civ. P. 85 (cite as "JCRCP")
- Nev. Rev. Stat. 220.170(4) (2000) (cite as "NRS")

New Hampshire

- N.H. Sup. Ct. R. 12-D(3) (citation of orders)
- N.H. Sup. Ct. R. 16(9) (citation of cases)
- N.H. Sup. Ct. R. 25(5) (citation of summary dispositions)
- <u>Preface</u> to <u>New Hampshire Revised Statutes Annotated</u> volumes (cite as "RSA __")

New Jersey

- N.J. Ct. R. 1:1-3 (cite as "R. __")
- N.J. R. App. Prac. 2:6-2(a)(5) (citation of cases)
- N.J. R. Evid. 1103 (cite as "N.J.R.E.")
- <u>Preface</u> to <u>New Jersey Statutes Annotated</u> volumes (cite as "N.J.S.A. __")
- Paul Axel-Lute & Molly Brownfield, <u>New Jersey Legal Research Handbook</u> (5th ed. 2008)
- <u>New Jersey Manual on Style for Judicial Opinions</u> (2004), <u>available at</u> http://www.judiciary.state.nj.us/appdiv/manualonstyle.pdf

New Mexico

- N.M. R. App. P. 12-213(E) (citation of N.M. cases and other authorities)
- N.M. Sup. Ct. R. 23-112 (citation of N.M. authorities; required use of <u>Bluebook</u> for other authorities)
- N.M. Dist. Ct. R. Crim. P. 5-101(D) (cite as "NMRA, Rule 5-__")
- N.M. Magis. Ct. R. Civ. P. 2-101(D) (cite as "NMRA, Rule 2-__")

> N.M. Magis. Ct. R. Crim. P. 6-101(D) (cite as "NMRA, Rule 6-__")

> N.M. Metro. Ct. R. Civ. P. 3-101(D) (cite as "NMRA, Rule 3-__")

> N.M. Metro. Ct. R. Crim. P. 7-101(D) (cite as "NMRA, Rule 7-__")

> N.M. Mun. Ct. R.P. 8-101(D) (cite as "NMRA, Rule 8-__")

> N.M. Child. Ct. R. 10-101(E) (cite as "Rule 10-__ NMRA")

New York

> N.Y. C.P.L.R. 5529(e) (McKinney 2003) (citation of N.Y. cases; citation of other decisions)

> N.Y. Ct. App. R. 500.1(g), 510.1(a) (citation of N.Y. cases)

> N.Y. Sup. Ct. App. Div. 1st Dept. R. 600.10(a)(11) (citation of cases)

> N.Y. Sup. Ct. App. Div. 4th Dept. R. 1000.4(f)(7) (citation of cases)

> Preface to McKinney's Consolidated Laws of New York Annotated volumes (cite to volume name and section number)

> Elizabeth G. Adelman & Suzanne E. Rowe, New York Legal Research app. A (2008)

> William H. Manz, Gibson's New York Legal Research Guide (3d ed. 2004)

> New York State Law Reporting Bureau, Official Reports Style Manual (2007), available at http://www.courts.state.ny.us/reporter/New_Styman.htm

> St. John's L. Rev. Ass'n, New York Rules of Citation (William H. Manz ed., 5th ed. 2005)

North Carolina

> N.C. R. App. P. 30(e)(3) (citation of unpublished opinions)

> N.C. R. App. P. 1(a) (cite as "N.C. R. App. P. __")

> N.C. R. App. P. app. B. (required use of most recent ed. of Bluebook; inclusion of citation to official state reporters)

North Dakota

> N.D. R. Ct. 11.6 (public domain case citations)

> N.D. R. Ct. 11.7 (cite as "N.D.R.Ct.")

> N.D. R. Civ. P. 85 (cite as "N.D.R.Civ.P.")

> N.D. R. Crim. P. 60 (cite as "N.D.R.Crim.P.")

> N.D. R. App. P. 48 (cite as "N.D.R.App.P.")

> N.D. R. Evid. 1103 (cite as "N.D.R.Ev.")

> N.D. Admis. Prac. R. 18 (cite as "Admission to Practice R.")

> N.D. R. C.L.E. 9 (cite as "N.D.R. Continuing Legal Ed.")

> N.D. R. J. Conduct Comm. 30 (cite as "R. Jud. Conduct Comm.")

> N.D. R. Lawyer Disc. 6.8 (cite as "N.D.R. Lawyer Discipl.")

> N.D. R. Ltd. Prac. X (cite as "R. Ltd. Practice of Law by Law Students")

> N.D. R. Loc. Ct. § 15 (cite as "N.D.R. Local Ct. P.R.")

> N.D. R. Proc. R. § 17 (cite as "N.D.R.Proc.R.")

> N.D. R. Prof'l Conduct 9.1 (cite as "N.D.R. Prof. Conduct")

> N.D. Sup. Ct. Admin. R. 42 (cite as "N.D. Sup. Ct. Admin. R.")

> N.D. Sup. Ct. Admin. Order 10 (cite as "N.D. Sup. Ct. Admin. Order")

N.D. Supreme Court, <u>North Dakota Supreme Court Citation Manual</u>, <u>available at</u> http://www.court.state.nd.us/citation

Ohio

Ohio R. Civ. P. 85 (cite as "Civ. R. ___")

Ohio Crim. R. 60 (cite as "Crim. R. ___")

Ohio R. Evid. 1103 (cite as "Evid. R. ___")

Ohio R. App. P. 42 (cite as "Appellate Rules" or "App. R. ___")

Ohio R. Juv. P. 48 (cite as "Juvenile Rules" or "Juv. R. ___")

Ohio R. Prof'l Conduct Form of Citation (cite as "Prof. Cond. Rule ___")

Ohio Sup. Ct. Prac. R. 21 (cite as "S. Ct. Prac. R. ___")

Ohio Sup. Ct. R. Gov. Bar 20 § 1 (cite as "Gov. Bar R. ___")

Ohio Sup. Ct. R. Rep. Ops. 4(B)-(C) (citation of Ct. App. decisions)

Ohio Sup. Ct. R. Rep. Ops. 9(B) (citation of Ohio opinions)

Ohio Sup. Ct. R. Rep. Ops. 7(A)-(B) (required use of <u>Manual of Citations</u>; citation of cases)

Ohio 1st Dist. Ct. App. R. 6(D)(1)-(3) (citation of cases; required use of <u>Manual of Citations</u>)

Ohio 3d Dist. Ct. App. R. 7(C) (citation of various types of legal authority)

Ohio 6th Dist. Ct. App. R. 23 (cite as "6th Dist.Loc.App.R. ___")

Ohio 8th Dist. Ct. App. Foreword (cite as "Loc.App.R. ___")

Ohio 9th Dist. Ct. App. R. 7(G) (citation of cases; required use of <u>Manual of Citations</u>)

Ohio 10th Dist. Ct. App. R. 7(A)(4) (required use of <u>Manual of Citations</u>)

Ohio 11th Dist. Ct. App. R. 16(B)(4) (citation of cases; required use of <u>Manual of Citations</u>)

Ohio 12th Dist. Ct. App. R. 11(C) (citation of cases)

Ohio Superintendence Ct. R. 1(C) (cite as "Sup. R. ___")

Ohio Mayor's Ct. Ed. & P. R. 1(B) (cite as "May. R. ___")

<u>Preface</u> to <u>Baldwin's Ohio Revised Code Annotated</u> court rules volumes (citation of various rules)

<u>User's Guide, Baldwin's Ohio Rev. Code Ann.</u> at xxxi (2004) (cite Baldwin's Ohio Rev. Code Ann. as "OHIO REV. CODE ANN. § x (Baldwin 20xx)" and <u>Baldwin's Ohio Legis. Serv. Ann.</u> as "20xx Ohio Legis. Serv. Ann. xxx (Baldwin)")

Ohio Supreme Court Reporter's Office, <u>Manual of Citations</u> (1992), <u>available at</u> http://www.sconet.state.oh.us/rod/MANCITEmain.pdf

Ohio Supreme Court Reporter's Office, <u>Revisions to the Manual of Citations</u> (2002), <u>available at</u> http://www.sconet.state.oh.us/rod/Rev_Manual_Cit_02.pdf

Katherine L. Hall & Sara Sampson, <u>Ohio Legal Research</u> ch. 12 (2009)

Oklahoma

Okla. R. Crim. App. 1.0(D) (cite as "Rule ___, Rules of the Oklahoma Court of Criminal Appeals, Title 22, Ch.18, App. (year)")

Okla. Sup. Ct. R. 1.1(a) (cite as "Okla.Sup.Ct.R. ___")

▸ Okla. Sup. Ct. R. 1.11(l) (citation of various types of legal authority)

▸ Okla. Sup. Ct. R. 1.200(b)-(d) (citation of various types of opinions)

▸ Okla. Sup. Ct. R. 1.200(e) (citation of cases; public domain citation)

▸ Okla. Ct. Crim. App. R. 3.5(C) (citation of Okla. Ct. Crim. App., U.S. Sup. Ct., and Okla. Unif. Jury Instr.; citation of unpublished opinions)

▸ <u>Preface</u> to <u>Oklahoma Statutes Annotated</u> volumes (cite as "___ Okl. St. Ann. § ___")

Oregon

▸ Or. R. Civ. P. 1(F) (cite as "ORCP")

▸ Or. R. App. P. 1.10(1) (cite as "ORAP")

▸ Or. R. App. P. 5.20(5) (citation of memorandum opinions)

▸ Or. R. App. P. 5.35(3) (required use of <u>Oregon Appellate Courts Style Manual</u>)

▸ Or. Unif. Trial Ct. R. 1.070(1) (cite as "UTCR")

▸ Or. Unif. Trial Ct. R. 1.070(2) (citation of supplementary rules)

▸ Or. Unif. Trial Ct. R. 2.010(13) (citation of Oregon cases)

▸ Or. Tax Ct. Reg. Div. R. 61 (citation of cases)

▸ <u>Preface</u> to Or. Tax Ct. Reg. Div. R. (cite as "TCR")

▸ <u>Preface</u> to Or. Tax Ct. Magis. Div. R. (cite as "TCR-MD")

▸ <u>Preface</u> to vol. 1, Or. Rev. Stat. at x (2007) (cite as "ORS ___")

▸ Suzanne E. Rowe, <u>Oregon Legal Research</u> app. A (2d ed. 2007)

▸ Or. Judicial Dep't, <u>Oregon Appellate Court Style Manual</u> (2002), <u>available at</u> http://www.publications.ojd.state.or.us/Style%20 Manual%202002.pdf

Pennsylvania

▸ Pa. R. Civ. P. 51 (cite as "Pa.R.C.P. No. ___")

▸ Pa. R. App. P. 101 (cite as "Pa.R.A.P. ___")

▸ Pa. R. App. P. 2119(b) (citation of various types of legal authority)

▸ Pa. Super. Ct. Internal Operating P. § 65.37 (citation of unpublished Super. Ct. decisions)

▸ Pa. Super. Ct., Notice to the Bar, <u>available at</u> http://www.superior. court.state.pa.us/notice_to_the_bar.htm

▸ Frank Y. Liu et al., <u>Pennsylvania Legal Research Handbook</u> (2008)

▸ Pa. Bar Inst., <u>PAstyle: A Pennsylvania Stylebook and Citation Guide for Legal Writing</u> (3d ed. 2008)

Rhode Island

▸ R.I. R. Prac. 1.1 (cite as "R.P.")

▸ R.I. R. Dom. Rel. P. 85 (cite as "R. Dom. Rel. P.")

▸ R.I. R. Juv. P. 36 (cite as "R. Juv. P.")

▸ R.I. Super. Ct. R. Civ. P. 1 (cite as "Super. R. Civ. P.")

▸ R.I. Super. Ct. R. Crim. P. 60 (cite as "Super. R. Crim. P.")

▸ R.I. Super. Ct. R. Prac. 1.1 (cite as "R.P.")

▸ R.I. Dist. Ct. Civ. R. 85 (cite as "D.C.R.")

▸ R.I. Dist. Ct. R. Crim. P. 60 (cite as "Dist. R. Crim. P.")

South Carolina

- S.C. R. Civ. P. 85(a) (cite as "Rule __, SCRCP")
- S.C. R. Crim. P. 38 (cite as "Rule __, SCRCrimP")
- S.C. R. Evid. 1103 (cite as "Rule __, SCRE")
- S.C. App. Ct. R. 101(b) (cite as "Rule __, SCACR")
- S.C. App. Ct. R. 220(a) (citation of memorandum opinions)
- S.C. App. Ct. R. 268 (citation of S.C. authority)
- S.C. Fam. Ct. R. 1 (cite as "Rule __, SCRFC")
- Paula Gail Benson & Deborah Ann Davis, <u>A Guide to South Carolina Legal Research and Citation</u> (1991)

South Dakota

- S.D. R. Civ. P. § 15-6-85 (cite as "RCP")
- S.D. R. App. P. § 15-26A-69.1 (citation of S.D. cases; public domain citation)
- S.D. R. App. P. § 15-26A-93 (cite as "S.D.R.C. App.P. Rule __")
- <u>Preface</u> to <u>South Dakota Codified Laws</u> volumes (cite as "SDCL § __")

Tennessee

- Tenn. R. Crim P. 60 (cite as "Tenn. R. Crim. P.")
- Tenn. R. App. P. 27(h) (citation of various types of legal authority)
- Tenn. Sup. Ct. R. 1 (cite Tennessee Rules of Appellate Procedure as "T.R.A.P." or "Tenn.R.App.P.")
- Tenn. Sup. Ct. R. 4(E)(2) (citation of unpublished opinions)
- Tenn. Sup. Ct. R. 8(Scope)(10) (cite Rules of Professional Conduct as "Tenn. Sup. Ct. R. 8, RPC __")
- Tenn. Sup. Ct. R. 28 § 12 (cite Tennessee Rules of Post-Conviction Procedure as "Tenn. Sup. Ct. R. 28, § __")
- Tenn. Ct. App. R. 12 (citation of unpublished opinions)
- Tenn. Ct. Crim. App. R. 19.4 (citation of unpublished opinions)
- Tenn. 3d J. Dist. Ch. Ct. R. § 1.05 (cite as "Local Rules of Practice, Section __")
- Tenn. 3d J. Dist. Cir. Ct. R. § 1.05 (cite as "Circuit Court Local Rules of Practice, Section __" or "Circuit Court Local Rules of Practice")
- Tenn. 4th J. Dist. Ch. Ct. § 1.05 (cite as "Local Rules of Practice, 4th District, Chancery Court Section __")
- Tenn. 11th J. Dist. R. Civ. Prac. § 1.04 (cite as "LRCP")
- Tenn. 11th J. Dist. Crim. Ct. R. 1 (cite as "L. R. Crim. P.")
- Tenn. 13th J. Dist. Ch. Ct. R. § 1.05 (cite as "Local Rules of Chancery Practice" or "L.R.C.P.")
- Tenn. 13th J. Dist. Cir. Ct. R. § 1.05 (cite as "L.R.P. __")
- Tenn. 16th J. Dist. R. 1.03 (cite as "Rule __ Local Rules of Practice, 16th Judicial District")
- Tenn. 18th J. Dist. R. 1.05 (cite as "Local Rules of Practice, 18th Judicial District")
- Tenn. Code Ann. § 1-2-101(a) (2008) (cite as "Tenn. Code Ann." or "T.C.A.")

Texas

Tex. R. App. P. 47.7 (citation of unpublished Ct. App. opinions)

Tex. Loc. R. 4th Ct. App. 8 cmt. (required use of <u>Bluebook</u> and <u>Texas Rules of Form</u>)

<u>Preface</u> to Tex. Loc. R. 5th Ct. App. (cite as "5th Tex.App. (Dallas) Loc.R.")

<u>Preface</u> to Tex. Loc. R. 8th Ct. App. (cite as "8th Tex.App. (El Paso) Loc.R.")

Tex. Loc. R. 8th Ct. App. 38.1(b) (required use of <u>Bluebook</u> and <u>Texas Rules of Form</u>)

Tex. Loc. R. 10th Ct. App. 12(b) (citation of cases)

Brandon D. Quarles & Matthew C. Cordon, <u>Researching Texas Law</u> ch. 14 (3d ed. 2012)

Tex. L. Rev., <u>The Greenbook: Texas Rules of Form</u> (12th ed. 2010)

Utah

Utah R. Civ. P. 85 (cite as "U.R.C.P.")

Utah Code Jud. Admin. R. 1-101(1)(E) (cite as "CJA")

Utah Supreme Court Standing Order No. 4 (effective Jan. 18, 2000) (citation of Utah opinions released on or after Jan. 1, 1999)

Vermont

Vt. R. Civ. P. 85 (cite as "V.R.C.P.")

Vt. R. App. P. 28.2(b)-(d) (citation of Vermont opinions; citation of other opinions)

Vt. R. App. P. 48 (cite as "V.R.A.P.")

Vt. R. Prob. P. 85 (cite as "V.R.P.P.")

Vt. R. Small Cl. P. 14 (cite as "V.R.S.C.P.")

Vt. Env. Ct. Proc. R. 7 (cite as "V.R.E.C.P.")

<u>Preface</u> of <u>Vermont Statutes Annotated volumes</u> (cite as "__ V.S.A. § __")

Virginia

Va. Sup. Ct. R. 5:17(c)(1), 5:28(a), 5A:20(a), 5A:21(a) (citation of authorities)

Leah F. Chanin et al., <u>Legal Research in the District of Columbia, Maryland and Virginia</u> app. XI (2d ed. 2000)

Washington

Wash. Civ. R. Ct. Ltd. J. 85 (cite as "CRLJ")

Wash. Crim. R. Ct. Ltd. J. 1.8 (cite as "CrRLJ")

Wash. R. App. P. 18.21 (cite as "RAP")

Wash. R. App. Dec. Cts. Ltd. J. 11.9 (cite as "RALJ")

Wash. R. Evid. 1103 (cite as "ER")

Wash. Infraction R. Ct. Ltd. J. 6.3 (cite as "IRLJ")

Wash. Gen. Application Ct. R. 14 app. 1 (general principles of citation)

Wash. Gen. Application Ct. R. 14.1 (citation of unpublished cases)

Wash. Super. Ct. Civ. R. 85 (cite as "CR")

Wash. Super. Ct. Mandatory Arb. R. 8.4 (cite as "MAR")

> Wash. Super. Ct. Spec. P. R. Explanation (cite as "SPR")

> Wash. Juv. Ct. R. 11.21 (cite as "JuCR")

> Office of Reporter of Decisions, <u>Style Sheet</u>, <u>available at</u> http://www.courts.wa.gov/appellate_trial_courts/supreme/?fa=atc_supreme.style

> Wash. Rev. Code Ann. § 1.04.040 (West 2004) (cite as "RCW")

West Virginia

> W. Va. R. Evid. 1102 (cite as "WVRE")

Wisconsin

> Wis. R. App. P. 809.19(1)(e) (citation of authorities; required use of <u>Bluebook</u>)

> Wis. Sup. Ct. R. 80.02 (citation of Wis. cases)

> Wis. Sup. Ct. R. 99.03 (cite as "SCR")

> Wisconsin Supreme Court, <u>Wisconsin Supreme Court Style and Procedures Manual</u> (2004)

> Theodore A. Potter et al., <u>Legal Research in Wisconsin</u> ch. 1.2 (2d ed. 2008)

Wyoming

> Wyo. R. Civ. P. Cir. Ct. 1.01 (cite as "W.R.C.P.C.C.")

> Wyo. R. Crim. P. 60 (cite as "W.R.Cr.P.")

> Wyo. R. Evid. 1103 (cite as "WRE")

> Wyo. Cir. Ct. Unif. R. 1.01 (cite as "U.R.C.C.")

> Order Amending Citation Format (Wyo. Aug. 19, 2005)

BT2.3 Territories

Guam

> <u>How to Cite Guam Law</u> (Sandra E. Cruz comp., 3d ed. 2002), <u>available at</u> http://www.jurispacific.com/public/cite_guamlaw.htm

> Guam Code Ann. tit. 1, § 101(b) (2006) (cite as "GCA")

Northern Mariana Islands

> Gen. Order in re Adoption of Universal Citations for App. Opinions Without Such Citations, no. 2004-100 (N. Mar. I. Jun. 22, 2004)

> Northern Mariana Islands Supreme and Superior Courts, <u>Northern Mariana Islands Style Manual for Judicial Decisions</u> (2002), <u>available at</u> http://www.cnmilaw.org/pdf/style_manual/style_manual.pdf

Puerto Rico

> P.R. Sup. Ct. R. 44(d) (citation of unpublished opinions improper)

> Resolution of P.R. Sup. Ct., June 11, 1999 (citation of electronically distributed Sup. Ct. opinions)

> <u>Preface</u> to <u>Laws of Puerto Rico Annotated</u> volumes (cite as "__ L.P.R.A. § __")

Virgin Islands

> V.I. R. App. P. 15(b) (citation in briefs, motions, and papers; required use of <u>Bluebook</u>)

> V.I. Code Ann. tit. 1, § 1(b) (cite as "__ V.I.C. __")

STRUCTURE AND USE OF CITATIONS 1

Provide citations to authorities so that readers may identify and find those authorities for future research. Citations are made in citation sentences and clauses (rule 1.1) and are introduced by signals. Signals organize authorities and show how those authorities support or relate to a proposition given in the text (rule 1.2). Citation sentences and clauses may contain more than one signal. Order signals according to rule 1.3. Within each signal, arrange authorities according to rule 1.4. Parentheticals may be necessary to explain the relevance of a particular authority to the proposition given in the text (rule 1.5). Certain additional information, specific to that authority, may also be appended according to rule 1.6.

Citation Sentences and Clauses in Law Reviews 1.1

Citations may be made in one of two ways: in citation sentences or in citation clauses. In law review pieces, all citations appear in footnotes appended to the portions of the text to which they refer. For an explanation of citation sentences and clauses in practitioners' documents, see Bluepages B2.

(a) Text. Citations to authorities that support (or contradict) a proposition made in the main text (as opposed to footnote text) are placed in footnotes. A footnote call number should appear at the end of a textual sentence if the cited authority supports (or contradicts) the entire sentence. In contrast, a call number should appear within the sentence next to the portion it supports if the cited authority supports (or contradicts) only that part of the sentence. The call number comes after any punctuation mark—such as a comma, semicolon, or period—with the exception of a dash or a colon. In addition to citation to authorities, a footnote may include textual sentences that are related to the main text to which the footnote is appended.

> ▶ This is sentence one.[1] Sentence two contains two call numbers;[2] however, only one of these — this one[3] — is surprising. Recall one thing[4]: call numbers precede dashes.

(b) Footnotes. If a footnote itself contains an assertion requiring support, a citation to the relevant authority should appear directly after the assertion as either a citation sentence or a citation clause.

(i) **Citation sentences.** Authorities that support (or contradict) an entire footnote sentence are cited in a separate citation sentence immediately after the sentence they support (or contradict). The citation sentence starts with a capital letter and ends with a period.

(ii) **Citation clauses.** Authorities that support (or contradict) only part of a sentence within a footnote are cited in clauses, set off by commas, that immediately follow the proposition they support (or contradict).

(c) Example. The following excerpt illustrates the use of citation sentences and clauses in a law review piece:

> ▶ Some American jurisdictions place the burden of sustaining criminal defenses on the accused.[1] States have required defendants to prove both insanity[2] and self-defense.[3] In several jurisdictions the defendant must even establish that a homicide was accidental.[4]

¹ *See* John Calvin Jeffries, Jr. & Paul B. Stephan III, *Defenses, Presumptions, and Burden of Proof in the Criminal Law*, 88 YALE L.J. 1325, 1329–30 (1979). The authors point out that the use of affirmative defenses may relieve the state of its duty to prove a sufficient factual basis for punishment, *id.* at 1357, and argue that the reasonable doubt standard should not be limited to those facts formally identified as elements of the offense charged, *id.* at 1327.

² *E.g.*, State v. Caryl, 543 P.2d 389, 390 (Mont. 1975); State v. Hinson, 172 S.E.2d 548, 551 (S.C. 1970).

³ *See, e.g.*, Quillen v. State, 110 A.2d 445, 449 (Del. 1955); State v. Skinner, 104 P. 223, 224 (Nev. 1909). *See generally* WAYNE R. LAFAVE & AUSTIN W. SCOTT, JR., HANDBOOK ON CRIMINAL LAW § 8.1, at 704–06 (2d ed. 1986) (discussing the origin of embezzlement and false pretense).

⁴ *See, e.g.*, Chandle v. State, 198 S.E.2d 289, 290 (Ga. 1973); State v. Enlow, 536 S.W.2d 533, 541 (Mo. Ct. App. 1976).

1.2 Introductory Signals

(a) Signals that indicate support.

[no signal] Cited authority (i) directly states the proposition, (ii) identifies the source of a quotation, or (iii) identifies an authority referred to in the text. Use no signal, for example, when directly quoting an authority or when restating numerical data from an authority.

E.g., Cited authority states the proposition; other authorities also state the proposition, but citation to them would not be helpful or is not necessary. "*E.g.*," may be used alone or attached to any other signal (whether supportive or not). When it is attached to another signal, it should be preceded by an italicized comma and followed by a non-italicized comma.

See, e.g.,
But see, e.g.,

Accord "*Accord*" is commonly used when two or more sources state or clearly support the proposition, but the text quotes or refers to only one; the other sources are then introduced by "*accord*." Similarly, the law of one jurisdiction may be cited as being in accord with the law of another.

See Cited authority clearly supports the proposition. "*See*" is used instead of "[no signal]" when the proposition is not directly stated by the cited authority but obviously follows from it; there is an inferential step between the authority cited and the proposition it supports.

See also Cited authority constitutes additional source material that supports the proposition. "*See also*" is commonly used to cite an authority supporting a proposition when authorities that state or directly support the proposition already have been cited or discussed. The use of a parenthetical explanation of the source's relevance (rule 1.5) following a citation introduced by "*see also*" is encouraged.

Cf.   Cited authority supports a proposition different from the main proposition but sufficiently analogous to lend support. Literally, "*cf.*" means "compare." The citation's relevance will usually be clear to the reader only if it is explained. Parenthetical explanations (rule 1.5), however brief, are therefore strongly recommended.

(b) Signal that suggests a useful comparison.

Compare...   Comparison of the authorities cited will offer support for or illus-
[and]...   trate the proposition. When used as a signal, "*Compare*" must be
with...   used in conjunction with "*with*"; the "*with*" is preceded by a
[and]...   comma, as is "*and*" when used. The relevance of the comparison will usually be clear to the reader only if it is explained. Parenthetical explanations (rule 1.5) following each authority are therefore strongly recommended.

> *Compare* Michael H. v. Gerald D., 491 U.S. 110, 121 (1989) (rejecting the claim by a putative natural father of the right to visit his child conceived by a married woman), *and* CATHARINE A. MACKINNON, FEMINISM UNMODIFIED 49 (1987) (contending that what connects all women is their oppression in a sexual hierarchy), *with* Loving v. Virginia, 388 U.S. 1, 12 (1967) (naturalizing language about marriage), Doe v. McConn, 489 F. Supp. 76, 80 (S.D. Tex. 1980) (holding a cross-dressing ordinance unconstitutional as applied to individuals undergoing therapy for sex-reassignment surgery), *and* Kenneth L. Karst, *The Freedom of Intimate Association*, 89 YALE L.J. 624, 631 (1980) ("The denial of the society of an intimate may be partial, as in the case of a parent who loses a contest over child custody but is allowed visitation rights, or virtually total, as when a noncustodial parent is denied visitation rights.").

(c) Signals that indicate contradiction.

Contra   Cited authority directly states the contrary of the proposition. "*Contra*" is used where "[no signal]" would be used for support.

But see   Cited authority clearly supports a proposition contrary to the main proposition. "*But see*" is used where "*see*" would be used for support.

But cf.   Cited authority supports a proposition analogous to the contrary of the main proposition. The use of a parenthetical explanation of the source's relevance (rule 1.5) following a citation introduced by "*but cf.*" is strongly recommended.

"*But*" should be omitted from "*but see*" and "*but cf.*" whenever one of these signals follows another negative signal:

> *Contra* Blake v. Kline, 612 F.2d 718, 723–24 (3d Cir. 1979); *see* CHARLES ALAN WRIGHT, LAW OF FEDERAL COURTS § 48 (4th ed. 1983).

(d) Signal that indicates background material.

See generally Cited authority presents helpful background material related to the proposition. The use of a parenthetical explanation of the source material's relevance (rule 1.5) following each authority introduced by "*see generally*" is encouraged.

(e) Signals as verbs. In footnotes, signals may be used as the verbs of textual sentences. When using signals in this way, include material that would otherwise be included in a parenthetical explanation as part of the sentence itself. Signals should not be italicized when used as verbs in textual sentences (rule 2.1(d)).

Thus:

▶ *See* Christina L. Anderson, Comment, *Double Jeopardy: The Modern Dilemma for Juvenile Justice*, 152 U. PA. L. REV. 1181, 1204–07 (2004) (discussing four main types of restorative justice programs).

becomes:

▶ See Christina L. Anderson, Comment, *Double Jeopardy: The Modern Dilemma for Juvenile Justice*, 152 U. PA. L. REV. 1181, 1204–07 (2004), for a discussion of restorative justice as a reasonable replacement for retributive sanctions.

"*Cf.*" becomes "compare" and "*e.g.*" becomes "for example" when used in this manner.

1.3 Order of Signals

When more than one signal is used, the signals (along with the authorities they introduce) should appear in the order in which those signals are listed in rule 1.2. When "*e.g.*," is used in conjunction with another signal, the other signal's position in rule 1.2 should be used. Note that the order of authorities within each signal must conform to rule 1.4. Signals of the same basic type—supportive, comparative, contradictory, or background (rule 1.2(a)–(d))—must be strung together within a single citation sentence and separated by semicolons. Signals of different types, however, must be grouped in different citation sentences. For example:

▶ *See* Mass. Bd. of Ret. v. Murgia, 427 U.S. 307 (1976) (per curiam); *cf.* Palmer v. Ticcione, 433 F. Supp. 653 (E.D.N.Y. 1977) (upholding a mandatory retirement age for kindergarten teachers). *But see, e.g.*, Gault v. Garrison, 569 F.2d 993 (7th Cir. 1977) (holding that a classification of public school teachers based on age violated equal protection absent a showing of justifiable and rational state purpose). *See generally* Comment, O'Neil v. Baine: *Application of Middle-Level Scrutiny to Old-Age Classifications*, 127 U. PA. L. REV. 798 (1979) (advocating a new constitutional approach to old-age classifications).

Within a citation clause (rule 1.1), however, citation strings may contain signals of more than one type, separated by semicolons.

1.4 Order of Authorities Within Each Signal

Authorities within each signal are separated by semicolons.

If one authority is considerably more helpful or authoritative than the other authorities cited within a signal, it should precede the others. Except in this situation, cite authorities in the order in which they are listed below. Authorities cited in short form are ordered as though cited in full.

(a) Constitutions and other foundational documents are cited in the following order:

    (1) federal

    (2) state (alphabetically by state)

    (3) foreign (alphabetically by jurisdiction)

    (4) foundational documents of the United Nations, the League of Nations, and the European Union, in that order

Constitutions of the same jurisdiction are cited in reverse chronological order.

(b) Statutes are cited according to jurisdiction in the following order:

Federal:

    (1) statutes in U.S.C., U.S.C.A., or U.S.C.S. (by progressive order of U.S.C. title)

    (2) statutes currently in force but not in U.S.C., U.S.C.A., or U.S.C.S. (by reverse chronological order of enactment)

    (3) rules of evidence and procedure

    (4) repealed statutes (by reverse chronological order of enactment)

State (alphabetically by state):

    (5) statutes in the current codification (by order in the codification)

    (6) statutes currently in force but not in the current codification (by reverse chronological order of enactment)

    (7) rules of evidence and procedure

    (8) repealed statutes (by reverse chronological order of enactment)

Foreign (alphabetically by jurisdiction):

    (9) codes or statutes in the current codification (by order in the codification)

    (10) statutes currently in force but not in codes or the current codification (by reverse chronological order of enactment)

    (11) repealed statutes (by reverse chronological order of enactment)

(c) Treaties and other international agreements (other than the foundational documents of the United Nations, the League of Nations, and the European Union) are cited in reverse chronological order.

(d) Cases are arranged within a signal according to the courts issuing the cited opinions. Subsequent and prior histories are irrelevant to the order of citation, as is whether the opinion is published or unpublished. Cases decided by the same court are arranged in reverse chronological order; for this purpose, all United States circuit courts of appeals are treated as one court (including the District of Columbia and Federal Circuits), and all federal district courts are treated as one court. The ordering system is as follows:

Federal:

    (1) Supreme Court

    (2) courts of appeals, Emergency Court of Appeals, and Temporary Emergency Court of Appeals

    (3) Court of Claims, Court of Customs and Patent Appeals, and bankruptcy appellate panels

    (4) district courts, Judicial Panel on Multidistrict Litigation, and Court of International Trade (previously the Customs Court)

    (5) district bankruptcy courts and Railroad Reorganization Court

(6) Court of Federal Claims (previously the trial division for the Court of Claims), Court of Appeals for the Armed Forces (previously the Court of Military Appeals), and Tax Court (previously the Board of Tax Appeals)

(7) administrative agencies (alphabetically by agency)

State:

(8) courts (alphabetically by state and then by rank within each state)

(9) agencies (alphabetically by state and then alphabetically by agency within each state)

Foreign:

(10) courts (alphabetically by jurisdiction and then by rank within each jurisdiction)

(11) agencies (alphabetically by jurisdiction and then alphabetically by agency within each jurisdiction)

International:

(12) International Court of Justice, Permanent Court of International Justice

(13) other international tribunals and arbitral panels (alphabetically by name)

(e) Legislative materials are cited in the following order:

(1) bills and resolutions

(2) committee hearings

(3) reports, documents, and committee prints

(4) floor debates

Cite materials within each classification in reverse chronological order.

(f) Administrative and executive materials are cited in the following order:

Federal:

(1) Executive Orders

(2) current Treasury Regulations, proposed Treasury Regulations

(3) all other regulations currently in force (by progressive order of C.F.R. title)

(4) proposed rules not yet in force (by progressive order of future C.F.R. title, if any; otherwise by reverse chronological order of proposal)

(5) all materials repealed (by reverse chronological order of promulgation)

State:

(6) state (alphabetically by state), currently in force, then repealed

Foreign:

(7) foreign (alphabetically by jurisdiction), currently in force, then repealed

(g) Resolutions, decisions, and regulations of intergovernmental organizations are cited in the following order:

(1) United Nations and League of Nations, in reverse chronological order by issuing body (General Assembly, then Security Council, then other organs in alphabetical order)

(2) other organizations (alphabetically by name of organization)

(h) Records, briefs, and petitions are cited in that order, and within each classification by order of the court in which filed (see **rule 1.4(d)**). Briefs within the same case and court are cited in the following order: plaintiff/petitioner, defendant/respondent, and then amicus curiae in alphabetical order by first word of the amicus party's name.

(i) Secondary materials are cited in the following order:

(1) uniform codes, model codes, and restatements, in that order (in reverse chronological order by category)

(2) books, pamphlets, and shorter works in a collection of a single author's works (alphabetically by last name of author; if none, by first word of title)

(3) works in journals (not magazines or newspapers), including forthcoming works and shorter works in a collection of various authors' works (alphabetically by last name of author)

(4) book reviews not written by students (alphabetically by last name of reviewer)

(5) student-written law review materials including book reviews (alphabetically by last name of author; if none, by first word of title; if none, by periodical as abbreviated in citation)

(6) annotations (in reverse chronological order)

(7) magazine and newspaper articles (alphabetically by last name of author; if none, by first word of title)

(8) working papers (alphabetically by last name of author; if none, by first word of title)

(9) unpublished materials not forthcoming (alphabetically by last name of author; if none, by first word of title)

(10) electronic sources, including Internet sources (alphabetically by last name of author; if none, by first word of title)

When not addressed above, for the purposes of alphabetizing within each classification, use only the name of the first author listed (if any) and then proceed to use the title.

(j) Cross-references to the author's own text or footnotes.

Parenthetical Information   1.5

(a) Substantive information. Use parentheticals, as needed, to explain the relevance of a particular authority to the proposition given in the text. Parenthetical information is recommended when the relevance of a cited authority might not otherwise be clear to the reader (see **rule 1.2**). Explanatory information takes the form of a present participial phrase, a quoted sentence, or a short statement that is appropriate in context.

(i) **Phrases not quoting the authority.** Explanatory parenthetical phrases not directly quoting the authority usually begin with a present participle and should never begin with a capital letter:

> ▶ *See generally* Akhil Reed Amar, *Reports of My Death Are Greatly Exaggerated: A Reply*, 138 U. PA. L. REV. 1651 (1990) (arguing that the author and the two-tier theory of federal jurisdiction are still viable).

When a complete participial phrase is unnecessary in context, a shorter parenthetical may be substituted:

> ▶ Such standards have been adopted to address a variety of environmental problems. *See, e.g.*, H.B. Jacobini, *The New International Sanitary Regulations*, 46 AM. J. INT'L L. 727, 727–28 (1952) (health-related water quality); Robert L. Meyer, Travaux Préparatoires *for*

the UNESCO World Heritage Convention, 2 EARTH L.J. 45, 45–81 (1976) (conservation of protected areas).

(ii) **Phrases quoting the authority.** If, however, the parenthetical information quotes one or more full sentences or a portion of material that reads as a full sentence, it should begin with a capital letter and include appropriate closing punctuation:

> ► 3 *Consequences of Changing U.S. Population: Hearing Before the H. Select Comm. on Population*, 95th Cong. 11 (1978) (statement of Dr. David Birch) ("[T]here are more mayors of Rockville, Maryland, than there are mayors of Detroit.").

> ► Mari J. Matsuda, *Public Response to Racist Speech: Considering the Victim's Story*, 87 MICH. L. REV. 2320, 2381 (1989) ("We are a legalized culture. If law is where racism is, then law is where we must confront it . . . . [L]et us present a competing ideology . . . .").

> Not: Mari J. Matsuda, *Public Response to Racist Speech: Considering the Victim's Story*, 87 MICH. L. REV. 2320, 2381 (1989) (explaining that "[w]e are a legalized culture. If law is where racism is, then law is where we must confront it . . . . [L]et us present a competing ideology . . . .").

When directly quoting only a short phrase from an authority, follow **rule 1.5(a)(i)**:

> ► *But see* Flanagan v. United States, 465 U.S. 259, 264 (1989) (explaining that the final judgment rule reduces the potential for parties to "clog the courts" with a succession of time-consuming appeals).

(b) Order of parentheticals within a citation. When a citation requires multiple parentheticals, place them in the following order:

> ► (date) [hereinafter short name] (en banc) (Lastname, J., concurring) (plurality opinion) (per curiam) (alteration in original) (emphasis added) (footnote omitted) (citations omitted) (quoting another source) (internal quotation marks omitted) (citing another source), *available at* http://www.domainname.com (explanatory parenthetical), prior or subsequent history.

In direct citations to Internet sources (**rule 18.2.2**), the "hereinafter" parenthetical should immediately follow the URL or, if there is one, the "last visited" parenthetical.

Note that explanatory parentheticals precede any citation of subsequent history or other related authority (**rule 1.6**):

> ► Atl. Richfield Co. v. Fed. Energy Admin., 429 F. Supp. 1052, 1061–62 (N.D. Cal. 1976) ("[N]ot every person aggrieved by administrative action is necessarily entitled to the protections of due process."), *aff'd*, 556 F.2d 542 (Temp. Emer. Ct. App. 1977).

> ► Louis Loss, *The Conflict of Laws and the Blue Sky Laws*, 71 HARV. L. REV. 209 (1957) (discussing the bewildering array of state laws then governing interstate securities transactions), *reprinted in* LOUIS LOSS & EDWARD M. COWETT, BLUE SKY LAW 180 (1958).

Related Authority   1.6

When citing a work, citations to related authorities may be helpful to aid in locating the primary work or to provide relevant information not reflected in the primary citation. Citations to related authority may be appended to the primary citation with the use of an italicized explanatory phrase.

(a) Related authority intended to increase access.

(i) **"In."** When citing a shorter work such as an article, essay, or speech originally published in a volume collecting such works, use *"in"* to introduce the collection as a whole (see rule 15.5):

> ▶ Kay Deaux & Brenda Major, *A Social-Psychological Model of Gender, in* THEORETICAL PERSPECTIVES ON SEXUAL DIFFERENCES 89, 93 (Deborah L. Rhode ed., 1990).

(ii) **"Reprinted in."** A work that conveniently reprints a source originally published elsewhere may be introduced by *"reprinted in."* As far as possible, provide a complete citation for the original work, followed by *"reprinted in"* and the citation of the volume containing the reprint (see rule 15.5.2):

> ▶ Louis Loss, *The Conflict of Laws and the Blue Sky Laws*, 71 HARV. L. REV. 209 (1957), *reprinted in* LOUIS LOSS & EDWARD M. COWETT, BLUE SKY LAW 180 (1958).

> ▶ Thomas Jefferson, Kentucky Resolutions of 1798 and 1799, *reprinted in* 4 DEBATES ON THE ADOPTION OF THE FEDERAL CONSTITUTION 540 (Jonathan Elliot ed., 2d ed., Philadelphia, J.B. Lippincott 1888).

To indicate excerpts or partial reprints, add the word *"as."*

> ▶ S. REP. NO. 95-181, at 14 (1977), *as reprinted in* 1977 U.S.C.C.A.N. 3401, 3414.

(iii) **Other phrases.** Other phrases may be used by analogy to rule 1.6(a)(i) and (ii), as appropriate (e.g., *"available at"* (see rule 18), *"microformed on"* (see rule 18.5.1), or *"translated in"* (see rule 20.2.5)).

(b) Relevant history. The prior or subsequent history of a case (rule 10.7) or of a statute (rule 12.7) may be appended to the main citation for that case or statute. See rules 10.7 and 12.7 for circumstances in which the subsequent history of a case or statute *must* be indicated.

> ▶ Matthews v. Konieczny, 488 A.2d 5 (Pa. Super. Ct. 1985), *rev'd*, 527 A.2d 508 (Pa. 1987).

(c) Commentary. Works that discuss or quote the primary authority may also be appended to the citation without parentheses as related authorities when particularly relevant or when locating the original source may be difficult. Use italicized phrases such as *"noted in," "construed in," "quoted in," "reviewed by," "cited with approval in,"* and *"questioned in"* to introduce these works. Works that the primary authority discusses, cites, or otherwise mentions, however, should be indicated parenthetically. Thus:

> ▶ Filled Milk Act § 1, 21 U.S.C. § 61 (2006), *construed in* Milnot Co. v. Richardson, 350 F. Supp. 221 (S.D. Ill. 1972).

> But: Milnot Co. v. Richardson, 350 F. Supp. 221 (S.D. Ill. 1972) (construing Filled Milk Act § 1, 21 U.S.C. § 61 (2006)).

2   TYPEFACES FOR LAW REVIEWS

Legal writing uses four typefaces, though choice of font may vary (e.g., Times New Roman, Courier, etc.):

Ordinary Roman (Plain Text)
Underlined
Italicized
LARGE AND SMALL CAPITALS

Law reviews use two sets of typeface conventions—one for law review text (either main text or footnote text) (**rule 2.2**) and one for law review citations (**rule 2.1**). Unless otherwise noted, the examples in *The Bluebook* correspond to the convention for law review footnotes.

For an explanation of the typeface conventions commonly used in other forms of legal writing, see **Bluepages B1**. Practitioners can make ready use of the examples in *The Bluebook* by substituting the typeface conventions outlined in the **Bluepages** for those found in the examples throughout the rest of the book.

For example, a practitioner's brief might look like this:

▶ Directors manage the business and affairs of a corporation. *See Revlon, Inc. v. MacAndrews & Forbes Holdings, Inc.*, 506 A.2d 173, 179 (Del. 1986); *see also* Del. Code. Ann. tit. 8, § 141(a) (2000). In *Guth v. Loft*, the court held that directors also owe a duty of loyalty to the shareholders. 5 A.2d 503, 510 (Del. 1939) (holding that directors' duty of loyalty demands that "there shall be no conflict between duty and self-interest").

A similar section of a law review article might read:

▶ Directors manage the business and affairs of a corporation.[1] In *Guth v. Loft*, the court held that directors also owe a duty of loyalty to the shareholders.[2]

▶ [1] *See* Revlon, Inc. v. MacAndrews & Forbes Holdings, Inc., 506 A.2d 173, 179 (Del. 1986); *see also* DEL. CODE. ANN. tit. 8, § 141(a) (2000).

▶ [2] 5 A.2d 503, 510 (Del. 1939) (holding that directors' duty of loyalty demands that "there shall be no conflict between duty and self-interest").

For additional guidance, see **rule 2.1**, **rule 2.2**, and **Bluepages B1**.

2.1   Typeface Conventions for Citations

Most law reviews use three different typefaces in citations:

▶ Ordinary Roman (Plain Text), *Italics*, and LARGE AND SMALL CAPITALS

Some replace large and small capitals with ordinary roman type. Thus:

▶ Colin S. Diver, *The Optimal Precision of Administrative Rules*, 93 YALE L.J. 65 (1983).

becomes:

> ► Colin S. Diver, *The Optimal Precision of Administrative Rules*, 93
> Yale L.J. 65 (1983).

Other law reviews replace some italics, as well as all large and small capitals, with ordinary roman type:

> ► Colin S. Diver, The Optimal Precision of Administrative Rules, 93
> Yale L.J. 65 (1983).

The examples in this book follow the first convention, using all three typefaces. The following list explains the more important typeface conventions used in law review citations:

(a) Case names (rules 10.2, 14.3.1, 18.3.1, 20.3, 21.5, and 21.6). Use ordinary roman type for case names in full citations, except for procedural phrases, which are always italicized:

> ► Lochner v. New York, 198 U.S. 45 (1905).

> ► State *ex rel.* Scott v. Zinn, 392 P.2d 417 (N.M. 1964).

When a case name appears within an article title in a citation, do not italicize it:

> ► Thomas J. Madden et al., *Bedtime for* Bivens: *Substituting the
> United States as Defendant in Constitutional Tort Suits*, 20 HARV. J.
> ON LEGIS. 469 (1983).

Use italics for the short form of case citations:

> ► *Lochner*, 198 U.S. at 50.

(b) Books (rule 15). Use large and small capitals for both authors and titles:

> ► RICHARD KLUGER, SIMPLE JUSTICE (1976).

(c) Periodicals (rule 16). Italicize article titles and use large and small capitals for periodical names. Authors' names should appear in ordinary roman type:

> ► Katherine K. Baker, *Once a Rapist? Motivational Evidence and
> Relevancy in Rape Law*, 110 HARV. L. REV. 563 (1997).

> ► Cass R. Sunstein, Lochner's *Legacy*, 87 COLUM. L. REV. 873 (1987).

> ► David E. Bernstein, *Lochner's* Legacy's *Legacy*, 82 TEX. L. REV. 1
> (2003).

(d) Introductory signals (rule 1.2). Italicize all introductory signals when they appear within citation sentences or clauses:

> ► *See, e.g.*, Parker Drilling Co. v. Ferguson, 391 F.2d 581 (5th Cir.
> 1968).

Do not, however, italicize a signal word when it serves as the verb of an ordinary sentence:

> ► For an analysis of risk allocation rules under the UCC, see Roger S.
> Goldman, Note, *Risk of Loss in Commercial Transactions: Efficiency
> Thrown into the Breach*, 65 VA. L. REV. 557, 563–72 (1979).

(e) Explanatory phrases (rules 1.6, 10.7, and 12.7). Italicize all explanatory phrases:

> ► Oreck Corp. v. Whirlpool Corp., 579 F.2d 126, 131 (2d Cir.) (en banc),
> *cert. denied*, 439 U.S. 946 (1978).

Note, however, that phrases in related authority parentheticals, such as "(quoting . . .)," "(citing . . .)," and "(translating . . .)" are not italicized.

(f) Punctuation. Italicize commas, semicolons, and other punctuation marks only when they constitute part of the italicized material, and not when they are merely an element of the sentence or citation in which they appear. For clarity, the italicized items in the examples below appear in blue:

► *See, e.g., id.*; Sabine Towing & Transp. Co. v. Zapata Ugland Drilling, Inc. (*In re* M/V Vulcan), 553 F.2d 489 (5th Cir.) (per curiam), *cert. denied*, 434 U.S. 855 (1977).

► Nancy Reagan, Editorial, *Just Say "Whoa,"* WALL ST. J., Jan. 23, 1996, at A14.

2.2   Typeface Conventions for Textual Material

(a) Main text. The main text of law review pieces does not contain citations and uses only ordinary roman and italics. Most material appears in ordinary roman type. Only the following are italicized:

(i) **Case names.** Italicize case names, including the "*v.*" and all procedural phrases such as "*In re*" and "*ex rel.*":

► *Missouri ex rel. Gaines v. Canada*

(ii) **Titles of publications, speeches, or articles.** Thus:

► The library has a copy of *The Path of the Law,* which was published in the *Harvard Law Review,* a complete set of the *Federal Supplement,* and today's *Wall Street Journal.* It does not have a copy of *Hearings on S. 776* or *Alaska Statutes.*

(iii) **Style.** Italicize words for emphasis or other stylistic purposes (rule 7). Also italicize words that are emphasized in quoted matter (rule 5.2).

(b) Footnote text. Unlike in the main text, a sentence in footnote text may contain citations, which are placed in citation clauses embedded in the sentence (rule 1.1(b)).

(i) **Case names.** When a case name is grammatically part of the sentence in which it appears, it should be italicized:

► In *Loving v. Virginia,* the Court invalidated Virginia's antimiscegenation statute.

► In *Loving v. Virginia,* 388 U.S. 1 (1967), the Court invalidated Virginia's antimiscegenation statute.

When the case name is not grammatically part of the sentence, but rather used in a citation clause embedded in the footnote text, use the typeface conventions for citations (rule 2.1(a)):

► The Court has upheld race-specific statutes that disadvantage a racial minority, *e.g.,* Korematsu v. United States, 323 U.S. 214 (1944), but those decisions have been severely criticized.

► Justice Harlan quipped that "one man's vulgarity is another's lyric," Cohen v. California, 403 U.S. 15, 25 (1971), but failed to provide further explanation.

(ii) **All other authorities.** When referring to any other type of authority, whether or not the reference is grammatically part of the sentence, use the typeface conventions for citations if the full citation or a short form citation (rule 4) is given:

> ► A different view is expressed in LEARNED HAND, THE BILL OF RIGHTS (1958), and HOLMES, *supra* note 2.

If the reference appears without the full or shortened citation information, follow the typeface conventions for the main text of law reviews (rule 2.2(a)(ii)):

> ► Judge Hand explained his philosophy of judicial review in *The Bill of Rights*.

(iii) **Explanatory parentheticals.** In explanatory parentheticals, follow the typeface convention for case names in citation text when a full citation clause is included:

> ► Nat'l R.R. Passenger Corp. v. Morgan, 536 U.S. 101, 110 (2002) (citing Chevron U.S.A. Inc. v. Natural Res. Def. Council, Inc., 467 U.S. 837 (1984)).

> ► Nat'l R.R. Passenger Corp. v. Morgan, 536 U.S. 101, 110 (2002) (addressing an argument based upon Chevron U.S.A. Inc. v. Natural Res. Def. Council, Inc., 467 U.S. 837 (1984)).

> ► Nat'l R.R. Passenger Corp. v. Morgan, 536 U.S. 101, 110 (2002) (addressing an argument based upon *Chevron*).

(c) **Punctuation.** Italicize commas, semicolons, etc., only when they constitute part of italicized material, and not when they are merely an element of the citation or sentence in which they appear. For purposes of clarity, the italicized punctuation marks in the examples below appear in blue:

> ► When it decided *Sabine Towing*, the Fifth Circuit presented a somewhat different rationale for its holding.

> ► Brannon Denning's article, *Reforming the New Confirmation Process: Replacing "Despise and Resent" with "Advise and Consent,"* suggests amendments to the Senate's procedural rules.

> **Not:** Brannon Denning's article, *Reforming the New Confirmation Process: Replacing "Despise and Resent" with "Advise and Consent,"* suggests amendments to the Senate's procedural rules.

3 SUBDIVISIONS

Most subdivisions (such as columns or sections) in citations are abbreviated. See table T16 for a list of subdivision abbreviations.

3.1 Volumes, Parts, and Supplements

A single work often appears in separately paginated (or sectioned or paragraphed) volumes, parts, or supplements. A citation to material that appears in one such volume, part, or supplement must identify the separately paginated subdivision in which the material appears.

(a) Volumes. When the volumes are numbered, cite the volume number in Arabic numerals. If the author of the entire work (all volumes) is cited, the volume number precedes the author's name:

▶ 2 FREDERICK POLLOCK & FREDERIC WILLIAM MAITLAND, THE HISTORY OF ENGLISH LAW 205-06 (2d ed. 1911).

▶ 2 SUBCOMM. ON LABOR OF THE S. COMM. ON LABOR & PUBLIC WELFARE, 92D CONG., LEGISLATIVE HISTORY OF THE EQUAL EMPLOYMENT OPPORTUNITY ACT OF 1972, at 1007 (1972).

Otherwise, the volume number precedes the volume's title:

▶ Donald H. Zeigler, *Young Adults as a Cognizable Group in Jury Selection*, 76 MICH. L. REV. 1045, 1047 (1978).

If no volume number is given but the volume is readily identifiable by year, use the year of the volume as the volume number and omit the year after the pincite:

▶ Thomas R. McCoy & Barry Friedman, *Conditional Spending: Federalism's Trojan Horse*, 1988 SUP. CT. REV. 85, 88.

▶ Donald A. Dripps, *Delegation and Due Process*, 1988 DUKE L.J. 657.

If the volume designation includes words, use brackets to avoid confusion:

▶ [1977–1978 Transfer Binder] Bankr. L. Rep. (CCH) ¶ 66,472

If volumes are numbered in a new series each year, give both the year and volume number, bracketing the year and placing it before the volume number to avoid confusion:

▶ [1943] 2 K.B. 154

(b) Separately paginated numbered parts. When a work is divided into separately paginated (or sectioned or paragraphed) series, books, chapters, or other parts, include the relevant subdivisions in the citation:

▶ 26 CONG. REC. app. at 156 (1894) (statement of Rep. Hicks).

▶ ser. 14, pt. 2, at 150

▶ pt. 3, § 4, at 15

(c) Supplements. When citing a separately paginated (or sectioned or paragraphed) supplement, identify the supplement and its date in parentheses:

▶ HAW. REV. STAT. § 296-46.1 (Supp. 1984).

▶ GEORGE GLEASON BOGERT, THE LAW OF TRUSTS AND TRUSTEES § 496 (rev. 2d ed. Supp. 1985).

To cite both the main volume and the supplement, use an ampersand:

▶ 42 U.S.C. § 1397b (1982 & Supp. I 1983).

Pages, Footnotes, Endnotes, and Graphical Materials 3.2

(a) Pages.

Give the page number or numbers before the date parenthetical, without any introductory abbreviation ("p." and "pp." are used only in internal cross-references (rule 3.5)):

- ARTHUR E. SUTHERLAND, CONSTITUTIONALISM IN AMERICA 45 (1965).
- H.R. REP. NO. 82-353, at 4–5 (1951).

Use "at" if the page number may be confused with another part of the citation; use a comma to set off "at." Use this form, for example, when the title of a work ends with an Arabic numeral or when the work uses Roman numerals for pagination:

- BIOGRAPHICAL DIRECTORY OF THE GOVERNORS OF THE UNITED STATES 1978–1983, at 257 (Robert Sobel & John W. Raimo eds., 1983).
- Thomas I. Emerson, *Foreword* to CATHARINE A. MACKINNON, SEXUAL HARASSMENT OF WORKING WOMEN, at vii, ix (1979).

If an article, case, or other source within a larger source is not separately paginated, cite the page on which the item begins:

- Bernard L. Diamond, *The Psychiatric Prediction of Dangerousness*, 123 U. PA. L. REV. 439 (1974).
- United States v. Bruno, 144 F. Supp. 593 (N.D. Ill. 1955).
- Government Employees Training Act, Pub. L. No. 85-507, 72 Stat. 327 (1958).

When referring to specific material within such a source, include both the page on which the source begins and the page on which the specific material appears (a pincite), separated by a comma:

- Matthew Roskoski, Note, *A Case-by-Case Approach to Pleading Scienter Under the Private Securities Litigation Reform Act of 1995*, 97 MICH. L. REV. 2265, 2271–75 (1999).
- CATHARINE A. MACKINNON, *On Exceptionality: Women as Women in Law*, *in* FEMINISM UNMODIFIED 70, 76–77 (1987).

When referring specifically to material on the first page of a source, repeat the page number:

- Christina M. Fernández, Note, *Beyond* Marvin: *A Proposal for Quasi-Spousal Support*, 30 STAN. L. REV. 359, 359 (1978).

When citing material within a concurring or dissenting opinion, give only the initial page of the case and the page on which the specific material appears, not the initial page of the concurring or dissenting opinion:

- Baker v. Carr, 369 U.S. 186, 297 (1962) (Frankfurter, J., dissenting).

When citing material that spans more than one page, give the inclusive page numbers, separated by an en dash (–) or hyphen (-). Always retain the last two digits, but drop other repetitious digits:

- Edward L. Rubin, Note, *Fairness, Flexibility, and the Waiver of Remedial Rights by Contract*, 87 YALE L.J. 1057, 1065–69 (1978).

If a hyphen or dash would be ambiguous because of the page numbering system, use the word "to":

- BORIS I. BITTKER & JAMES S. EUSTICE, FEDERAL INCOME TAXATION OF CORPORATIONS AND SHAREHOLDERS ¶ 5.06, at 5-31 to -32 (5th abr. ed. 1987).

Cite nonconsecutive pages by giving the individual page numbers separated by commas:

▶ Kleppe v. New Mexico, 426 U.S. 529, 531, 546 (1976).

If a source uses star paging (such as "*3"), drop the star in the ending page number of a page range, but keep the star in all references to nonconsecutive pages.

▶ 2 WILLIAM BLACKSTONE, COMMENTARIES *152, *155-56.

When a point is often repeated throughout the entire source, use "*passim*" rather than citing specific pages. Do not insert a comma after the initial page number:

▶ Linda S. Mullenix, *The Constitutionality of the Proposed Rule 23 Class Action Amendments*, 39 ARIZ. L. REV. 615 passim (1997).

(b) Footnotes. To cite a footnote, give the page on which the footnote appears, "n.," and the footnote number, with no space between "n." and the number:

▶ Akhil Reed Amar, *The Two-Tiered Structure of the Judiciary Act of 1789*, 138 U. PA. L. REV. 1499, 1525 n.80 (1990).

To cite a footnote that spans more than one page, cite only the page on which the footnote begins, "n.," and the footnote number:

▶ Akhil Reed Amar, *The Two-Tiered Structure of the Judiciary Act of 1789*, 138 U. PA. L. REV. 1499, 1560 n.222 (1990).

When referring only to specific pages of a footnote that spans more than one page, cite only the specific pages, rather than the page on which the footnote begins:

▶ Akhil Reed Amar, *The Two-Tiered Structure of the Judiciary Act of 1789*, 138 U. PA. L. REV. 1499, 1561–62 n.222 (1990).

Cite multiple footnotes (or endnotes) by using "nn.":

▶ 141 nn.180–86

Treat nonconsecutive footnotes (or endnotes) like nonconsecutive pages, but (except for internal cross-references) substitute an ampersand for the last comma:

▶ 350 n.12, 355 n.18
▶ 291 nn.14 & 18, 316 nn.4, 6 & 8–9

To refer to both a page in the text and a footnote that begins on that page, use an ampersand between the page and the note number:

▶ Irene Merker Rosenberg, Winship *Redux: 1970 to 1990*, 69 TEX. L. REV. 109, 123 & n.90 (1990).

(c) Endnotes. To cite an endnote, give the page on which the endnote appears (not the page on which the call number appears), "n.," and the endnote number, with no space between "n." and the number:

▶ JOHN HART ELY, DEMOCRACY AND DISTRUST 215 n.85 (1980).

To refer to both a page in text and an endnote whose call appears on that page, use an ampersand between the text page and the page on which the endnote appears. In the following example, the cited text is on p. 61 and the endnote is on p. 215:

▶ JOHN HART ELY, DEMOCRACY AND DISTRUST 61 & 215 n.85 (1980).

Otherwise, cite endnotes in the same manner as footnotes.

(d) Graphical materials. When citing tables, figures, charts, graphs, or other graphical materials, give the page number on which the graphical material appears and the designation, if any, provided in the source, with no space between the abbreviation and the number. Use the abbreviations in **table T16**:

▶ Kevin M. Clermont & Theodore Eisenberg, Commentary, *Xenophilia in American Courts*, 109 HARV. L. REV. 1120, 1131 tbl.2 (1996).

▶ Jennifer Gerarda Brown & Ian Ayres, *Economic Rationales for Mediation*, 80 VA. L. REV. 323, 397 fig.6 (1994).

To refer to multiple charts, tables, figures, etc., on the same page, pluralize the abbreviated designation according to **table T16**. Use commas and ampersands, not en dashes, to separate:

▶ 9 figs.3 & 4

▶ 1236 tbls.1, 2 & 3

Sections and Paragraphs   3.3

If an authority is organized by section (§) or paragraph (¶), cite to these subdivisions:

▶ 15 U.S.C. § 18 (1982).

▶ 6 JAMES WM. MOORE ET AL., MOORE'S FEDERAL PRACTICE ¶ 56.07 (3d ed. 1997).

A page number may also be provided if useful in locating specific matter within the section or paragraph:

▶ LAURENCE H. TRIBE, AMERICAN CONSTITUTIONAL LAW § 15-4, at 1314, § 15-6, at 1320 (2d ed. 1988).

If an authority is organized in part by indented paragraphs not introduced by paragraph symbols (¶), do not cite such paragraphs with the symbol. Instead use the written abbreviation (**para.**):

▶ THE DECLARATION OF INDEPENDENCE para. 2 (U.S. 1776).

Do not cite indented paragraphs if the authority is ordinarily cited by page:

▶ *Mandela Trial Scheduled Today*, USA TODAY, Feb. 4, 1991, at A4.

Do not use "at" before a section or paragraph symbol:

▶ *Id.* § 7.

Not: *Id.* at § 7.

▶ MOORE ET AL., *supra* note 5, ¶ 56.07.

Not: MOORE ET AL., *supra* note 5, at ¶ 56.07.

Rule 6.2(c) discusses the use of section and paragraph symbols.

To cite session laws amending prior acts that are divided into sections within sections, see **rule 12.4(d)**.

(a) Subsections. If the source contains punctuation separating sections from subsections, use the original punctuation:

▶ N.M. STAT. ANN. § 4-44-7(G) (1983).

Not: N.M. STAT. ANN. § 4(44)(7)(G) (1983).

If the source contains no such separating punctuation, separate the subsection designations using parentheses, not decimals, hyphens, or other marks. Thus, place "1" and "a." in parentheses ("(1)" and "(a)"), but not ".01" or "-32."

(b) Multiple sections and subsections. When citing multiple sections, use two section symbols (§§). Give inclusive numbers; do not use "*et seq.*" Identical digits or letters preceding a punctuation mark may be omitted, unless doing so would create confusion. Otherwise retain all digits.

> WASH. REV. CODE ANN. §§ 18.51.005–.52.900 (West 1989 & Supp. 1991).
> DEL. CODE ANN. tit. 9, §§ 817–819 (1989).

Note that letters are sometimes used to designate sections, rather than subsections, and that section designations may contain punctuation within them:

> 42 U.S.C. §§ 1396a–1396d (2006).

If an en dash or hyphen would be ambiguous, use the word "to":

> 42 U.S.C. §§ 1973aa-2 to -4 (1994).
> MONT. CODE ANN. §§ 75-1-301 to -324 (1989).

When citing scattered sections, separate the sections with commas:

> N.J. STAT. ANN. §§ 18A:54-1, -3, -6 (West 1989).

Repeat digits if necessary to avoid confusion:

> N.J. STAT. ANN. §§ 18A:58-17, :58-25, :64A-22.1, :64A-22.6 (West 1989).

When citing multiple subsections within a *single* section, use only one section symbol:

> 28 U.S.C. § 105(a)(3)–(b)(1) (2006).
> 19 U.S.C. § 1485(a)(1)–(3) (2006).
> DEL. CODE ANN. tit. 9, § 6910(a), (c) (1989).

But when citing multiple subsections within *different* sections, use two section symbols:

> 19 U.S.C. §§ 1485(a), 1486(b) (2006).

(c) Multiple paragraphs. Multiple paragraphs should be treated like multiple sections, following rule 3.3(b):

> 1 Blue Sky L. Rep. (CCH) ¶¶ 4471–4474.
> MOORE ET AL., *supra* note 5, ¶¶ 54.32–.35.

3.4   Appended Material

Indicate an appendix or appended note or comment by placing the appropriate abbreviation (see table T16) after the citation to the largest full subdivision to which the item is appended, whether page, section, paragraph, chapter, title, or volume:

> James Edwin Kee & Terrence A. Moan, *The Property Tax and Tenant Equality*, 89 HARV. L. REV. 531 app. (1976).
> RESTATEMENT (SECOND) OF TORTS § 623A cmt. a (1977).

Cite a particular page, section, or other subdivision in an appendix as follows:

> ► 50 U.S.C. app. § 454 (2006).

> ► Samuel Issacharoff & George Loewenstein, *Second Thoughts About Summary Judgment*, 100 YALE L.J. 73 app. at 124–25 (1990).

Other types of appended material that serve as commentary on the material to which they are appended, or that further discuss a point related to the textual discussion, should be cited as notes or appendices:

> ► FED. R. EVID. 702 advisory committee's note.

> ► RESTATEMENT (SECOND) OF PROP. § 2.1 cmt. c, illus. 2 (1977).

Further information necessary to identify which of several named notes is cited may be added parenthetically:

> ► 42 U.S.C. § 1862 note (1988) (Denial of Financial Assistance to Campus Disrupters).

> ► N.Y. BUS. CORP. LAW § 624 note (McKinney 1963) (Legislative Studies and Reports).

Appendices that reprint materials normally cited to another source should be cited according to **rule 1.6(a)**:

> ► An Act for the Prevention of Frauds and Perjuries, 1677, 29 Car. 2, c. 2, § 17 (Eng.), *reprinted in* JOHN P. DAWSON, WILLIAM BURNETT HARVEY & STANLEY D. HENDERSON, CASES AND COMMENTS ON CONTRACTS app. 1, at 942 (5th ed. 1988).

Internal Cross-References   3.5

Portions of text, footnotes, and groups of authorities within the piece may be cited using "*supra*" or "*infra*." Use *supra* to refer back to material that has already appeared within the piece. Use *infra* to refer to material that appears later in the piece.

"Part" and "note" are used to refer to parts (when parts are specifically designated) and footnotes within the same piece; "p." and "pp." are used to refer to other pages within the same piece; "Figure" and "Table" are used to refer to figures and tables within the same piece. A variety of forms may be used. For example:

> ► *See supra* text accompanying notes 305–07.

> ► *See supra* notes 12–15, 92–97 and accompanying text.

> ► *See* cases cited *supra* note 22.

> ► *But see* sources cited *supra* note 24.

> ► *See* discussion *infra* Parts II.B.2, III.C.1.

> ► *See supra* Part IV.A–B.

> ► *See infra* pp. 106–07.

> ► *See infra* p. 50 and note 100.

> ► *See supra* Figure 2.

> ► *See infra* Table 3.

Note that "*supra*" is also used in short form citations for certain types of sources (see **rule 4.2**).

4 SHORT CITATION FORMS

This rule provides general guidance for all short forms. For guidance as to specific short forms see the following rules:

Cases . . . . rule 10.9

Constitutions . . . . rule 11

Statutes. . . . . rule 12.10

Legislative Materials . . . . rule 13.8

Regulations. . . . . rule 14.4

Books, Reports, and Other Nonperiodic Materials . . . . rule 15.10

Periodical Materials . . . . rule 16.9

Unpublished and Forthcoming Sources. . . . . rule 17.6

Internet, Electronic Media, and Other Nonprint Resources . . . rule 18.8

Services . . . . rule 19.2

Foreign Materials . . . . rule 20.7

International Materials . . . . rule 21.16

For additional guidance on the use of short forms in court documents and legal memoranda, see Bluepages B5.2, B7.2, B8.2, B9.2, and B10.2.

4.1 "*Id.*"

"*Id.*" may be used in citation sentences and clauses for any kind of authority except internal cross-references (as described in rule 3.5). In court documents and legal memoranda, use "*id.*" when citing the immediately preceding authority, *but only when the immediately preceding citation contains only one authority.* In law review footnotes, use "*id.*" when citing the immediately preceding authority within the same footnote or within the immediately preceding footnote *when the preceding footnote contains only one authority.* Note that the period at the end of "*id.*" is always italicized.

Indicate where a subsequent citation varies from the former, such as the specific page number being cited. If the first citation refers only to a shorter work contained within an authority, do not use "*id.*" for a subsequent citation to the entire authority. Instead, use the "*supra*" form (see rule 4.2(a)).

The following examples illustrate the use of "*id.*" to refer to a variety of commonly cited materials:

▸ [1] Chalfin v. Specter, 233 A.2d 562, 562 (Pa. 1967).

▸ [2] *Id.* at 563.

▸ [3] 42 U.S.C. § 1983 (1994).

▸ [4] *See id.* § 1981.

▸ [5] U.C.C. § 3-302(2) (1977); *see also id.* § 3-303(a).

▸ [6] Dupuy v. Dupuy, [1977–1978 Transfer Binder] Fed. Sec. L. Rep. (CCH) ¶ 96,048, at 91,701 (5th Cir. May 9, 1977).

► ⁷ *Id.* ¶ 96,052, at 91,705; *see also* U.S. Const. art. I, § 8, cl. 10 (giving Congress the power to punish "Offences against the Law of Nations").

► ⁸ Fleming James, Jr. & Geoffrey C. Hazard, Jr., Civil Procedure §§ 1.3–.5 (3d ed. 1985).

► ⁹ *See id.* § 1.7.

► ¹⁰ 3 William Holdsworth, A History of English Law 255 (3d ed. 1927).

► ¹¹ 1 *id.* at 5–17 (2d ed. 1914).

► ¹² Thomas C. Schelling, A Process of Residential Segregation: Neighborhood Tipping 2, *reprinted in* Economic Foundations of Property Law 307, 308 (Bruce A. Ackerman ed., 1975).

► ¹³ *Id.* at 3.

► ¹⁴ James & Hazard, *supra* note 8, § 1.5.

► ¹⁵ *See id.*

"*Id.*" may not be used to refer to one authority in a preceding footnote if the preceding footnote cites more than one source:

► ¹⁶ *See* Robert B. Reich, *Toward a New Consumer Protection*, 128 U. Pa. L. Rev. 1 (1979); Note, *Direct Loan Financing of Consumer Purchases*, 85 Harv. L. Rev. 1409, 1415–17 (1972); *see also* Chalfin v. Specter, 233 A.2d 562 (Pa. 1967).

► ¹⁷ *See Chalfin*, 233 A.2d at 570.

Not: ¹⁷ *See id.* at 570.

Sources identified in explanatory parentheticals, explanatory phrases, or prior/subsequent history, however, are ignored for the purposes of this rule. Thus, the following examples are correct:

► ¹⁸ Tuten v. United States, 460 U.S. 660, 663 (1983) (quoting Ralston v. Robinson, 454 U.S. 201, 206 (1981)).

► ¹⁹ *See id.* at 664.

► ²⁰ Dillon v. Gloss, 256 U.S. 368, 376 (1921), *quoted in* Nixon v. United States, 506 U.S. 224, 230 (1993).

► ²¹ *See id.* at 374.

► ²² Kohler v. Tugwell, 292 F. Supp. 978, 985 (E.D. La. 1968), *aff'd per curiam*, 393 U.S. 531 (1969).

► ²³ *See id.* at 980.

"*Id.*" may not be used to refer to an internal cross-reference:

► ²⁴ *See supra* text accompanying note 2.

► ²⁵ *See supra* text accompanying note 2.

Not: ²⁵ *See supra id.*

4.2 "*Supra*" and "Hereinafter"

"*Supra*" and "hereinafter" may be used to refer to legislative hearings; court filings; books; pamphlets; reports; unpublished materials; nonprint resources; periodicals; services; treaties and international agreements; regulations, directives, and decisions of intergovernmental organizations; and internal cross-references. "*Supra*" and "hereinafter" should not be used to refer to cases, statutes, constitutions, legislative materials (other than hearings), restatements, model codes, or regulations, except in extraordinary circumstances, such as when the name of the authority is extremely long:

> ▶ 26 *In re* Multidistrict Private Civil Treble Damage Antitrust Litig. Involving Motor Vehicle Air Pollution Control Equip., 52 F.R.D. 398 (C.D. Cal. 1970) [hereinafter *Air Pollution Control Antitrust Case*].

Appropriate short forms for cases, statutes, and legislative materials (other than hearings) are provided in their respective rules.

(a) "*Supra*." When an authority has been fully cited previously, the "*supra*" form may be used (unless "*id.*" is appropriate or "*supra*" is inappropriate for that authority). The "*supra*" form generally consists of the last name of the author of the work, followed by a comma and the word "*supra*." Indicate any particular manner in which the subsequent citation differs from the former.

If the author is an institutional author, use the full institutional name. If no author is cited, use the title of the work; for unsigned student-written law review materials, use the appropriate designation (see **rule 16.7.1(b)**).

Indicate the footnote in which the full citation can be found, unless the full citation is in the same footnote, in which case "*supra*" should be used without any cross-reference. Indicate any particular manner in which the subsequent citation differs from the former. Volume, paragraph, section, or page numbers may be added to refer to specific material:

> ▶ 27 Reich, *supra* note 16, at 6.

> ▶ 28 2 HOLDSWORTH, *supra* note 10, at 6.

> ▶ 29 JAMES & HAZARD, *supra* note 8, § 7.21; W. PAGE KEETON ET AL., PROSSER AND KEETON ON THE LAW OF TORTS § 1, at 2 (5th ed. 1984); *see also supra* text accompanying note 7.

> ▶ 30 KEETON ET AL., *supra* note 29, § 2, at 4; Note, *supra* note 16, at 1416.

> ▶ 31 *Cf.* SCHELLING, *supra* note 12, at 3.

Note that citation of a second item or work found within a volume of collected materials already cited takes the form:

> ▶ 32 CATHARINE A. MACKINNON, *On Exceptionality: Women as Women in Law, in* FEMINISM UNMODIFIED 70, 70 (1987).

> ▶ 33 CATHARINE A. MACKINNON, *Desire and Power, in* FEMINISM UNMODIFIED, *supra* note 32, at 46, 47.

(b) "Hereinafter." For authority that would be cumbersome to cite with the usual "*supra*" form or for which the regular shortened form may confuse the reader, the author may establish a specific shortened form. After the first citation of the authority, but before any explanatory parenthetical, place the word "hereinafter" and the shortened form in brackets. The shortened form should appear in the same typeface as in the full citation. In subsequent citations, cite the authority using the shortened form followed by a comma and the appropriate "*supra*" cross-reference (**rule 4.2(a)**):

▶ 34 *Proposed Amendments to the Federal Rules of Criminal Procedure: Hearings Before the Subcomm. on Criminal Justice of the H. Comm. on the Judiciary*, 95th Cong. 92–93 (1977) [hereinafter *Hearings*] (statement of Prof. Wayne LaFave).

▶ 35 RICHARD H. FALLON, JR. ET AL., HART AND WECHSLER'S THE FEDERAL COURTS AND THE FEDERAL SYSTEM 330 (5th ed. 2003).

▶ 36 *Hearings*, *supra* note 34, at 33 (statement of Hon. Edward Becker).

Do not use the "hereinafter" form when a simple "*supra*" form is adequate:

▶ 37 FALLON ET AL., *supra* note 35, at 343.

The "hereinafter" form, however, should be used to distinguish two authorities appearing in the same footnote if the simple "*supra*" form would be confusing:

▶ 38 *See* Edward B. Rock, *Saints and Sinners: How Does Delaware Corporate Law Work?*, 44 UCLA L. REV. 1009, 1016–17 (1997) [hereinafter Rock, *Saints and Sinners*]; Edward B. Rock, *The Logic and (Uncertain) Significance of Institutional Shareholder Activism*, 79 GEO. L.J. 445 (1991) [hereinafter Rock, *Shareholder Activism*].

▶ 39 *See* Rock, *Saints and Sinners*, *supra* note 38, at 1019; Rock, *Shareholder Activism*, *supra* note 38, at 459–63.

5   QUOTATIONS

5.1   Formatting of Quotations

(a) Quotations of fifty or more words.

(i) **Indentation and quotation marks.** The quotation should be indented on the left and right without quotation marks, and quotation marks within a block quotation should appear as they do in the original:

> ▶ [T]his presumptive privilege must be considered in light of our historic commitment to the rule of law. This is nowhere more profoundly manifest than in our view that "the twofold aim [of criminal justice] is that guilt shall not escape or inno-cence suffer." We have elected to employ an adversary system of criminal justice in which the parties contest all issues before a court of law . . . . The ends of criminal justice would be defeated if judgments were to be founded on a partial or speculative presentation of the facts. The very integrity of the judicial system and public confidence in the system depend on full disclosure of all the facts, within the framework of the rules of evidence. To ensure that justice is done, it is imperative to the function of courts that compul-sory process be available for the production of evidence needed either by the prosecution or by the defense.

> United States v. Nixon, 418 U.S. 683, 708–09 (1974) (second alter-ation in original) (citation omitted). The Court then balanced this interest against the evils of forced disclosure. *Id.* at 710.

(ii) **Footnote and citation placement.** In law review text (in which citations are not permitted), the footnote number should appear after the final punctuation of the quotation. In law review footnotes, court documents, and legal memoranda (in which citations are permitted), the citation should not be indented but should begin at the left margin on the line immediately following the quotation. In law review footnotes, where the quotation is placed within a parenthetical, it should be enclosed in quotation marks and not otherwise set off from the rest of the text.

(iii) **Paragraph structure.** The paragraph structure of an indented quotation should be indicated by further indenting the first line of each paragraph. The first sentence of the first quoted paragraph is only indented, however, if the first word of the quoted passage is also the first word of a paragraph in the source being quoted. If language at the beginning of the first paragraph is omitted, do not indent the first line or use an ellipsis. To indicate omission at the beginning of subsequent paragraphs, insert and indent an ellipsis. Indicate the omission of one or more entire paragraphs by inserting and indenting four periods (". . . .") on a new line. The following example illustrates these rules:

> ▶   On appeal to the federal courts via a habeas petition, McClesky alleged that Georgia's capital sentencing process was administered in a racially discriminatory manner in violation of the Equal Protection clause of the Fourteenth Amendment. McClesky based his claims on a study, con-ducted by respected law and economics Professors Baldus, Pulaski, and Woodworth . . . . The Baldus study examined roughly 2,500 murder cases . . . .

. . . .

     . . . Professors Baldus, Pulaski, and Woodworth also sub jected their data to an extensive statistical analysis.

In law review footnotes, when the quotation is placed within a parenthetical, it should be enclosed in quotation marks and not otherwise set off from the rest of the text.

(b) Quotations of forty-nine or fewer words.

(i) **Indentation and quotation marks.** The quotation should be enclosed in quotation marks but not otherwise set off from the rest of the text. Quotation marks around material quoted inside another quote should appear as single marks within the quotation in keeping with the standard convention.

(ii) **Footnote and citation placement.** The footnote number or citation should follow immediately after the closing quotation mark unless it is more accurate to place it elsewhere shortly before or after the quotation.

(iii) **Paragraph structure.** Do not indicate the original paragraph structure of quotations of forty-nine or fewer words except when the material quoted would commonly be set off from the text, such as lines of poetry or dialogue from a play. In this case, the quotation may appear as a block quote per **rule 5.1(a)(iii)**, regardless of its length.

(iv) **Punctuation.** Always place commas and periods inside the quotation marks; place other punctuation marks inside the quotation marks only if they are part of the original text.

Alterations and Quotations Within Quotations   5.2

(a) Substitution of letters or words. When a letter must be changed from upper to lower case, or vice versa, enclose it in brackets. Substituted words or letters and other inserted material should also be bracketed:

> ► "[P]ublic confidence in the [adversary] system depend[s upon] full disclosure of all the facts, within the framework of the rules of evidence."

(b) Omission of letters. Indicate the omission of letters from a common root word with empty brackets ("judgment[]").

(c) Mistakes in original. Significant mistakes in the original should be followed by "[sic]" and otherwise left as they appear in the original:

> ► "This list of statutes are [sic] necessarily incomplete."

(d) Changes to citations.

(i) Use a parenthetical clause after the citation to indicate when the source quoted contains any addition of emphasis, alteration to the original in the quoted text, or omission of citations, emphasis, internal quotation marks, or footnote call numbers. When a citation requires multiple parentheticals, place them in the order indicated in **rule 1.5(b)**:

> ► "The fact that individuals define themselves in a significant way through their sexual relationships suggests . . . that much of the richness of a relationship will come from the freedom to *choose* the form and nature of these *intensely personal bonds*." Bowers v.

Hardwick, 478 U.S. 186, 205 (1986) (Blackmun, J., dissenting) (second emphasis added).

> ▶ The Court of Appeals recognized the city's substantial interest in limiting the sound emanating from the band-shell. The court concluded, however, that the city's sound-amplification guideline was not narrowly tailored to further this interest, because "it has not [been] shown . . . that the requirement of the use of the city's sound system and technician was the *least intrusive means* of regulating the volume."

Ward v. Rock Against Racism, 491 U.S. 781, 797 (1989) (alteration in original) (citation omitted).

(ii) Do not indicate the omission of a citation or footnote call number that follows the last word quoted.

(iii) Do not indicate that emphasis in the quotation appears in the original.

(e) Quotations within quotations. Whenever possible, a quotation within a quotation should be attributed to its original source. Insert a parenthetical following any parenthetical required by **rule 5.2(d)**:

> ▶ Chief Judge Skelly Wright noted Congress's "*firm resolve* to insure that the CIA's 'power that flows from money and stealth' could not be turned loose in domestic investigations of Americans." Marks v. CIA, 590 F.2d 997, 1008 (D.C. Cir. 1978) (Wright, C.J., concurring in part and dissenting in part) (emphasis added) (quoting Weissman v. CIA, 565 F.2d 692, 695 (D.C. Cir. 1977)).

Note that sources included in parentheticals pursuant to this rule should be formatted as though they appear in citation clauses (see **rules 2.1** and **2.2(b)(iii)**).

5.3   Omissions

Omission of a word or words is generally indicated by the insertion of an ellipsis, three periods separated by spaces and set off by a space before the first and after the last period ("•.•.•.•"), to take the place of the word or words omitted. Note that "•" indicates a space.

An ellipsis should never be used to begin a quotation; nor should it be used when individual words are merely altered (**rules 5.1(a)(iii)** and **5.2**).

(a) When using quoted language as a phrase or clause. Do not indicate omission of matters before or after a quotation:

> ▶ Chief Justice Burger wrote that the availability of compulsory process is "imperative to the function of courts" and that "[t]he very integrity of the judicial system and public confidence in the system depend on full disclosure of all the facts."

However, indicate omission of matter within such a phrase or clause with an ellipsis:

> ▶ Chief Justice Burger wrote that the availability of compulsory process is "imperative to•.•.•courts" and that "[t]he•.•.•judicial system and public confidence in the system depend on full disclosure of all the facts."

(b) When using quoted language as a full sentence. For example, assume the text of the original language is as follows:

> National borders are less of a barrier to economic exchange now than at almost any other time in history. As economic activity continues its relentless drive toward world-wide scope, trademarks become even more important. Why, then, are certain scholars advocating less comprehensive trademark protection? In fact, this seems counterintuitive.

(i) Where the *beginning of* the quoted sentence is being omitted, capitalize the first letter of the quoted language and place it in brackets if it is not already capitalized:

> "[B]orders are less of a barrier to economic exchange now than at almost any other time in history."

(ii) Where the *middle* of a quoted sentence is being omitted, insert an ellipsis where the language is omitted:

> "National borders are less of a barrier . . . now than at almost any other time in history."

(iii) Where the *end* of a quoted sentence is being omitted, insert an ellipsis between the last word being quoted and the final punctuation of the sentence being quoted:

> "National borders are less of a barrier to economic exchange now than at almost any other time . . . ."

(iv) Do not indicate the deletion of matter after the period or other final punctuation that concludes the last quoted sentence.

> "National borders are less of a barrier to economic exchange now than at almost any other time in history."

(v) Where language *after the end* of a quoted sentence is deleted and is followed by further quotation, retain the punctuation at the end of the quoted sentence and insert an ellipsis before the remainder of the quotation.

> "National borders are less of a barrier to economic exchange now than at almost any other time in history. . . . [E]conomic activity continues its relentless drive toward world-wide scope, [so] trademarks become even more important."

(vi) If language both *at the end* and *after the end* of a quoted sentence is omitted and followed by further quoted material, use only one ellipsis to indicate both of the omissions:

> "National borders are less of a barrier . . . . [E]conomic activity continues its relentless drive toward world-wide scope, [so] trademarks become even more important."

Note that the punctuation at the end of the first sentence should follow the ellipsis:

> "Why, then, are certain scholars advocating less . . . ? [T]his seems counterintuitive."

(c) When omitting a footnote or citation. Indicate omission of footnotes or citations with the parenthetical phrase "(footnote omitted)" or "(citation omitted)" immediately following the citation to the quoted source. Do not insert an ellipsis for an omitted footnote or citation.

6   ABBREVIATIONS, NUMERALS, AND SYMBOLS

6.1   Abbreviations

Tables at the end of this book contain lists of specific abbreviations for arbitral reporters (T5), case names (T6), court names (T7), explanatory phrases (T8), legislative documents (T9), geographical terms (T10), judges and officials (T11), months (T12), periodicals (T13), publishing terms (T14), services (T15), and subdivisions (T16).

Abbreviations not listed in this book should be avoided unless substantial space will be saved and the resulting abbreviation is unambiguous.

Note that in legal writing the same word may be abbreviated differently for different uses:

> ► F. and Fed.
> ► app. and App'x

(a) Spacing. In general, close up all adjacent single capitals:

> ► N.W.
> ► S.D.N.Y.

But do not close up single capitals with longer abbreviations:

> ► D. Mass.
> ► S. Ct.

In abbreviations of periodical names (see table T13), close up all adjacent single capitals except when one or more of the capitals refers to the name of an institutional entity, in which case set the capital or capitals referring to the entity off from other adjacent single capitals with a space. Thus:

> ► GEO. L.J.
> ► B.C. L. REV.
> ► N.Y.U. L. REV.
> ► S. ILL. U. L.J.

Individual numbers, including both numerals and ordinals, are treated as single capitals:

> ► F.3d
> ► S.E.2d
> ► A.L.R.4TH

But, insert a space adjacent to any abbreviation containing two or more letters:

> ► So. 2d
> ► Cal. App. 3d
> ► F. Supp. 2d

Close up initials in personal names:

> ► W.C. Fields

(b) Periods.

Generally, every abbreviation should be followed by a period, except those in which the last letter of the original word is set off from the rest of the abbreviation by an apostrophe. Thus:

► Ave.

► Bldg.

But:

► Ass'n

► Dep't

Some entities with widely recognized initials, e.g., AARP, CBS, CIA, FCC, FDA, FEC, NAACP, NLRB, are commonly referred to in spoken language by their initials rather than by their full names; such abbreviations may be used without periods in text, in case names, and as institutional authors. Do not, however, omit the periods when the abbreviations are used as reporter names, in names of codes, or as names of courts of decision. Thus:

► NLRB v. Baptist Hosp., Inc., 442 U.S. 773 (1979).

But: E. Belden Corp., 239 N.L.R.B. 776 (1978).

United States may be abbreviated to "U.S." only when used as an adjective (do not omit the periods):

► U.S. history

But: history of the United States

In addition to the abbreviation "U.S.," always retain periods in abbreviations not commonly referred to in speech as initials (e.g., N.Y., S.D.).

Numerals and Symbols   6.2

(a) Numerals. In general, spell out the numbers zero to ninety-nine in text and in footnotes; for larger numbers use numerals. This general rule is subject, however, to the following exceptions:

(i) Any number that *begins a sentence* must be spelled out.

(ii) "Hundred," "thousand," and similar *round numbers* may be spelled out, if done so consistently.

(iii) When a series includes numbers both less than 100 and greater than or equal to 100, numerals should be used for the entire series:

► The plaintiffs gained, respectively, 117, 6, and 28 pounds.

(iv) Numerals should be used if the number includes a decimal point.

(v) Where material repeatedly refers to percentages or dollar amounts, numerals should be used for those percentages or amounts.

(vi) Numerals should be used for section or other subdivision numbers.

(vii) In numbers containing five or more digits, use commas to separate groups of three digits. Thus:

▶ 1,234,567

But: 9876

Do not employ this convention in citations to Internet database locators, docket numbers, the U.S. Code, or other sources whose classification systems do not themselves include commas:

▶ United States v. Walker, No. 00-40098-JAR, 2003 WL 131711 (D. Kan. Jan. 6, 2003).

(b) Ordinals.

(i) Unless part of a citation, ordinal numbers appearing in text and footnotes are controlled by **rule 6.2(a)**. If part of a citation, figures are used for all ordinal numbers. Do not use superscripts:

▶ 41st Leg.

▶ 4th ed.

(ii) In textual sentences, where **rule 6.2(a)** requires that the numeral be used, use "2nd" or "3rd" for figures representing ordinal numbers ending in two or three. But, in citations, for figures representing ordinal numbers ending in the number two or three, use "2d" or "3d," not "2nd" or "3rd." Do not use superscripts in any case. Thus:

▶ The 102nd Congress could not pass a rule that would bind the 103rd Congress.

But, in citations:

▶ 103d Cong.

▶ 2d ed.

(c) Section (§) and paragraph (¶) symbols. The first word of any sentence must be spelled out. In addition, spell out the words "section" and "paragraph" in the text (whether main text or footnote text) of law review pieces and other documents, except when referring to a provision in the U.S. Code (see **rule 12.10**) or a federal regulation (see **rule 14.4**). In citations, the symbols should be used (except when citing session laws amending prior acts as noted in **rule 12.4(d)**). When the symbols are used, insert a space between "§" or "¶" and the numeral. See **rules 3.3(b)** and **3.3(c)** when citing to multiple sections or paragraphs.

(d) Dollar ($) and percent (%) symbols. These symbols should be used wherever numerals are used, and the words should be spelled out wherever numbers are spelled out, but a symbol should never begin a sentence. There should *not* be a space between "$" or "%" and the numeral.

ITALICIZATION FOR STYLE AND IN UNIQUE CIRCUMSTANCES

7

See rule 2 for a general discussion on the uses of typefaces. The conventions below apply to italicization for emphasis, italicization of foreign words and phrases, and italicization in other unique circumstances.

(a) Emphasis. Words and phrases may be italicized for emphasis.

(b) Foreign words and phrases. Italicize non-English words and phrases unless they have been incorporated into common English usage. Latin words and phrases that are often used in legal writing are considered to be in common English usage and should not be italicized. However, very long Latin phrases and obsolete or uncommon Latin words and phrases should remain italicized. For example:

- ► *expressio unius est exclusio alterius*
- ► *ignorantia legis neminem excusat*
- ► *sero sed serio*
- ► *ex dolo malo non oritur actio*

But:

- ► e.g.
- ► res judicata
- ► amicus curiae
- ► corpus juris
- ► obiter dictum
- ► modus operandi
- ► non obstante verdicto
- ► mens rea

- ► i.e.
- ► quid pro quo
- ► certiorari
- ► ab initio
- ► de jure
- ► habeas corpus
- ► prima facie
- ► en banc

Note, however, that "*id.*" is always italicized. Note also that other typeface rules may control. For example, when "**e.g.**" is used as a signal it should be italicized as per rule 2.1(d). Similarly, always italicize procedural phrases in case names, such as "*In re* " or "*ex rel.*," under rule 10.2.1(b).

(c) Letters representing hypothetical parties, places, or things. Italicize and capitalize individual letters when used to represent the names of hypothetical parties, places, or things:

- ► *A* went to bank *B* in state *X*.

(d) The lowercase letter "l." Italicize the lowercase letter "*l*" when used as a subdivision, as in a statute or rule, to distinguish it from the numeral "1":

- ► § 23 (*l*)
- ► cmt. *l*

(e) Mathematical expressions. Italicize mathematical formulas and variables:

- ► $E = mc^2$
- ► $a > 2b$

8   CAPITALIZATION

(a) Headings and titles. Capitalize words in a heading or title, including the initial word and any word that immediately follows a colon. Do not capitalize articles, conjunctions, or prepositions when they are four or fewer letters, unless they begin the heading or title, or immediately follow a colon.

(b) Internet main page titles and URLs. Capitalize URLs and words in an Internet main page title in accordance with the actual capitalization of the source.

(c) Text. Except for headings, titles, and Internet main page titles and URLs, capitalize according to this rule. When this rule does not address a particular question of capitalization, refer to a style manual such as the *Chicago Manual of Style* or the *Government Printing Office Style Manual*. Practitioners should also refer to **Bluepages B7.3** for further advice on capitalization. Additional words that should be capitalized in legal writing include:

(i) Nouns that identify specific persons, officials, groups, government offices, or government bodies.

These words and phrases should always be capitalized according to the following examples.

► the Social Security Administrator

   The plaintiff was declared disabled by the Social Security Administrator and was awarded benefits.

► the Administrator

   For fifty years, the statute has provided that the Administrator make all necessary determinations.

► the FDA

   The FDA has approved the salts as safe and effective.

► the Agency

   The Agency reported that all areas of the country met the standard for nitrogen dioxide.

► Congress

   Members of Congress are immune from false imprisonment claims under certain circumstances.

► the President

   A sitting President's executive power allows him or her to pardon convicted criminals.

But:

► the congressional hearings

   The congressional hearings were held on the potential cumulative effects of these three rules.

► the presidential veto

   The presidential veto does not confer such power upon the President.

(ii) **Exceptions.** Certain words are exceptions to the above rule and should be capitalized according to the following rules:

Act	Capitalize when referring to a specific legislative act:

▶ A union has a statutory duty of fair representation under the National Labor Relations Act.

▶ The record of the hearing shows that the Act required operators to pay for their own retirees.

Circuit	Capitalize when used with a circuit's name or number:

▶ We have decided to follow the Fifth Circuit and District of Columbia Circuit in that regard, rather than this circuit's unclear precedent.

Code	Capitalize when referring to a specific code:

▶ At least one court considered the significance of the change between the 1939 and 1954 Codes.

Commonwealth	Capitalize if it is a part of the full title of a state, if the word it modifies is capitalized, or when referring to a state as a governmental actor or a party to a litigation:

▶ The Commonwealth of Massachusetts sued several companies.

▶ The Commonwealth may not relitigate the issue in a post-conviction hearing.

Constitution	Capitalize when naming any constitution in full or when referring to the U.S. Constitution, but do not capitalize the adjective form "constitutional." Also, capitalize nouns that identify specific parts of the U.S. Constitution when referring to them in textual sentences, but not in citations:

▶ Students in this class have studied the full faith and credit clause of the Pennsylvania Constitution. The students agree that the clause in that constitution is substantially similar to the Full Faith and Credit Clause in the U.S. Constitution.

But: He claims his constitutional rights were violated.

▶ Of all the amendments in the U.S. Constitution, the Fifth Amendment may be the most complex.

▶ Accordingly, there was no violation of Article I, Section 8, Clause 17 of the Constitution.

But: *See* U.S. CONST. art. I, § 8, cl. 17 (granting Congress the power to "exercise exclusive Legislation in all Cases whatsoever . . . over all Places purchased" by the United States).

Court	Capitalize when naming any court in full or when referring to the United States Supreme Court (with some exceptions for court documents and legal memoranda, see **Bluepages B7.3**):

▶ The California Supreme Court found no violation in such a case.

▶ The argument in the state supreme court concerning the lack of prior notice was based solely on state authorities.

▶ When the Court approves the argument, it becomes constitutional doctrine for the entire country.

▶ The court of appeals reversed the trial court.

▶ The Court of Appeals for the Fifth Circuit affirmed.

Federal   Capitalize when the word it modifies is capitalized:

▶ The Federal Constitution provides for three branches of government.

▶ A higher level of clarity is required in statutes that require federal spending.

Judge, Justice   Capitalize when giving the name of a specific judge or justice or when referring to a Justice of the United States Supreme Court:

▶ In one of the first decisions on point, Judge Cedar-baum rejected a group appointment.

▶ This era of constitutional non-interference ended when the Justices proclaimed a profound national commitment to the principle that debate on public issues should be uninhibited.

▶ The justices of the state's highest court will hear oral arguments on the issue of gay marriage at the end of the month.

State   Capitalize if it is a part of the full title of a state, if the word it modifies is capitalized, or when referring to a state as a governmental actor or as a party to a litigation:

▶ The principal issue is whether the State of Kansas may impose its motor fuel tax. The State Commissioner adopted a broad-based policy.

▶ The State brought this action two years ago.

Term   Capitalize when referring to a Term of the United States Supreme Court:

▶ The United States Supreme Court considered this issue in this Term and in four other Terms since the 1978 Term.

▶ The central common law courts sat only four times a year, but customarily the year began with Michaelmas term.

TITLES OF JUDGES, OFFICIALS, AND TERMS OF COURT   9

(a) Justices and judges. Justices are referred to as "Justice Ginsburg" and "Chief Justice Roberts." Parenthetical references are to "Brennan, J.," "Scalia, J.," and "Brennan & Scalia, JJ." Capitalize "justice" and "chief justice" according to **rule 8(c)(ii)**. Judges are referred to as "Judge Surrick" and "Chief Judge Scirica." For parenthetical references, abbreviate titles of judges and officials as indicated in **table T11**.

(b) Ordering. As a matter of etiquette, lists of judges should be in the order indicated at the beginning of each volume of the official reporter for the court. Justices of the United States Supreme Court are always listed with the Chief Justice first and then in order of seniority.

(c) Term of court. A term of court currently in progress may be referred to as "this term." The immediately preceding term, no longer in progress at the time of publication, should be referred to as "last term." Any term may be indicated by year:

▶ the 1999 term

The Supreme Court Term should be indicated by the year in which the Term began, not the year it ended. Capitalize "term" according to **rule 8(c)(ii)**.

CASES   10

Citation of a U.S. Supreme Court case:

Citation of a case decided by the U.S. Court of Appeals for the Fourth Circuit, later reversed by the U.S. Supreme Court, with parenthetical information about the Fourth Circuit decision:

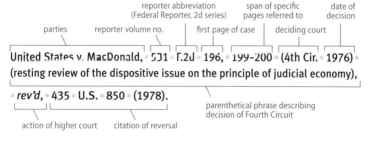

Short form for the above case after it has been cited in full:

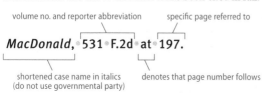

Main Elements

Case Names . . . . Rule 10.2

Reporters and Other Sources . . . . Rule 10.3

Court and Jurisdiction . . . . Rule 10.4

Date or Year . . . . Rule 10.5

Parenthetical Information . . . . Rule 10.6

Prior and Subsequent History . . . . Rule 10.7

10.1 Basic Citation Forms

Filed but not decided	Tice v. Philbrick, No. 90-345 (D. Mass. filed Sept. 18, 1990).
Unpublished interim order	Mishra v. Yee, No. 90-345 (D. Mass. Oct. 25, 1990) (order granting preliminary injunction).
Published interim order	Haber v. Scotten, 725 F. Supp. 1395 (D. Mass. 1990) (order granting preliminary injunction).
Unpublished decision	Kitchens v. Grohman, No. 90-345, slip op. at 6 (D. Mass. Dec. 4, 1990).
Decision published in service only	Tice v. Scotten, 1990 Fed. Sec. L. Rep. (CCH) ¶ 102,342 (D. Mass. Dec. 4, 1990).
Decision published in newspaper only	Mishra v. Grohman, N.Y. L.J., Dec. 5, 1990, at 1 (D. Mass. Dec. 4, 1990).
Decision available in electronic database	Yee v. Kitchens, No. 90-345, 1990 U.S. Dist. LEXIS 20837, at *6–8, *10 (D. Mass. Dec. 4, 1990).
Decision available in electronic database after revision	Phibrick v. Haber, No. 90-345, 1990 U.S. Dist. LEXIS 20837, at *4 (D. Mass. Dec. 4, 1990, revised Jan. 3, 1991).
Published decision	Tice v. Haber, 727 F. Supp. 1407, 1412 (D. Mass. 1990).
Appeal docketed	Yee v. Grohman, 727 F. Supp. 1407 (D. Mass. 1990), *appeal docketed*, No. 90-567 (1st Cir. Dec. 20, 1990).
Brief, record, or appendix	Brief for Appellant at 7, Kitchens v. Scotten, 925 F.2d 314 (1st Cir. 1991) (No. 90-567).
Disposition on appeal	Philbrick v. Mishra, 925 F.2d 314, 335 (1st Cir. 1991).
Disposition in lower court showing subsequent history	Haber v. Yee, 727 F. Supp. 1407, 1412 (D. Mass. 1990), *aff'd*, 925 F.2d 314 (1st Cir. 1991).

Petition for certiorari filed	Grohman v. Tice, 925 F.2d 314 (1st Cir. 1991), *petition for cert. filed*, 60 U.S.L.W. 3422 (U.S. Jan. 14, 1992) (No. 92-212).
Petition for certiorari granted	Scotten v. Kitchens, 925 F.2d 314 (1st Cir. 1991), *cert. granted*, 60 U.S.L.W. 3562 (U.S. Jan. 21, 1992) (No. 92-212).
Disposition in Supreme Court published only in service	Charlesworth v. Mack, 60 U.S.L.W. 4420, 4421 (U.S. Feb. 4, 1992), *vacating as moot* 925 F.2d 314 (1st Cir. 1991).

Case Names 10.2

The only significant differences between case names in textual sentences and case names in citations are the italicization (rule 2) and the extent to which the case name is abbreviated. The provisions of rule 10.2.1 apply to every case name, whether in text or citations, but case names in citations are further abbreviated according to rule 10.2.2. Thus:

► In *Southern Pacific Co. v. Jensen*, 244 U.S. 205 (1917), Justice McReynolds stressed the value of uniform laws.

► *Southern Pacific* also indicates the breadth of federal lawmaking power under the admiralty jurisdiction.

Not: In *S. Pac. Co. v. Jensen*, 244 U.S. 205 (1917), Justice McReynolds stressed the value of uniform laws.

But: in citations:

► *See, e.g.*, S. Pac. Co. v. Jensen, 244 U.S. 205, 225–26 (1917) (Pitney, J., dissenting).

Note that the examples throughout rule 10.2 employ the typeface conventions for law review citations. For an explanation of typeface conventions, see rule 2. For typeface conventions in court documents and legal memoranda, see Bluepages B1.

....

General Rules for Case Names 10.2.1

Use the case name that appears at the beginning of the opinion in the cited reporter as modified by the paragraphs below. If no name appears in the cited reporter, use a popular name or cite as "Judgment of <date>":

► Shelley's case

► Judgment of Oct. 11, 2008

Always retain in full the first word in each party's name (including a relator) except as provided below. In extremely long case names, omit words not necessary for identification; the running head (the short identifier printed at the top of each page of the case) may serve as a guide. Make the following modifications where applicable:

(a) Actions and parties cited. If the case is a consolidation of two or more actions, cite only the first listed:

> ► Shelley v. Kraemer

Not: Shelley v. Kraemer, McGhee v. Sipes

Omit all parties other than the first listed on each side. Do not omit the first-listed relator or any portion of a partnership name:

> ► Fry v. Mayor of Sierra Vista

Not: Fry v. Mayor & City Council of Sierra Vista

But:

> ► Massachusetts *ex rel.* Alison v. Pauly

> ► Eisen v. Spradlin, Lincoln & Amorosi

Omit words indicating multiple parties, such as "et al." Also omit alternative names given for the first-listed party on either side:

> ► Cheng v. Seinfeld

Not: Cheng et al. v. Seinfeld d/b/a The Man, Inc.

Similarly, for in rem jurisdiction cases, omit all but the first-listed item or group of items:

> ► *In re* Three Pink Cadillacs

Not: *In re* Three Pink Cadillacs, Two Turtle Doves, and a Partridge in a Pear Tree

Where real property is a party, use its common street address, if available:

> ► United States v. 6109 Grubb Road

Not: United States v. Parcel of Real Property Known as 6109 Grubb Road, Millcreek Township, Erie County, Pennsylvania

In bankruptcy and similar cases, the case name might contain both an adversary and a nonadversary name. If both appear at the beginning of the opinion, cite the adversary name first, followed by the nonadversary name in parentheses. Include a procedural phrase such as "*In re*" or "*ex rel.*" before the nonadversary name, followed by a descriptive or introductory phrase such as "Estate of" or "Interest of," if any. If only an adversary name or only a nonadversary name appears at the beginning of the opinion, cite the name supplied:

> ► Wallingford's, Inc. v. Waning (*In re* Waning), 120 B.R. 607, 611 (Bankr. D. Me. 1990).

> ► *In re* Drexel Burnham Lambert Group, Inc., 120 B.R. 724 (Bankr. S.D.N.Y. 1990).

> ► *In re* Estate of Benson, No. C7-95-2185, 1996 WL 118367 (Minn. Ct. App. Mar. 19, 1996).

> ► State v. Powers (*In re* Interest of Powers), 493 N.W.2d 167 (Neb. 1992).

(b) Procedural phrases. Abbreviate "on the relation of," "for the use of," "on behalf of," "as next friend of," and similar expressions to "*ex rel.*" Abbreviate "in the matter of," "petition of," "application of," and similar expressions to "*In re.*" Omit all procedural phrases except the first. When adversary parties are named, omit all procedural phrases except "*ex rel.*":

► Gorman v. Bruh

Not: *In re* Gorman v. Bruh

But:

► Massachusetts *ex rel.* Kennedy v. Armbruster

► *Ex parte* Young

Include any introductory or descriptive phrases such as "**Accounting of**," "**Estate of**," and "**Will of**." Thus:

► *In re* Will of Holt

► Estate of Haas v. Commissioner

Procedural phrases should always be italicized, regardless of whether the rest of the case name is italicized. Thus, in law review text:

► *Ex parte Young*

(c) Abbreviations. In textual sentences, whether in main text or in footnote text, abbreviate only widely known acronyms under **rule 6.1(b)** and these eight words: "**&**," "**Ass'n**," "**Bros.**," "**Co.**," "**Corp.**," "**Inc.**," "**Ltd.**," and "**No.**" If one of these eight begins a party's name, however, do not abbreviate it.

► Philadelphia Electric Co. v. Hirsch

Not: PECO v. Hirsch

But: NAACP v. Kaminski

For abbreviations in citations, see **rule 10.2.2**.

(d) "The." Omit "The" as the first word of a party's name, except as part of the name of the object of an in rem action or in cases in which "**The King**" or "**The Queen**" is a party. Thus:

► Miami Herald v. Sercus

But:

► *In re* The Clinton Bridge

► The King v. Broadrup

Do not omit "The" in an established popular name, except when referring to the case textually. Thus:

► *See* The Civil Rights Cases, 109 U.S. 3 (1883).

But: Neither of the *Civil Rights Cases* opinions was correct.

Not: Neither of *The Civil Rights Cases* opinions was correct.

(e) Descriptive terms. Omit terms such as "**administrator**," "**appellee**," "**executor**," "**licensee**," and "**trustee**" that describe a party already named:

► Burns v. McMillen

Not: Burns v. McMillen, Administrator

But: Trustees of Dartmouth College v. Garodnick

(f) Geographical terms. Omit "State of," "Commonwealth of," and "People of," except when citing decisions of the courts of that state, in which case only "State," "Commonwealth," or "People" should be retained:

▶ Blystone v. Pennsylvania, 494 U.S. 299 (1990).

Not: Blystone v. Commonwealth of Pennsylvania, 494 U.S. 299 (1990).

But: Commonwealth v. Ferrone, 448 A.2d 637 (Pa. Super. Ct. 1982).

Omit "City of," "County of," "Village of," "Township of," and like expressions unless the expression begins a party name:

▶ Mayor of New York v. Clinton

Not: Mayor of the City of New York v. Clinton

But: Butts v. City of New York

Omit all prepositional phrases of location not following "City," or like expressions, unless the omission would leave only one word in the name of a party or the location is part of the full name of a business or similar entity:

▶ Surrick v. Bd. of Wardens

Not: Surrick v. Bd. of Wardens of the Port of Philadelphia

But: Planned Parenthood of Se. Pa. v. Casey

Not: Planned Parenthood v. Casey

▶ Shapiro v. Bank of Harrisburg

▶ Eimers v. Mutual of Omaha

Include designations of national or larger geographical areas except in union names (**rule 10.2.1(i)**). Omit "of America" after "United States":

▶ Flatow v. Islamic Republic of Iran

▶ United States v. Aluminum Co. of America

Retain all geographical designations not introduced by a preposition:

▶ Billman v. Indiana Department of Corrections

(g) Given names or initials. Generally, omit given names or initials of individuals, but not in names of business firms or where a party's surname is abbreviated:

▶ Meyer v. Gordon

Not: Jennifer Cannon Meyer v. Daniel S. Gordon

But:

▶ Tanya Bartucz, Inc. v. Virginia J. Wise & Co.

▶ Linda R.S. v. Richard D.

Do not omit any part of a surname made up of more than one word:

▶ Van der Velt v. Standing Horse

▶ Abdul Ghani v. Subedar Shoedar Khan

Given names that follow a surname should be retained. Thus, retain the full name where the name is *entirely* in a language in which the surname is given first, such as Chinese, Korean, or Vietnamese:

- Yao Zhen Guang v. Yeh Zhi An
- Chow v. Ha Quang Jin

Not: Timothy Chow v. Ha Quang Jin

Similarly, if a party's name is of Spanish or Portuguese derivation, cite the surname and all names following:

- Ortega y Gasset v. Alcala de Larosa

If in doubt, use the name under which the party appears in the index of the reporter cited.

(h) Business firm designations. Omit "Inc.," "Ltd.," "L.L.C.," "N.A.," "F.S.B.," and similar terms if the name also contains a word such as "Ass'n," "Bros.," "Co.," "Corp.," or "R.R.," clearly indicating that the party is a business firm:

- Wisconsin Packing Co. v. Indiana Refrigerator Lines, Inc.

Not: Wisconsin Packing Co., Inc. v. Indiana Refrigerator Lines, Inc.

This rule should be read narrowly. The omission of the business firm designation is only appropriate if the name of the business could not *possibly* be mistaken for the name of some other entity, such as a natural person.

(i) Union and local union names. Cite a union name exactly as given in the official reporter. This general rule is subject, however, to the following exceptions:

(i) Only the smallest unit should be cited:

- NLRB v. Radio & Television Broadcast Engineers Local 1212

Not: NLRB v. Radio & Television Broadcast Engineers Local 1212, IBEW, AFL-CIO

(ii) All craft or industry designations, except the first *full* such designation, should be omitted:

- Douds v. Local 294, International Brotherhood of Teamsters

Not: Douds v. Local 294, International Brotherhood of Teamsters, Chauffeurs, Warehousemen & Helpers

But: International Union of Doll & Toy Workers v. Local 379

(iii) A widely recognized abbreviation of the union's name (e.g., UAW) may be used in accordance with **rules 6.1(b)** and **10.2.1(c)**.

(iv) All prepositional phrases of location, including those of national or larger areas, should be omitted.

(j) Commissioner of Internal Revenue. Cite simply as "Commissioner" or, in citations, "Comm'r."

(k) Common names different from name in reporter. For cases not known by the name that appears in the reporter, but known instead by a common name, the common name must either be substituted for the reporter name in its entirety, or indicated parenthetically in the same type as the case name in the reporter:

- The Brig Amy Warwick (The Prize Cases), 67 U.S. (2 Black) 635 (1863).

▶ The Prize Cases, 67 U.S. (2 Black) 635 (1863).

Not: The Prize Cases (The Brig Amy Warwick), 67 U.S. (2 Black) 635 (1863).

For cases known by the name in the reporter, but also commonly known by a *short* name different from that appearing in the reporter, the common name may *not* be substituted for the reporter name in its entirety in a full citation, but it may be indicated parenthetically in *italics*:

▶ Youngstown Sheet & Tube Co. v. Sawyer (*Steel Seizure*), 343 U.S. 579 (1952).

Not: *Steel Seizure*, 343 U.S. 579 (1952).

Similarly, for mandamus actions against courts where the case is known by the name of the judge against whom the writ is sought, the name may be indicated parenthetically in *italics*:

▶ United States v. U.S. District Court (*Keith*), 407 U.S. 297 (1972).

And, for cases with multiple dispositions, a helpful identifier of the number of the decision may be indicated parenthetically in *italics*:

▶ Hamdi v. Rumsfeld (*Hamdi III*), 316 F.3d 450 (4th Cir. 2003).

This parenthetical identifier is given only when a case is cited as the primary citation. Once given, the parenthetical identifier alone may be used as the case name when the case is cited again, even in circumstances where a full citation would otherwise be required.

▶ [1] Fox Television Stations, Inc. v. FCC (*Fox I*), 280 F.3d 1027 (D.C. Cir.), *modified on reh'g*, 293 F.3d 537 (D.C. Cir. 2002).

▶ [2] Fox Television Stations, Inc. v. FCC (*Fox II*), 293 F.3d 537, 540 (D.C. Cir. 2002) (quoting *Fox I*, 280 F.3d at 1043).

In conformity with **rule 2.1(f)**, when citing cases according to the above rule, the parentheses themselves should never be italicized in either main text or footnote text.

10.2.2 Additional Rules for Case Names in Citations

Cite case names in citations according to the rules given above, but with the following further modifications:

Always abbreviate any word listed in **table T6**, even if the word is the first word in a party's name:

▶ S. Consol. R.R. v. Consol. Transp. Co.

▶ *In re* Acad. Answering Serv. Inc.

▶ McGaugh v. Comm'r

Abbreviate states, countries, and other geographical units as indicated in **table T10** unless the geographical unit is the entire name of the party (as opposed to just a part thereof). This includes "United States." Thus:

▶ *In re* W. Tex. Pepper Co.

▶ LeBeau v. Univ. of Md.

But: Staub v. District of Columbia

▶ Ctr. for Nat'l Sec. Studies v. U.S. Dep't of Justice

But: Alvarez-Machain v. United States

Abbreviate other words of eight letters or more if *substantial* space is thereby saved and the result is unambiguous.

Reporters and Other Sources   10.3

Parallel Citations and Which Source(s) to Cite   10.3.1

The federal and state jurisdictions table (table T1) indicates which reporters to cite for the decisions of most courts. Note that many state court decisions are published in two or more sources.

(a) Parallel citations in state court documents. In documents submitted to state courts, all case citations must be to the source(s) required by local rules. Many state rules require that citations to state court decisions include a citation to the official state reporter, *followed* by a parallel citation to a regional reporter. Thus, these local rules, and *not* the citation rules set forth in table T1, govern state court filings. See Bluepages B4.1.3 and table BT2 for further guidance concerning jurisdiction-specific citation rules.

(b) Case citations in all other documents. In all other documents, including *ordinary legal memoranda* and *law review pieces*, cite the relevant regional reporter, if the decision is found therein. For example:

▶ Swedloff v. Phila. Transp. Co., 187 A.2d 152 (Pa. 1963).

If the decision is available as an official public domain citation (also referred to as medium-neutral citation), that citation must be provided, as well as a parallel citation to the regional reporter, if available.

If the decision is not found in a regional reporter or available as a public domain citation, cite the other sources indicated in table T1. Cite decisions of unlisted courts as you would those of courts listed in the table. If a case is not available in an official or preferred unofficial reporter or as a public domain citation, cite another unofficial reporter, a widely used computer database (rule 18.3.1), a service (rule 19), a slip opinion (rule 10.8.1(b)), an Internet source (rule 18.2.2), or a newspaper (rule 16.6), in that order of preference:

▶ United States v. Carlisle, No. 90-2465SI, 1991 U.S. App. LEXIS 5863, at *3 (8th Cir. Apr. 10, 1991) (per curiam).

▶ *In re* Smithfield Estates, Inc., [1985–1986 Transfer Binder] Bankr. L. Rep. (CCH) ¶ 70,707 (Bankr. D.R.I. Aug. 9, 1985).

▶ Simmons v. Brothers, No. 90-627 (D. Mass. Dec. 19, 1990).

▶ State v. McArthur, No. C4-99-502 (Minn. Ct. App. Sept. 28, 1999), http://www.lawlibrary.state.mn.us/archive/ctapun/9909/502.htm.

▶ United States v. Palermo, N.Y. TIMES, Aug. 27, 1957, at 24 (S.D.N.Y. Aug. 26, 1957).

For citation to administrative reporters, see rule 14.3.2.

10.3.2 Reporters

Bound publications that print only cases (or cases and annotations) are considered reporters and are cited in roman type. A citation to a reporter consists of a volume designation (rule 3.1), the abbreviated name of the reporter (as shown in table T1), and the page on which the case report begins (rule 3.2). For rules on spacing in reporter abbreviations, see rule 6.1(a).

▸ Burt v. Rumsfeld, 322 F. Supp. 2d 189 (D. Conn. 2004).

Early American reporters were often named after their editors rather than after the courts whose cases they reported. Subsequently, official editor-named series have been combined into jurisdiction-named series with continuous volume numbering. Such reporters are now generally cited by the official series name and number only; the name of the reporter's editor is omitted:

▸ Cobb v. Davenport, 32 N.J.L. 369 (Sup. Ct. 1867).

Not: 3 Vroom 369

But for United States Supreme Court reporters through 90 U.S. (23 Wall.) and a few early state reporters (see table T1.3), give the name of the reporter's editor and the volume of that series. If the pagination of the official jurisdiction-named reprints and the original reporters is the same, use the following form:

▸ Green v. Biddle, 21 U.S. (8 Wheat.) 1 (1823).

▸ Hall v. Bell, 47 Mass. (6 Met.) 431 (1843).

If the pagination differs, give parallel citations to the reprints and the original reporters:

▸ Wadsworth v. Ruggles, 23 Mass. 62, 6 Pick. 63 (1828).

Some very early Pennsylvania federal and state court decisions are reported in the initial volumes of the *United States Reports*. Where this occurs, include the cite to "U.S.," along with a parallel cite to the appropriate lower court reporter.

▸ Barnes's Lessee v. Irwin, 2 U.S. (2 Dall.) 199, 1 Yeates 221 (Pa. 1793) (mem.).

▸ United States v. Fries, 3 U.S. (3 Dall.) 515, 9 F. Cas. 826 (C.C.D. Pa. 1799) (No. 5126).

....

10.3.3 Public Domain Format

When citing a decision available in public domain format (also referred to as medium-neutral format), if the jurisdiction's format can be cited in the following form (see table T1), provide the case name, the year of decision, the state's two-character postal code, the table T7 court abbreviation (unless the court is the state's highest court), the sequential number of the decision, and, if the decision is unpublished, a capital "U" after the sequential number of the decision. When referencing specific material within the decision, a pinpoint citation should be made to the paragraph number at which the material appears. If available, a parallel citation to the appropriate regional reporter must be provided.

The following examples are representative of the recommended public domain citation format:

- Beck v. Beck, 1999 ME 110, ¶ 6, 733 A.2d 981, 983.
- Gregory v. Class, 1998 SD 106, ¶ 3, 584 N.W.2d 873, 875.
- Jones v. Fisher, 1998 OK Civ. App. 120U.

If a jurisdiction adopts a public domain format that differs from the above, the requirements of the jurisdiction's format should be observed (**table T1**):

- Cannon v. Am. Bowling Cong., 94-0647, p.1 (La. 4/29/94); 637 So. 2d 463.
- Morton v. New Orleans Police Dep't, 96-1799 (La. App. 4 Cir. 2/5/97); 687 So. 2d 699.
- Sullivan v. State, 98-KA-00521-SCT (¶ 23) (Miss. 1999).
- State v. Brennan, 1998-NMCA-176, ¶ 7, 126 N.M. 389, 970 P.2d 161.

Court and Jurisdiction   10.4

Every case citation must indicate which court decided the case. In American and other common law citations, give the name of the court and its geographical jurisdiction (abbreviated according to **tables T1** or **T2** if included therein and according to **tables T7** and **T10** in all other cases) in the parenthetical phrase that immediately follows the citation and includes the date or year of decision. For court names that include ordinals, format and abbreviate the ordinals in accordance with **rule 6.2(b)**:

- Commonwealth v. Virelli, 620 A.2d 543 (Pa. Super. Ct. 1992).
- United States v. Andolschek, 142 F.2d 503 (2d Cir. 1944).

For citations to foreign cases, see **rule 20.3** and **table T2**.

A more detailed court designation than those specified by the following paragraphs may be given if necessary.

(a) Federal courts. In citations to *United States Law Week*, the United States Supreme Court is indicated with "U.S." In citations to the *Supreme Court Reporter* and the *United States Reports*, omit the Supreme Court's name. When a Supreme Court Justice sits alone in his or her capacity as a Circuit Justice, cite the decision as:

- Russo v. Byrne, 409 U.S. 1219 (Douglas, Circuit Justice 1972).

United States courts of appeals for numbered circuits, regardless of year, are indicated:

- 2d Cir.

Not: C.C.A.2d

Not: CA2

When citing the United States Court of Appeals for the District of Columbia Circuit and its predecessors, or when citing the Federal Circuit, use the following abbreviations:

- D.C. Cir.
- Fed. Cir.

For district court cases, give the district but not the division:

> ▶ D.N.J.
> ▶ D.D.C.
> ▶ C.D. Cal.

Not: C.D. Cal. E.D.

Cite the old circuit courts (abolished 1912):

> ▶ C.C.S.D.N.Y.
> ▶ C.C.E.D. Mo.

Cite the Judicial Panel on Multidistrict Litigation:

> ▶ J.P.M.L.

Cite the Foreign Intelligence Surveillance Court and Court of Review, respectively:

> ▶ FISA Ct., FISA Ct. Rev.

Cite decisions of bankruptcy courts and bankruptcy appellate panels:

> ▶ Bankr. E.D. Va.
> ▶ B.A.P. 9th Cir.

(b) State courts. In general, indicate the state and court of decision. However, do not include the name of the court if the court of decision is the highest court of the state:

> ▶ People v. Armour, 590 N.W.2d 61 (Mich. 1999).

Not: People v. Armour, 590 N.W.2d 61 (Mich. Sup. Ct. 1999).

Omit the jurisdiction and the court abbreviation if unambiguously conveyed by the reporter title:

> ▶ DiLucia v. Mandelker, 493 N.Y.S.2d 769 (App. Div. 1985).

Not: DiLucia v. Mandelker, 493 N.Y.S.2d 769 (N.Y. App. Div. 1985).

> ▶ Dubreuil v. Witt, 80 Conn. App. 410 (2003).

Not: Dubreuil v. Witt, 80 Conn. App. 410 (App. Ct. 2003).

Thus, when a decision is rendered by the highest court in a particular jurisdiction and the name of the reporter is the same as the name of that jurisdiction, neither the name of the court nor the name of the state need be given:

> ▶ Bates v. Tappan, 99 Mass. 376 (1868).

Do not indicate the department or district in citing decisions of intermediate state courts unless that information is of particular relevance:

> ▶ Schiffman v. Corsi, 50 N.Y.S.2d 897 (Sup. Ct. 1944).

When the department or district is of particular relevance, that information should be indicated as follows:

> ▶ Schiffman v. Corsi, 50 N.Y.S.2d 897 (Sup. Ct. N.Y. Cnty. 1944).
> ▶ Lee v. Perez, 120 S.W.3d 463 (Tex. App. 14th 2003).

Date or Year   10.5

(a) Decisions published in reporters. If possible, provide the year of decision; use the year of the term of court only if the year of decision is unavailable. In ambiguous cases, follow the year given in the running head (at the top of each page) in the reporter. Before Volume 108 of the U.S. Reports (1882), opinions do not usually list their date of decision but list only the term in which they were decided. For the dates of these opinions, refer to the Librarian of the Supreme Court's list of dates, available at http://www.supremecourt.gov/opinions/datesofdecisions.pdf.

(b) Decisions published in other sources. Give the exact date for all unreported cases and for all cases cited to a looseleaf service, a slip opinion, an electronic database, or a newspaper.

> ► Charlesworth v. Mack, No. 90-567, slip op. 3458 (1st Cir. Jan. 19, 1991).

Per **rule 10.5(a)**, the exact date is *not* necessary for cases that are labeled "unpublished" but are nevertheless reported, including cases reported in the *Federal Appendix* and "unpublished" cases reported in the appropriate reporter for the jurisdiction.

> ► United States v. Tando, 68 F. App'x 85 (9th Cir. 2003).

(c) Pending cases and cases dismissed without opinion. Use the date or year of the most recent major disposition. "Major dispositions" include *only*: the initial filing, whether in the trial court or on appeal (e.g., "filed," "*appeal docketed*," "*petition for cert. filed*"), oral argument ("argued"), and, for cases dismissed without opinion, the dismissal ("dismissed"). Indicate the significance of the date within a parenthetical phrase, unless its significance is explained elsewhere:

> ► Charlesworth v. Mack, No. 90-567 (1st Cir. argued Jan. 10, 1991).

Otherwise no special notation is necessary:

> ► Charlesworth v. Mack, 725 F. Supp. 1407 (D. Mass. 1990), *appeal docketed*, No. 90-567 (1st Cir. Dec. 20, 1990).

(d) Multiple decisions within a single year. When citing a case with several different decisions in the same year, include the year only with the last-cited decision in that year:

> ► United States v. Eller, 114 F. Supp. 284 (M.D.N.C.), *rev'd*, 208 F.2d 716 (4th Cir. 1953).

However, if the exact date of decision is required in either case, include both dates:

> ► DiNapoli v. Ne. Reg'l Parole Comm'n, 764 F.2d 143 (2d Cir. 1985), *petition for cert. filed*, 54 U.S.L.W. 3146 (U.S. Aug. 29, 1985) (No. 85-335).

10.6 Parenthetical Information Regarding Cases

10.6.1 Weight of Authority

(a) Generally. Information regarding the weight of the authority (e.g., en banc; in banc; 2-1 decision; mem.; per curiam; Brandeis, J.; unpublished table decision) may be added in a separate parenthetical phrase following the date of decision.

> ► Webb v. Baxter Healthcare Corp., 57 F.3d 1067 (4th Cir. 1995) (unpublished table decision).

When a case is cited for a proposition that is not the single, clear holding of a majority of the court (e.g., alternative holding; by implication; dictum; dissenting opinion; plurality opinion; holding unclear), indicate that fact parenthetically:

> ► Parker v. Randolph, 442 U.S. 62, 84 (1979) (Stevens, J., dissenting).

> ► Garcia v. San Antonio Metro. Transit Auth., 469 U.S. 528, 570 (1985) (5-4 decision) (Powell, J., dissenting).

Information regarding related authority (**rule 1.6**) or prior or subsequent history (**rule 10.7**) that can properly be indicated with an explanatory phrase (**table T8**) should not be given parenthetically. Thus:

> ► Wersba v. Seiler, 393 F.2d 937 (3d Cir. 1968) (per curiam).

> But: Wersba v. Seiler, 263 F. Supp. 838, 843 (E.D. Pa. 1967), *aff'd per curiam*, 393 F.2d 937 (3d Cir. 1968).

(b) "Mem." and "per curiam." The abbreviation "mem." stands for the word "memorandum" and should be used in a parenthetical if, and only if, a court disposition is issued without an opinion. District court and other opinions denominated "memorandum decision" are not designated "mem." in citations. The phrase "per curiam" refers to an opinion issued "by the court" as an institution as opposed to a decision issued by a particular judge. "Per curiam" is used in a parenthetical to describe an opinion so denominated by the court.

(c) Seriatim opinions. Prior to the Marshall Court (which began February 4, 1801), the U.S. Supreme Court followed the traditional British practice of each Justice writing his own opinion rather than producing a majority opinion for the Court. To cite such an opinion, include the parenthetical "(opinion of Lastname, J.)."

10.6.2 Quoting/Citing Parentheticals in Case Citations

When a case cited as authority itself quotes or cites another case for that point, a "quoting" or "citing" parenthetical is appropriate per **rule 1.6(c)**. Within the parenthetical, the same rules regarding typeface, pincites, and short forms apply to the quoted or cited authority as if it were the direct source:

> ► Zadvydas v. Davis, 533 U.S. 678, 719 (2001) (Kennedy, J., dissenting) (citing Shaughnessy v. United States *ex rel.* Mezei, 345 U.S. 206 (1953)).

Note, however, that only one level of recursion is required. Thus, if a case quotes a case, which itself quotes another case, only one level of "quoting" or "citing" parentheticals is necessary. An additional level of parenthetical information may be used if the information conveyed is particularly relevant.

Order of Parentheticals

10.6.3

Parenthetical phrases should be placed in the following order: (i) weight of authority parentheticals; (ii) "quoting" and "citing" parentheticals; (iii) explanatory parentheticals. For more detailed information, see **rule 1.5(b)**. Thus:

> ► Wolf v. Colorado, 338 U.S. 25, 47 (1949) (Rutledge, J., dissenting) (rejecting the Court's conception of the exclusionary rule), *aff' g* 187 P.2d 926 (Colo. 1947), *overruled by* Mapp v. Ohio, 367 U.S. 643 (1961).

If an explanatory parenthetical contains text that *itself* requires a "quoting" or "citing" parenthetical, the two parentheticals should be nested:

> ► Kansas v. Crane, 534 U.S. 407, 409 (2002) ("[T]he statutory criterion for confinement embodied in the statute's words 'mental abnormality or personality disorder' satisfied '"substantive" due process' requirements.'" (quoting Kansas v. Hendricks, 521 U.S. 346, 356 (1997))).

> ► Fullilove v. Klutznick, 448 U.S. 448, 519 (1980) (Marshall, J., concurring) (noting that conventional strict scrutiny is "strict in theory, but fatal in fact" (citing Regents of the Univ. of Cal. v. Bakke, 438 U.S. 265, 362 (1978))).

Prior and Subsequent History

10.7

Whenever a decision is cited in full, give the entire *subsequent* history of the case, but omit denials of certiorari or denials of similar discretionary appeals, unless the decision is less than two years old or the denial is particularly relevant. Omit also the history on remand or any denial of a rehearing, unless relevant to the point for which the case is cited. Finally, omit any disposition withdrawn by the deciding authority, such as an affirmance followed by reversal on rehearing. Thus:

> ► Cent. Ill. Pub. Serv. Co. v. Westervelt, 342 N.E.2d 463 (Ill. App. Ct. 1976), *aff'd*, 367 N.E.2d 661 (Ill. 1977).

> Not: Cent. Ill. Pub. Serv. Co. v. Westervelt, 342 N.E.2d 463 (Ill. App. Ct. 1976), *aff'd*, 367 N.E.2d 661 (Ill. 1977), *cert. denied*, 434 U.S. 1070 (1978).

> ► Cheng v. GAF Corp., 631 F.2d 1052 (2d Cir. 1980), *vacated*, 450 U.S. 903 (1981).

> Not: Cheng v. GAF Corp., 631 F.2d 1052 (2d Cir. 1980), *vacated*, 450 U.S. 903, *remanded to* 659 F.2d 1058 (2d Cir. 1981).

Give *prior* history only if significant to the point for which the case is cited or if the disposition cited does not intelligibly describe the issues in the case, as in a Supreme Court "mem." Give separate decisions of other issues in the case with their prior and subsequent history only if relevant.

....

10.7.1 Explanatory Phrases and Weight of Authority

A partial list of explanatory phrases (as abbreviated) appears in **table T8**.

(a) Prior or subsequent history. Append the prior or subsequent history of a case to the primary citation. Introduce and explain each decision with italicized words between each citation:

> ► Cooper v. Dupnik, 924 F.2d 1520, 1530 & n.20 (9th Cir. 1991), *rev'd en banc*, 963 F.2d 1220 (9th Cir. 1992).

If a subsequent disposition occurred in the same year as the primary citation, omit the year from the primary citation's parenthetical.

If subsequent history itself has subsequent history, append the additional subsequent history with another explanatory phrase. For example, in the following case the Supreme Court reversed the Second Circuit, which had reversed the Southern District of New York:

> ► Herbert v. Lando, 73 F.R.D. 387 (S.D.N.Y.), *rev'd*, 568 F.2d 974 (2d Cir. 1977), *rev'd*, 441 U.S. 153 (1979).

To show both prior and subsequent history, give the prior history first:

> ► Kubrick v. United States, 581 F.2d 1092 (3d Cir. 1978), *aff' g* 435 F. Supp. 166 (E.D. Pa. 1977), *rev'd*, 444 U.S. 111 (1979).

Citations to prior or subsequent history should follow any parenthetical information given for the primary citation (**rule 1.5(b)**).

(b) Significance of disposition. Give the reason for a disposition if the disposition does not carry the normal substantive significance:

> ► *vacated as moot*,

> ► *appeal dismissed per stipulation*,

(c) Overruled, abrogated, and superseded cases. Also note cases that have been overruled, abrogated, or superseded by statute or constitutional amendment:

(i) **Overruled cases.** Indicate cases where a later decision by the same court (or a court with appellate jurisdiction over the original court) *explicitly* repudiates its earlier decision with the phrase "*overruled by*":

> ► Nat'l League of Cities v. Usery, 426 U.S. 833 (1976), *overruled by* Garcia v. San Antonio Metro. Transit Auth., 469 U.S. 528 (1985).

Also, when one case is overruled by multiple subsequent decisions by the same court (i.e., separate decisions overrule separate parts of the holding), include "*and*" between the citations to each of the overruling cases:

> ► Olmstead v. United States, 277 U.S. 438 (1928), *overruled by* Katz v. United States, 389 U.S. 347 (1967), *and* Berger v. New York, 388 U.S. 41 (1967).

(ii) **Abrogated cases.** Cases that are effectively (but not explicitly) overruled or departed from by a later decision of the same court are indicated with the phrase "*abrogated by*":

> ► Ahrens v. Clark, 335 U.S. 188 (1948), *abrogated by* Braden v. 30th Judicial Circuit Court, 410 U.S. 484 (1973).

(iii) **Cases superseded by statute or constitutional amendment.** When citing cases where a statute or amendment was enacted with the specific intent of reversing the outcome of the initial case, the statute or amendment *must* always be cited, and a later case recognizing such *may* be cited for support, as long as the later case is decided by the same court (or a court with appellate jurisdiction over the original court) as the superseded case:

► Wards Cove Packing Co. v. Atonio, 490 U.S. 642 (1989), *superseded by statute*, Civil Rights Act of 1991, Pub. L. No. 102-166, 105 Stat. 1074, *as recognized in* Raytheon Co. v. Hernandez, 540 U.S. 44 (2003).

► Dred Scott v. Sandford, 60 U.S. (19 How.) 393 (1857), *superseded by constitutional amendment*, U.S. Const. amend. XIV.

Statutes cited according to this rule should be cited to the session laws (**rule 12.4**) wherever possible, and, if appropriate, specific sections of the statute superseding the case may be cited.

(d) Multiple dispositions. Multiple dispositions by the same court following a primary case citation should be connected with the word "*and*" in italics:

► United States v. Baxter, 492 F.2d 150 (9th Cir.), *cert. dismissed*, 414 U.S. 801 (1973), *and cert. denied*, 416 U.S. 940 (1974).

....

Different Case Name on Appeal   10.7.2

(a) Name changes in subsequent history. When the name of a case differs in subsequent history, the new name must be given, introduced by the phrase "*sub nom.*":

► Great W. United Corp. v. Kidwell, 577 F.2d 1256 (5th Cir. 1978), *rev'd sub nom.* Leroy v. Great W. United Corp., 443 U.S. 173 (1979).

This rule applies even when the difference in the name is slight, such as a change in only the procedural phrases:

► Padilla *ex rel.* Newman v. Rumsfeld, 243 F. Supp. 2d 42 (S.D.N.Y.), *aff'd in part, rev'd in part sub nom.* Padilla v. Rumsfeld, 352 F.3d 695 (2d Cir. 2003), *rev'd*, 542 U.S. 426 (2004).

(b) Name changes in prior history. To indicate a different name in prior history, use the following form:

► Rederi v. Isbrandtsen Co., 342 U.S. 950 (1952) (per curiam), *aff'g by an equally divided court* Isbrandtsen Co. v. United States, 96 F. Supp. 883 (S.D.N.Y. 1951).

(c) Exceptions. Do not provide a different case name (i) when the parties' names are merely reversed; (ii) when the citation in which the difference occurs is to a denial of certiorari or rehearing; (iii) when, in the appeal of an administrative action, the name of the private party remains the same; or (iv) when the change is simply stylistic (e.g., "State" to "California"):

► United Dairy Farmers Coop. Ass'n, 194 N.L.R.B. 1094, *enforced*, 465 F.2d 1401 (3d Cir. 1972).

But: Perma Vinyl Corp., 164 N.L.R.B. 968 (1967), *enforced sub nom.* U.S. Pipe & Foundry Co. v. NLRB, 398 F.2d 544 (5th Cir. 1968).

10.8 Special Citation Forms

10.8.1 Pending and Unreported Cases

(a) Cases available on electronic media. When a case is unreported but available on a widely used electronic database, it may be cited to that database. Provide the case name, docket number, database identifier, court name, and full date of the most recent major disposition of the case. Cite to the case docket number exactly as it appears. If the database contains codes or numbers that uniquely identify the case (as do LEXIS and Westlaw), these must be given. Screen or page numbers, if the database assigns them, should be preceded by an asterisk; paragraph numbers, if assigned, should be preceded by a paragraph symbol:

▶ Gibbs v. Frank, No. 02-3924, 2004 U.S. App. LEXIS 21357, at *18–19 (3d Cir. Oct. 14, 2004).

▶ Chavez v. Metro. Dist. Comm'n, No. 3:02CV458(MRK), 2004 U.S. Dist. LEXIS 11266, at *5 n.3 (D. Conn. June 1, 2004).

▶ Int'l Snowmobile Mfrs. Ass'n v. Norton, No. 00-CV-229-B, 2004 WL 2337372, at *3, *7 (D. Wyo. Oct. 14, 2004).

▶ Shelton v. City of Manhattan Beach, No. B171606, 2004 WL 2163741, at *1 (Cal. Ct. App. Sept. 28, 2004).

If the name of the database is not clear from the database identifier, include it parenthetically at the end of the citation:

▶ Staats v. Brown, No. 65681-9, 2000 WA 0042007, ¶ 25 (Wash. Jan. 6, 2000) (VersusLaw).

Citations to cases that have not been assigned unique database identifiers should include all relevant information, such as the specific collection within the database in which the case can be found:

▶ Frankel v. Banco Nacional de Mex., S.A., No. 82 Civ. 6547 (S.D.N.Y. May 31, 1983) (LEXIS, Genfed Library, Dist. File).

▶ Lindquist v. Hart, 1 CA-CV 98-0323 (Ariz. Ct. App. July 15, 1999) (Loislaw, Ariz. Case Law).

(b) Cases available in slip opinions. When a case is unreported but available in a separately printed slip opinion, give the docket number, the court, and the full date of the most recent major disposition of the case:

▶ Groucho Marx Prods. v. Playboy Enters., No. 77 Civ. 1782 (S.D.N.Y. Dec. 30, 1977).

Note any renumbering of the docket:

▶ United States v. Johnson, 425 F.2d 630 (9th Cir. 1970), *cert. granted*, 403 U.S. 956 (1971) (No. 577, 1970 Term; renumbered No. 70-8, 1971 Term).

Always give the full docket number:

▶ No. 75-31

Not: No. 31

If the date given does not refer to the date of decision and the significance of the date is not indicated elsewhere, indicate that significance within the parenthetical phrase containing the date:

▶ Charlesworth v. Mack, No. 90-345 (D. Mass. filed Sept. 18, 1990).

To cite a particular page of a separately paginated slip opinion, use the form:

▶ Charlesworth v. Mack, No. 90-345, slip op. at 6 (D. Mass. Dec. 4, 1990).

If the case is not separately paginated, cite the page on which the case begins as well as the page on which any particular material appears:

▶ Charlesworth v. Mack, No. 90-567, slip op. 3458, 3465 (1st Cir. Jan. 19, 1991).

In pending or unreported adversary proceedings in bankruptcy, supply both the case number of the underlying nonadversary proceeding and the case number of the adversary proceeding:

▶ Brown v. Sachs (*In re* Brown), Ch. 7 Case No. 84-00170-G, Adv. No. 85-1190, slip op. at 5 (E.D. Mich. Jan. 24, 1986).

(c) Other pending and unreported cases. Cases that are not available in slip opinions or on electronic databases may be cited to services (**rule 19**), periodicals (**rule 16**), or the Internet (**rule 18.2.2**).

(d) Depublished cases. A number of jurisdictions allow their decisions to be "depublished," usually when review is denied, and generally without a reported order. When there is no reported order depublishing the lower court decision, the fact that the case was depublished should be indicated parenthetically:

▶ Mitchell v. Cal. Fair Plan Ass'n, 260 Cal. Rptr. 3 (Ct. App. 1989) (depublished).

If the order depublishing a case *is* reported, the order should be indicated as subsequent history pursuant to **rule 10.7**, introduced with the explanatory phrase "*depublished by*."

Fifth Circuit Split   10.8.2

On October 1, 1981, the Fifth Circuit of the United States Courts of Appeals was divided to create the new Fifth and Eleventh Circuits. Cite cases decided during the transitional period leading to this reorganization according to the following rules: (i) cite decisions rendered in 1981 and labeled "5th Cir." by month; (ii) give unit information whenever available; (iii) designate as "Former 5th" any nonunit judgment labeled as a Former Fifth judgment and rendered after September 30, 1981:

▶ Birl v. Estelle, 660 F.2d 592 (5th Cir. Nov. 1981).

▶ Haitian Refugee Ctr. v. Smith, 676 F.2d 1023 (5th Cir. Unit B 1982).

▶ Trailways, Inc. v. ICC, 676 F.2d 1019 (5th Cir. Unit A Aug. 1981) (per curiam).

▶ McCormick v. United States, 680 F.2d 345 (Former 5th Cir. 1982).

10.8.3 Briefs, Court Filings, and Transcripts

Citation for a petitioner's brief in a U.S. Supreme Court case:

In general, all court filings follow the same general form. The full name of the document, as it appears on the filing, must come first, abbreviated according to **rule 10.2.1(c)**, followed by a pinpoint citation, if any. The full case citation and the docket number should follow the name of the document and the pinpoint citation. If no decision has yet been rendered on the filing cited, cite the case according to **rule 10.5(c)**, but the date in the parenthetical should be the date *on which the filing was made*, regardless of subsequent dispositions (e.g., oral argument). If a decision has been rendered, cite the case according to **rule 10.5(a)**.

> ► Complaint at 17, Kelly v. Wyman, 294 F. Supp. 893 (S.D.N.Y. 1968) (No. 68 Civ. 394).

Always include the docket number, whether parenthetically (when there *is* a reported citation) or *as* the citation (when there is no reported citation):

> ► Brief of Petitioner-Appellant at 48, United States v. Al-Marri, No. 03-3674 (7th Cir. Nov. 12, 2003).

The document number assigned by the court, such as that found on PACER for federal cases, may also be included, but is not necessary unless it is essential to finding the document:

> ► Amended Complaint & Demand for Jury Trial, Viola v. Am. Brands, Inc., No. 85-2496-G (D. Mass. Aug. 1, 1985), ECF No. 14.

With court-produced documents, including oral argument transcripts and transcripts of record, the same general rules apply:

> ► Transcript of Oral Argument at 11, Ayers v. Belmontes, 127 S. Ct. 469 (2006) (No. 05-493).

> ► Transcript of Record at 16–17, Johnson v. Eisentrager, 339 U.S. 763 (1950) (No. 306).

With amicus briefs, the same general rules apply, with the sole exception that if there are more than two signatories to the brief, "et al." may be used:

> ► Brief for Ringling Bros.-Barnum & Bailey Combined Shows, Inc. et al. as Amici Curiae Supporting Respondents, Moseley v. V Secret Catalogue, Inc., 537 U.S. 418 (2003) (No. 01-1015).

Further, though the above information is sufficient, a parallel citation to an electronic database or a website may be provided, if helpful:

> ► Brief for Ringling Bros.-Barnum & Bailey Combined Shows, Inc. et al. as Amici Curiae Supporting Respondents, Moseley v. V Secret Catalogue, Inc., 537 U.S. 418 (2003) (No. 01-1015), 2002 WL 1987618.

Such parallel citations *must* include a pinpoint citation to the electronic database where one is required for the primary document, and vice versa.

With audio recordings of court proceedings, including oral arguments and oral dissents, the same general rules apply, except that the title may be a description of the recording. Timestamps should be used for designating pinpoint citations. If the recording is available online, append a URL pursuant to **rule 18.7.3**.

► Oral Argument at 11:38, Roe v. Wade, 410 U.S. 113 (1973) (No. 70-18), *available at* http://www.oyez.org/cases/1970-1979/1971/1971_70_18/argument.

► Oral Dissent of Justice Ginsburg at 4:25, Ledbetter v. Goodyear Tire & Rubber Co., 127 S. Ct. 2162 (2007) (No. 05-1074), *available at* http://www.oyez.org/cases/2000-2009/2006/200_05_908/opinion.

For purposes of short forms (**rule 10.9**), a citation to a court document including a case citation suffices as a citation to the case itself. Where the case may be cited in short form per **rule 10.9**, it may be cited in short form in the citation to the court document, but the docket number must still be provided.

► ¹ Brief for the Petitioner, Demore v. Kim, 538 U.S. 510 (2003) (No. 01-1491).

► ² Petition for Writ of Certiorari, *Demore*, 538 U.S. 510 (No. 01-1491).

Further, the court document itself may be cited using a *supra* form, unlike the case, which may not. A *supra* form for the court document, however, does not count for purposes of the "five footnote" rule. The document title will suffice so long as it does not create confusion. Hereinafter forms may also be used (**rule 4.2(b)**), if helpful.

► ³ Brief for the Petitioner, *supra* note 1, at 12.

....

Court Administrative Orders 10.8.4

Cite the official reporter, if therein; give the title of the order, if any:

► Order Discharging the Advisory Committee, 352 U.S. 803 (1956).

Short Forms for Cases 10.9

(a) Footnotes. In law review footnotes, a short form for a case may be used if it clearly identifies a case that (1) is already cited in the *same footnote* or (2) is cited (in either full or short form, including "*id.*") in *one of the preceding five footnotes*. Otherwise a full citation is required. Thus in the following example, the use of the short form in footnotes 4 and 7–8 is correct:

► ¹ United States v. Montoya de Hernandez, 473 U.S. 531 (1985).

► ² *Id.* at 537–38.

► ³ *See* United States v. Martinez-Fuerte, 428 U.S. 543, 557 (1976); Cal. Bankers Ass'n v. Shultz, 416 U.S. 21, 62 (1974); Zimmermann v. Jenkins (*In re* GGM, P.C.), 165 F.3d 1026, 1027 (5th Cir. 1999); Cohen v. Drexel Burnham Lambert Grp. (*In re* Drexel Burnham Lambert Grp.), 138 B.R. 687, 702 (Bankr. S.D.N.Y. 1992); *In re* Draughon Training Inst., Inc., 119 B.R. 921, 926 (Bankr. W.D. La. 1990).

▶ 4 *See Martinez-Fuerte*, 428 U.S. at 550; *In re Draughon Training*, 119 B.R. at 930.

▶ 5 New York v. Belton, 453 U.S. 454, 457 (1981).

▶ 6 *See id.* at 456.

▶ 7 *See Montoya de Hernandez*, 473 U.S. at 540; *Cohen*, 138 B.R. at 707.

▶ 8 *See Martinez-Fuerte*, 428 U.S. at 550; *Cal. Bankers*, 416 U.S. at 55; *In re* GGM, P.C., 165 F.3d at 1030.

(i) **Generally.** Use of only one party's name (or a readily identifiable shorter version of one party's name) in a short form citation is permissible if the reference is unambiguous. When only one party's name (or a short form thereof) is used, it should be italicized. Acceptable short forms include:

▶ Youngstown Sheet & Tube Co. v. Sawyer, 343 U.S. at 585.

▶ *Youngstown Sheet & Tube Co.*, 343 U.S. at 585.

▶ *Youngstown*, 343 U.S. at 585.

▶ 343 U.S. at 585.

▶ *Id.* at 585.

Omit the case name as in the last two examples only if the reader will have no doubt about the case to which the citation refers.

Per **rule 10.2.1(k)**, cases may also be cited in short form by different names than that which appears in the reporter, so long as the full citation includes both versions:

▶ Youngstown Sheet & Tube Co. v. Sawyer (*Steel Seizure*), 343 U.S. 579, 585 (1952).

becomes: *Steel Seizure*, 343 U.S. at 585.

When citing an entire decision, and not a pinpoint therein, in short form, you must include the shorter version of the case name, the volume number, reporter designation, and first page; but do *not* include a jurisdiction/date parenthetical:

▶ *Steel Seizure*, 343 U.S. 579.

When using only one party name in a short form citation, avoid using the name of a geographical or governmental unit, a governmental official, or other common litigant. Thus:

▶ NAACP v. Alabama *ex rel.* Patterson, 357 U.S. 449, 464 (1958).

becomes: *Patterson*, 357 U.S. at 464.

Not: *NAACP*, 357 U.S. at 464.

Not: *Alabama*, 357 U.S. at 464.

▶ Reno v. Bossier Parish Sch. Bd., 520 U.S. 471 (1997).

becomes: *Bossier Parish Sch. Bd.*, 520 U.S. at 480.

Not: *Reno*, 520 U.S. at 480.

(ii) **Commercial electronic databases.** For cases that are available on an electronic database (**rule 10.8.1**), use a unique database identifier, if one has been assigned, in constructing a short form:

> ► Clark v. Homrighous, No. CIV.A.90-1380-T, 1991 WL 55402, at *3 (D. Kan. Apr. 10, 1991).

becomes: *Clark*, 1991 WL 55402, at *3.

> ► Albrecht v. Stanczek, No. 87-C9535, 1991 U.S. Dist. LEXIS 5088, at *1 (N.D. Ill. Apr. 18, 1991).

becomes: *Albrecht*, 1991 U.S. Dist. LEXIS 5088, at *1.

> ► Lindquist v. Hart, 1 CA-CV 98-0323, at *2 (Ariz. Ct. App. July 15, 1999) (Loislaw.com, Ariz. Case Law).

becomes: *Lindquist*, at *2 (Loislaw.com, Ariz. Case Law).

(b) Two exceptions when using "id." There are two exceptions when using "*id.*" as a short form for case citations: (i) citations to the same case, but to a different opinion therein; and (ii) citation to the same case where the case citation includes parallel authorities.

(i) **"Id." for different opinions.** When an "*id.*" refers to the same case, and to the same opinion cited in the preceding citation, no parenthetical is necessary. But when the "*id.*" refers to a *different* opinion, that fact *must* be indicated parenthetically, even if the second opinion cited is the majority opinion. Thus, the following examples are all correct:

> ► [1] Youngstown Sheet & Tube Co. v. Sawyer (*Steel Seizure*), 343 U.S. 579 (1952).

> ► [2] *Id.* at 584.

> ► [3] *Id.* at 635 (Jackson, J., concurring).

> ► [4] *Id.* at 638.

> ► [5] *Id.* at 589 (Frankfurter, J., concurring).

> ► [6] *Id.* at 582 (majority opinion).

(ii) **"Id." for parallel citations.** For cases in which a parallel citation is required, the "*id.*" form looks slightly different (to avoid confusion). Thus,

> ► Chalfin v. Specter, 426 Pa. 464, 465, 233 A.2d 562, 563 (1967).

becomes. *Id.* at 465, 233 A.2d at 563.

Not: *Id.* at 465.

Not: *Id.* at 465, 563.

(c) Text. A case that has been cited in full in the same general discussion may be referred to (in main text or footnote text) by one of the parties' names without further citation:

> ► The issue presented in *Bakke* has not been fully resolved.

11 CONSTITUTIONS

Citation of Section 2 of the Fourteenth Amendment to the U.S. Constitution:

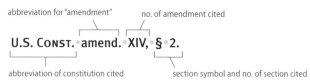

Cite the United States federal and state constitutions by "U.S." or the abbreviated name of the state (as indicated in **table T10**) and the word "CONST." Abbreviate the subdivisions of constitutions, such as article and clause, according to **table T16**:

▶ U.S. CONST. art. I, § 9, cl. 2.
▶ U.S. CONST. amend. XIV, § 2.
▶ U.S. CONST. pmbl.
▶ LA. CONST. art. X, pt. IV.

Cite constitutional provisions currently in force without a date. If the cited provision has been repealed, either indicate parenthetically the fact and year of repeal or cite the repealing provision in full:

▶ U.S. CONST. amend. XVIII (repealed 1933).
▶ U.S. CONST. amend. XVIII, *repealed by* U.S. CONST. amend. XXI.

When citing a provision that has been subsequently amended, either indicate parenthetically the fact and year of amendment or cite the amending provision in full:

▶ U.S. CONST. art. I, § 3, cl. 1 (amended 1913).
▶ U.S. CONST. art. I, § 3, cl. 1, *amended by* U.S. CONST. amend. XVII.

Cite constitutions that have been totally superseded or are otherwise no longer in effect by year of adoption; if the specific provision cited was adopted in a different year, give that year parenthetically:

▶ ARTICLES OF CONFEDERATION of 1781, art. IX, para. 1.
▶ ARK. CONST. of 1868, art. III, § 2 (1873).

When citing a constitution contained in an electronic database, indicate parenthetically the name of the publisher, editor, or compiler unless the constitution is published, edited, compiled by, or under the supervision of, federal or state officials. Also indicate the name of the database and information regarding the currency of the database as provided by the database itself:

▶ WASH. CONST. art. I, § 2 (West, Westlaw through Nov. 2003 amendments).

Do not use a short citation form (other than "*id.*") for constitutions.

	Citation	Text
U.S. Constitution	U.S. CONST. art. IV, § 1	Article IV, Section 1 or the Full Faith and Credit Clause
State constitution	S.C. CONST. art. I, § 12	article I, section 12 or the double jeopardy clause

For foreign constitutions, see **rule 20.4**.

STATUTES 12

Citation of an entire statute, the Comprehensive Environmental Response, Compensation, and Liability Act, as codified in the *United States Code:*

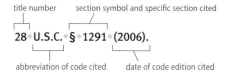

Citation of an individual provision of the *United States Code:*

title number   section symbol and specific section cited

28 U.S.C. § 1291 (2006).

abbreviation of code cited   date of code edition cited

Basic Citation Forms 12.1

Official and unofficial codes arrange statutes currently in force by subject matter. Official and privately published session laws report statutes in chronological order of enactment. Cite secondary sources—such as looseleaf services, the CIS microform service, periodicals, newspapers, or electronic databases—only when the above listed sources are not available.

Rule 12.2 explains when to use each of these basic citation forms. The next four rules discuss the citation forms for official and unofficial codes (**rule 12.3**), session laws (**rule 12.4**), electronic media and online sources (**rule 12.5**), and other secondary sources (**rule 12.6**). **Rule 12.7** explains when the prior or subsequent history of a statute may or must be cited, and **rule 12.8** discusses the use of explanatory parenthetical phrases with respect to statute citations. **Rule 12.9** outlines special citation forms for the Internal Revenue Code, ordinances, rules of evidence and procedure, uniform acts, model codes, restatements of the law, standards, sentencing guidelines, and the ABA Code of Professional Responsibility. **Rule 12.10** provides short forms for statutes.

Table T1 lists citation forms for the codes and session laws of the federal and state governments, and other United States jurisdictions.

Citing current official code	42 U.S.C. § 1983 (2006).
	National Environmental Policy Act of 1969 § 102, 42 U.S.C. § 4332 (2006).
	Consumer Credit Code, OKLA. STAT. tit. 14A, § 6-203 (1996).
Citing current unofficial code	12 U.S.C.A. § 1426 (West 2010).
	Parking Authority Law, 53 PA. STAT. ANN. tit. 53, § 342 (West 2010).
Citing official session laws	National Environmental Policy Act of 1969, Pub. L. No. 91-190, § 102, 83 Stat. 852, 853 (1970) (prior to 1975 amendment).
Citing privately published session laws	Uniform Commercial Code—General, Provisions, 2004 Minn. Sess. Law Serv., ch. 162, art. 1, § 16 (West) (to be codified at MINN. STAT. ANN. § 336.1-301).
	Uniting and Strengthening America by Providing Appropriate Tools Required to Intercept and Obstruct Terrorism Act, Pub. L. No. 107-56, 2001 U.S.C.C.A.N. (115 Stat.) 272 (2001).
Citing commercial electronic database	10 U.S.C.A. § 10173 (West, Westlaw through P.L. 111-4 (excluding P.L. 111-3)).
Citing secondary source	Social Security Amendments of 1983, Pub. L. No. 98-21, 51 U.S.L.W. 203 (1983).

12.2   Choosing the Proper Citation Form

12.2.1   General Rule

(a) Statutes currently in force. If possible, cite statutes currently in force to the current official code or its supplement. Otherwise, cite a current unofficial code or its supplement, the official session laws, privately published session laws (e.g., *United States Code Congressional and Administrative News*), a commercial electronic database, a looseleaf service, an Internet source, or a newspaper—in that order of preference:

▶ National Environmental Policy Act of 1969 § 102, 42 U.S.C. § 4332 (2006).

For example, a new main edition of the official *United States Code* is published every six years, and an annual cumulative supplement is published for each intervening year. An exact copy of the *United States Code* in PDF format may be found at http://www.gpo.gov/fdsys/browse/collectionUScode.action?collectionCode=USCODE; these versions may be cited as if they were the print code. Codified federal statutes enacted subsequent to the latest edition or supplement of the Code should be cited to an unofficial code (e.g., West's *United States Code Annotated*) until published in the *United States Code*.

(b) Statutes no longer in force. Cite statutes no longer in force to the current official or unofficial code if they still appear therein. Otherwise, cite the last edition of the official or unofficial code in which the statute appeared, the session laws, or a secondary source—in that order of preference. In any case, the fact of invalidation, repeal, or amendment must be noted parenthetically according to **rules 12.7.1, 12.7.2**, and **12.7.3**:

▶ Law of June 1, 1895, ch. 4322, § 23, 1895 Fla. Laws 3, 20–21 (repealed 1969).

▶ Clayton Act, ch. 323, § 7, 38 Stat. 730, 731–32 (1914) (current version at 15 U.S.C. § 18 (2006)).

(c) Private laws. Cite private laws to the session laws if therein; otherwise cite a secondary source:

▶ Priv. L. No. 94-75, 90 Stat. 2985 (1976).

Exceptions

12.2.2

(a) Scattered statutes. Cite the session laws if a statute appears in so many scattered sections or titles that no useful citation to the code is possible. Indicate parenthetically the general location of the codified sections. Thus:

▶ Tax Reduction Act of 1975, Pub. L. No. 94-12, 89 Stat. 26 (codified as amended in scattered sections of 26 U.S.C.).

But: Robinson-Patman Act, 15 U.S.C. §§ 13–13b, 21a (2006).

If the current version of a statute is split between the main body and the supplement of a code, it should be cited according to **rule 3.1(c)**:

▶ 42 U.S.C. § 1397b (1982 & Supp. I 1983).

If the current version of a statute can be determined only by reference to multiple sources (not just a code and its supplement), it should be cited according to **rule 12.7.3**:

▶ 31 U.S.C. § 3724 (1988), *amended by* Act of Dec. 7, 1989, 31 U.S.C.S. § 3724 (Law. Co-op. Supp. 1990).

(b) Historical fact. The historical fact of enactment, amendment, or repeal should be cited to the session laws. A parenthetical reference to the current version (see **rules 12.7.3** and **12.8**) may be added:

▶ Two years later, Congress passed the Voting Rights Act of 1965, Pub. L. No. 89-110, 79 Stat. 445 (codified as amended at 42 U.S.C. §§ 1971, 1973 to 1973bb-1 (2006)).

▶ The Sarbanes-Oxley Act of 2002 increased criminal penalties for mail and wire fraud. *See* Pub. L. No. 107-204, § 903(a)-(b), 2002 U.S.C.C.A.N. (116 Stat.) 745, 805 (to be codified at 18 U.S.C. §§ 1341, 1343).

(c) Materially different language. If the language in the current code (including its supplement) differs materially from the language in the session laws and the relevant title has not been enacted into positive law, cite the session laws. A parenthetical reference to the code version, introduced by the phrase "codified with some differences in language at" may be given. If differences in the language merely reflect subsequent amendments, however, cite the current code.

Cite the official code wherever possible. A current list of federal code titles that have been enacted into positive law appears in the preface to the latest edition or supplement of the *United States Code*. Similarly, state codes should indicate whether the titles contained therein have been enacted into positive law.

12.3 Current Official and Unofficial Codes

Cite the *United States Code* (U.S.C.), the official federal code, whenever possible. Unofficial federal codes include the *United States Code Annotated* (U.S.C.A.) and the *United States Code Service* (U.S.C.S.). Official and unofficial codes for each state (where they exist) are listed in table T1.3.

All citations to codes contain the abbreviated name of the code found in table T1 printed in large and small capitals; the section, paragraph, or article number(s) of the statute; and the year of the code (determined according to rule 12.3.2):

▶ N.C. GEN. STAT. § 1-181 (2003).

12.3.1 Additional Information

Additional information may be required as follows:

(a) Name and original section number. Give the statute's name and original section number (as it appears in the appropriate session laws) only if the statute is commonly cited that way or if the information would otherwise aid in identification. Omit "The" as the first word of a statute's name. Include the year of the statute if it is in the official title. An official name, a popular name, or both may be used:

▶ Labor Management Relations (Taft-Hartley) Act § 301(a), 29 U.S.C. § 185(a) (2006).

▶ Family Medical Leave Act (FMLA) of 1993, 29 U.S.C. § 2601 (2006).

(b) Title, chapter, or volume. If a code is divided into separately sectioned or paragraphed titles, chapters, or volumes, the title, chapter, or volume number must be indicated. When citing the federal code, give the title number before the name of the code:

▶ 42 U.S.C. § 1983 (2006).

▶ 12 U.S.C.S. § 1710 (LexisNexis 1993 & Supp. 2004).

The form for citation to state codes varies; table T1.3 indicates whether and in what manner to identify the title, chapter, or volume number of a state code. For example:

▶ DEL. CODE ANN. tit. 13, § 1301 (1999).

▶ NEV. REV. STAT. § 28.501 (1998).

If each title, chapter, or volume of a code contains differently numbered sections or paragraphs, then the volume, chapter, or title number need not be given separately:

▶ GA. CODE ANN. § 21-2-16 (2003).

(c) Subject-matter codes. If a separately sectioned or paragraphed portion of
a code is identified by subject matter rather than by a title, volume, or chapter
number, give that subject-matter name as part of the code:

> ► CAL. VEH. CODE § 11506 (West 2000).

> ► TEX. FAM. CODE ANN. § 5.01 (Vernon 2002 & Supp. 2004–2005).

Table T1.3 indicates which state codes require this treatment.

(d) Publisher, editor, or compiler. Unless a code is published, edited, compiled
by, or under the supervision of, federal or state officials, give the name of the
publisher, editor, or compiler in the parenthetical phrase containing the year of
the code:

> ► 42 U.S.C.A. § 300a-7 (West 2001).

> ► 18 U.S.C.S. § 1307 (LexisNexis 1994 & Supp. 2004).

> ► CAL. VEH. CODE § 11509 (West 2000).

> Not: CAL. VEH. CODE § 11509 (Cal. 2000).

Table T1 indicates which federal and state codes require this information.

(e) Supplements. Cite material appearing in supplements (including pocket
parts) according to **rule 3.1(c)**:

> ► 18 U.S.C. § 510(b) (Supp. I 1983).

> ► 12 U.S.C. § 1455 (1982 & Supp. I 1983).

(f) Compilations of uncodified laws. If a code contains uncodified laws
printed in a separate compilation, cite in this manner:

> ► N.Y. UNCONSOL. LAW § 751 (McKinney 2000).

(g) Appendices. If a statute appears in an appendix to a code, and the statute is
numbered and otherwise printed as if it were part of that code, cite according to
rule 3.4:

> ► 50 U.S.C. app. § 5 (2006).

If the statute is not printed as if it were part of a code, cite the session laws and
add an explanatory phrase (see **rule 1.6(a)(ii)**) indicating that the statute is
reprinted in the code's appendix:

> ► Act of Aug. 31, 1970, ch. 842, 1970 Mass. Acts 732, *reprinted in*
> MASS. GEN. LAWS ANN. ch. 40 app. at 180 (West 1985).

Year of Code
12.3.2

When citing a bound volume of the current official or unofficial code, provide
parenthetically the year that appears on the spine of the volume, the year that
appears on the title page, or the latest copyright year—in that order of preference.
If the date on the spine or title page spans more than one year, give all years
covered. If the volume is a replacement of an earlier edition, use the year of the
replacement volume, not the year of the original:

> ► NEB. REV. STAT. § 33-114 (1998).

When citing a provision that appears in a supplement or pocket part, give the year that appears on the title page of the supplement or pocket part. If there is none, give the latest copyright year of the supplement or pocket part. In either case, if the date spans more than one year, give all years included:

▶ IND. CODE ANN. § 29-1-5-3.1 (West Supp. 2003).

To cite material that appears in both the main volume and a supplement or pocket part, give both years according to **rule 3.1(c)**:

▶ VT. STAT. ANN. tit. 12, § 892 (2002 & Supp. 2004).

If a code is published in looseleaf form, give the year that appears on the page on which the provision is printed or the year that appears on the first page of the subdivision in which the provision appears—in that order of preference—rather than the years indicated above:

▶ ALASKA STAT. § 28.01.010 (2002).

Other dates (such as the date on which an act becomes effective) may also be given parenthetically according to **rule 12.8**:

▶ OKLA. STAT. tit. 10, § 7303-1.7 (1998 & Supp. 2005) (effective July 1, 2002).

12.4   Session Laws

(a) Name. When citing session laws, always give the name of the statute and the public law or chapter number. Omit "The" as the first word of a statute's name. An official name, a popular name, or both may be used:

▶ White-Slave Traffic (Mann) Act, ch. 395, 36 Stat. 825 (1910) (codified as amended at 18 U.S.C. §§ 2421–2424 (2006)).

▶ Foreign Assistance Act of 1961, Pub. L. No. 87-195, 75 Stat. 424.

If the statute has no official or popular name, identify the act with a full date. Use the form "Act of [date of enactment]," or, if that information is unavailable, "Act effective [date of effectiveness]." Other identifying information may be added parenthetically:

▶ Act of Aug. 21, 1974, ch. 85, 1974 N.J. Laws 385 (providing unemployment compensation for jurors).

Not: An Act concerning unemployment compensation for persons serving on jury duty, and amending R.S. 43:21-4, ch. 85, 1974 N.J. Laws 385.

(b) Volume. Give the volume number (or, if none, the year) of the session laws, followed by the abbreviated name of the session laws in ordinary roman type. The official federal session laws, *Statutes at Large*, are abbreviated "Stat." Abbreviations for official and privately published state session laws appear in **table T1.3**. When citing state session laws, begin the abbreviated title of the session laws with the name of the state abbreviated according to **table T10**, even if the state name is not part of the official title; omit words in the official title not necessary for identification:

▶ 1978 Ark. Acts.

▶ 1935–1936 Ill. Laws 4th Spec. Sess.

▶ 1878 Minn. Laws.

Not: 1878 Laws of Minn.

(c) Pages and sections. When citing an entire act, give the page of the session laws on which the act begins:

▶ National Environmental Policy Act of 1969, Pub. L. No. 91-190, 83 Stat. 852 (1970).

When citing only part of an act, give the section(s) or subsection(s) cited, the page on which the act begins, and the page(s) on which the relevant section(s) or subsection(s) appear(s):

▶ National Environmental Policy Act of 1969, Pub. L. No. 91-190, § 102, 83 Stat. 852, 853–54 (1970).

▶ Act of June 15, 1995, No. 302, § 3602(11), 1995 La. Sess. Law Serv. 344, 344 (West).

(d) Session laws amending prior acts. Session laws amending prior acts are often divided into sections within sections; that is, the session law is divided into primary sections, and these sections, in turn, contain sections of the amended act. Cite the bill's sections by abbreviation (sec.) and the amended act's sections by symbol (§):

▶ Labor-Management Relations Act, ch. 120, sec. 101, § 8(a)(3), 61 Stat. 136, 140–41 (1947).

(e) Year or date. Give parenthetically the year in which the statute was passed by the legislature. If no date of enactment is identified, give the date on which the statute became effective:

▶ McCarran-Ferguson Act, ch. 20, 59 Stat. 33 (1945) (codified as amended at 15 U.S.C. §§ 1011–1015 (2006)).

Omit the year of the statute's passage if the same year is part of the name of the statute or of the session laws:

▶ Securities Act of 1933, ch. 38, 48 Stat. 74 (codified as amended at 15 U.S.C. §§ 77a–77aa (2006)).

▶ Act of Apr. 25, 1978, No. 515, § 3, 1978 Ala. Acts 569, 569 (codified as amended at ALA. CODE § 9-3-12 (1987)).

(f) Codification information. If a statute has been or will ultimately be codified and the code location is known, give that information parenthetically.

▶ Act of July 12, 1985, ch. 223, § 3, 1985 Cal. Legis. Serv. 239, 241 (West) (to be codified at CAL. INS. CODE § 11589.5).

Electronic Media and Online Sources   12.5

(a) Commercial electronic databases. When citing a code contained in an electronic database, give parenthetically the name of the database and information regarding the currency of the database as provided by the database itself (rather than the year of the code according to rule 12.3.2). In accordance with rule 12.3.1(d), also give the name of the publisher, editor, or compiler unless the code is published, edited, compiled by, or under the supervision of, federal or state officials:

- CAL. BUS. & PROF. CODE § 1670 (Deering, LEXIS through 1995 Sess.).

- CAL. BUS. & PROF. CODE § 1670 (West, Westlaw through 1995 portion of 1995-1996 Legis. Sess.).

- WASH. REV. CODE § 13.64.060 (VersusLaw through 1999 legislation).

- WIS. STAT. § 19.43 (LEXIS through 1994 legislation).

- WIS. STAT. § 19.43 (Loislaw through 1997-1998 Legis. Sess.).

- WIS. STAT. ANN § 19.43 (West, Westlaw through 1995 Act 26).

(b) Internet and online sources. When states and municipalities only publish their official statutes or ordinances online, the online source may be directly cited.

- BELLINGHAM, WASH., MUN. CODE § 16.60.060 (2008), http://www.cob.org/web/bmcode.nsf/CityCode?OpenView.

Authenticated, official, or exact copies of a source available online can be cited as if to the original print source (**rule 18.2.1(a)**).

- NEB. REV. STAT. § 2-1247 (2007)

Unofficial online sources are cited in accordance with **rule 18.2.3**.

- HAW. REV. STAT. § 142-23.5 (2009), *available at* http://www.capitol.hawaii.gov/hrscurrent/Vol03_Ch0121-0200D/HRS0142/HRS_0142-0023_0005.htm.

12.6   Other Secondary Sources

When citing a statute to any source other than a code, session laws, or electronic database, give the name of the act and public law or chapter number as if citing to session laws (**rule 12.4**). When referring to a particular provision, give the section or subsection number after the public law or chapter number. If possible, cite federal statutes (particularly those enacted after 1974) to the *United States Code Congressional and Administrative News*, indicating the volume number (and page number, if known) of the *Statutes at Large* where the statute will appear (note that the page numbers in these two sources often differ):

- Act of July 19, 1985, Pub. L. No. 99-68, 1985 U.S.C.C.A.N. (99 Stat.) 166.

- Act of Aug. 13, 1954, ch. 731, 1954 U.S.C.C.A.N. (68 Stat. 717) 833.

When citing an entire act, give the page on which the act begins. When citing part of an act, give both the page on which the act begins and the pages on which the cited material appears. If the statute has been or will ultimately be codified and the code location is known, give that information parenthetically:

- Act of July 9, 1985, Pub. L. No. 99-61, § 110, 1985 U.S.C.C.A.N. (99 Stat.) 113, 115 (to be codified at 31 U.S.C. § 5112).

Cite other secondary sources according to **rule 19** (services) or **16** (periodicals) in that order of preference. Give the date or year appropriate for the cited source. If the name of a statute cited to a service includes the year, and the service was published in that year, the year of the service may be omitted. If the future location of the act in either a code or session laws is known, give that information parenthetically according to **rule 12.8**:

> ► Presidential and Executive Office Accountability Act of 1996, Pub.
> L. No. 104-331, [1 Lab. Rel.] Lab. L. Rep. (CCH) ¶ 660 (1997).

If a recent statute has not yet been published in any source, give only the name of the act; the public law or chapter number; the section or subsection number if referring to only part of the statute; the full date of enactment or, if none, the date of approval by the executive or effective date; and the future location, if known, in a code or session laws:

> ► Alabama Corporate Income Tax Reform Act, No. 85-515 (May 8, 1985).

Invalidation, Repeal, Amendment, and Prior History   12.7

Invalidation   12.7.1

When citing a statute invalidated or declared unconstitutional by a case, indicate this fact by citing the case in full:

> ► Religious Freedom Restoration Act (RFRA) of 1993, Pub. L. No. 103-141, 1993 U.S.C.C.A.N. (107 Stat.) 1488, *invalidated by* City of Boerne v. Flores, 521 U.S. 507 (1997).

Repeal   12.7.2

When citing a statute no longer in force, indicate the fact and date of repeal parenthetically, or include a full citation to the repealing statute when particularly relevant:

> ► Law of June 1, 1895, ch. 4322, § 23, 1895 Fla. Laws ch. 3, 20–21 (repealed 1969).

> ► Act of Jan. 24, 1923, ch. 42, 42 Stat. 1174, 1208, *repealed by* Budget and Accounting Procedures Act of 1950, ch. 946, § 301(97), 64 Stat. 832, 844.

Amendment   12.7.3

When citing a version of a statute that has since been amended, indicate the fact and date of amendment parenthetically, cite the amending statute in full, or cite the current amended version parenthetically:

> ► Supplemental Appropriation Act of 1955, Pub. L. No. 663, § 1311, 68 Stat. 800, 830 (1954) (amended 1959).

> ► 33 U.S.C. § 1232 (1982), *amended by* 33 U.S.C. § 1232(f) (Supp. I 1983).

> ► Clayton Act, ch. 323, § 7, 38 Stat. 730, 731–32 (1914) (current version at 15 U.S.C. § 18 (2000)).

Prior History   12.7.4

When citing the current version of a statute, prior history may be given parenthetically according to **rule 12.8** if relevant:

- ▶ 33 U.S.C. § 1232(f) (Supp. I 1983) (amending 33 U.S.C. § 1232 (1982)).
- ▶ 28 U.S.C. § 1652 (2006) (originally enacted as Act of June 25, 1948, ch. 646, § 1652, 62 Stat. 869, 944).
- ▶ 28 U.S.C. § 1652 (2006) (corresponds to the Judiciary Act of 1789, ch. 20, § 34, 1 Stat. 73, 92).
- ▶ Clayton Act § 7, 15 U.S.C. § 18 (2006) (original version at ch. 323, § 7, 38 Stat. 730, 731–32 (1914)).

12.8 Explanatory Parenthetical Phrases

Explanatory parenthetical phrases are used to show the code location of statutes cited to session laws (**rules 12.2.2** and **12.4**) or secondary sources (**rule 12.6**); to identify useful dates, such as the effective date of a statute (**rules 12.3.2** and **12.4(e)**); and to indicate the invalidation (**rule 12.7.1**), repeal (**rule 12.7.2**), amendment (**rule 12.7.3**), or prior history (**rule 12.7.4**) of a statute. In addition, explanatory parenthetical phrases may be used to give any other relevant information about a statute:

- ▶ 5 U.S.C. § 553(b) (2006) (requiring agencies to publish notice of proposed rulemaking in the *Federal Register*).

See generally **rule 1.5** (parenthetical information).

12.9 Special Citation Forms

12.9.1 Internal Revenue Code

In citations to the Internal Revenue Code, "26 U.S.C." may be replaced with "I.R.C." Thus:

- ▶ 26 U.S.C. § 61 (2006).

becomes: I.R.C. § 61 (2006).

In law review citations, the year of the current *United States Code* or its supplement (as appropriate) should always be given (**rule 12.3.2**). Citations to the Internal Revenue Code as it appears in an unofficial code should identify the unofficial code by placing the publisher's name in the parenthetical phrase containing the year of the version cited. Thus, citations to U.S.C.A. should appear:

- ▶ I.R.C. § 1371 (West Supp. 1991).
- ▶ I.R.C. § 1247 (West 1988).

See also **rule 12.10** regarding short form citation of statutes. For special citation forms for federal taxation materials in court documents and legal memoranda, see **Bluepages B5.1.5**.

12.9.2 Ordinances

Cite ordinances analogously to statutes. Always give the name of the political subdivision (such as a city or county) and the abbreviated state name at the beginning of the citation. Do not abbreviate the name of the political subdivision unless it is abbreviated in **table T10**. If the ordinance is codified, give the name of the code (abbreviated according to **table T1**), the section or other subdivision, and the year of the code (determined according to **rule 12.3.2**). Print the political subdivision, state, and code names in large and small capitals:

► MONTGOMERY, ALA., CODE § 3A-11 (1971).

► PORTLAND, OR., POLICE CODE art. 30 (1933).

► FORT WORTH, TEX., REV. ORDINANCES ch. 34, art. I, § 15 (1950).

► S.F., CAL., POLICE CODE art. 16, div. 1, § 1076(a) (2000).

If the ordinance is uncodified, give its number (or, if none, its name) and, in a parenthetical, the exact date of adoption. Print the political subdivision, state, and ordinance name in ordinary roman type:

► San Jose, Cal., Ordinance 16,043 (Jan. 17, 1972).

► Halifax County, Va., Ordinance To Regulate the Solicitation of Membership in Organizations (Aug. 6, 1956).

Rules of Evidence and Procedure

12.9.3

Citation of a Federal Rule of Civil Procedure:

number of rule cited

FED. R. CIV. P. 11.

abbreviation of set of rules cited

Cite current or uniform rules of evidence or procedure in large and small capitals, without any date. Use abbreviations such as the following or abbreviations suggested by the rules themselves:

► FED. R. CIV. P. 12(b)(6).

► FED. R. CRIM. P. 42(a).

► FED. R. APP. P. 2.

► 1ST CIR. R. 6(a).

► DEL. CT. C.P.R. 8(f).

► FED. R. EVID. 410.

► UNIF. R. EVID. 404(b).

► SUP. CT. R. 17.

When citing rules no longer in force, give the most recent official source in which they appear and indicate the date of repeal parenthetically:

► SUP. CT. R. 8, 306 U.S. 690 (1939) (repealed 1954).

Uniform Acts

12.9.4

When citing a uniform act as the law of a particular state, cite as a state statute:

► OKLA. STAT. tit. 12A, § 2-314 (2004).

When not citing to the law of a particular state, cite as a separate code:

▶ U.C.C. § 2-314 (1977).

When citing a uniform act to the *Uniform Laws Annotated* (U.L.A.), provide the title of the act using abbreviations in **table T6**, the section number, the year of amendment or repeal (if any), the appropriate volume of the U.L.A., the page number on which the relevant section appears, and the year of publication:

▶ UNIF. ADOPTION ACT § 10, 9 U.L.A. 45 (1988).

Give the year in which the uniform act was last amended, even if the section referred to was not amended at that time. If a uniform act or section has been withdrawn, superseded, or amended, indicate that fact parenthetically according to **rule 12.7**:

▶ UNIF. PROBATE CODE § 2-706 (amended 1993), 8 U.L.A. 171 (Supp. 1995).

12.9.5 Model Codes, Restatements, Standards, and Sentencing Guidelines

Cite model codes, restatements, standards, sentencing guidelines, and similar materials in large and small capitals, by section, rule, or other relevant subdivision. For restatements, give the year in which the restatement was published. For model codes, standards, and sentencing guidelines, give the year in which the code, set of standards, or guidelines manual was adopted, unless the version cited indicates that it incorporates subsequent amendments. In that case, give the year of the last amendment, even when citing a portion not amended at that time. Usually the cover or title page of the source will indicate the date of the most recent amendments incorporated. When naming the code, restatement, or set of standards, use abbreviations listed in **table T6** (abbreviation of case names) or suggested by the source itself:

▶ MODEL BUS. CORP. ACT § 57 (1979).

▶ RESTATEMENT (THIRD) OF UNFAIR COMPETITION § 3 (1995).

▶ STANDARDS RELATING TO APP. CTS. § 3.12 (1977).

▶ U.S. SENTENCING GUIDELINES MANUAL § 2D1.1(c) (2004).

If a code, restatement, set of standards, or sentencing guidelines manual is a tentative or proposed draft, indicate that fact parenthetically as it appears on the publication and give the draft number (if available) and the year of the draft:

▶ MODEL LAND DEV. CODE § 2-402(2) (Proposed Official Draft 1975).

▶ RESTATEMENT (SECOND) OF TORTS § 847A (Tentative Draft No. 17, 1974).

If a restatement contains a subtitle, retain the subtitle in the citation:

▶ RESTATEMENT (THIRD) OF PROP.: DONATIVE TRANSFERS § 2 (2000).

Indicate the author's name parenthetically, unless the work was authored by the American Bar Association, the American Law Institute, the National Conference of Commissioners on Uniform State Laws, or a federal or state sentencing commission. Abbreviate the author's name according to **rule 15.1(c)** (institutional authors):

▶ MODEL CHILDREN'S CODE § 3.9B(2) (Am. Indian Law Ctr. 1976).

▶ STANDARDS FOR INMATES' LEGAL RIGHTS 18 (Nat'l Sheriffs' Ass'n, Tentative Draft 1974).

Cite Generally Accepted Auditing Standards and Generally Accepted Accounting Principles as follows:

▶ CODIFICATION OF ACCOUNTING STANDARDS AND PROCEDURES, Statement on Auditing Standards No. 1, § 150 (Am. Inst. of Certified Pub. Accountants 1972).

▶ RESEARCH AND DEV. ARRANGEMENTS, Statement of Fin. Accounting Standards No. 68, § 32 (Fin. Accounting Standards Bd. 1982).

Comments, notes, and other addenda should be cited according to **rule 3.4**:

▶ MODEL PENAL CODE § 223.6 note on status of section (Proposed Official Draft 1962).

▶ RESTATEMENT (SECOND) OF CONFLICT OF LAWS § 305 cmt. b, illus. 1 (1971).

▶ STANDARDS FOR TRAFFIC JUSTICE § 4.2 cmt. at 9 (1975).

▶ RESTATEMENT (SECOND) OF CONTRACTS ch. 16, topic 3, intro. note (1981).

Cite application notes, background commentary, introductory commentary, and appendices to sentencing guidelines as follows:

▶ U.S. SENTENCING GUIDELINES MANUAL § 3D1.5 cmt. n.1 (2004).

▶ U.S. SENTENCING GUIDELINES MANUAL § 2D1.2 cmt. background (2004).

▶ U.S. SENTENCING GUIDELINES MANUAL ch. 3, pt. D, introductory cmt. (2004).

▶ U.S. SENTENCING GUIDELINES MANUAL app. C (2004).

When citing a version of a code, restatement, or set of standards that has been withdrawn or amended, indicate that fact according to **rule 12.7.2** or **12.7.3**:

▶ MODEL BUS. CORP. ACT § 2(f) (1969) (amended 1973).

ABA Code of Professional Responsibility and Opinions on Ethics
12.9.6

Cite the old *Model Code of Professional Responsibility* and the new *Model Rules of Professional Conduct* according to **rule 12.9.5**:

▶ MODEL CODE OF PROF'L RESPONSIBILITY Canon 2 (1980).

▶ MODEL RULES OF PROF'L CONDUCT r. 3.12 (Discussion Draft 1983).

Cite ethical considerations and disciplinary rules as follows:

▶ MODEL CODE OF PROF'L RESPONSIBILITY EC 7-36 (1980).

▶ MODEL CODE OF PROF'L RESPONSIBILITY DR 8-101 (1980).

Cite notes or other commentary according to **rule 3.4**:

▶ MODEL RULES OF PROF'L CONDUCT r. 1.15 cmt. (1983).

Cite formal and informal opinions of the Committee on Ethics and Professional Responsibility (or the older Committees on Professional Ethics (1958-1971) and on Professional Ethics and Grievances (1919-1958)) by issuing body, opinion number, and year. Abbreviate according to **table T6**; "American Bar Association" may be abbreviated "ABA" for these documents.

> ► ABA Comm. on Prof'l Ethics & Grievances, Formal Op. 35 (1931).

> ► ABA Comm. on Ethics & Prof'l Responsibility, Informal Op. 1414 (1978).

The subject of the opinion may be given parenthetically:

> ► ABA Comm. on Ethics & Prof'l Responsibility, Formal Op. 338 (1974) (discussing the use of credit cards for the payment of legal services and expenses).

12.10 Short Forms for Statutes

(a) Text. In law review text and footnote text, use the forms listed in the "Text" column of the table below to refer to statutes. Provide a citation (in full or short form according to **rule 12.10(b)**) in an accompanying footnote when appropriate.

(b) Citations. In law review citations, use any of the forms listed in the "Short Citation" column of the table below that clearly identifies a statute if the statute is already cited (in either full or short form, including "*id.*") in either the *same footnote* or in a manner such that it can be readily found in *one of the preceding five footnotes*, again including "*id.*" Otherwise, use the "Full Citation" form.

	Full Citation	Text	Short Citation
Named Statutes	Administrative Procedure Act § 1, 5 U.S.C. § 551 (2006)	section 1 of the Administrative Procedure Act or section 1	§ 1 or 5 U.S.C. § 551 or Administrative Procedure Act § 1
U.S. Code Provisions	42 U.S.C. § 1983 (2006)	42 U.S.C. § 1983 or § 1983	42 U.S.C. § 1983 or § 1983
State Code Provisions (numbered codes)	DEL. CODE ANN. tit. 28, § 1701 (1999)	title 28, section 1701 of the Delaware Code or section 1701	tit. 28, § 1701 or § 1701
State Code Provisions (named codes)	CAL. EDUC. CODE § 48222 (West 2008)	section 48222 of the California Education Code or section 48222	EDUC. § 48222
Session Laws	National Environmental Policy Act of 1969, Pub. L. No. 91-190, § 102, 83 Stat. 852, 853–54 (1970)	section 102 of the National Environmental Policy Act or section 102	§ 102 or National Environmental Policy Act § 102 or § 102, 83 Stat. at 853–54

(c) "Section." Note that except when referring to *United States Code* provisions, the word "section" should be spelled out in law review text and footnote text, although the symbol "§" may be used in citations. See **rule 6.2(c)**.

(d) Electronic sources. For materials available on an electronic database, use the name of the database in constructing a short form:

▶ WIS. STAT. ANN. § 19.43 (West, Westlaw through 2007 Act 242).

becomes: § 19.43 (Westlaw).

For materials available only online, use the normal short form appropriate for the source. A URL need not be repeated after a full citation.

▶ UTAH CODE § 4-29-2 (2008), http://le.utah.gov/code/TITLE04/ htm/04_29_000200.htm.

becomes: § 4-29-2.

13 LEGISLATIVE MATERIALS

Besides statutes (**rule 12**), the legislative process generates bills and resolutions (**rule 13.2**); committee hearings (**rule 13.3**); reports, documents, and committee prints (**rule 13.4**); floor debates (**rule 13.5**); and, sometimes, separately bound legislative histories (**rule 13.6**). When citing any United States legislative material except debates, include the title (if relevant), the abbreviated name of the house, the number of the Congress, the number assigned to the material, and the year of publication. State legislative materials are cited similarly except when indicated otherwise. Abbreviations for commonly used words in legislative materials are listed in **table T9**.

In addition, include parenthetically the session number for House and Senate documents published before the 60th Congress (1907), House Reports published before the 47th Congress (1881), and Senate Reports published before the 40th Congress (1867). For House and Senate materials published after these dates, the session number can be inferred from the year of publication: First sessions always fall in odd-numbered years, while second sessions always fall in even-numbered years. On rare occasions, Congress holds a third session. When citing materials produced during a third session, provide this information parenthetically.

13.1 Basic Citation Forms

Federal bill (unenacted)	Privacy Protection Act of 1998, H.R. 3224, 105th Cong. § 2(a) (1998).
	H.R. 119, 54th Cong. (1st Sess. 1896).
Federal resolution (unenacted)	H.R.J. Res. 79, 106th Cong. (1999).
State bill	H.R. 124, 179th Leg., 1st Spec. Sess. (Pa. 1995).
State resolution	S.J. Res. 836, 118th Leg., 3d Spec. Sess. (Me. 1999).
Committee hearing	*Background and History of Impeachment: Hearing Before the Subcomm. on the Constitution of the H. Comm. on the Judiciary*, 105th Cong. 22–23 (1998) (statement of Rep. Hutchinson, Member, H. Comm. on the Judiciary).
Federal report	H.R. REP. NO. 101-524, at 10 (1990), *reprinted in* 1990 U.S.C.C.A.N. 1448, 1451.
Federal document	H.R. DOC. NO. 102-399, at 3 (1992).
Committee print	STAFF OF H. COMM. ON THE JUDICIARY, 93D CONG., CONSTITUTIONAL GROUNDS FOR PRESIDENTIAL IMPEACHMENT 38 (Comm. Print 1974).
Congressional debate	145 CONG. REC. H1817 (daily ed. Apr. 12, 1999) (statement of Rep. Pease).
Source reprinted in separately bound legislative history	S. COMM. ON LABOR AND PUB. WELFARE, LABOR-MANAGEMENT REPORTING AND DISCLOSURE ACT OF 1959, S. REP. NO. 86-187, at 4 (1959), *reprinted in* 1959 U.S.C.C.A.N. 2318, 2320, *and in* 1 NLRB, LEGISLATIVE HISTORY OF THE LABOR-MANAGEMENT REPORTING AND DISCLOSURE ACT OF 1959, at 397, 400 (1959).

Bills and Resolutions 13.2

(a) Unenacted federal bills and resolutions. When citing federal bills, include the name of the bill (if relevant), the abbreviated name of the house, the number of the bill, the number of the Congress, the section (if any), and the year of publication:

▶ S. 516, 105th Cong. § 2 (1997).

▶ H.R. 422, 106th Cong. (1999).

▶ Clear Skies Act, S. 485, 108th Cong. (2003).

▶ Protection from Personal Intrusion Act, H.R. 2448, 105th Cong. § 2(a) (1997).

A parenthetical indicating the date and stage of the bill may be provided in order to distinguish among multiple versions of the same bill in the same Congress. Subcommittee and committee names may be abbreviated according to **tables T6, T9,** and **T10:**

▶ S. 593, 101st Cong. § 2 (as passed by Senate, May 31, 1989).

▶ S. 593, 101st Cong. § 2 (as reported by S. Comm. on the Judiciary, May 12, 1989).

Cite resolutions analogously, using the following abbreviations:

House Resolution	▶ H.R. Res.
Senate Resolution	▶ S. Res.
House Concurrent Resolution	▶ H.R. Con. Res.
Senate Concurrent Resolution	▶ S. Con. Res.
House Joint Resolution	▶ H.R.J. Res.
Senate Joint Resolution	▶ S.J. Res.
Senate Executive Resolution	▶ S. Exec. Res.

Thus:

▶ H.R.J. Res. 124, 105th Cong. (1998).

A parallel citation to a published committee hearing, a legislative report, or the *Congressional Record* may also be provided if it would assist the reader in locating the bill (**rules 13.3, 13.4,** and **13.5**).

(b) Enacted federal bills and resolutions. Enacted bills and joint resolutions are statutes (**rule 12**). They are cited as statutes except when used to document legislative history, in which case they are cited as unenacted bills.

Enacted simple resolutions, which bind only one house of Congress, and enacted concurrent resolutions, which bind either one or both houses of Congress, should be cited as unenacted bills. Unless otherwise clear in context, the fact of enactment should be noted parenthetically:

▶ S. Res. 141, 106th Cong. (1999) (enacted).

▶ H.R. Con. Res. 196, 106th Cong. (1999) (enacted).

▶ H.R. Res. 811, 108th Cong. (2004) (enacted).

A parallel citation to the *Congressional Record* (for simple resolutions) or to the *Statutes at Large* (for concurrent resolutions) may be provided if it would assist the reader in locating the enacted resolution. Because only enacted resolutions are printed in the *Statutes at Large* ("Stat."), a parenthetical noting enactment is not necessary when a parallel citation to Stat. is given:

▶ S. Res. 218, 83d Cong., 100 CONG. REC. 2972 (1954) (enacted).

▶ S. Con. Res. 97, 94th Cong., 90 Stat. 3024 (1976).

(c) State bills and resolutions. When citing state bills and resolutions, include the name of the legislative body, abbreviated according to **tables T6, T9,** and **T10,** the number of the bill or resolution, the number of the legislative body (or, if not numbered, the year of the body), and the number or designation of the legislative session. Parenthetically indicate the name of the state, abbreviated according to **table T10,** and the year of enactment (for an enacted bill or resolution) or the year of publication (for an unenacted bill or resolution).

▶ H.D. 636, 1999 Leg., 413th Sess. (Md. 1999).

▶ H.R. 189, 145th Gen. Assemb., Reg. Sess. (Ga. 1999).

A parallel citation to state session laws may be provided if it would assist the reader in locating an enacted resolution.

▶ H.R.J. Res. 1, 40th Leg., 2d Spec. Sess., 1974 Utah Laws 7.

13.3 Hearings

(a) Federal committee hearings. When citing federal committee hearings, always include the entire subject matter title as it appears on the cover, the bill number (if any), the subcommittee name (if any), the committee name, the number of the Congress, the page number of the particular material being cited (if any), and the year of publication. Subcommittee and committee names may be abbreviated according to tables **T6, T9,** and **T10.** Cite as follows:

▶ *Protection from Personal Intrusion Act and Privacy Protection Act of 1998: Hearing on H.R. 2448 and H.R. 3224 Before the H. Comm. on the Judiciary,* 105th Cong. 56–57 (1998) (statement of Richard Masur, President, Screen Actors Guild).

▶ *Copyright Protection for Semiconductor Chips: Hearing on H.R. 1028 Before the Subcomm. on Courts, Civil Liberties, & the Admin. of Justice of the H. Comm. on the Judiciary,* 98th Cong. 14 (1983) (statement of Jon A. Baumgarten, Copyright Counsel, Association of American Publishers).

Titles of the individuals providing statements may be abbreviated according to **table T11:**

▶ *Tribal Energy Self-Sufficiency Act and the Native American Energy Development and Self-Determination Act: Hearing on S. 424 and S. 522 Before the S. Comm. on Indian Affairs,* 108th Cong. 1 (2003) (statement of Sen. Ben Nighthorse Campbell, Chairman, S. Comm. on Indian Affairs).

▶ *Transforming the Federal Government To Protect America from Terrorism: Hearing Before the H. Select Comm. on Homeland Sec.,* 107th Cong. 23–25 (2002) (statement of John Ashcroft, Att'y Gen. of the United States).

(b) State committee hearings. When citing state committee hearings, follow the same form, but also include the number of the legislative session:

> *Tax Credit for Cost of Providing Commuter Benefits to Employees: Hearing on H.D. 636 Before the H. Comm. on Ways & Means*, 1999 Leg., 413th Sess. 5-8 (Md. 1999) (statement of Del. Paul Carlson, Member, H. Comm. on Ways & Means).

Reports, Documents, and Committee Prints   13.4

(a) Numbered federal reports and documents. Citations to numbered federal reports should include the name of the house, the number of the Congress connected by a hyphen to the number of the report, the part and/or page number on which material being cited appears, and the year of publication. Use large and small caps for the house, abbreviation of report, and abbreviation of number:

> H.R. REP. NO. 99-253, pt. 1, at 54 (1985).

> S. REP. NO. 84-2, at 7 (1955).

Cite conference reports using the following format:

> H.R. REP. NO. 98-1037, at 3 (1984) (Conf. Rep.).

> S. REP. NO. 95-601, at 5 (1977) (Conf. Rep.).

Cite numbered federal documents analogously, using the following abbreviations:

House Document	H.R. DOC. NO.
Senate Document	S. DOC. NO.
House Miscellaneous Document	H.R. MISC. DOC. NO.

The following citation formats are often used to designate international agreements to which the United States is a party (**rule 21.4.5(a)**):

| Senate Executive Document | S. EXEC. DOC. NO. |
| Senate Treaty Document | S. TREATY DOC. NO. |

When possible (and particularly for documents published after 1974), give a parallel citation to the permanent edition of *United States Code Congressional and Administrative News* (**rule 12.6**):

> S. REP. NO. 95-797, at 4 (1978), *as reprinted in* 1978 U.S.C.C.A.N. 9260, 9263.

(b) Titles and authors. Titles of numbered reports or documents may be indicated; if the title is given, the author should also be named (see **rule 15.1(c)** regarding institutional authors):

> CARLTON KOEPGE, THE ROAD TO INDUSTRIAL PEACE, H.R. DOC. NO. 82-563, at 29–30 (1953).

> U.S. IMMIGRATION COMM'N, IMMIGRATION LEGISLATION, S. DOC. NO. 61-758, at 613 (3d Sess. 1911).

(c) Unnumbered federal documents and committee prints. Committee prints and unnumbered documents must be cited as works of institutional authors (**rule 15.1(c)**). Note that the number of the Congress is part of the author's name:

> ► STAFF OF S. COMM. ON THE JUDICIARY, 81ST CONG., REP. ON
>   ANTITRUST LAW 17 (Comm. Print 1950).

If the document or committee print is primarily the work of specific persons, that fact may be noted parenthetically.

(d) Federal legislative agency reports. Legislative reports, like those of the Congressional Research Service (CRS) and the Government Accountability Office (GAO), must be cited as works of institutional authors (**rule 15.1(c)**); include the report number (as given by the agency) as part of the title.

> ► LOUIS FISHER, CONG. RESEARCH SERV., RL31340, MILITARY
>   TRIBUNALS: THE QUIRIN PRECEDENT 30 (2002).

> ► U.S. GOV'T ACCOUNTABILITY OFFICE, GAO-08-751, FOOD AND DRUG
>   ADMINISTRATION: APPROVAL AND OVERSIGHT OF THE DRUG MIFEPREX
>   27 (2008).

(e) Federal legislative journals. Cite congressional journals according to the following model:

> ► S. JOURNAL, 24th Cong., 2d Sess. 123-24 (1836).

(f) State materials. Citations to state legislative reports, documents, and similar materials must include the name of the legislative body abbreviated according to **tables T6, T9,** and **T10,** the number of the legislative body connected by a hyphen to the number of the report or document, the number of the legislative session, the part or page number on which the material being cited appears, and the year of publication. Unless it is clear from the title or author information appearing in the citation, provide the name of the state abbreviated according to **table T10** parenthetically:

> ► S. 178-247, 1st Sess., at 4 (Pa. 1994).

Titles of numbered reports or documents may be indicated; if the title is given, the author should also be named (see **rule 15.1(c)** regarding institutional authors):

> ► COMMONWEALTH OF PA. DEP'T OF AGRIC., ANNUAL REPORT OF THE
>   STATE FOOD PURCHASE PROGRAM, S. 178-247, 1st Sess., at 4 (1994).

13.5 Debates

Cite congressional debates after 1873 to the *Congressional Record;* use the daily edition only for matter not yet appearing in the permanent edition. The primary ways in which the *Congressional Record* differs from the daily edition are continuous pagination, altered text, and the dropping of the prefixes H, S, and E before page numbers:

> ► 123 CONG. REC. 17,147 (1977).

> ► 131 CONG. REC. S11,465–66 (daily ed. Sept. 13, 1985) (statement of
>   Sen. Wallop).

Cite congressional debates through 1873 according to the following models:

1837-1873	► CONG. GLOBE, 36th Cong., 1st Sess. 1672 (1860).
1824-1837	► 10 REG. DEB. 3472 (1834).
1789-1824	► 38 ANNALS OF CONG. 624 (1822).

For volume one of the *Annals* give the name(s) of the editor(s) and year of publication in parentheses:

▶ 1 ANNALS OF CONG. 486 (1789) (Joseph Gales ed., 1834).

Separately Bound Legislative Histories 13.6

The legislative histories of several important acts are published separately (e.g., the Administrative Procedure Act, titles VII and IX of the Civil Rights Act of 1964, the Clean Air Act Amendments of 1970, the Equal Employment Opportunity Act, the Internal Revenue Acts, the National Labor Relations Act, the Occupational Safety and Health Act of 1970, and the Securities Exchange Act of 1934). If it would aid the reader in locating the source, a parallel citation may be given to such a separate publication. Cite these publications according to **rule 15** (books, reports, and other nonperiodic materials):

▶ H.R. REP. NO. 80-245, at 6 (1947), *reprinted in* 1 NLRB, LEGISLATIVE HISTORY OF THE LABOR-MANAGEMENT RELATIONS ACT, 1947, at 292, 297 (1948).

▶ Internal Revenue Amendments, Pub. L. No. 87-834, § 15(a), 76 Stat. 960, 1041–42 (1962) (codified at I.R.C. § 1248(a) (2000)), *reprinted in* JOINT COMM. ON INTERNAL REVENUE TAXATION, 90TH CONG., LEGISLATIVE HISTORY OF THE INTERNAL REVENUE CODE OF 1954, at 473–74 (1967).

Electronic Media and Online Sources 13.7

(a) Commercial electronic databases. When citing to materials contained in a commercial electronic database, give the name of the database and any identifying codes or numbers that uniquely identify the material. If the name of the database is not clear from the database identifier, include it parenthetically at the end of the citation:

Federal bill (unenacted) H.R. 3781, 104th Cong. § 2(b) (1996), 1996 CONG US HR 3781 (Westlaw).

Federal report H.R. REP. NO. 92-98 (1971), *reprinted in* 1971 U.S.C.C.A.N. 1017, 1971 WL 11312.

Congressional debate 142 CONG. REC. H11,460 (daily ed. Sept. 27, 1996) (statement of Rep. Tanner), 142 Cong Rec H 11452, at *H11, 460 (LEXIS).

(b) Internet and online sources. Where a print version is accessible, citation should be made to the print source. Where, however, the print source is difficult or impossible to obtain or the governing authority has designated the electronic source as the official version, citation should be made to the electronic source with consideration of the general principles in **rule 18** regarding authentication and preferred document formats. The URL should be appended to the end of the citation in accordance with **rule 18.2.2(d)**:

▶ An Act Prohibiting Writing a Text Message While Driving, H.R. 34, 2009 Sess. (N.H. 2009), http://www.gencourt.state.nh.us/legislation/2009/HB0034.html.

13.8 Short Forms for Legislative Materials

(a) Main text. In law review text, use the forms listed in the "Text" column of the table below to refer to legislative materials. Provide a citation in full or short form according to rule 13.8(c) in an accompanying footnote when appropriate.

(b) Footnote text. Similarly, when referring to legislative materials in law review footnote text, use the forms listed in the "Text" column of the table below. Provide a citation in full or short form according to rule 13.8(c) in an accompanying citation clause or sentence when appropriate.

(c) Citations. In law review citations, use any of the forms listed in the "Short Citation" column of the table below that clearly identifies the legislative material if the legislative material is already cited (in either full or short form, including *id.*) in either the *same footnote* or in a manner such that it can be readily found in *one of the preceding five footnotes.* Otherwise, use the "Full Citation" form. See rule 4.2(a) regarding the use of "*supra*."

	Full Citation	Text	Short Citation
Federal Bill (unenacted)	H.R. 3055, 94th Cong. (1976)	House Bill 3055	H.R. 3055
State Resolution	S. Res. 20, 37th Leg., 2d Sess. (Okla. 1979)	Oklahoma Senate Resolution 20	Okla. S. Res. 20
Federal Report	H.R. REP. NO. 92-98 (1971)	House Report 98	H.R. REP. NO. 92-98
Federal Document	H.R. DOC. NO. 94-208 (1975)	House Document 208	H.R. DOC. NO. 94-208

(d) Electronic sources. For materials available in an electronic database, use a unique database identifier, if one has been assigned, in constructing a short form:

▶ H.R. 3781, 104th Cong. § 1 (1996), 1996 Cong US HR 3781 (Westlaw).

becomes: H.R. 3781 § 1, 1996 Cong US HR 3781 (Westlaw).

For materials available only online, use the normal short form appropriate for the source. A URL need not be repeated after a full citation.

ADMINISTRATIVE AND EXECUTIVE MATERIALS   14

Administrative agencies and other executive institutions produce a tremendous variety of official materials. This rule provides guidance for the most common forms of existing materials. Consult table T1.2 for information regarding specific federal organizations that use unique citation formats. As with courts, practitioners should comply with an agency's conventions for citation when authoring submissions to that agency, if that convention varies from the rule established herein. Cite state materials by analogy to the federal examples given in this rule.

Basic Citation Forms   14.1

Federal regulation cited to the *Code of Federal Regulations*	FTC Credit Practices Rule, 16 C.F.R. § 444.1 (1999).
Federal regulation cited to the *Federal Register*	Importation of Fruits and Vegetables, 60 Fed. Reg. 50,379 (Sept. 29, 1995) (to be codified at 7 C.F.R. pt. 300).
Administrative adjudication	Reichhold Chems., Inc., 91 F.T.C. 246 (1978).
Arbitration	Charles P. Ortmeyer, 23 Indus. Arb. 272 (1980) (Stern, Arb.).

Rules, Regulations, and Other Publications   14.2

Citation of a particular provision of a regulation in the *Code of Federal Regulations*:

C.F.R. title no.   section symbol and specific section cited

7 C.F.R. § 319.76 (1999).

abbreviation of set of regulations cited   date of code edition cited

(a) Final rules and regulations. Whenever possible, cite federal rules and regulations to the *Code of Federal Regulations* (C.F.R.) by title, section or part, and year:

▶ 47 C.F.R. § 73.609 (1999).

Each title of the *Code of Federal Regulations* is revised at least once a year; cite the most recent edition. Give the name of the rule or regulation only if the rule or regulation is commonly cited that way or the information would otherwise aid in identification. The abbreviated name of the issuing body may also be included if helpful:

▶ FCC Broadcast Radio Services, 47 C.F.R. § 73.609 (2009).

▶ FTC Credit Practices Rule, 16 C.F.R. § 444.1 (2009).

▶ Credit Practices Rule, 16 C.F.R. § 444.1 (2009).

Certain titles of the *Code of Federal Regulations* focused on specific subjects have unique citations. For citation to Title 26, *Treasury Regulations*, see **Table 1.2**. Title 48, the *Federal Acquisition Regulations*, may be cited as "**FAR**."

> ▶ FAR 52.249-2(e) (2008).

The *Federal Register* (Fed. Reg.) publishes rules and regulations before they are entered into the *Code of Federal Regulations*. Citations to rules or regulations in the *Federal Register* should give any commonly used name of the rule or regulation, the volume and page on which the rule or regulation (or any preceding discussion thereof) begins, and the date of the rule or regulation. When citing a part of a rule or regulation, give both the page on which the rule or regulation (or preceding discussion) begins and the page(s) on which the cited material appears. When the *Federal Register* indicates where the rule or regulation will appear in the *Code of Federal Regulations*, give that information parenthetically:

> ▶ Importation of Fruits and Vegetables, 60 Fed. Reg. 50,379, 50,381 (Sept. 29, 1995) (to be codified at 7 C.F.R. pt. 300).

> ▶ Federal Acquisition Regulations for National Aeronautics and Space Administration, 55 Fed. Reg. 52,782 (Dec. 21, 1990) (to be codified at 48 C.F.R. pt. 1).

Prohibitively long titles may be shortened as long as the result is unambiguous:

> ▶ Order Approving NYSE and NASDAQ Proposed Rule Changes Relating to Equity Compensation Plans

> Not: Self-Regulatory Organizations; New York Stock Exchange, Inc. and National Association of Securities Dealers, Inc.; Order Approving NYSE and NASDAQ Proposed Rule Changes and NASDAQ Amendment No. 1 and Notice of Filing and Order Granting Accelerated Approval to NYSE Amendments No. 1 and 2 and NASDAQ Amendments No. 2 and 3 Thereto Relating to Equity Compensation Plans

(b) Proposed rules and other notices. Administrative notices that are not transferred to the *Code of Federal Regulations* should be cited to the *Federal Register*. When citing notices of proposed rules and regulations, follow the form for final rules, but add the status to the date parenthetical:

> ▶ Control of Air Pollution from New Motor Vehicles and New Motor Vehicle Engines, 56 Fed. Reg. 9754 (proposed Mar. 7, 1991) (to be codified at 40 C.F.R. pt. 86).

Cite notices pertaining to administrative adjudications according to **rule 14.3**. Cite other administrative notices by volume, page, and date. The citation may begin with a description or a commonly used name:

> ▶ Meeting Notice, 65 Fed. Reg. 3415 (Jan. 21, 2000).

For rules and announcements not appearing in the *Code of Federal Regulations* or the *Federal Register* cite a service (**rule 19**), the original form of issuance, or an agency or governmental website (**rule 18.2**).

(c) Regular reports. Cite in the same manner as periodicals (**rule 16**). Always give the abbreviated agency name first and then use the abbreviations for periodical names given in **table T13**:

- ► 4 NLRB Ann. Rep. 93 (1939).

- ► 1942 Att'y Gen. Ann. Rep. 22.

- ► 1955–1956 Mich. Att'y Gen. Biennial Rep. pt. 1, at 621.

(d) Other publications. Cite as a work by an institutional author (**rule 15.1(c)**), including a serial number, if any (**rule 15.7**), unless issued as a congressional document (**rule 13.4**):

- ► Office of Mgmt. & Budget, Exec. Office of the President, OMB Bull. No. 99-04, Revised Statistical Definitions of Metropolitan Areas (MAs) and Guidance on Uses of MA Definitions (1999).

- ► U.S. Gov't Accountability Office, GAO-01-1163T, Commercial Aviation: A Framework for Considering Federal Financial Assistance (1998).

Administrative Adjudications and Arbitrations   14.3

Citations to administrative cases and arbitrations should conform to **rule 10**, except as follows:

Names   14.3.1

(a) Administrative adjudications. Cite by the reported name of the first-listed private party (abbreviated according to **rule 10.2**) or by the official subject-matter title. Omit all procedural phrases:

- ► Trojan Transp., Inc., 249 N.L.R.B. 642 (1980).

Not: In the Matter of Trojan Transp., Inc., 249 N.L.R.B. 642 (1980).

Not: *In re* Trojan Transp., Inc., 249 N.L.R.B. 642 (1980).

Subject-matter titles may sometimes indicate the nature and stage of an adjudicatory proceeding. It is permissible to shorten such titles, and, if the nature and stage of the proceeding are not clear from the context, such information may be included in a parenthetical phrase at the end of the citation. The parenthetical phrase may consist of terms such as "notice," "initiation," "prelim. neg.," or "determination," or may be more elaborate.

- ► Bottled Green Olives from Spain, 50 Fed. Reg. 28,237 (Dep't of Commerce July 11, 1985) (final admin. review).

Not: Bottled Green Olives from Spain, Final Results of Admin. Review of Countervailing Duty Order, 50 Fed. Reg. 28,237 (Dep't of Commerce July 11, 1985).

(b) Arbitrations. Cite as court cases if adversary parties are named and as administrative adjudications if they are not. The arbitrator's name should be indicated parenthetically:

- ► Kroger Co. v. Amalgamated Meat Cutters, Local 539, 74 Lab. Arb. Rep. (BNA) 785, 787 (1980) (Doering, Arb.).

- ► Charles P. Ortmeyer, 23 Indus. Arb. 272 (1980) (Stern, Arb.).

14.3.2 Which Source(s) to Cite

(a) Official reporters. Cite the official reporter of the agency if the opinion appears therein:

> ► Tennessee Intrastate Rates & Charges, 286 I.C.C. 41 (1952).

For the official reporters of many federal agencies, see table T1.2.

(b) Official releases and slip opinions. If the opinion does not appear in an official reporter, cite the official release or slip opinion. Provide the full date, any helpful publication number, and the number of the case or investigation:

> ► Iron Construction Castings from Brazil, Canada, India, and the People's Republic of China, Inv. No. 701-TA-249, USITC Pub. 1720 (June 1985).

If the opinion will later be published in an official bound volume, provide the volume number and the initial page number, if available; if the initial page number is not available, retain the case number:

> ► Rosenberg Library Ass'n, 269 N.L.R.B. No. 197 (Apr. 24, 1984).

Whenever possible, append a parallel citation to an unofficial reporter, service, or other source, in that order of preference:

> ► Rosenberg Library Ass'n, 269 N.L.R.B. No. 197, 1983–1984 NLRB Dec. (CCH) ¶ 16,238 (Apr. 24, 1984).

Once the official reporter is issued, however, cite only to that reporter:

> ► Rosenberg Library Ass'n, 269 N.L.R.B. 1173 (1984).

(c) Services and electronic databases. Where an agency decision is only available from a service or on the agency's website, cite according to rule 19 (for services) or rule 18.2 (for Internet sources).

> ► Carr, [1990-1992 Transfer Binder] Comm. Fut. L. Rep. (CCH) ¶ 24,933 (Oct. 2, 1990).

> ► MatchNet PLC v. Gordon, Case No. AF-001060 (eResolution Dec. 4, 2001), http://www.disputes.org/decisions/1060.htm.

Many agencies have adopted unique citation formats for opinions not listed in official reporters. Consult table T1.2 for agency-specific citation formats. For a list of services and service abbreviations, see table T15.

14.3.3 Issuing Agency

If the name of the issuing agency is not apparent from the name of the source, include the name of the agency abbreviated according to rule 15.1(d) in the parenthetical containing the date:

> ► Gen. Dynamics Corp., 50 Fed. Reg. 45,949 (U.S. Dep't of Labor Nov. 5, 1985).

4.4   Short Forms for Regulations

(a) Main text. In law review text, use the forms listed in the "Text" column of the table below to refer to regulations. Provide a citation (in full or short form according to rule 14.4(c)) in an accompanying footnote when appropriate.

(b) Footnote text. Similarly, when referring to regulations in law review footnote text, use the forms listed in the "Text" column of the table below. Provide a citation (in full or short form according to rule 14.4(c)) in an accompanying citation clause or sentence when appropriate.

(c) Citations. In law review citations, use any of the forms listed in the "Short citation" column of the table below that clearly identifies the regulation if the regu-

	Full citation	Text	Short citation
Code of Federal Regulations	FTC Credit Practices Rule, 16 C.F.R. § 444.1 (2009)	16 C.F.R. § 444.1	16 C.F.R. § 444.1 or § 444.1
Federal Register	Importation of Fruits and Vegetables, 60 Fed. Reg. 50,379, 50,381 (Sept. 29, 1995) (to be codified at 7 C.F.R. pt. 300)	Importation of Fruits and Vegetables	Importation of Fruits and Vegetables, 60 Fed. Reg. at 50,381

lation is already cited (in full or short form) in either the same footnote or in a manner such that it can be readily found (including "*id.*") in one of the preceding five footnotes or the same general textual discussion. Otherwise, use the "Full citation" form.

(d) Electronic sources. See rule 18.8.

15 BOOKS, REPORTS, AND OTHER NONPERIODIC MATERIALS

This rule governs the citation of books, treatises, reports, white papers, dictionaries, encyclopedias, and all other nonperiodic materials.

Citation of a particular page within the sixth edition of Francis Carey's *Organic Chemistry*:

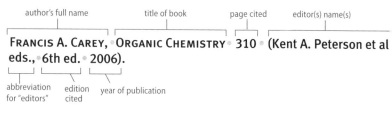

author's full name   title of book   page cited   editor(s) name(s)

FRANCIS A. CAREY, ORGANIC CHEMISTRY 310 (Kent A. Peterson et al eds., 6th ed. 2006).

abbreviation for "editors"   edition cited   year of publication

Main Elements:

Author . . . . rule 15.1

Editor or translator . . . . rule 15.2

Title . . . . rule 15.3

Page, section, or paragraph
(if only part of a work is cited) . . . . rules 3.2 and 3.3

Edition . . . . rule 15.4

Publisher . . . . rule 15.4

Date . . . . rule 15.4

15.1 Author

The first time a work is cited, always give the author's full name as it appears on the publication, including any designation such as "JR." or "III" (inserting a comma before the designation only if the author does). Do not include a designation such as "Dr." or "Prof." even if it appears on the title page. Use large and small capitals:

▶ HAROLD W. FUSON, JR., TELLING IT ALL: A LEGAL GUIDE TO THE EXERCISE OF FREE SPEECH 57–58 (1995).

When citing a single volume of a multivolume work, give only the author(s) of the volume cited. Include the volume number, if any, at the beginning of the citation:

▶ 4 CHARLES ALAN WRIGHT & ARTHUR R. MILLER, FEDERAL PRACTICE AND PROCEDURE § 1006 (2d ed. 1987).

(a) Two authors. List the authors' names in the order in which they appear on the title page, separated by an ampersand:

▶ A. LEO LEVIN & MEYER KRAMER, NEW PROVISIONS IN THE KETUBAH: A LEGAL OPINION 3–4 (1955).

If the title page establishes an alternative relationship between the two authors, e.g., "WITH" or "AS TOLD TO," use this phrase to separate the authors' names:

▶ EARVIN "MAGIC" JOHNSON WITH WILLIAM NOVAK, MY LIFE 39 (1993).

(b) More than two authors. Either use the first author's name followed by "ET AL." or list all of the authors' names. The first method is appropriate where saving space is desired, including short form citations. The second method is appropriate when listing all of the authors' names is particularly relevant. When listing all of the authors' names, separate the names with commas, except the final name, which should be set off with an ampersand (and without a comma).

► A. LEO LEVIN ET AL., DISPUTE RESOLUTION DEVICES IN A DEMOCRATIC SOCIETY 77 (1985).

► 14 CHARLES ALAN WRIGHT, ARTHUR R. MILLER & EDWARD H. COOPER, FEDERAL PRACTICE AND PROCEDURE § 3637 (3d ed. 1998).

► RICHARD H. FALLON, JR. ET AL., HART AND WECHSLER'S THE FEDERAL COURTS AND THE FEDERAL SYSTEM 330 (6th ed. 2009).

► RICHARD H. FALLON, JR., JOHN F. MANNING, DANIEL J. MELTZER & DAVID L. SHAPIRO, HART AND WECHSLER'S THE FEDERAL COURTS AND THE FEDERAL SYSTEM 330 (6th ed. 2009).

(c) Institutional authors. Citations to works by institutional authors begin with the author's complete name. Abbreviate according to **rule 15.1(d)**:

► CITY OF NEW HAVEN, RECYCLE NOW NEW HAVEN (1991).

When an individual author is credited on behalf of an institution, use the individual's name and then the institution's name. Only include subdivisions of the institution if particularly relevant:

► JUDITH A. LHAMON, NAT'L ASS'N FOR LAW PLACEMENT, A FAIR SHAKE: LAWFUL AND EFFECTIVE INTERVIEWING 3 (1987).

► S. ELIZABETH GIBSON, FED. JUDICIAL CTR., CASE STUDIES OF MASS TORT LIMITED FUND CLASS ACTION SETTLEMENTS & BANKRUPTCY REORGANIZATIONS 39–45 (2000).

Not: S. ELIZABETH GIBSON, FED. JUDICIAL CTR., WORKING GROUP ON MASS TORTS, CASE STUDIES OF MASS TORT LIMITED FUND CLASS ACTION SETTLEMENTS & BANKRUPTCY REORGANIZATIONS 39–45 (2000).

When no individual author is credited, use the smallest subdivision that prepared the work and then the overall body of which that subdivision is a part:

► STATISTICAL ANALYSIS CTR., STATE CRIME COMM'N, CRIME IN GEORGIA 41 (1980).

(d) Abbreviations. Abbreviate the name of an institutional author only if the result will be completely unambiguous. When abbreviating, use the abbreviations found in **tables T6** and **T10**. "United States" should be abbreviated to "U.S." Omit "Inc.," "Ltd.," and similar terms if the name also contains a word such as "Ass'n," "Bros.," "Co.," or "Corp.," clearly indicating that the institution is a business firm:

► CONSUMER DEPUTY PROGRAM, U.S. CONSUMER PROD. SAFETY COMM'N, CHILDREN'S SLEEPWEAR 7 (1975).

► NAT'L MUN. LEAGUE, A MODEL ELECTION SYSTEM 3 (1973).

Editor or Translator   15.2

(a) Basic format. Always give the full name of an editor and/or translator according to **rule 15.1**, followed by "**ed.**," or "**trans.**," in that order if both apply, in the parenthetical containing information about the edition, publisher, and date (see rule 15.4). A comma should separate the designation of an editor and/or translator from other publication information:

> ▶ MICHEL FOUCAULT, DISCIPLINE AND PUNISH 30–31 (Alan Sheridan trans., Vintage Books 2d ed. 1995) (1977).

> ▶ ETHICS OF CONSUMPTION: THE GOOD LIFE, JUSTICE, AND GLOBAL STEWARDSHIP 118–19 (David A. Crocker & Toby Linden eds., 1998).

> ▶ AIDS AND THE LAW (Harlon L. Dalton et al. eds., 1987).

> ▶ KARL MARX & FREDERICH ENGELS, THE COMMUNIST MANIFESTO (Joseph Katz ed., Samuel Moore trans., Washington Square Press 1964) (1848).

(b) Institutional editors. Follow rule 15.1(c), substituting the name of the institution for the name of the individual editor. Abbreviate the institutional editor's name according to rule 15.1(d):

> ▶ THE ROLE OF MEDIATION IN DIVORCE PROCEEDINGS 33 (Vt. Law Sch. Dispute Resolution Project ed., 1987).

> ▶ THE BLUEBOOK: A UNIFORM SYSTEM OF CITATION (Columbia Law Review Ass'n et al. eds., 19th ed. 2010).

(c) No named parties. If a work has no named author, editor, or translator, then the work may be designated by the publisher of the edition (rule 15.4). Abbreviate the publisher's name according to rule 15.1(d).

15.3 Title

Cite the full main title as it appears on the title page, but capitalize according to rule 8 (unless the title is not in English, in which case follow rule 20.2.2(b)). Give a subtitle only if it is particularly relevant. Do not abbreviate words or omit articles in the title. Use large and small capitals:

> ▶ CAPITAL FLOWS IN THE APEC REGION (Mohsin S. Khan & Carmen M. Reinhart eds., 1995).

> ▶ 6 JAMES WM. MOORE ET AL., MOORE'S FEDERAL PRACTICE ¶ 56.10 (3d ed. 1999).

When citing a single volume of a multivolume work, give the main title of the volume cited. If the title of a work ends with a numeral, or if distinguishing between the title and page number could otherwise be confusing, the page number should be set off by a comma and the word "at" (see rule 3.2(a)):

> ▶ J.A.S. GRENVILLE, THE MAJOR INTERNATIONAL TREATIES, 1914–1973, at 114–15 (1974).

15.4 Edition, Publisher, and Date

(a) Editions. Always cite the latest edition of a work that supports the point under discussion, unless an earlier edition would be particularly relevant or authoritative.

(i) Single edition. When citing a work that has been published in only one edition, indicate the year of publication in parentheses. In general, cite by the date of the edition rather than the date of a particular printing:

▶ DEBORAH L. RHODE, JUSTICE AND GENDER 56 (1989).

▶ AIDS AND THE LAW (Harlon L. Dalton et al. eds., 1987).

If a printing differs in a respect relevant to the purposes of the citation, however, give the printing designation and the date of printing instead:

▶ (6th prtg. 1980)

If the title of the work incorporates the date of the work, do not omit the date of publication, even if it is the same date:

▶ HUMAN RIGHTS WATCH, WORLD REPORT 2004: HUMAN RIGHTS AND ARMED CONFLICT 148 (2004).

(ii) **Multiple editions by the same publisher.** When citing a work that has been published by the same publisher in more than one edition, indicate the edition and the year the edition was published. Follow the publisher's terminology when designating an edition (see **table T14** for a list of publishing abbreviations):

▶ FLEMING JAMES, JR. ET AL., CIVIL PROCEDURE § 2.3 (4th ed. 1992).

▶ 1 WILLIAM MEADE FLETCHER ET AL., FLETCHER CYCLOPEDIA OF THE LAW OF PRIVATE CORPORATIONS § 7.05 (perm. ed., rev. vol. 1999).

▶ LARRY BERGER, MANEK MISTRY, PAUL ROSSI, MICHAEL COLTON & ADAM JED, UP YOUR SCORE: THE UNDERGROUND GUIDE TO THE SAT 34 (1999-2000 ed. 1998).

▶ ARISTOTLE, NICOMACHEAN ETHICS bk. IV, at 15-16 (G.P. Goold ed., H. Rackham trans., Harvard Univ. Press rev. ed. 1934) (c. 384 B.C.E.).

(iii) **Editions not by the original publisher.** When citing a work that has been published by someone other than the original publisher, indicate the editor and/or translator if any (**rule 15.2**), the publisher, the edition cited if not the first, and the date of publication of the edition cited (in that order). Abbreviate the publisher's name according to **rule 15.1(d)**. Unless the work is one that is regularly updated or revised, add a second parenthetical indicating the date of publication of the original edition:

▶ CHARLES DICKENS, BLEAK HOUSE 49–55 (Norman Page ed., Penguin Books 1971) (1853).

▶ JOHN C.H. WU, THE GOLDEN AGE OF ZEN 214–15 (Image Books 1996) (1975).

▶ SIMONE DE BEAUVOIR, THE SECOND SEX, at xvi–xvii (H.M. Parshley ed. & trans., Bantam Books 1961) (1949).

▶ THE CHICAGO MANUAL OF STYLE ¶ 8.191 (15th ed. 2003).

(b) **Photoduplicated reprints.** Cite photoduplicated reprints to the original, indicating in parentheses the existence of a reprint and the date of the reprint, followed by the publication date of the original in separate parentheses:

▶ PAUL W. GATES, HISTORY OF PUBLIC LAND LAW DEVELOPMENT 1 (photo. reprint 1979) (1968).

(c) **Pre-1900 works.** Cite works published before 1900 to a scholarly modern edition, according to **rule 15.4(a)**:

▶ JOHN LOCKE, TWO TREATISES OF GOVERNMENT 137–39 (Peter Laslett ed., Cambridge Univ. Press 1988) (1690).

If there is no modern edition, cite the first edition whenever possible. When citing a pre-1900 edition, indicate the place of publication and the publisher, separated by a comma:

> ▶ 1 JAMES FITZJAMES STEPHEN, A HISTORY OF THE CRIMINAL LAW OF ENGLAND 156–57 (London, MacMillan & Co. 1883).

If the place or date of publication is not available, use the abbreviation "n.p." for "no place" or "n.d." for "no date."

(d) Supplements. Cite pocket parts and bound supplements according to **rule 3.1(c)**:

> ▶ 4 SYDNEY C. SCHWEITZER & JOSEPH RASCH, CYCLOPEDIA OF TRIAL PRACTICE § 895 (2d ed. Supp. 1984).

> ▶ 5 SAMUEL WILLISTON & RICHARD A. LORD, A TREATISE ON THE LAW OF CONTRACTS § 11:8 (4th ed. 1993 & Supp. 1999).

15.5 Shorter Works in Collection

Cite essays and articles in collections according to **rule 15.5.1**. Cite collections of other materials, such as letters, speeches, manuscripts, diaries, debates, newspaper articles, tracts, etc., according to **rule 15.5.2**.

15.5.1 Works in Collection Generally

(a) Works by various authors. To cite an individual shorter work within a volume of collected works by various authors, list the author's full name according to **rule 15.1** in ordinary roman type followed by the title of the shorter work in italics, the word "*in*" in italics, the volume number, if any (**rule 3.1(a)**), and the name of the volume as a whole in large and small capitals. Always note the page on which the shorter work begins as well as any pages on which specific material appears (**rule 3.2(a)**). Editors, translators, edition, publisher, and date should be noted parenthetically according to **rules 15.2** and **15.4**:

> ▶ Andrew G. Ferguson, *Continuing Seizure: Fourth Amendment Seizure in Section 1983 Malicious Prosecution Cases*, *in* 15 NAT'L LAWYERS GUILD, CIVIL RIGHTS LITIGATION AND ATTORNEY FEES ANNUAL HANDBOOK 54-1 (Steven Saltzman ed., 1999).

> ▶ Kay Deaux & Brenda Major, *A Social-Psychological Model of Gender*, *in* THEORETICAL PERSPECTIVES ON SEXUAL DIFFERENCE 89, 89 (Deborah L. Rhode ed., 1990).

(b) Works by the same author. If all the shorter works within a volume are by the same author, use the same form as above, but print the author's name in large and small capitals and place the volume number, if any, before the author's name (**rule 3.1(a)**):

> ▶ OLIVER WENDELL HOLMES, *Law in Science and Science in Law*, *in* COLLECTED LEGAL PAPERS 210, 210 (1920).

> ▶ ADRIENNE RICH, *Transcendental Etude*, *in* THE FACT OF A DOOR-FRAME 264, 267–68 (1984).

Collected Documents

(a) Documents originally published. Use the "*reprinted in*" form (**rule 1.6(a)(ii)**) to cite collected materials that were previously published. As far as possible, provide a complete citation for the original work followed by "*reprinted in*" and the citation of the volume containing the reprint:

> ► MARQUIS DE CONDORCET, ESSAY ON THE APPLICATION OF MATHE-MATICS TO THE THEORY OF DECISION-MAKING (1785), *reprinted in* CONDORCET: SELECTED WRITINGS 33, 48–49 (Keith M. Baker ed., 1976).

(b) Documents originally unpublished. Cite letters, speeches, manuscripts, diaries, and other similar works that have never been published except in collection as you would any other shorter work in collection (**rule 15.5.1**), but print the name or description of the document in ordinary roman type following **rule 17**. The date of the particular document or other identifying information, if available, may be included in a parenthetical following the document title:

> ► Letter from Virginia Woolf to Vita Sackville-West (Dec. 22, 1925), *in* 3 THE LETTERS OF VIRGINIA WOOLF, 1923–1928, 223, 224 (Nigel Nicolson & Joanne Trautmann eds., 1st Am. ed. 1978) (1977).

> ► John Adams, Argument and Report, *in* 2 LEGAL PAPERS OF JOHN ADAMS 285, 322–35 (L. Kinvin Wroth & Hiller B. Zobel eds., 1965).

Prefaces, Forewords, Introductions, and Epilogues   15.6

Cite a preface, foreword, introduction, or epilogue by someone other than the author as follows:

> ► L. Maria Child, *Introduction* to HARRIET A. JACOBS, INCIDENTS IN THE LIFE OF A SLAVE GIRL 3, 3–4 (L. Maria Child & Jean F. Yellin eds., Harvard Univ. Press 1987) (1861).

> ► Henry M. Hart & Herbert Wechsler, *Preface to the First Edition* of PAUL M. BATOR ET AL., HART AND WECHSLER'S THE FEDERAL COURTS AND THE FEDERAL SYSTEM, at xxvii, xxx (3d ed. 1988).

Cite to similar material by the author of the work without special designation:

> ► JOHN HART ELY, DEMOCRACY AND DISTRUST, at vii (1980).

Serial Number   15.7

(a) Series issued by the author. When citing a publication that is one of a series issued by the author (other than U.N. documents (**rule 21.7**)), include the serial number as part of the title. The serial number indicator may be abbreviated according to **table T16**:

> ► BUREAU OF INTELLIGENCE & RESEARCH, U.S. DEP'T OF STATE, PUB. NO. 8732, WORLD STRENGTH OF THE COMMUNIST PARTY ORGANIZA-TIONS 65 (1973).

> ► WOMEN'S BUREAU, U.S. DEP'T OF LABOR, LEAFLET NO. 55, A WORKING WOMAN'S GUIDE TO HER JOB RIGHTS 4 (1978).

(b) Series issued by one other than the author. To cite a publication that is one of a series issued by someone other than the author, indicate the series and number parenthetically, abbreviating institutional entities according to **rule 15.1(d)**:

> ► Anne C. Vladeck, *Counseling a Plaintiff During Litigation*, in EMPLOYMENT LITIGATION 1990, at 77, 80–82 (PLI Litig. & Admin. Practice, Course Handbook Ser. No. 386, 1990).

15.8 Special Citation Forms

(a) Frequently cited works. A few frequently cited works require special citation forms:

> ► BALLENTINE'S LAW DICTIONARY 1190 (3d ed. 1969).

> ► BLACK'S LAW DICTIONARY 712 (9th ed. 2009).

> ► 88 C.J.S. *Trial* § 192 (1955).

> ► 17 AM. JUR. 2D *Contracts* § 74 (1964).

(b) Star edition. In a very few well-known works, the page of the original edition (star page) is indicated, usually by an asterisk (*), in either the margin or the text of all recent editions. In such cases the date and edition may be omitted and the citation may be made to the star page, unless the material cited was inserted by the editor of the cited edition. There is no space between the asterisk and the page number:

> ► 2 WILLIAM BLACKSTONE, COMMENTARIES *152, *155–56.

(c) Other named works.

(i) The Federalist. When citing an entire *Federalist* paper, include the author's name parenthetically and do not indicate a specific edition:

> ► THE FEDERALIST NO. 23 (Alexander Hamilton).

Group together papers written by the same author:

> ► THE FEDERALIST NOS. 23, 78 (Alexander Hamilton), NOS. 10, 51 (James Madison).

When citing particular material within a paper, however, list the usual publication information for the edition cited:

> ► THE FEDERALIST NO. 5, at 53 (John Jay) (Clinton Rossiter ed., 1961).

(ii) Manual for Complex Litigation. Citations to the *Manual for Complex Litigation* prepared by the Federal Judicial Center are as follows:

> ► MANUAL FOR COMPLEX LITIGATION (THIRD) § 33.2 (1995).

> ► MANUAL FOR COMPLEX LITIGATION § 2.10 (5th ed. 1982).

However, when citing an edition other than the edition prepared by the Federal Judicial Center, identify the source and publication date of the edition cited:

> ► MANUAL FOR COMPLEX LITIGATION § 4.52 (1982) (supplement to CHARLES ALAN WRIGHT & ARTHUR R. MILLER, FEDERAL PRACTICE AND PROCEDURE (1969–1985)).

(iii) The Bible. Cite the Bible as follows:

> ► 2 *Kings* 12:19.

The version may be indicated parenthetically if relevant:

▶ *Mark* 9:21 (King James).

(iv) **Shakespeare.** A Shakespearean play may be cited as follows:

▶ WILLIAM SHAKESPEARE, THE SECOND PART OF KING HENRY THE SIXTH act 2, sc. 2.

To cite particular lines, a specific edition should be indicated according to **rule 15.4**.

(v) **The Bluebook.** *The Bluebook* is cited as follows:

▶ THE BLUEBOOK: A UNIFORM SYSTEM OF CITATION R. 1.4(e), at 58 (Columbia Law Review Ass'n et al. eds., 19th ed. 2010).

▶ THE BLUEBOOK: A UNIFORM SYSTEM OF CITATION 293 tbl.T.10 (Columbia Law Review Ass'n et al. eds., 16th ed. 9th prtg. 1999).

Electronic Media and Online Sources 15.9

(a) Commercial electronic databases. When citing secondary materials to a database, provide a complete citation to the document according to **rule 15** and a citation to the database. If the database assigns a unique identifier or code to the document, include that identifier or code to assist the reader in locating the document cited.

When a source is available both in print and in a commercial electronic database, a parallel citation to the database using "*available at*" may be supplied:

▶ ABBEY G. HAIRSTON, LEAVE AND DISABILITY COORDINATION HANDBOOK ¶ 110 (2009), *available at* Westlaw LDCHBK.

(b) Internet and online sources. Because e-books may differ in format from the print version, the two sources should not be treated interchangeably unless the online source is an exact copy of the original as dictated by **rule 18.2.1(a)**. If a book or report is only available online, cite to it directly in accordance with **rule 18.2.2**.

▶ U.S. DEP'T OF JUSTICE, LEGAL AUTHORITIES SUPPORTING THE ACTIVITIES OF THE NATIONAL SECURITY AGENCY DESCRIBED BY THE PRESIDENT 25 (2006) [hereinafter NSA WHITE PAPER], *available at* http://fl1.findlaw.com/news.findlaw.com/hdocs/docs/nsa/dojnsa 11906.pdf.

▶ *Lampoon Definition*, DICTIONARY.COM, http://dictionary.reference.com/browse/lampoon (last visited Feb. 22, 2009).

Short Citation Forms 15.10

Once a book, report, or other nonperiodic material has been cited in full in a law review footnote, a short form employing either "*id.*" or "*supra*" may be used to refer to the work in subsequent citations. Never use "*infra*" to refer to these materials. In general, follow **rule 4** for short citation forms; however, use **rule 15.10.1** when referring to a shorter work in collection or the collection as a whole.

15.10.1 Short Forms for Works in Collection

To cite an essay, article, or document found within a volume of collected shorter works when the shorter work has already been cited in full, you may use "*id.*" to refer to the shorter work if it was cited as the immediately preceding authority within the same footnote or as the sole authority within the immediately preceding footnote. Do not use "*id.*" to refer to the collection as a whole when citing another shorter work within the collection.

Use a "*supra*" form to refer to the collection as a whole. The "*supra*" form for the entire volume should include the title of the collection (rather than an author) regardless of whether the collected pieces have a single author or multiple authors.

Use a "*supra*" form to refer to the shorter work if it was not cited as the immediately preceding authority in the same footnote or as the sole authority in the immediately preceding footnote. The "*supra*" form for the individual work should include the last name of the author or authors, or, if none, the title of the shorter work:

> ▶ [1] FEMINISM/POSTMODERNISM (Linda J. Nicholson ed., 1990); *see also* THOMAS SCHELLING, A PROCESS OF RESIDENTIAL SEGREGATION: NEIGHBORHOOD TIPPING, *reprinted in* ECONOMIC FOUNDATIONS OF PROPERTY LAW 307, 308 (Bruce A. Ackerman ed., 1975).

> ▶ [2] Letter from Virginia Woolf to Vita Sackville-West (Dec. 22, 1925), *in* 3 THE LETTERS OF VIRGINIA WOOLF, 1923–1928, at 224 (N. Nicolson & Joanne Trautmann eds., 1st Am. ed. 1978); *cf.* Judith Butler, *Gender Trouble, Feminist Theory, and Psychoanalytic Discourse*, *in* FEMINISM/POSTMODERNISM, *supra* note 1, at 324, 324–25; Andreas Huyssen, *Mapping the Postmodern*, *in* FEMINISM/POSTMODERNISM, *supra* note 1, at 234, 234–35. Butler does not think "woman" can be adequately defined, Butler, *supra*, at 325, but Woolf's observations are especially compelling, Letter from Virginia Woolf to Vita Sackville-West, *supra*.

> ▶ [3] A wholly different perspective is presented in AYN RAND, *The Cashing-In: The Student "Rebellion,"* *in* THE NEW LEFT 13, 20–24 (1971). *But see* Huyssen, *supra* note 2, at 234–35 (questioning whether postmodern transformation has generated genuinely new forms).

> ▶ [4] *E.g.*, SCHELLING, *supra* note 1, at 310.

> ▶ [5] *Id.*; *see also* THE FEDERALIST NO. 81, at 393 (Alexander Hamilton) (Terrence Ball ed., 2003). *But see* AYN RAND, *The Comprachicos*, *in* THE NEW LEFT, *supra* note 3, at 152, 203 (arguing that the educational establishment teaches ideas that destroy children's minds).

> ▶ [6] *See* RAND, *supra* note 3, at 99; RAND, *supra* note 5, at 201.

> ▶ [7] 4 RICHARD R. POWELL, POWELL ON REAL PROPERTY ¶ 513[3], at 41–42 (Patrick J. Rohan ed., 1995).

> ▶ [8] 2 *id.* ¶ 203, at 20–17; *see also* THE FEDERALIST NO. 5, *supra* note 5, at 17 (John Jay).

For materials available only online, use the normal short form appropriate for the source. A URL need not be repeated after a full citation.

PERIODICAL MATERIALS

16

Citation of particular pages within a law review article with parenthetical information about what appears on those pages:

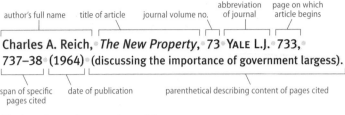

Citation of an entire magazine article:

Citation of a signed newspaper article:

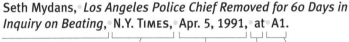

Basic Citation Forms

16.1

Article in consecutively paginated journal	Elizabeth F. Emens, *Integrating Accommodation*, 156 U. Pa. L. Rev. 839, 894 (2008).
Article in nonconsecutively paginated journal or magazine	Benjamin Wittes, *Without Precedent*, Atlantic Monthly, Sept. 2005, at 39, 40.
Newspaper article	Scott Martelle, *ID Law Keeps Nuns, Students from Polls*, L.A. Times, May 7, 2008, at A14.
Online newspaper article	Pamela Mendels, *A Case of Spam and Free Speech at Intel*, N.Y. Times, Dec. 11, 1998, http://www.nytimes.com/library/tech/98/12/cyber/cyberlaw/11law.html.

Signed student-written law review note	Bradford R. Clark, Note, *Judicial Review of Congressional Section Five Action: The Fallacy of Reverse Incorporation*, 84 COLUM. L. REV. 1969, 1986 (1984).
Unsigned student-written comment	Case Comment, *Fairness Standards for SEC Approval of Mergers:* Collins v. SEC, 90 HARV. L. REV. 453 (1976).
Student-written book review	Sharon Dolovich, Book Note, *Leaving the Law Behind*, 20 HARV. WOMEN'S L.J. 313, 329 (1997) (reviewing PATRICIA J. WILLIAMS, THE ROOSTER'S EGG: ON THE PERSISTENCE OF PREJUDICE (1995)).
Non-student-written book review	Jane E. Stromseth, *Understanding Constitutional War Powers Today: Why Methodology Matters*, 106 YALE L.J. 845 (1996) (reviewing LOUIS FISHER, PRESIDENTIAL WAR POWER (1995)).
Symposium	Symposium, *The Presidency and Congress: Constitutionally Separated and Shared Powers*, 68 WASH. U. L.Q. 485, 640–51 (1990).
Specially designated article in consecutively paginated journal	John M. Golden, Commentary, *"Patent Trolls" and Patent Remedies*, 85 TEX. L. REV. 2111, 2113 (2007).
Noncommercially distributed newsletter	Douglas Gary Lichtman, *Patent Holdouts in the Standard-Setting Process*, ACAD. ADVISORY COUNCIL BULL. (Progress & Freedom Found., D.C.), May 2006, at 4.

Follow **rule 16.4** or **rule 16.5** to cite articles, essays, commentaries, and all other materials contained within periodicals. Where the periodical is organized by volume, and page numbers continue throughout the volume, it is a consecutively paginated periodical and should be cited according to **rule 16.4**. Where the periodical is paginated separately for each issue and the first page of every issue is 1, it is a nonconsecutively paginated periodical and should be cited according to **rule 16.5**.

Cite newspapers according to **rule 16.6**.

Special citation forms for non-student-written book reviews, student-written law review materials, symposia, colloquia, surveys, commentaries and other special designations, multipart articles, annotations, proceedings, regular publications by institutes, ABA Section Reports, and noncommercially distributed periodicals such as newsletters are given in **rule 16.7**.

Cite sources in electronic media and online sources using **rule 16.8**.

Follow **rule 16.9** for short citation forms.

Capitalize the titles of works cited according to **rule 8(a)**.

The name of the periodical should appear in large and small capitals whether it is a journal, magazine, or newspaper, and should be abbreviated according to **tables T13** (periodical abbreviations) and **T10** (geographic abbreviations).

For purposes of this rule, the date of the publication is the cover date of the periodical.

Author   16.2

For signed materials appearing in periodicals (including student-written materials), follow **rule 15.1**, but print in ordinary roman type. Thus:

- ► Kim Lane Scheppele, *Foreword: Telling Stories*, 87 Mɪᴄʜ. L. Rᴇᴠ. 2073, 2082 (1989).

- ► Robert P. Inman & Michael A. Fitts, *Political Institutions and Fiscal Policy: Evidence from the U.S. Historical Record*, 6 J.L. Eᴄᴏɴ. & Oʀɢ. 79, 79–82 (1990).

- ► Paul Butler et al., *Race, Law and Justice: The Rehnquist Court and the American Dilemma*, 45 Aᴍ. U. L. Rᴇᴠ. 567, 569 (1996).

- ► Georgette C. Poindexter, LizabethAnn Rogovoy & Susan Wachter, *Selling Municipal Property Tax Receivables: Economics, Privatization, and Public Policy in an Era of Urban Distress*, 30 Cᴏɴɴ. L. Rᴇᴠ. 157 (1997).

- ► R. Gregory Cochran, Comment, *Is the Shrink's Role Shrinking? The Ambiguity of Federal Rule of Criminal Procedure 12.2 Concerning Government Psychiatric Testimony in Negativing Cases*, 147 U. Pᴀ. L. Rᴇᴠ. 1403 (1999).

- ► Peter Carlson, *Tales Out of Law School; Repeat After Us: It's Nothing Like 'L.A. Law,'* Wᴀsʜ. Pᴏsᴛ, July 2, 1989, (Magazine), at W13.

Title   16.3

Cite the full periodical title as it appears on the title page, but capitalize according to **rule 8** (unless the title is not in English, as described in **rule 20.2.2(b)**). Do not abbreviate words or omit articles in the title. Use italics:

- ► Edward B. Rock, *The Logic and (Uncertain) Significance of Institutional Shareholder Activism*, 79 Gᴇᴏ. L.J. 445 (1991).

- ► Cecilia Lacey O'Connell, Comment, *The Role of the Objector and the Current Circuit Court Confusion Regarding Federal Rule of Civil Procedure 23.1: Should Non-Named Shareholders Be Permitted To Appeal Adverse Judgements?*, 48 Cᴀᴛʜ. U. L. Rᴇᴠ. 939, 943–46 (1999).

When the title contains a reference to material that would be italicized when appearing in the main text according to **rule 2.2(a)**, such material should appear in ordinary roman type:

- ► Nathaniel A. Vitan, Book Note, *Grounded Paratroopers: On Collins and Skover's* The Death of Discourse, 13 J.L. & Pᴏʟ. 207, 210 (1997).

- ► Seth F. Kreimer, *Does Pro-Choice Mean Pro-Kevorkian? An Essay on* Roe, Casey, *and the Right To Die*, 44 Aᴍ. U. L. Rᴇᴠ. 803, 812 (1995).

16.4 Consecutively Paginated Journals

Cite works found within periodicals that are consecutively paginated throughout an entire volume by author, title of work, volume number, periodical name, first page of the work, page or pages on which specific material appears (rule 3.2(a)), and year enclosed in parentheses at the end of the citation. Consult tables T10 and T13 to abbreviate the names of periodicals:

> ► David Rudovsky, *Police Abuse: Can the Violence Be Contained?*, 27 HARV. C.R.-C.L. L. REV. 465, 500 (1992).

> ► Richard A. Epstein, *The Supreme Court, 1987 Term—Foreword: Unconstitutional Conditions, State Power, and the Limits of Consent*, 102 HARV. L. REV. 4, 44 (1988).

> ► Kenneth W. Tsang et al., *A Cluster of Cases of Severe Acute Respiratory Syndrome in Hong Kong*, 348 NEW ENG. J. MED. 1977, 1977 (2003).

> ► Pauline M. Ippolito & Alan D. Mathios, *New Food Labeling Regulations and the Flow of Nutrition Information to Consumers*, 12 J. PUB. POL'Y & MARKETING 188 (1993).

Some journals maintain separate but consecutive pagination with different page numbering systems. Cite these journals as indicated above, but include the special numbering:

> ► Kenneth R. Feinberg, *Mediation—A Preferred Method of Dispute Resolution*, 16 PEPP. L. REV. S5, S14 n.19 (1989).

Some journals publish special annual issues that do not conform to their consecutive pagination system. Cite these as indicated above, but indicate the special issue designation parenthetically and use the numbering from the special issue:

> ► John Ferejohn & Charles Shipan, *Congressional Influence on Bureaucracy*, 6 J.L. ECON. & ORG. (SPECIAL ISSUE) 1 (1990).

> ► George A. Akerlof, *Procrastination and Obedience*, 81 AM. ECON. REV. (PAPERS & PROC.) 1 (1991).

If the periodical has no volume number but is nonetheless consecutively paginated throughout each volume, use the year of publication as the volume number and omit the parenthetical reference to the year:

> ► Thomas R. McCoy & Barry Friedman, *Conditional Spending: Federalism's Trojan Horse*, 1988 SUP. CT. REV. 85, 100.

> ► Stephen D. Sugarman, *Using Private Schools To Promote Public Values*, 1991 U. CHI. LEGAL F. 171.

16.5 Nonconsecutively Paginated Journals and Magazines

Works appearing in periodicals that are separately paginated within each issue should be cited by author, title of work, periodical name, date of issue as it appears on the cover, the word "at" (rule 3.2(a)), first page of work, and, if applicable, page or pages on which specific material appears. If there is no author listed, begin the citation with the title of the piece. Consult tables T10 and T13 to abbreviate the names of periodicals:

> ▶ Barbara Ward, *Progress for a Small Planet*, Harv. Bus. Rev., Sept.–Oct. 1979, at 89, 90.

> ▶ Barbara Ehrenreich, *Iranscam: The Real Meaning of Oliver North*, Ms., May 1987, at 24, 24.

> ▶ Joan B. Kelly, *Mediated and Adversarial Divorce: Respondents' Perceptions of Their Processes and Outcomes*, Mediation Q., Summer 1989, at 71.

> ▶ *Damages for a Deadly Cloud: The Bhopal Tragedy Will Cost Union Carbide $470 Million*, Time, Feb. 27, 1989, at 53.

If no date of issue is available, provide the issue number in its place, and indicate the volume number before the title of the periodical per **rule 16.4**; also include the year and month of copyright, if available:

> ▶ Charles E. Mueller, *The American Who Wants To Give Away His Country but Doesn't Know That's What He's Voting for*, 34 Antitrust L. & Econ. Rev., no. 1, 2008, at 1, 7.

Newspapers   16.6

(a) In general. Materials appearing in newspapers are generally cited in the same manner as those found in nonconsecutively paginated periodicals (**rule 16.5**) with three exceptions: (i) when appropriate, designate the work as an "Editorial," "Op-Ed.," or "Letter to the Editor," in ordinary roman type, after the author's name but before the title, or at the beginning of the citation if there is no author; (ii) after the date, give the designation of the section in which the piece is found in a parenthetical if necessary to identify the page unambiguously; and (iii) give only the first page of the piece and do not indicate the location of specific material. Substitute "Letter to the Editor" or another designation for the title when no separate title is provided. Citations to signed articles should include the author's full name (**rule 16.2**); citations to unsigned pieces should begin with the title of the piece:

> ▶ Ari L. Goldman, *O' Connor Warns Politicians Risk Excommunication over Abortion*, N.Y. Times, June 15, 1990, at A1.

> ▶ *Cop Shoots Tire, Halts Stolen Car*, S.F. Chron., Oct. 10, 1975, at 43.

> ▶ Jane Gross, *Silent Right: Lawyer Defends Principles from Her Jail Cell*, Chi. Trib., Mar. 3, 1991, § 6, at 6.

> ▶ Nancy Reagan, Editorial, *Just Say "Whoa,"* Wall St. J., Jan. 23, 1996, at A14.

> ▶ William J. Clinton, Op-Ed., *AIDS Is Not a Death Sentence*, N.Y. Times, Dec. 1, 2002, § 4, at 9.

> ▶ Editorial, *Pricing Drugs*, Wash. Post, Feb. 17, 2004, at A18.

> ▶ Michael Harwood, *The Ordeal: Life as a Medical Resident*, N.Y. Times, June 3, 1984, § 6 (Magazine), at 38.

(b) Place of publication. Include the place of publication in ordinary roman type in parentheses following the name of the newspaper if not clear from the name:

> ▶ *Trial Judge Will Not Give Enquiry Evidence*, Times (London), June 13, 1990, at 3.

▶ Nancy Johnson, Letter to the Editor, CHRON. HIGHER EDUC. (D.C.), Oct. 8, 2004, at A55.

(c) Consecutively paginated newspapers. Cite an article in a newspaper paginated consecutively by volume according to **rule 16.4**:

▶ *New York County Lawyers Association: Edwin M. Otterbourg To Represent the Association in House of Delegates of American Bar Association*, 124 N.Y. L.J. 1221 (1950).

(d) Wire services. Articles derived from wire services should be cited to a print newspaper in which they are published (**rule 16.6(a)**), a commercial electronic database (**rule 16.6(e)**), or a webpage (**rule 16.6(f)**). Include the name of the wire service (in large and small caps) only if the citation is to the wire service itself.

▶ Richard Carelli, *Judges' Financial Reports Hit Web*, ASSOCIATED PRESS, June 22, 2000, *available at* 2000 WL 23358974.

▶ Kevin Drawbaugh, *Obama, Edwards Hit Lobbyists on Private Equity Tax*, REUTERS, Oct. 9, 2007, *available at* http://www.reuters.com/ article/politicsNews/idUSN0942219020071009.

But: *Record Labels Sue LimeWire for Enabling Music File-Sharing*, FOXNEWS.COM, Aug. 6, 2007, http://www.foxnews.com/story/ 0,2933,207287,00.html.

(e) Commercial electronic databases. News reports published in electronic databases may be cited according to **rule 16.8**.

▶ *Justice Minister Calls for Solving Int' l Legal Conflicts*, JAPAN ECON. NEWSWIRE PLUS, Apr. 22, 1991, at 1, *available at* DIALOG, File No. 612.

▶ *InfoUSA Tells Shareholders To Ignore Hedge Fund*, REUTERS, May 4, 2006, *available at* Factiva, Doc. No. LBA000020060504e254001vp.

(f) Internet and online newspapers. Online newspapers are often used in place of print newspapers. Because the titles, content, and publication date online may be different from the print version, the two sources should not be treated interchangeably unless the online source is an exact copy of the original as dictated by **rule 18.2.1(a)**. If an article is only available online, cite to it directly in accordance with **rule 18.2.2**; pagination can be included if available but is not necessary.

▶ John M. Broder, *Geography Is Dividing Democrats over Energy*, N.Y. TIMES, Jan. 27, 2009, at A1.

becomes: John M. Broder, *Geography Is Dividing Democrats over Energy*, N.Y. TIMES, Jan. 27, 2009, http://www.nytimes.com/2009/ 01/27/science/earth/27coal.html.

Special Citation Forms   16.7

....

Student-Written Law Review Materials   16.7.1

(a) Signed, student-written materials. Signed and titled notes, comments, projects, etc. are cited in the same manner as any other signed article in a law review (rule 16.4), with the author's full name in ordinary roman type at the beginning of the citation (rule 16.2), except that the designation of the piece should appear before the title of the work (rule 16.3) to indicate that it is student-written. Cite student-written book reviews according to rule 16.7.1(c).

A student work is considered signed if a student is credited with writing or contributing to the piece anywhere within the issue in which the work appears—on the first page of the piece, at the end of the piece, or in the table of contents. If a student work is signed only with initials, it is considered unsigned:

> ► Ellen London, Comment, *A Critique of the Strict Liability Standard for Determining Child Support in Cases of Male Victims of Sexual Assault and Statutory Rape*, 152 U. PA. L. REV. 1957, 1959–63 (2004).

> ► B. George Ballman, Jr., Note, *Amended Rule 6.1: Another Move Towards Mandatory Pro Bono? Is That What We Want?*, 7 GEO. J. LEGAL ETHICS 1139, 1162 n.155 (1994).

> ► Barry I. Pershkow, Recent Development, Maryland v. Craig: *A Child Witness Need Not View the Defendant During Testimony in Child Abuse Cases*, 65 TUL. L. REV. 935, 938, 941 (1991).

Signed, student-written commentary that is shorter, that falls under a designation such as "Recent Case," "Recent Statute," "Recent Decision," "Case Note," "Recent Development," or "Abstract," and that carries no title or merely a digest-like heading should be cited by author followed by the designation of the piece as provided in the periodical, both in ordinary roman type. When appearing in the title, a case or statute citation should be formatted according to the typeface conventions in rule 16.3. Thus:

> ► Catherine Hauber, Note, 30 U. KAN. L. REV. 611 (1982).

> ► Sally Anne Moore, Recent Case, H.L. v. Matheson, *101 S. Ct. 1164 (1981)*, 50 U. CIN. L. REV. 867, 868 (1981).

> Not: Sally Anne Moore, Recent Case, *Constitutional Law—Right of Privacy—Abortion—Family Law—Parent and Child—Standing—As Applied to Immature, Unemancipated and Dependent Minors, a State Statute Requiring a Physician To Notify a Pregnant Minor's Parents Prior to the Performing of an Abortion Is Constitutional—* H.L. v. Matheson, *101 S. Ct. 1164 (1981)*, 50 U. CIN. L. REV. 867, 868 (1981).

(b) Unsigned, student-written materials. Cite unsigned notes, comments, and shorter commentary by the designation given by the periodical, such as "Note," "Comment," "Case Comment," "Project," "Recent Case," "Case Note," etc., in ordinary roman type, followed by the title of the piece, if any, in italics:

> ► Note, *The Death of a Lawyer*, 56 COLUM. L. REV. 606 (1956).

▶ Case Comment, *Evidentiary Use of a Criminal Defendant's Reading Habits and Political Conversations:* United States v. Giese, 93 HARV. L. REV. 419, 425–27 (1979).

▶ Recent Case, 24 VAND. L. REV. 148, 151–52 (1970).

When there is no separable designation, italicize the entire title:

▶ *Developments in the Law—The Law of Cyberspace*, 112 HARV. L. REV. 1577, 1624 n.95 (1999).

▶ *The Supreme Court, 1998 Term—Leading Cases*, 113 HARV. L. REV. 368, 378 n.60 (1999).

(c) Student-written book reviews. If a review is written and signed by a student, include the author's name and the designation "Book Note" (regardless of the journal's designation) to indicate that it is student-written, followed by the title, if any. Add a parenthetical indicating the work under review if relevant to the purpose of the citation and not clear from the surrounding discussion:

▶ William Dubinsky, Book Note, 90 MICH. L. REV. 1512 (1992) (reviewing DANIEL A. FARBER & PHILIP P. FRICKEY, LAW AND PUBLIC CHOICE (1991)).

▶ Nathaniel A. Vitan, Book Note, *Irons vs. Rehnquist: A Critical Review of Peter Irons'* Brennan vs. Rehnquist, 12 J.L. & POL. 141 (1995).

An unsigned, student-written book review should be cited in the same manner as other unsigned student works, with a parenthetical citing the work under review if relevant:

▶ Book Note, *Let Us Reason Together*, 112 HARV. L. REV. 958 (1999) (reviewing PIERRE SCHLAG, THE ENCHANTMENT OF REASON (1998)).

16.7.2 Non-Student-Written Book Reviews

Give the full name of the reviewer according to **rule 16.2**, and the title of the review in italics. Include a second parenthetical after the date parenthetical indicating, if relevant to the purpose of the citation and if not clear from the surrounding discussion, the author, title, and publication date of the book reviewed. If it is unnecessary to identify the book under review, simply include the words "book review" in the second parenthetical:

▶ Colin S. Diver, *Second Governance and Sound Law*, 89 MICH. L. REV. 1436 (1991) (reviewing CHRISTOPHER F. EDLEY, JR., ADMINISTRATIVE LAW: RETHINKING JUDICIAL CONTROL OF BUREAUCRACY (1990)).

▶ Bruce Ackerman, *Robert Bork's Grand Inquisition*, 99 YALE L.J. 1419, 1422–25 (1990) (book review).

If a non-student-written review is untitled, cite it by the designation "Book Review"; it is unnecessary to include a second parenthetical unless there is a need to identify the book under review:

▶ Howard C. Westwood, Book Review, 45 U. CHI. L. REV. 255 (1977).

Symposia, Colloquia, and Surveys

When citing a symposium, colloquium, or colloquy as a unit, do not give any author, but include "**Symposium**," "**Colloquium**," or "**Colloquy**" in roman type before the title unless made clear by the title. Cite the first page of the first piece:

► Symposium, *Changing Images of the State*, 107 HARV. L. REV. 1179 (1994).

► *The Brennan Center Symposium on Constitutional Law*, 87 CALIF. L. REV. 1059 (1999).

If an article is part of a survey of the law of one jurisdiction, the title of the article should incorporate the title of the survey as follows:

► Alain A. Levasseur, *Sales, The Work of the Louisiana Appellate Courts for the 1977–1978 Term*, 39 LA. L. REV. 705 (1979).

Cite an individual article within a symposium, colloquium, colloquy, or survey in the same manner as any other article:

► Eric A. Posner, *Law, Economics, and Inefficient Norms*, 144 U. PA. L. REV. 1697 (1996).

► Kevin R. Vodak, Comment, *A Plainly Obvious Need for New-Fashioned Municipal Liability: The Deliberate Indifference Standard and* Board of County Commissioners of Bryan County v. Brown, 48 DEPAUL L. REV. 785 (1999).

Commentaries and Other Special Designations

When citing a "**Commentary**," "**Tribute**," "**In Memoriam**," or other special article designation, the designation should appear in roman type after the author's name but before the title. If the author is unnamed or if the journal's editors are listed as the authors, the designation should appear at the beginning of the citation. "**Commentary**" should not be confused with "**Comment**," a term frequently used to describe student-written pieces (**rule 16.7.1**).

► Alvin C. Warren, Jr., Commentary, *Financial Contract Innovation and Income Tax Policy*, 107 HARV. L. REV. 460 (1993).

► Sandra Day O'Connor, Dedication, *Lending Light to Countless Lamps: A Tribute to Judge Norma Levy Shapiro*, 152 U. PA. L. REV. 1 (2003).

► Marguerite A. Driessen, Response, *Not for the Sake of Punishment Alone: Comments on* Viewing the Criminal Sanction Through Latter-day Saint Thought, 2003 BYU L. REV. 941.

Multipart Articles

To cite an entire article that appears in more than one part, identify the numbers of the parts in parentheses after the article's main title and give the volume number, first page, and publication year for each part:

► Harlan F. Stone, *The Equitable Rights and Liabilities of Strangers to a Contract* (pts. 1 & 2), 18 COLUM. L. REV. 291 (1918), 19 COLUM. L. REV. 177 (1919).

If all of the parts appear in one volume, use the shortened form:

> ► L.L. Fuller, *Legal Fictions* (pts. 1–3), 25 ILL. L. REV. 363, 513, 877 (1930–1931).

To cite only some parts of a multipart article, indicate which part or parts are cited and give only the volume number(s), page number(s), and publication year(s) of the part(s) cited:

> ► L.L. Fuller, *Legal Fictions* (pt. 2), 25 ILL. L. REV. 513, 514 (1931).

16.7.6 Annotations

Cite discussions in selective case reporters (such as *American Law Reports* and *Lawyer's Reports Annotated*) by the author's full name, followed by the designation "Annotation" in ordinary roman type and the title of the work in italics:

> ► William B. Johnson, Annotation, *Use of Plea Bargain or Grant of Immunity as Improper Vouching for Credibility of Witness in Federal Cases*, 76 A.L.R. FED. 409 (1986).

16.7.7 Proceedings, Regular Publications by Institutes, and ABA Section Reports

Cite as periodicals, abbreviating according to **tables T10** and **T13**:

> ► Herbert F. Goodrich, *Annual Report of Adviser on Professional Relations*, 16 A.L.I. PROC. 48 (1939).

> ► George Vranesh, *Water Planning for Municipalities*, 24 ROCKY MTN. MIN. L. INST. 865 (1978).

If the volumes are unnumbered, use either the number of the institute (or proceedings) or the year of publication as a volume number; in the latter case omit the parenthetical reference to the year:

> ► David J. Beck, *Crude Oil Issues*, 30 INST. ON OIL & GAS L. & TAX'N 1 (1979).

> ► Julius L. Sackman, *Landmark Cases on Landmark Law*, 1979 INST. ON PLAN. ZONING & EMINENT DOMAIN 241.

> ► William J. Curtin, *Reverse Discrimination and Affirmative Action: Practical Considerations for the Utilities Industry*, 1978 A.B.A. SEC. PUB. UTIL. L. REP. 26.

If the publication is organized by paragraph or section numbers, use those numbers in citations:

> ► Max Gutierrez, Jr., *Estate Planning for the Unmarried Cohabitant*, 13 INST. ON EST. PLAN. ¶ 1600 (1979).

To cite part of an article identified by paragraph or section number, cite both the first paragraph or section number of the article and the paragraph or section number(s) where the relevant material appears. Add a page citation if necessary for further identification (see **rule 3.3**):

> ► Walter F. O'Connor, *Taxation of Foreign Investors*, 38 INST. ON FED. TAX'N § 22.01, § 22.04, at 22-10 (1980).

Newsletters and Other Noncommercially Distributed Periodicals

Materials appearing in newsletters and other similar periodicals not commercially distributed should be cited in the same manner as nonconsecutively paginated journals and magazines (**rule 16.5**), except that a parenthetical should follow the title of the publication indicating the issuing group or organization and its location. Abbreviate the name of the periodical according to **tables T10** and **T13** and abbreviate the name of the issuing institution according to **rule 15.1(d)**:

> ▶ *Indictment of Pregnant Woman for Drug Use Dismissed*, REPROD. RTS. UPDATE (ACLU/Reprod. Freedom Project, New York, N.Y.), Oct. 26, 1990, at 5.

> ▶ *Recent Grants*, FCD UPDATE (Found. for Child Dev., New York, N.Y.), Dec. 1990, at 1, 7.

Electronic Media and Online Sources

16.8

(a) Commercial electronic databases. When citing periodical materials to a database, provide a complete citation to the document according to **rule 16** and a citation to the database. If the database assigns a unique identifier or code to each document within the database, include that identifier or code to assist the reader in locating the document cited.

Some sources are available in two forms, electronic and paper. To facilitate access to the source, it is permissible to include a parallel citation to a commercial electronic database using "*available at*":

> ▶ T.R. Fehrenbach, *TV's Alamo Tale Fairly Accurate*, SAN ANTONIO EXPRESS-NEWS, Mar. 17, 1996, at A1, *available at* 1996 WL 282423.

(b) Internet and online sources. Where a print version is accessible, citation should be made to the print source. Where, however, the print source is difficult or impossible to obtain or the governing authority has designated the electronic source as the official version, citation should be made to the electronic source with consideration of **rule 18**'s principles on authentication. If a periodical source is only available online, cite to it directly in accordance with **rule 18.2.2**.

Short Citation Forms

16.9

Once a work in a periodical has been cited in full, use "*id.*" or "*supra*" to refer to it in subsequent citations.

(a) *Id.* If the work is cited as the immediately preceding authority within the same footnote or as the sole authority within the immediately preceding footnote, use "*id.*" and indicate any difference in page number:

> ▶ [1] Lynn Hirschberg, *The Misfit*, VANITY FAIR, Apr. 1991, at 158.

> ▶ [2] *See id.*; Recent Case, 24 VAND. L. REV. 148, 148 (1970).

> ▶ [3] *See generally* Abram S. Benenson et al., *Reporting the Results of Human Immunodeficiency Virus Testing*, 262 JAMA 3435 (1989) (stating that actual laboratory results are often obscured by incorrect information).

> ▶ [4] *Id.* at 3437.

▶ [5] *See, e.g.*, Bruce Ackerman, *Robert Bork's Grand Inquisition*, 99 YALE L.J. 1419 (1990) (book review). *Compare id.* (arguing against constitutional transformation by judicial appointment), *with* Book Note, *Manual Labor, Chicago Style*, 101 HARV. L. REV. 1323 (1988) (arguing against stylistic transformation by self-appointment).

(b) Supra. Include the author's last name before "*supra*"; when there is no author, use the title of the piece, or, if listed before or instead of a title, the designation of the piece. However, if the first citation to the work gives a hereinafter form (**rule 4.2(b)**), use the hereinafter form in place of the author's name, title, or designation. Give the footnote in which the full citation appears unless the full citation is in the same footnote, in which case "*supra*" may be used without a footnote reference. In using a "*supra*" form, always indicate the page or pages cited except when citing the work in its entirety:

▶ [6] Ackerman, *supra* note 5, at 1425; *see also* Note, *The Death of a Lawyer*, 56 COLUM. L. REV. 606, 607 (1956); *New York County Lawyers Association: Edwin M. Otterbourg To Represent the Association in House of Delegates of American Bar Association*, 124 N.Y. L.J. 1221 (1950) [hereinafter *Otterbourg To Represent*] (describing internal politics).

▶ [7] Recent Case, *supra* note 2, at 150. *But see* Randy E. Barnett, *A Consent Theory of Contract*, 86 COLUM. L. REV. 269, 275 (1986) (noting circularity of reliance theory of contract); Jennifer Roback, *Southern Labor Law in the Jim Crow Era: Exploitative or Competitive?*, 51 U. CHI. L. REV. 1161, 1164–65 (1984) (describing the importance of interaction between a competitive market and a racially biased government).

▶ [8] *Cf.* David Margolick, *At the Bar: Elitist Yale Breaks Precedent and Invites a Symbol of Populism To Preside at a Legal Rite*, N.Y. TIMES, Apr. 12, 1991, at B16 (describing the reaction to students' decision to invite Judge Wapner to preside over a mock-trial competition at Yale). *See generally* Roback, *supra* note 7, at 1163 (outlining four basic types of legislation that aided enforcement of the labor-market cartel under Jim Crow laws).

▶ [9] See Book Note, *supra* note 5, for a cogent analysis of the more significant flaws in the competing theory.

▶ [10] *Otterbourg To Represent*, *supra* note 6; *see also* Note, *supra* note 6 (discussing problems that arise upon the death of a lawyer). *But see Cop Shoots Tire, Halts Stolen Car*, S.F. CHRON., Oct. 10, 1975, at 43 (discussing the legal ramifications of the officer's action).

For materials available only online, use the normal short form appropriate for the source. A URL need not be repeated after a short citation.

UNPUBLISHED AND FORTHCOMING SOURCES   17

Basic Citation Forms   17.1

Unpublished manuscript	Jennifer Arlen, Public Versus Private Enforcement of Securities Fraud 12–19 (June 22, 2007) (unpublished manuscript) (on file with the Columbia Law Review).
Unpublished student work	Alexander J. Blenkinsopp, Honesty vs. Expedience: The Deficient Jurisprudence of Punishment and the Legal Labeling Game (Nov. 1, 2005) (unpublished A.B. thesis, Harvard University) (on file with the Harvard University Library system).
Letter, memorandum, or press release	Memorandum from President Franklin Roosevelt for Attorney Gen. Robert H. Jackson (July 1, 1939) (on file with the Harvard Law School Library).
E-mail correspondence	E-mail from Makau Mutua, Chairman, Kenya Human Rights Comm'n, to author (Dec. 28, 2006, 16:18 EST) (on file with author).
Forthcoming publication	Eduardo Peñalver, *Land Virtues*, 94 CORNELL L. REV. (forthcoming May 2009).
Working paper	Dan Black et al., *Demographics of the Gay and Lesbian Population in the United States: Evidence from Available Systemic Date Sources* 9 (Ctr. for Policy Research, Working Paper No. 12, 1999).

Unpublished Materials   17.2

In general, cite unpublished materials not scheduled for publication by author; title or description; page or pages, if applicable; the most precise writing date available; and, if possible, information as to where the work can be located. Use ordinary roman type. Refer to **rule 10.8.1** when citing pending and unreported cases and **rule 12.6** when citing statutes too recent to appear in any published source. If unpublished materials are subsequently collected and published, cite according to **rule 15.5.2(b)**.

Manuscripts   17.2.1

Cite unpublished (or not formally published) manuscripts not scheduled for publication in ordinary roman type, beginning with the author's full name (**rule 16.2**). The title of the work as it appears on the title page should follow, capitalized according to **rule 8(a)** (unless the title is not in English, in which case follow **rule 20.2.2(b)**). Provide a subtitle only if it is particularly relevant. Do not abbreviate words or omit articles in the title. The full date of the manuscript should be enclosed in parentheses after the title of the work or the pincite. Append parentheticals indicating that the work is unpublished and describing where it can be found:

> ▶ Anatoliy Bizhko, Capitalism and Democracy 25 (Feb. 29, 2000) (unpublished manuscript) (on file with author).

Also use this format for student-written comments and notes written under faculty supervision for a law journal, but not selected for publication, with the second parenthetical indicating the type of work:

> ▶ Victoria E. Anderson, Company Outing: How Consensual Relationship Agreements Adversely Affect Homosexual Employees 12 (Mar. 15, 2004) (unpublished comment) (on file with the University of Pennsylvania Journal of Labor and Employment Law).

17.2.2 Dissertations and Theses

Cite unpublished student-written materials, such as dissertations and theses, in the same manner as other unpublished manuscripts (**rule 17.2.1**), but add a parenthetical after the date to indicate the type of work and the institution that awarded the degree:

> ▶ Barbara G. Ryder, Incremental Data Flow Analysis Based on a Unified Model of Elimination Algorithms (Aug. 15, 1982) (unpublished Ph.D. dissertation, Rutgers University) (on file with author).

> ▶ Kathryn Arcario, Identifying Potential Response: Croat- and Serb-American Diasporas to the Dissolution of Yugoslavia (May 11, 2003) (unpublished A.B. thesis, Princeton University) (on file with Mudd Library, Princeton University).

17.2.3 Letters, Memoranda, and Press Releases

When citing unpublished letters, memoranda, and press releases, the description of the document should identify the nature of the document, and the writer and addressee (if any) by name, title, and institutional affiliation. Abbreviate title and institutional affiliation according to **tables T6 and T10**.

> ▶ Letter from Pierre Arsenault, Exec. Editor, Harvard Law Review, to Bryan M. Killian, Supreme Court Chair, Harvard Law Review (Apr. 2, 2004) (on file with the Harvard Law School Library).

> ▶ Memorandum from the Ad Hoc Comm. on Women and Clerkships to the Faculty of Yale Law Sch. 14 (Feb. 13, 1991) (on file with author).

> ▶ Press Release, Screen Actors Guild, Screen Actors Guild Hails Passage of California Privacy Law (Sept. 30, 1998) (on file with author).

To cite a letter written to the author of the work in which the letter is being cited, omit the addressee's name and use "to author":

> ▶ Letter from Emily Turner to author (Oct. 14, 2008) (on file with author).

17.2.4 E-Mail Correspondence and Listserv Postings

When citing personal e-mail messages, analogize to unpublished letters (**rule 17.2.3**). The date of the message and the time stamp may be needed for specific identification of the message. Archival information may be included parenthetically and is recommended. The e-mail addresses of the sender and recipient are not required, although they may be included if there is a reason for doing so:

> ► E-mail from Mary Miles Prince, Assoc. Dir., Vanderbilt Law Library, to Edward C. Brewer, III, Assistant Professor of Law, Salmon P. Chase Coll. of Law (Sept. 26, 1999, 06:15 CST) (on file with author).

Postings to listservs should follow a similar format, but should include the author's e-mail address and the address of the listserv:

> ► Posting of Archie Leach, aleach@act.org, to Art-Law@zealot.org (Apr. 14, 2000) (on file with author).

Interviews 17.2.5

When citing an in-person or telephone interview, include the name, title, and institutional affiliation (if any) of the interviewee and the date of the interview. For an in-person interview, provide the location of the interview before the date. Abbreviate title, institutional affiliation, and location according to **tables T6** and **T10**.

> ► Interview with Patricia Keane, Editor-in-Chief, UCLA Law Review, in L.A., Cal. (Mar. 2, 2000).
> ► Telephone Interview with John J. Farrell, Senior Partner, Hildebrand, McLeod & Nelson (Nov. 11, 1999).

When the author has not personally conducted the interview, provide the name of the interviewer:

> ► Interview by Lauren Brook Eisen with Shane Spradlin, CEO, Nextel Commc'ns, in Potomac, Md. (Mar. 1, 2000).

Speeches and Addresses 17.2.6

When citing speeches and addresses (including those made at panels and conference presentations), identify the speaker by name. Add the speaker's title and institutional affiliation if they are included in the description or transcript of the document, or if they would be particularly helpful to the reader. The title of the speech or address, pincite where available, and date of the speech should follow. Abbreviate the speaker's title and institutional affiliation according to **tables T6** and **T10**.

> ► Bradley Smith, Chairman, Fed. Election Comm'n, Keynote Address at the University of Pennsylvania Law Review Symposium: The Law of Democracy (Feb. 6, 2004).

If the speech or address does not have a formal title, provide a description with identifying information:

> ► Senator Hubert Humphrey, Address at the Harvard Law Review Annual Banquet (Mar. 29, 1958).

If the speech or address has been transcribed but not published, include the location of the transcript in a second parenthetical:

> ► Herbert Wechsler, Remarks at the Meeting of the Bar of the Supreme Court of the United States in Memory of Chief Justice Stone 5 (Nov. 12, 1947) (transcript available in the Columbia Law School Library).

If the speech or address has been published, cite using an "*in*" form according to rules **1.6(a)(i)** and **15.5.2(b)**:

> ► James A. Baker III, U.S. Sec'y of State, Principles and Pragmatism: American Policy Toward the Arab-Israeli Conflict, Address Before the American Israel Public Affairs Committee (May 22, 1989), *in* Dep't St. Bull., July 1989, at 24, 24–25.

17.3 Forthcoming Publications

Cite a book, article, or other work scheduled for publication in the same manner as the published piece would be cited, with the same typefaces, except: (i) do not include a pincite following the title of the journal or book; (ii) add the designation "forthcoming" in the date parenthetical; and (iii) include the month of publication, if available, in addition to the year in the date parenthetical:

> ► Sarah Greenberger, Comment, *Enforceable Rights, No Child Left Behind, and Political Patriotism: A Case for Open-Minded Section 1983 Jurisprudence*, 153 U. Pa. L. Rev. (forthcoming Jan. 2005).

> ► Sarah Barringer Gordon, The Twin Relics of Barbarism (forthcoming 2001).

To cite a particular page of a forthcoming publication, add a second parenthetical with the manuscript page cite and the location of the forthcoming document. Omit volume number, if not yet available:

> ► F. Brandon Baer & James M. Feldman, *We're Low on Vermouth: The Trials and Tribulations of Two Summer Associates*, 1 J.L. & Oppression (forthcoming 2001) (manuscript at 3) (on file with authors).

17.4 Working Papers

When citing an unpublished work designated as a working paper, provide a parenthetical indicating the name of the sponsoring organization, the working paper designation and number, and the year. Abbreviate institutional entities according to rule **15.1(d)**:

> ► Alan J. Auerbach & Laurence J. Kotlikoff, *National Savings, Economic Welfare, and the Structure of Taxation* 24–33 (Nat'l Bureau of Econ. Research, Working Paper No. 729, 1981).

> ► Richard Briffault, *The Political Parties and Campaign Finance Reform* 16–17 (Columbia Law Sch. Pub. Law & Legal Theory Working Paper Grp., Paper No. 12, 2000), *available at* http://papers.ssrn.com/sol3/papers.cfm?abstract_id=223729.

When a work is designated as a working paper, but is not numbered, cite according to rule **17.2.1**.

17.5 Electronic Media and Online Sources

(a) Commercial electronic databases. When citing unpublished and forthcoming materials to a database, provide a complete citation to the document according to rule **17**, and a citation to the database. If the database assigns a unique identifier or code to each document within the database, include that identifier or code to assist the reader in locating the document cited.

> ► Barbara G. Ryder, Incremental Data Flow Analysis Based on a Unified Model of Elimination Algorithms (Aug. 15, 1982) (unpublished Ph.D. dissertation, Rutgers University), 23 PQDT 5467.

Some sources are available in two forms, electronic and paper. To facilitate access to the source, it is permissible to include a parallel citation to a commercial electronic database using "*available at*":

> ► Cass R. Sunstein, *Clear Statement Principles and National Security:* Hamdan *and Beyond*, 2006 SUP. CT. REV. (forthcoming 2007) (manuscript at 17), *available at* http://ssrn.com/abstract _id=922406.

(b) Internet and online sources. Where a print version is accessible, citation should be made to the print source. Where, however, the print source is difficult or impossible to obtain, or the governing authority has designated the electronic source as the official version, citation should be made to the electronic source as described in **rule 18**'s general principles regarding authentication. If a source is only available online, cite to it directly in accordance with **rule 18.2.2**.

> ► *See* Press Release, House Speaker Nancy Pelosi, Pelosi Statement on Hate Crimes Legislation (Dec. 6, 2007), http://speaker.gov/ newsroom/pressreleases?id=0432.

Short Citation Forms 17.6

Use the "*id.*" and "*supra*" forms in the same manner as they are employed for materials appearing in periodicals (**rule 16.9**) and non-periodicals (**rule 15.10**), substituting the name of the source in place of an author when no author is listed, and enclosing a page citation to the manuscript version of a forthcoming publication in parentheses:

> ► [1] Interview with Frank Van Dusen, President, Van Dusen Indus., Inc., in Rye, N.Y. (Feb. 15, 2000).

> ► [2] *Id.*; *see also* J. Paul Oetken, Note, *Form and Substance in Critical Legal Studies*, 100 YALE L.J. (forthcoming May 2001) (manuscript at 17) (on file with author). Oetken points out inherent contradictions in CLS rhetoric. *See id.* (manuscript at 10–12); *see also* Adrienne D. Davis, African American Literature and the Law: Revising and Revisiting Freedom 3–4 (Dec. 1989) (unpublished manuscript) (on file with The Yale Law Journal) (describing depiction of the law in slave literature).

> ► [3] *See* Oetken, *supra* note 2 (manuscript at 15); Davis, *supra* note 2, at 12; Press Release, Children's Def. Fund, 2.8 Million Children of Mexican Heritage Are Among Nearly 4 Million Latino Children Living in Poverty in the United States (May 5, 2004) (on file with author).

> ► [4] Interview with Frank Van Dusen, *supra* note 1; *see* Letter from Asma Hasan to Michael Cannon 2 (Mar. 15, 2000) (on file with author).

> ► [5] *See* Letter from Asma Hasan to Michael Cannon, *supra* note 4, at 3.

> ► [6] *See* Press Release, Children's Def. Fund, *supra* note 3.

For materials available only online, use the normal short form appropriate for the source. A URL need not be repeated after a short citation.

18   THE INTERNET, ELECTRONIC MEDIA, AND OTHER NONPRINT RESOURCES

This rule covers citation of information found on the Internet (**rule 18.2**); widely used commercial databases such as Westlaw and LEXIS (**rule 18.3**); CD-ROMs (**rule 18.4**); microforms (**rule 18.5**); films, broadcasts, and noncommercial video-tapes (**rule 18.6**); and audio recordings (**rule 18.7**).

18.1   Basic Citation Forms

(a) Internet Sources (rule 18.2)

authenticated or official documents	OFFICE OF MGMT. & BUDGET, A NEW ERA OF RESPONSIBILITY: RENEWING AMERICA'S PROMISE (2009).
unaltered scanned copies of print source	United States v. Grigg, 498 F.3d 1070, 1072–73 (9th Cir. 2007).
documents for which print copy is practically unavailable	Conference Report, German Soc'y for Contemporary Theatre and Drama in English, Mediated Drama/Dramatized Media: From Boards to Screens to Cyberspace (June 17–20, 1999), http://fb14. uni-mainz.de/projects/CDE/conf/1999/.
electronic version improving reader access to source also available in print	SANTA MONICA, CAL., MUN. CODE ch. 3.20 (1976), *available at* http://qcode.us/codes/ santamonica/.
online-only sources	BEN & JERRY'S HOMEMADE ICE CREAM, http://www.benjerry.com (last visited Oct. 6, 2008).
subheadings linked from main page of website	David S. Cloud, *Gates Budget Eyes Next Gen. Warfare*, POLITICO (Apr. 12, 2009, 3:54 PM), http://www.politico.com/news/stories/0409/ 21123.html.
dynamic webpages, such as blogs	Asahi Shimbun, *A-Bomb Disease Ruling*, JAPANESE L. BLOG (Mar. 27, 2009, 9:29 PM), http://japaneselaw.blogspot.com.
online source requiring form, query, or unwieldy URL	Driving Directions from N.Y. to New Haven, CT, GOOGLE MAPS, http://maps.google.com (follow "Get Directions" hyperlink; then search "A" for "New York, NY" and search "B" for "New Haven, CT"; then follow "Get Directions" hyperlink).
online source that preserves original pagination, such as a PDF	Kenneth W. Simons, *Retributivists Need Not and Should Not Endorse the Subjectivist Account of Punishment*, 109 COLUM. L. REV. SIDEBAR 1, 3 (2009), http://www.columbialawreview.org/ Sidebar/volume/109/1_Simons.pdf.

(b) Non-Internet Electronic Sources (rules 18.3–.7)

commercial electronic databases	Bissinger v. City of New York, Nos. 06 Civ. 2325(WHP), 06 Civ. 2326(WHP), 2007 WL 2826756, at *3 (S.D.N.Y. Sept. 24, 2007).
electronic storage media	46 C.F.R. § 57.105(a) (Westlaw Desk Code of Federal Regulations CD-ROM, current through July 1, 1999).
microform collections	Petition for Writ of Certiorari for Defendant-Appellant, Cosman v. United States, 471 U.S. 1102 (1985) (No. 84-1585), *microformed on* U.S. Supreme Court Records and Briefs (Microform, Inc.).
films and broadcasts	ON THE WATERFRONT (Columbia Pictures 1954).
commercial audio recordings	THE GRATEFUL DEAD, AMERICAN BEAUTY (Warner Bros. 1970).
non-commercial recordings	Videotape: Andrew Haber Monologue Series (Scarsdale A/V Services 2008) (on file with author).
podcasts	*This American Life: Mistakes Were Made*, CHICAGO PUBLIC RADIO (Apr. 13, 2009) (downloaded using iTunes).

The Internet   18.2

The Bluebook requires the use and citation of traditional printed sources when available, unless there is a digital copy of the source available that is authenticated, official, or an exact copy of the printed source, as described in **rule 18.2.1**.

The rules that follow offer guidance in formatting Internet citations. **Rule 18.2.1** lays out general principles applicable to all Internet citations. **Rule 18.2.2** sets out rules for direct citations to Internet sources. **Rule 18.2.3** discusses parallel Internet citations introduced by "*available at*." E-mails should be treated as unpublished letters per **rule 17.2.4**.

....

General Internet Citation Principles   18.2.1

(a) Sources that can be cited as if to the original print source. When an authenticated, official, or exact copy of a source is available online, citation can be made as if to the original print source (without any URL information appended). Many states have begun to discontinue printed official legal resources, instead relying on online versions as the official resource for administrative or legislative documents. The federal government is also moving toward increasing access to online versions of legal documents, though it continues to publish official print versions.

(i) **Authenticated documents.** When citing to such materials, *The Bluebook* encourages citation to "authenticated" sources: those that use an encryption-based authentication method, such as digital signatures and public key infrastructure, to ensure the accuracy of the online source. Generally, an authenticated document will have a certificate or logo indicating that a government entity verified that the document is complete and unaltered.

(ii) **Official Versions.** Some states have designated, either by legislation or other official mechanism, that the online source is the "official" source for a particular legal document. Some online publishers similarly make a distinction as to whether the document has been approved by, contributed by, or harvested from an official source by the content originator, designating such a document "official." Generally, *The Bluebook* prefers citation to an authenticated source, or if none is available, to the "official" source.

(iii) **Exact Copies.** An exact copy is one that is an unaltered copy of the printed source in a widely used format that preserves pagination and other attributes of the printed work (such as Adobe's portable document format, or "PDF").

(b) Sources where the URL should be appended. If the cited information is available in print but such copies are so obscure as to be practically unavailable, citation should be made as if to the printed source, but indicating the online location of the copy used by appending the URL directly to the end of the citation.

(c) Sources using "available at" to indicate where access is available online. Even if a printed source is available, a parallel citation to an electronic source as related authority (**rule 1.6**) may be appropriate where it would substantially improve access to the relevant information. In this case, citation should be made first to the printed source and then separately to the electronic source, introduced with the explanatory phrase "*available at.*"

....

18.2.2 Direct Citations to Internet Sources

An Internet source may be cited directly when it does not exist in a traditional printed format or when a traditional printed source, such as a letter or unpublished dissertation, exists but cannot be found or is so obscure that it is practically unavailable. All efforts should be made to cite to the most stable electronic location available. The Internet citation should include information designed to facilitate the clearest path of access to the cited reference, including the title, pagination, and publication date as they appear on the webpage. The Internet URL should be separated by a comma and appended to the end of the citation (that is, not preceded by "*available at*" or "*at*").

(a) Author. When available, provide author information in ordinary roman type. When no author is clearly announced, omit author information from the citation unless there is a clear institutional owner of the domain. Abbreviate the name of an institutional author according to **rule 15.1(d)**:

▶ Eric Posner, *More on Section 7 of the Torture Convention*, VOLOKH CONSPIRACY (Jan. 29, 2009, 10:04 AM), http://www.volokh.com/posts/1233241458.shtml.

▶ *Pavement Planning New Album Release*, GLIDE MAG. (Nov. 6, 2009), http://www.glidemagazine.com/articles/55317/pavement-planning-new-album-release.html.

If domain ownership is clear from the website's title, omit the name of the institutional author:

▶ Dᴜɴᴋɪɴ' Dᴏɴᴜᴛs, http://www.dunkindonuts.com (last visited Feb. 1, 2009).

▶ *The Butterfly Conservatory*, Aᴍ. Mᴜsᴇᴜᴍ Nᴀᴛ. Hɪsᴛ., http://www.amnh.org/exhibitions/butterflies/?src=h_h (last visited Nov. 25, 2009).

For postings and comments, cite using the username of the poster. Comments should include the author of the comment when available but need not include the author of the original post:

▶ Martinned, Comment to *More on Section 7 of the Torture Convention*, Vᴏʟᴏᴋʜ Cᴏɴsᴘɪʀᴀᴄʏ (Jan. 29, 2009, 11:02 AM), http://www.volokh.com/posts/1233241458.shtml.

(b) Titles. Titles should be used to indicate the location of the page being viewed in relation to the rest of the site. Titles should be taken either from the "title bar" at the top of the browser or from any clearly announced heading identifying the page as it appears in the browser. All efforts should be made to include a title that sufficiently identifies the page but that is not unwieldy, long, uninformative, or confusing:

▶ *Weird and Dumb International Laws*, JᴜsᴛɪᴄᴇDᴀɪʟʏ.ᴄᴏᴍ, http://www.justicedaily.com/weird/part2.html (last visited May 21, 2004).

Not: *Weird Law and Dumb Law—Legal Jokes, Lawyer Jokes, Humor, Law*, JᴜsᴛɪᴄᴇDᴀɪʟʏ.ᴄᴏᴍ, http://www.justicedaily.com/weird/part2.html (last visited May 21, 2004).

(i) Main page titles. The citation should always include the homepage or domain name of which the particular citation is a part, referred to here as a "main page title." The website's main page title should be cited using small caps. Capitalization should conform to the title as it appears on the site. Main page titles should be abbreviated in accordance with **table T13**:

▶ Dᴀɪʟʏ Kᴏs (Jan. 19, 2009), http://www.dailykos.com.

(ii) Titles for pages other than the main page. The title of the specific pages within the domain name and linked from the main page, for example postings or comments to postings, should also be included where relevant. Titles to subheadings should appear in italics. Follow standard rules for capitalizing the titles of sources in accordance with **rule 8**, even if the title bar uses nonstandard capitalization. Where appropriate, subheadings should include language indicating the page's relation to the page to which it responds:

▶ David Waldman, *This Week in Congress*, Dᴀɪʟʏ Kᴏs (Jan. 19, 2009, 6:30:04 AM), http://www.dailykos.com/storyonly/2009/1/18/235223/489/683/685802.

▶ Packerland Progressive, *How Is Sec 115 Constitutional Under* INS v. Chadha?, Comment to *This Week in Congress*, Dᴀɪʟʏ Kᴏs (Jan. 19, 2009, 9:20 AM), http://www.dailykos.com/storyonly/2009/1/18/235223/489/683/685802.

(iii) Descriptive titles. If the page's headings are not sufficiently clear, a descriptive title can be used. Do not italicize descriptive titles:

▶ Archive of Columns by William Safire, N.Y. TIMES,
http://www.nytimes.com/top/opinion/editorialsandoped/oped/c
olumnists/williamsafire/ (last visited Jan. 17, 2004).

▶ Review of *The Hitchhiker's Guide to the Galaxy: Collector's
Edition*, ROTTEN TOMATOES, http://www.rottentomatoes.com/
m/hitchhikers_guide_to_the_galaxy_the_collectors_edition (last
visited Jan. 6, 2004).

(c) Date and time. The date should be provided as it appears on the Internet
site. Use only dates that refer clearly to the material cited. The date should be indicated after the main page title and any pinpoint citation:

▶ Ashby Jones, *Activists, Research Facilities Taking Disclosure
Battles to Court*, WALL ST. J. L. BLOG (Feb. 26, 2009, 9:40 AM),
http://blogs.wsj.com/law/2009/02/26/activists-research-facili-
ties-taking-disclosure-battles-to-the-courts.

If there is no date associated with the specific subject matter of the citation, "last
updated" or "last modified" dates should be supplied in a parenthetical after the
URL. "Last updated" or "last modified" dates or copyright designations that refer
to a site as a whole should not be used for dynamic sites that are updated regularly:

▶ Dale Fast, *History of Biology and Medicine*, SAINT XAVIER U.,
http://faculty.sxu.edu/~fast/general_biology/history.htm (last
updated Oct. 31, 2001).

When material is otherwise undated, the date that the website was last visited
should be placed in a parenthetical after the URL:

▶ YAHOO!, http://www.yahoo.com (last visited Dec. 15, 2004).

Blogs and other dynamic sites that are updated frequently should include a time-
stamp whenever possible. Especially when the citation is for a comment to a
posting or is otherwise easily identifiable by the time of its posting, the time-
stamp listed on the subheading should be included with the date:

▶ Donn Zaretsky, *Ruling Is a Setback for Sports Artist*, ART L. BLOG
(Aug. 26, 2009, 10:51 AM), http://theartlawblog.blogspot.com.

(d) The URL. A site's Internet address, or URL, should point readers directly to
the source cited rather than to an intervening page of links. If the URL is straight-
forward, then cite the entire URL as it appears in the address bar of the browser:

▶ Stanley Kubrick—Biography, YAHOO! MOVIES, http://movies.yahoo
.com/shop?d=hc&id=1800011072&cf=biog&intl=us (last visited
Nov. 24, 2009)

Not: Biography of Stanley Kubrick, YAHOO! MOVIES, http://movies
.yahoo.com/ (search "Search Yahoo! Movies" for "Stanley
Kubrick"; then follow "Stanley Kubrick" hyperlink under "Top
Matching Cast and Crew"; then follow "Biography" hyperlink) (last
visited Nov. 24, 2009).

Alternatively, the root URL of the site from which information is accessed may be
used if (1) the URL is long, unwieldy, or full of nontextual characters (such as
question marks, percentage signs, or ampersands); or (2) the source may only be
obtained by submitting a form or query. If the root URL is used and the site's
format is not clear from the rest of the citation, a clarifying parenthetical should

be added to explain how to access the specific information to which the citation refers:

▶ http://fjsrc.urban.org/noframe/wqs/q_data_1.htm#2001 (follow "2001: AOUSC out" hyperlink; then follow "Offenses: TTSECMO" hyperlink)

Not: http://fjsrc.urban.org/noframe/wqs/q_e.cfm?cat=3&year=2001 &agency=AOUSC&saf=out&var1=TTSECMSO.

Note that some URLs are case sensitive, so cite URLs as they appear in the Internet browser.

(e) Multiple URLs. Some popular sites are served by more than one URL. In these cases, a proper citation should use the primary URL rather than a URL that links to an alternate server:

▶ Yahoo!, http://www.yahoo.com (last visited Nov. 24, 2009).

Not: Yahoo!, http://www1.yahoo.com (last visited Nov. 24, 2009).

(f) Document format. If a document is available both in HTML format and in a widely used format that preserves pagination and other attributes of printed work (such as Adobe's portable document format, or "PDF"), the latter should always be cited in lieu of an HTML document:

▶ Elizabeth McNichol & Iris J. Lav, *New Fiscal Year Brings No Relief from Unprecedented State Budget Problems*, CENTER ON BUDGET & POL'Y PRIORITIES 1 (Sept. 3, 2009), http://www.cbpp.org/9-8-08sfp.pdf.

Not: Elizabeth McNichol & Iris J. Lav, *New Fiscal Year Brings No Relief from Unprecedented State Budget Problems*, CENTER ON BUDGET & POL'Y PRIORITIES 1 (Sept. 3, 2009), http://www.cbpp.org/9-8-08sfp.htm.

(g) Pinpoint citations. If the cited document is rendered in a format (such as a PDF file) that preserves the pagination of a print version, pinpoint citations should be provided where appropriate. Page numbers should always refer to the numbers that appear on the document itself. Do not use "screen numbers" or other numbers that may appear in a software viewing window or scroll bar. When there is pagination information available, it should be included between the domain name and the date or URL, whichever comes first.

(h) Archival. Printing or downloading copies of Internet sources is encouraged. It is not, however, necessary to indicate the location of an archival copy in the citation. When citing to a past version of an Internet page, include an explanatory parenthetical:

▶ Tom Goldstein, *Somewhat Significant Settlement*, SCOTUSBLOG (Feb. 7, 2005, 8:54 PM), http://web.archive.org/web/20050208081922/www.scotusblog.com/movabletype (accessed by searching for SCOTUSblog in the Internet Archive index).

Parallel Citations to Internet Sources   18.2.3

(a) Generally. Even when a source is available in a traditional printed medium, a parallel citation to an Internet source with identical content may be provided if it will substantially improve access to the source cited. The citation to the primary source should be formatted according to **rules 10–17** and **rules 19–21**, and the parallel Internet citation should then be introduced with the explanatory phrase "*available at*":

> ▶ Am. Mining Cong. v. U.S. Army Corps of Eng'rs, No. CIV.A.93-1754 SSH (D.D.C. Jan. 23, 1997), *available at* http://www.wetlands.com/fed/tulloch1.htm.

> ▶ Marcel Kahan & Edward B. Rock, *Corporate Constitutionalism: Antitakeover Charter Provisions as Pre-Commitment*, 152 U. PA. L. REV. (forthcoming Dec. 2003), *available at* http://ssrn.com/abstract=416605.

(b) Author, title, pagination, and publication data. The author, title, pagination, and publication data of the original printed source should be used, even if the Internet source renders this information slightly differently. If the information available on the Internet differs materially from the information in the traditional printed source, then a parallel citation should not be used:

> ▶ Letter from John Brady Kiesling, U.S. Diplomat, to Colin L. Powell, U.S. Sec'y of State (Feb. 27, 2003) (on file with author), *available at* http://www.truthout.org/article/us-diplomat-john-brady-kiesling-letter-resignation-secretary-state-colin-l-powell.

> Not: Letter from John Brady Kiesling, U.S. Diplomat, to Colin L. Powell, U.S. Sec'y of State (on file with author), *available at* http://www.truthout.org/article/us-diplomat-john-brady-kiesling-letter-resignation-secretary-state-colin-l-powell (last modified Jan. 15, 2004).

Online sources do not need to be archived (**rule 18.2.2(h)**) when they are used only in parallel citations. In the event that a website becomes inaccessible, readers may always consult the traditional printed source instead.

(c) Order of authorities and parentheticals. A parallel citation does not affect the order of authorities under **rule 1.4**. The source is ordered in the same way that the traditional printed source would be:

> ▶ *See* Marcel Kahan & Edward B. Rock, *Corporate Constitutionalism: Antitakeover Charter Provisions as Pre-Commitment*, 152 U. PA. L. REV. (forthcoming Dec. 2003), *available at* http://ssrn.com/abstract=416605; Interview with Morris Kramer, Partner, Skadden, Arps, Slate, Meagher & Flom, in N.Y., N.Y. (Mar. 14, 1997) (discussing the limitations of shareholder rights plans).

When a parallel citation requires multiple parentheticals, place them in the order indicated in **rule 1.5(b)**. Thus, a parallel citation introduced by "*available at*" should follow format-related parenthetical information (such as "on file with author," "unpublished manuscript," "emphasis added," or "internal quotation marks omitted") and related authority parentheticals (such as "citing" or "quoting"), but precede explanatory parentheticals:

> ▶ Polly J. Price, *Precedent and Judicial Power After the Founding*, 42 B.C. L. REV. 81, 84 (2000) (emphasis added) (citing GUIDO CALABRESI, A COMMON LAW FOR THE AGE OF STATUTES 4 (1982)), *available at* http://www.bc.edu/schools/law/lawreviews/meta-elements/journals/bclawr/42_1/02_FMS.htm (discussing precedent in the context of statutory construction).

Commercial Electronic Databases 18.3

Because of the reliability and authoritativeness of LEXIS, Westlaw, Bloomberg Law and other commercial electronic databases such as Dialog, cite such sources, if available, in preference to the other sources covered by rule 18. Citations to these electronic databases should be consistent with this present rule regardless of whether the databases are accessed through proprietary software or through a website such as http://www.westlaw.com or http://www.lexis.com.

Cases 18.3.1

When a case is unreported but available on a widely used electronic database, it may be cited to that database. Provide the case name, docket number, database identifier, court name, and full date of the most recent major disposition of the case. If the database contains codes or numbers that uniquely identify the case (as LEXIS, Westlaw, and Bloomberg Law do), these must be given. Screen or page numbers, if assigned, should be preceded by an asterisk; paragraph numbers, if assigned, should be preceded by a paragraph symbol:

▶ Gibbs v. Frank, No. 02-3924, 2004 U.S. App. LEXIS 21357, at *18 (3d Cir. Oct. 14, 2004).

▶ Chavez v. Metro. Dist. Comm'n, No. 3:02CV458(MRK), 2004 U.S. Dist. LEXIS 11266, at *5 n.3 (D. Conn. June 1, 2004).

▶ Ortho-McNeil Pharm., Inc. v. Teva Pharm. Indus., Ltd., No. 2008-1549, 2009 BL 181480, at *4 (Fed. Cir. Aug. 26, 2009).

▶ Shelton v. City of Manhattan Beach, No. B171606, 2004 WL 2163741, at *1 (Cal. Ct. App. Sept. 28, 2004).

If the name of the database is not clear from the database identifier, include it parenthetically at the end of the citation:

▶ Staats v. Brown, No. 65681-9, 2000 WA 0042007, ¶ 25 (Wash. Jan. 6, 2000) (VersusLaw).

Citations to cases that have not been assigned unique database identifiers should include all relevant information, such as the specific collection within the database in which the case can be found:

▶ Frankel v. Banco Nacional de Mex., S.A., No. 82 Civ. 6547 (S.D.N.Y. May 31, 1983) (LEXIS, Genfed Library, Dist. File).

▶ Lindquist v. Hart, 1 CA-CV 98-0323 (Ariz. Ct. App. July 15, 1999) (Loislaw, Ariz. Case Law).

Constitutions and Statutes 18.3.2

Cite codes and session laws according to rules 12.3 and 12.4. In addition, when citing a code contained in an electronic database, give parenthetically the name of the database and information regarding the currency of the database as provided by the database itself (rather than the year of the code according to rule 12.3.2). In accordance with rule 12.3.1(d), also give the name of the publisher, editor, or compiler unless the code is published, edited, compiled by, or under the supervision of, federal or state officials:

> ▶ WASH. CONST. art. I, § 2 (West, Westlaw through Nov. 2003 amendments).

> ▶ CAL. BUS. & PROF. CODE § 1670 (Deering, LEXIS through 1995 Sess.).

> ▶ CAL. BUS. & PROF. CODE § 1670 (West, Westlaw through 1995 portion of 1995–1996 Legis. Sess.).

> ▶ WASH. REV. CODE § 13.64.060 (VersusLaw through 1999 legislation).

> ▶ WIS. STAT. § 19.43 (LEXIS through 1994 legislation).

> ▶ WIS. STAT. § 19.43 (Loislaw through 1997–1998 Legis. Sess.).

> ▶ WIS. STAT. ANN. § 19.43 (West, Westlaw through 1995 Act 26).

18.3.3 **Legislative, Administrative, and Executive Materials**

Cite legislative, administrative, and executive materials according to **rules 13** and **14**. In addition, when citing to materials contained in a commercial electronic database, give the name of the database and any identifying codes or numbers that uniquely identify the material. If the name of the database is not clear from the database identifier, include it parenthetically at the end of the citation:

federal bill (unenacted)	H.R. 3781, 104th Cong. § 2(b) (1996), 1996 CONG US HR 3781 (Westlaw).
federal report	H.R. REP. NO. 92-98 (1971), *reprinted in* 1971 U.S.C.C.A.N. 1017, 1971 WL 11312.
congressional debate	142 CONG. REC. H11,460 (daily ed. Sept. 27, 1996) (statement of Rep. Tanner), 142 Cong Rec H11452, at *H11,460 (LEXIS).
federal regulation cited to *Code of Federal Regulations*	FTC Credit Practices Rule, 16 C.F.R. § 444.1 (2000), WL 16 CFR s 444.1.
administrative adjudication	Reichhold Chems., Inc., 91 F.T.C. 246 (1978), 1978 WL 206094.
formal advisory opinion	39 Op. Att'y Gen. 484 (1940), 1940 US AG LEXIS 16.
revenue ruling	Rev. Rul. 86-71, 1986-1 C.B. 102, 1986 IRB LEXIS 189.

18.3.4 **Books, Periodicals, and Other Secondary Materials**

When citing secondary materials to a database, provide a complete citation to the document according to **rules 15–17** and a citation to the database. If the database assigns a unique identifier or code to each document within the database, include that identifier or code to assist the reader in locating the document cited.

Some sources are available in two forms, electronic and paper. To increase ease of access to the source, it is permissible to include a parallel citation to a commercial electronic database using "*available at*":

► T.R. Fehrenbach, *TV's Alamo Tale Fairly Accurate*, SAN ANTONIO EXPRESS-NEWS, Mar. 17, 1996, at A1, *available at* 1996 WL 2824823.

► *Justice Minister Calls for Solving Int' l Legal Conflicts*, JAPAN ECON. NEWSWIRE PLUS, Apr. 22, 1991, at 1, *available at* DIALOG, File No. 612.

CD-ROM and Other Electronic Storage Media   18.4

(a) Print form preferred. Information found on CD-ROM or other medium of electronic distribution (flash drive, etc.) is usually available in print form, and citation to the print form is preferred. If the information is accessed by electronic storage medium, however, it should be cited to that medium.

(b) Citation format. When citing CD-ROM or other similar media, include the title of the material, the publisher of the CD-ROM, the version searched, and the date of the material, if available, or the date of the version searched. The information may be provided in a source-date parenthetical or, if the information is voluminous, as related authority (**rule 1.6**):

► 7 LAWRENCE P. KING, COLLIER ON BANKRUPTCY ¶ 700.02 (Matthew Bender Authority Bankruptcy Law CD-ROM, rel. 13, Aug. 1999).

Microform   18.5

Microform Collections Reproducing Preexisting Materials   18.5.1

In general, when a document is reproduced in microform, it is not necessary to indicate this fact unless it would otherwise be difficult for a reader to identify and obtain the source. When citing material as "*microformed on*" a service, provide a complete citation to the original document and a citation to the microform in accordance with **rule 1.6** regarding citations to related authority. If the microform service assigns a unique identifier or code to each document reproduced, include that identifier to assist the reader in locating the document cited. Include the name of the publisher of the microform series in parentheses, abbreviated according to **rule 15.1(d)**:

► CAL. CODE REGS. tit. 26, § 23-2631(g) (Barclay's 1990), *microformed on* Cal. Code of Reg. 1990 Revised Format, Fiche 143 (Univ. Microforms Int'l).

► APPLICATION OF EMPLOYER SANCTIONS TO LONGSHORE WORK, H.R. REP. NO. 101-208 (1989), *microformed on* CIS No. 89-H523-17 (Cong. Info. Serv.).

► S. 1237, 99th Cong. § 505 (1985), *microformed on* Sup. Docs. No. Y 1.4/1:99-1237 (U.S. Gov't Printing Office).

18.5.2 Microform Collections Containing Original Materials

When a microform collection contains materials original to that collection, identify the microform set and its publisher, and use the publisher's system for identifying individual forms within the set. Use **rule 18.5.1** as a guide.

18.6 Films, Broadcasts, and Noncommercial Video Materials

Cite films in large and small capitals, and television or radio broadcasts in italics, by title, episode name (if available), and exact date (if available). Include the name of the company or network that produced the film or broadcast. If there is no information as to the producer of the broadcast, include the name of the company or network that aired the broadcast:

> ▶ AIRPLANE! (Paramount Pictures 1980).

> ▶ *Law & Order: Tabula Rasa* (NBC television broadcast Apr. 21, 1999).

Cite video materials containing images that have not been commercially displayed or broadcast by the medium of the material, the title of the video or DVD (if any), the name of the person or institution that produced the video, and the year of production. Timestamps may be used for designating pinpoint citations, but they are not required:

> ▶ Videotape: Installing Your CLS-2009 (Emily Weiss Electric Co. 1995) (on file with the Arlington Public Library).

> ▶ DVD: 2004 Yale Law Revue (Yale Media Services 2004) (on file with author).

When a television broadcast is also available online, a parallel citation to the online source is acceptable in accordance with **rule 18.2.3**.

If the video was originally broadcast online, cite per **rule 18.2.2** for dynamic websites. Consistent with the general principles of this rule, all efforts should be made to cite to the distinct URL for the specific video. Use the creator of the video as the author if available; otherwise treat the person who posted the video as the author. When the site indicates that the video contains contents from another source, use an explanatory parenthetical to indicate that source:

> ▶ Periodicvideos, *Chocolate and Roses – Periodic Table of Videos*, YOUTUBE (Feb. 10, 2009), http://www.youtube.com/watch?v=3ALAZdsguO8&feature=dir.

18.7 Audio Recordings

18.7.1 Commercial Recordings

Cite commercial recordings by artist and title, providing the name of the recording company and the date of release (if available):

> ▶ COWBOY MOUTH, ARE YOU WITH ME? (MCA Records 1996).

> ▶ THE BEATLES, SGT. PEPPER'S LONELY HEARTS CLUB BAND (Capitol Records 1990) (1967).

If a particular song or musical work is referred to, cite it by analogy to shorter works in a collection according to **rule 15.5.1**. Timestamps may be used for designating pinpoint citations, but they are not required:

> ▶ Don Henley, *The Boys of Summer, on* Building the Perfect Beast (Geffen Records 1984).

Noncommercial Recordings   18.7.2

If the recording referred to is not commercially available, use ordinary roman type and indicate parenthetically where a copy may be obtained. Timestamps may be used for designating pinpoint citations, but they are not required:

> ▶ Audio tape: Conference on Business Opportunities in Space, held by the Center for Space Policy, Inc., and the Commonwealth of Massachusetts (Mar. 3–5, 1986) (on file with author).

Podcasts and Recordings Available Online   18.7.3

If the audio recording was accessed online, a parallel citation to its location is suggested per **rule 18.2.3**. If the recording is only available online, it should be cited using the principles of **rule 18.2.2**. If there is no stable URL available to facilitate access to the source, an explanatory parenthetical should be added explaining how the source should be accessed. Timestamps may be used for designating pinpoint citations, but they are not required:

> ▶ *War of Words: Judith Thurman Discusses Scrabble, Both Online and Off,* The New Yorker (Jan. 19, 2009), http://www.newyorker.com/online/2009/01/19/0901190n_audio_thurman.

> ▶ *Splitting Verbs, Grammar Girl's Quick and Dirty Tips for Better Writing* (Feb. 26, 2009) (downloaded using iTunes).

Short Citation Forms   18.8

(a) Internet. When citing to a previously referenced Internet site, use a "*supra*" form with the last name of the author, if any, or the title or description of the document. "*Id.*" may also be used in accordance with **rule 4**. If various subsections of a website with no author are cited or if more than one posting by a given author is cited, include the subsection title. A URL need not be repeated after a full citation:

> ▶ [1] *See* Douglas Gantenbein, *Mad Cows Come Home,* Slate (Jan. 5, 2004, 12:10 PM), http://slate.msn.com/id/2093396.

> ▶ [2] Pfizer, Inc., http://www.pfizer.com (last visited Jan. 17, 2004).

> ▶ [3] Gantenbein, *supra* note 1; Pfizer, Inc., *supra* note 2.

(b) Commercial electronic databases. For materials available on an electronic database, use a unique database identifier, if one has been assigned, in constructing a short form:

> ▶ Int'l Snowmobile Mfrs. Ass'n v. Norton, No. 00-CV-229-B, 2004 WL 2337372, at *3 (D. Wyo. Oct. 14, 2004).

becomes: *Int'l Snowmobile,* 2004 WL 2337372, at *3.

► Chavez v. Metro. Dist. Comm'n, No. 3:02CV458(MRK), 2004 U.S. Dist. LEXIS 11266, at *5 n.3 (D. Conn. June 1, 2004).

becomes: *Chavez*, 2004 U.S. Dist. LEXIS 11266, at *5 n.3.

(c) CD-ROM and microform. When citing a separately published document available on CD-ROM or microform, use the short form appropriate for the original document; it is not necessary to indicate the source once it has been given in the first full citation.

(d) Films, broadcasts, and audio recordings. When citing films, broadcasts, and audio recordings, "*id.*" and "*supra*" may be used according to **rule 4**:

► [4] *Nightline: Microsoft Monopoly* (ABC television broadcast Apr. 3, 2000) (transcript on file with the Columbia Law Review).

► [5] *Id.*

► [6] *See id.*; MEAT LOAF, *For Crying Out Loud, on* BAT OUT OF HELL (Epic Records 1977).

► [7] MEAT LOAF, *supra* note 6; *see also Nightline: Microsoft Monopoly*, *supra* note 4 (describing Microsoft's response to the court ruling).

SERVICES   19

Cases, administrative materials, and brief commentaries are often published unofficially in topical compilations called "services," which appear in looseleaf form initially and are sometimes published later as bound volumes. Consult *Legal Looseleafs in Print*, which is updated annually, for a comprehensive listing of services. **Rule 19.1** provides rules for citing services. Some services are no longer published in print or are otherwise available online. When citation is made to an online service publication, indicate that the version is online in the title of the publication.

Citation Form for Services   19.1

Cite services by volume, abbreviated title in ordinary roman type, publisher, subdivision, and date. If the source is a case, include the abbreviated name of the court in the same parenthetical as the date, as you would under **rule 10.4**. Consult **table T15** for service and publisher abbreviations; if a service is not listed, refer to **table T13** to abbreviate the words that make up its title:

> ► *In re* Smithfield Estates, Inc., [1985–1986 Transfer Binder] Bankr. L. Rep. (CCH) ¶ 70,707 (Bankr. D.R.I. Aug. 9, 1985).
> ► SEC v. Tex. Int'l Airlines, 29 Fed. R. Serv. 2d (West) 408 (D.D.C. 1979).
> ► Kovacs v. Comm'r, 74 A.F.T.R.2d (RIA) 354 (6th Cir. 1994).

When citing looseleaf material that will eventually be bound, add the name of the bound form in parentheses if it is different from the name of the looseleaf form; include the volume of the bound form if available:

> ► Marietta Concrete Co., 3 Lab. Rel. Rep. (BNA) (84 Lab. Arb. Rep.) 1158 (May 7, 1985).

(a) Volume. The volume designation of a service may be a number, a year, a descriptive subtitle from the volume's spine, or a combination of these. If the volume designation includes words or a year, use brackets to avoid confusion:

> ► 5 Trade Reg. Rep.
> ► 1979-1 Trade Cas.
> ► [Current Developments] Hous. & Dev. Rep.
> ► [1979] 8 Stand. Fed. Tax Rep.
> ► [2 Wages-Hours] Lab. L. Rep.
> ► [1 Estate & Gift] U.S. Tax Rep.

In citing a transfer binder, the volume designation should indicate the years of material included in that binder:

> ► [1994–1995 Transfer Binder] Fed. Sec. L. Rep.

See generally **rule 3.1(a)** (designation of volumes and use of brackets).

(b) Publisher. Every citation to a service, whether looseleaf or bound, must indicate the publisher. Enclose an abbreviation of the publisher's name in parentheses following the service's title. Consult **table T15** for a list of service publisher abbreviations; if a publisher is not listed, abbreviate according to **rule 15.1(d)**.

> ► 4 Lab. L. Rep. (CCH) ¶ 9046.
> ► [1982] 12 Envtl. L. Rep. (Envtl. Law Inst.).

(c) Subdivision. Cite services by paragraph or section number if possible, otherwise by page number. See generally **rule 3.2** (pages, footnotes, endnotes, and graphical materials) and **rule 3.3** (sections and paragraphs). Additionally, a report number may be given if it will assist the reader in locating the cited material:

> ▸ *Rhode Island Insurance Agents Agree Not To Rig Bids*, [Jan.–June] Antitrust & Trade Reg. Rep. (BNA) No. 967, at D-11 (June 5, 1980).

> ▸ *Domination of Markets, AMA Report Finds Consumers Have Few Options*, [Jan.–Feb.] Antitrust & Trade Reg. Rep. Online (BNA) No. 96, at 88 (2008).

(d) Date. When citing a case reported in a service, give the exact date (for looseleaf services) or year (for bound services) of the case (**rule 10.5**):

> ▸ Defenders of Wildlife, Inc. v. Watt, [1982] 12 Envtl. L. Rep. (Envtl. Law Inst.) 20,210 (D.D.C. May 28, 1981).

When citing a statute or regulation, give the exact date of its enactment or promulgation unless the exact date is indicated elsewhere in the citation:

> ▸ Act of Sept. 26, 1980, Food Drug Cosm. L. Rep. (CCH) ¶ 653.

Citations to other material (such as articles or commentary) should give the exact date, if available. When citing otherwise undated material in a looseleaf service, give the date of the page on which the material is printed or the date of the subsection in which it is printed:

> ▸ *ERISA Preemption Bills Draw Praise from Labor and Criticism from Business*, [Aug. 1991–June 1993] Pens. Plan Guide (CCH) ¶ 26,263, at 27,037-40 (Aug. 2, 1991).

19.2 Short Citation Forms

(a) Cases. For cases, use short citation forms as provided by **rule 10.9**. Include the complete volume designation for the service binder and substitute paragraph or section numbers for page numbers where appropriate. If a case has page numbers as well as paragraph or section numbers, you may cite individual pages instead of the paragraph or section number in the short form to identify specific material. To cite the entire case in short form, give the paragraph or section number of the case or the first page number of the case, without using "at":

> ▸ [1] *In re* Looney, [1987–1989 Transfer Binder] Bankr. L. Rep. (CCH) ¶ 72,447, at 93,590 (Bankr. W.D. Va. Sept. 9, 1988).

> ▸ [2] *Id.*

> ▸ [3] *Id.* at 93,591.

> ▸ [4] Defenders of Wildlife, Inc. v. Watt, [1982] 12 Envtl. L. Rep. (Envtl. Law Inst.) 20,210, 20,211 (D.D.C. May 28, 1981).

> ▸ [5] *In re Looney*, [1987–1989 Transfer Binder] Bankr. L. Rep. (CCH) at 93,591.

> ▸ [6] *Defenders of Wildlife*, [1982] 12 Envtl. L. Rep. (Envtl. Law Inst.) at 20,212.

> ▸ [7] This was the approach taken in *Looney*. *See* [1987–1989 Transfer Binder] Bankr. L. Rep. (CCH) ¶ 72,447.

(b) Other materials. Short form citations for other materials found in services, such as statutes, regulations, articles, and commentary, should follow the relevant citation rules as described elsewhere in *The Bluebook*.

FOREIGN MATERIALS   20

Table T2 contains jurisdiction-specific citation examples and is the primary source for the citation of foreign materials. For sources not present in **table T2**, follow the respective country's own citation rules for the sources as modified by these general rules:

Jurisdiction   20.1

When citing any non-U.S. source, whether in English or in another language, indicate parenthetically the jurisdiction issuing the source, abbreviated according to **table T10**, unless the jurisdiction is otherwise clear from the other elements of the citation.

► Chase v. Campbell, [1962] S.C.R. 425 (Can.).

► *Berry v Dorsey* (1975) 101 ALR 35 (Austl.).

This parenthetical may be omitted if the jurisdiction is clear from the context.

► Spain has enacted a separate code governing legal procedure in employment cases.[1]

► [1] Labor Procedure Law (R.C.L. 1990, 922).

The parenthetical is located at the end of the citation but before any parallel citations, unless otherwise indicated in **table T2**.

► Canada Act, 1982, c.11 (U.K.), *reprinted in* R.S.C. 1985, app. II, no. 5 (Can.).

► Control of Fishing for Salmon Order 2008 (S.I. No. 098/2008) (Ir.), *available at* http://www.attorneygeneral.ie/esi/2008/B26061.pdf.

Non-English-Language Documents   20.2

Documents Appearing in More than One Language   20.2.1

Unless otherwise required by the citation, always cite the most official or authoritative version of the document. The document itself should clarify which version(s) is authoritative. For documents published in multiple languages, use the English-language version whenever it is as authoritative as (or more authoritative than) other versions. If the document is silent on the issue of authority, always cite the English-language version unless the purpose served by the citation requires otherwise.

Titles and Names of Documents in Languages   20.2.2
Other than English

(a) **Original language and translation.** When citing a document in a language other than English, always give the document's full title or name in the original language the first time the document is cited. If desired, the original-language title may be followed by brackets containing its shortened or full-length English title in the same typeface as the original:

▶ Verdrag tot het Vermijden van Dubbele Belasting [Agreement for the Avoidance of Double Taxation]

(b) Capitalization. Capitalize names and titles in languages other than English as they appear on the page. Capitalize translations according to **rule 8**.

20.2.3 Abbreviations in Languages Other than English

The abbreviations of reporters, codes, statutes, statutory collections, constitutions, and periodicals in languages other than English may be unfamiliar to the reader. Therefore, the full form should be given the first time the source is cited, and the abbreviation should be given in brackets. Thereafter for the whole piece, the abbreviated form may be used without cross-reference.

Abbreviations for many legal materials in languages other than English are given in **table T2**; for periodicals, see **rule 20.6**. When abbreviating foreign legal materials for which an abbreviation is not provided, follow the usage of the source.

▶ [1] BÜRGERLICHES GESETZBUCH [BGB] [CIVIL CODE] art. 13 (Ger.).

▶ [2] Bundesgerichtshof [BGH] [Federal Court of Justice] Apr. 16, 2008, 140 ENTSCHEIDUNGEN DES BUNDESGERICHTSHOFES IN ZIVILSACHEN [BGHZ] 245 (Ger.).

▶ [3] BGB art. 12 (Ger.); *see also* BGH Mar. 3, 2009, 141 BGHZ 245 (250) (Ger.).

20.2.4 Languages That Do Not Use the Roman Alphabet

Transliterate all titles, names, or words cited that are not in the Roman alphabet, using a standard transliteration system (for example, the ALA-LC Romanization Tables).

(a) Languages generally. For instructions regarding transliteration that are specific to particular countries, check the relevant entries in **table T2**.

(b) Chinese language.

(i) **Chinese language romanization.** For citations to Chinese language sources, regardless of jurisdiction or place of publication, always provide romanization as instructed here. Whenever possible, also provide Chinese characters for authors, titles, and case names. Do not use Chinese characters without accompanying romanization, as some publishers or databases may drop them from citations. Use simplified or traditional characters to reflect the usage of the source. Generally, add an English translation or shortened form in English as provided in **rule 20.2.2**. Do not cite a Chinese language source in English only.

For romanization of Chinese language citations, use the Pinyin romanization system as set forth in the international standard, *Hanyu Pinyin Fang' an* (1958), and related documents. Do not include tone marks. Do not use "v" to represent "ü." Competing standards exist for word division in Pinyin. Follow commonly accepted guidelines for word division in scholarly publications as summarized in the examples below and in **table T2**. Note that the Pinyin standard used in many libraries differs with regard to word division and separates most syllables, so when searching for sources in library catalogs, it may be necessary to break up compound words into separate syllables.

For capitalization in Pinyin romanization, follow **rule 8** and related guidelines. Do not capitalize the possessive "de" (的).

▶ 邓小平	Deng Xiaoping
▶ 对外贸易经济合作部	Duiwai Maoyi Jingji Hezuo Bu
▶ 行政院	Xingzhengyuan
▶ 香港法例	Xianggang Fali
▶ 臺北地方法院	Taibei Difang Fayuan

(ii) **Chinese personal names.** When citing a Chinese author or editor's name, regardless of jurisdiction or place of publication, follow **rules 15.1** and **16.2**, giving the full name in the order it appears on the document. Repeat the full name in subsequent short citations to the source. For Chinese personal names in case citations, follow **rule 10.2.1(g)**.

(A) **Chinese language sources.** In Chinese language texts the surname is always given first. Transcribe authors and editors of Chinese texts in Pinyin, joining multiple syllables of surname and/or forename without hyphens or commas.

▶ Chen Hongyi (陈弘毅), Fazhi Qimeng yu Xiandai Fa de Jingshen (法制启蒙与现代法的精神) (1998).

▶ Wang Taisheng (王泰升), Taiwan Falü de Duanlie yu Lianxu (台灣法律的斷裂與連續) (2002).

(B) **English language sources.** Chinese names in English texts may follow either Chinese (surname first) or English (surname last) word order. They also may or may not be spelled according to the Pinyin system and may vary in fullness. Transcribe the full name in the order and in the spelling in which it appears on the document.

▶ ALBERT HUNG-YEE CHEN, AN INTRODUCTION TO THE LEGAL SYSTEM OF THE PEOPLE'S REPUBLIC OF CHINA (3d ed., LexisNexis 2004) (1992).

▶ TAY-SHENG WANG, LEGAL REFORM IN TAIWAN UNDER JAPANESE COLONIAL RULE (2000).

▶ ZHU SANZHU, SECURITIES REGULATION IN CHINA 8–13 (2001).

▶ Guanghua Yu, *Towards a Market Economy: Security Devices in China*, 8 PAC. RIM L. & POL'Y J. 1 (1999).

Citations to Translations of Non-English-Language Documents 20.2.5

If desired, a work that conveniently reprints the primary authority in translation may be cited when referring to a foreign-language source that is not widely available to researchers in the United States. In such cases, provide the citation to the original source in accordance with **rules 20** and **21**, and provide a parallel citation to the translated version, according to **rule 1.6(a)**, introduced by "*translated in*":

▶ Ley Federal de Derechos de Autor [LFDA] [Authors' Rights Law], Diario Oficial de la Federación [DO], 21 de Diciembre de 1963 (Mex.), *translated in* COPYRIGHT LAWS AND TREATIES OF THE WORLD 521 (U.N. Educ., Scientific & Cultural Org. et al. eds., 1992).

R20

20.3 Cases

Cite foreign cases according to **rule 10** as modified by the following instructions.

20.3.1 Common Law Cases

If the reporter does not clearly indicate the court deciding the case, indicate the court parenthetically:

▶ R v. Lockwood, (1782) 99 Eng. Rep. 379 (K.B.).

But if the court involved is the highest court in the jurisdiction, only the jurisdiction needs to be identified unless the jurisdiction is otherwise clear from context:

▶ Chase v. Campbell, [1962] S.C.R. 425 (Can.).

20.3.2 Civil Law and Other Non-Common-Law Cases

Cite cases from non-common-law countries according to **table T2** as modified by the following instructions.

(a) Name of the court. Identify courts as indicated in **rule 20.1**. If not otherwise clear from the context, include an English translation of the court designation:

▶ Bundesgerichtshof [BGH] [Federal Court of Justice] Apr. 7, 2003, 154 ENTSCHEIDUNGEN DES BUNDESGERICHTSHOFES IN ZIVILSACHEN [BGHZ] 53 (126) (Ger.).

(b) Source. Cite the sources listed, with their abbreviations, in **table T2**. As required by **rule 20.2.3**, give the full form the first time a source is cited, indicating in brackets the abbreviation that will be used subsequently.

Many civil law decisions do not appear in official reporters. If a case cited does not appear in an official source, cite a journal or periodical, issued within the jurisdiction if possible, or a reprint or translation of the decision according to **rules 1.6(a)** or **20.2.5** respectively.

(c) Jurisdiction. If the national jurisdiction is not evident from the citation or the context, include the jurisdiction, abbreviated according to **table T10**, in parentheses at the end of the citation, as required by **rule 20.1**.

(d) Annotations. Annotations to civil law cases are cited according to **rule 3.4**:

▶ Cass. 1e civ., Dec. 14, 1982, D. 1983, 416, note Aynès (Fr.).

20.4 Constitutions

Cite all foreign constitutions by name. If the nature of the document is not otherwise clear from the context, include "Constitution" in brackets following the document name or abbreviation in the first citation. Successive citations may exclude this note. If the country is unclear from the title of the constitution, include the country abbreviation in a parenthetical at the end of the citation.

▶ BUNDESVERFASSUNG [BV] [CONSTITUTION] Apr. 18, 1999, SR 101, art. 29 (Switz.).

Statutes   20.5

Statutes in Common Law Systems   20.5.1

Cite like U.S. statutes (rule 12) if the jurisdiction's statutes appear in a codification or other compilation:

► Extradition Law, 5714–1954, 8 LSI 144 (1953–1954) (Isr.).

Otherwise, cite like statutes of the United Kingdom (table T2.42 United Kingdom), noting the jurisdiction parenthetically at the end of the citation if not otherwise clear from the context:

► Emergency Powers Act (Act No. 3/1976) (Ir.).

Statutes in Civil Law and Other Non-Common-Law Jurisdictions   20.5.2

Cite generally according to rules found in table T2. When citing a code, do not indicate the year of the code unless citing a version no longer in force. In accordance with rule 20.2.3, use the full publication name the first time the publication is cited, indicating in brackets the abbreviation that will be used subsequently. Thereafter, the abbreviated form may be used:

► CODE CIVIL [C. CIV.] art. 1112 (Fr.).

Give the publisher or editor and date of privately published sources only when citing an annotation rather than the code itself:

► CODE CIVIL [C. CIV.] art. 1098 (64th ed. Petits Codes Dalloz 1965) (Fr.).

Non-English-Language and Foreign Periodicals   20.6

(a) In general. For all foreign periodicals, including both English- and non-English-language sources, include the country of origin in a parenthetical if not otherwise clear from the context.

► Catherine Labrusse-Riou, *La filiation et la médecine moderne*, 38 REVUE INTERNATIONALE DE DROIT COMPARÉ [R.I.D.C.] 419 (1986) (Fr.).

For foreign newspapers, cite according to rule 16.6.

► Marianne Kearney, *Indonesia Risks Becoming Like Balkans: Mega*, STRAITS TIMES (Sing.), Oct. 29, 2001, at 3.

If the title of the periodical is not listed in table T13, and it is not unduly long, the whole title may be used throughout. If the title of the periodical is long, and no abbreviation is given for it in table T13, abbreviate the title in such a way as to provide enough information to uniquely identify the source.

(b) Foreign-language sources. Cite foreign-language periodicals according to rule 16, as modified by rule 20.2. Give the author; title in the original language, followed by a translation or shortened name in English, if desired (rule 20.2.2); the volume number of the periodical if appropriate (rule 16.4); the full name of the periodical, if it is being cited for the first time, followed by the official abbreviation in brackets (rule 20.2.3); the page number(s); the year (rules 16.4 and

16.5); and the abbreviation of the country of publication, if not otherwise clear from the context. A hereinafter form, provided in brackets at the end of the citation, may be given if desired.

> [1] Marie-Thérèse Meulders-Klein, *Le droit de l' enfant face au droit à l' enfant et les procréations médicalement assistées* [*The Right of a Child Versus the Right To Have a Child and Medically Assisted Procreation*], 87 REVUE TRIMESTRIELLE DE DROIT CIVIL [REV. TRIM. DR. CIV.] 645, 657 (1988) (Fr.).

> [2] *Aktuelle Fragen der Schutzbereichsbestimmung im deutschen und europäischen Patentrecht* [*Current Issues in Identifying the Scope of Protection in German and European Patent Law*], 2003 GEWERBLICHER RECHTSSCHUTZ UND URHEBERRECHT [GRUR] 905 (Ger.) [hereinafter *Scope of Protection*].

> [3] *Scope of Protection*, *supra* note 2, at 906; *see also* Benjamin Taibleson & Rebecca Krauss, *Embracing Convergence: Forty Countries in Comparative Perspective*, 106 REV. TRIM. DR. CIV. 119 (2007) (Fr.).

20.7 Short Citation Forms

(a) **Cases.** For common law citations, use short forms analogous to those provided in **rule 10.9**, when permitted. For civil law citation forms, the short form should include enough information to uniquely identify the original source and any additional information that would be helpful to the reader.

(b) **Constitutions.** Do not use a short form, other than "*id.*," for constitutions.

(c) **Statutes.** Use short forms analogous to those provided in **rule 12.10**, when permitted. Otherwise, include enough information to uniquely identify the original source and any additional information that would be helpful to the reader. The jurisdiction parenthetical may be included in the short form if it is not evident from either the elements of the short form citation or the context.

> [1] Loi 85-699 du 11 juillet 1985 tendant à la constitution d'archives audiovisuelles de la justice [Law 85-699 of July 11, 1985 for the Formation of Audiovisual Archives of the Judiciary], JOURNAL OFFICIEL DE LA RÉPUBLIQUE FRANÇAISE [J.O.] [OFFICIAL GAZETTE OF FRANCE], July 12, 1985, p. 7885.

> [2] Ley No. 217, 2 May 1996, Ley General del Medio Ambiente y los Recursos Naturales [Ley del Medio Ambiente] [Environmental and Natural Resources Law] tit. III, ch. II, sec. I, LA GACETA, DIARIO OFICIAL [L.G.], 6 June 1996 (Nicar.).

> [3] Law 85-699 of July 11, 1985, art. 4 (Fr.); Environmental and Natural Resources Law, tit. III, ch. II, sec. II (Nicar.).

(d) **Periodicals.** Use short forms analogous to those provided in **rule 16.9**.

INTERNATIONAL MATERIALS

Basic Citation Forms   21.1

(a) Treaties and other international agreements. (rule 21.4)

Bilateral	Treaty of Friendship, Commerce and Navigation, U.S.-Japan, art. X, Apr. 2, 1953, 4 U.S.T. 2063.
	Agreement Concerning Payments for Certain Losses Suffered During World War II, U.S.-Fr., Jan. 18, 2001, Temp. State Dep't No. 01-36, 2001 WL 416465.
	Treaty of Neutrality, Hung.-Turk., Jan. 5, 1929, 100 L.N.T.S. 137.
Multilateral	Geneva Convention Relative to the Treatment of Prisoners of War art. 3, Aug. 12, 1949, 6 U.S.T. 3316, 75 U.N.T.S. 135.
	Police Convention, Feb. 29, 1920, 127 L.N.T.S. 433.
	North American Free Trade Agreement, U.S.-Can.-Mex., Dec. 17, 1992, 32 I.L.M. 289 (1993).

(b) International law cases. (rule 21.5)

World Court	Military and Paramilitary Activities in and Against Nicaragua (Nicar. v. U.S.), 1986 I.C.J. 14 (June 27).
	Fisheries Jurisdiction (U.K. v. Ice.), Interim Protection Order, 1972 I.C.J. 12 (Aug. 17).
	Diversion of Water from Meuse (Neth. v. Belg.), 1937 P.C.I.J. (ser. A/B) No. 70, at 7 (June 28).
	Reservations to Convention on Prevention and Punishment of Crime of Genocide, Advisory Opinion, 1951 I.C.J. 15 (May 28).
Court of Justice of the European Union	Case C-213/89, The Queen v. Sec'y of State for Transp. *ex parte* Factortame Ltd., 1990 E.C.R. I-2433.
European Court of Human Rights	Kampanis v. Greece, 318 Eur. Ct. H.R. 29, 35 (1995).
	Ireland v. United Kingdom, 23 Eur. Ct. H.R. (ser. B) at 23 (1976).
Inter-American Commission on Human Rights	Tortrino v. Argentina, Case 11.597, Inter-Am. Comm'n H.R., Report No. 7/98, OEA/Ser.L./V/II.98, doc. 7 rev. ¶ 15 (1997).
Inter-American Court of Human Rights	Restrictions to the Death Penalty (Arts. 4(2) and 4(4) American Convention on Human Rights), Advisory Opinion OC-3/83, Inter-Am. Ct. H.R. (ser. A) No. 3, ¶ 70 (Sept. 8, 1983).

International Tribunal for the Law of the Sea	M/V Saiga (No. 2) (St. Vincent v. Guinea), Case No. 2, Order of Jan. 20, 1998, 2 ITLOS Rep. 4, 5.
International Criminal Tribunals	Prosecutor v. Tadic, Case No. IT-94-1-I, Decision on Defence Motion for Interlocutory Appeal on Jurisdiction, ¶ 70 (Int'l Crim. Trib. for the Former Yugoslavia Oct. 2, 1995).
	Prosecutor v. Kayishema & Ruzindana, Case No. ICTR 95-1-T, Judgment, ¶ 126 (May 21, 1999).
	Prosecutor v. Jean-Pierre Bemba Gombo, Case No. ICC-01/05-01/08, Warrant of Arrest, ¶ 22 (May 23, 2008), http://www.icc-cpi.int/iccdocs/doc/doc535163.pdf.

(c) International arbitrations. (rule 21.6)

	Amoco Int'l Fin. Corp. v. Iran, 15 Iran-U.S. Cl. Trib. Rep. 189 (1987).
	Savarkar (Fr. v. Gr. Brit.), Hague Ct. Rep. (Scott) 275 (Perm. Ct. Arb. 1911).

(d) United Nations materials. (rule 21.7)

Verbatim and Summary Meeting Records	U.N. GAOR, 57th Sess., 42d plen. mtg. at 3, U.N. Doc. A/57/PV.42 (Nov. 1, 2002).
U.N. Charter	U.N. Charter art. 2, para. 4.
Resolutions	G.A. Res. 832 (IX), U.N. GAOR, 9th Sess., Supp. No. 21, U.N. Doc. A/2890, at 19 (Oct. 21, 1954).
	G.A. Res. 47/1, ¶ 2, U.N. Doc. A/RES/47/1 (Sept. 22, 1992).
Reports	U.N. Secretary-General, *An Agenda for Peace: Preventive Diplomacy, Peacemaking and Peace-Keeping: Rep. of the Secretary-General*, ¶ 14, U.N. Doc. A/47/277-S/24111 (June 17, 1992).

(e) European Union materials. (rule 21.9)

	Council Directive 2001/18, 2001 O.J. (L 106) 1 (EC).

(f) World Trade Organization materials. (rule 21.11)

Panel decisions	Panel Report, *United States—Sections 301–310 of the Trade Act of 1974*, WT/DS152/R (Dec. 22, 1999).
Appellate Body decisions	Appellate Body Report, *Brazil—Export Financing Programme for Aircraft*, ¶ 19, WT/DS46/AB/R (Aug. 2, 1999).
Founding Agreements	Marrakesh Agreement Establishing the World Trade Organization, Apr. 15, 1994, 1867 U.N.T.S. 154.
Ministerial documents	World Trade Organization, Ministerial Declaration of 14 November 2001, WT/MIN(01)/DEC/1, 41 I.L.M. 746 (2002).

Non-English-Language Documents 21.2

See **rule 20.2** regarding non-English-language documents.

Jurisdiction Not Evident from Context 21.3

When citing any non-U.S. source, whether in English or another language, indicate parenthetically the jurisdiction issuing the source, abbreviated according to tables **T3** and **T10**, unless the jurisdiction is otherwise clear from the context or the other elements of the citation:

▶ Council Directive 66/45 art. 15, 1965–1966 O.J. SPEC. ED. 265, 268 (Euratom).

Treaties and Other International Agreements 21.4

Citation of a treaty between two parties:

name of agreement

Convention for the Avoidance of Double Taxation and the Prevention of Fiscal Evasion with Respect to Taxes on Estates, Inheritances, and Gifts, U.S.-Fr., Nov. 24, 1978, 32 U.S.T. 1935.

abbreviated names of parties to agreement   date of signing   one U.S. treaty source

Citation of a treaty among more than two parties:

name of agreement   subdivision cited   date of signing   one U.S. treaty source

North Atlantic Treaty art. 5, Apr. 4, 1949, 63 Stat. 2241, 34 U.N.T.S. 243.

one international treaty source

Citation of a convention published by an international organization:

▶ Organization of American States, American Convention on Human Rights, Nov. 22, 1969, O.A.S.T.S. No. 36, 1144 U.N.T.S. 123.

▶ United Nations Convention on the Law of the Sea, Dec. 10, 1982, 1833 U.N.T.S. 397.

Citation of a founding document or statute resulting in the creation of a new institution:

▶ U.N. Charter art. 2, para. 4.

▶ Statute of the International Tribunal for the Law of the Sea art. 2, Dec. 10, 1982, 1833 U.N.T.S. 561.

A citation to a treaty or other international agreement—other than the U.N. Charter and the League of Nations Covenant—should include the agreement's name (**rule 21.4.1**); parties, if applicable (**rule 21.4.2**); the subdivision referred to, if applicable (**rule 21.4.3**); the date of signing (**rule 21.4.4**); and the source(s) in which the treaty can be found (**rule 21.4.5**).

21.4.1 Name of the Agreement

Use the English-language version of a treaty name when possible. See **rule 20.2.2** regarding the treatment of treaties whose names are not in English.

(a) First citation. The first citation to a treaty should contain its full name, including both its form (**rule 21.4.1(a)(i)**) and its subject matter (**rule 21.4.1(a)(ii)**), in either order:

▶ Convention for the Suppression of Unlawful Seizure of Aircraft, Dec. 16, 1970, 22 U.S.T. 1641, 860 U.N.T.S. 105.

(i) **Form of agreement.** The title of the treaty should indicate the form of agreement (e.g., Agreement, Convention, Memorandum, Protocol, Treaty, Understanding). Use only the first form designation that appears on the title page. Omit all others:

▶ Convention

Not: Convention & Supplementary Protocol

Cite lesser-included documents as subdivisions (**rule 21.4.3**).

(ii) **Subject matter.** Use the subject-matter description that appears as part of the title of the agreement:

▶ Kyoto Protocol to the United Nations Framework Convention on Climate Change

(b) Subsequent citations. If a treaty's name is very long, or if the treaty is commonly known by a popular name, the first citation to the treaty should end with a "**hereinafter**" short-form citation (**rule 4.2(b)**) to be used in all subsequent citations. The short-form citation must be in the same typeface as the original:

▶ [1] Protocol for the Prohibition of the Use in War of Asphyxiating, Poisonous or Other Gases, and of Bacteriological Methods of Warfare, June 17, 1925, 26 U.S.T. 571 [hereinafter Geneva Protocol].

▶ [3] Geneva Protocol, *supra* note 1, at 572.

21.4.2 Parties to the Agreement

When citing an agreement between two parties, indicate both parties, abbreviating their names according to **table T10**:

▶ U.S.-Japan

▶ Fr.-Ger.

If the United States is a named party, it should appear first. Other parties' names should appear in alphabetical order and abbreviated according to **table T10** unless otherwise indicated by the treaty itself.

For multilateral treaties, names of parties may, but need not, be provided:

▶ North American Free Trade Agreement, U.S.-Can.-Mex., Dec. 17, 1992, 32 I.L.M. 289 (1993).

Subdivisions   21.4.3

When citing only part of an agreement, or when citing an appended document, give the subdivision or appended document:

▶ Treaty on Commerce and Navigation, U.S.-Iraq, art. III, ¶ 2, Dec. 3, 1938, 54 Stat. 1790.

▶ Declaration on the Neutrality of Laos, Protocol, July 23, 1962, 14 U.S.T. 1104, 456 U.N.T.S. 301.

When citing a subdivision, it is not necessary to include a pinpoint cite for the treaty series; the article, paragraph, or section number is sufficient. For a discussion of citations to subdivisions and appendices, see **rules 3.3** and **3.4**.

Date of Signing   21.4.4

Give the exact date of signing:

▶ Protocol to Amend the Convention for the Suppression of the Traffic in Women and Children, Nov. 12, 1947, 53 U.N.T.S. 13.

When multiple dates of signing are given for an agreement or exchange of notes between two parties, give the first and last dates of signing:

▶ Agreement on Weather Stations, U.S.-Colom., Apr. 27–May 13, 1964, 15 U.S.T. 1355.

If a treaty is not signed on a single date, use the date on which the treaty is opened for signature, done, approved, ratified, or adopted, and indicate the significance of the date in italics:

▶ Treaty on the Non-Proliferation of Nuclear Weapons, *opened for signature* July 1, 1968, 21 U.S.T. 483, 729 U.N.T.S. 161.

The date on which a treaty entered into force or other such date may be added parenthetically at the end of the citation if it is of particular relevance:

▶ U.N. Convention on the Law of the Sea, *opened for signature* Dec. 10, 1982, 1833 U.N.T.S. 397 (entered into force Nov. 16, 1994).

For abbreviations of the months of the year, see **table T12**.

Treaty Sources   21.4.5

See **table T4** for a listing of international treaty sources. Treaty sources of some foreign states are listed with the other materials of those states in **table T2**. Dates in the tables refer to the years of the treaties contained in the source, not to the years in which the source was published.

(a) Agreements to which the United States is a party.

(i) **Bilateral treaties.** For agreements between the United States and another party, cite *one* of the following sources, in the following order of preference: U.S.T. (or Stat.); T.I.A.S. (or T.S., or E.A.S.); U.N.T.S.; Senate Treaty Documents or Senate Executive Documents; the Department of State Dispatch; Department of State Press Releases. If the agreement has not appeared in one of these official sources, cite an unofficial source (**rule 21.4.5(c)**):

- ► Treaty on the Limitation of Anti-Ballistic Missile Systems, U.S.-U.S.S.R., May 26, 1972, 23 U.S.T. 3435.
- ► Agreement on Defense and Economic Cooperation, U.S.-Greece, at 4, Sept. 8, 1983, T.I.A.S. No. 10,814.
- ► Tax Convention, U.S.-Fin., Sept. 21, 1989, S. TREATY DOC. No. 101-11 (1990).
- ► Migratory Birds Protection Agreement, U.S.-Can., at 3, Jan. 30, 1979, S. EXEC. DOC. W, 96-2 (1980).
- ► Memorandum of Understanding Regarding Bilateral Verification Experiment and Data Exchange Related to Prohibition of Chemical Weapons, U.S.-U.S.S.R., art. V(1), Sept. 23, 1989, DEP'T ST. BULL., Nov. 1989, at 18 [hereinafter Chemical Weapons MOU].
- ► Cuban-American Treaty, U.S.-Cuba, art. I, Feb. 16–23, 1903, T.S. No. 418.
- ► Agreement Regarding Mutual Assistance Between Their Customs Administrations, U.S.-Ir., art. 3, Sept. 16, 1996, 2141 U.N.T.S. 51.

(ii) **Multilateral treaties.** For agreements among three or more parties to which the United States is a party, cite one of the U.S. domestic sources listed in **rule 21.4.5(a)(i)**, if therein. Additionally, a parallel citation may be added from one source published by an international organization (e.g., U.N.T.S., L.N.T.S., O.A.S.T.S., Pan-Am. T.S., O.J., E.T.S., or C.E.T.S.), if therein:

- ► North Atlantic Treaty art. 5, Apr. 4, 1949, 63 Stat. 2241, 34 U.N.T.S. 243.

If either of these official sources cannot be obtained, provide a citation to one unofficial treaty source (**rule 21.4.5(c)**) or another reliable source where the treaty can be found.

(b) Agreements to which the United States is not a party. Cite one source published by an international organization (**rule 21.4.5(a)(ii)**), if therein:

- ► Treaty of Neutrality, Hung.-Turk., Jan. 5, 1929, 100 L.N.T.S. 137.
- ► Agreement for the Avoidance of Double Taxation, Neth.-Swed., art. 4, Apr. 25, 1952, 163 U.N.T.S. 131.

If not, cite the official source of one signatory, if therein, indicating parenthetically the jurisdiction whose source is cited according to **rule 21.3** if it is not clear from the context. If the treaty is not found in a signatory's treaty source, cite to an unofficial treaty source (**rule 21.4.5(c)**):

- ► Agreement on Trade, Economic, and Technical Cooperation, Austl.-Oman, Oct. 20, 1981, [1982] A.T.S. 4.

(c) Unofficial treaty sources. When a treaty does not appear in a required source listed in **rule 21.4.5(a)(i)** or **21.4.5(a)(ii)**, provide a citation to International Legal Materials (I.L.M.), if therein:

- ► Olivos Protocol for the Settlement of Disputes in Mercosur art. 6, Feb. 18, 2002, 42 I.L.M. 2.

If a treaty is not found in I.L.M., cite to another unofficial treaty source. These sources include the websites of governments and intergovernmental organizations, electronic databases, and sources such as Consol. T.S., Hein's microfiche treaty service, and Martens Nouveau Recueil:

► Agreement Concerning Payments for Certain Losses Suffered During World War II, U.S.-Fr., Jan. 18, 2001, Temp. State Dep't No. 01-36, 2001 WL 416465.

If no other citation is available, cite a book (**rule 15**) or periodical (**rule 16**).

International Law Cases   **21.5**

Cite according to **rule 10** as modified by the following instructions. If no authoritative English-language source is available, cite foreign-language sources according to **rule 20.2**.

....

The International Court of Justice and the Permanent Court   21.5.1
of International Justice (The World Court)

The International Court of Justice (I.C.J.) replaced the Permanent Court of International Justice (P.C.I.J.) when it was dissolved in 1946.

Cite a case before the International Court of Justice or the Permanent Court of International Justice by the case name (**rule 21.5.1(a)**); the names of the parties, if any (**rule 21.5.1(b)**); the type of court document (such as **Preliminary Objection, Provisional Measure, Advisory Opinion, Judgment**, etc.), if relevant; the volume and name of the publication in which the decision is found (**rule 21.5.1(c)**); the page or case number (**rule 21.5.1(d)**); the pincite, if any, with preference for paragraph number when available; and the date (**rule 21.5.1(e)**):

► Military and Paramilitary Activities in and Against Nicaragua (Nicar. v. U.S.), 1986 I.C.J. 14, 181 (June 27) (separate opinion of Judge Ago).

► Reservations to Convention on Prevention and Punishment of Crime of Genocide, Advisory Opinion, 1951 I.C.J. 15 (May 28).

► Diversion of Water from Meuse (Neth. v. Belg.), 1937 P.C.I.J. (ser. A/B) No. 70, at 7 (June 28).

► Delimitation of Maritime Boundary in Gulf of Maine Area (Can./U.S.), 1982 I.C.J. 560, ¶ 22 (Nov. 5).

Cite pleadings according to **rule 21.5.1(f)** and court rules and acts according to **rule 21.5.1(g)**. If necessary, cite yearbooks and annual reports of the World Court according to **rules 21.14** and **21.15**.

(a) Case name. Give the case name as found on the first pages of the report. Omit articles, such as "the." Include the word "**Case**" only if the case name is a person's name. Do not abbreviate the names of countries where they appear in case names:

► Continental Shelf

Not: Case Concerning the Continental Shelf

Note that an application may appear as the case name:

► Application of Convention on Prevention and Punishment of Crime of Genocide (Bosn. & Herz. v. Serb. & Montenegro), 1996 I.C.J. 595, ¶ 31 (July 11).

(b) Parties' names. Give the names of the parties involved in a parenthetical phrase immediately following the case name. Abbreviate the names of countries according to **table T10**, but not when the country's name is in the title of the case. When a dispute is brought before the court by a unilateral application of one country against another, the countries' names are separated by "**v.**" If the case is brought on the basis of a special agreement between two countries, the names of the parties are separated instead by a slash:

▶ (Nicar. v. U.S.)

▶ (Indon./Malay.)

In advisory opinions, no parties are listed:

▶ Interpretation of Peace Treaties with Bulgaria, Hungary and Romania, Advisory Opinion, 1950 I.C.J. 65 (Mar. 30).

▶ Polish Postal Service in Danzig, Advisory Opinion, 1925 P.C.I.J. (ser. B) No. 11, at 6 (May 16).

(c) Volume number and name of publication. Identify the volume by the date, as required by **rule 3.1(a)**. The International Court of Justice publishes its opinions in *Reports of Judgments, Advisory Opinions and Orders* (I.C.J.):

▶ 1950 I.C.J. 65

Decisions and other documents of the P.C.I.J. were published in seven series (lettered A through F, including A/B). Indicate the series in any citation to P.C.I.J. documents:

▶ 1925 P.C.I.J. (ser. B) No. 11

(d) Page or case number. Cite I.C.J. cases to the page on which they begin. Cite cases of the P.C.I.J. by number:

▶ 2006 I.C.J. 107

▶ 1937 P.C.I.J. (ser. A/B) No. 70

Use pinpoint citations to refer to specific pages or paragraphs. Note that when use of paragraph numbers will substantially improve specificity, they should be used instead of page numbers. See **rule 3.3** for more information about paragraph numbers:

▶ 1986 I.C.J. 14, ¶ 15

▶ 1933 P.C.I.J. (ser. C) No. 62, at 12

(e) Date. Provide the month and day:

▶ Nuclear Tests (N.Z. v. Fr.), Interim Protection Order, 1973 I.C.J. 135 (June 22).

(f) Separately published pleadings. Cite separately published pleadings by the designation given on the document itself, followed by the name of the case (**rule 21.5.1(a)**); the names of the parties in a parenthetical phrase (**rule 21.5.1(b)**); the volume number and name of the publication (**rule 21.5.1(c)**); and the full date, since the year of publication often will not correspond to the year of the pleading. Separately published pleadings before the I.C.J. are published in *Pleadings, Oral Arguments, Documents* (I.C.J. Pleadings), while P.C.I.J. rules and acts were published in P.C.I.J.:

► Memorial of United Kingdom, Corfu Channel (U.K. v. Alb.), 1949 I.C.J. Pleadings 19 (Sept. 30, 1947).

► Memorial of Denmark, Legal Status of Eastern Greenland (Den. v. Nor.), 1933 P.C.I.J. (ser. C) No. 62, at 12 (Oct. 31, 1931).

(g) Court rules and acts. Cite court rules and acts by title, volume number and name of publication, and page or document number. I.C.J. rules and acts are published in *Acts and Documents Concerning the Organization of the Court* (abbreviated I.C.J. Acts & Docs.), while those adjudicated by the P.C.I.J. were published in P.C.I.J.:

► Travel and Subsistence Regulations of the International Court of Justice, 1947 I.C.J. Acts & Docs. 94.

► Revised Rules of the Court, 1926 P.C.I.J. (ser. D) No. 1, at 33.

(h) Online materials. Recent I.C.J. materials that have not yet been published may be cited to International Legal Materials (I.L.M.) (**rule 21.4.5(c)**) or to the I.C.J. Website (http://www.icj-cij.org) (**rule 18.1**):

► Maritime Delimitation in Black Sea (Rom. v. Ukr.), Judgment, ¶ 5 (Feb. 3, 2009), *available at* http://www.icj-cij.org/docket/files/132/14987.pdf.

Some older pleadings are unavailable in a print publication, and online versions must be used pursuant to **rule 18.1**. For oral pleadings, the date parenthetical should include the specific date and session time:

► LaGrand Case (Ger. v. U.S.), Verbatim Record, ¶¶ 5.1–5.19 (Nov. 14, 2000, 3 p.m.), http://www.icj-cij.org/docket/files/104/4663.pdf.

European Union Courts   21.5.2

Cite a case before the Court of Justice of the European Union (formerly the Court of Justice of the European Communities) or the General Court (formerly the Court of First Instance) by case number; the names of the parties, abbreviated according to **rule 10.2** and **table T6**; and a citation to the official reports of the Court, including the year of decision (**rule 21.5.2(a)**). A parallel citation to a private service may be made, if necessary (**rule 21.5.2(b)**).

For cases lodged before the Court of Justice since 1989, the case number will contain the prefix "C"; older cases will not have a prefix. Cases lodged before the General Court, created in 1989, will carry the prefix "T." Where the Commission, Council, or Parliament of the European Union is one of the parties, give its name as "Commission," "Council," or "Parliament" only, as appropriate:

► Case T-198/98, Micro Leader Bus. v. Comm'n, 1999 E.C.R. II-3989.

► Case C-213/89, The Queen v. Sec'y of State for Transp. *ex parte* Factortame Ltd., 1990 E.C.R. I-2433.

► Case 58/69, Elz v. Comm'n, 16 E.C.R. 507 (1970).

Cases on European Union law are often decided in the courts of member states. These cases should be cited to the reporters of the particular member state. If necessary, such cases may also be cited to one of the unofficial reporters collecting materials regarding the European Union (see **rule 21.5.8**). When citing such a case to European Union materials, always indicate the court, as well as the jurisdiction if not clear from context, as provided by **rule 20.1**.

(a) Official reports. For pre-1990 cases, cite the *Report of Cases Before the Court of Justice of the European Communities* (E.C.R.); post-1990 cases are cited to the *Report of Cases Before the Court of Justice and the Court of First Instance* (also abbreviated E.C.R.). Place the year designation before the reporter abbreviation. Beginning with Part I, 1990, page numbers in the E.C.R. begin with a "I," "II," or "III" before the number:

- Case C-286/01, Comm'n v. France, 2002 E.C.R. I-5463.
- Case 30/79, Land Berlin v. Wigei, 1980 E.C.R. 151.
- Joined Cases 56 & 58/64, Établissements Consten, S.A.R.L. v. Comm'n, 1966 E.C.R. 299.

If an official report is not available in print, cite to the official Website of the Court of Justice of the European Union (http://curia.europa.eu) (**rule 18.1**), an electronic database (**rule 18.3.1**), or a private service (**rule 21.5.2(b)**):

- Case C-279/06, CEPSA v. LV Tobar, 2008 EUR-Lex CELEX LEXIS 2099 (Sept. 11, 2008).

(b) Private services. If necessary, provide a parallel citation to one of the private services providing selected reports of the court's opinions. *Common Market Law Reports* (C.M.L.R.) is preferred. When citing to volumes through 1973, include the full volume number; when citing to volumes for 1974 and later, include the issue number to reflect cessation of continuous issue numbering. Otherwise, use *Common Market Reporter* (Common Mkt. Rep. (CCH)) (through 1988) or *European Community Cases* (CEC (CCH)). See **rule 19** for treatment of CCH looseleaf services:

- Case 148/78, Pubblico Ministero v. Ratti, 1979 E.C.R. 1629, 1 C.M.L.R. 96 (1980).
- Case 48/69, Imperial Chem. Indus. v. Comm'n, 18 E.C.R. 619, [1971–1973 Transfer Binder] Common Mkt. Rep. (CCH) ¶ 8161 (1972).

21.5.3 European Court of Human Rights

Cite cases before the European Court of Human Rights to *European Court of Human Rights, Reports of Judgments and Decisions* (Eur. Ct. H.R.). Cite cases before the court by case name (abbreviated according to **rule 10.2**); volume number; reporter; page number, where applicable; and year. Recent volumes are numbered by year of publication and do not require a separate reference to the year. Older decisions may also be cited to *Publications of the European Court of Human Rights*, which was issued in multiple series (e.g., Eur. Ct. H.R. (ser. A)) or *Yearbook of the European Convention on Human Rights* (Y.B. Eur. Conv. on H.R.):

- Papon v. France (No. 2), 2001-XII Eur. Ct. H.R. 235.
- Kampanis v. Greece, 318 Eur. Ct. H.R. 29, 35 (1995).

Recent volumes contain several cases, but some earlier volumes contain only one case. Where a volume contains only one case, citation to a beginning page is unnecessary, and all page numbers may be indicated directly by "at":

- Ireland v. United Kingdom, 23 Eur. Ct. H.R. (ser. B) at 23 (1976).

Until 1999, cases were also heard before the now-defunct European Commission on Human Rights. These cases should be cited to *Collections of Decisions of the European Commission on Human Rights* (Eur. Comm'n H.R. Dec. & Rep.) or Y.B. Eur. Conv. on H.R., if therein. If not, cite *European Human Rights Reports* (Eur. H.R. Rep.). When citing Y.B. Eur. Conv. on H.R., indicate parenthetically whether the case was before the Commission or the Court. Indicate both the parties and the application number for the case:

- ► Y. v. Netherlands, App. No. 7245/32, 32 Eur. Comm'n H.R. Dec. & Rep. 345, 358 (1982).

- ► Smith v. Belgium, App. No. 3324/76, 8 Eur. H.R. Rep. 445, 478 (1982).

- ► Iversen v. Norway, App. No. 1468/62, 1963 Y.B. Eur. Conv. on H.R. 278 (Eur. Comm'n on H.R.).

If a case before the European Court is not available in print, materials may be cited to an unofficial printed source or to the Court's official website, HUDOC (http://www.echr.coe.int) (**rule 18.1**).

Inter-American Commission on Human Rights   21.5.4

Cite cases before the Inter-American Commission on Human Rights to the *Annual Report of the Inter-American Commission on Human Rights* (Inter-Am. Comm'n H.R.). The citation should include the case name; the case number; the volume name; the report number, which includes the year of the decision; the series and docket numbers; the paragraph number, if applicable; and the year of the reporter:

- ► Tortrino v. Argentina, Case 11.597, Inter-Am. Comm'n H.R., Report No. 7/98, OEA/Ser.L./V/II.98, doc. 7 rev. ¶ 15 (1997).

- ► Calderón v. Colombia, Case 10.454, Inter-Am. Comm'n H.R., Report No. 32/92, OEA/Ser.L./V/II.83, doc. 14 (1992–1993).

Cite to the English version unless necessary for the citation. If an official report is not yet available, cite the Commission's official website (http://www.cidh.org) (**rule 18.1**).

Inter-American Court of Human Rights   21.5.5

For cases before the Inter-American Court of Human Rights, cite to *Inter-American Court of Human Rights, Decisions and Judgments* (Inter-Am. Ct. H.R.). The citation should include the case name; the volume number; the series; the case number; the page number, if needed; and the date. Cite to the English version unless necessary for the citation.

Cite cases before the Inter-American Court of Human Rights (Inter-Am. Ct. H.R.) to Series (ser.), Annual Reports of the Inter-American Court of Human Rights (Rep. Inter-Am. Ct. H.R.), or to the Court's official website (http://www.corteidh.or.cr).

(a) **Advisory Opinions.** Cite Advisory Opinions by the name of the opinion; "Advisory Opinion" and opinion code; the report and volume number; the pincite, if any; and the date. Always cite to Series A:

► Restrictions to the Death Penalty (Arts. 4(2) and 4(4) American Convention on Human Rights), Advisory Opinion OC-3/83, Inter-Am. Ct. H.R. (ser. A) No. 3, ¶ 70 (Sept. 8, 1983).

(b) Contentious Cases. Cite Contentious Cases by the name of the case; the matter of decision; the type of opinion; the report and volume number; the pincite, if any; and date. Always cite to Series C:

► Baldeon-Garcia v. Peru, Merits, Reparations, and Costs, Judgment, Inter-Am. Ct. H.R. (ser. C) No. 147, ¶ 169 (Apr. 6, 2006).

(c) Provisional Measures. Cite Provisional Measures by the name of the case or matter; "Provisional Measures"; and the type of opinion. When citing to the print reports, cite to the Series E report with the volume number and first page of the decision; the section name in quotes; the pincite, if any; and the date. When citing to an online version, cite to the section name in quotes; the pincite, if any; the court and date; and the URL (**rule 18.1**):

► Bámaca Velázquez v. Guatemala, Provisional Measures, Order of the Court, Inter-Am. Ct. H.R. (ser. E) No. 4, 1, "Decides," ¶ 2 (Sept. 5, 2001).

► Mendoza Prisons Regarding Argentina, Provisional Measures, Order of the President of the Court, "Having Seen," ¶ 21 (Inter-Am. Ct. H.R. Aug. 22, 2007), *available at* www.corteidh.or.cr/docs/medidas/penitenciariamendoza_se_04_ ing.pdf.

(d) Compliances with Judgment. Cite Compliances with Judgment by the name of the case; "Monitoring Compliance with Judgment"; and the type of opinion. When citing to the print reports, cite to the volume number, the report name, and first page of the decision; the section name in quotes; pincite, if any; and date. When citing to an online version, cite to the section name in quotes; the pincite, if any; the court and date; and the URL (**rule 18.1**):

► Genie Lacayo v. Nicaragua, Monitoring Compliance with Judgment, Order of the Court, 1998 Rep. Inter-Am. Ct. H.R. 335, "Resolves," ¶ 1 (Aug. 29, 1998).

► Baena Ricardo et al. v. Panama, Monitoring Compliance with Judgment, Order of the President of the Court, "Considering," ¶ 14 (Inter-Am. Ct. H.R. Feb. 11, 2008), *available at* www.corteidh.or.cr/docs/supervisiones/baena_11_02_08_ing.pdf.

21.5.6 **International Tribunal for the Law of the Sea**

Cite cases of the International Tribunal for the Law of the Sea to the *International Tribunal for the Law of the Sea Reports of Judgments, Advisory Opinions and Orders* (ITLOS Rep.). Cite cases before the Tribunal by the case name and the names of the parties in a parenthetical phrase abbreviated according to **table T10**; the case number; the type of ruling and date; the volume number, name of the publication, and page number; and the pincite, if any, with preference for paragraph numbers when available:

► M/V Saiga (No. 2) (St. Vincent v. Guinea), Case No. 2, Order of Jan. 20, 1998, 2 ITLOS Rep. 4, 5.

When print reports are unavailable, cite to the Tribunal's official website (http://www.itlos.org) (**rule 18.1**).

International Criminal Tribunals 21.5.7

Cite cases of the International Criminal Court, the International Criminal Tribunal for the Former Yugoslavia, the International Criminal Tribunal for Rwanda, the Extraordinary Chambers in the Courts of Cambodia, and the Special Court for Sierra Leone by case name; case number; type of ruling; paragraph number, if necessary; and date. When the tribunal is not clear from the case number, add the name of the tribunal before the date:

▶ Prosecutor v. Tadic, Case No. IT-94-1-I, Decision on Defence Motion for Interlocutory Appeal on Jurisdiction, ¶ 70 (Int'l Crim. Trib. for the Former Yugoslavia Oct. 2, 1995).

▶ Prosecutor v. Kayishema & Ruzindana, Case No. ICTR 95-1-T, Judgment, ¶ 126 (May 21, 1999).

Many cases can be found on official websites and should be cited pursuant to **rule 18.1**:

▶ Prosecutor v. Jean-Pierre Bemba Gombo, Case No. ICC-01/05-01/08, Warrant of Arrest, ¶ 22 (May 23, 2008), http://www.icc-cpi.int/iccdocs/doc/doc535163.pdf.

▶ Prosecutor v. Simba, Case No. ICTR-01-76-T, Judgement and Sentence, ¶ 23 (Dec. 13, 2005), http://www.ictr.org/ENGLISH/cases/Simba/Judgement/simba131205.pdf.

▶ Prosecutor v. Lukić & Lukić, Case No. IT-98-32/1-T, Order to Disclose Portions of the Transcript (Int'l Crim. Trib. for the Former Yugoslavia Jan. 22, 2009), http://www.icty.org/x/cases/milan_lukic_sredoje_lukic/tord/en/090122.pdf.

Other Multinational Courts 21.5.8

If cases cannot be found in official reports, cite to *International Law Reports* (I.L.R.) (1950–present) or *Annual Digest and Reports of Public International Law Cases* (Ann. Dig.) (1919–49). Volume numbers, rather than years, should be used; early volumes of Annual Digest have been renumbered according to tables appearing in all volumes after volume 25. Include the name of the court and the year of the decision in a parenthetical:

▶ Loomba v. Food & Agric. Org. of the United Nations, 47 I.L.R. 382 (Int'l Lab. Org. Admin. Trib. 1970).

▶ Mayras v. Secretary-General of the League of Nations, 13 Ann. Dig. 199 (Admin. Trib. of the League of Nations 1946).

International Cases in National Courts 21.5.9

If an international case is decided by a national court whose reporter is not indicated in **table T2**, cite to I.L.R., Ann. Dig., C.M.L.R., Common Mkt. Rep. (CCH), a yearbook (**rule 21.14**) or an online source (**rule 18.1**). Indicate the country and court of origin parenthetically if not otherwise clear from the citation:

▶ Abdul Ghani v. Subedar Shoedar Khan, 38 I.L.R. 3 (W. Pak. High Ct. 1964).

▶ Ko Maung Tin v. U Gon Man, 14 Ann. Dig. 233 (High Ct. 1947) (Burma).

21.6 International Arbitrations and Claims Commissions

Cite arbitral decisions and claims commission decisions by analogy to **rule 21.5**, modified as follows. If adversarial parties are named, give the names as if it were a court case:

▶ Massaut v. Stupp

Otherwise, cite by the name of the first-party plaintiff or by the subject matter if no name is given. Indicate parenthetically the countries involved, when available, if not otherwise evident:

▶ N. Atl. Coast Fisheries (U.K. v. U.S.), 11 R.I.A.A. 167, 196 (Perm. Ct. Arb. 1910).

Cite arbitration awards to the official source, if possible, unless that source is a pamphlet containing only a single judgment. Consult **table T5** for frequently cited arbitral reporters and claims commissions. Unless the court or tribunal is identified unambiguously in the name of the reporter, it should be indicated parenthetically:

▶ Amoco Int'l Fin. Corp. v. Iran, 15 Iran-U.S. Cl. Trib. Rep. 189 (1987).

▶ Massaut v. Stupp, 9 Trib. Arb. Mixtes 316 (Ger.-Belg. 1929).

▶ Savarkar (Fr. v. Gr. Brit.), Hague Ct. Rep. (Scott) 275 (Perm. Ct. Arb. 1911).

▶ Case No. 5428 of 1988, 14 Y.B. Comm. Arb. 146 (ICC Int'l Ct. Arb.).

The International Centre for Settlement of Investment Disputes (ICSID), part of the World Bank, includes the full diplomatic name of each country involved, when relevant, in the case name. After the case number, include a description of the type of decision or ruling, when relevant:

▶ Société Générale de Surveillance S.A. v. Republic of the Phil., ICSID Case No. ARB/02/6, Objections to Jurisdiction, ¶ 154 (Jan. 29, 2004), 8 ICSID Rep. 518 (2005).

When decisions do not appear in a traditional printed source, an internet source may be used pursuant to **rule 18.1**:

▶ *In re* Account of Gafner, Case No. CV96-4849, Certified Award, at 2 (Claims Resolution Trib. 2006), http://www.crt-ii.org/_awards/ _apdfs/Gafner_Elisabeth.pdf.

21.7 United Nations Sources

Frequently cited U.N. documents will often be drawn from the Official Records, masthead documents, or Internet sources; U.N. websites are favored over all other Internet sites. The Official Records are the preferred source for citations, but masthead documents and documents drawn from U.N. websites are acceptable. Press releases, sales documents, yearbooks, and periodicals should be cited only when preferred sources are unavailable or when the purpose of the citation so requires.

Many users will refer to the masthead version of the document. As such, paragraph and article numbers, rather than page numbers in the Official Records, should be used for pinpoint citations whenever possible. Some documents utilize both unnumbered and numbered paragraphs, referred to as preambular and operative paragraphs, respectively; cite language in preambular paragraphs by page number and language in the numbered operative paragraphs by paragraph number. For resolutions of the General Assembly and Security Council, cite the Official Records and provide a parallel citation to document symbols for the individual resolution.

This section covers the principal organs of the United Nations and several subsidiaries of the General Assembly. Subsidiaries of organs or committees should be included in citations whenever appropriate. Other organs and committees not specifically covered by this section should be cited analogously to the examples in this rule. If a committee is known by an abbreviation, write out the committee's full name in the first instance and include the proper abbreviation in brackets. The abbreviation may then be used in subsequent instances.

Verbatim and Summary Records 21.7.1

Verbatim records of the Security Council, the General Assembly, and the Trusteeship Council are kept in the Official Records of those organs. The Economic and Social Council and the Trade and Development Board do not keep verbatim records. All citations to verbatim and summary records should be to the Official Records whenever possible.

Include in the citation the Official Records title; the subdivision of the organ, if necessary; the session and meeting number; the pinpoint citation, if necessary; the U.N. document symbol; and the date:

▶ U.N. GAOR, 56th Sess., 1st plen. mtg. at 3, U.N. Doc. A/56/PV.1 (Sept. 12, 2001).

▶ U.N. SCOR, 59th Sess., 4893d mtg. at 2, U.N. Doc. S/PV.4893 (Jan. 15, 2004).

Resolutions and Decisions 21.7.2

The final, authorized versions of resolutions appear in the Official Records. However, it has become customary to cite the electronic versions found in the Official Document System (ODS) of the United Nations using resolution symbols. Cite resolutions either to the Official Records or using resolution symbols. For pinpoint citations to material within a resolution, use paragraph or article numbers.

(a) General Assembly. After 1976, General Assembly resolution symbols are designated as session number/resolution number. The first resolution adopted during the forty-seventh General Assembly would thus be G.A. Res. 47/1.

Prior to 1976, the resolution symbols continued increasing from year to year and the session number was indicated as a Roman numeral in parentheses after the resolution number.

(i) **Citation to the Official Record.** General Assembly resolutions and decisions are published in the supplements to the Official Records (GAOR). The Official Records are documents and have their own symbols, different from the symbol of the resolutions. General Assembly decisions are not published as individual documents, but have numbers similar to resolutions and are published only in the supplements to the Official Records.

- ► G.A. Res. 832 (IX), U.N. GAOR, 9th Sess., Supp. No. 21, U.N. Doc. A/2890, at 19 (Oct. 21, 1954).

- ► G.A. Res. 47/163, ¶ 5, U.N. GAOR, 47th Sess., Supp. No. 49, (Vol. I), U.N. Doc. A/47/49 (Vol. I), at 120 (Dec. 18, 1992).

- ► G.A. Dec. 62/557, U.N. GAOR, 62d Sess., Supp. No. 49, (Vol. III), U.N. Doc. A/63/49 (Vol. III), at 106 (Sept. 15, 2008).

(ii) **Citation to electronic version found in the Official Document System (ODS).** To cite to the electronic versions of resolutions, use resolution symbols. To create resolution symbols, insert "A/RES/" before the resolution number.

- ► G.A. Res. 47/1, ¶ 2, U.N. Doc. A/RES/47/1 (Sept. 22, 1992).

- ► G.A. Res. 62/228, ¶ 35, U.N. Doc. A/RES/62/228 (Dec. 22, 2007).

- ► G.A. Res. 2262 (XXII), ¶ 12, U.N. Doc. A/6884 (Nov. 3, 1967).

- ► G.A. Res. 133 (II), at 43, U.N. Doc. A/519 (Nov. 17, 1947).

(iii) **General Assembly resolutions known by a popular name.** For General Assembly resolutions better known by title (e.g., the Universal Declaration of Human Rights), put the title at the beginning of the citation:

- ► Universal Declaration of Human Rights, G.A. Res. 217 (III) A, U.N. Doc. A/RES/217(III) (Dec. 10, 1948).

- ► 2005 World Summit Outcome, G.A. Res. 60/1, U.N. Doc. A/RES/60/1 (Sept. 16, 2005).

- ► Declaration on the Rights of Persons Belonging to National or Ethnic, Religious and Linguistic Minorities, G.A. Res. 47/135, Annex, U.N. GAOR, 47th Sess., Supp. No. 49 (Vol. I), U.N. Doc. A/47/49 (Vol. 1), at 210 (Dec. 18, 1992).

(b) Security Council resolutions. Cite Security Council resolutions in accordance with either **rule 21.7.2(a)(i)** or **21.7.2(a)(ii)**. Resolution symbols are created by inserting "S/RES/" prior to the resolution number. Security Council presidential statements may be cited in a similar manner.

- ► S.C. Res. 508, para. 3, U.N. SCOR, 37th Year, U.N. Doc. S/INF/38, at 5 (June 5, 1982).

- ► S.C. Res. 1325, para. 8, U.N. Doc. S/RES/1325 (Oct. 31, 2000).

- ► S.C. Pres. Statement 2008/48, U.N. Doc. S/PRST/2008/48 (Dec. 22, 2008).

(c) Resolutions issued by other organs. Resolutions issued by other U.N. organs should be cited analogously to General Assembly and Security Council resolutions.

- ► E.S.C. Res. 1990/26, U.N. Doc. E/RES/1990/90 (May 24, 1990).

- ► T.C. Res. 2014 (XXVI), U.N. TCOR, 26th Sess., Supp. No. 1, U.N. Doc. T/1549, at 2 (June 1, 1960).

(d) Resolutions by subsidiary bodies. Resolutions issued by subsidiary bodies of the principal U.N. organs should be cited by the name of the subsidiary body and resolution number; the title, session, and date of the document where the resolution is found; the title of the Official Records; the supplement number; the U.N. document symbol; the pinpoint cite, if any; and the date:

- Human Rights Council Res. 5/1, Rep. of the Human Rights Council, 5th Sess., June 11-18, 2007, U.N. GAOR, 62d Sess., Supp. No. 53, A/62/53, at 48 (June 18, 2007).

(e) Short form. Resolutions can subsequently be cited in short form, abbreviating the name of the body where practical, giving the name of the resolution, and providing the pinpoint citation:

- S.C. Res. 508, *supra* note 1, ¶ 2.

- H.R.C. Res. 5/1, *supra* note 2, ¶ 1.

....

U.N. Reports   21.7.3

(a) In general. Reports from U.N. organs, committees, or the Secretariat should include the name of the body and the subcommittee, if any (both abbreviated according to **rule 15.1(d)**); the title of the report; the pinpoint cite, if any; the document symbol; and the date. If a personal author is given along with the institutional author, the author should be included in a parenthetical at the end of the citation.

(b) Reports of subsidiary bodies to parent organs. Reports of subsidiary bodies to parent organs are usually part of the Official Records of the parent organ, as are the reports of the principal organs to the General Assembly. Include the title of the report; the name of the body; the session number; dates of the session; the pinpoint cite, if any; the document symbol; the Official Record supplement number; and the date of publication.

- U.N. S.C. Rep. of the Security Council, Aug. 1, 2007–July 31, 2008, U.N. Doc. A/63/2; GAOR, 63d Sess., Supp. No. 2 (2008).

- Comm. on the Peaceful Uses of Outer Space, Legal Subcomm., Rep. on its 24th Sess., Mar. 18–Apr. 4, 1985, U.N. Doc. A/AC.105/352 (Apr. 11, 1985).

- Rep. of the Int'l Law Comm'n, 60th Sess., May 5–June 6, July 7–Aug. 8, 2008, U.N. Doc. A/63/10; GAOR, 63d Sess., Supp. No. 10 (2008).

- U.N. Group of Experts on Côte d'Ivoire, Rep., transmitted by letter dated Oct. 17, 2007 from the Chairman of the Security Council Comm. established pursuant to resolution 1572 (2004) concerning Côte d'Ivoire addressed to the President of the Security Council, ¶¶ 61-80, U.N. Doc. S/2007/611 (Oct. 18, 2007).

(c) Reports from the Secretary-General or other officials. When citing a report published by the Secretary-General, or anyone acting in an official capacity as a committee chair, representative, envoy, etc., include in the citation: the author of the report; the title of the report; the pinpoint cite, if any; the body to which the document is delivered, if needed; the document symbol; and the date. List the author's official capacity and not his or her name. If a personal author is given along with the institutional author, the author should be included in a parenthetical at the end of the citation.

- U.N. Secretary-General, *An Agenda for Peace: Preventive Diplomacy, Peacemaking and Peace-Keeping: Rep. of the Secretary-General*, ¶ 14, U.N. Doc. A/47/277-S/24111 (June 17, 1992).

▶ Executive Chairman of the U.N. Monitoring, Verification and Inspection Comm'n (UNMOVIC), *8th Quarterly Rep. of the Executive Chairman of the U.N. Monitoring, Verification and Inspection Commission in Accordance with Paragraph 12 of Security Council Resolution 1284* (1999), *transmitted by Note of the Secretary-General*, U.N. Doc. S/2002/195 (Feb. 26, 2002).

▶ Special Rapporteur on the Expulsion of Aliens, *Fourth Rep. on the Expulsion of Aliens*, Int'l Law Comm'n, U.N. Doc. A/CN.4/594 (Mar. 24, 2008) (by Maurice Kamto).

(d) Reports from conferences. If the report is the product of a conference or a series of conferences, include in the citation: the conference name; the name of this particular meeting of the conference, if it is in a series; the place of the conference, unless it occurs at the headquarters of the organizing agency; the dates of the conference; the report title; the pinpoint cite, if any; the document symbol, when available; and the official document date, if different from the conference date:

▶ World Conference on Human Rights, June 14–25, 1993, *Vienna Declaration and Programme of Action*, ¶ 37, U.N. Doc. A/CONF.157/23 (July 12, 1993).

▶ United Nations Conference on Environment and Development, Rio de Janeiro, Braz., June 3-14, 1992, *Rio Declaration on Environment and Development*, U.N. Doc. A/CONF.151/26/Rev.1 (Vol. I), Annex I (Aug. 12, 1992).

(e) Short forms. Reports often have very long names. It is appropriate to list a short form in brackets at the end of the citation (**rule 4.2(b)**).

21.7.4   Masthead Documents

Most U.N. documents are issued as masthead documents. Some documents originally published in masthead form, such as resolutions of the General Assembly and Security Council, are subsequently issued in the Official Records. Always cite to the Official Record, when possible. Masthead documents should be cited by the name of the institutional author, if any (**rule 21.7.4(a)**); the title of the document (**rule 21.7.4(b)**); pinpoint cite, if any; the document symbol (**rule 21.7.4(c)**); and the date of publication.

▶ U.N. Secretary-General, Letter dated Mar. 2, 2006 from the Secretary-General addressed to the President of the General Assembly, U.N. Doc. A/60/706 (Mar. 3, 2006).

▶ U.N. President of the S.C., Letter dated Dec. 9, 2008 from the President of the Security Council to the Secretary-General, U.N. Doc. S/2008/757 (Dec. 9, 2008).

▶ Prevention Through Education, Ministerial Declaration of the 1st Meeting of the Ministers of Health and Education to Stop HIV/AIDS and Sexually Transmitted Infections in Latin America and the Caribbean, in letter dated Aug. 15, 2008 from the Chargé d'affaires a.i. of the Permanent Mission of Mexico to the United Nations addressed to the Secretary-General, U.N. Doc. A/63/307 (Aug. 19, 2008).

► Permanent Rep. of Somalia to the U.N., Letter dated May 12, 2008 from the Permanent Rep. of Somalia to the United Nations addressed to the President of the Security Council, U.N. Doc. S/2008/323 (May 14, 2008).

► U.N. Secretariat, Expulsion of Aliens, Memorandum by the Secretariat, ¶¶ 702-44, Int'l Law Comm'n, U.N. Doc. A/CN.4/565 (July 10, 2006).

(a) Author. Include the name of the author, as listed on the cover page of the document:

► U.N. Secretary-General, Letter dated Mar. 2, 2006 from the Secretary-General addressed to the President of the General Assembly, U.N. Doc. A/60/706 (Mar. 3, 2006).

► United Nations, Econ. & Soc. Council, Comm. on Arrangements for Consultation with Non-Governmental Orgs., Dev. of Tourism on the African Continent, Statement Submitted by the Int'l Union of Official Travel Orgs., U.N. Doc. E/C.2/562 (1960).

(b) Title. Capitalize the title in accordance with **rule 8.**

(c) United Nations document symbol. Include the U.N. document symbol (**rule 21.7.1**), if available.

U.N. Press Releases and Memoranda   21.7.5

Cite U.N. press releases and memoranda according to **rule 17.2.3**, but also include the U.N. press release symbol:

► Press Release, Security Council, Security Council Takes Up Report on Diamonds, Arms in Sierra Leone; Expert Panel Says Council Sanctions Broken 'with Impunity,' U.N. Press Release SC/6997 (Jan. 25, 2001).

Adjudicatory Bodies Established by the United Nations   21.7.6

The International Criminal Tribunals for the Former Yugoslavia and Rwanda, the Special Court for Sierra Leone, and all other ad hoc and regional tribunals should be cited according to **rule 21.5.7.** The U.N. Administrative Tribunal should be cited to *Judgments of the U.N. Administrative Tribunal* (Judgments U.N. Admin. Trib.) by judgment number:

► Eldridge v. Secretary-General of the United Nations, Judgments U.N. Admin. Trib., No. 32, at 144, U.N. Doc. AT/DEC/32 (1953).

Sales Publications   21.7.7

Numerous U.N. agencies publish, for sale to the public, documents other than Official Records. These sales publications may take many forms, such as reports, studies, or proceedings. Every citation to a sales publication must include the author and/or title (**rule 21.7.7(a)**); the page(s) or paragraph(s) (**rule 21.7.7(b)**); the U.N. document symbol, if available (**rule 21.7.7(c)**); the sales number (**rule 21.7.7(d)**); and the year (**rule 21.7.7(e)**).

(a) Author and title. Include the author and/or title according to **rules 15.1** and 15.3. Include the name of the author only if it is not apparent from the title of the document:

> ► U.N. Dep't of Int'l Econ. & Soc. Affairs, U.N. Model Double Taxation Convention Between Developed and Developing Countries, at 243, U.N. Doc. ST/ESA/102, U.N. Sales No. E.80.XVI.3 (1980).

> ► U.N. Dep't of Econ. & Soc. Affairs, Comm. for Dev. Policy, Handbook on the Least Developed Country Category: Inclusion, Graduation and Special Support Measures, U.N. Sales No. E.07.II.A.9 (2008).

(b) Page(s) or paragraph(s). The volume and subdivision designations should be followed by the page(s) or paragraph(s) to which reference is intended. Introduce page numbers with the word "at."

(c) United Nations document symbol. Include the U.N. document symbol **(rule 21.7.1)**, if available.

(d) United Nations sales number. Include the U.N. sales number:

> ► U.N. Dep't of Int'l Econ. & Soc. Affairs, World Economic Survey 1977, at I-19, U.N. Doc. ST/ESA/82, U.N. Sales No. E.78.II.C.1 (1977).

(e) Year. Give the year of publication.

....

21.7.8 **Yearbooks and Periodicals**

United Nations yearbooks and periodicals collect summaries of the work of subsidiary organizations and related documents. Citations should include the author and/or title of the document or separately designated article (if any); the name of the yearbook or periodical (abbreviated according to **rule 16.4**); and the U.N. document symbol or, if none, the U.N. sales number **(rule 21.7.7(d))**. For example:

> ► *Summary Records of the 1447th Meeting*, [1977] 1 Y.B. Int'l L. Comm'n 175, U.N. Doc. A/CN.4/SER.A/1977.

> ► *Human Rights in the Union of Burma in 1953*, 1953 Y.B. on H.R. 31, U.N. Sales No. 1955.XIV.1.

> ► 1981 U.N. Jurid. Y.B. 41, U.N. Doc. ST/LEG/SER.C/19.

> ► 1985 U.N.Y.B. 1391, U.N. Sales No. E.84.I.1.

Material reprinted in yearbooks from other U.N. documents should be cited to the original source or to the official records of a U.N. organ:

> ► *Report of the International Law Commission to the General Assembly*, 19 U.N. GAOR Supp. No. 9, at 1, U.N. Doc. A/5509 (1963), *reprinted in* [1963] 2 Y.B. Int'l L. Comm'n 187, U.N. Doc. A/CN.4/SER.A/1963/Add.1.

Regional Organization Documents   21.7.9

Resolutions, reports, and other similar documents produced by regional organizations, such as the Organization of American States or the African Union, should be cited analogously to the U.N. document citation methods.

....

U.N. Charter   21.7.10

See rule 21.4:

> ▸ U.N. Charter art. 2, para. 4.

....

U.N. Internet Materials   21.7.11

Only provide citations to a URL for materials without document or press release symbols. United Nations websites are preferred to all other websites. Cite materials in accordance with rule 21.7.4 and format them pursuant to rule 18.1:

> ▸ U.N. Secretary-General, High-Level Event on the Millennium Development Goals 25 September 2008: Committing to Action: Achieving the Millennium Development Goals: Background Note by the Secretary-General (July 25, 2008), http://www.un.org/millenniumgoals/2008highlevel/pdf/commiting.pdf.

> ▸ Letter from the President of the General Assembly to all Permanent Representatives and Permanent Observers to the U.N. (Dec. 16, 2008), http://www.un.org/ga/president/63/letters/peacebuilding 161208.pdf.

> ▸ U.N. President of the G.A., Remarks on the Work to Date of the Sixty-Third Session of the United Nations General Assembly (Dec. 23, 2008), http://www.un.org/ga/president/63/statements/ ga231208.shtml.

League of Nations   21.8

Cite the League of Nations Covenant as:

> ▸ League of Nations Covenant art. 15, para. 6.

Cite conventions and treaties promulgated by the League of Nations according to rule 21.4.

Cite other League of Nations materials by issuing body (if not included in the title); title; document number; and year:

> ▸ *Reports Presented by the Comm. of Technical Experts on Double Taxation and Tax Evasion*, League of Nations Doc. C.216M.85 1927 II (1927).

European Union and European Community   21.9

(a) Acts of the Council and Commission.

(i) **Sources.** Cite publications of the Council and of the Commission published beginning February 1, 2003, to the *Official Journal of the European Union* (O.J.). Cite documents published between January 1, 1973, and January 31, 2003, to the *Official Journal of the European Communities* (also abbreviated O.J.). Cite documents published before January 1, 1973, to the Special Edition of the *Official Journal of the European Communities* (O.J. SPEC. ED.), if available; otherwise cite to the *Journal Officiel des Communautés Européennes* (J.O.).

Beginning with the 1998 editions, the O.J. is available at the European Union's official website, http://eur-lex.europa.eu/en/index.htm. The online editions are updated daily and may be used when paper versions are not available.

Cite volumes of O.J. and J.O. by year. J.O. volumes published prior to 1968 were numbered in a single series. Since 1968, O.J. and J.O. have been published in parallel series, paginated separately by issue. Legislative acts appear in the "L" series, while other documents appear in the "C" series. Citations to O.J. and J.O. since 1968 must include the series and issue number; citations to J.O. before 1968 must include the issue number:

▶ 1971 J.O. (L 20) 1

▶ 1975 O.J. (L 337) 7

▶ 1964 J.O. (234) 5

Citations to the O.J. SPEC. ED. must indicate the period covered by the issue:

▶ 1965-1966 O.J. SPEC. ED. 265

(ii) **Legislative acts of the Council and Commission.** Cite Regulations, Directives, and Decisions of the Council and Commission by the issuing institution, type of legislation, number, and any subdivision cited. If it is unclear from the context that the source is a European Union (EU) or European Community (EC) act, indicate this with a parenthetical at the end of the citation (**rule 20.1**). If the act was not issued under the Treaty on the Functioning of the European Union, indicate the authority for the promulgation of the act:

▶ Council Directive 90/476, art. 5, 1990 O.J. (L 266) 1, 2 (EC).

▶ Council Directive 66/45, art. 15, 1965-1966 O.J. SPEC. ED. 265, 268 (Euratom).

▶ Commission Regulation 725/67, 1967 J.O. (253) 1.

If desired, all or part of the full name of the legislation may be given, with or without the date. Even though the Commission and the Council frequently do not capitalize the titles of legislation, capitalize them according to **rule 8**:

▶ Commission Regulation 2751/90, Fixing the Import Levies on Compound Feeding Stuffs, Annex, 1990 O.J. (L 264) 37, 38.

▶ Directive 2001/18, of the European Parliament and of the Council of 12 March 2001 on the Deliberate Release into the Environment of Genetically Modified Organisms and Repealing Council Directive 20/220/EEC, 2001 O.J. (L 106) 1, 3.

(iii) **Other publications of the Council and Commission.** Cite proposed Regulations, Directives, and Decisions, as well as conclusions, resolutions, and other notices of the Council and Commission, by issuing institution and title, as given at the beginning of the item.

For Common Positions, the complete date and the title, either complete or in short form, may be included:

▶ Council Common Position (EC) No. 57/2003 of 25 June 2003, art. 2, 2003 O.J. (C 277) 1, 2.

> ▶ Administrative Commission on Social Security for Migrant Workers, 2009 O.J. (C 213) 6, 8.

(iv) **COM and SEC documents.** "COM" documents are proposed legislation and other Commission communications to other European institutions, and the Commission's preparatory papers. "SEC" documents are internal documents concerning the operations of Commission departments. Cite "COM" and "SEC" documents by issuing body (unless clear from the title); title; pinpoint cite, if any; the "COM" or "SEC" number, which includes the year of publication in parentheses and the running number assigned to the document; the word "final" (unless the version cited is not final); and the date:

> ▶ *Commission Proposal for a Directive of the European Parliament and of the Council To Establish a New Financial Services Committee Organisational Structure*, at 11, COM (2003) 659 final (Nov. 5, 2003).

> ▶ *Proposal for a Regulation of the European Parliament and of the Council Concerning the Registration, Evaluation, Authorisation and Registration of Chemicals (Reach)*, COM (2003) 644 final (Oct. 29, 2003).

(b) Documents of the European Parliament.

(i) **Debates.** Debates of the European Parliament are bound and published in the *European Parliamentary Debates* (Eur. Parl. Deb.). The debates are also published in the annex to the *Official Journal of the European Union*. It is acceptable to cite debates to the O.J. before they are bound. Include in the citation the name of the speaker, the document number, and the exact date. If the context of the debate is unclear, provide an explanatory parenthetical at the end of the citation:

> ▶ Remarks of Mr. Kuijpers, Eur. Parl. Deb. (378) 4 (May 24, 1989).

> ▶ Remarks of President Ortoli, 1975 O.J. (Annex 193) 123 (July 9, 1975) (European Parliament debates).

(ii) **Documents.** Cite documents to *European Parliament Session Documents* (Eur. Parl. Doc.) (entitled *European Parliament Working Documents* prior to 1988), if therein; otherwise cite to *Parlement Européen Documents de Séance* (Parl. Eur. Doc.). Include the document number:

> ▶ Eur. Parl. Doc. (COM 258) 5 (1973).

> ▶ Parl. Eur. Doc. (SEC 64) 6 (1963).

If desired, the name may be included as well:

> ▶ Resolution on Action Required Internationally To Provide Effective Protection for Indigenous Peoples, Eur. Parl. Doc. PV 58(II) (1994).

(c) Founding treaties. Cite sources as indicated in **rule 21.4.5**:

> ▶ Treaty of Lisbon Amending the Treaty on European Union and the Treaty Establishing the European Community, Dec. 13, 2007, 2007 O.J. (C 306) 1 [hereinafter Treaty of Lisbon].

> ▶ Consolidated Version of the Treaty on the Functioning of the European Union art. 15, May 9, 2008, 2008 O.J. (C 115) 47 [hereinafter TFEU].

> ► Treaty of Amsterdam Amending the Treaty on European Union, the Treaties Establishing the European Communities and Certain Related Acts, Oct. 2, 1997, 1997 O.J. (C 340) 1.

Subsequent citations should use the appropriate short form alone:

> ► TFEU art. 177.

> ► Treaty of Lisbon arts. 4–5.

> ► Euratom Treaty art. 4.

The Treaty of Lisbon has significantly amended the EC Treaty, the TEU, and certain other documents, resulting in the renaming of the Treaty Establishing the European Community (EC Treaty) to the Treaty on the Functioning of the European Union (TFEU) and a renumbering of the articles. For current references to the founding treaty, cite to the TFEU, incorporating amendments to the 1957 EEC Treaty by the 1987 Single European Act (SEA), the 1992 Treaty on European Union (TEU), the Treaty of Amsterdam, the Treaty of Nice, and the Treaty of Lisbon.

Current citations should be to the article number as amended by the Treaty of Lisbon. To cite to previous versions of the EC Treaty, EEC Treaty, or the TEU, do not cite to the TFEU; instead cite to the treaty as named on that date, indicate the date of the version cited, and state in parentheses the current number of the article in the TFEU, if still active:

> ► EC Treaty art. 49 (as in effect 2005) (now TFEU art. 56).

> ► EC Treaty art. 53 (as in effect 1994) (repealed by the Treaty of Amsterdam).

> ► EEC Treaty art. 30 (as in effect 1958) (now TFEU art. 34).

(d) International treaties and agreements. Cite according to rule 21.4.

(e) Reports, Green Papers, and White Papers. Cite reports from any institution or working group within the European Union or the European Communities according to rule 21.7.3. Green Papers and White Papers should be cited as reports. Include in the citation of reports the issuing body and the committee, division, or group that produced the report, if applicable. If a report is not given a document number, give the information necessary to locate the document:

> ► *Commission White Paper on European Governance*, at 17, COM (2001) 482 final (July 25, 2001).

> ► *Initial Report of the Committee of Wise Men on the Regulation of European Securities Markets*, at 4 (Nov. 9, 2000), *available at* http://ec.europa.eu/internal_market/securities/docs/lamfalussy /wisemen/initial-report-wise-men_en.pdf.

The comments, notices, opinions, and remarks on reports, proposals, White Papers, and Green Papers should also be cited as reports.

> ► *Opinion of the Committee of the Regions on the ʻCoR Proposals for the Intergovernmental Conference,ʼ* 2004 O.J. (C 32) 1, 2.

If it is unclear whether a source should be cited according to rule 21.9.2(a)(iii) or 21.9(e), the form and documentation should govern. If the source takes a form analogous to other reports and is not given the type of document number that Commission and Council acts are given (e.g., Council Directive (EC) No.

2504/90), then it should be cited as a report.

(f) Press releases, Presidency Conclusions, and memoranda. European Union and European Community press releases and memoranda should be cited according to **rule 17.2.3**. Treat the Presidency Conclusions of the Council like press releases and include the exact date as well as the meeting place of the Council:

> ▸ Presidency Conclusions, Brussels European Council (Dec. 12, 2003).

(g) Court of Justice materials. Cite European Court of Justice materials according to **rule 21.5.2**.

(h) Recent materials. Recent European Union materials can be found at the European Union's official website (http://europa.eu) (**rule 18.1**).

Council of Europe   21.10

Cite debates of the Parliamentary Assembly, formerly the Consultative Assembly, to the official reports:

> ▸ Eur. Consult. Ass. Deb. 10th Sess. 639 (Oct. 16, 1958).

> ▸ Eur. Parl. Ass. Deb. 23d Sess. 499 (Sept. 30, 1980).

Cite documents as follows:

> ▸ Eur. Consult. Ass., *Reply of the Comm. of Ministers*, 12th Sess., Doc. No. 1126 (1960).

Recent Council of Europe materials can be found on the Council of Europe's official website (http://assembly.coe.int) (**rule 18.1**).

World Trade Organization   21.11

If it is ever unclear from the context that the citation refers to a WTO or GATT document, explain the reference in a parenthetical following the citation.

(a) WTO panel and Appellate Body materials. Cite reports of WTO panels and the Appellate Body by their official document symbol:

> ▸ Panel Report, *United States—Sections 301–310 of the Trade Act of 1974*, WT/DS152/R (Dec. 22, 1999) [hereinafter Section 301 Panel Report].

> ▸ Appellate Body Report, *Brazil—Export Financing Programme for Aircraft*, ¶ 19, WT/DS46/AB/R (Aug. 2, 1999).

Give the date the report was issued, not the date it was adopted by the Dispute Settlement Body, unless the latter date is necessary to the purpose served by the citation. In those cases, place the italicized word "*adopted*" and the date in parentheses at the end of the citation:

> ▸ Appellate Body Report, *European Communities—Measures Concerning Meat and Meat Products*, WT/DS26/AB/R, WT/DS48/AB/R (Jan. 16, 1998) (*adopted* Feb. 13, 1998).

Cite communications of panels and the Appellate Body, as well as members' communications to panels and the Appellate Body, in a like format:

- Preliminary Ruling by the Panel, *Canada—Measures Relating to Exports of Wheat and Treatment of Imported Grain*, ¶ 23, WT/DS276/12 (July 21, 2003).

- Request for Consultations by the United States, *European Communities—Measures Affecting the Approval and Marketing of Biotech Products*, WT/DS291/1 (May 20, 2003).

- Request for the Establishment of a Panel by Brazil, *United States—Subsidies on Upland Cotton*, WT/DS267/7 (Feb. 7, 2003).

Members' written submissions and oral statements to panels and the Appellate Body are made public at the discretion of the individual member. Because these documents are not normally publicly available, include precise information regarding their location:

- First Written Submission of the United States, *United States—Subsidies on Upland Cotton*, WT/DS267 (July 11, 2003), *available at* http://www.ustr.gov/webfm_send/578.

(b) General Agreement on Tariffs and Trade (GATT) panel decisions. Cite to *Basic Instruments and Selected Documents* (B.I.S.D.), if therein. Include the title; case number if listed; document date; ordinal number of the supplement (annual volume); page; and year of publication.

- Report of the Panel, *Japan—Restrictions on Imports of Certain Agricultural Products*, ¶ 5.2.2, L/6253 (Feb. 2, 1988), GATT B.I.S.D. (35th Supp.) at 163, 229 (1989).

- *Netherlands Measure of Suspension of Obligations to the United States* (Nov. 8, 1952), GATT B.I.S.D. (1st Supp.) at 32 (1953).

(c) Reports. Cite reports from the WTO Secretariat and other bodies as you would those from the United Nations (**rule 21.7.3**):

- Council for Trade-Related Aspects of Intellectual Property Rights, *Note by the Secretariat: Available Information on the Existence of Patents in Regard to the Diseases Referred to in the Declaration on the TRIPS Agreement and Public Health*, IP/C/W/348 (June 11, 2002).

- Special Session of the Council for Trade in Services, *Guidelines and Procedures for the Negotiations on Trade in Services*, S/L/93 (Mar. 29, 2001).

- GATT Secretariat, *An Analysis of the Proposed Uruguay Round Agreement, with Particular Emphasis on Aspects of Interest to Developing Countries*, MTN.TNC/W/122 (Nov. 29, 1993).

(d) Founding agreements. Cite sources as indicated in **rule 21.4.5**:

- Marrakesh Agreement Establishing the World Trade Organization, Apr. 15, 1994, 1867 U.N.T.S. 154 [hereinafter Marrakesh Agreement].

- General Agreement on Tariffs and Trade, Oct. 30, 1947, 61 Stat. A-11, 55 U.N.T.S. 194 [hereinafter GATT].

The Marrakesh Agreement concluded the Uruguay Round, which resulted in a set of agreements and appended annexes, some of which constitute agreements on separate trade issues. Indicate to which other part of the agreements they attach, if any:

► Understanding on Rules and Procedures Governing the Settlement of Disputes art. 1, Apr. 15, 1994, Marrakesh Agreement Establishing the World Trade Organization, Annex 2, 1869 U.N.T.S. 401 [hereinafter DSU].

GATT-era side agreements should be cited to an unofficial treaty source, such as B.I.S.D.:

► Agreement Regarding International Trade in Textiles, Dec. 20, 1973, GATT B.I.S.D. (21st Supp.) at 4 (1975).

Subsequent citations should use the appropriate short form alone, citing only to articles or paragraphs:

► Marrakesh Agreement ¶ 5.

► DSU art. 3.7.

(e) Ministerial documents. Cite ministerial documents by document number and to an unofficial source, such as International Legal Materials, if therein:

► World Trade Organization, Ministerial Declaration of 14 November 2001, WT/MIN(01)/DEC/1, 41 I.L.M. 746 (2002) [hereinafter Doha Declaration].

(f) Other documents. Cite ICSID international arbitration documents according to rule 21.6.

Cite press releases according to rule 17.2.3.

Some documents can be found on the WTO's website, and should be cited in accordance with rule 18.1.

Other Intergovernmental Organizations 21.12

Generally, cite by analogy to United Nations materials (rule 21.7) and to the forms in rules 21.8-21.11. See rule 20.2 regarding citation of materials in languages other than English. Citations should include the name of the issuing institution, which should be written out on first reference and followed by the proper abbreviation from table T3 in brackets. The abbreviation may then be used in all subsequent instances. The citation should also include the title; the resolution number, if any; the pinpoint citation; the document number; and the date. Indicate parenthetically any other relevant information. Always provide enough information to locate the source with minimal effort:

► Int'l Atomic Energy Agency [IAEA], *Supply Agreement for a Research Reactor in Romania*, at 3, IAEA Doc. INFCIRC/206 (June 12, 1974).

► IAEA, *Assessment of Members' Contributions to the Regular Budget*, Gen. Conf. Res. 434, IAEA Doc. GC(XXVIII)/RES/434 (Sept. 28, 1984).

► Int'l Civil Aviation Org. [ICAO], *Manual of All-Weather Operations*, at 2-2, ICAO Doc. 9365-AN/910 (1st ed. 1982).

► ICAO, *Condemnation of the Policies of Apartheid and Racial Discrimination of South Af*rica, Assemb. Res. A15-7 (1964), *compiled in Assembly Resolutions in Force*, at I-21, ICAO Doc. 9509 (Oct. 10, 1986).

> ▶ Int'l Telecomm. Union [ITU], *Geographical Distribution of ITU Staff*, ITU Admin. Council Res. No. 580 (1981), *compiled in* Resolutions and Decisions of the Administrative Council of the International Telecommunication Union 2.1.1 (gen. rev. 1979 plus supps.).

A citation to a source that is particularly difficult to locate should include a parenthetical explaining its availability:

> ▶ Int'l Maritime Org. [IMO], *Provision of Facilities in Ports for the Reception of Oily Wastes from Ships*, IMO Assemb. Res. A. 585 (14) (Nov. 20, 1985) (on file with the Harvard International Law Journal).

21.13 International Committee of the Red Cross and International Non-Governmental Organizations

Certain organizations and international NGOs have special responsibilities with regard to international law. The International Committee of the Red Cross, for example, is the only body that can produce authoritative commentaries and interpretations of the Geneva Conventions. Other NGOs are so deeply involved in the process of creating international law that they are frequently cited in cases and academic materials.

Cite materials from international NGOs analogously to United Nations materials in **rule 21.7**. Include in the citation the name of the organization, including the appropriate abbreviation according to **rule 21.12**; the title of the document; the document number, if any; and the date:

> ▶ Amnesty Int'l, *Sierra Leone: Ending Impunity an Opportunity Not To Be Missed*, AI Index AFR 51/061/2000 (July 26, 2000).

21.14 Yearbooks

Citations to yearbooks should be avoided whenever a more official source is available. Cite United Nations yearbooks according to **rule 21.7.8**. Cite other international yearbooks or annual reports as periodicals (**rule 16**). Italicize article titles, but do not italicize the names of materials not ordinarily italicized (such as case names in footnotes). Give the yearbook title in the original language (abbreviated according to **tables T3** and **T13**, and **rule 20.2.3**) and, if not obvious, the name of the issuing organization. For example:

> ▶ Ronald Graveson, *The Inequality of the Applicable Law*, 1980 Brit. Y.B. Int'l L. 231, 233.

> ▶ Revised Staff Regulations, 1922–1925 P.C.I.J. Ann. Rep. (ser. E) No. 1, at 81 (1925).

> ▶ X. v. Belgium, 1961 Y.B. Eur. Conv. on H.R. (Eur. Comm'n of H.R.) 224.

> ▶ Jean Boulouis, *Cour de Justice des Communautés Européennes*, 1965 Annuaire Français de Droit International (Centre National de la Recherche Scientifique) 333.

> ▶ *Recommendations of the Customs Co-Operation Council on the Customs Treatment of Products Imported for Testing*, 1972 Eur. Y.B. (Council of Eur.) 429.

21.15 Digests

Citations to digests should be avoided whenever a more official source is available.

(a) Annual digests. Since 1973, the United States Department of State has published an annual Digest of United States Practice in International Law. These volumes are organized by topic and contain analysis and excerpts of documents in the field. In general, each section contains many subdivisions with individual subtitles. Provide the title for the entire section, the year of the digest, the section number, and the page(s), if citing to particular pages within the section:

▶ Diplomatic Relations and Recognition, 1975 DIGEST § 3, at 36.

Provide subdivision titles, separated by colons, only if particularly relevant:

▶ Extradition: Double Criminality: Bigamy, 1980 DIGEST § 5, at 226 (stating that when divorce in the United States is valid, no crime of bigamy has been committed under U.S. law and double criminality is absent).

(b) Named digests. Earlier digests were multiple-volume sets edited by a single editor and known by that person's name. For these digests, provide the title of the section (including subtitles only if particularly relevant, as under **rule 15.3**), the volume cited, the editor's name followed by the word DIGEST, the section number, and the page reference, if any:

▶ Source: Custom, 1 Hackworth DIGEST § 3, at 16.

▶ Access to Courts, 8 Whiteman DIGEST § 7, at 408.

(c) Foreign digests. When citing the digests of another country, cite analogously to those published in the United States. If the digest is published as an annual series, cite according to **rule 21.15(a)**; if it is identified by its editor's name, cite according to **rule 21.15(b)**. The first time a digest is cited, always provide the complete title, followed by the abbreviation in brackets, similar to **rule 20.2.3**.

(d) Digests published as periodical sections. When a digest appears as an annual or periodical section of a journal, cite as a periodical under **rule 16**:

▶ Arthur W. Rovine, *Contemporary Practice of the United States Relating to International Law,* 67 AM. J. INT'L L. 760, 767 (1973) (describing discussions of terrorism in the U.N. Security Council).

Short Citation Forms   21.16

(a) Treaties and other international agreements. Subsequent citations to treaties and other international agreements may use both "*id.*" and "*supra.*" Provide the full name of the treaty, followed by "*supra*," and the pages on which the cited material appears:

▶ Convention for the Avoidance of Double Taxation, *supra* note 6, at 25.

▶ Treaty on the Non-Proliferation of Nuclear Weapons, *supra* note 1, 21 U.S.T. at 486, 729 U.N.T.S. at 167.

If the original citation provided a "**hereinafter**" short title, use that title in a subsequent "*supra*" reference, as provided by **rule 21.4.1(b)**.

(b) International law cases and arbitrations. Use short forms analogous to those provided in **rule 10.9**, when permitted by that rule.

(c) United Nations and other intergovernmental organizations materials. Subsequent citations to materials of intergovernmental organizations may use both "*id.*" and "*supra*":

> ▶ G.A. Res. 832, *supra* note 4, at 22.

> ▶ *Permanent Missions to the U.N.: Report of the Secretary-General, supra* note 6, at 18.

If the first citation to the document included a "hereinafter" reference, use that form for subsequent "*supra*" cites:

> ▶ Completing the Internal Market, *supra* note 12, at 9.

(d) Yearbooks and digests. Subsequent citations to articles in yearbooks and digests should follow the short forms for periodicals (**rule 16.9**). Subsequent citations may be made using both "*id.*" and "*supra*."

T1   UNITED STATES JURISDICTIONS

The abbreviations and citation conventions listed in this table, except as noted, are primarily intended to serve a national audience. Practitioners should adhere to local citation rules (see Bluepages table BT2). The preferred sources of citation are suggested when relevant. In the absence of such preference, the user may cite to any listed sources, as appropriate. Official URLs have been listed where official print sources are no longer published at the time of this edition's publication. In general, when citing to online sources, be sure to cite to stable URLs of the specific provision cited in accordance with the principles of rule 18.

T1.1   Federal Judicial and Legislative Materials

For more information about the federal court system, including a list of the district courts and the territorial jurisdiction of the courts of appeals, access http://www.uscourts.gov.

Supreme Court (U.S.): Cite to U.S., if therein; otherwise, cite to S. Ct., L. Ed., or U.S.L.W., in that order of preference.

- ► United States Reports

► 91 U.S. to date	1875–date	U.S.
► Wallace	1863–1874	e.g., 68 U.S. (1 Wall.)
► Black	1861–1862	e.g., 66 U.S. (1 Black)
► Howard	1843–1860	e.g., 42 U.S. (1 How.)
► Peters	1828–1842	e.g., 26 U.S. (1 Pet.)
► Wheaton	1816–1827	e.g., 14 U.S. (1 Wheat.)
► Cranch	1801–1815	e.g., 5 U.S. (1 Cranch)
► Dallas	1790–1800	e.g., 1 U.S. (1 Dall.)
► Supreme Court Reporter	1882–date	S. Ct.
► United States Supreme Court Reports, Lawyers' Edition	1790–date	L. Ed., L. Ed. 2d
► United States Law Week	1933–date	U.S.L.W.

Circuit Justices (e.g., Rehnquist, Circuit Justice): Cite to U.S., if therein; otherwise, cite to S. Ct., L. Ed., or U.S.L.W., if therein, in that order of preference.

► United States Reports	1893–date	U.S.
► Supreme Court Reporter	1893–date	S. Ct.
► United States Supreme Court Reports, Lawyers' Edition	1790–date	L. Ed., L. Ed. 2d
► United States Law Week	1933–date	U.S.L.W.

Some cases presided over by Circuit Justices are found in other reporters and should be cited as follows:

- ► Halperin v. Kissinger, 807 F.2d 180 (Scalia, Circuit Justice, D.C. Cir. 1986).
- ► United States v. Benson, 31 F. 896 (Field, Circuit Justice, C.C.D. Cal. 1887).

Courts of Appeals (e.g., 2d Cir., D.C. Cir.), previously **Circuit Courts of Appeals** (e.g., 2d Cir.), and **Court of Appeals of/for the District of Columbia** (D.C. Cir.): Cite to F., F.2d, or F.3d, if therein.

▸ Federal Reporter	1891-date	F., F.2d, F.3d
▸ Federal Appendix	2001-date	F. App'x

Circuit Courts (e.g., C.C.S.D.N.Y., C.C.D. Cal.) (abolished 1912): Cite to F. or F. Cas.

▸ Federal Reporter	1880-1912	F.
▸ Federal Cases	1789-1880	F. Cas.

Citations to F. Cas. should give the case number parenthetically.

> ▸ Oelrich v. Pittsburgh, 18 F. Cas. 598 (C.C.W.D. Pa. 1859) (No. 10,444).

Temporary Emergency Court of Appeals (Temp. Emer. Ct. App.) (created 1971, abolished 1993), **Emergency Court of Appeals** (Emer. Ct. App.) (created 1942, abolished 1961), and **Commerce Court** (Comm. Ct.) (created 1910, abolished 1913): Cite to F. or F.2d.

▸ Federal Reporter	1910-1993	F., F.2d

United States Court of Appeals for the Federal Circuit (Fed. Cir.) (created 1982), successor to the **United States Court of Customs and Patent Appeals** (C.C.P.A.) (previously the **Court of Customs Appeals** (Ct. Cust. App.)) and the appellate jurisdiction of the **Court of Claims** (Ct. Cl.): Cite to F., F.2d, or F.3d, if therein; otherwise, cite to the respective official reporter.

▸ Federal Reporter	1910-date	F., F.2d, F.3d
▸ Court of Claims Reports	1956-1982	Ct. Cl.
▸ Court of Customs and Patent Appeals Reports	1929-1982	C.C.P.A.
▸ Court of Customs Appeals Reports	1910-1929	Ct. Cust.

United States Court of Federal Claims (Fed. Cl.) (created 1992), formerly **United States Claims Court** (Cl. Ct.) (created 1982), and successor to the original jurisdiction of the **Court of Claims** (Ct. Cl.): Cite to one of the following reporters:

▸ Federal Claims Reporter	1992-date	Fed. Cl.
▸ United States Claims Court Reporter	1983-1992	Cl. Ct.
▸ Federal Reporter	1930-1932	F.2d
	1960-1982	F.2d
▸ Federal Supplement	1932-1960	F. Supp.
▸ Court of Claims Reports	1863-1982	Ct. Cl.

United States Court of International Trade (Ct. Int'l Trade) (created 1980), formerly **United States Customs Court** (Cust. Ct.) (created 1926): Cite to the official reporters, if possible; if unavailable, cite to F. Supp. or F. Supp. 2d, to Cust. B. & Dec. (an official publication), or to I.T.R.D. (BNA), in that order of preference.

▸ Court of International Trade Reports	1980-date	Ct. Int'l Trade
▸ Customs Court Reports	1938-1980	Cust. Ct.
▸ Federal Supplement	1980-date	F. Supp., F. Supp. 2d
▸ Customs Bulletin and Decisions	1967-date	Cust. B. & Dec.
▸ International Trade Reporter Decisions	1980-date	I.T.R.D. (BNA)

District Courts (e.g., D. Mass., S.D.N.Y.): For cases after 1932, cite to F. Supp., F. Supp. 2d, F.R.D., or B.R., if therein; otherwise, cite to Fed. R. Serv., Fed. R. Serv. 2d, or Fed. R. Serv. 3d. For prior cases, cite to F., F.2d, or F. Cas., if therein.

▸ Federal Supplement	1932–date	F. Supp., F. Supp. 2d
▸ Federal Rules Decisions	1938–date	F.R.D.
▸ West's Bankruptcy Reporter	1979–date	B.R.
▸ Federal Rules Service	1938–date	Fed. R. Serv. (Callaghan), Fed. R. Serv. 2d (Callaghan), Fed. R. Serv. 3d (West)
▸ Federal Reporter	1880–1932	F., F.2d
▸ Federal Cases	1789–1880	F. Cas.

Citations to F. Cas. should give the case number parenthetically.

   ▸ *Ex parte* McKean, 16 F. Cas. 186 (E.D. Va. 1878) (No. 8848).

Bankruptcy Courts (e.g., Bankr. N.D. Cal.) and **Bankruptcy Appellate Panels** (e.g., B.A.P. 1st Cir.): Cite to B.R., if therein; otherwise, cite to a service (**rule 19**).

▸ Bankruptcy Reporter	1979–date	B.R.

Judicial Panel on Multidistrict Litigation (J.P.M.L.) (created 1968) and **Special Court, Regional Rail Reorganization Act** (Reg'l Rail Reorg. Ct.) (created 1973): Cite to F. Supp. or F. Supp. 2d.

▸ Federal Supplement	1968–date	F. Supp., F. Supp. 2d

Tax Court (T.C.) (created 1942), previously **Board of Tax Appeals** (B.T.A.): Cite to T.C. or B.T.A., if therein; otherwise, cite to T.C.M. (CCH), T.C.M. (P-H), T.C.M. (RIA), or B.T.A.M. (P-H).

▸ United States Tax Court Reports	1942–date	T.C.
▸ Reports of the United States Board of Tax Appeals	1924–1942	B.T.A.
▸ Tax Court Memorandum Decisions	1942–date 1942–1991 1991–date	T.C.M. (CCH) T.C.M. (P-H) T.C.M. (RIA)
▸ Board of Tax Appeals Memorandum Decisions	1928–1942	B.T.A.M. (P-H)

United States Court of Appeals for Veterans Claims (Vet. App.), previously **United States Court of Veterans Appeals** (Vet. App.) (created 1988): Cite to Vet. App., if therein.

▸ West's Veterans Appeals Reporter	1990–date	Vet. App.

United States Court of Appeals for the Armed Forces (C.A.A.F.), previously **United States Court of Military Appeals** (C.M.A.): Cite to C.M.A., if therein.

▸ Decisions of the United States Court of Military Appeals	1951–1975	C.M.A.
▸ West's Military Justice Reporter	1978–date	M.J.
▸ Court Martial Reports	1951–1975	C.M.R.

Military Service Courts of Criminal Appeals (A. Ct. Crim. App., A.F. Ct. Crim. App., C.G. Ct. Crim. App., N-M. Ct. Crim. App.), previously **Courts of Military Review** (e.g., A.C.M.R.), previously **Boards of Review** (e.g., A.B.R.):

For cases after 1950, cite to **M.J.** or **C.M.R.** For earlier cases, cite to the official reporter.

▸ West's Military Justice Reporter	1975–date	**M.J.**
▸ Court Martial Reports	1951–1975	**C.M.R.**

Statutory compilations: Cite to **U.S.C.**, if therein.

▸ United States Code (26 U.S.C. may be abbreviated as I.R.C.)	‹tit. no.› **U.S.C.** § x (‹year›)
▸ United States Code Annotated	‹tit. no.› **U.S.C.A.** § x (West ‹year›)
▸ United States Code Service	‹tit. no.› **U.S.C.S.** § x (LexisNexis ‹year›)
▸ Gould's United States Code Unannotated	‹tit. no.› **U.S.C.U.** § x (Gould ‹year›)

Session laws

▸ United States Statutes at Large	‹vol. no.› **Stat.** ‹page no.› (‹year›)

(Cite public laws before 1957 by chapter number; cite subsequent acts by public law number.)

T1.2   Federal Administrative and Executive Materials

The following is a non-exclusive table of administrative agency and executive materials, with an emphasis on citation forms that vary from **rule 14**. Where an agency entry only lists that agency's official publications, no unique citation format is used and agency materials can be cited following **rule 14**.

Armed Services Board of Contract Appeals (ASBCA)

Decisions: Cite decisions as: ‹case name›, ASBCA No. ‹decision number›, ‹citation to service›. Note that in citations to the *Board of Contract Appeals Decisions* (BCA), published by Commerce Clearing House, the publisher is not indicated and the volume number serves to indicate the year of the decision.

> ▸ KAMP Sys., Inc., ASBCA No. 55317, 08-1 BCA ¶ 33,748.

Civilian Board of Contract Appeals (CBCA)

Decisions: Cite in the same manner as decisions of the Armed Services Board of Contract Appeals, but include the opposing agency in the case name.

> ▸ Flathead Contractors, LLC v. Dep't of Agric., CBCA 118-R, 07-2 BCA ¶ 33,688.

Department of Agriculture (USDA)

Decisions: Cite to the Agriculture Decisions (Agric. Dec.).

> ▸ Western Cattle Co., 47 Agric. Dec. 992, 1052 (U.S.D.A. 1988).

Directives: Numerous organizations within the USDA issue directives. These should be cited as: ‹issuing agency abbreviated according to table below› Directive ‹directive number›, ‹directive title› (U.S.D.A. ‹year›).

> ▸ FSIS Directive 7160.3, Advanced Meat Recovery Using Beef Vertebral Raw Materials (U.S.D.A. 2002).

▸ Agricultural Marketing Service	AMS
▸ Agricultural Research Service	ARS

- ▸ Animal and Plant Health Inspection Service — APHIS
- ▸ Center for Nutrition Policy and Promotion — CNPP
- ▸ Cooperative State Research, Education, and Extension Service — CSREES
- ▸ Economic Research Service — ERS
- ▸ Farm Service Agency — FSA
- ▸ Food and Nutrition Service — FNS
- ▸ Food Safety and Inspection Service — FSIS
- ▸ Foreign Agricultural Service — FAS
- ▸ Forest Service — FS
- ▸ Grain Inspection, Packers, and Stockyards Administration — GIPSA
- ▸ National Agricultural Library — NAL
- ▸ National Agricultural Statistics Service — NASS
- ▸ National Resources Conservation Service — NRCS
- ▸ Risk Management Agency — RMA
- ▸ Rural Development — RD

Department of Commerce, National Oceanic and
Atmospheric Administration (NOAA)

Decisions in Consistency Appeals Under the Coastal Zone Management Act: Cite decisions of the Secretary of Commerce under the Coastal Zone Management Act as: Decision and Findings in the Consistency Appeal of ‹party name›, from an objection by ‹state or relevant state agency's name› (Sec'y of Commerce ‹date›). To date these decisions are not published in an official reporter; indicate the source where the decision is located.

- ▸ Decision and Findings in the Consistency Appeal of the Va. Elec. and Power Co., from an objection by the N.C. Dep't of Envtl., Health and Natural Res. (Sec'y of Commerce May 19, 1994), http://www.ogc.doc.gov/ogc/czma/vepc.pdf.

Other NOAA Decisions: Cite decisions of administrative law judges in civil administrative law cases to the *Ocean Resources and Wildlife Reporter* (O.R.W.), if therein. Otherwise cite to an appropriate secondary source.

- ▸ J.H. Miles & Co., 4 O.R.W. 223 (NOAA 1985).
- ▸ Rio San Marcos, Inc., 2008 WL 642099 (NOAA Feb. 12, 2008).

Decisions of the Administrator for Appeals (NOAA App.) should so specify.

- ▸ Lars Vinjerud Fisheries, Inc., 6 O.R.W. 210 (NOAA App 1990).

Department of Commerce, Patent and Trademark Office (USPTO)

Decisions: Cite decisions of the Commissioner of Patents to *Decisions of the Commissioner of Patents* (Dec. Comm'r Pat.) following rule 14.3, except that if the party name includes a procedural phrase, it should be included.

- ▸ *Ex parte* Latimer, 1889 Dec. Comm'r Pat. 123.

Cite decisions by the Board of Patent Appeals and Interferences (B.P.A.I.) as: ‹party name›, No. ‹docket number›, ‹citation to secondary source if available› (B.P.A.I. ‹date›).

- ▸ *Ex parte* Baggett, No. 2007-2648 (B.P.A.I. Mar. 10, 2008).
- ▸ *Ex parte* Fallaux, No. 2008-2251, 2008 WL 2463014 (B.P.A.I. June 17, 2008).

Cite decisions of the Trademark Trial and Appeal Board (T.T.A.B.) as: ‹case name›, ‹citation to secondary source› (T.T.A.B. ‹year›).

▶ Bos. Red Sox Baseball Club, Ltd. v. Sherman, 88 U.S.P.Q.2d (BNA) 1581 (T.T.A.B. 2008).

Patents: Cite the patent number and the date the patent was filed.

▶ U.S. Patent No. 4,405,829 (filed Dec. 14, 1977).

The patent name and/or issuing date may be included if relevant.

▶ Cryptographic Commc'ns Sys. & Method, U.S. Patent No. 4,405,829 (filed Dec. 14, 1977) (issued Sept. 20, 1983).

To cite a specific field of the title page, include the field code in brackets.

▶ U.S. Patent No. 4,405,829, at [75] (filed Dec. 14, 1977).

Cite a specific portion of patent text, a patent figure, or an item within a figure according to the following examples:

▶ U.S. Patent No. 4,405,829 col. 2 l. 30 (filed Dec. 14, 1977).
▶ U.S. Patent No. 4,405,829 fig.3 (filed Dec. 14, 1977).
▶ U.S. Patent No. 4,405,829 fig.3, item 22 (filed Dec. 14, 1977).

The short form for a patent includes an apostrophe followed by the last three digits of the patent number.

▶ '829 Patent.

Trademarks: Cite registered trademarks as ‹TRADEMARK NAME›, Registration No. ‹registration number›.

▶ INTERNATIONAL WALKIE TALKIE, Registration No. 3,016,449.

Cite trademarks that have been filed, but not approved, as U.S. Trademark Application Serial No. ‹Serial Number› (filed ‹date›).

▶ U.S. Trademark Application Serial No. 77,341,910 (filed Dec. 1, 2007).

Official Publications:

▶ Official Gazette of the United States Patent Office (1872-1971)	Off. Gaz. Pat. Office
▶ Official Gazette of the United States Patent and Trademark Office (1975-2002)	Off. Gaz. Pat. & Trademark Office
▶ Trademark Manual of Examining Procedure	TMEP (5th ed. Sept. 2007)
▶ Manual of Patent Examining Procedure	MPEP (8th ed. Rev. 7, Sept. 2008)

Nuclear Regulatory Commission (NRC)

Cite decisions of the Nuclear Regulatory Commission to the *Nuclear Regulatory Commission Issuances* (N.R.C.). Cite decisions of its predecessor, the Atomic Energy Commission (1956-1975) to the *Atomic Energy Commission Reports* (A.E.C.).

Department of Homeland Security, Bureau of Customs and Border Protection

The Bureau of Customs and Border Protection and its predecessors have two official reporters: *Administrative Decisions Under Immigration and Nationality Laws* (I. & N. Dec.) and the *Customs Bulletin and Decisions* (Cust. B. & Dec.).

Department of Justice

Advisory Opinions: Cite published, formal advisory opinions in the same manner as adjudications under **rule 14.3**. Cite Attorney General opinions to *Opinions of the Attorneys General* (Op. Att'y Gen.) and opinions from the Office of Legal Counsel to *Opinions of the Office of Legal Counsel of the Department of Justice* (Op. O.L.C.).

- ► Legality of Revised Phila. Plan, 42 Op. Att'y Gen. 405 (1969).
- ► Applicability of Exec. Order No. 12,674 to Pers. of Reg'l Fishery Mgmt. Councils, 17 Op. O.L.C. 150, 154 (1993).

Department of Labor

Decisions in Petition for Modification Cases Under Section 101(c) of the Mine Act, 30 U.S.C. § 811(c): At the time of publication, these decisions were not reported in any official reporter or service. Cite as: ‹description of decision›, ‹case name›, Docket No. ‹docket number› (Dep't of Labor ‹date›).

- ► Administrator's Proposed Decision and Order, RAG Emerald Res., Docket No. 2002-MSA-3 (Dep't of Labor Aug. 6, 2002).
- ► ALJ's Decision and Order, RAG Emerald Res., Docket No. 2002-MSA-3 (Dep't of Labor May 16, 2003).

Decisions in Enforcement Actions Brought by the Office of Federal Contract Compliance Programs: At the time of publication, these decisions were not reported in any official reporter or service. Cite as: ‹case name›, ‹docket number›, ‹description of decision› (Dep't of Labor ‹date›).

- ► OFCCP v. Greenwood Mills, Inc., 89-OFC-39, Secretary's Decision and Order of Remand (Dep't of Labor Nov. 20, 1995).
- ► OFCCP v. S. Pac. Transp. Co., 79-OFC-10A, ALJ's Recommended Decision (Dep't of Labor Nov. 9, 1982).

Decisions by the Benefits Review Board: Cite to a service following **rule 19**.

- ► P.M.N. v. Bajkowski Coal Co., 33 Black Lung Rep. (Juris) 1-10 (Ben. Rev. Bd. 2009).
- ► T.M. v. Reinhalter Shipping Co., 44 Ben. Rev. Bd. Serv. (MB) 21, 23 (2009).

Department of the Interior

Cite agency decisions to *Interior Decisions* (Interior Dec.) or *Interior and General Land Office Cases Relating to Public Lands* (Pub. Lands Dec.), if published therein, as per **rule 14.3**.

Where a board within the agency issues the opinion, note the board in the same parenthetical as the date, using the abbreviations below:

- ► Fortune Oil Co., 90 Interior Dec. 84 (IBLA 1983).

► Interior Board of Land Appeals	IBLA
► Interior Board of Indian Appeals	IBIA
► Interior Board of Contract Appeals	IBCA

Department of the Treasury

Regulations: Although Department of Treasury regulations are published under title 26 of the C.F.R., cite as ‹**Treas. Reg.**›. For unamended regulations, cite to the year of promulgation. If the regulation is a temporary regulation, indicate such:

▶ Treas. Reg. § 1.72-16(a) (1963).

▶ Temp. Treas. Reg. § 1.338-4T(k) (1985).

Citations to specific questions and answers should be cited as:

▶ Treas. Reg. § 1.72-16(a), Q&A (3)(a) (1963).

If any subsection of the cited section has been amended or for some other reason appears in substantially different versions, give the year of the last amendment. Follow this form even if the particular subsection cited has never been amended.

▶ Treas. Reg. § 1.61-2(c) (as amended in 1995).

When the source of the amendment is relevant, indicate it.

▶ Treas. Reg. § 1.61-2(c) (as amended by T.D. 8607, 1995-36 I.R.B. 8).

Cite proposed Treasury regulations to the *Federal Register*.

▶ Prop. Treas. Reg. § 1.704-1, 48 Fed. Reg. 9871, 9872 (Mar. 9, 1983).

Treasury Determinations: Cite Revenue Rulings, Revenue Procedures, and Treasury Decisions to the *Cumulative Bulletin* (C.B.) or its advance sheet, the *Internal Revenue Bulletin* (I.R.B.), or to *Treasury Decisions Under Internal Revenue Laws* (Treas. Dec. Int. Rev.), in that order of preference.

▶ Rev. Rul. 83-137, 1983-2 C.B. 41.

▶ Rev. Proc. 85-47, 1985-37 I.R.B. 10.

▶ T.D. 2747, 20 Treas. Dec. Int. Rev. 457 (1918).

The *Cumulative Bulletin* has been numbered in three series: by volume number from 1919 to 1921, by volume number and part number from 1921 to 1936, and by year and part number from 1937 to date.

▶ T.B.R. 29, 1 C.B. 230 (1919).

▶ I.T. 2624, 11-1 C.B. 122 (1932).

▶ T.D. 7522, 1978-1 C.B. 59.

The abbreviations used in the above examples and other abbreviations are explained in the introductory pages of each volume of the *Cumulative Bulletin*.

Private Letter Rulings: Cite by number and the date issued, if available.

▶ I.R.S. Priv. Ltr. Rul. 86-01-012 (Sept. 30, 1985).

Technical Advice Memoranda: Cite by number and the date issued, if available.

▶ I.R.S. Tech. Adv. Mem. 85-04-005 (Sept. 28, 1984).

General Counsel Memoranda: Cite by number and the date on which the memorandum was approved.

▶ I.R.S. Gen. Couns. Mem. 39,417 (Sept. 30, 1985).

Other Treasury Determinations: Cite all other Treasury materials, including Delegation Orders (Deleg. Order), Treasury Orders (Treas. Order), Treasury Directives (Treas. Dir.), Notices, Announcements, and News Releases to the *Cumulative Bulletin*, *Internal Revenue Bulletin*, or *Internal Revenue Manual* (IRM), if therein. Otherwise cite by number and date issued.

▶ I.R.S. Deleg. Order 1-35 (Rev. 1), IRM 1.2.40.17 (June 19, 2008).

▶ I.R.S. Notice 84-9, 1984-1 C.B. 341.

▶ I.R.S. News Release IR-84-111 (Oct. 19, 1984).

Cases: Cite the names of Tax Court and Board of Tax Appeals decisions as those of a court (rule 10.2), not as those of an agency.

▶ Benson v. Comm'r, 80 T.C. 789 (1983).

▶ Price v. Comm'r, 46 T.C.M. (CCH) 657 (1983).

If the Commissioner of the Internal Revenue Service has published an acquiescence (*acq.*), acquiescence in result only (*acq. in result*), or nonacquiescence (*nonacq.*) in a decision of the Tax Court or Board of Tax Appeals, that fact may be indicated in the citation of the case.

▶ N.M. Bancorp. v. Comm'r, 74 T.C. 1342 (1980), *acq. in result*, 1983-2 C.B. 1.

Similarly, an action on decision (*action on dec.*) may be cited as subsequent history by appending its identifying number, if any, and its full date.

▶ Keller v. Comm'r, 79 T.C. 7 (1982), *action on dec.*, 1984-037 (Apr. 23, 1984).

See generally rule 10.7 (prior and subsequent history of cases).

Environmental Protection Agency (EPA)

Decisions: Cite decisions to *Environmental Administrative Decisions* (E.A.D.), if therein. Indicate whether the Environmental Appeals Board (EAB) or an administrative law judge made the decision, if not obvious from the source.

▶ Solutia, Inc., 10 E.A.D. 193, 214 (EAB 2001)

▶ Geron Furniture, Inc., 1994 EPA ALJ LEXIS 53.

Equal Employment Opportunity Commission (EEOC)

Decisions: Most EEOC decisions do not have readily identifiable titles, and should therefore be cited using the decision number in place of the title, and otherwise per rule 14.3.

▶ EEOC Decision No. 71-24444, 4 Fair Empl. Prac. Cas. (BNA) 18 (1971).

EEOC Federal Sector decisions have party names and should therefore be cited in accordance with rule 14.3.

Executive Office of the President

Executive Orders, Presidential Proclamations, and Reorganization Plans: Cite by page number to 3 C.F.R. as per rule 14.2 except that, because all executive orders are not reprinted in successive years of the C.F.R., the original year of promulgation, rather than the most recent edition of the C.F.R., must be cited. Append a parallel citation to the U.S.C. if also therein.

▶ Exec. Order No. 11,609, 3 C.F.R. § 586 (1971–1975), *reprinted as amended in* 3 U.S.C. § 301 app. at 404–07 (2006).

Cite to the *Federal Register* if the material is not in the C.F.R.

▶ Proclamation No. 5366, 50 Fed. Reg. 37,635 (Sept. 14, 1985).

A parallel citation to the *Statutes at Large* may also be given.

▶ Reorganization Plan No. 1 of 1978, 3 C.F.R. 321 (1978), *reprinted in* 5 U.S.C. app. at 1366 (2006), *and in* 92 Stat. 3781 (1978).

Other Presidential Papers: Cite to the *Public Papers of the Presidents* (PUB. PAPERS) if therein. For material not recorded in the *Public Papers*, cite the *Weekly Compilation of Presidential Documents* (WEEKLY COMP. PRES. DOC.), published from 1965 to January 29, 2009, the *Daily Compilation of Presidential Documents* (DAILY COMP. PRES. DOC.), published from January 29, 2009 to date, or the *U.S. Code Congressional and Administrative News* (U.S.C.C.A.N.) (**rule 12.6**).

▶ Memorandum on New Tools To Help Parents Balance Work and Family, 1 PUB. PAPERS 841 (May 24, 1999).

▶ Presidential Statement on Signing the Consolidated Appropriations Resolution 2003, 39 WEEKLY COMP. PRES. DOC. 225 (Feb. 20, 2003).

▶ Remarks on the National Economy, 2009 DAILY COMP. PRES. DOC. 2 (Feb. 4, 2009).

Budgets: Cite governmental budgets as books (**rule 15**).

▶ OFFICE OF MGMT. & BUDGET, EXEC. OFFICE OF THE PRESIDENT, BUDGET OF THE UNITED STATES GOVERNMENT, FISCAL YEAR 2003 (2002).

Federal Aviation Administration (FAA)

Decisions: Cite decisions of administrative law judges in civil penalty enforcement matters adjudicated under 14 C.F.R. Part 13, Section 13.16 and subpart G, as slip opinions following **rule 14.3.2(b)**.

▶ Siddall, Docket No. CP05WP0016 (FAA Oct. 7, 2008).

Decisions of the Administrator or his delegate are cited using an order number rather than a docket number.

▶ Alaska Airlines, Inc., FAA Order No. 2004-8, 2004 WL 319820 (Oct. 4, 2004).

Decisions of the Office of Dispute Resolution for Acquisition (ODRA) adjudicated under 14 C.F.R. Part 17 should incorporate the type of dispute in the citation.

▶ Protest of the United Parcel Service, Docket No. 08-ODRA-0400 (Sept. 12, 1999).

Citations to other FAA decisions and orders should indicate the nature of the decision preceding the date.

▶ Paul D. Asmus & P.D. Aviation Consulting v. Haw. Dep't of Transp., Docket No. 16-05-11, Determination of the Director of Compliance and Field Operations (Apr. 12, 2006).

▶ Steere v. County of San Diego, FAA Docket No. 16-99-15, Final Agency Decision (Dec. 7, 2004).

Federal Communications Commission (FCC)

Cite to the *Federal Communications Commission Reports* (F.C.C., F.C.C.2d), published 1934–1986, or the *Federal Communications Commission Record* (FCC Rcd.), published since 1986.

Federal Energy Regulatory Commission (FERC)

Cite decisions to the *Federal Energy Guidelines: FERC Reports* (FERC).

Federal Labor Relations Authority (FLRA)

Cite decisions to the *Decisions of the Federal Labor Relations Authority* (F.L.R.A.).

Federal Mine Safety and Health Review Commission (FMSHRC)

Cite decisions to the *Federal Mine Safety and Health Review Commission Decisions* (FMSHRC).

Federal Reserve System

Enforcement Actions: Cite written agreements resulting from enforcement actions as: Written Agreement between ‹private bank name› and ‹Federal Reserve Bank name›, Docket no. ‹docket number› (‹date›).

▸ Written Agreement Between Ridgedale State Bank and Federal Reserve Bank of Minneapolis, Docket No. 03-024-WA/RB-SM (July 29, 2003).

Federal Trade Commission (FTC)

Cite decisions to the *Federal Trade Commission* (F.T.C.).

Government Accountability Office (GAO)

Bid Protest Decisions: Cite to *Decisions of the Comptroller General of the United States* (Comp. Gen.), if therein.

▸ Astrophysics Research Corp., 66 Comp. Gen. 211 (1987).

Cite unpublished decisions to a readily accessible source, as follows: ‹protesting party›, ‹docket number›, ‹volume number or year› ‹source› ‹location within source volume or year› (Comp. Gen. ‹date›). Note that when citing these cases to the *Comptroller General's Procurement Decisions*, published by West, the publisher is not indicated:

▸ Def. Sys. Group, B-240295, 1990 WL 293536 (Comp. Gen. Nov. 6, 1990).
▸ Info. Ventures, Inc., B-232094, 88-2 CPD ¶ 443 (Comp. Gen. Nov. 4, 1988).

Where a decision resolves multiple bid protests, each of which has its own docket number, indicate this by inserting "*et al.*" after the docket number.

▸ Midland Supply, Inc., B-298720 *et al.*, 2007 CPD ¶ 2 (Comp. Gen. Nov. 29, 2006).

International Trade Commission (USITC)

Trade Remedy Investigations: Cite as: ‹investigation name›, Inv. No. ‹number›, USITC Pub. ‹number› (‹date›) (‹status›). Where a single decision contains multiple investigation numbers, this should be indicated.

▸ Certain Tissue Paper Prods. from China, Inv. No. 731-TA-1070B, USITC Pub. 3758 (Mar. 25, 2005) (Final).
▸ Grain-Oriented Elec. Steel from It. & Japan, Inv. Nos. 701-TA-355, 731-TA-659-660, USITC Pub. 3396 (Feb. 7, 2001) (Preliminary).

Merit Systems Protection Board (MSPB)

Cite decisions to the *Decisions of the United States Merit Systems Protection Board* (M.S.P.R.).

National Labor Relations Board (NLRB)

Cite decisions and orders to the *Decisions and Orders of the National Labor Relations Board* (N.L.R.B.).

National Mediation Board (NMB)

Cite decisions to the *Decisions of the National Mediation Board* (N.M.B.).

National Transportation Safety Board (NTSB)

Cite decisions to the *National Transportation Safety Board Decisions* (N.T.S.B.), published from 1967–1977, if therein.

Occupational Safety and Health Review Commission (OSHRC)

Decisions: Cite commission decisions reported in a service as: ‹party name›, ‹service volume number› ‹publisher› ‹service, abbreviated as below› ‹page/paragraph number› (No. ‹docket number›, ‹year›).

▶ Burkes Mech., Inc., 21 BNA OSHC 2136 (No. 04-0475, 2007).

or: Burkes Mech., Inc., 2007 CCH OSHD ¶ 32,922 (No. 04-0475, 2007).

Where an administrative law judge, rather than the commission itself, issued the decision, indicate this parenthetically at the end of the citation.

▶ Pike Elec., Inc., 21 BNA OSHC 2153 (No. 06-0166, 2007) (ALJ).

OSHRC uses abbreviations for services reporting its decisions that vary from table T15:

▶ Occupational Safety & Health Cases (BNA)   OSHC
▶ Occupational Safety & Health Decisions   OSHD

Where a decision is not cited in any service or database, it may be cited as a slip opinion using rule 14.3.2(b).

▶ Z & P Builders, No. 08-0930 (OSHRC Dec. 19, 2008).

Securities and Exchange Commission (SEC)

Interpretive Letters, No-Action Letters, and Exemptive Letters: Cite a service (rule 19) or an electronic database (rule 18.3). Include the full name of the correspondent and the full date on which the letter became publicly available.

▶ Union Carbide Corp., SEC No-Action Letter, [1994–1995 Transfer Binder] Fed. Sec. L. Rep. (CCH) ¶ 76,911 (Apr. 15, 1994).

▶ Squadron, Ellenoff, Plesent & Lehrer, SEC Interpretive Letter, 1992 WL 55818 (Feb. 28, 1992).

Releases: Cite the *Federal Register*, SEC Docket, or a service (rule 19). If the release has a subject-matter title, it may be presented in a shortened form. Include the act under which the release was issued, the release number, and the full date.

▶ Customer Limit Orders, Exchange Act Release No. 34,753, [1994-1995 Transfer Binder] Fed. Sec. L. Rep. (CCH) ¶ 85,434 (Sept. 29, 1994).

▶ Regulation of Securityholder Communications, Exchange Act Release No. 29,315, 49 SEC Docket 147 (June 17, 1991).

If the release is an adjudication, abbreviate the parties' names according to rule 14.3.1(a).

▶ Am. Kiosk Corp., Exchange Act Release No. 58504, 2008 WL 2574438 (June 27, 2008).

If the adjudication occurred before an administrative law judge, indicate this fact in the date parenthetical.

▶ Am. Kiosk Corp., Exchange Act Release No. 57866, 2008 WL 2229644 (ALJ May 30, 2008) (default order).

If a particular release is issued under the Securities Act, the Exchange Act, or the Investment Company Act, a parallel citation should be given in that order.

▶ Implementation of Standards of Professional Conduct for Attorneys, Securities Act Release No. 8150, Exchange Act Release No. 46,868, Investment Company Act Release No. 25,829, 67 Fed. Reg. 71,670 (proposed Dec. 2, 2002).

Staff Interpretations: Cite SEC Staff Accounting Bulletins, Staff Legal Bulletins, and Telephone Interpretations as follows:

▶ SEC Staff Accounting Bulletin No. 56, 49 Fed. Reg. 4936 (May 23, 1984).

SEC Filings: For annual reports, proxy statements, and other company filings required under federal securities laws, provide the name of the company (abbreviated according to rule 15.1(d)), the title as given in the document, the form type in parentheses, the page number if applicable, and the full date of filing with the SEC.

▶ Coca-Cola Co., Annual Report (Form 10-K) (Feb. 27, 2004).
▶ Sony Music Entm't Inc., Statement of Changes in Beneficial Ownership (Form 4/A) (Jan. 23, 2004).

If citing annual reports, proxy statements, or other documents in a form other than that filed with the SEC, treat as books under rule 15.

▶ COCA-COLA CO., 2003 SUMMARY ANNUAL REPORT 7 (2004).

Small Business Administration (SBA)

Decisions: Cite decisions as: ‹party name›, SBA No. ‹docket number› (‹date›).

▶ Ace Technical, LLC, SBA No. SDBA-178 (Apr. 17, 2008).

The docket number indicates the type of decision:

▶ Small disadvantaged business	SDBA
▶ Size determination	SIZ
▶ Service disabled veteran owned business	VET
▶ Business development program	BDP
▶ North American Industry Classification System	NAICS

Social Security Administration (SSA)

Rulings and Acquiescence Rulings: Cite to the *Social Security Rulings, Cumulative Edition* (S.S.R. Cum. Ed.), if therein. If not located therein, cite to another official source, such as the *Code of Federal Regulations* or the *Federal Register*. Otherwise, cite a commercial database or other readily available source. Cite Social Security Rulings as SSR and Social Security Acquiescence Rulings as SSAR.

▶ SSAR 92-2(6), 57 Fed. Reg. 9262 (Mar. 17, 1992).
▶ SSR 00-4p, 2000 WL 1898704 (Dec. 4, 2000).

Surface Transportation Board (STB)

Cite materials from the Surface Transportation Board to the *Surface Transportation Board Reporter* (S.T.B.). Cite materials from its predecessor, the Interstate Commerce Commission (ICC), to the *Interstate Commerce Commission Reporter* (I.C.C., I.C.C. 2d).

For unpublished decisions, the official date is the date on which the STB (or ICC) served the decision on the parties or otherwise filed it, not the date of the decision itself.

T1.3   States and the District of Columbia

Alabama (AL)

http://www.judicial.state.al.us

Supreme Court (Ala.): Cite to So., So. 2d, or So. 3d, if therein.

▶ Southern Reporter	1886–date	So., So. 2d, So. 3d
▶ Alabama Reports	1840–1976	Ala.
▶ Porter	1834–1839	Port.
▶ Stewart and Porter	1831–1834	Stew. & P.
▶ Stewart	1827–1831	Stew.
▶ Minor	1820–1826	Minor

Court of Civil Appeals (Ala. Civ. App.) and **Court of Criminal Appeals** (Ala. Crim. App.), before 1969 **Court of Appeals** (Ala. Ct. App.): Cite to So., So. 2d, or So. 3d, if therein.

▶ Southern Reporter	1911–date	So., So. 2d, So. 3d
▶ Alabama Appellate Courts Reports	1911–1974	Ala. App.

Statutory compilations: Cite to ALA. CODE (published by West), if therein.

▶ Code of Alabama, 1975 (West)	ALA. CODE § x-x-x (‹year›)
▶ Michie's Alabama Code, 1975 (LexisNexis)	ALA. CODE § x-x-x (LexisNexis ‹year›)

Session laws: Cite to Ala. Laws, if therein.

▶ Alabama Laws	‹year› Ala. Laws ‹page no.›
▶ West's Alabama Legislative Service	‹year› Ala. Legis. Serv. ‹page no.› (West)
▶ Michie's Alabama Code ‹year› Advance Legislative Service (LexisNexis)	‹year›-‹pamph. no.› Ala. Adv. Legis. Serv. ‹page no.› (LexisNexis)

Administrative compilation
- Alabama Administrative Code   ALA. ADMIN. CODE r. x-x-x.x (‹year›)

Administrative register
- Alabama Administrative Monthly   ‹vol. no.› Ala. Admin. Monthly
                                       ‹page no.› (‹month day, year›)

....

Alaska (AK)

http://www.state.ak.us/courts

Supreme Court (Alaska): Cite to P.2d or P.3d.
- Pacific Reporter   1960–date   P.2d, P.3d

Court of Appeals (Alaska Ct. App.): Cite to P.2d or P.3d.
- Pacific Reporter   1980–date   P.2d, P.3d

District Courts of Alaska (D. Alaska): These courts had local jurisdiction from 1884 to 1959. Cite to F. Supp., F., or F.2d, if therein; otherwise, cite to Alaska or Alaska Fed., in that order of preference.
- Federal Supplement   1946–1959   F. Supp.
- Federal Reporter   1886–1932   F., F.2d
- Alaska Reports   1887–1958   Alaska
- Alaska Federal Reports   1869–1937   Alaska Fed.

United States District Courts for California and Oregon, and **District Courts of Washington** (D. Cal., D. Or., D. Wash.): These courts had local jurisdiction in Alaska until 1884. Cite to F. or F. Cas.
- Federal Reporter   1880–1884   F.
- Federal Cases   1867–1880   F. Cas.

(Citations to F. Cas. should give the case number parenthetically. e.g., The Ocean Spray, 18 F. Cas. 558 (D. Or. 1876) (No. 10,412).)
- Alaska Federal Reports   1869–1937   Alaska Fed.

Statutory compilations: Cite to ALASKA STAT., if therein.
- Alaska Statutes (LexisNexis)   ALASKA STAT. § x.x.x (‹year›)
- West's Alaska Statutes Annotated   ALASKA STAT. ANN. § x.x.x (West ‹year›)

Session laws: Cite to Alaska Sess. Laws, if therein.
- Session Laws of Alaska   ‹year› Alaska Sess. Laws ‹page no.›
- Alaska Statutes ‹year› Advance   ‹year›-‹pamph. no.› Alaska Adv. Legis.
  Legislative Service (LexisNexis)   Serv. ‹page no.› (LexisNexis)
- West's Alaska Legislative Service   ‹year› Alaska Legis. Serv. ‹page no.›
                                       (West)

Administrative compilation
- Alaska Administrative Code   ALASKA ADMIN. CODE tit. x, § x.x
  (LexisNexis)   (‹year›)

Arizona (AZ)

http://www.supreme.state.az.us

Supreme Court (Ariz.): Cite to P., P.2d, or P.3d, if therein.
- ► Pacific Reporter   1883-date   P., P.2d, P.3d
- ► Arizona Reports   1866-date   Ariz.

Court of Appeals (Ariz. Ct. App.): Cite to P.2d or P.3d, if therein.
- ► Pacific Reporter   1965-date   P.2d, P.3d
- ► Arizona Reports   1976-date   Ariz.
- ► Arizona Appeals Reports   1965-1977   Ariz. App.

Tax Court (Ariz. Tax Ct.): Cite to P.2d or P.3d, if therein.
- ► Pacific Reporter   1988-date   P.2d, P.3d

Statutory compilations: Cite to ARIZ. REV. STAT. ANN., if therein.
- ► Arizona Revised Statutes Annotated   ARIZ. REV. STAT. ANN. § x-x (‹year›)
  (West)
- ► Arizona Revised Statutes (LexisNexis) ARIZ. REV. STAT. § x-x (LexisNexis ‹year›)

Session laws: Cite to ARIZ. SESS. LAWS, if therein.
- ► Session Laws, Arizona   ‹year› Ariz. Sess. Laws ‹page no.›
- ► Arizona Legislative Service (West)   ‹year› Ariz. Legis. Serv. ‹page no.›
  (West)

Administrative compilation
- ► Arizona Administrative Code   ARIZ. ADMIN. CODE § x-x-x (‹year›)

Administrative register
- ► Arizona Administrative Register   ‹vol. no.› Ariz. Admin. Reg. ‹page no.› (‹month day, year›)

Arkansas (AR)

http://www.courts.state.ar.us

Public domain citation format: Arkansas has adopted a public domain citation format for cases after February 13, 2009. The format is:
- ► Smith v. Hickman, 2009 Ark. 12, at 1, 273 S.W.3d 340, 343.
- ► Doe v. State, 2009 Ark. App. 318, at 7, 2009 WL 240613, at *8.

For additional instruction, consult Arkansas Supreme Court Rule 5-2.

Supreme Court (Ark.): Cite to S.W., S.W.2d, or S.W.3d, if therein.
- ► South Western Reporter   1886-date   S.W., S.W.2d, or S.W.3d
- ► Arkansas Reports   1837-2009   Ark.

Court of Appeals (Ark. Ct. App.): Cite to S.W.2d or S.W.3d, if therein.
- ► South Western Reporter   1979-date   S.W.2d, S.W.3d
- ► Arkansas Appellate Reports   1981-2009   Ark. App.
- ► Arkansas Reports   1979-1981   Ark.

Statutory compilations: Cite to ARK. CODE ANN. (published by LexisNexis), if therein.

- ▸ Arkansas Code of 1987 Annotated (LexisNexis) — ARK. CODE ANN. § x-x-x (‹year›)
- ▸ West's Arkansas Code Annotated — ARK. CODE ANN. § x-x-x (West ‹year›)

Session laws: Cite to Ark. Acts, if therein.

- ▸ Acts of Arkansas (West) — ‹year› Ark. Acts ‹page no.›
- ▸ Arkansas Code of 1987 Annotated ‹year› Advance Legislative Service (LexisNexis) — ‹year›-‹pamph. no.› Ark. Adv. Legis. Serv. ‹page no.› (LexisNexis)
- ▸ West's Arkansas Legislative Service — ‹year› Ark. Legis. Serv. ‹page no.› (West)

Administrative compilation

- ▸ Code of Arkansas Rules (LexisNexis) — x-x-x ARK. CODE R. § x (LexisNexis ‹year›)

Administrative registers: Cite to Ark. Reg., if therein.

- ▸ Arkansas Register — ‹vol. no.› Ark. Reg. ‹page no.› (‹month year›)
- ▸ Arkansas Government Register — ‹iss. no.› Ark. Gov't Reg. ‹page no.› (LexisNexis ‹month year›)

California (CA)
http://www.courtinfo.ca.gov

Supreme Court (Cal.): Cite to P., P.2d, or P.3d, if therein.

- ▸ Pacific Reporter — 1883–date — P., P.2d, P.3d
- ▸ California Reports — 1850–date — Cal., Cal. 2d, Cal. 3d, Cal. 4th
- ▸ West's California Reporter — 1959–date — Cal. Rptr., Cal. Rptr. 2d, Cal. Rptr. 3d
- ▸ California Unreported Cases — 1855–1910 — Cal. Unrep.

Court of Appeal (Cal. Ct. App.), previously **District Court of Appeal** (Cal. Dist. Ct. App.): Cite to P. or P.2d (before 1960) or Cal. Rptr., Cal. Rptr. 2d, or Cal. Rptr. 3d (after 1959), if therein.

- ▸ West's California Reporter — 1959–date — Cal. Rptr., Cal. Rptr. 2d, Cal. Rptr. 3d
- ▸ Pacific Reporter — 1905–1959 — P., P.2d
- ▸ California Appellate Reports — 1905–date — Cal. App., Cal. App. 2d, Cal. App. 3d, Cal. App. 4th

Appellate Divisions of the Superior Court (Cal. App. Dep't Super. Ct.): Cite to P. or P.2d (before 1960) or to Cal. Rptr., Cal. Rptr. 2d, or Cal. Rptr. 3d (after 1959), if therein.

- ▸ West's California Reporter — 1959–date — Cal. Rptr., Cal. Rptr. 2d, Cal. Rptr. 3d
- ▸ Pacific Reporter — 1929–1959 — P., P.2d
- ▸ California Appellate Reports Supplement (bound with Cal. App.) — 1929–date — Cal. App. Supp., Cal. App. 2d Supp., Cal. App. 3d Supp., Cal. App. 4th Supp.

Statutory compilations: Cite to either the West or the Deering subject-matter code, if therein.

▸ West's Annotated California Codes   Cal. ‹Subject› Code § x (West ‹year›)

▸ Deering's California Codes,   Cal. ‹Subject› Code § x (Deering ‹year›)
    Annotated (LexisNexis)

▸ Agricultural (renamed   Agric.
    "Food and Agricultural" in 1972)

▸ Business and Professions   Bus. & Prof.

▸ Civil   Civ.

▸ Civil Procedure   Civ. Proc.

▸ Commercial   Com.

▸ Corporations   Corp.

▸ Education   Educ.

▸ Elections   Elec.

▸ Evidence   Evid.

▸ Family   Fam.

▸ Financial   Fin.

▸ Fish and Game   Fish & Game

▸ Food and Agricultural   Food & Agric.
    (formerly "Agricultural")

▸ Government   Gov't

▸ Harbors and Navigation   Harb. & Nav.

▸ Health and Safety   Health & Safety

▸ Insurance   Ins.

▸ Labor   Lab.

▸ Military and Veterans   Mil. & Vet.

▸ Penal   Penal

▸ Probate   Prob.

▸ Public Contract   Pub. Cont.

▸ Public Resources   Pub. Res.

▸ Public Utilities   Pub. Util.

▸ Revenue and Taxation   Rev. & Tax.

▸ Streets and Highways   Sts. & High.

▸ Unemployment Insurance   Unemp. Ins.

▸ Vehicle   Veh.

▸ Water   Water

▸ Welfare and Institutions   Welf. & Inst.

Session laws: Cite to Cal. Stat., if therein.

▸ Statutes of California   ‹year› Cal. Stat. ‹page no.›

▸ West's California Legislative Service   ‹year› Cal. Legis. Serv. ‹page no.› (West)

▸ Deering's California Advance   ‹year›-‹pamph. no.› Cal. Adv. Legis.
    Legislative Service (LexisNexis)   Serv. ‹page no.› (LexisNexis)

Administrative compilation

▸ California Code of Regulations   Cal. Code Regs. tit. x, § x (‹year›)
    (West)

Administrative register

▸ California Regulatory Notice   ‹iss. no.› Cal. Regulatory Notice Reg.
    Register   ‹page no.› (‹month day, year›)

Colorado (CO)

http://www.courts.state.co.us

Supreme Court (Colo.): Cite to P., P.2d, or P.3d, if therein; otherwise, cite to Colo., if therein, or to Colo. Law. or Brief Times Rptr.

▸ Pacific Reporter	1883–date	P., P.2d, P.3d
▸ Colorado Reports	1864–1980	Colo.
▸ Colorado Lawyer	1972–date	Colo. Law.
▸ Brief Times Reporter	1977–1996	Brief Times Rptr.
▸ Colorado Journal	1996–2002	Colo. J.
▸ Law Week Colorado	2002–date	L. Week Colo.

Court of Appeals (Colo. App.): Cite to P., P.2d, or P.3d, if therein; otherwise, cite to Colo. App., if therein, or else to one of the other reporters listed below.

▸ Pacific Reporter	1970–date	P.2d, P.3d
	1912–1915	P.
	1891–1905	P.
▸ Colorado Court of Appeals Reports	1891–1905	Colo. App.
	1912–1915	Colo. App.
	1970–1980	Colo. App.
▸ Colorado Lawyer	1972–date	Colo. Law.
▸ Brief Times Reporter	1977–1996	Brief Times Rptr.
▸ Colorado Journal	1996–2002	Colo. J.
▸ Law Week Colorado	2002–date	L. Week Colo.

Statutory compilations: Cite to COLO. REV. STAT., if therein.

▸ Colorado Revised Statutes (LexisNexis)	COLO. REV. STAT. § x-x-x ‹year›
▸ West's Colorado Revised Statutes Annotated	COLO. REV. STAT. ANN. § x-x-x (West ‹year›)

Session laws: Cite to Colo. Sess. Laws, if therein.

▸ Session Laws of Colorado (LexisNexis)	‹year› Colo. Sess. Laws ‹page no.›
▸ Colorado Legislative Service (West)	‹year› Colo. Legis. Serv. ‹page no.› (West)

Administrative compilations: Cite to COLO. CODE REGS., if therein.

▸ Colorado Code of Regulations http://www.sos.state.co.us/CCR/Welcome.do	COLO. CODE REGS. § x-x ‹year›
▸ Code of Colorado Regulations (LexisNexis)	‹vol. no.› COLO. CODE REGS. § x-x (LexisNexis ‹year›)

Administrative register

▸ Colorado Register	‹iss. no.› Colo. Reg. ‹page no.› (‹month year›)

....

Connecticut (CT)

http://www.jud.state.ct.us

Supreme Court (Conn.), previously **Supreme Court of Errors** (Conn.): Cite to A., A.2d, or A.3d, if therein.

▸ Atlantic Reporter	1885-date	A., A.2d, A.3d
▸ Connecticut Reports	1814-date	Conn.
▸ Day	1802-1813	Day
▸ Root	1789-1798	Root
▸ Kirby	1785-1789	Kirby

Appellate Court (Conn. App. Ct.): Cite to A.2d or A.3d, if therein.

▸ Atlantic Reporter	1983-date	A.2d, A.3d
▸ Connecticut Appellate Reports	1983-date	Conn. App.

Superior Court (Conn. Super. Ct.) and **Court of Common Pleas** (Conn. C.P.): Cite to A.2d or A.3d, if therein; otherwise, cite to Conn. Supp., if therein, or else to one of the other reporters listed below.

▸ Atlantic Reporter	1954-date	A.2d, A.3d
▸ Connecticut Supplement	1935-date	Conn. Supp.
▸ Connecticut Law Reporter	1990-date	Conn. L. Rptr.
▸ Connecticut Superior Court Reports	1986-1994	Conn. Super. Ct.

Circuit Court (Conn. Cir. Ct.): Cite to A.2d or A.3d, if therein.

▸ Atlantic Reporter	1961-1974	A.2d, A.3d
▸ Connecticut Circuit Court Reports	1961-1974	Conn. Cir. Ct.

Statutory compilations: Cite to CONN. GEN. STAT., if therein.

▸ General Statutes of Connecticut	CONN. GEN. STAT. § x-x (‹year›)
▸ Connecticut General Statutes Annotated (West)	CONN. GEN. STAT. ANN. § x-x (West ‹year›)

Session laws: Cite to Conn. Acts, Conn. Pub. Acts, or Conn. Spec. Acts, if therein.

▸ Connecticut Public & Special Acts	1972-date	‹year› Conn. Acts ‹page no.› ([Reg. or Spec.] Sess.)
▸ Connecticut Public Acts	1650-1971	‹year› Conn. Pub. Acts ‹page no.›
▸ Connecticut Special Acts	1789-1971	‹year› Conn. Spec. Acts ‹page no.›

(published under various titles—i.e., Resolves & Private Laws, Private & Special Laws, Special Laws, Resolves & Private Acts, Resolutions & Private Acts, Private Acts & Resolutions, and Special Acts & Resolutions—and with various volume designations—i.e., by year or volume number)

▸ Connecticut Legislative Service (West)	‹year› Conn. Legis. Serv. ‹page no.› (West)

Administrative compilation

▸ Regulations of Connecticut State Agencies	CONN. AGENCIES REGS. § x-x-x (‹year›)

Administrative registers: Cite to Conn. L.J., if therein.

▸ Connecticut Law Journal	‹vol. no.› Conn. L.J. ‹page no.› (‹month day, year›)

▸ Connecticut Government   ‹iss. no.› Conn. Gov't Reg. ‹page no.›
  Register (LexisNexis)   (LexisNexis ‹month year›)

....

Delaware (DE)

http://www.courts.state.de.us

Supreme Court (Del.), previously **Court of Errors and Appeals** (Del.): Cite to A., A.2d, or A.3d, if therein.

▸ Atlantic Reporter	1886-date	A., A.2d, A.3d
▸ Delaware Reports		
▸ 31 Del. to 59 Del.	1919-1966	Del.
▸ Boyce	1909-1920	e.g., 24 Del. (1 Boyce)
▸ Pennewill	1897-1909	e.g., 17 Del. (1 Penne.)
▸ Marvel	1893-1897	e.g., 15 Del. (1 Marv.)
▸ Houston	1855-1893	e.g., 6 Del. (1 Houst.)
▸ Harrington	1832-1855	e.g., 1 Del. (1 Harr.)
▸ Delaware Cases	1792-1830	Del. Cas.

Court of Chancery (Del. Ch.): Cite to A., A.2d, or A.3d, if therein.

▸ Atlantic Reporter	1886-date	A., A.2d, A.3d
▸ Delaware Chancery Reports	1814-1968	Del. Ch.
▸ Delaware Cases	1792-1830	Del. Cas.

Superior Court (Del. Super. Ct.), previously **Superior Court and Orphans' Court** (Del. Super. Ct. & Orphans' Ct.): Cite to A.2d or A.3d, if therein; otherwise, cite to one of the official reporters listed under Supreme Court.

▸ Atlantic Reporter	1951-date	A.2d, A.3d

Family Court (Del. Fam. Ct.): Cite to A.2d or A.3d.

▸ Atlantic Reporter	1977-date	A.2d, A.3d

Statutory compilations: Cite to DEL. CODE ANN., if therein.

▸ Delaware Code Annotated (LexisNexis)	DEL. CODE ANN. tit. x, § x (‹year›)
▸ West's Delaware Code Annotated	DEL. CODE ANN. tit. x, § x (West ‹year›)

Session laws: Cite to Del. Laws, if therein.

▸ Laws of Delaware	‹vol. no.› Del. Laws ‹page no.› (‹year›)
▸ Delaware Code Annotated ‹year› Advance Legislative Service (LexisNexis)	‹year›-‹pamph. no.› Del. Code. Ann. Adv. Legis. Serv. ‹page no.› (Lexis-Nexis)
▸ West's Delaware Legislative Service	‹year› Del. Legis. Serv. ‹page no.› (West)

Administrative compilations: Cite to DEL. ADMIN. CODE, if therein.

▸ Delaware Administrative Code	x-x-x DEL. ADMIN. CODE § x (‹year›)
▸ Code of Delaware Regulations (LexisNexis)	x-x-x DEL. CODE REGS. § x (LexisNexis ‹year›)

Administrative registers: Cite to Del. Reg. Regs., if therein.

▸ Delaware Register of Regulations	‹vol. no.› Del. Reg. Regs. ‹page no.› (‹month day, year›)
▸ Delaware Government Register (LexisNexis)	‹iss. no.› Del Gov't Reg. ‹page no.› (LexisNexis ‹month year›)

District of Columbia (DC)

http://www.dccourts.gov

Court of Appeals (D.C.), previously **Municipal Court of Appeals** (D.C.): Cite to A.2d or A.3d.

▸ Atlantic Reporter	1943-date	A.2d, A.3d

United States Court of Appeals for the District of Columbia Circuit (D.C. Cir.), previously **Court of Appeals of/for the District of Columbia** (D.C. Cir.), previously **Supreme Court of the District of Columbia** (D.C.): Cite to F., F.2d, or F.3d, if therein.

▸ Federal Reporter	1919-date	F., F.2d, F.3d
▸ United States Court of Appeals Reports	1941-date	U.S. App. D.C.
▸ Appeal Cases, District of Columbia	1893-1941	App. D.C.
▸ District of Columbia Reports		
▸ Tucker and Clephane	1892-1893	21 D.C. (Tuck. & Cl.)
▸ Mackey	1880-1892	12–20 D.C. (Mackey 1–9) e.g., 12 D.C. (1 Mackey)
▸ MacArthur and Mackey	1879-1880	11 D.C. (MacArth. & M.)
▸ MacArthur	1873-1879	8–10 D.C. (MacArth. 1–3) e.g., 8 D.C. (1 MacArth.)
▸ District of Columbia Reports (reported by Mackey)	1863-1872	6–7 D.C. e.g., 6 D.C.
▸ Hayward & Hazleton, Circuit Court (Circuit Court Reports, vols. 6-7)	1840-1863	1–2 Hay. & Haz. e.g., 1 Hay. & Haz.
▸ Cranch, Circuit Court	1801-1840	1–5 D.C. (Cranch 1–5) e.g., 2 D.C. (2 Cranch)

Statutory compilations: Cite to D.C. CODE, if therein.

▸ District of Columbia Official Code (West)	D.C. CODE § x-x (‹year›)
▸ Lexis District of Columbia Code (LexisNexis)	D.C. CODE § x-x (LexisNexis ‹year›)

Session laws: Cite to Stat., if therein.

▸ United States Statutes at Large	‹vol. no.› Stat. ‹page no.› (‹year›)
▸ District of Columbia Register	‹vol. no.› D.C. Reg. ‹page no.› (‹month day, year›)
▸ Lexis District of Columbia Code ‹year›-‹year› Advance Legislative Service	‹year›-‹pamph. no.› D.C. Code Adv. Leg. Serv. ‹page no.› (LexisNexis)
▸ District of Columbia Legislative Service (West)	‹year› D.C. Legis. Serv. ‹page no.› (West)

Municipal regulations: Cite to D.C. MUN. REGS., if therein.

▸ District of Columbia Municipal Regulations	D.C. MUN. REGS. tit. x, § x (‹year›)
▸ Code of District of Columbia Municipal Regulations (LexisNexis)	D.C. CODE MUN. REGS. tit. x § x (LexisNexis ‹year›)

Administrative register

▸ District of Columbia Register	‹vol. no.› D.C. Reg. ‹page no.› (‹month day, year›)

Florida (FL)

http://www.flcourts.org

Supreme Court (Fla.): Cite to So., So. 2d, or So. 3d, if therein.

▸ Southern Reporter	1886-date	So., So. 2d, So. 3d
▸ Florida Reports	1846-1948	Fla.
▸ Florida Law Weekly	1978-date	Fla. L. Weekly

District Court of Appeal (Fla. Dist. Ct. App.): Cite to So. 2d or So. 3d, if therein.

▸ Southern Reporter	1957-date	So. 2d, So. 3d
▸ Florida Law Weekly	1978-date	Fla. L. Weekly

Circuit Court (Fla. Cir. Ct.), **County Court** (e.g., Fla. Orange County Ct.), **Public Service Commission** (Fla. P.S.C.), and other lower courts of record: Cite to Fla. Supp. or Fla. Supp. 2d, if therein.

▸ Florida Supplement	1950-1991	Fla. Supp., Fla. Supp. 2d
▸ Florida Law Weekly Supplement	1992-date	Fla. L. Weekly Supp.

Statutory compilations: Cite to FLA. STAT., if therein.

▸ Florida Statutes	FLA. STAT. § x.x (‹year›)
▸ West's Florida Statutes Annotated	FLA. STAT. ANN. § x.x (West ‹year›)
▸ LexisNexis Florida Statutes Annotated	FLA. STAT. ANN. § x.x (LexisNexis ‹year›)

Session laws: Cite to Fla. Laws, if therein.

▸ Laws of Florida	‹year› Fla. Laws ‹page no.›
▸ West's Florida Session Law Service	‹year› Fla. Sess. Law Serv. ‹page no.› (West)

Administrative compilation

▸ Florida Administrative Code Annotated (LexisNexis)	FLA. ADMIN. CODE ANN. r. x-x.x (‹year›)

Administrative register

▸ Florida Administrative Weekly (LexisNexis)	‹vol. no.› Fla. Admin. Weekly ‹page no.› (‹month day, year›)

Georgia (GA)

http://www.georgiacourts.org

Supreme Court (Ga.): Cite to S.E. or S.E.2d, if therein.

▸ South Eastern Reporter	1887-date	S.E., S.E.2d
▸ Georgia Reports	1846-date	Ga.

Court of Appeals (Ga. Ct. App.): Cite to S.E. or S.E.2d, if therein.

▸ South Eastern Reporter	1907-date	S.E., S.E.2d
▸ Georgia Appeals Reports	1907-date	Ga. App.

Statutory compilations: Cite to GA. CODE ANN. (published by LexisNexis), if therein.

▸ Official Code of Georgia Annotated (LexisNexis)	GA. CODE ANN. § x-x-x (‹year›)

▸ West's Code of Georgia Annotated   GA. CODE ANN. § x-x-x (West ‹year›)

Session laws: Cite to GA. Laws, if therein.

▸ Georgia Laws	‹year› Ga. Laws ‹page no.›
▸ Georgia ‹year› Advance Legislative Service (LexisNexis)	‹year›-‹pamph. no.› Ga. Code Ann. Adv. Legis. Serv. ‹page no.› (LexisNexis)
▸ West's Georgia Legislative Service	‹year› Ga. Code Ann. Adv. Legis. Serv. ‹page no.› (West)

Administrative compilation

▸ Official Compilation Rules and Regulations of the State of Georgia	GA. COMP. R. & REGS. x-x-x.x (‹year›)

Administrative register

▸ Georgia Government Register (LexisNexis)	‹iss. no.› Ga. Gov't Reg. ‹page no.› (LexisNexis ‹month year›)

Hawaii (HI)

http://www.courts.state.hi.us

Supreme Court (Haw.): Cite to P.2d or P.3d, if therein.

▸ Pacific Reporter	1959-date	P.2d, P.3d
▸ West's Hawaii Reports (begins with vol. 76)	1994-date	Haw.
▸ Hawaii Reports (ends with vol. 75)	1847-1994	Haw.

Intermediate Court of Appeals (Haw. Ct. App.): Cite to P.2d or P.3d, if therein.

▸ Pacific Reporter	1980-date	P.2d, P.3d
▸ West's Hawaii Reports (begins with vol. 76)	1994-date	Haw.
▸ Hawaii Appellate Reports	1980-1994	Haw. App.

Statutory compilations: Cite to HAW. REV. STAT., if therein.

▸ Hawaii Revised Statutes	HAW. REV. STAT. § x-x (‹year›)
▸ Michie's Hawaii Revised Statutes Annotated (LexisNexis)	HAW. REV. STAT. ANN. § x-x (LexisNexis ‹year›)
▸ West's Hawai'i Revised Statutes Annotated	HAW. REV. STAT. § x-x (West ‹year›)

Session laws: Cite to HAW. SESS. LAWS, if therein.

▸ Session Laws of Hawaii	‹year› Haw. Sess. Laws ‹page no.›
▸ Michie's Hawaii Revised Statutes Annotated Advance Legislative Service (LexisNexis)	‹year›-‹pamph. no.› Haw. Rev. Stat. Ann. Adv. Legis. Serv. ‹page no.› (LexisNexis)
▸ West's Hawai'i Legislative Service	‹year› Haw. Legis. Serv. ‹page no.› (West)

Administrative compilation

▸ Code of Hawaii Rules (LexisNexis)	HAW. CODE R. § x-x-x (LexisNexis ‹year›)

Administrative register

▸ Hawaii Government Register (LexisNexis)	‹iss. no.› Haw. Gov't Reg. ‹page no.› (LexisNexis ‹month year›)

Idaho (ID)

http://www.isc.idaho.gov

Supreme Court (Idaho): Cite to P., P.2d, or P.3d, if therein.

▸ Pacific Reporter	1883-date	P., P.2d, P.3d
▸ Idaho Reports	1866-date	Idaho

Court of Appeals (Idaho Ct. App.): Cite to P.2d or P.3d, if therein.

▸ Pacific Reporter	1982-date	P.2d, P.3d
▸ Idaho Reports	1982-date	Idaho

Statutory compilations: Cite to IDAHO CODE ANN. (published by LexisNexis), if therein.

▸ Idaho Code Annotated (LexisNexis)	IDAHO CODE ANN. § x-x (‹year›)
▸ West's Idaho Code Annotated	IDAHO CODE ANN. § x-x (West ‹year›)

Session laws: Cite to Idaho Sess. Laws, if therein.

▸ Idaho Session Laws	‹year› Idaho Sess. Laws ‹page no.›
▸ Idaho Code Annotated Advance Legislative Service (LexisNexis)	‹year›-‹pamph. no.› Idaho Code Ann. Adv. Legis. Serv. ‹page no.› (LexisNexis)
▸ West's Idaho Legislative Service	‹year› Idaho Legis. Serv. ‹page no.› (West)

Administrative compilation

▸ Idaho Administrative Code	IDAHO ADMIN. CODE r. x.x.x.x (‹year›)

Administrative register

▸ Idaho Administrative Bulletin	‹vol. no.› Idaho Admin. Bull. ‹page no.› (‹month day, year›)

Illinois (IL)

http://www.state.il.us/court

Supreme Court (Ill.): Cite to N.E. or N.E.2d, if therein.

▸ North Eastern Reporter	1884-date	N.E., N.E.2d
▸ Illinois Reports		
▸ 11 Ill. to date	1849-date	Ill., Ill. 2d
▸ Gilman	1844-1849	e.g., 6 Ill. (1 Gilm.)
▸ Scammon	1832-1843	e.g., 2 Ill. (1 Scam.)
▸ Breese	1819-1831	1 Ill. (Breese)
▸ West's Illinois Decisions	1976-date	Ill. Dec.

Appellate Court (Ill. App. Ct.): Cite to N.E.2d, if therein.

▸ North Eastern Reporter	1936-date	N.E.2d
▸ Illinois Appellate Court Reports	1877-date	Ill. App., Ill. App. 2d, Ill. App. 3d
▸ West's Illinois Decisions	1976-date	Ill. Dec.

Court of Claims (Ill. Ct. Cl.): Cite to Ill. Ct. Cl.

▸ Illinois Court of Claims Reports	1889-date	Ill. Ct. Cl.

Statutory compilations: Cite to ILL. COMP. STAT., if therein.

▸ Illinois Compiled Statutes   ‹ch. no.› ILL. COMP. STAT. ‹act no.› / ‹sec. no.› (‹year›)

▸ West's Smith-Hurd Illinois Compiled Statutes Annotated   ‹ch. no.› ILL. COMP. STAT. ANN. ‹act no.› / ‹sec. no.›(West ‹year›)

▸ Illinois Compiled Statutes Annotated (LexisNexis)   ‹ch. no.› ILL. COMP. STAT. ANN. ‹act no.› / ‹sec. no.› (LexisNexis ‹year›)

Session laws: Cite to Ill. Laws, if therein.

▸ Laws of Illinois   ‹year› Ill. Laws ‹page no.›

▸ Illinois Legislative Service (West)   ‹year› Ill. Legis. Serv. ‹page no.› (West)

▸ Illinois Compiled Statutes Annotated Advance Legislative Service (LexisNexis)   ‹year›-‹pamph. no.› Ill. Comp. Stat. Ann. Adv. Legis. Serv. ‹page no.› (LexisNexis)

Administrative compilations: Cite to ILL. ADMIN. CODE, if therein.

▸ Illinois Administrative Code   ILL. ADMIN. CODE tit. x, § x (‹year›)

▸ Code of Illinois Rules (LexisNexis)   ‹vol. no.› ILL. CODE R. ‹rule no.› (LexisNexis ‹year›)

Administrative register

▸ Illinois Register   ‹vol. no.› Ill. Reg. ‹page no.› (‹month day, year›)

Indiana (IN)

http://www.in.gov/judiciary

Supreme Court (Ind.): Cite to N.E. or N.E.2d, if therein.

▸ North Eastern Reporter	1885–date	N.E., N.E.2d
▸ Indiana Reports	1848–1981	Ind.
▸ Blackford	1817–1847	Blackf.

Court of Appeals (Ind. Ct. App.), previously **Appellate Court** (Ind. App.): Cite to N.E. or N.E.2d, if therein.

▸ North Eastern Reporter	1891–date	N.E., N.E.2d
▸ Indiana Court of Appeals Reports (prior to 1972, Indiana Appellate Court Reports)	1890–1979	Ind. App.

Tax Court (Ind. T.C.): Cite to N.E.2d, if therein.

▸ North Eastern Reporter	1886–date	N.E., N.E.2d

Statutory compilations: Cite to IND. CODE, if therein.

▸ Indiana Code   IND. CODE § x-x-x-x (‹year›)

▸ West's Annotated Indiana Code   IND. CODE ANN. § x-x-x-x (West ‹year›)

▸ Burns Indiana Statutes Annotated (LexisNexis)   IND. CODE ANN. § x-x-x-x (LexisNexis ‹year›)

Session laws: Cite to Ind. Acts, if therein.

▸ Acts, Indiana   ‹year› Ind. Acts ‹page no.›

▸ West's Indiana Legislative Service   ‹year› Ind. Legis. Serv. ‹page no.› (West)

▸ Burns Indiana Statutes Annotated Advance Legislative Service (LexisNexis)   ‹year›-‹pamph. no.› Ind. Stat. Ann. Adv. Legis. Serv. ‹page no.› (LexisNexis)

Administrative compilations: Cite to IND. ADMIN. CODE, if therein.

▸ Indiana Administrative Code	‹tit. no.› IND. ADMIN. CODE ‹rule no.› (year)
▸ West's Indiana Administrative Code	‹tit. no.› IND. ADMIN. CODE ‹rule no.› (West year)

Administrative register

▸ Indiana Register	‹vol. no.› Ind. Reg. ‹page no.› (‹month day, year›)

Iowa (IA)

http://www.iowacourts.gov

Supreme Court (Iowa): Cite to N.W. or N.W.2d, if therein.

▸ North Western Reporter	1879-date	N.W., N.W.2d
▸ Iowa Reports (Cite to edition published by Clarke for vols. 1-8.)	1855-1968	Iowa
▸ Greene	1847-1854	Greene
▸ Morris	1839-1846	Morris
▸ Bradford	1838-1841	Bradf.

Court of Appeals (Iowa Ct. App.): Cite to N.W.2d.

▸ North Western Reporter	1977-date	N.W.2d

Statutory compilations: Cite to IOWA CODE, if therein.

▸ Code of Iowa	IOWA CODE § x.x (‹year›)
▸ West's Iowa Code Annotated	IOWA CODE ANN. § x.x (West ‹year›)

Session laws: Cite to Iowa Acts, if therein.

▸ Acts of the State of Iowa	‹year› Iowa Acts ‹page no.›
▸ Iowa Legislative Service (West)	‹year› Iowa Legis. Serv. ‹page no.› (West)

Administrative compilation

▸ Iowa Administrative Code	IOWA ADMIN. CODE r. x-x.x (‹year›)

Administrative register

▸ Iowa Administrative Bulletin	‹vol. no.› Iowa Admin. Bull. ‹page no.› ‹month day, year›

Kansas (KS)

http://www.kscourts.org

Supreme Court (Kan.): Cite to P., P.2d, or P.3d, if therein.

▸ Pacific Reporter	1883-date	P., P.2d, P.3d
▸ Kansas Reports	1862-date	Kan.
▸ McCahon	1858-1868	McCahon

Court of Appeals (Kan. Ct. App.): Cite to P., P.2d, or P.3d, if therein.

▸ Pacific Reporter	1895-1901	P.
	1977-date	P.2d, P.3d
▸ Kansas Court of Appeals Reports	1895-1901	Kan. App.
	1977-date	Kan. App. 2d

Statutory compilations: Cite to KAN. STAT. ANN., if therein.

- ▸ Kansas Statutes Annotated — KAN. STAT. ANN. § x-x (‹year›)
- ▸ West's Kansas Statutes Annotated — KAN. STAT. ANN. § x-x (West ‹year›)

Session laws: Cite to KAN. SESS. LAWS, if therein.

- ▸ Session Laws of Kansas — ‹year› Kan. Sess. Laws ‹page no.›
- ▸ West's Kansas Legislative Service — ‹year› Kan. Legis. Serv. ‹page no.› (West)

Administrative compilation

- ▸ Kansas Administrative Regulations (updated by supplements) — KAN. ADMIN. REGS. § x-x-x (‹year›)

Administrative register

- ▸ Kansas Register — ‹vol. no.› Kan. Reg. ‹page no.› (‹month day, year›)

Kentucky (KY)

http://courts.ky.gov

Supreme Court (Ky.): before 1976 the **Court of Appeals** (Ky.) was the highest state court. Cite to S.W., S.W.2d, or S.W.3d, if therein.

▸ South Western Reporter	1886-date	S.W., S.W.2d, S.W.3d
▸ Kentucky Reports		
▸ 78 Ky. to 314 Ky.	1879-1951	Ky.
▸ Bush	1866-1879	e.g., 64 Ky. (1 Bush)
▸ Duvall	1863-1866	e.g., 62 Ky. (1 Duv.)
▸ Metcalf	1858-1863	e.g., 58 Ky. (1 Met.)
▸ Monroe, Ben	1840-1857	e.g., 40 Ky. (1 B. Mon.)
▸ Dana	1833-1840	e.g., 31 Ky. (1 Dana)
▸ Marshall, J.J.	1829-1832	e.g., 24 Ky. (1 J.J. Marsh.)
▸ Monroe, T.B.	1824-1828	e.g., 17 Ky. (1 T.B. Mon.)
▸ Littell	1822-1824	e.g., 11 Ky. (1 Litt.)
▸ Littell's Selected Cases	1795-1821	e.g., 16 Ky. (1 Litt. Sel. Cas.)
▸ Marshall, A.K.	1817-1821	e.g., 8 Ky. (1 A.K. Marsh.)
▸ Bibb	1808-1817	e.g., 4 Ky. (1 Bibb)
▸ Hardin	1805-1808	3 Ky. (Hard.)
▸ Sneed	1801-1805	2 Ky. (Sneed)
▸ Hughes	1785-1801	1 Ky. (Hughes)
▸ Kentucky Opinions	1864-1886	Ky. Op.
▸ Kentucky Law Reporter	1880-1908	Ky. L. Rptr.
▸ Kentucky Appellate Reporter	1994-2000	Ky. App.
▸ Kentucky Attorneys Memo	2001-2007	Ky. Att'y Memo
▸ Kentucky Law Summary	1966-date	Ky. L. Summ.

Court of Appeals (Ky. Ct. App.) (for decisions before 1976, see **Kentucky Supreme Court**): Cite to S.W.2d or S.W.3d, if therein.

▸ South Western Reporter	1976-date	S.W.2d, S.W.3d
▸ Kentucky Appellate Reporter	1994-2000	Ky. App.
▸ Kentucky Attorneys Memo	2001-2007	Ky. Att'y Memo
▸ Kentucky Law Summary	1966-date	Ky. L. Summ.

Statutory compilations: Cite to one of the following codes.

▶ Baldwin's Kentucky Revised Statutes Annotated (West)	Ky. Rev. Stat. Ann. § x.x (West ‹year›)
▶ Michie's Kentucky Revised Statutes Annotated (LexisNexis)	Ky. Rev. Stat. Ann. § x.x (LexisNexis ‹year›)

Session laws: Cite to Ky. Acts, if therein.

▶ Acts of Kentucky	‹year› Ky. Acts ‹page no.›
▶ Kentucky Revised Statutes and Rules Service (West)	‹year› Ky. Rev. Stat. & R. Serv. ‹page no.› (West)
▶ Michie's Kentucky Revised Statutes Advance Legislative Service (LexisNexis)	‹year›-‹pamph. no.› Ky. Rev. Stat. Adv. Legis. Serv. ‹page no.› (LexisNexis)

Administrative compilation

▶ Kentucky Administrative Regulations Service	‹tit. no.› Ky. Admin. Regs. ‹rule no.› (‹year›)

Administrative register

▶ Administrative Register of Kentucky	‹vol. no.› Ky. Admin. Reg. ‹page no.› (‹month year›)

Louisiana (LA)

http://www.lasc.org

Public domain citation format: Louisiana has adopted a public domain citation format for cases after December 31, 1993. The format is:

- ▶ State v. Ray, 97-1093 (La. App. 3 Cir. 2/4/98); 705 So. 2d 1295.
- ▶ State v. Ray, 97-1093, p. 2 (La. App. 3 Cir. 2/4/98); 705 So. 2d 1295, 1296.
- ▶ State v. Fleury, 2001-0871, p. 5 (La. 10/16/01); 799 So. 2d 468, 472.

For additional information, consult Rules of the Supreme Court of Louisiana, part G, section 8.

Supreme Court (La.), before 1813 the **Superior Court of Louisiana** (La.) and the **Superior Court of the Territory of Orleans** (Orleans): Cite to So., So. 2d, or So. 3d, if therein.

▶ Southern Reporter	1886–date	So., So. 2d, So. 3d
▶ Louisiana Reports	1901–1972	La.
▶ Louisiana Annual Reports	1846–1900	La. Ann.
▶ Robinson	1841–1846	Rob.
▶ Louisiana Reports	1830–1841	La.
▶ Martin (Louisiana Term Reports)	1809–1830	Mart. (o.s.), Mart. (n.s.)

Court of Appeal (La. Ct. App.): Cite to So., So. 2d, or So. 3d, if therein.

▶ Southern Reporter	1928–date	So., So. 2d, So. 3d
▶ Louisiana Court of Appeals Reports	1924–1932	La. App.
▶ Peltier's Decisions, Parish at Orleans	1917–1924	Pelt.
▶ Teissier, Orleans Court of Appeals	1903–1917	Teiss.
▶ Gunby's Reports	1885	Gunby
▶ McGloin	1881–1884	McGl.

Statutory compilations: Cite to one of the following codes.

- ► LexisNexis Louisiana Revised Annotated Statutes — LA. REV. STAT. ANN. § x:x (‹year›)
- ► West's Louisiana Revised Statutes Annotated — LA. REV. STAT. ANN. § x:x (‹year›)
- ► West's Louisiana Children's Code Annotated — LA. CHILD. CODE ANN. art. x (‹year›)
- ► West's Louisiana Civil Code Annotated — LA. CIV. CODE ANN. art. x (‹year›)
- ► West's Louisiana Code of Civil Procedure Annotated — LA. CODE CIV. PROC. ANN. art. x (‹year›)
- ► West's Louisiana Code of Criminal Procedure Annotated — LA. CODE CRIM. PROC. ANN. art. x (‹year›)
- ► West's Louisiana Code of Evidence Annotated — LA. CODE EVID. ANN. art. x (‹year›)

Session laws: Cite to La. Acts, if therein.

- ► State of Louisiana: Acts of the Legislature — ‹year› La. Acts ‹page no.›
- ► West's Louisiana Session Law Service — ‹year› La. Sess. Law Serv. ‹page no.› (West)
- ► LexisNexis Louisiana Annotated Statutes <year> Advance Legislative Service — ‹year›-‹pamph. no.› La. Ann. Stat. Adv. Legis. Serv. ‹page no.› (LexisNexis)

Administrative compilations: Cite to LA. ADMIN. CODE, if therein.

- ► Louisiana Administrative Code — LA. ADMIN. CODE tit. x, § x (‹year›)

Administrative register

- ► Louisiana Register — ‹vol. no.› La. Reg. ‹page no.› (‹month day, year›)

Maine (ME)

http://www.courts.state.me.us

Public domain citation format: Maine has adopted a public domain citation format for cases after December 31, 1996. The format is:

- ► Bangor Publ'g Co. v. Union St. Mkt., 1998 ME 37, 706 A.2d 595.
- ► Bangor Publ'g Co. v. Union St. Mkt., 1998 ME 37, ¶ 3, 706 A.2d 595, 595.

For additional information, consult Administrative Order of the Supreme Judicial Court—New Citation Form (Aug. 20, 1996).

Supreme Judicial Court (Me.): Cite to A., A.2d, or A.3d, if therein.

► Atlantic Reporter	1885–date	A., A.2d, A.3d
► Maine Reports	1820–1965	Me.

Statutory compilations: Cite to Me. Rev. Stat., if therein.

- ► West's Maine Revised Statutes — ME. REV. STAT. tit. x, § x (‹year›)
- ► Maine Revised Statutes Annotated (West) — ME. REV. STAT. ANN. tit. x, § x (‹year›)

Session laws: Cite to Me. Laws, if therein.

- ► Laws of the State of Maine — ‹year› Me. Laws ‹page no.›
- ► Maine Legislative Service (West) — ‹year› Me. Legis. Serv. ‹page no.› (West)

Administrative compilation

▸ Code of Maine Rules (LexisNexis)　　x-x-x ME. CODE R. § x (LexisNexis ‹year›)

Administrative register

▸ Maine Government Register (LexisNexis)　‹iss. no.› Me. Gov't Reg. ‹page no.› (LexisNexis ‹month year›)

Maryland (MD)

http://www.courts.state.md.us

Court of Appeals (Md.): Cite to A., A.2d, or A.3d, if therein.

▸ Atlantic Reporter	1885-date	A., A.2d, A.3d
▸ Maryland Reports	1851-date	Md.
▸ Gill	1843-1851	Gill
▸ Gill and Johnson	1829-1842	G. & J.
▸ Harris and Gill	1826-1829	H. & G.
▸ Harris and Johnson	1800-1826	H. & J.
▸ Harris and McHenry	1770-1774 1780-1799	H. & McH.

Court of Special Appeals (Md. Ct. Spec. App.): Cite to A.2d or A.3d, if therein.

▸ Atlantic Reporter	1967-date	A.2d, A.3d
▸ Maryland Appellate Reports	1967-date	Md. App.

Statutory compilations: Cite by subject to either Michie's MD. CODE ANN. or West's MD. CODE ANN., if therein.

▸ Michie's Annotated Code of Maryland (LexisNexis)　MD. CODE ANN., ‹subject› § x-x (LexisNexis ‹year›)

▸ West's Annotated Code of Maryland　MD. CODE ANN., ‹subject› § x-x (West ‹year›)

▸ Agriculture	AGRIC.
▸ Business Occupations and Professions	BUS. OCC. & PROF.
▸ Business Regulation	BUS. REG.
▸ Commercial Law	COM. LAW
▸ Corporations and Associations	CORPS. & ASS'NS
▸ Correctional Services	CORR. SERVS.
▸ Courts and Judicial Proceedings	CTS. & JUD. PROC.
▸ Criminal Law	CRIM. LAW
▸ Criminal Procedure	CRIM. PROC.
▸ Economic Development	ECON. DEV.
▸ Education	EDUC.
▸ Election Law	ELEC. LAW
▸ Environment	ENVIR.
▸ Estates and Trusts	EST. & TRUSTS
▸ Family Law	FAM. LAW
▸ Financial Institutions	FIN. INST.
▸ Health-General	HEALTH–GEN.
▸ Health Occupations	HEAlTH OCC.
▸ Housing and Community Development	HOUS. & CMTY. DEV.
▸ Human Services	HUM. SERVS.

▸ Insurance	Ins.
▸ Labor and Employment	Lab. & Empl.
▸ Natural Resources	Nat. Res.
▸ Public Safety	Pub. Safety
▸ Public Utility Companies	Pub. Util. Cos.
▸ Real Property	Real Prop.
▸ State Finance and Procurement	State Fin. & Proc.
▸ State Government	State Gov't
▸ State Personnel and Pensions	State Pers. & Pens.
▸ Tax-General	Tax–Gen.
▸ Tax-Property	Tax–Prop.
▸ Transportation	Transp.

Session laws: Cite to Md. Laws, if therein.

▸ Laws of Maryland	‹year› Md. Laws ‹page no.›
▸ Michie's Annotated Code of Maryland Advance Legislative Service (LexisNexis)	‹year›-‹pamph. no.› Md. Code Ann. Adv. Legis. Serv. ‹page no.› (LexisNexis)
▸ West's Maryland Legislative Service	‹year› Md. Legis. Serv. ‹page no.› (West)

Administrative compilation

▸ Code of Maryland Regulations	Md. Code Regs. ‹reg. no.› (‹year›)

Administrative register

▸ Maryland Register	‹vol. no.› Md. Reg. ‹page no.› (‹month day, year›)

....

Massachusetts (MA)

http://www.mass.gov/courts

Supreme Judicial Court (Mass.): Cite to N.E. or N.E.2d, if therein.

▸ North Eastern Reporter	1885–date	N.E., N.E.2d
▸ Massachusetts Reports		
▸ 97 Mass. to date	1867–date	Mass.
▸ Allen	1861–1867	e.g., 83 Mass. (1 Allen)
▸ Gray	1854–1860	e.g., 67 Mass. (1 Gray)
▸ Cushing	1848–1853	e.g., 55 Mass. (1 Cush.)
▸ Metcalf	1840–1847	e.g., 42 Mass. (1 Met.)
▸ Pickering	1822–1839	e.g., 18 Mass. (1 Pick.)
▸ Tyng	1806–1822	e.g., 2 Mass. (1 Tyng)
▸ Williams	1804–1805	1 Mass. (1 Will.)

Appeals Court (Mass. App. Ct.): Cite to N.E.2d, if therein.

▸ North Eastern Reporter	1972–date	N.E.2d
▸ Massachusetts Appeals Court Reports	1972–date	Mass. App. Ct.

Lower Courts (Mass. Dist. Ct., Bos. Mun. Ct.): Cite to Mass. App. Div., if therein; otherwise cite to Mass. Supp. or Mass. App. Dec., if therein.

▸ Reports of Massachusetts Appellate Division	1936–1950 1980–date	Mass. App. Div.
▸ Massachusetts Reports Supplement	1980–1983	Mass. Supp.

| ▸ Massachusetts Appellate Decisions | 1941-1977 | Mass. App. Dec. |
| ▸ Appellate Division Advance Sheets | 1975-1979 | ‹year› Mass. App. Div. Adv. Sh. ‹page no.› |

Statutory compilations: Cite to MASS. GEN. LAWS, if therein.

▸ General Laws of Massachusetts (Mass. Bar Ass'n/West)	MASS. GEN. LAWS ch. x, § x (‹year›)
▸ Massachusetts General Laws Annotated (West)	MASS. GEN. LAWS ANN. ch. x, § x (West ‹year›)
▸ Annotated Laws of Massachusetts (LexisNexis)	MASS. ANN. LAWS ch. x, § x (LexisNexis ‹year›)

Session laws: Cite to Mass. Acts, if therein.

▸ Acts and Resolves of Massachusetts	‹year› Mass. Acts ‹page no.›
▸ Massachusetts Legislative Service (West)	‹year› Mass. Legis. Serv. ‹page no.› (West)
▸ Massachusetts Advance Legislative Service (LexisNexis)	‹year›-‹pamph. no.› Mass. Adv. Legis. Serv. ‹page no.› (LexisNexis)

Administrative compilations: Cite to official MASS. CODE REGS., if therein.

| ▸ Code of Massachusetts Regulations | ‹tit. no.› MASS. CODE REGS. ‹sec. no.› (‹year›) |
| ▸ Code of Massachusetts Regulations (LexisNexis) | ‹tit. no.› MASS. CODE REGS. ‹sec. no.› (LexisNexis ‹year›) |

Administrative register

| ▸ Massachusetts Register | ‹iss. no.› Mass. Reg. ‹page no.› (‹month day, year›) |

Michigan (MI)

http://courts.mi.gov

Supreme Court (Mich.): Cite to N.W. or N.W.2d, if therein.

▸ North Western Reporter	1879-date	N.W., N.W.2d
▸ Michigan Reports	1847-date	Mich.
▸ Douglass	1843-1847	Doug.
▸ Blume, Unreported Opinions	1836-1843	Blume Unrep. Op.
▸ Blume, Supreme Court Transactions	1805-1836	Blume Sup. Ct. Trans.

Court of Appeals (Mich. Ct. App.): Cite to N.W.2d, if therein.

| ▸ North Western Reporter | 1965-date | N.W.2d |
| ▸ Michigan Appeals Reports | 1965-date | Mich. App. |

Court of Claims (Mich. Ct. Cl.): Cite to Mich. Ct. Cl.

| ▸ Michigan Court of Claims Reports | 1939-1942 | Mich. Ct. Cl. |

Statutory compilations: Cite to MICH. COMP. LAWS, if therein.

▸ Michigan Compiled Laws (1979)	MICH. COMP. LAWS § x.x (‹year›)
▸ Michigan Compiled Laws Annotated (West)	MICH. COMP. LAWS ANN. § x.x (West ‹year›)
▸ Michigan Compiled Laws Service (LexisNexis)	MICH. COMP. LAWS SERV. § x.x (LexisNexis ‹year›)

Session laws: Cite to Mich. Pub. Acts, if therein.

▸ Public and Local Acts of the Legislature of the State of Michigan	‹year› Mich. Pub. Acts ‹page no.›
▸ Michigan Legislative Service (West)	‹year› Mich. Legis. Serv. ‹page no.› (West)
▸ Michigan Advance Legislative Service (LexisNexis)	‹year›-‹pamph no.› Mich. Adv. Legis. Serv. ‹page no.› (LexisNexis)

Administrative compilation

▸ Michigan Administrative Code	MICH. ADMIN. CODE r. x.x (‹year›)

Administrative register

▸ Michigan Register	‹iss. no.› Mich. Reg. ‹page no.› (‹month day, year›)

Minnesota (MN)
http://www.mncourts.gov

Supreme Court (Minn.): Cite to N.W. or N.W.2d, if therein.

▸ North Western Reporter	1879–date	N.W., N.W.2d
▸ Minnesota Reports	1851–1977	Minn.

Court of Appeals (Minn. Ct. App.): Cite to N.W.2d.

▸ North Western Reporter	1983–date	N.W.2d

Statutory compilations: Cite to MINN. STAT., if therein.

▸ Minnesota Statutes	MINN. STAT. § x.x (‹year›)
▸ Minnesota Statutes Annotated (West)	MINN. STAT. ANN. § x.x (West ‹year›)

Session laws: Cite to Minn. Laws, if therein.

▸ Laws of Minnesota	‹year› Minn. Laws ‹page no.›
▸ Minnesota Session Law Service (West)	‹year› Minn. Sess. Law Serv. ‹page no.› (West)

Administrative compilation

▸ Minnesota Rules	MINN. R. ‹rule no.› (‹year›)

Administrative register

▸ Minnesota State Register	‹vol. no.› Minn. Reg. ‹page no.› (‹month day, year›)

Mississippi (MS)
http://www.mssc.state.ms.us

Public domain citation format: Mississippi has adopted a public domain citation format for cases after July 1, 1997. The format is:

▸ Pro-Choice Miss. v. Fordice, 95-CA-00960-SCT (Miss. 1998).

▸ Pro-Choice Miss. v. Fordice, 95-CA-00960-SCT (¶ 1) (Miss. 1998).

For additional information, consult Mississippi Rules of Appellate Procedure, Rule 28(e).

Supreme Court (Miss.): Cite to So., So. 2d, or So. 3d, if therein.

▸ Southern Reporter	1886–date	So., So. 2d, So. 3d
▸ Mississippi Reports		
▸ 23 Miss. to 254 Miss.	1851–1966	Miss.

▸ Smedes and Marshall	1843–1850	e.g., 9 Miss. (1 S. & M.)
▸ Howard	1834–1843	e.g., 2 Miss. (1 Howard)
▸ Walker	1818–1832	1 Miss. (1 Walker)
▸ Mississippi Decisions	1820–1885	Miss. Dec.

Court of Appeals (Miss. Ct. App.): Cite to So. 2d or So. 3d.

▸ Southern Reporter	1995–date	So. 2d, So. 3d

Statutory compilations: Cite to MISS. CODE ANN. (published by LexisNexis), if therein.

▸ Mississippi Code 1972 Annotated (LexisNexis)	MISS. CODE ANN. § x-x-x (‹year›)
▸ West's Annotated Mississippi Code	MISS. CODE ANN. § x-x-x (West ‹year›)

Session laws: Cite to Miss. Laws, if therein.

▸ General Laws of Mississippi	‹year› Miss. Laws ‹page no.›
▸ Mississippi General Laws Advance Sheets (LexisNexis)	‹year›-‹pamph. no.› Miss. Laws Adv. Sh. ‹page no.› (LexisNexis)
▸ West's Mississippi Legislative Service	‹year› Miss. Legis. Serv. ‹page no.› (West)

Administrative compilation

▸ Code of Mississippi Rules (LexisNexis)	‹tit. no.›-‹ch. no.› MISS. CODE R. § x (LexisNexis ‹year›)

Administrative register

▸ Mississippi Government Register (LexisNexis)	‹iss. no.› Miss. Gov't Reg. ‹page no.› (LexisNexis ‹month year›)

Missouri (MO)

http://www.courts.mo.gov

Supreme Court (Mo.): Cite to S.W., S.W.2d, or S.W.3d, if therein.

▸ South Western Reporter	1886–date	S.W., S.W.2d, S.W.3d
▸ Missouri Reports	1821–1956	Mo.

Court of Appeals (Mo. Ct. App.): Cite to S.W., S.W.2d, or S.W.3d, if therein.

▸ South Western Reporter	1902–date	S.W., S.W.2d, S.W.3d
▸ Missouri Appeals Reports	1876–1954	Mo. App.

Statutory compilations: Cite to MO. REV. STAT., if therein.

▸ Missouri Revised Statutes	MO. REV. STAT. § x.x (‹year›)
▸ Vernon's Annotated Missouri Statutes (West)	MO. ANN. STAT. § x.x (West ‹year›)

Session laws: Cite to Mo. Laws, if therein.

▸ Laws of Missouri	‹year› Mo. Laws ‹page no.›
▸ Missouri Legislative Service (West)	‹year› Mo. Legis. Serv. ‹page no.› (West)

Administrative compilation

▸ Missouri Code of State Regulations Annotated	MO. CODE REGS. ANN. tit. x, § x-x.x (‹year›)

Administrative register

▸ Missouri Register	‹vol. no.› Mo. Reg. ‹page no.› (‹month day, year›)

Montana (MT)

http://www.montanacourts.org

Public domain citation format: Montana has adopted a public domain citation format for cases after December 31, 1997. The format is:

> ► Mont. Envtl. Info. Ctr. v. Dep't of Envtl. Quality, 1999 MT 248, 296 Mont. 207, 988 P.2d 1236.

> ► Mont. Envtl. Info. Ctr. v. Dep't of Envtl. Quality, 1999 MT 248, ¶ 21, 296 Mont. 207, 988 P.2d 1236.

For additional instruction, consult Order In re: Opinion Forms and Citation Standards of the Supreme Court of Montana; and the Adoption of Public Domain and Neutral-Format Citation (Dec. 16, 1997), and Order in the Matter of Amending Citations Standards for the Montana Supreme Court (Jan. 22, 2009).

Supreme Court (Mont.): Cite to P., P.2d, or P.3d, if therein.

► Pacific Reporter	1883–date	P., P.2d, P.3d
► Montana Reports	1868–date	Mont.
► State Reporter	1945–date	State Rptr.

Statutory compilation: Cite to MONT. CODE ANN., if therein.

► Montana Code Annotated	MONT. CODE ANN. § x-x-x (‹year›)
► West's Montana Code Annotated	MONT. CODE ANN. § x-x-x (West ‹year›)

Session laws

► Laws of Montana	‹year› Mont. Laws ‹page no.›

Administrative compilation

► Administrative Rules of Montana	MONT. ADMIN. R. ‹rule no.› (‹year›)

Administrative register

► Montana Administrative Register	‹iss. no.› Mont. Admin. Reg. ‹page no.› (‹month day, year›)

Nebraska (NE)

http://court.nol.org

Supreme Court (Neb.): Cite to N.W. or N.W.2d, if therein.

► North Western Reporter	1879–date	N.W., N.W.2d
► Nebraska Reports	1860–date	Neb.

Court of Appeals (Neb. Ct. App.): Cite to N.W.2d, if therein.

► North Western Reporter	1992–date	N.W.2d
► Nebraska Court of Appeals Reports	1992–date	Neb. App.

Statutory compilations: Cite to NEB. REV. STAT., if therein.

► Revised Statutes of Nebraska	NEB. REV. STAT. § x-x (‹year›)
► Revised Statutes of Nebraska Annotated (LexisNexis)	NEB. REV. STAT. ANN. § x-x (LexisNexis ‹year›)
► West's Revised Statutes of Nebraska Annotated	NEB. REV. STAT. ANN. § x-x (West ‹year›)

Session laws: Cite to Neb. Laws, if therein.

► Laws of Nebraska	‹year› Neb. Laws ‹page no.›
► West's Nebraska Legislative Service	‹year› Neb. Legis. Serv. ‹page no.› (West)

Administrative compilation:
- Nebraska Administrative Code ⟨tit. no.⟩ NEB. ADMIN. CODE § x-x (⟨year⟩)

Nevada (NV)

http://www.nevadajudiciary.us

Supreme Court (Nev.): Cite to P., P.2d, or P.3d, if therein.
- Pacific Reporter   1883–date   P., P.2d, P.3d
- Nevada Reports   1865–date   Nev.

Statutory compilations: Cite to NEV. REV. STAT., if therein.
- Nevada Revised Statutes   NEV. REV. STAT. § x.x (⟨year⟩)
- Michie's Nevada Revised Statutes Annotated (LexisNexis)   NEV. REV. STAT. ANN. § x.x (Lexis-Nexis ⟨year⟩)
- West's Nevada Revised Statutes Annotated   NEV. REV. STAT. ANN. § x.x (West ⟨year⟩)

Session laws: Cite to Nev. Stat., if therein.
- Annotated Statutes of Nevada   ⟨year⟩ Nev. Stat. ⟨page no.⟩
- Annotated West's Nevada Legislative Service   ⟨year⟩ Nev. Legis. Serv. ⟨page no.⟩ (West)

Administrative compilation
- Nevada Administrative Code   NEV. ADMIN. CODE § x.x (⟨year⟩)

Administrative register
- Nevada Register of Administrative Regulations   ⟨vol. no.⟩ Nev. Reg. Admin. Regs. ⟨reg. no.⟩ (⟨month day, year⟩)

New Hampshire (NH)

http://www.courts.state.nh.us

Supreme Court (N.H.): Cite to A., A.2d, or A.3d, if therein.
- Atlantic Reporter   1885–date   A., A.2d, A.3d
- New Hampshire Reports   1816–date   N.H.

Statutory compilations: Cite to N.H. REV. STAT. ANN. (published by West), if therein.
- New Hampshire Revised Statutes Annotated (West)   N.H. REV. STAT. ANN. § x:x (⟨year⟩)
- Lexis New Hampshire Revised Statutes Annotated   N.H. REV. STAT. ANN. § x:x (LexisNexis ⟨year⟩)

Session laws: Cite to N.H. Laws, if therein.
- Laws of the State of New Hampshire   ⟨year⟩ N.H. Laws ⟨page no.⟩
- Lexis New Hampshire Revised Statutes Annotated ⟨year⟩ Advance Legislative Service (LexisNexis)   ⟨year⟩-⟨pamph. no.⟩ N.H. Rev. Stat. Ann. Adv. Legis. Serv. ⟨page no.⟩ (LexisNexis)

Administrative compilations: Cite to N.H. CODE ADMIN. R. ANN., if therein.
- New Hampshire Code of Administrative Rules Annotated (LexisNexis)   N.H. CODE ADMIN. R. ANN. ⟨dep't name as abbreviated in Rules⟩ ⟨rule no.⟩ (⟨year⟩)

▸ Code of New Hampshire Rules (LexisNexis)   N.H. CODE R. ‹dep't name as abbreviated in Rules› ‹rule no.› (LexisNexis ‹year›)

Administrative registers: Cite to N.H. Rulemaking Reg., if therein.

▸ New Hampshire Rulemaking Register   ‹vol. no.› N.H. Rulemaking Reg. ‹page no.› (‹month day, year›)

▸ New Hampshire Government Register (LexisNexis)   ‹iss. no.› N.H. Gov't Reg. ‹page no.› (LexisNexis ‹month year›)

New Jersey (NJ)
http://www.judiciary.state.nj.us

Supreme Court (N.J.), previously **Court of Errors and Appeals** (N.J.): Cite to A., A.2d, or A.3d, if therein.

▸ Atlantic Reporter	1885–date	A., A.2d, A.3d
▸ New Jersey Reports	1948–date	N.J.
▸ New Jersey Law Reports	1790–1948	N.J.L.
▸ New Jersey Equity Reports	1845–1948	N.J. Eq.
▸ New Jersey Miscellaneous Reports	1923–1948	N.J. Misc.

Superior Court (N.J. Super. Ct. App. Div., N.J. Super. Ct. Ch. Div., N.J. Super. Ct. Law Div.), previously **Court of Chancery** (N.J. Ch.), **Supreme Court** (N.J. Sup. Ct.), and **Prerogative Court** (N.J. Prerog. Ct.): Cite to A., A.2d, or A.3d, if therein.

▸ Atlantic Reporter	1885–date	A., A.2d, A.3d
▸ New Jersey Superior Court Reports	1948–date	N.J. Super.
▸ New Jersey Law Reports	1790–1948	N.J.L.
▸ New Jersey Equity Reports	1830–1948	N.J. Eq.
▸ New Jersey Miscellaneous Reports	1923–1948	N.J. Misc.

County Court (e.g., Essex County Ct.) and other lower courts: Cite to A.2d, if therein; otherwise, cite to another of the reporters.

Tax Court (N.J. Tax Ct.): Cite to N.J. Tax.

▸ New Jersey Tax Court Reports	1979–date	N.J. Tax

Statutory compilations: Cite to N.J. STAT. ANN., if therein.

▸ New Jersey Statutes Annotated (West)   N.J. STAT. ANN. § x:x (West ‹year›)

▸ New Jersey Revised Statutes (1937)   N.J. REV. STAT. § x:x (‹year›)

Session laws: Cite to N.J. Laws, if therein.

▸ Laws of New Jersey   ‹year› N.J. Laws ‹page no.›

▸ New Jersey Session Law Service (West)   ‹year› N.J. Sess. Law Serv. ‹page no.› (West)

Administrative compilation

▸ New Jersey Administrative Code (LexisNexis)   N.J. ADMIN. CODE § x:x-x.x (‹year›)

Administrative register

▸ New Jersey Register (LexisNexis)   ‹vol. no.› N.J. Reg. ‹page no.› (‹month day, year›)

Administrative reports

▸ New Jersey Administrative Reports	1982–date	N.J. Admin., N.J. Admin. 2d

New Mexico (NM)

http://www.nmcourts.gov

Public domain citation format: New Mexico has adopted a public domain citation format for cases after December 31, 1995. The format is:

- ▶ Atlixco Coal. v. Maggiore, 1998-NMCA-134, 125 N.M. 786, 965 P.2d 370.
- ▶ Atlixco Coal. v. Maggiore, 1998-NMCA-134, ¶ 14, 125 N.M. 786, 965 P.2d 370.

For additional information, consult New Mexico Supreme Court Rule 23-112 (effective June 4, 2004).

Supreme Court (N.M.): Cite to P., P.2d, or P.3d, if therein.

▶ Pacific Reporter	1883–date	P., P.2d, P.3d
▶ New Mexico Reports	1852–2012	N.M.

Court of Appeals (N.M. Ct. App.): Cite to P.2d or P.3d, if therein.

▶ Pacific Reporter	1967–date	P.2d, P.3d
▶ New Mexico Reports	1967–2012	N.M.

Statutory compilations: Cite to N.M. STAT. ANN. (published by Conway Greene), if therein.

▶ New Mexico Statutes Annotated 1978 (Conway Greene)	N.M. STAT. ANN. § x-x-x (‹year›)
▶ West's New Mexico Statutes Annotated	N.M. STAT. ANN. § x-x-x (West ‹year›)
▶ Michie's Annotated Statutes of New Mexico (LexisNexis)	N.M. STAT. ANN. § x-x-x (LexisNexis ‹year›)

Session laws: Cite to N.M. Laws, if therein.

▶ Laws of the State of New Mexico	‹year› N.M. Laws ‹page no.›
▶ New Mexico Advance Legislative Service (Conway Greene)	‹year› N.M. Adv. Legis. Serv. ‹page no.›
▶ West's New Mexico Legislative Service	‹year› N.M. Legis. Serv. ‹page no.› (West)

Administrative compilations

▶ Code of New Mexico Rules (LexisNexis)	N.M. CODE R. § x.x.x.x (LexisNexis ‹year›)

Administrative register

▶ New Mexico Register	‹vol. no.› N.M. Reg. ‹page no.› (‹month day, year›)

New York (NY)

http://www.courts.state.ny.us

Court of Appeals (N.Y.) after 1847: Cite to N.E. or N.E.2d, if therein.

▶ North Eastern Reporter	1885–date	N.E., N.E.2d
▶ New York Reports	1847–date	N.Y., N.Y.2d
▶ West's New York Supplement	1956–date	N.Y.S.2d

(The first series of N.Y. is reprinted in N.Y.S. and N.Y.S.2d without separate pagination. Do not include a parallel cite to N.Y.S. or N.Y.S.2d in citations to the first series of N.Y.)

Court for the Correction of Errors (N.Y.) and **Supreme Court of Judicature** (N.Y. Sup. Ct.) (highest state courts of law before 1848): Cite to one of the following reporters.

▸ Lockwood's Reversed Cases	1799–1847	Lock. Rev. Cas.
▸ Denio's Reports	1845–1848	Denio
▸ Hill and Denio Supplement (Lalor)	1842–1844	Hill & Den.
▸ Hill's Reports	1841–1844	Hill
▸ Edmond's Select Cases	1834–1853	Edm. Sel. Cas.
▸ Yates' Select Cases	1809	Yates Sel. Cas.
▸ Anthon's Nisi Prius Cases	1807–1851	Ant. N.P. Cas.
▸ Wendell's Reports	1828–1841	Wend.
▸ Cowen's Reports	1823–1829	Cow.
▸ Johnson's Reports	1806–1823	Johns.
▸ Caines' Reports	1803–1805	Cai.
▸ Caines' Cases	1796–1805	Cai. Cas.
▸ Coleman & Caines' Cases	1794–1805	Cole. & Cai. Cas.
▸ Johnson's Cases	1799–1803	Johns. Cas.
▸ Coleman's Cases	1791–1800	Cole. Cas.

Court of Chancery (N.Y. Ch.) (highest state court of equity before 1848): Cite to one of the following reporters.

▸ Edwards' Chancery Reports	1831–1850	Edw. Ch.
▸ Barbour's Chancery Reports	1845–1848	Barb. Ch.
▸ Sandford's Chancery Reports	1843–1847	Sand. Ch.
▸ Saratoga Chancery Sentinel	1841–1847	Sarat. Ch. Sent.
▸ Paige's Chancery Reports	1828–1845	Paige Ch.
▸ Clarke's Chancery Reports	1839–1841	Cl. Ch.
▸ Hoffman's Chancery Reports	1839–1840	Hoff. Ch.
▸ Hopkins' Chancery Reports	1823–1826	Hopk. Ch.
▸ Lansing's Chancery Reports	1824–1826	Lans. Ch.
▸ Johnson's Chancery Reports	1814–1823	Johns. Ch.
▸ New York Chancery Reports Annotated	1814–1847	N.Y. Ch. Ann.

Supreme Court, Appellate Division (N.Y. App. Div.), previously **Supreme Court, General Term** (N.Y. Gen. Term): Cite to N.Y.S. or N.Y.S.2d, if therein.

▸ West's New York Supplement	1888–date	N.Y.S., N.Y.S.2d
▸ Appellate Division Reports	1896–date	A.D., A.D.2d, A.D.3d
▸ Supreme Court Reports	1874–1896	N.Y. Sup. Ct.
▸ Lansing's Reports	1869–1873	Lans.
▸ Barbour's Supreme Court Reports	1847–1877	Barb.

Other lower courts (e.g., N.Y. App. Term, N.Y. Sup. Ct., N.Y. Ct. Cl., N.Y. Civ. Ct., N.Y. Crim. Ct., N.Y. Fam. Ct.): Cite to N.Y.S. or N.Y.S.2d, if therein.

▸ West's New York Supplement	1888–date	N.Y.S., N.Y.S.2d
▹ New York Miscellaneous Reports	1892–date	Misc., Misc. 2d

Other lower courts before 1888: Cite to one of the following reporters.

▸ Abbott's New Cases	1876–1894	Abb. N. Cas.
▸ Abbott's Practice Reports	1854–1875	Abb. Pr., Abb. Pr. (n.s.)
▸ Howard's Practice Reports	1844–1886	How. Pr., How. Pr. (n.s.)

Statutory compilations: Cite to one of the following sources, if therein.

▸ McKinney's Consolidated Laws of New York Annotated (West)	N.Y. ‹SUBJECT› LAW § x (McKinney ‹year›)
▸ New York Consolidated Laws Service (LexisNexis)	N.Y. ‹SUBJECT› LAW § x (Consol. ‹year›)
▸ Gould's New York Consolidated Laws Unannotated (LexisNexis)	N.Y. ‹SUBJECT› LAW § x (Gould ‹year›)
▸ Abandoned Property	ABAND. PROP.
▸ Agriculture and Markets	AGRIC. & MKTS.
▸ Alcoholic Beverage Control	ALCO. BEV. CONT.
▸ Alternative County Government	ALT. COUNTY GOV'T
▸ Arts and Cultural Affairs	ARTS & CULT. AFF.
▸ Banking	BANKING
▸ Benevolent Orders	BEN. ORD.
▸ Business Corporation	BUS. CORP.
▸ Canal	CANAL
▸ Civil Practice Law and Rules	N.Y. C.P.L.R. ‹rule no.› (McKinney ‹year›) or: N.Y. C.P.L.R. ‹rule no.› (Consol. ‹year›)
▸ Civil Rights	CIV. RIGHTS
▸ Civil Service	CIV. SERV.
▸ Commerce	COM.
▸ Cooperative Corporations	COOP. CORP.
▸ Correction	CORRECT.
▸ County	COUNTY
▸ Criminal Procedure	CRIM. PROC.
▸ Debtor and Creditor	DEBT. & CRED.
▸ Domestic Relations	DOM. REL.
▸ Economic Development	ECON. DEV.
▸ Education	EDUC.
▸ Elder	ELDER
▸ Election	ELEC.
▸ Eminent Domain Procedure	EM. DOM. PROC.
▸ Employers' Liability	EMPL'RS LIAB.
▸ Energy	ENERGY
▸ Environmental Conservation	ENVTL. CONSERV.
▸ Estates, Powers and Trusts	EST. POWERS & TRUSTS
▸ Executive	EXEC.
▸ General Associations	GEN. ASS'NS
▸ General Business	GEN. BUS.
▸ General City	GEN. CITY
▸ General Construction	GEN. CONSTR.
▸ General Municipal	GEN. MUN.
▸ General Obligations	GEN. OBLIG.

▸ Highway	High.
▸ Indian	Indian
▸ Insurance	Ins.
▸ Judiciary Court Acts	Jud. Ct. Acts
▸ Labor	Lab.
▸ Legislative	Legis.
▸ Lien	Lien
▸ Limited Liability Company	Ltd. Liab. Co.
▸ Local Finance	Local Fin.
▸ Mental Hygiene	Mental Hyg.
▸ Military	Mil.
▸ Multiple Dwelling	Mult. Dwell.
▸ Multiple Residence	Mult. Resid.
▸ Municipal Home Rule and Statute of Local Governments	Mun. Home Rule
▸ Navigation	Nav.
▸ Not-for-Profit Corporation	Not-for-Profit Corp.
▸ Optional County Government	Opt. Cnty. Gov't
▸ Parks, Recreation and Historic Preservation	Parks Rec. & Hist. Preserv.
▸ Partnership	P'ship
▸ Penal	Penal
▸ Personal Property	Pers. Prop.
▸ Private Housing Finance	Priv. Hous. Fin.
▸ Public Authorities	Pub. Auth.
▸ Public Buildings	Pub. Bldgs.
▸ Public Health	Pub. Health
▸ Public Housing	Pub. Hous.
▸ Public Lands	Pub. Lands
▸ Public Officers	Pub. Off.
▸ Public Service	Pub. Serv.
▸ Racing, Pari-Mutuel Wagering and Breeding	Rac. Pari-Mut. Wag. & Breed.
▸ Railroad	R.R.
▸ Rapid Transit	Rapid Trans.
▸ Real Property	Real Prop.
▸ Real Property Actions and Proceedings	Real Prop. Acts.
▸ Real Property Tax	Real Prop. Tax
▸ Religious Corporations	Relig. Corp.
▸ Retirement and Social Security	Retire. & Soc. Sec.
▸ Rural Electric Cooperative	Rural Elec. Coop.
▸ Second Class Cities	Second Class Cities
▸ Social Services	Soc. Serv.
▸ Soil and Water Conservation Districts	Soil & Water Conserv. Dist.
▸ State	State
▸ State Administrative Procedure Act	A.P.A.

▸ State Finance	STATE FIN.
▸ State Printing and Public Documents	STATE PRINT. & PUB. DOCS.
▸ State Technology	STATE TECH.
▸ Statutes	STAT.
▸ Surrogate's Court Procedure Act	SURR. CT. PROC. ACT
▸ Tax	TAX
▸ Town	TOWN
▸ Transportation	TRANSP.
▸ Transportation Corporations	TRANSP. CORP.
▸ Unconsolidated	UNCONSOL.
▸ Uniform Commercial Code	U.C.C.
▸ Vehicle and Traffic	VEH. & TRAF.
▸ Village	VILLAGE
▸ Volunteer Ambulance Workers' Benefit	VOL. AMBUL. WORKERS' BEN.
▸ Volunteer Firefighters' Benefit	VOL. FIRE. BEN.
▸ Workers' Compensation	WORKERS' COMP.

Uncompiled laws: Cite to one of the following sources, if therein. For the user's convenience, the McKinney's volume in which the law appears is indicated parenthetically below.

▸ McKinney's Consolidated Laws	N.Y. ‹LAW› § x (McKinney ‹year›)
▸ Consolidated Laws Service	N.Y. ‹LAW› § x (Consol. ‹year›)
▸ Gould's New York Consolidated Laws Unannotated	N.Y. ‹LAW› § x (Gould ‹year›)
▸ New York City Civil Court Act (29A)	CITY CIV. CT. ACT
▸ New York City Criminal Court Act (29A)	CITY CRIM. CT. ACT
▸ Code of Criminal Procedure (11A)	CODE CRIM. PROC.
▸ Court of Claims Act (29A)	CT. CL. ACT
▸ Family Court Act (29A)	FAM. CT. ACT
▸ Uniform City Court Act (29A)	UNIFORM CITY CT. ACT
▸ Uniform District Court Act (29A)	UNIFORM DIST. CT. ACT
▸ Uniform Justice Court Act (29A)	UNIFORM JUST. CT. ACT

Session laws: Cite to official **N.Y. Laws**, if therein; otherwise, cite to **N.Y. Sess. Laws**, if therein.

▸ Laws of New York	‹year› N.Y. Laws ‹page no.›
▸ McKinney's Session Laws of New York (West)	‹year› N.Y. Sess. Laws ‹page no.› (McKinney)
▸ New York Consolidated Laws Service Advance Legislative Service (LexisNexis)	‹year›-‹pamph. no.› N.Y. Consol. Laws Adv. Legis. Serv. ‹page no.› (LexisNexis)

Administrative compilation

▸ Official Compilation of Codes, Rules & Regulations of the State of New York (West)	N.Y. COMP. CODES R. & REGS. tit. x, § x (‹year›)

Administrative register

▸ New York State Register	‹vol. no.› N.Y. Reg. ‹page no.› (‹month day, year›)

North Carolina (NC)

http://www.nccourts.org

Supreme Court (N.C.): Cite to S.E. or S.E.2d, if therein.

► South Eastern Reporter	1887-date	S.E., S.E.2d
► North Carolina Reports		
► 63 N.C. to date	1868-date	N.C.
► Phillips' Equity	1866-1868	62 N.C. (Phil. Eq.)
► Phillips' Law	1866-1868	61 N.C. (Phil.)
► Winston	1863-1864	60 N.C. (Win.)
► Jones' Equity (54-59)	1853-1863	e.g., 54 N.C. (1 Jones Eq.)
► Jones' Law (46-53)	1853-1862	e.g., 46 N.C. (1 Jones)
► Busbee's Equity	1852-1853	45 N.C. (Busb. Eq.)
► Busbee's Law	1852-1853	44 N.C. (Busb.)
► Iredell's Equity (36-43)	1840-1852	e.g., 36 N.C. (1 Ired. Eq.)
► Iredell's Law (23-35)	1840-1852	e.g., 23 N.C. (1 Ired.)
► Devereux & Battle's Equity (21-22)	1834-1839	e.g., 21 N.C. (1 Dev. & Bat. Eq.)
► Devereux & Battle's Law (18-20)	1834-1839	e.g., 20 N.C. (3 & 4 Dev. & Bat.)
► Devereux's Equity (16-17)	1826-1834	e.g., 16 N.C. (1 Dev. Eq.)
► Devereux's Law (12-15)	1826-1834	e.g., 12 N.C. (1 Dev.)
► Hawks (8-11)	1820-1826	e.g., 8 N.C. (1 Hawks)
► Murphey (5-7)	1804-1813 1818-1819	e.g., 5 N.C. (1 Mur.)
► Taylor's North Carolina Term Reports	1816-1818	4 N.C. (Taylor)
► Carolina Law Repository	1813-1816	4 N.C. (Car. L. Rep.)
► Haywood (2-3)	1789-1806	e.g., 2 N.C. (1 Hayw.)
► Conference by Cameron & Norwood	1800-1804	1 N.C. (Cam. & Nor.)
► Taylor	1798-1802	1 N.C. (Tay.)
► Martin	1778-1797	1 N.C. (Mart.)

Court of Appeals (N.C. Ct. App.): Cite to S.E.2d, if therein.

► South Eastern Reporter	1968-date	S.E.2d
► North Carolina Court of Appeals Reports	1968-date	N.C. App.

Statutory compilations: Cite to N.C. GEN. STAT. (published by LexisNexis), if therein.

► General Statutes of North Carolina (LexisNexis)	N.C. GEN. STAT. § x-x (‹year›)
► West's North Carolina General Statutes Annotated	N.C. GEN. STAT. ANN. § x-x (West ‹year›)

Session laws: Cite to N.C. SESS. LAWS, if therein.

► Session Laws of North Carolina	‹year› N.C. Sess. Laws ‹page no.›
► North Carolina ‹year› Advance Legislative Service (LexisNexis)	‹year›-‹pamph. no.› N.C. Adv. Legis. Serv. ‹page no.› (LexisNexis)
► North Carolina Legislative Service (West)	‹year› N.C. Legis. Serv. ‹page no.› (West)

Administrative compilation

▶ North Carolina Administrative Code   ‹tit. no.› N.C. ADMIN. CODE ‹rule
  (West)   no.› (‹year›)

Administrative register

▶ North Carolina Register (LexisNexis)   ‹vol. no.› N.C. Reg. ‹page no.›
                                          (‹month day, year›)

North Dakota (ND)

http://www.ndcourts.gov

Public Domain Citation Format: North Dakota has adopted a public domain
citation format for cases after December 31, 1996. The format is:

▶ Kautzman v. Kautzman, 2003 ND 140, 668 N.W.2d 59.

▶ Kautzman v. Kautzman, 2003 ND 140, ¶ 9, 668 N.W.2d 59, 63.

For additional information, consult North Dakota Rules of Court, Rule 11.6.

Supreme Court (N.D.): Cite to **N.W.** or **N.W.2d**, if therein.

▶ North Western Reporter	1890-date	N.W., N.W.2d
▶ North Dakota Reports	1890-1953	N.D.

Supreme Court of Dakota (Dakota): Cite to **N.W.**, if therein.

▶ North Western Reporter	1879-1889	N.W.
▶ Dakota Reports	1867-1889	Dakota

Court of Appeals of North Dakota (N.D. Ct. App.): Cite to **N.W.2d**.

▶ North Western Reporter	1987-date	N.W.2d

Statutory compilations: Cite to **N.D. CENT. CODE**, if therein.

▶ North Dakota Century Code (LexisNexis)   N.D. CENT. CODE § x-x-x (‹year›)

▶ West's North Dakota Century Code   N.D. CENT. CODE ANN. § x-x-x
  Annotated   (West ‹year›)

Session laws: Cite to **N.D. Laws**, if therein.

▶ Laws of North Dakota   ‹year› N.D. Laws ‹page no.›

▶ North Dakota Century Code ‹year›   ‹year›-‹pamph. no.› N.D. Cent.
  Advance Legislative Service (LexisNexis)   Code Adv. Legis. Serv. ‹page no.›
                                      (LexisNexis)

▶ West's North Dakota Legislative Service   ‹year› N.D. Legis. Serv. ‹page
                                      no.› (West)

Administrative compilation

▶ North Dakota Administrative Code   N.D. ADMIN. CODE ‹rule no.› (‹year›)

Ohio (OH)

http://www.sconet.state.oh.us

Public Domain Citation Format: Ohio has adopted a public domain citation
format for cases decided after April 30, 2002. The format is:

▶ State v. Lynch, 98 Ohio St. 3d 514, 2003-Ohio-2284, 787 N.E.2d
1185.

▶ State v. Lynch, 98 Ohio St. 3d 514, 2003-Ohio-2284, 787 N.E.2d
1185, at ¶ 3.

For additional information, consult Revisions to the Manual of Citations, 96 Ohio
St. 3d CXLIX-CLVII (2002).

Supreme Court (Ohio): Cite to N.E. or N.E.2d, if therein.

▸ North Eastern Reporter	1885-date	N.E., N.E.2d
▸ Ohio State Reports	1852-date	Ohio St., Ohio St. 2d, Ohio St. 3d
▸ Ohio Reports	1821-1851	Ohio
▸ Wilcox's Condensed Reports	1821-1831	Wilc. Cond. Rep.
▸ Wright	1831-1834	Wright
▸ Ohio Unreported Cases	1809-1899	Ohio Unrep. Cas.

Court of Appeals (Ohio Ct. App.): Cite to N.E. or N.E.2d, if therein.

▸ North Eastern Reporter	1926-date	N.E., N.E.2d
▸ Ohio Appellate Reports	1913-2012	Ohio App., Ohio App. 2d, Ohio App. 3d
▸ Ohio Circuit Court Reports	1914-1917	Ohio C.C.
▸ Ohio Courts of Appeals Reports	1916-1922	Ohio Ct. App.

Other law courts: Cite to Ohio Misc. or Ohio Misc. 2d, if therein; otherwise, cite to another reporter in the following order of preference.

▸ Ohio Miscellaneous	1962-date	Ohio Misc., Ohio Misc. 2d
▸ Ohio Bar Reports	1982-1987	Ohio B.
▸ Ohio Opinions	1934-1982	Ohio Op., Ohio Op. 2d, Ohio Op. 3d
▸ Ohio Law Abstract	1922-1964	Ohio Law Abs.
▸ Ohio Nisi Prius Reports	1903-1934	Ohio N.P., Ohio N.P. (n.s.)
▸ Ohio Decisions	1900-1921	Ohio Dec.
▸ Ohio Decisions, Reprint	1840-1893	Ohio Dec. Reprint
▸ Ohio Circuit Decisions	1885-1923	Ohio Cir. Dec.
▸ Ohio Circuit Court Decisions	1901-1923	e.g., 13-23 Ohio C.C. Dec.
▸ Ohio Circuit Court Reports	1885-1902	Ohio C.C.
▸ Ohio Law Bulletin	1876-1921	Ohio L. Bull.
▸ Ohio Circuit Court Reports, New Series	1903-1917	Ohio C.C. (n.s.)
▸ Ohio Law Reporter	1903-1934	Ohio L.R.
▸ Tappen's Reports	1816-1819	Tapp. Rep.
▸ Anderson's Unreported Ohio Appellate Cases	1990	Ohio App. Unrep.

Statutory compilations: Cite to one of the following codes.

▸ Page's Ohio Revised Code Annotated (LexisNexis)	OHIO REV. CODE ANN. § x.x (LexisNexis ‹year›)
▸ Baldwin's Ohio Revised Code Annotated (West)	OHIO REV. CODE ANN. § x.x (West ‹year›)

Session laws: Cite to Ohio Laws, if therein.

▸ State of Ohio: Legislative Acts Passed and Joint Resolutions Adopted	‹year› Ohio Laws ‹page no.›
▸ Page's Ohio Legislative Bulletin (LexisNexis)	‹year› Ohio Legis. Bull. ‹page no.› (LexisNexis)
▸ Baldwin's Ohio Legislative Service Annotated (West)	‹year› Ohio Legis. Serv. Ann. ‹page no.› (West)

Administrative compilation

▸ Baldwin's Ohio Administrative Code (West)	OHIO ADMIN. CODE ‹rule no.› (‹year›)

Administrative and executive registers: Cite to one of the following registers.

▸ Baldwin's Ohio Monthly Record	1977-date	Ohio Monthly Rec. ‹page no.› (‹month year›)
▸ Ohio Government Reports	1965-1976	Ohio Gov't ‹page no.› (‹month day, year›)
▸ Ohio Department Reports	1914-1964	Ohio Dep't ‹page no.› (‹month day, year›)

Oklahoma (OK)

http://www.oscn.net

Public domain citation format: Oklahoma has adopted a public domain citation format for cases after May 1, 1997. The format is:

▸ Herbert v. Okla. Christian Coal., 1999 OK 90, 992 P.2d 322.

▸ Herbert v. Okla. Christian Coal., 1999 OK 90, ¶ 2, 992 P.2d 322, 325.

For additional information, consult Oklahoma Supreme Court Rule 1.200(e) and Oklahoma Criminal Appeals Rule 3.5(c).

Supreme Court (Okla.): Cite to P., P.2d, or P.3d, if therein.

▸ Pacific Reporter	1890-date	P., P.2d, P.3d
▸ Oklahoma Reports	1890-1953	Okla.

Court of Appeals of Indian Territory (Indian Terr.): Cite to S.W., if therein.

▸ South Western Reporter	1896-1907	S.W.
▸ Indian Territory Reports	1896-1907	Indian Terr.

Court of Criminal Appeals (Okla. Crim. App.), before 1959 **Criminal Court of Appeals** (Okla. Crim. App.): Cite to P., P.2d, or P.3d, if therein.

▸ Pacific Reporter	1908-date	P., P.2d, P.3d
▸ Oklahoma Criminal Reports	1908-1953	Okla. Crim.

Court of Civil Appeals (Okla. Civ. App.): Cite to P.2d or P.3d.

▸ Pacific Reporter	1971-date	P.2d, P.3d

Statutory compilations: Cite to OKLA. STAT., if therein.

▸ Oklahoma Statutes (West)	OKLA. STAT. tit. x, § x (‹year›)
▸ Oklahoma Statutes Annotated (West)	OKLA. STAT. ANN. tit. x, § x (West ‹year›)

Session laws: Cite to one of the following sources.

▸ Oklahoma Session Laws (West)	‹year› Okla. Sess. Laws ‹page no.›
▸ Oklahoma Session Law Service (West)	‹year› Okla. Sess. Law Serv. ‹page no.› (West)

Administrative compilation

▸ Oklahoma Administrative Code	OKLA. ADMIN. CODE § x:x-x-x (‹year›)

Administrative registers: Cite to one of the following sources.

▸ Oklahoma Register	1983-date	‹vol. no.› Okla. Reg. ‹page no.› (‹month day, year›)
▸ Oklahoma Gazette	1962-1983	‹vol. no.› Okla. Gaz. ‹page no.› (‹month day, year›)

Oregon (OR)

http://courts.oregon.gov/OJD

Supreme Court (Or.): Cite to P., P.2d, or P.3d, if therein.

▸ Pacific Reporter	1883–date	P., P.2d, P.3d
▸ Oregon Reports	1853–date	Or.

Court of Appeals (Or. Ct. App.): Cite to P.2d or P.3d, if therein.

▸ Pacific Reporter	1969–date	P.2d, P.3d
▸ Oregon Reports, Court of Appeals	1969–date	Or. App.

Tax Court (Or. T.C.): Cite to Or. Tax.

▸ Oregon Tax Reports	1962–date	Or. Tax

Statutory compilations: Cite to OR. REV. STAT., if therein.

▸ Oregon Revised Statutes	OR. REV. STAT. § x.x ‹year›
▸ West's Oregon Revised Statutes Annotated	OR. REV. STAT. ANN. § x.x (West ‹year›)

Session laws: Cite to Or. Laws, if therein. When citing statutes repealed during or after 1953, indicate parenthetically the former OR. REV. STAT. sections.

▸ Oregon Laws and Resolutions	‹year› Or. Laws ‹page no.›
	‹year› Or. Laws Spec. Sess. ‹page no.›
	‹year› Or. Laws Adv. Sh. No. x, ‹page no.›
▸ West's Oregon Legislative Service	‹year› Or. Legis. Serv. ‹page no.› (West)

Administrative compilation

▸ Oregon Administrative Rules	OR. ADMIN. R. ‹rule no.› (‹year›)

Administrative register

▸ Oregon Bulletin	‹vol. no.› Or. Bull. ‹page no.› (‹month day, year›)

Pennsylvania (PA)

http://www.courts.state.pa.us

Supreme Court (Pa.): Cite to A., A.2d, or A.3d, if therein.

▸ Atlantic Reporter	1885–date	A., A.2d, A.3d
▸ Pennsylvania State Reports	1845–date	Pa.
▸ Monaghan	1888–1890	Monag.
▸ Sadler	1885–1889	Sadler
▸ Walker	1855–1885	Walk.
▸ Pennypacker	1881–1884	Pennyp.
▸ Grant	1814–1863	Grant
▸ Watts and Sergeant	1841–1845	Watts & Serg.
▸ Wharton	1835–1841	Whart.
▸ Watts	1832–1840	Watts
▸ Rawle	1828–1835	Rawle
▸ Penrose and Watts	1829–1832	Pen. & W.
▸ Sergeant and Rawle	1814–1828	Serg. & Rawle
▸ Binney	1799–1814	Binn.
▸ Yeates	1791–1808	Yeates

► Addison	1791–1799	Add.
► Dallas	1754–1806	Dall.
► Alden	1754–1814	Ald.

Superior Court (Pa. Super. Ct.): Cite to A., A.2d, or A.3d, if therein. For cases decided after December 31, 1998, use the following public domain citation format:

> ► Rapagnani v. Judas Co., 1999 PA Super 203.

► Atlantic Reporter	1931–date	A., A.2d, A.3d
► Pennsylvania Superior Court Reports	1895–1997	Pa. Super.

Commonwealth Court (Pa. Commw. Ct.): Cite to A.2d or A.3d, if therein.

► Atlantic Reporter	1970–date	A.2d, A.3d
► Pennsylvania Commonwealth Court Reports	1970–1994	Pa. Commw.

Other lower courts: Cite to Pa. D. & C., Pa. D. & C.2d, Pa. D. & C.3d, or Pa. D. & C.4th, if therein. Not all lower court decisions are reproduced in the reporters listed below, and it may be necessary, on occasion, to cite to the legal reporter for an individual county, if available. For a comprehensive list of Pennsylvania county court reports, consult chapter seven, appendix four, FRANK Y. LIU ET AL., PENNSYLVANIA LEGAL RESEARCH HANDBOOK (2008).

► Pennsylvania District and County Reports	1921–date	Pa. D. & C., Pa. D. & C.2d, Pa. D. & C.3d, Pa. D. & C.4th
► Pennsylvania District Reports	1892–1921	Pa. D.
► Pennsylvania County Court Reports	1870–1921	Pa. C.

Statutory compilations: Pennsylvania is undertaking its first official codification, PA. CONS. STAT. (79 titles); the old, unofficial compilation is Purdon's PA. STAT. ANN. (79 titles), which uses a different numbering system. Purdon is also reprinting the new, official codification as PA. CONS. STAT. ANN., which is currently bound with PA. STAT. ANN. Cite to PA. CONS. STAT. or PA. CONS. STAT. ANN., in that order of preference. If the statute is contained in neither source, cite to PA. STAT. ANN. These publications should not be confused with PA. CODE, which is a code of regulations, not of legislation.

► Pennsylvania Consolidated Statutes	‹tit. no.› PA. CONS. STAT. § x (‹year›)
► Purdon's Pennsylvania Consolidated Statutes Annotated (West)	‹tit. no.› PA. CONS. STAT. ANN. § x (West ‹year›)
► Purdon's Pennsylvania Statutes Annotated (West)	‹tit. no.› PA. STAT. ANN. § x (West ‹year›)

Session laws: Cite to Pa. Laws, if therein.

► Laws of Pennsylvania	‹year› Pa. Laws ‹page no.›
► Purdon's Pennsylvania Legislative Service (West)	‹year› Pa. Legis. Serv. ‹page no.› (West)

Administrative compilation

► Pennsylvania Code (Fry Communications)	‹tit. no.› PA. CODE § x.x (‹year›)

Administrative register

► Pennsylvania Bulletin (Fry Communications)	‹vol. no.› Pa. Bull. ‹page no.› (‹month day, year›)

Rhode Island (RI)

http://www.courts.state.ri.us

Supreme Court (R.I.): Cite to **A.**, **A.2d**, or **A.3d**, if therein.

▸ Atlantic Reporter	1885–date	A., A.2d, A.3d
▸ Rhode Island Reports	1828–1980	R.I.

Statutory compilations: Cite to **R.I. GEN. LAWS**, if therein.

▸ General Laws of Rhode Island (LexisNexis)	R.I. GEN. LAWS § x-x-x ‹year›
▸ West's General Laws of Rhode Island Annotated	R.I. GEN. LAWS ANN. § x-x-x (West ‹year›)

Session laws: Cite to **R.I. Pub. Laws**, if therein.

▸ Public Laws of Rhode Island and Providence Plantations	‹year› R.I. Pub. Laws ‹page no.›
▸ Acts and Resolves of Rhode Island and Providence Plantations	‹year› R.I. Acts & Resolves ‹page no.›
▸ Rhode Island General Laws Advance Legislative Service (LexisNexis)	‹year›-‹pamph. no.› R.I. Gen. Laws Adv. Legis. Serv. ‹page no.› (LexisNexis)
▸ West's Rhode Island General Laws Advance Legislative Service	‹year› R.I. Gen. Laws Adv. Legis. Serv. ‹page no.› (West)

Administrative compilation

▸ Code of Rhode Island Rules (LexisNexis)	‹tit. no.›-‹ch. no.› R.I. CODE R. § x (LexisNexis ‹year›)

Administrative register

▸ Rhode Island Government Register (LexisNexis)	‹iss. no.› R.I. Gov't Reg. ‹page no.› (LexisNexis ‹month year›)

South Carolina (SC)

http://www.judicial.state.sc.us

Supreme Court after 1868 (S.C.): Cite to **S.E.** or **S.E.2d**, if therein.

▸ South Eastern Reporter	1887–date	S.E., S.E.2d
▸ South Carolina Reports	1868–date	S.C.

Court of Appeals (S.C. Ct. App.): Cite to **S.E.2d**, if therein.

▸ South Eastern Reporter	1983–date	S.E.2d
▸ South Carolina Reports	1983–date	S.C.

Courts of law before 1868: Cite to **S.C.L.**

▸ South Carolina Law Reports

▸ Richardson (37–49)	1850–1868	e.g., 37 S.C.L. (3 Rich.)
▸ Strobhart (32–36)	1846–1850	e.g., 32 S.C.L. (1 Strob.)
▸ Richardson (30–31)	1844–1846	e.g., 30 S.C.L. (1 Rich.)
▸ Speers (28–29)	1842–1844	e.g., 28 S.C.L. (1 Speers)
▸ McMullan (26–27)	1840–1842	e.g., 26 S.C.L. (1 McMul.)
▸ Cheves	1839–1840	25 S.C.L. (Chev.)
▸ Rice	1838–1839	24 S.C.L. (Rice)
▸ Dudley	1837–1838	23 S.C.L. (Dud.)
▸ Riley	1836–1837	22 S.C.L. (Ril.)

▸ Hill (19–21)	1833–1837	e.g., 19 S.C.L. (1 Hill)
▸ Bailey (17–18)	1828–1832	e.g., 17 S.C.L. (1 Bail.)
▸ Harper	1823–1824	16 S.C.L. (Harp.)
▸ McCord (12–15)	1821–1828	e.g., 12 S.C.L. (1 McCord)
▸ Nott and McCord (10–11)	1817–1820	e.g., 10 S.C.L. (1 Nott & McC.)
▸ Mill (Constitutional) (8–9)	1817–1818	e.g., 8 S.C.L. (1 Mill)
▸ Treadway (6–7)	1812–1816	e.g., 6 S.C.L. (1 Tread.)
▸ Brevard (3–5)	1793–1816	e.g., 3 S.C.L. (1 Brev.)
▸ Bay (1–2)	1783–1804	e.g., 1 S.C.L. (1 Bay)

Courts of equity before 1868: Cite to S.C. Eq.

▸ South Carolina Equity Reports

▸ Richardson's Equity (24–35)	1850–1868	e.g., 24 S.C. Eq. (3 Rich. Eq.)
▸ Strobhart's Equity (20–23)	1846–1850	e.g., 20 S.C. Eq. (1 Strob. Eq.)
▸ Richardson's Equity (18–19)	1844–1846	e.g., 18 S.C. Eq. (1 Rich. Eq.)
▸ Speers' Equity	1842–1844	17 S.C. Eq. (Speers Eq.)
▸ McMullan's Equity	1840–1842	16 S.C. Eq. (McMul. Eq.)
▸ Cheves' Equity	1839–1840	15 S.C. Eq. (Chev. Eq.)
▸ Rice's Equity	1838–1839	14 S.C. Eq. (Rice Eq.)
▸ Dudley's Equity	1837–1838	13 S.C. Eq. (Dud. Eq.)
▸ Riley's Chancery	1836–1837	12 S.C. Eq. (Ril. Eq.)
▸ Hill's Chancery (10–11)	1833–1837	e.g., 10 S.C. Eq. (1 Hill Eq.)
▸ Richardson's Cases	1831–1832	9 S.C. Eq. (Rich. Cas.)
▸ Bailey's Equity	1830–1831	8 S.C. Eq. (Bail. Eq.)
▸ McCord's Chancery (6–7)	1825–1827	e.g., 6 S.C. Eq. (1 McCord Eq.)
▸ Harper's Equity	1824	5 S.C. Eq. (Harp. Eq.)
▸ Desaussure's Equity (1–4)	1784–1817	e.g., 1 S.C. Eq. (1 Des. Eq.)

Statutory compilation

▸ Code of Laws of South Carolina 1976 Annotated	S.C. CODE ANN. § x-x-x (‹year›)

Session laws

▸ Acts and Joint Resolutions, South Carolina	‹year› S.C. Acts ‹page no.›

Administrative compilation: Administrative regulations appear in volumes 23–27 of S.C. CODE ANN.

▸ Code of Laws of South Carolina 1976 Annotated: Code of Regulations (West)	S.C. CODE ANN. REGS. ‹reg no.› (‹year›)

Administrative register

▸ South Carolina State Register	‹vol. no.› S.C. Reg. ‹page no.› (‹month day, year›)

....

South Dakota (SD)

http://www.sdjudicial.com

Public domain citation format: South Dakota has adopted a public domain citation format for cases after December 31, 1996. The format is:

- ▸ Wulf v. Senst, 2003 SD 105, 669 N.W.2d 135.
- ▸ Wulf v. Senst, 2003 SD 105, ¶ 14, 669 N.W.2d 135, 141.

For additional information, consult South Dakota Rules of Civil Procedure § 15-26A-69.1.

Supreme Court (S.D.): Cite to **N.W.** or **N.W.2d**, if therein.

▸ North Western Reporter	1890-date	**N.W., N.W.2d**
▸ South Dakota Reports	1890-1976	**S.D.**

Supreme Court of Dakota (Dakota): Cite to **N.W.**, if therein.

▸ North Western Reporter	1879-1889	**N.W.**
▸ Dakota Reports	1867-1889	**Dakota**

Statutory compilation

▸ South Dakota Codified Laws (West)	S.D. CODIFIED LAWS § x-x-x (‹year›)

Session laws: Cite to **S.D. Sess. Laws**, if therein.

▸ Session Laws of South Dakota	‹year› S.D. Sess. Laws ‹page no.›

Administrative compilation

▸ Administrative Rules of South Dakota	S.D. ADMIN. R. ‹rule no.› (‹year›)

Administrative register

▸ South Dakota Register	‹vol. no.› S.D. Reg. ‹page no.› (‹month day, year›)

. . . .

Tennessee (TN)

http://www.tsc.state.tn.us

Supreme Court (Tenn.): Cite to **S.W., S.W.2d,** or **S.W.3d**, if therein.

▸ South Western Reporter	1886-date	**S.W., S.W.2d, S.W.3d**
▸ Tennessee Reports		
▸ 60 Tenn. to 225 Tenn.	1872-1972	**Tenn.**
▸ Heiskell	1870-1874	e.g., **48 Tenn. (1 Heisk.)**
▸ Coldwell	1860-1870	e.g., **41 Tenn. (1 Cold.)**
▸ Head	1858-1860	e.g., **38 Tenn. (1 Head)**
▸ Sneed	1853-1858	e.g., **33 Tenn. (1 Sneed)**
▸ Swan	1851-1853	e.g., **31 Tenn. (1 Swan)**
▸ Humphreys	1839-1851	e.g., **20 Tenn. (1 Hum.)**
▸ Meigs	1838-1839	**19 Tenn. (Meigs)**
▸ Yerger	1818-1837	e.g., **9 Tenn. (1 Yer.)**
▸ Martin & Yerger	1825-1828	**8 Tenn. (Mart. & Yer.)**
▸ Peck	1821-1824	**7 Tenn. (Peck)**
▸ Haywood	1814-1818	e.g., **4 Tenn. (1 Hayw.)**
▸ Cooke	1811-1814	**3 Tenn. (Cooke)**
▸ Overton	1791-1815	e.g., **1 Tenn. (1 Overt.)**

Court of Appeals (Tenn. Ct. App.): Cite to **S.W.2d** or **S.W.3d**, if therein.

▸ South Western Reporter	1932-date	**S.W.2d, S.W.3d**
▸ Tennessee Appeals Reports	1925-1971	**Tenn. App.**

Court of Criminal Appeals (Tenn. Crim. App.): Cite to **S.W.2d** or **S.W.3d**, if therein.

▸ South Western Reporter	1967-date	**S.W.2d, S.W.3d**
▸ Tennessee Criminal Appeals Reports	1967-1971	**Tenn. Crim. App.**

Statutory compilations: Cite to TENN. CODE ANN. (published by LexisNexis), if therein.

▸ Tennessee Code Annotated (LexisNexis)	TENN. CODE ANN. § x-x-x (‹year›)
▸ West's Tennessee Code Annotated	TENN. CODE ANN. § x-x-x (West ‹year›)

Session laws: Cite to Tenn. Pub. Acts or Tenn. Priv. Acts, if therein.

▸ Public Acts of the State of Tennessee	‹year› Tenn. Pub. Acts ‹page no.›
▸ Private Acts of the State of Tennessee	‹year› Tenn. Priv. Acts ‹page no.›
▸ Tennessee Code Annotated Advance Legislative Service (LexisNexis)	‹year›-‹pamph. no.› Tenn. Code Ann. Adv. Legis. Serv. ‹page no.› (LexisNexis)
▸ West's Tennessee Legislative Service	‹year› Tenn. Legis. Serv. ‹page no.› (West)

Administrative compilation

▸ Official Compilation Rules & Regulations of the State of Tennessee	TENN. COMP. R. & REGS. ‹rule no.› (‹year›)

Administrative register

▸ Tennessee Administrative Register	‹vol. no.› Tenn. Admin. Reg. ‹page no.› (‹month year›)

Texas (TX)

http://www.courts.state.tx.us

Supreme Court (Tex.): Cite to S.W., S.W.2d, or S.W.3d, if therein.

▸ South Western Reporter	1886–date	S.W., S.W.2d, S.W.3d
▸ Texas Reports	1846–1962	Tex.
▸ Synopses of the Decisions of the Supreme Court of Texas Arising from Restraints by Conscript and Other Military Authorities (Robards)	1862–1865	Robards (no vol. number)
▸ Texas Law Review (containing previously unpublished cases from the 1845 term)	1845–1846	65 TEX. L. REV. [e.g., Lamar v. Houston (Tex. 1845), 65 TEX. L. REV. 382 (Paulsen rep. 1986)]
▸ Digest of the Laws of Texas (Dallam's Opinions)	1840–1844	Dallam (no vol. number)
▸ Texas Supreme Court Journal	1957–date	TEX. SUP. CT. J.

Court of Criminal Appeals (Tex. Crim. App.), previously **Court of Appeals** (Tex. Ct. App.): Cite to S.W., S.W.2d, or S.W.3d, if therein.

▸ South Western Reporter	1892–date	S.W., S.W.2d, S.W.3d
▸ Texas Criminal Reports	1892–1962	Tex. Crim.
▸ Texas Court of Appeals Reports	1876–1892	Tex. Ct. App.
▸ Condensed Reports of Decisions in Civil Causes in the Court of Appeals (White & Willson vol. 1) (Willson vols. 2-4)	1876–1883 1883–1892	White & W. Willson

Commission of Appeals (Tex. Comm'n App.): Cite to S.W. or S.W.2d, if therein.

▸ South Western Reporter	1886–1892 1918–1945	S.W. S.W.2d

▸ Texas Reports	1879–1892	Tex.
	1918–1945	
▸ Texas Unreported Cases (Posey)	1879–1884	Posey
▸ Condensed Reports of Decisions in Civil Causes in the Court of Appeals (White & Willson)	1879–1883	White & W.

Officially published opinions of the Commission of Appeals from 1879 to 1892 were adopted by the Supreme Court and should be cited as opinions of the Supreme Court. Opinions of the Commission of Appeals from 1918 to 1945 have a notation from the Supreme Court that usually appears in the final paragraph of the opinion, e.g., opinion adopted, holding approved, or judgment adopted. Commission opinions that were adopted by the Supreme Court should be cited as opinions of the Supreme Court. "Holding approved" and "judgment adopted" opinions are cited by using "holding approved" or "judgm't adopted," e.g., Savage v. Cowen, 33 S.W.2d 433 (Tex. Comm'n App. 1930, judgm't adopted).

Courts of Appeals (Tex. App.), previously **Courts of Civil Appeals** (Tex. Civ. App.): Cite to S.W., S.W.2d, or S.W.3d, if therein.

| ▸ South Western Reporter | 1892–date | S.W., S.W.2d, S.W.3d |
| ▸ Texas Civil Appeals Reports | 1892–1911 | Tex. Civ. App. |

For additional information on the history and structure of Texas courts and on local citation rules, the following sources are suggested: TEXAS LAW REVIEW ASS'N, THE GREENBOOK: TEXAS RULES OF FORM (12th ed. 2010); LYDIA M.V. BRANDT, TEXAS LEGAL RESEARCH (1995); and A REFERENCE GUIDE TO TEXAS LAW AND LEGAL HISTORY (Karl T. Gruben & James E. Hambleton eds., 2d ed. 1987).

Statutory compilations: Texas is nearing the completion of a recodification of its laws. Cite to the new subject-matter TEX. CODE ANN., if therein; otherwise, cite to TEX. REV. CIV. STAT. ANN. or to one of the independent codes contained in the series *Vernon's Texas Civil Statutes* or *Vernon's Texas Statutes Annotated*. Note that the independent codes are not part of the new subject-matter TEX. CODE ANN.

▸ Vernon's Texas Codes Annotated	TEX. ‹SUBJECT› CODE ANN. § x (West ‹year›)
▸ Agriculture	AGRIC.
▸ Alcoholic Beverage	ALCO. BEV.
▸ Business and Commerce	BUS. & COM.
▸ Business Organizations (effective Jan. 1, 2006)	BUS. ORGS.
▸ Civil Practice and Remedies	CIV. PRAC. & REM.
▸ Education	EDUC.
▸ Election	ELEC.
▸ Family	FAM.
▸ Finance	FIN.
▸ Government	GOV'T
▸ Health and Safety	HEALTH & SAFETY
▸ Human Resources	HUM. RES.
▸ Labor	LAB.
▸ Local Government	LOC. GOV'T

▸ Natural Resources	Nat. Res.
▸ Occupations	Occ.
▸ Parks and Wildlife	Parks & Wild.
▸ Penal	Penal
▸ Property	Prop.
▸ Special District Local Laws	Spec. Dists.
▸ Tax	Tax
▸ Transportation	Transp.
▸ Utilities	Util.
▸ Water	Water
▸ Vernon's Texas Revised Civil Statutes Annotated (West)	Tex. Rev. Civ. Stat. Ann. art. x, § x (West ‹year›)
▸ Vernon's Texas Business Corporation Act Annotated (West)	Tex. Bus. Corp. Act Ann. art. x (West ‹year›)
▸ Vernon's Texas Code of Criminal Procedure Annotated (West)	Tex. Code Crim. Proc. Ann. art. x (West ‹year›)
▸ Vernon's Texas Insurance Code Annotated (West)	Tex. Ins. Code Ann. art. x (West ‹year›)
▸ Vernon's Texas Probate Code Annotated (West)	Tex. Prob. Code Ann. § x (West ‹year›)

Session laws: Cite to Tex. Gen. Laws, if therein.

▸ General and Special Laws of the State of Texas	‹year› Tex. Gen. Laws ‹page no.›
▸ Vernon's Texas Session Law Service (West)	‹year› Tex. Sess. Law Serv. ‹page no.› (West)
▸ Laws of the Republic of Texas	‹year› Repub. Tex. Laws ‹page no.›

Session laws passed before 1941 must be cited according to the exact title, e.g., Tex. Loc. & Spec. Laws, Tex. Gen. & Spec. Laws, and Tex. Gen. Laws. The Revised Statutes were enacted and published separately in 1879, 1895, 1911, and 1925 and should be cited as ‹year› Tex. Rev. Civ. Stat. xxx. The Code of Criminal Procedure and Penal Code were enacted and published separately in 1856, 1879, 1895, 1911, and 1925 and should be cited as ‹year› Tex. Crim. Stat. xxx.

Administrative compilation

▸ Texas Administrative Code (West)	‹tit. no.› Tex. Admin. Code § x.x (‹year›)

Administrative register

▸ Texas Register (LexisNexis)	‹vol. no.› Tex. Reg. ‹page no.› (‹month day, year›)

....

Utah (UT)

http://www.utcourts.gov

Public domain citation format: Utah has adopted a public domain citation format for cases after December 31, 1998. The format is:

▸ Wickham v. Galetka, 2002 UT 72, 61 P.3d 979.

▸ Gilley v. Blackstock, 2002 UT App 414, ¶ 10, 61 P.3d 305.

For additional information, consult Utah Supreme Court Standing Order No. 4 (effective Jan. 18, 2000).

Supreme Court (Utah): Cite to P., P.2d, or P.3d, if therein.

▸ Pacific Reporter	1881–date	P., P.2d, P.3d
▸ Utah Reports	1873–1974	Utah, Utah 2d

Court of Appeals (Utah Ct. App.): Cite to P.2d or P.3d.

▸ Pacific Reporter	1987–date	P.2d, P.3d

Statutory compilations: Cite to one of the following codes, if therein.

▸ Utah Code Annotated (LexisNexis)	UTAH CODE ANN. § x-x-x (LexisNexis ‹year›)
▸ West's Utah Code Annotated	UTAH CODE ANN. § x-x-x (West ‹year›)

Session laws: Cite to Utah Laws, if therein.

▸ Laws of Utah	‹year› Utah Laws ‹page no.›
▸ Utah Code ‹year› Advance Legislative Service (LexisNexis)	‹year›-‹pamph. no.› Utah Adv. Legis. Serv. ‹page no.› (LexisNexis)
▸ Utah Legislative Service (West)	‹year› Utah. Legis. Serv. ‹page no.› (West)

Administrative compilation

▸ Utah Administrative Code	UTAH ADMIN. CODE r. x-x-x (‹year›)

Administrative register

▸ Utah State Bulletin	‹iss. no.› Utah Bull. ‹page no.› (‹month day, year›)

Vermont (VT)

http://www.vermontjudiciary.org

Public domain citation format: Vermont has adopted a public domain citation format for cases after December 31, 2002. The format is:

▸ Charbonneau v. Gorczyk, 2003 VT 105, ¶ 3, 176 Vt. 140, 838 A.2d 117.

For additional information, consult Vt. R. App. P. 28.2.

Supreme Court (Vt.): Cite to A., A.2d, or A.3d, if therein.

▸ Atlantic Reporter	1885–date	A., A.2d, A.3d
▸ Vermont Reports	1826–date	Vt.
▸ Aikens	1825–1828	Aik.
▸ Chipman, D.	1789–1824	D. Chip.
▸ Brayton	1815–1819	Brayt.
▸ Tyler	1800–1803	Tyl.
▸ Chipman, N.	1789–1791	N. Chip.

Statutory compilations: Cite to VT. STAT. ANN. (published by LexisNexis), if therein.

▸ Vermont Statutes Annotated (LexisNexis)	VT. STAT. ANN. tit. x, § x (‹year›)
▸ West's Vermont Statutes Annotated	VT. STAT. ANN. tit. x, § x (West ‹year›)

Session laws: Cite to Vt. Acts & Resolves, if therein.

▸ Acts and Resolves of Vermont	‹year› Vt. Acts & Resolves ‹page no.›
▸ Vermont ‹year› Advance Legislative Service (LexisNexis)	‹year›-‹pamph. no.› Vt. Adv. Legis. Serv. ‹page no.› (LexisNexis)
▸ West's Vermont Legislative Service	‹year› Vt. Legis. Serv. ‹page no.› (West)

Administrative compilation

▸ Code of Vermont Rules (LexisNexis) ‹tit. no.›-‹ch. no.› Vt. Code R. § x (‹year›)

Administrative and executive register

▸ Vermont Government Register   ‹iss. no.› Vt. Gov't Reg. ‹page no.›
  (LexisNexis)   (LexisNexis ‹month year›)

Virginia (VA)

http://www.courts.state.va.us

Supreme Court (Va.), previously **Supreme Court of Appeals** (Va.): Cite to S.E. or S.E.2d, if therein.

▸ South Eastern Reporter	1887–date	S.E., S.E.2d
▸ Virginia Reports		
▸ 75 Va. to date	1880–date	Va.
▸ Grattan	1844–1880	e.g., 42 Va. (1 Gratt.)
▸ Robinson	1842–1844	e.g., 40 Va. (1 Rob.)
▸ Leigh	1829–1842	e.g., 28 Va. (1 Leigh)
▸ Randolph	1821–1828	e.g., 22 Va. (1 Rand.)
▸ Gilmer	1820–1821	21 Va. (Gilmer)
▸ Munford	1810–1820	e.g., 15 Va. (1 Munf.)
▸ Hening & Munford	1806–1810	e.g., 11 Va. (1 Hen. & M.)
▸ Call	1779–1825	e.g., 5 Va. (1 Call)
▸ Virginia Cases, Criminal	1789–1826	e.g., 3 Va. (1 Va. Cas.)
▸ Washington	1790–1796	e.g., 1 Va. (1 Wash.)

Court of Appeals (Va. Ct. App.): Cite to S.E.2d, if therein.

▸ South Eastern Reporter	1985–date	S.E.2d
▸ Virginia Court of Appeals Reports	1985–date	Va. App.

Circuit Court (Va. Cir. Ct.): Cite to Va. Cir.

▸ Virginia Circuit Court Opinions	1957–date	Va. Cir.

Statutory compilations: Cite to Va. Code Ann. (published by LexisNexis), if therein.

▸ Code of Virginia 1950 Annotated   Va. Code Ann. § x-x (‹year›)
  (LexisNexis)
▸ West's Annotated Code of Virginia Va. Code Ann. § x-x (West ‹year›)

Session laws: Cite to Va. Acts, if therein.

▸ Acts of the General Assembly of the   ‹year› Va. Acts ‹page no.›
  Commonwealth of Virginia
▸ Virginia ‹year› Advance Legislative ‹year›-‹pamph. no.› Va. Adv. Legis.
  Service (LexisNexis)   Serv. ‹page no.› (LexisNexis)
▸ West's Virginia Legislative Service ‹year› Va. Legis. Serv. ‹page no.›
                (West)

Administrative compilation

▸ Virginia Administrative Code (West) ‹tit. no.› Va. Admin. Code § x-x-x
                (‹year›)

Administrative register

▸ Virginia Register of Regulations   ‹vol. no.› Va. Reg. Regs. ‹page no.›
  (LexisNexis)   (‹month day, year›)

Washington (WA)

http://www.courts.wa.gov

Supreme Court (Wash.): Cite to P., P.2d, or P.3d, if therein.

▶ Pacific Reporter	1880–date	P., P.2d, P.3d
▶ Washington Reports	1889–date	Wash., Wash. 2d
▶ Washington Territory Reports	1854–1888	Wash. Terr.

Court of Appeals (Wash. Ct. App.): Cite to P.2d or P.3d, if therein.

▶ Pacific Reporter	1969–date	P.2d, P.3d
▶ Washington Appellate Reports	1969–date	Wash. App.

Statutory compilations: Cite to WASH. REV. CODE, if therein.

▶ Revised Code of Washington	WASH. REV. CODE § x.x.x (‹year›)
▶ West's Revised Code of Washington Annotated	WASH. REV. CODE ANN. § x.x.x (West ‹year›)
▶ Annotated Revised Code of Washington (LexisNexis)	WASH. REV. CODE ANN. § x.x.x (LexisNexis ‹year›)

Session laws: Cite to Wash. Sess. Laws, if therein.

▶ Session Laws of Washington	‹year› Wash. Sess. Laws ‹page no.›
▶ West's Washington Legislative Service	‹year› Wash. Legis. Serv. ‹page no.› (West)

Administrative compilation

▶ Washington Administrative Code	WASH. ADMIN. CODE § x-x-x (‹year›)

Administrative register

▶ Washington State Register	‹iss. no.› Wash. Reg. ‹page no.› (‹month day, year›)

West Virginia (WV)

http://www.state.wv.us/wvsca

Supreme Court of Appeals (W. Va.): Cite to S.E. or S.E.2d, if therein.

▶ South Eastern Reporter	1886–date	S.E., S.E.2d
▶ West Virginia Reports	1864–date	W. Va.

Statutory compilations: Cite to W. VA. CODE, if therein.

▶ West Virginia Code	W. VA. CODE § x-x-x (‹year›)
▶ Michie's West Virginia Code Annotated (LexisNexis)	W. VA. CODE ANN. § x-x-x (LexisNexis ‹year›)
▶ West's Annotated Code of West Virginia	W. VA. CODE ANN. § x-x-x (West ‹year›)

Session laws: Cite to W. Va. Acts, if therein.

▶ Acts of the Legislature of West Virginia	‹year› W. Va. Acts ‹page no.›
▶ West Virginia ‹year› Advance Legislative Service (LexisNexis)	‹year›-‹pamph. no.› W. Va. Adv. Legis. Serv. ‹page no.› (LexisNexis)
▶ West's West Virginia Legislative Service	‹year› W. Va. Legis. Serv. ‹page no.›

Administrative compilation

▶ West Virginia Code of State Rules	W. VA. CODE R. § x-x-x (‹year›)

Administrative register

▸ West Virginia Register   ‹vol. no.› W. Va. Reg. ‹page no.›
                                     (‹month day, year›)

Wisconsin (WI)

http://wicourts.gov

Public domain citation format: Wisconsin has adopted a public domain citation format for cases decided after December 31, 1999. The format is:

▸ Glaeske v. Shaw, 2003 WI App 71, 261 Wis. 2d 549, 661 N.W.2d 72.
▸ Glaeske v. Shaw, 2003 WI App 71, ¶ 9, 261 Wis. 2d 549, 661 N.W.2d 72.

For additional information, consult Wisconsin Supreme Court Rule 80.

Supreme Court (Wis.): Cite to **N.W.** or **N.W.2d**, if therein.

▸ North Western Reporter	1879-date	N.W., N.W.2d
▸ Wisconsin Reports	1853-date	Wis., Wis. 2d
▸ Pinney	1839-1852	Pin.
▸ Chandler	1849-1852	Chand.
▸ Burnett	1842-1843	Bur.
▸ Burnett (bound with session laws for Dec. 1841)	1841	Bur.

Court of Appeals (Wis. Ct. App.): Cite to **N.W.2d**, if therein.

▸ North Western Reporter	1978-date	N.W.2d
▸ Wisconsin Reports	1978-date	Wis. 2d

Statutory compilations: Cite to **Wis. Stat.**, if therein.

▸ Wisconsin Statutes   **Wis. Stat.** § x.x (‹year›)
▸ West's Wisconsin Statutes Annotated   **Wis. Stat. Ann.** § x.x (West ‹year›)

Session laws: Cite to **Wis. Sess. Laws**, if therein.

▸ Wisconsin Session Laws   ‹year› **Wis. Sess. Laws** ‹page no.›
▸ West's Wisconsin Legislative Service   ‹year› **Wis. Legis. Serv.** ‹page no.›
                                    (West)

Administrative compilation

▸ Wisconsin Administrative Code   **Wis. Admin. Code** ‹agency
                                    abbreviation› § x-x (‹year›)

Administrative register

▸ Wisconsin Administrative Register   ‹iss. no.› Wis. Admin. Reg. ‹page no.›
                                    (‹month day, year›)

Wyoming (WY)

http://courts.state.wy.us

Public domain citation format: Wyoming has adopted a public domain citation format for cases decided after December 31, 2003. The format is:

▸ CLC v. Wyoming, 2004 WY 2, 82 P.3d 1235 (Wyo. 2004).
▸ CLC v. Wyoming, 2004 WY 2, ¶ 4, 82 P.3d 1235, 1236 (Wyo. 2004).

For additional information, consult Order Amending Citation Format (Aug. 19, 2005).

Supreme Court (Wyo.): Cite to P., P.2d, or P.3d, if therein.

▸ Pacific Reporter	1883-date	P., P.2d, P.3d
▸ Wyoming Reports	1870-1959	Wyo.

Statutory compilations: Cite to Wyo. Stat. Ann. (published by LexisNexis), if therein.

▸ Wyoming Statutes Annotated (LexisNexis)	Wyo. Stat. Ann. § x-x-x (‹year›)
▸ West's Wyoming Statutes Annotated	Wyo. Stat. Ann. § x-x-x (West ‹year›)

Session laws: Cite to Wyo. Sess. Laws, if therein.

▸ Session Laws of Wyoming	‹year› Wyo. Sess. Laws ‹page no.›
▸ West's Wyoming Legislative Service	‹year› Wyo. Legis. Serv. ‹page no.› (West)

Administrative compilation

▸ Code of Wyoming Rules (LexisNexis)	‹tit. no.›-‹ch. no.› Wyo. Code R. § x (LexisNexis ‹year›)

Administrative register

▸ Wyoming Government Register (LexisNexis)	‹iss. no.› Wyo. Gov't Reg. ‹page no.› (LexisNexis ‹month year›)

T1.4   Other United States Jurisdictions

American Samoa

http://www.asbar.org

High Court of American Samoa (Am. Samoa): Cite to Am. Samoa, Am. Samoa 2d, or Am. Samoa 3d.

▸ American Samoa Reports	1900-date	Am. Samoa, Am. Samoa 2d, Am. Samoa 3d

Statutory compilation

▸ American Samoa Code Annotated	Am. Samoa Code Ann. § x (‹year›)

Administrative compilation

▸ American Samoa Administrative Code	Am. Samoa Admin. Code § x (‹year›)

Canal Zone (CZ)

(now part of Panama)

United States District Court for the Eastern District of Louisiana (E.D. La.): This court has jurisdiction over litigation pending as of Apr. 1, 1982, in the United States District Court for the District of the Canal Zone. Cite to F. Supp.

▸ Federal Supplement	1982-1983 F. Supp.

United States District Court for the District of the Canal Zone (D.C.Z.): This court ceased to exist on Mar. 31, 1982. Cite to F. Supp.

▸ Federal Supplement	1946-1982 F. Supp.

Statutory compilation

▸ Panama Canal Code	C.Z. Code tit. x, § x (‹year›)

(enacted as Canal Zone Code, Pub. L. No. 87-845, 76A Stat. 1 (1962), and redesignated and continued partially in force by the Panama Canal Act of 1979, Pub. L. No. 96-70, § 3303(b), 93 Stat. 452, 499).

Guam (GU)

http://www.justice.gov.gu

Guam cases that cannot be located in paper form may be available at one of the following locations:
- http://www.jurispacific.com
- http://www.justice.gov.gu/supreme.html

Supreme Court of Guam (Guam): Cite using the following public domain format:

- Adams v. Duenas, 1998 Guam 15.
- Adams v. Duenas, 1998 Guam 15 ¶ 2.

District Court of Guam (D. Guam): Cite to F. Supp. or F. Supp. 2d, if therein.

▸Federal Supplement	1951–date	F. Supp., F. Supp. 2d
▸Guam Reports	1955–1980	Guam

Statutory compilation

▸Guam Code Annotated	‹tit. no.› GUAM CODE ANN. § x (‹year›)

Session laws

▸Guam Session Laws	Guam Pub. L. ‹law no.› (‹year›)

Administrative compilation

▸Administrative Rules & Regulations of the Government of Guam	‹tit. no.› GUAM ADMIN. R. & REGS. § x (‹year›)

Navajo Nation

http://www.navajo.org

Supreme Court (Navajo), previously **Court of Appeals** (Navajo): Cite to Navajo Rptr.

▸ Navajo Reporter	1969–date	Navajo Rptr.

District Court (Navajo D. Ct.): Cite to Navajo Rptr.

▸ Navajo Reporter	1969–date	Navajo Rptr.

Statutory compilation

▸ Navajo Nation Code Annotated (West)	NAVAJO NATION CODE ANN. tit. x, § x (‹year›)

Northern Mariana Islands

http://www.cnmilaw.org

Public domain citation format: The Commonwealth of the Northern Mariana Islands has adopted a public domain citation format for cases after June 15, 1996. The format is:

- Lifoifoi v. Lifoifoi-Aldan, 1996 MP 14.

Supreme Court (N. Mar. I.): Cite to N. Mar. I.

▸ Northern Mariana Islands Reporter   1989-date   N. Mar. I.

District Court for the Northern Mariana Islands, Trial and Appellate Divisions (D. N. Mar. I. and D. N. Mar. I. App. Div.), and **Commonwealth Superior Court** (N. Mar. I. Commw. Super. Ct.), previously **Commonwealth Trial Court** (N. Mar. I. Commw. Trial Ct.): Cite to F. Supp. or F. Supp. 2d, if therein.

▸ Federal Supplement   1979-date   F. Supp., F. Supp. 2d
▸ Northern Mariana Islands   1979-date   N. Mar. I. Commw.
   Commonwealth Reporter

Statutory compilation

▸ Northern Mariana Islands   ‹tit. no.› N. MAR. I. CODE § x (‹year›)
   Commonwealth Code

Session laws

▸ Northern Mariana Islands Session Laws   ‹year› N. Mar. I. Pub. L. ‹law no.›

Administrative compilation

▸ Northern Mariana Islands   ‹tit. no.› N. MAR. I. ADMIN. CODE § x
   Administrative Code   (‹year›)

Administrative register

▸ Northern Mariana Islands   ‹vol. no.› N. Mar. I. Reg. ‹page no.›
   Commonwealth Register   (‹month day, year›)

Oklahoma Native Americans

Tribal Courts, Courts of Indian Offenses (Appellate Division), Courts of Indian Appeals, and **Courts of Indian Offenses**: Cite to Okla. Trib.

▸ Oklahoma Tribal Court Reports   1979-date   Okla. Trib.

Puerto Rico (PR)

http://www.ramajudicial.pr (in Spanish)

Public domain citation format: Puerto Rico has adopted a public domain citation format for cases decided after December 31, 1997. The format is:

▸ Spanish: Guzman Rosario v. Departamento de Hacienda, 98 TSPR 148.
▸ English: Guzman Rosario v. Departamento de Hacienda, 98 PRSC 148.

Supreme Court (P.R.): Cite to P.R. or P.R. Offic. Trans., if therein; otherwise, cite to P.R. Dec. or P.R. Sent., in that order of preference.

▸ Puerto Rico Reports   1899-1978   P.R.
▸ Official Translations of the Opinions   1978-date   P.R. Offic. Trans.
   of the Supreme Court of Puerto Rico
▸ Decisiones de Puerto Rico   1899-date   P.R. Dec.
▸ Sentencias del Tribunal Supremo de   1899-1902   P.R. Sent.
   Puerto Rico

Circuit Court of Appeals (P.R. Cir.): Cite to T.C.A.

▸ Decisiones del Tribunal de Circuito de   1995-date   T.C.A.
   Apelaciones de Puerto Rico

Statutory compilation

▸ Laws of Puerto Rico Annotated (LexisNexis)   P.R. LAWS ANN. tit. x, § x (‹year›)

Session laws

▸ Laws of Puerto Rico   ‹year› P.R. Laws ‹page no.›

....

Virgin Islands (VI)

http://www.visupremecourt.org

All courts: Cite to V.I.

▸ Virgin Islands Reports   1917–date   V.I.

Statutory compilation

▸ Virgin Islands Code Annotated   1962–date   V.I. CODE ANN. tit. x,
  (LexisNexis)   § x-x ‹year›

Session laws: Cite to V.I. Sess. Laws, if therein.

▸ Session Laws of the Virgin Islands   ‹year› V.I. Sess. Laws ‹page no.›
▸ Virgin Islands Code Annotated Advance ‹year›-‹pamph. no.› V.I. Code Ann.
  Legislative Service (LexisNexis)   Adv. Legis. Serv. ‹page no.›
                                        (LexisNexis)

Administrative compilation

▸ Code of U.S. Virgin Island Rules   ‹tit. no.›-‹ch. no.› V.I. CODE R. § x-x
  (LexisNexis)   (LexisNexis ‹year›)

Administrative register

▸ Virgin Islands Government Register   ‹iss. no.› V.I. Gov't Reg. ‹page no.›
  (LexisNexis)   (LexisNexis ‹month year›)

T2   FOREIGN JURISDICTIONS

T2.1   Argentine Republic

(Civil Law)

....

Cases

Citation format: ‹court name› [‹court abbreviation›][‹English translation of court name›], ‹date in day/month/year format›, "‹case name› / ‹type of case›," ‹name of publication› [‹abbreviation of publication›] (‹year›-‹volume›-‹page number›) (‹country abbreviation if not evident from context›).

The party names are separated by "c.," which refers to "contra," the Spanish translation of "versus."

▸ Corte Suprema de Justicia de la Nación [CSJN][National Supreme
  Court of Justice], 18/7/2001, "Frenquel, Adolfo c. Centro de
  Ortopedias / recurso extraordinario," La Ley [L.L.] (2001-D-22)
  (Arg.).

Federal jurisdiction: **Corte Suprema de Justicia de la Nación** (CSJN) (National Supreme Court of Justice: highest court on constitutional and federal matters): Cite to Fallos, if therein; otherwise cite to L.L., E.D., or J.A.; **Cámara Nacional de Casación Penal** (C.N.C.P.) (National Court of Appeal on Criminal Matters: highest federal court on criminal matters): Cite to L.L., E.D., or J.A.; **Cámara Federal de Apelaciones** (CFed.) (federal courts of appeals) and

Juzgado Federal (Juzg. Fed.) (lower federal courts): Cite to L.L., E.D., or J.A., appending the specific jurisdiction to the court name and court abbreviation.

▸ Colección Oficial de Fallos de la Corte Suprema de Justicia de la Nación	1863–date	e.g., Fallos (1997-299-142)
▸ Revista Jurídica Argentina—La Ley	1936–date	e.g., L.L. (1985-E-292)
▸ El Derecho	1962–date	e.g., E.D. (1972-42-934)
▸ Jurisprudencia Argentina	1918–date	e.g., J.A. (1961-VI-332)

Ordinary jurisdiction: **Provincial courts: Corte de Justicia** (CJ) (Court of Justice: highest provincial court in the provinces of Catamarca (Cat.), Salta (Sta.), and San Juan (SJn.)), **Corte Suprema de Justicia** (CSJ) (Supreme Court of Justice: highest provincial court in the provinces of Santa Fe (SFe.) and Tucumán (Tuc.)), **Superior Tribunal de Justicia** (STJ) (Superior Tribunal of Justice: highest provincial court in the provinces of Chaco (Cha.), Chubut (Cht.), Corrientes (Ctes.), Entre Ríos (ERs.), Formosa (For.), Jujuy (Juj.), La Pampa (LPa.), Misiones (Mis.), Río Negro (RNg.), San Luis (SLs.), Santiago del Estero (Sgo.), and Tierra del Fuego (TFg.)), **Suprema Corte de Justicia** (SCJ) (Supreme Court of Justice: highest provincial court in the provinces of Buenos Aires (BAs.) and Mendoza (Mza.)), **Tribunal Superior de Justicia** (Trib. Sup.) (Superior Tribunal of Justice: highest provincial court in the provinces of Córdoba (Cba.), La Rioja (LRj.), Neuquén (Nqn.), and Santa Cruz (SCz.)), **Cámara de Apelaciones en lo Civil y Comercial** (CApel.CC) (provincial courts of appeals in civil and commercial matters), **Cámara de Apelaciones en lo Penal** (CApel. Penal) (provincial courts of appeals in criminal matters), **Cámara del Trabajo** (CTrab.) (provincial courts of appeals in labor matters), and **Juzgado de Primera Instancia** (1a Inst.) (provincial lower courts of ordinary jurisdiction): Cite to L.L., E.D., or J.A., adding the name of the province or region when the report is local.

Append the specific province to the court name and court abbreviation. Include the sala (section or panel), if applicable, after the court and province name.

▸ Civ. y Com. Mendoza, sala 4a, 14/4/1980, Rep. LL XL-1724, n. 50.

Courts with jurisdiction over the federal district of Buenos Aires: Cámara Nacional de Apelaciones en lo Civil de la Capital Federal (CNCiv.) (National Court of Civil Appeals of the Federal Capital: court of appeals in civil matters, divided into sections A, B, C, etc.), **Cámara Nacional de Apelaciones en lo Comercial de la Capital Federal** (CNCom.) (National Court of Commercial Appeals of the Federal Capital: court of appeals in commercial matters, divided into sections A, B, C, etc.), **Cámara Nacional de Apelaciones Especial Civil y Comercial de la Capital Federal** (CNEspecial Civ. y Com.) (National Court of Special Civil and Commercial Appeals of the Federal Capital: court of appeals in civil and commercial matters), **Cámara Nacional de Apelaciones en lo Penal Económico de la Capital Federal** (CNPenal Económico) (National Court of Economic Criminal Appeals of the Federal Capital: court of appeals in economic criminal matters), **Cámara Nacional de Apelaciones del Trabajo de la Capital Federal** (CNTrab.) (National Court of Labor Appeals of the Federal Capital: court of appeals in labor matters), **Cámara Nacional de Apelaciones en lo Federal y Contenciosoadministrativo de la Capital Federal** (CNFed.) (National Court of Appeals in Federal and Administrative Litigation of the Federal Capital: court of appeals in administrative matters), and **Juzgado Nacional de Primera Instancia** (1a Inst.) (lower courts of ordinary jurisdiction): Cite to L.L., E.D., or J.A.

Constitution

- ► Constitución Nacional   Const. Nac.
  - ► Art. 4, Constitución Nacional [Const. Nac.] (Arg.).

Codes

- ► Código Civil (Civil Code)   Cód. Civ.
- ► Código de Comercio (Commercial Code)   Cód. Com.
- ► Código Penal (Criminal Code)   Cód. Pen.
- ► Código Procesal Civil y Comercial de la   Cód. Proc. Civ. y Com.
  Nación (Civil and Commercial Procedure Code)
- ► Código Procesal Penal de la Nación (Criminal   Cód. Proc. Pen.
  Procedure Code)

Include publication information for the version cited, if available:

- ► Código Penal [Cód. Pen.] [Criminal Code] art. 22 (Abeledo Perrot, Buenos Aires, 1971) (Arg.).

Statutes and decrees

Citation format: Law No. ‹law number›, ‹province abbreviation, if relevant›, ‹promulgation date›, [‹volume number›] ‹reporter abbreviation› ‹first page› (‹country abbreviation if not evident from context›).

- ► Law No. 23098, Oct. 19, 1984, [XLIV-D] A.D.L.A. 3733 (Arg.).

Cite to one of the following:

- ► Boletín Oficial   B.O.
- ► Anales de Legislación Argentina   A.D.L.A.
- ► El Derecho—Legislación Argentina   E.D.L.A.
- ► Anuario de Legislación   A.L.J.A.

Periodicals

- ► Revista Juridica La Ley   L.L.
- ► Lexis Nexis Jurisprudencia Argentina   J.A.
- ► El Derecho   E.D.

Internet sources

http.//www.bolctinoficial.gov.ar (Official Gazette; paid subscription and free access to current issue)

http://www.diariojudicial.com.ar (legal portal with free subscription)

http://www.laley.com.ar/laley (paid subscription)

http://www.abeledoperrot.com (paid subscription)

http://www.saij.jus.gov.ar (database of the Ministry of Justice; paid subscription includes national, provincial, and municipal legislation, court decisions, and scholarly sources)

http://www.infoleg.gov.ar (Ministry of Economy Database of legislation in PDF format; free access)

http://www.legalmania.com.ar/marco_home.htm (portal of legal information; free subscription)

http://www.colabogados.org.ar/publicaciones/larevista.php (*Revista del Colegio de Abogados de la Ciudad de Buenos Aires* online; free access)

T2.2   Australia

(Common Law)

Cases

Reported decisions: Citation format: ‹case name, in italics› (‹year of publication, when different from volume number›) ‹volume number› ‹reporter abbreviation› ‹first page›, ‹page(s) of specific material, if desired› (‹country abbreviation if not evident from context›).

Or: ‹case name, in italics› [‹year of volume, if it constitutes volume number›] ‹part number, if applicable› ‹reporter abbreviation› ‹first page›, ‹page(s) of specific material, if desired› (‹country abbreviation if not evident from context›).

> *Mabo v Queensland (No. 2)* (1992) 175 CLR 1, 5 (Austl.).

Only the name of the first plaintiff and first defendant should be cited. Note that all case names are in italics, and the abbreviation "v" for "versus" is not followed by a period. Case names may be abbreviated according to **tables T6** and **T10**. For example:

> *GA v Dep't of Educ. & Training* [2004] NSWADT 2 (Austl.).

Where the Commonwealth of Australia is a party, retain only "Commonwealth" as the party name. Where a state or territory is a party, omit "State of" or "Territory of" and retain only the state or territory name as the party name (for example, "Queensland" rather than "State of Queensland"). Where the Department of Public Prosecutions is a party, cite as "DPP" (with the relevant jurisdiction short abbreviation in parentheses). For example:

> *Silbert v DPP (WA)* [2004] HCA 9 (Austl.).

Jurisdiction short abbreviations are as follows: **Commonwealth** (Cth), **New South Wales** (NSW), **Victoria** (Vic), **South Australia** (SA), **Western Australia** (WA), **Tasmania** (Tas), **Queensland** (Qld), **Northern Territory** (NT), and **Australian Capital Territory** (ACT). The Crown is abbreviated as "R" except as a respondent, when it is cited as either "The Queen" or "The King."

In some reporters, the year acts as the volume number, so there is no separate volume number and parentheses should not be placed around the year. When the year is the volume number, the year is cited in square brackets. The volume year should be cited even when it differs from the year of the decision. When more than one part is issued per volume, the part number is cited after the volume number. For example:

> *Perini Corp. v Commonwealth* [1969] 2 NSWLR 530 (Austl.).

In some instances, a reporter uses paragraph references or other indicia rather than page numbers. In such instances, cite to the subdivision reference used by the reporter. For example:

▶ *Hart v Herron* [1984] Aust Torts Report ¶¶ 80-201 (Austl.).

The best available report of a case should be cited. When available, an official reporter should be cited. A generalist reporter is preferred to a subject specific reporter. When including more than one citation, cite the official reporter first. The correct abbreviation for a reporter will be included in the front of the reporters. Official reporters include the *Commonwealth Law Reports* (CLR), the *Federal Court Reports* (FCR), the *Victorian Reports* (VR), the *New South Wales Law Reports* (NSWLR), and the *Family Law Reports* (Fam LR).

If relevant, the court may be cited in parentheses subsequent to a citation. For example:

▶ *Aldrick v EM Invs. (Qld) Pty. Ltd.* [2000] 2 Qd R 346 (Court of Appeal) (Austl.).

Courts

High Court of Australia (the final court of appeal with both original and appellate jurisdiction since 1903): Cite to CLR, if therein. An avenue of appeal to the **Privy Council** (P.C.) was previously permitted, but limited in 1968 and abolished in 1975. All appeals from state and territory courts were abolished in the 1980s. For Privy Council decisions, cite to a reporter listed under **table T2.42 United Kingdom**, if therein; otherwise, cite to an official Australian reporter.

Federal Court of Australia (established in 1977, sits in each state and in the Australian Capital Territory and the Northern Territory, with original jurisdiction and appellate jurisdiction from single judges of the Federal Court, decisions (other than family law decisions) of the Federal Magistrates Court, and some decisions of State and Territory Supreme Courts): Cite to FCR, if therein.

Family Court of Australia (established in 1975, with original and appellate jurisdiction regarding family and child support disputes (other than in Western Australia)): Cite to Fam LR, if therein.

Federal Magistrates Court (established in 2000, hears less complex disputes): Cite to FCR, if therein.

Cite to a reporter below, in the following order of preference (* indicates an authorized reporter):

▶ Commonwealth Law Reports*	1903-date	CLR
▶ Federal Court Reports*	1984-date	FCR
▶ Family Law Reports*	1976-date	Fam LR
▶ Australian Argus Law Reports (previously the Argus Law Reports (Vic) (1895-1959) (ALR) and continues as Australian Law Reports (ALR))	1960-1973	AALR
▶ Australian Law Reports	1973-date	ALR
▶ Federal Law Reports	1956-date	FLR
▶ Australian Law Journal Reports	1927-date	ALJR
▶ Administrative Law Decisions	1976-date	ALD
▶ Australian Criminal Reports	1979-date	A Crim R
▶ Commonwealth Arbitration Reports	1906-1994	CAR
▶ Commonwealth Public Service Arbitration Reports	1921-1984	CPSAR
▶ Australian Company Law Reports	1974-1989	ACLR
▶ Australian Corporations and Securities Reports	1989-date	ACSR

▸ Australian Bankruptcy Cases	1928–1964	ABC
▸ Intellectual Property Reports	1982–date	IPR
▸ Australasian Tax Reports	1970–1990	ATR
▸ Australian Tax Reports	1990–date	ATR
▸ Australian and New Zealand Income Tax Reports	1940–1969	AITR
▸ Australian Tax Cases	1969–date	ATC
▸ Commonwealth Taxation Board of Review Decisions	1950–1986	CTBR (NS)
▸ Decisions of the Income Tax Board of Review, Commonwealth	1925–1937	CTBR
▸ Decisions of the Board of Review, Commonwealth Taxation Board of Review Decisions	1937–1950	CTBR

Unreported decisions: When the court has adopted it, cite in medium neutral format as: ‹case name, in italics› [‹year›] ‹unique court identifier› ‹case number or reference assigned by the court; if none assigned, then court name›, **(Unreported,** ‹references to judges›, ‹date of judgment›) ‹page(s) of specific material, if desired› (‹country abbreviation if not evident from context›).

Otherwise, cite unreported decisions as: ‹case name, in italics› (Unreported, ‹court name›, ‹date of judgment›) ‹page(s) of specific material, if desired› (‹country abbreviation if not evident from context›).

> ▸ *R v Diamond* (Unreported, Court of Criminal Appeal, 18 Feb. 1993) (Austl.).

References to judicial officers

Abbreviations are as follows:

▸ Chief Justice	CJ
▸ Acting Chief Justice	ACJ
▸ Justice(s)	J, JJ
▸ Acting Justice	AJ
▸ Judge	Judge
▸ Justice(s) of Appeal	JA, JJA
▸ Magistrate	Magistrate
▸ Master	Master
▸ President	P
▸ Vice-President	VP

Constitution

The enacting legislation for the Australian Constitution is the Commonwealth of Australia Act, 1900 (Imp), 63 & 64 Victoria, c. 12, § 9 (U.K.). Citation may be made directly to the Australian Constitution. For example:

> ▸ AUSTRALIAN CONSTITUTION S 51.

Statutes and regulations

Citation format for statutes: ‹short title of the act, in italics› ‹year of passage, in italics› (‹jurisdiction short abbreviation›) ‹subdivision, if relevant› (‹country abbreviation if not evident from context›).

(Statutes of the Australian Capital Territory and the Northern Territory were referred to as ordinances prior to self-government.)

The short title of an act is found within the act. When an act does not have a short title, the long title should be used. For example:

▶ *Trade Practices Act 1974* (Cth) s 2 (Austl.).

Subdivisions of acts and corresponding abbreviations include the following:

▶ section(s)	s, ss
▶ schedule(s)	sch, schs
▶ part(s)	pt, pts
▶ division(s)	div, divs
▶ paragraph(s)	para, paras

Acts cited are presumed to be as amended. Amending acts do not need to be cited unless the amending statute is being directly cited. Reference to year should be to the year the act was originally passed, not the year of amendment.

Citation format for delegated legislation (regulations, orders, etc.): ‹name of delegated legislation, in italics› ‹year of passage, in italics› (‹jurisdiction short abbreviation›) ‹subdivision, if relevant› (‹country abbreviation if not evident from context›).

▶ *Family Law Regulations 1984* (Cth) reg 20(3) (Austl.).

Provisions within a regulation are simply referred to as regulations. Subdivisions with corresponding abbreviations include the following:

▶ regulation(s)	reg, regs
▶ chapter(s)	ch, chs
▶ order	O
▶ rule(s)	r, rr
▶ sub-regulation(s)	sub-reg, sub-regs
▶ sub-rule(s)	sub-r, sub-rr

Citation format for bills: ‹bill name› ‹year of submission› (‹jurisdiction short abbreviation›) (‹country abbreviation if not evident from context›). Note that the titles of bills are not italicized.

▶ Interactive Gambling Bill 2001 (Cth) (Austl.).

Copies of bills are available from the relevant parliament's website. For example, Commonwealth bills are available at **http://www.aph.gov.au/bills**.

Citation format for explanatory memoranda of bills: Explanatory Memorandum, ‹bill name› ‹year of submission› (‹jurisdiction short abbreviation›) ‹page(s) of specific material, if desired› (‹country abbreviation if not evident from context›).

Citation format for parliamentary debates (Hansard): ‹jurisdiction short abbreviation›, Parliamentary Debates, ‹legislative chamber›, ‹date of debate in day month year format›, ‹page(s) of specific material, if desired› (‹full name of speaker and position if applicable›) (‹country abbreviation if not evident from context›).

▶ Cth, Parliamentary Debates, House of Representatives, 25 June 2008, 5823 (Robert McClelland, Attorney-General) (Austl.).

Copies of parliamentary debates are available from the relevant parliament's website. For example, copies of Commonwealth parliament debates are available at **http://www.aph.gov.au/hansard**.

Treaties

Citation format for treaties in the Australian Treaty Series: ‹treaty name›, [‹year›] ATS ‹reference number› (‹country abbreviation if not evident from context›).

▶ Treaty on Judicial Assistance in Civil and Commercial Matters Between Australia and the Republic of Korea, [2000] ATS 5 (Austl.).

Internet sources

There are several free Internet sources for primary legal materials.

ComLaw is owned by the Australian Commonwealth Attorney-General's Department and is intended to provide low or no-cost access to the law. ComLaw includes Commonwealth primary legislation (and ancillary documents) and the Federal Register of Legislative Instruments (FRLI) (established in January 2005 under the Legislative Instruments Act 2003). Acts on ComLaw are not authoritative. The PDF version of a legislative instrument on the Federal Register of Legislative Instruments is authoritative. ComLaw is accessible at **http://www.comlaw.gov.au**.

AustLII, the Australasian Legal Information Institute, is a joint facility of the University of Technology Sydney and the University of New South Wales. AustLII contains primary and secondary materials, including Commonwealth and state and territory legislation and case law. AustLII is not an authoritative source. It does not always contain the most up-to-date legislation, although it usually contains the most recent cases as well as oral argument transcripts from the High Court of Australia. AustLII is available at **http://www.austlii.edu.au**.

All Australian states and territories publish their statutes on the Internet, as indicated below. Not all databases are comprehensive.

http://www.legislation.act.gov.au (Australian Capital Territory Legislation Register)

http://www.parliament.nsw.gov.au/prod/parlment/nswbills.nsf/V3BillsHome (New South Wales Bills and Explanatory Notes)

http://www.legislation.nsw.gov.au (New South Wales legislation)

http://www.legislation.qld.gov.au/OQPChome.htm (Queensland legislation and bills)

http://www.parliament.sa.gov.au/BillsMotions (South Australia bills)

http://www.legislation.sa.gov.au/index.aspx (South Australia bills since 2005 and legislation)

http://www.thelaw.tas.gov.au/index.w3p (current Tasmania bills and legislation)

http://www.legislation.vic.gov.au (Victoria legislation and bills)

http://www.slp.wa.gov.au/legislation/statutes.nsf/default.html (Western Australia legislation and bills)

http://www.nt.gov.au/dcm/legislation/current.html (Northern Territory legislation)

http://www.nt.gov.au/dcm/legislation/register.html (Northern Territory bills)

http://www.info.gov.nf (Norfolk Island legislation)

Some Australian courts also publish judgments on the Internet (sometimes via AustLII). Databases may not be comprehensive. For example:

http://www.austlii.edu.au/au/cases/cth/HCA (High Court of Australia)

http://www.fedcourt.gov.au (Federal Court of Australia)

http://www.lawlink.nsw.gov.au (Supreme Court of New South Wales)

http://www.supremecourt.vic.gov.au (Supreme Court of Victoria)

http://www.supremecourt.tas.gov.au (Supreme Court of Tasmania)

http://www.supremecourt.wa.gov.au (Supreme Court of Western Australia)

http://www.sclqld.org.au (Supreme Court of Queensland)

http://www.supremecourt.nt.gov.au (Supreme Court of the Northern Territory)

http://www.courts.act.gov.au (Supreme Court of the Australian Capital Territory since 2002)

Guides to online resources for Australian law are available at the following websites:

http://www.aph.gov.au/library/intguide/law/auslaw.htm (Federal Parliament's Parliamentary Library)

http://www.nla.gov.au/oz/law.html (National Library of Australia)

Other legal materials, including various secondary sources, are available from commercial publishers, including Westlaw Australia, the Lawbook Company, CCH, and Butterworths (LexisNexis).

The most recent guide to legal citation in Australia is the 2002 second edition of the *Australian Guide to Legal Citation*, available at **http://mulr.law.unimelb.edu.au/files/aglcdl.pdf**.

T2.2.1   Australian states and territories

Cases

Cite to a reporter below, in the following order of preference:

▸ New South Wales Law Reports	1971–date	NSWLR
▸ State Reports, New South Wales	1901 1970	SR (NSW)
▸ New South Wales Reports	1960–1970	NSWR
▸ New South Wales Supreme Court Reports, Equity	1862–1876	NSWSCR (Eq)
▸ New South Wales Supreme Court Reports, Law	1862–1876	NSWSCR (L)
▸ New South Wales Supreme Court Reports, New Series	1825–1879	NSWSCR NS
▸ Weekly Notes	1884–1970	WN (NSW)
▸ Industrial Arbitration Reports, New South Wales	1902–1911 1912–1926 1927–date	AR (NSW)
▸ New South Wales Industrial Gazette	1912–date	NSW Indus Gaz
▸ New South Wales Local Government Reports	1911–1956	LGR (NSW)

▸ Land Appeal Court Cases	1890-1921	LACC
▸ Land and Valuations Court Reports, New South Wales	1922-1970	NSW LVR
▸ New South Wales Worker's Compensation Reports	1926-date	WCR (NSW)
▸ Queensland Reports	1958-date	Qd R
▸ Queensland State Reports	1902-1957	QSR
▸ Queensland Law Journal and Reports	1879-1901	QLJ
▸ Queensland Law Reports by Beor	1876-1878	QLR (Beor)
▸ Queensland Supreme Court Reports	1860-1881	QSCR
▸ Queensland Lawyer, Reports	1973-date	Qld Lawyer Rep
▸ Queensland Justice of the Peace and Local Authorities' Journal, Reports	1907-1968	QJP Rep
▸ Queensland Land Court Reports	1974-date	QLCR
▸ Crown Lands Law Report, Queensland Land Court	1859-1973	CL (Q)
▸ South Australian State Reports	1921-1971 1971-date	SASR
▸ South Australian Law Reports	1867-1892 1899-1920	SALR
▸ South Australian Industrial Reports	1916-date	SAIR
▸ Tasmanian Reports	1979-date	Tas R
▸ Tasmanian State Reports	1941-1978	Tas SR
▸ Tasmanian Law Reports	1905-1940	Tas LR
▸ Victorian Reports	1957-date	VR
▸ Victorian Law Reports	1885-1956	VLR
▸ Victorian Law Reports, Equity	1875-1884	VLR (E)
▸ Victorian Law Reports, Insolvency, Probate and Matrimonial Causes	1875-1884	VLR (I)
▸ Victorian Law Reports, Law	1875-1884	VLR (L)
▸ Victorian Law Reports, Mining	1875-1884	VLR (M)
▸ Australian Jurist Reports	1870-1874	A Jur Rep
▸ Western Australian Reports	1960-date	WAR
▸ West Australian Law Reports	1899-1959	WALR
▸ State Reports, Western Australia	1980-date	SR (WA)

T2.3   Austria, Republic of

(Civil Law)

....

Cases

Citation format for first citation of decisions of courts of last resort: ‹court name› [‹court abbreviation›] [‹English translation of court name›] ‹date of decision›, **docket No.** ‹docket number›, ‹volume number, if desired› ‹reporter name› [‹reporter abbreviation›] **No.** ‹case number› (‹country abbreviation if not evident from context›).

> ▸ Oberster Gerichtshof [OGH] [Supreme Court] Jan. 16, 2001, docket No. 4 Ob 311/00i, 74 ENTSCHEIDUNGEN DES ÖSTERREICHISCHEN OBERSTEN GERICHTSHOFES IN ZIVILSACHEN [SZ] No. 5 (Austria).

Citation of lower court case to a special subject collection of decisions:

▶ Landesgericht für Zivilrechtssachen [LGZ] Wien, Apr. 2, 2002, docket No. 42 R 382/01z, 39 Ehe- und familienrechtliche Entscheidungen [EF-Slg] No. 102.649 (Austria).

Citation format for court decision in collection of decisions in a periodical: ‹court abbreviation›, ‹date of decision›, docket No. ‹docket number›, ‹name of collection of decisions› [‹abbreviation of collection of decisions›] ‹case number within collection›, *in* ‹volume number› ‹periodical name› ‹first page›, ‹page(s) of specific material, if desired› (‹year›) (‹country abbreviation if not evident from context›).

▶ OGH, Nov. 26, 2002, docket No. 1 Ob 268/02x, Evidenzblatt der Rechtsmitteletschedungen [EvBl] 2003/53, *in* 58 Österreichische Juristen-Zeitung 260 (2003) (Austria).

Ordinary jurisdiction

Oberster Gerichtshof (OGH) (Supreme Court): Cite to SZ for civil matters and to SSt for criminal matters, or to a periodical, special subject reporter, or electronic source; **Oberlandesgericht** (OLG) (higher regional court for appeals from a Landesgericht), **Landesgericht** (LG) (regional trial courts and courts of appeals from a Bezirksgericht), and **Bezirksgericht** (BG) (local trial courts): Cite to any available source, naming the court's location (e.g., OLG Wien or LG Salzburg). In Wien and Graz, the Landesgericht is split into a court for civil matters (LGZ) (e.g., LGZ Wien) and one for criminal cases (LGSt).

▶ Entscheidungen des Österreichischen Obersten Gerichtshofes in Zivilsachen	1919-1938 1946-date	SZ
▶ Entscheidungen des Obersten Gerichtshofes in Strafsachen	1921-1938 1946-date	SSt

Special jurisdiction

Arbeits-und Sozialgericht (ASG) (trial court for labor and social insurance matters): Cite to ArbRSlg for labor matters, and SVSlg for social insurance matters, if therein; **Handelsgericht** (HG) (trial court and court of appeals for commercial matters): Cite to HS, if therein; **Kartellobergericht** (OGH as KOG) (division of Supreme Court for antitrust matters) and **Kartellgericht** (KartG) (trial court for antitrust matters): Cite to the source where the decision is reprinted.

▶ Sammlung Arbeitsrechtlicher Entscheidungen	1973-date	Arb
▶ Sozialversicherungsrechtliche Entscheidungen	1945-date	SVSlg
▶ Handelsrechtliche Entscheidungen	1939-date	HS

Constitutional jurisdiction

Verfassungsgerichtshof (VfGH) (Constitutional Court): Cite to VfSlg, if therein.

▶ Erkenntnisse und Beschlüsse des Verfassungsgerichtshofes	1921-1933 1946-present	VfSlg

▶ Verfassungsgerichtshof [VfGH] [Constitutional Court], Oct. 15, 2004, Erkenntnisse und Beschlüsse des Verfassungsgerichtshofes [VfSlg] No. 17339/2004 (Austria).

Administrative jurisdiction

Format for first citation of administrative court decision: ‹court name› [‹court abbreviation›] [‹English translation of court name›] ‹date of decision›, docket No. ‹docket number›, ‹volume number› ‹reporter name› [‹reporter abbreviation›] No. ‹case number within collection› (‹country abbreviation if not evident from context›).

▶ Verwaltungsgerichtshof [VwGH] [Administrative Court] June 29, 2000, docket No. 96/01/1071, 55 ERKENNTNISSE UND BESCHLÜSSE DES VERWALTUNGSGERICHTSHOFES ADMINISTRATIVRECHTLICHER TEIL [VwSLG] No. 15 444 A (Austria).

▶ Verwaltungsgerichtshof [VwGH] [Administrative Court] Jan. 25, 1980, docket No. 1753/79, 35 ERKENNTNISSE UND BESCHLÜSSE DES VERWALTUNGSGERICHTSHOFES FINANZRECHTLICHER TEIL [VwSLG] No. 5453 F/1980 (Austria).

Verwaltungsgerichtshof (VwGH) (Administrative Court): Cite to VwSLG, distinguishing between administrative and fiscal decisions by the letters A or F after the case number.

▶ ERKENNTNISSE UND BESCHLÜSSE DES VERWALTUNGSGERICHTSHOFES ADMINISTRATIVRECHTLICHER TEIL	1946–date	VwSLG
▶ ERKENNTNISSE UND BESCHLÜSSE DES VERWALTUNGS-GERICHTSHOFES FINANZRECHTLICHER TEIL	1946–date	VwSLG

Electronic citations

Citation format: ‹case citation›, ‹"*available at*" if published in an official reporter, or "*at*" if decision is not reported in an official reporter› ‹database name› [‹database abbreviation›] ‹URL›, document No. ‹document number in the electronic source› (‹country abbreviation if not evident from context›).

▶ Verfassungsgerichtshof [VfGH] [Constitutional Court], Sept. 18, 2004, docket No. B292/04, *at* Bundeskanzleramt Rechtsinformationssystem [BKA/RIS] http://www.ris2.bka.gv.at, document No. JFR/09959072/04B00292/2 (Austria).

....

Constitution

Citation format: ‹constitution name› [‹constitution abbreviation›] [CONSTITUTION] ‹federal law gazette› [‹abbreviation›] No. ‹number›/‹year› ‹"as amended" or "as last amended by" and citation of amending law, if pertinent›, ‹article number, if desired›, ‹paragraph, if desired› (‹country abbreviation if not evident from context›).

▶ BUNDES-VERFASSUNGSGESETZ [B-VG] [CONSTITUTION] BGBl No. 1/1930, as last amended by Bundesverfassungsgesetz [BVG] BGBl I No. 2/2008, art. 147, ¶ 2 (Austria).

Cite federal statutes of constitutional rank and constitutional provisions in federal statutes and treaties of international law according to the format for these enactments.

▶ BUNDES-VERFASSUNGSGESETZ	B-VG
▶ Menschenrechtskonvention (European Convention on Human Rights)	MRK
▶ Staatsgrundgesetz über die allgemeinen Rechte der Staatsbürger (federal bill of rights)	StGG

....

Codes

Citation format: ‹name of code› [‹abbreviation of code›] [‹English translation of name of code›] ‹name of gazette of promulgation› [‹gazette abbrevia-

tion›] No. ‹number›/‹year›, as amended, ‹section, if desired› ‹paragraph,
if desired› (‹country abbreviation if not evident from context›).

> ▸ ALLGEMEINES BÜRGERLICHES GESETZBUCH [ABGB] [CIVIL CODE]
>   JUSTIZGESETZSAMMLUNG [JGS] No. 946/1816, as amended, § 841
>   (Austria).

▸ ALLGEMEINES BÜRGERLICHES GESETZBUCH (CIVIL CODE)	ABGB
▸ HANDELSGESETZBUCH (COMMERCIAL CODE)	HGB
▸ STRAFGESETZBUCH (PENAL CODE)	STGB
▸ STRAFPROZESSORDNUNG (CODE OF CRIMINAL PROCEDURE)	STPO
▸ ZIVILPROZESSORDNUNG (CIVIL PROCEDURE STATUTE)	ZPO

Statutes and regulations

Citation format: ‹full or short name› [‹abbreviation, if it exists›] [‹English
translation of name›] ‹date of promulgation (optional)› ‹gazette of promulgation› [‹gazette abbreviation›] No. ‹number›/‹year›, ‹"as amended,"
if applicable›, ‹section, paragraph, or other subdivision, if desired›
(‹country abbreviation if not evident from context›).

> ▸ RECHTSANWALTSORDNUNG [RAO] [ACT ON ATTORNEYS]
>   REICHSGESETZBLATT [RGBL] No. 96/1868, § 1 ¶ 2 letter D (Austria).
> ▸ STAATSDRUCKEREIGESETZ 1996 [ACT ON THE STATE PRINTING OFFICE
>   OF 1996] BUNDESGESETZBLATT [BGBL] No. 1/1997 (Austria).

The date of enactment is not required. The date of promulgation also is not
required, unless it is pertinent. The law or regulation becomes effective on the
day after promulgation in the gazette, unless otherwise specified.

Cite a Bundesverfassungsgesetz (BVG) (federal statute of constitutional rank),
Bundesgesetz (BG) (federal statute), or Verordnung (V) (regulation) to *Bundesgesetzblatt* (BGBL). Cite their predecessors, a Reichsgesetz (RG) or Gesetz (G), to
Reichsgesetzblatt (RGBL) or *deutsches Reichsgesetzblatt* (DRGBL), or a Staatsge-
setz (StG) or Gesetz (G) to *Staatsgesetzblatt* (STGBL).

Since 1997, the *Bundesgesetzblatt* is published in three parts: Teil I (statutes), Teil
II (regulations), and Teil III (treaties). For 1940-1945, the *deutsches Reichsgesetzblatt* consists of two parts: Teil I (statutes and regulations) and Teil II (treaties).
Since January 1, 2004, the electronic version of the *Bundesgesetzblatt*, which is
available at **http://www.ris.bka.gv.at/Bund**, is the authentic version. Since
January 1, 2007, no paper copy has been published. These changes, however,
have not changed the format or the citation.

▸ BUNDESGESETZBLATT I	1997-date	BGBL I
▸ BUNDESGESETZBLATT II	1997-date	BGBL II
▸ BUNDESGESETZBLATT III	1997-date	BGBL III
▸ BUNDESGESETZBLATT	1945-1996	BGBL
▸ DEUTSCHES REICHSGESETZBLATT I	1940-1945	DRGBL I
▸ DEUTSCHES REICHSGESETZBLATT II	1940-1945	DRGBL II
▸ GESETZBLATT FÜR DAS LAND ÖSTERREICH	1938-1940	GBLÖ
▸ BUNDESGESETZBLATT	1920-1938	BGBI
▸ STAATSGESETZBLATT	1918-1920	STGBL
▸ REICHSGESETZBLATT	1849-1918	RGBL

Periodicals

- EVIDENZBLATT DER RECHTSMITTELENTSCHEIDUNGEN IN ÖSTERREICHISCHE JURISTENZEITUNG — EvBl
- JURISTISCHE BLÄTTER — JBL
- ÖSTERREICHISCHE JURISTEN-ZEITUNG — ÖJZ
- ÖSTERREICHISCHES RECHT DER WIRTSCHAFT — RdW
- ÖSTERREICHISCHES BANK-ARCHIV — ÖBA
- ÖSTERREICHISCHE BLÄTTER FÜR GEWERBLICHEN RECHTSSCHUTZ UND URHEBERRECHT — ÖBL
- ECOLEX — ECOLEX
- ÖSTERREICHISCHE ZEITSCHRIFT FÜR WIRTSCHAFTSRECHT — ÖZW
- DER GESELLSCHAFTER — GESRZ
- ZEITSCHRIFT FÜR VERWALTUNG — ZFV

Legislative materials

Citation format: ‹legislative body name› [‹legislative body abbreviation›] [‹English translation of name›] ‹legislative period› [‹legislative period abbreviation›] ‹legislative period number› ‹materials name› [‹materials abbreviation›] **No.** ‹document number› (‹country abbreviation if not evident from context›).

- Nationalrat [NR] [National Council] Gesetzgebungsperiode [GP] 22 Beilage [Blg] No. 446 (Austria).

Internet sources

The Austrian Bundeskanzleramt (Federal Chancellery) maintains Rechtsinformationssystem, a free electronic legal database available at **http://www.ris.bka.gv.at**. Rechtsinformationssystem contains texts of the decisions of the courts of last resort, federal legislation, legislation of the Länder, and many other legal sources.

T2.3.1   Austrian Länder

Cases

All courts are federal courts, listed above.

Constitutions

- LANDESVERFASSUNG — LVG

Citation format: **LANDESVERFASSUNG [LVG] [STATE CONSTITUTION]**, ‹article number, if desired› (‹name of state›) (‹country abbreviation if not evident from context›).

- **LANDESVERFASSUNG [LVG] [STATE CONSTITUTION]**, art. 3 (Kärnten) (Austria).

Statutes and regulations

Cite a Landesverfassungsgesetz (LVG) (state constitutional statute), Landesgesetz (LG) (state statute), or Verordnung (V) (administrative regulation) to *Landesgesetzblatt* (LGBL). Cite by number/year.

- LANDESGESETZBLATT — LGBL

T2.4   Belgium, Kingdom of

(Civil Law)

All federal and regional statutes and legislative materials have official versions in French (the language in Wallonia) and Dutch (the language in Flanders). The same applies to the case law of the two highest courts in Belgium. Furthermore, the names of all Belgian courts exist in two languages, although decisions of lower courts are issued in one language only. It is customary in Belgian legal publishing to cite to the same language version as one is actually writing in, either Dutch or French. Belgian citation rules and customs differ slightly between the French- and Dutch-speaking parts of the country.

Cases

Citation format: ‹court name› [‹court abbreviation›] [‹English translation of court name›] ‹city, if applicable›, ‹chamber, if applicable› ‹date of decision in month day, year format›, ‹reporter or journal name› [‹reporter or journal abbreviation›] ‹year of publication›, ‹part number, if applicable›, ‹case number, if applicable›, ‹first page›, ‹author of case note, if applicable› (‹country abbreviation if not evident from context›).

- ▶ Tribunal de Première Instance [Civ.] [Tribunal of First Instance] Charleroi, 2e ch. Apr. 9, 2003, REVUE DE DROIT DE LA SANTÉ [Rev.dr.santé] 2003, 768 (Belg.).
- ▶ Tribunal de Commerce [Comm.] [Commerce Tribunal] Ostende, Réf, Oct. 12, 1987, REVUE DE DROIT COMMERCIAL BELGE [RDC] 1988, 268, note Verougstraete (Belg.).
- ▶ Hof van Beroep [HvB] [Court of Appeal] Antwerpen, Feb. 18, 2003, RECHTSKUNDIG WEEKBLAD [RW] 2003, 584 (Belg.).

Ordinary jurisdiction

Court of Cassation: Cour de Cassation (Cass.)/**Hof van Cassatie** (Cass.): Cite to PAS., or to ARR.CASS., if therein; otherwise, cite to the official online version, giving the date and docket number only, or cite to another Belgian law review.

▶ PASICRISIE BELGE (French)	1791–date	PAS.
▶ ARRESTEN VAN HET HOF VAN CASSATIE (Dutch)	1937–date	ARR.CASS.

Prior to 2003, the *Pasicrisie* was published in three parts: Part I, the Cour de Cassation decisions; Part II, a selection of courts of appeal cases; and Part III, a selection of lower court cases. In 2003, the publisher decided to maintain only Part I

- ▶ Hof van Cassatie [Cass.] [Court of Cassation], Dec. 24, 1993, ARR.CASS. 1993, 1117 (Belg.).
- ▶ Cour de Cassation [Cass.] [Court of Cassation], Oct. 3, 1986, PAS. 1987, I, No. 64, 886 (Belg.).
- ▶ Hof van Cassatie [Cass.] [Court of Cassation], Mar. 16, 2007, AR F050049N, http://www.cass.be (Belg.).

Cours d'Appel (CA)/**Hoven van Beroep** (HvB) (courts of appeal). There are five courts of appeal: Anvers/Antwerpen and Gand/Gent in Flanders, Liege/Luik and Mons/Bergen in Wallonia, and Bruxelles in the bilingual capital region Brussels.

Cour du Travail (Cour. Trav.)/**Arbeidshof** (Arbh.) (Labor Court: hears appeals in social law matters).

Cour d'Assises (Cour. ass.)/**Hof van Assisen** (Assisen) (Court of Assizes: court of original jurisdiction for very serious crimes, the only Belgian court with a jury).

Tribunaux de Première Instance/Rechtbanken van Eerste Aanleg (tribunals of first instance: ordinary courts of original jurisdiction, either in civil matters (Civ./Rb.); in commercial matters as **Tribunaux de Commerce** (Comm.)/**Rechtbanken van Koophandel** (Kh.) (commerce tribunals); in criminal matters as **Tribunaux Correctionels** (Corr.)/**Correctionele Recht-banken** (Corr.) (criminal tribunals); or in social justice matters as **Tribunaux du Travail** (Trib. Trav.)/**Arbeidsrechtbanken** (Arbrb.) (labor tribunals)).

Tribunaux des Juges de Paix (J.P.)/**Vredegerechten** (Vred.) (justices of the peace: hear civil and commercial low-value claims).

Tribunaux de Police (Pol.)/**Politierechtbanken** (Pol.) (police courts: deal with minor offenses).

Journals

Belgian law reviews are either in French, in Dutch, or bilingual. Most journals publish case law, and they are the main source for lower courts' case law. All types of cases are reported in these journals, and there is no preferred citation.

▸ Journal des Tribunaux	1882–date	JT
▸ Revue Critique de Jurisprudence Belge	1947–date	RCJB
▸ Nieuw Juridisch Weekblad	2002–date	NJW
▸ Algemeen Juridisch Tijdschrift	1994–2002	AJT
▸ Revue de Jurisprudence de Liège, Mons Bruxelles	1987–date	JLMB
▸ Jurisprudence de Liège	1888–1987	JL
▸ Rechtspraak Antwerpen Brussel Gent	2003–date	RABG
▸ Tijdschrift voor Belgisch Handelsrecht-Revue de Droit Commercial Belge	1968–date	TBH-RDC
▸ Revue Général de Droit Civil Belge-Tijdschrift voor Belgisch Burgerlijk Recht	1987–date	TBBR-RGDC

Administrative jurisdiction

Citation format for highest administrative court: ‹court name›[‹court abbreviation›][‹English translation of court name›] ‹date of decision›, ‹names of parties›, ‹case number›, ‹reporter name or website› [‹reporter abbreviation›], ‹year of publication›, ‹page› (‹country abbreviation if not evident from context›).

Conseil d'État (CE)/**Raad van State** (RvS) (Council of State): Cite to RACE or Arr.RvS for cases decided prior to 1994; cite to the official publication on the website of the Council for cases decided after 1994, using the date, names of parties, and docket number. The Council of State is the highest administrative court in Belgium, and serves as a court of first instance for judicial review of administrative acts and as a court of appeal for various administrative commissions.

▸ Recueil des Arrêts du Conseil d'État (French)	1948–1994	RACE
▸ Verzameling van Arresten van de Raad van State (Dutch)	1948–1994	Arr.RvS

> ▸ Conseil d'Etat [CE] [Council of State] June 3, 1975, Beeckman, No. 17.056, Recueil des Arrêts du Conseil d'État [RACE], 1975 (Belg.).

> ▶ Raad van State [RvS] [Council of State] Nov. 4, 1985, Vlaamse Gemeenschap, No. 25.797, Verzameling van Arresten van de Raad van State [Arr.RvS], 1985 (Belg.).

> ▶ Conseil d'État [CE] [Council of State] Nov. 25, 2004, Ingrosso, No. 137.642, http://www.conseildetat.be (Belg.).

Constitutional jurisdiction

Citation format: ‹court name› [‹court abbreviation›] [‹English translation of court name›] ‹case number›, ‹date of decision› ‹reporter name› [‹reporter abbreviation›] [‹English translation of reporter name›], ‹date of publication›, ‹page› (‹country abbreviation if not evident from context›).

Cour Constitutionnelle (CC)/**Grondwettelijk Hof** (GwH) (Constitutional Court (**Cour d'arbitrage/Arbitragehof** prior to 2007)): Cite to M.B. or B.S., if therein; otherwise, cite to the court's website, giving the date and docket number only.

▶ Moniteur Belge/Belgisch Staatsblad (Official Gazette of Belgium, case extracts only)	1845–2003 (print) 1997–date (online)	M.B./B.S.
▶ Recueil des Arrêts de la Cour Constitutionnelle/Arresten Grondwettelijk Hof (complete official versions of cases)	1986–date	ACC/Arr.GwH

> ▶ Cour Constitutionnelle [CC] [Constitutional Court] decision no 144/2008, Oct. 30, 2008, Moniteur Belge [MB] [Official Gazette of Belgium], Nov. 20, 2008, 61,692 (Belg.).

> ▶ Grondwettelijk Hof [GwH] [Constitutional Court] decision no 113/2007, July 26, 2007, http://www.grondwettelijkhof.be (Belg.).

....

Constitution

> ▶ La Constitution   Const.

Citation format: ‹year› Const. ‹article› (‹country abbreviation if not evident from context›).

The original 1831 constitution was amended on numerous occasions. The most recent version was published in 1994. If desired, cite by date:

> ▶ 1994 Const. art. 1 (Belg.).

....

Codes

Citation format: ‹code name› [‹code abbreviation›] ‹article› (‹country abbreviation if not evident from context›).

> ▶ Code Civil [C.Civ.] art. 235 (Belg.).

▶ Code Civil/Burgerlijk Wetboek	C.Civ./BW
▶ Code de Commerce/Wetboek van Koophandel	C.Comm./WKh
▶ Code d'Instruction Criminelle/Wetboek van Strafvordering	C.I.Cr./Sv.
▶ Code Judiciaire/Gerechtelijk Wetboek	C.Jud./Ger.W.
▶ Code Pénal/Strafwetboek	C.Pén./Sw.

....

Statutes and decrees

Citation format: ‹statute or decree name› [‹English translation of statute or decree name›] of ‹date of enactment›, ‹"Moniteur Belge" or "Belgisch

STAATSBLAD"] ["M.B." or "B.S."] [Official Gazette of Belgium], ‹date of publication›, ‹edition if applicable›, ‹first page, if not citing the online version› (‹country abbreviation if not evident from context›).

► Loi relative à la responsabilité du fait des produits défectueux [Product Liability Act] of Feb. 25, 1991, MONITEUR BELGE [M.B.] [Official Gazette of Belgium], Mar. 22, 1991, 5884.

► Wet houdende diverse bepalingen [Law Concerning Diverse Dispositions] of Dec. 27, 2006, BELGISCH STAATSBLAD [B.S.] [Official Gazette of Belgium], Dec. 28, 2006, 3d ed., http://www.staatsblad .be.

► MONITEUR BELGE/BELGISCH STAATSBLAD (Official Gazette of Belgium)	1845–2003 (print) 1997–date (online)	M.B./B.S.
► Bulletin Officiel des Lois et Arrêtés Royaux de Belgique	1788–1845	Bull.Off.

Treaties and conventions

Citation format: ‹name of law ratifying the treaty› [‹English translation of law name›] of ‹date of law›, ‹"MONITEUR BELGE" or "BELGISCH STAATSBLAD"› [‹"M.B." or "B.S."›] [Official Gazette of Belgium], ‹date of publication›, ‹first page› (‹country abbreviation if not evident from context›).

► Loi portant assentiment à la Convention de Budapest relative au contrat de transport de merchandises en navigation intérieure (CMNI), faite à Budapest le 22 juin 2001 [Law Ratifying the Budapest Convention on the Contract for the Carriage of Goods by Inland Waterway (CMNI), Done at Budapest on June 22, 2001] of June 29, 2008, MONITEUR BELGE [M.B.] [Official Gazette of Belgium], Oct. 10, 2008, 54,229.

Internet sources

http://www.belgiumlex.be (access to the constitution, codes, official gazette, consolidated legislation, court decisions, and other official publications)

http://www.just.fgov.be (Ministry of Justice)

http://www.lachambre.be (House of Representatives, providing access to recent legislation)

http://www.senaat.be (the Federal Senate, providing access to recent legislation)

http://www.vlaamsparlement.be (Flemish Parliament)

http://www.parlement-wallon.be (Walloon Parliament)

http://www.pcf.be (French Community Parliament)

http://www.parlbruparl.irisnet.be (Brussels Parliament)

http://www.juridat.be (the Judicial Power, providing a free searchable database of case law)

http://www.councilofstate.be (Council of State, providing access to a database of its judgments)

http://www.constitutionalcourt.be (Constitutional Court, providing access to a database of its judgments)

http://www.ejustice.just.fgov.be/cgi/welcome.pl (Official Gazette, providing access to back issues (2002–date))

http://www.ejustice.just.fgov.be/loi/loi.htm (consolidated legislation, providing access to federal and regional materials)

http://www.fisconet.fgov.be (federal tax legislation)

http://wallex.wallonie.be (Walloon legislation)

http://www.gallilex.be (French Community legislation)

http://www.codex.vlaanderen.be (Flemish legislation)

T2.5   Brazil, Federative Republic of

(Civil Law)

Cases

Citation format: ‹court abbreviation›-‹chamber/region number›, ‹docket number›, Relator: ‹relator name›, ‹judgment date in day.month.year format›, ‹volume number›, ‹reporter name› [‹reporter abbreviation›], ‹publication date in day.month.year format›, ‹first page›, ‹page(s) of specific material, if desired› (‹country abbreviation if not evident from context›).

> ▸ TRF-2, Ap. Crim. No. 1990.51.01.043265-8, Relator: Des. Fernando Marques, 14.11.2008, 232, Diário da Justiça [D.J.], 28.11.2008, 13 (Braz.).

> ▸ T.J.M.G., Ap. Civ. No. 1.0024.08.158530-9/001 Belo Horizonte, Relator: Des. Fernando Caldeira Brant, 26.11.2008, 136, Diário do Judiciário Eletrônico [D.J.e.], 09.12.2008, 147 (Braz.).

Official gazettes

▸ Diário Oficial da União (federal laws and cases from S.T.F.)	D.O.U.
▸ Diário da Justiça (higher court cases)	D.J.
▸ Diário Oficial dos Estados (state laws and cases)	D.O.E.
▸ e.g., Rio de Janeiro	D.O.E.R.J.
▸ e.g., São Paulo	D.O.E.S.P.
▸ e.g., Minas Gerais	D.O.E.M.G.

Higher courts

Supremo Tribunal Federal (S.T.F.) (highest court of appeals on constitutional matters): Cite to R.T.J., R.S.T.F., or S.T.F.J., if therein.

▸ Revista Trimestral de Jurisprudência	1956-date	e.g., R.T.J. 50/101
▸ Revista do Supremo Tribunal Federal	1914-1956	R.S.T.F.
▸ Supremo Tribunal Federal Jurisprudência (available at **http://www.stf.gov.br**)		S.T.F.J.

Superior Tribunal de Justiça (S.T.J.) (highest court of appeals on all non-constitutional matters): Cite to R.S.T.J., S.T.J.J., or R.T., if therein.

▸ Revista do Superior Tribunal de Justiça	1989-date	R.S.T.J.
▸ Superior Tribunal de Justiça Jurisprudência (available at **http://www.stj.jus.br**)		S.T.J.J.
▸ Revista dos Tribunais	1912-date	R.T.

Tribunal Superior do Trabalho (T.S.T.) (highest court of appeals on labor law): Cite to R.T.S.T. or T.S.T.J., if therein.

▸ Revista do Tribunal Superior do Trabalho   1946–date   R.T.S.T.
▸ Tribunal Superior do Trabalho Jurisprudência   T.S.T.J.
   (available at **http://www.tst.gov.br**)

Tribunal Superior Eleitoral (T.S.E.) (highest court of appeals on electoral law): Cite to T.S.E.J., if therein.

▸ Tribunal Superior Eleitoral Jurisprudência   T.S.E.J.
   (available at **http://www.tse.gov.br**)

Superior Tribunal Militar (S.T.M.) (highest court of appeals on military law): Cite to S.T.M.J., if therein.

▸ Superior Tribunal Militar Jurisprudência   S.T.M.J.
   (available at **http://www.stm.gov.br**)

Federal courts

Tribunal Regional Federal (TRF-‹region number›, e.g., TRF-1) (regional federal court of appeals on matters of federal interest): Cite to R.T.R.F., if therein.

▸ Revista do Tribunal Regional Federal (regions vary)   R.T.R.F.

Vara da Justiça Federal (J.F.) (federal district courts on matters of federal interest): Indicate number and city.

State courts

Tribunais de Justiça dos Estados (T.J. ‹state initials›, e.g., T.J.M.G. for Minas Gerais) (higher state courts of appeals): Cite to D.J.‹state initials› (e.g., D.J.M.G. for Minas Gerais), if therein.

▸ State's Judiciary Gazette (regions vary)   e.g., D.J.M.G.
▸ Revista dos Tribunais   1912–date   R.T.
▸ Revista Forense   1904–date   R.F.

Constitution

▸ Constituição Federal   C.F.

   ▸ Constituição Federal [C.F.] [Constitution] art. 3 (Braz.).

Codes

▸ Código de Águas   C.Ag.
▸ Código Civil   C.C.
▸ Código Comercial   C.Com.
▸ Código Eleitoral   C.E.
▸ Código Florestal   C.Flor.
▸ Código de Mineração   C.Min.
▸ Consolidação das Leis do Trabalho   C.L.T.
▸ Código Penal   C.P.
▸ Código Penal Militar   C.P.M.
▸ Código de Processo Civil   C.P.C.
▸ Código de Processo Penal   C.P.P.
▸ Código de Propriedade Industrial   C.P.I.
▸ Código de Proteção e Defesa do Consumidor   C.D.C.
▸ Código Tributário Nacional   C.T.N.
▸ Código Brasileiro de Telecomunicações   C.B.T.
▸ Código de Processo Penal Militar   C.P.P.M.
▸ Código de Caça   C.Ca.

- CÓDIGO BRASILEIRO DE AERONÁUTICA   C.B.A.
- ESTATUTO DA CRIANÇA E DO ADOLESCENTE   E.C.A.
- CÓDIGO DE TRÂNSITO BRASILEIRO   C.T.B.

Statutes and decrees

Citation format: ‹statute/decree number›, **de** ‹date of promulgation in Portuguese›, ‹official gazette name› [‹official gazette abbreviation›] **de** ‹date of publication in day.month.year format› (‹country abbreviation if not evident from context›).

Or: ‹statute/decree number›, **de** ‹date of promulgation in Portuguese›, ‹reporter name› [‹reporter abbreviation›], ‹volume number› (‹number›, **t.** ‹tomo number›): ‹page(s)› **de** ‹date of publication in day.month.year format› (‹country abbreviation if not evident from context›).

Use "**t.**" to refer to "tomo," which is Portuguese for "volume."

Official gazettes
- DIÁRIO OFICIAL DA UNIÃO (available at   1862–date D.O.U.
  http://portal.in.gov.br/in) (federal laws)
- DIÁRIO OFICIAL ‹of state name› (state laws, regions vary)   e.g., D.O.E.R.J.

  - Decreto No. 6.626, de 3 de Novembro de 2008, DIÁRIO OFICIAL DA UNIÃO [D.O.U.] de 4.11.2008 (Braz.).

  - Decreto No. 41.566, de 27 de Novembro de 2008, DIÁRIO OFICIAL DO RIO DE JANEIRO [D.O.E.R.J.] de 28.11.2008 (Braz.).

Alternate sources

Citation format: ‹statute/decree number›, **de** ‹date of promulgation in Portuguese›, ‹publication name› [‹publication abbreviation›], ‹date of publication› (‹country abbreviation if not evident from context›).

Or: ‹statute/decree number›, **de** ‹date of promulgation in Portuguese›, ‹reporter abbreviation›, ‹volume number› (‹number›, **t.**‹tomo number›): ‹page(s)›, ‹date of publication in month year format› (‹country abbreviation if not evident from context›).

- REVISTA LEX   LEX
- COLEÇÃO DAS LEIS   COL. LEIS REP. FED. BRASIL

  - Lei No. 9.215, de 22 de Dezembro de 1995, COL. LEIS REP. FED. BRASIL, 187 (12, t.1): 5388, Dezembro 1995 (Braz.).

Treaties and conventions

Coleção de Atos Internacionais	1927–1964	Col. Atos Internacionais, No. ‹treaty number›

Ministry of Foreign Affairs:

http://www2.mre.gov.br/dai/bilaterais.htm (international bilateral agreements by country)

http://www2.mre.gov.br/dai/quadros.htm (international bilateral agreements by topic and international multilateral agreements)

T2.6   Canada

(Common Law and Civil Law (Québec))

....

Cases

Privy Council (P.C.) (criminal appeals until 1935, civil appeals until 1949): Cite to reports listed under **table T2.42 United Kingdom** if therein; otherwise cite to Olms.

> ▶ Great Britain privy council judicial committee, decisions relating to   Olms.
>   the British North American Act, 1867, and the Canadian
>   Constitution 1867-1954, arranged by Richard A. Olmsted

Supreme Court of Canada (S.C.C.): Cite to S.C.R. if therein; otherwise cite to D.L.R.

▶ Canada: Supreme Court Reports	1876-date	S.C.R.
▶ Dominion Law Reports	1912-date	D.L.R.

Federal Court (Fed. Ct.) (formerly the **Exchequer Court**): Cite to F.C. or Ex. C.R. if therein; otherwise cite to D.L.R.

▶ Federal Court Reports	1971-date	F.C.
▶ Exchequer Court Reports	1875-1971	Ex. C.R.

Tax Court of Canada (Can. Tax Ct.): Cite to C.T.C. or Tax A.B.C. if therein; otherwise cite to D.T.C. or D.L.R.

▶ Canada Tax Cases	1985-date	C.T.C.
▶ Canada Tax Appeal Board Cases	1945-1972	Tax A.B.C.
▶ Dominion Tax Cases	1920-date	D.T.C.

There are six main citation styles for Canadian cases:

1) Reporters for which the year constitutes the volume number. The following reporters fit this description during the specified year ranges:

▶ Supreme Court Reports	1923-1974	S.C.R.
▶ Federal Court Reports	1971-1973	F.C.
▶ Ontario Reports	1931-1962	O.R.

Citation format: ‹case name›, [‹year of report›] ‹abbreviation of report› ‹first page› (‹country abbreviation› ‹province abbreviation, if applicable› ‹court abbreviation, if applicable›).

> ▶ Chase v. Campbell, [1962] S.C.R. 425 (Can.).

> ▶ Roméo Lafrance c. Hôpital St-Luc et Commission des affaires sociales, [1980] C.A. 497 (Can. Que.).

Always include the province abbreviation for decisions of provincial courts. Only include the court abbreviation when it is not apparent from the reporter. When citing French translations of Canadian cases, the party names are separated by "c.," which refers to "contre," the French translation of "versus."

2) Reporters that begin at volume one each year, and are thus organized by year first, then volume number. The following reporters fit this description during the specified year ranges:

▶ Supreme Court Reports	1975-date	S.C.R.
▶ Federal Court Reports	1974-2003	F.C.

► Federal Court Reports	2004-date	F.C.R.
► Ontario Reports	1963-1973	O.R.
► Dominion Law Reports	1923-1955	D.L.R.

Omit the year of decision when it is the same as the reporter year:

Citation format: ‹case name›, [‹reporter year›] ‹volume number› ‹reporter abbreviation› ‹first page› (‹country abbreviation› ‹province abbreviation, if applicable› ‹court abbreviation, if applicable›).

- ► R. v. Morgentaler, [1993] 3 S.C.R. 463 (Can.).
- ► Brockville Hotel Co. v. Aga Heat (Can.) Ltd., [1944] 2 D.L.R. 698 (Can. Ont. C.A.).

Include the year of decision when it is different from the reporter year:

Citation format: ‹case name› (‹year of decision›), [‹reporter year›] ‹volume number› ‹reporter abbreviation› ‹first page› (‹country abbreviation› ‹province abbreviation, if applicable› ‹court abbreviation, if applicable›).

- ► Swiss Bank Corp. v. Air Can. (1987), [1988] 1 F.C. 71 (Can. C.A.).

3) Reporters that are divided into series, and are thus organized by series first, then volume number. The following reporters fit this description during the specified year ranges:

| ► Ontario Reports (2d, 3d) | 1974-date | O.R. 2d, O.R. 3d |
| ► Dominion Law Reports (2d, 3d, 4th) | 1956-date | D.L.R. 2d, D.L.R. 3d, D.L.R. 4th |

Many other Canadian case reporters fit this description. In addition, some Canadian and provincial administrative tribunal reporters such as *Labour Arbitration Cases* (L.A.C.) fit this description.

Citation format: ‹case name› (‹year of decision›), ‹volume number› ‹reporter abbreviation› ‹series› ‹first page› (‹country abbreviation› ‹province abbreviation, if applicable› ‹court abbreviation, if applicable›).

- ► Weber v. Ont. Hydro (1992), 98 D.L.R. 4th 32 (Can. Ont. C.A.).
- ► De Zorzi Estate v. Read (2008), 38 E.T.R. 3d 318 (Can. Ont. Sup. Ct. J.).
- ► Ferrel v. Ontario (Att'y Gen.) (1998), 42 O.R. 3d 97 (Can. Ont. C.A.).
- ► Westfair Foods Ltd. v. U.F.C.W., Local 1400 (2008), 175 L.A.C. 4th 1 (Can. Ont.).

4) Reporters that are organized by volume only. The following reporters fit this description during the specified year ranges:

► Supreme Court Reports	1876-1922	S.C.R.
► Alberta Reports	1977-date	A.R.
► Ontario Reports	1882-1901	O.R.
► Ontario Law Reports	1901-1930/1931	O.L.R.
► Dominion Law Reports	1912-1922	D.L.R.
► Saskatchewan Reports	1979-date	Sask. R.
► Exchequer Court of Canada Report	1875-1922	Ex. C.R.

In addition, some Canadian and provincial administrative tribunal reporters such as the *Ontario Securities Commission Bulletin* (O.S.C. Bull.) and the *Canadian Human Rights Reporter* (C.H.R.R.) fit this description.

Citation format: ‹case name› (‹year of decision›), ‹volume number› ‹reporter abbreviation› ‹first page› (‹country abbreviation› ‹province abbreviation, if applicable› ‹court abbreviation, if applicable›).

▶ R. v. Chehimi (I.Y.) (2007), 419 A.R. 336 (Can. Alta. Q.B.).

▶ R. v. Moolla (M.) (2008), 310 Sask. R. 254 (Can. Sask. C.A.).

▶ Falconer v. The Queen (1889), 2 Ex. C.R. 82 (Can.).

▶ Leamy v. The King (1916), 54 S.C.R. 143 (Can.).

▶ St. John (Re) (1998), 21 O.S.C. Bull. 3851 (Can. Ont. Sec. Com.).

▶ Corren v. B.C. (Ministry of Educ.) (No. 2) (2005), 55 C.H.R.R. D/26 (Can. B.C. H.R.T.).

5) Neutral citations.

Since 1998, some Canadian courts and administrative tribunals have adopted neutral citations. A neutral citation is denoted by two main characteristics: the year of decision without brackets or parentheses, and the court abbreviation, not delineated by periods. Neutral citations are preferred over other citations. A neutral citation should always be placed before a parallel case citation.

Citation format: ‹case name›, ‹year of decision› ‹neutral citation court abbreviation› ‹document number›, ‹parallel citation, if desired› (‹country abbreviation if not evident from context› ‹province abbreviation, if applicable›).

▶ MacDonald v. Taubner, 2006 ABQB 138 (Can.).

▶ R. v. Fuhrer, 2007 ABQB 58, 413 A.R. 385 (Can.).

▶ R. v. Mann, 2004 SCC 52, [2004] 3 S.C.R. 59 (Can.).

▶ L. v. Fraser-Cascade Sch. Dist. No. 78, 2004 BCHRT 276 (Can.).

For further information, see Canadian Citation Commission, A Neutral Citation Standard for Case Law, which is available at **http://www.lexum.com/ccc-ccr/ neutr/neutr.jur_en.html**.

6) Case citations to electronic systems.

The two main electronic legal research systems for Canada are Westlaw Canada (WL) and Quicklaw (QL). WL assigns its own citations to decisions that it collects. WL citations are normally denoted by two main characteristics: the year of decision without brackets or parentheses, and the electronic reporter name that includes the word "Carswell." QL also assigns its own citations to decisions that it collects. QL citations are normally denoted by three main characteristics: the year of decision in brackets, the electronic reporter abbreviation that includes the letter "J," and the document number preceded by "No." Do not use a citation to electronic content if a neutral citation or a citation to a printed reporter is available.

WL citation format: ‹case name›, ‹year of decision› ‹online reporter name› ‹document number› (‹country abbreviation› ‹province abbreviation, if applicable› ‹court abbreviation, if applicable›) (WL).

▶ Apple Computer Inc. v. Mackintosh Computers Ltd., 1987 CarswellNat 675 (Can. F.T.C.D.) (WL).

QL citation format: ‹case name›, [‹year of decision›] ‹online reporter name› No. ‹document number› (‹country abbreviation› ‹province abbreviation, if applicable› ‹court abbreviation, if applicable›) (QL).

▶ Victorov v. Davison, [1988] O.J. No. 190 (Can. Ont. H.C.J.) (QL).

CanLII is a free, unofficial collection of Canadian cases, tribunal decisions, and law. CanLII provides its own citation system, denoted by three main characteristics: the year of decision without brackets or parentheses, CanLII as the reporter name, and the document number applied by CanLII.

▶ Doug Burns Excavation Contracting Ltd. v. Int'l Union of Operating Eng'rs, Local 721, 1999 CanLII 1081 (Can. N.S. S.C.).

Pinpoint citations

Generally, it is appropriate to provide a pinpoint citation to a specific page in the printed reporter. For cases published after 1996, provide a pinpoint citation to the specific paragraph instead, where available. Pinciting to a paragraph is also appropriate when referring to content from an online legal research service.

▶ Chase v. Campbell, [1962] S.C.R. 425, 426 (Can.).

▶ Brown v. Lefebvre (2007), 419 A.R. 347, para. 4 (Can. Alta. Q.B.).

▶ Bank of N.S. v. Visentin, [1996] O.J. No. 4563, para. 2 (Can. Ont. Gen. Div.) (QL).

▶ L. v. Fraser-Cascade Sch. Dist. No. 78, 2004 BCHRT 276, para. 4 (Can.).

Order of reporters

Neutral citations and citations to official and semi-official reporters are preferred over all other citations. *Dominion Law Reports* is the preferred unofficial reporter. Printed reporters are preferred over electronic reporters. Quicklaw and Westlaw Canada are preferred over CanLII or other free content on the Internet.

Official reporters

▶ Canada Supreme Court Reports	1876–1922	S.C.R.
▶ Canada Law Reports: Supreme Court of Canada	1923–1969	S.C.R.
▶ Canada Supreme Court Reports	1970–date	S.C.R.
▶ Exchequer Court of Canada Report	1875–1970	Ex. C.R.
▶ Canada Federal Court Reports	1971–2003	F.C.
	2004–date	F.C.R.

Case reporters from the provinces and territories

*denotes a reporter which is published under the auspices of a Law Society

▶ *Alberta Reports	1976–date	A.R.
▶ *Alberta Law Reports	1908–1932/1933	Alta. L.R.
▶ Alberta Law Reports (2d)	1977–1992	Alta. L.R. 2d
▶ Alberta Law Reports (3d)	1992–2002	Alta. L.R. 3d
▶ Alberta Law Reports (4th)	2002–date	Alta. L.R. 4th
▶ *British Columbia Reports	1867–1947	B.C.R.
▶ British Columbia Law Reports	1977–1986	B.C.L.R.
▶ British Columbia Law Reports (2d)	1986–1995	B.C.L.R. 2d
▶ British Columbia Law Reports (3d)	1995–2002	B.C.L.R. 3d
▶ British Columbia Law Reports (4th)	2002–date	B.C.L.R. 4th
▶ Manitoba Law Reports	1875–1883	Man. L.R.
▶ *Manitoba Reports	1883–1961	Man. R.

▸ Manitoba Reports (2d)	1979-date	Man. R. 2d
▸ Maritime Provinces Reports: Cases decided in the Supreme Courts of New Brunswick, Newfoundland, Nova Scotia and Prince Edward Island	1929-1968	M.P.R.
▸ New Brunswick Reports	1825-1929	N.B.R.
▸ *New Brunswick Reports (2d)	1969-date	N.B.R. 2d
▸ Newfoundland Law Reports	1817-1946	Nfld. L.R.
▸ *Newfoundland & Prince Edward Island Reports	1971-date	Nfld. & P.E.I.R.
▸ *Northwest Territories Reports	1983-1998	N.W.T.R.
▸ Nova Scotia Reports	1834-1929 1965-1969	N.S.R.
▸ *Nova Scotia Reports (2d)	1970-date	N.S.R. 2d
▸ Ontario Appeals Reports	1876-1900	O.A.R.
▸ Ontario Appeal Cases	1984-date	O.A.C.
▸ *Ontario Law Reports	1901-1931	O.L.R.
▸ *Ontario Weekly Notes	1909-1962	O.W.N.
▸ Ontario Reports	1882-1901	O.R.
▸ *Ontario Reports	1931-1973	O.R.
▸ *Ontario Reports (2d)	1974-1991	O.R. 2d
▸ *Ontario Reports (3d)	1991-date	O.R. 3d
▸ *Recueils de jurisprudence du Québec (continues C.A., C.S., C.P., C.S.P., T.J.)	1986-date	R.J.Q.
▸ *Recueils de jurisprudence du Québec: Cour d'appel	1970-1985	C.A.
▸ *Rapports judiciaires officiels de Québec: Cour supérieure	1892-1969 1970-1985	C.S.
▸ *Recueils de jurisprudence du Québec: Cour provinciale	1975-1985	C.P.
▸ *Recueils de jurisprudence du Québec: Cour des Sessions de la paix	1975-1985	C.S.P.
▸ *Recueils de jurisprudence du Québec: Tribunal de la jeunesse	1975-1985	T.J.
▸ *Rapports judiciaires officiels de Québec: Cour du Banc de la Reine/du Roi	1892-1969	B.R.
▸ *Recueils de jurisprudence du Québec: Cour du bien-être social	1975-1985	C.B.E.S.
▸ Québec Appeals Cases	1987-1995	Q.A.C.
▸ *Saskatchewan Law Reports	1907-1931	Sask. L.R.
▸ Saskatchewan Reports	1980-date	Sask. R.
▸ *Territories Law Reports	1885-1907	Terr. L.R
▸ *Yukon Reports	1987-1989	Y.R.

Other commonly cited reporters

▸ Atlantic Provinces Reports	1975-date	A.P.R.
▸ Dominion Law Reports	1912-1955	D.L.R.
▸ Dominion Law Reports (2d)	1956-1968	D.L.R. 2d
▸ Dominion Law Reports (3d)	1969-1984	D.L.R. 3d
▸ Dominion Law Reports (4th)	1984-date	D.L.R. 4th
▸ Eastern Law Reporter	1906-1914	E.L.R.
▸ Maritime Provinces Reports	1929-1968	M.P.R.
▸ National Reporter	1974-date	N.R.
▸ Western Law Reporter	1905-1916	W.L.R.
▸ Western Weekly Reports	1911-date	W.W.R.

Only some commonly cited reporters are listed here. For a full list of reporters for Canada, see McGill Law Journal, Canadian Guide to Uniform Legal Citation app. G (6th ed. 2006).

Constitutions

Canada's constitution consists of a series of United Kingdom enactments reprinted in the appendix to the *Revised Statutes of Canada* (R.S.C.). Cite to the U.K. statute following **table T2.42 United Kingdom** and, if desired, the relevant reprint in the R.S.C.

- ▶ Constitution Act, 1867, 30 & 31 Vict., c. 3 (U.K.), *reprinted in* R.S.C. 1985, app. II, no. 5 (Can.).

- ▶ Canada Act, 1982, c. 11 (U.K.), *reprinted in* R.S.C. 1985, app. II, no. 44 (Can.).

- ▶ Constitution Act, 1982, *being* Schedule B to the Canada Act, 1982, c. 11 (U.K.).

- ▶ Canadian Charter of Rights and Freedoms, Part I of the Constitution Act, 1982, *being* Schedule B to the Canada Act, 1982, c. 11 (U.K.).

Statutes

Consolidated statutes

Cite statutes appearing in the current national or provincial *Revision* (alphabetical consolidation of acts in force) analogously to codified United States statutes (**rule 12.3**). Note that the chapter numbers for federal statutes in the R.S.C. are labeled using a letter and a number (L-2), and the chapter numbers for Ontario statutes in the R.S.O. are labeled using a letter and a number (P.30). Individual provinces may have similar variations.

- ▶ Canada Labour Code, R.S.C. 1985, c. L-2.

- ▶ Province of Ontario Savings Office Act, R.S.O. 1990, c. P.30 (Can.).

- ▶ Code of Civil Procedure, R.S.Q., c. C-25 (Can.).

Always provide the country abbreviation unless it is clear from the context. Always provide a province abbreviation unless the province of origin is made clear in the title of the act or the publication abbreviation.

Session laws

For federal statutes passed subsequent to the most recent consolidation, cite to the annual *Statutes of Canada*, or provincial statutes to their annual volumes (for example, *Statutes of Alberta*, *Statutes of Québec*), in a manner similar to that used for United States session laws (**rule 12.4**):

- ▶ Antarctic Environmental Protection Act, S.C. 2003, c. 20 (Can.).

- ▶ Civil Code of Québec, S.Q. 1991, c. 64, art. 2 (Can.).

For Québec codes, include a pinpoint citation to the article number.

When citing an act appearing in the current *Revision* as well as the act's subsequent amendment, the name of the amendment need not be given:

- ▶ Freehold Mineral Rights Tax Act, R.S.A. 2000, c. F-26, amended by S.A. 2006, c. 21 (Can. Alta.).

Regulations

Federal and provincial regulations may be cited in two ways. Regulations that have been incorporated into a consolidation should be cited to the consolidation. Regulations that have been filed between consolidations should be cited by name and, for federal regulations, by SOR/‹year›-‹number› or SI/‹year›-‹document number›.

▶ Additional Legislative Powers Designation Order, C.R.C., c. 1235 (Can.).

▶ Passenger Information Regulations (Preclearance Act), SOR/2002-147 (Can.).

Provincial regulations have their own form of citation:

▶ Speed Limits, O. Reg. 383/08 (Can.).

▶ Nova Scotia Fresh Fruit and Vegetable Regulations, N.S. Reg. 84/79 (Can.).

Statutory and regulatory compilations

Federal

▶ Revised Statutes of Canada	R.S.C.
▶ Consolidated Regulations of Canada	C.R.C.

Provincial

▶ Revised Statutes of Alberta	R.S.A.
▶ Revised Statutes of British Columbia	R.S.B.C.
▶ Revised Statutes of Manitoba	R.S.M.
▶ Revised Statutes of New Brunswick	R.S.N.B.
▶ Revised Statutes of Newfoundland and Labrador	R.S.N.L.
▶ Revised Statutes of the Northwest Territories	R.S.N.W.T.
▶ Revised Statutes of Nova Scotia	R.S.N.S.
▶ Revised Statutes of Ontario	R.S.O.
▶ Revised Regulations of Ontario	R.R.O.
▶ Revised Statutes of Prince Edward Island	R.S.P.E.I.
▶ Revised Regulations of Prince Edward Island	R.R.P.E.I.
▶ Revised Statutes of Québec	R.S.Q.
▶ Revised Regulations of Québec	R.R.Q.
▶ Revised Statutes of Saskatchewan	R.S.S.
▶ Revised Statutes of Yukon	R.S.Y.

Session laws and regulations

Federal

▶ Statutes of Canada	S.C.
▶ Statutes of the Province of Canada	S. Prov. C.
▶ Canada Gazette	C. Gaz.

Provincial

▶ Statutes of Alberta	S.A.
▶ Alberta Gazette	A. Gaz.
▶ British Columbia Statutes	S.B.C.

► British Columbia Gazette	B.C. Gaz.
► Statutes of Manitoba	S.M.
► Manitoba Gazette	M. Gaz.
► Statutes of Newfoundland	S. Nfld.
► Statues of Newfoundland and Labrador	S.N.L.
► Ordinances of the Northwest Territories	O.N.W.T.
► Statutes of Nova Scotia	S.N.S.
► Statutes of Nunavut	S. Nu.
► Statutes of Ontario	S.O.
► Ontario Regulations	R.O.
► Statutes of Québec	S.Q.
► Statutes of Saskatchewan	S.S.
► Saskatchewan Gazette	S. Gaz.
► Statutes of Yukon	S.Y.

Treaties

► Canada Treaty Series	1925-date	‹year› Can. T.S. No. ‹treaty number›

Internet sources

http://www.loc.gov/law/help/guide/nations/canada.html (Library of Congress Guide to Law Online: Canada)

http://www.llrx.com/features/ca.htm (law and technology resources for legal professionals)

T2.7   Catholic Church

Codes before 1917: Cite by the name of the individual document or fragment, as in the examples below, not by the title of a collection that includes the material. For other examples, see the *Bulletin of Medieval Canon Law*.

► Gratian	c. 1140	
Part 1		e.g., D.33 c.1 (d.a.)
Part 2		e.g., C.9 q.3 c.1
Part 3		e.g., DE CONS. D.2 c.84
► Decretals of Gregory IX	1234	e.g., X 3.24.2
► Decretals of Boniface VIII	1298	e.g., VI 1.11.1
► Constitutions of Clement V	1317	e.g., CLEM. 3.5.7
► Extravagants of John XXII	1316-1334	e.g., EXTRAV. JO. 14.3
► Common Extravagants	1261-1484	e.g., EXTRAV. COM. 2.1.1

Codes after 1917: Cite to either the 1917 or 1983 *Codex Iuris Canonici*.

► Codex Iuris Canonici (1917)	1917-1983	e.g., 1917 CODE c.430, § 1
► Codex Iuris Canonici (1983)	1983-date	e.g., 1983 CODE c.515, § 3

T2.8   Chile, Republic of

(Civil Law)

Cases

Citation format: ‹court name› [‹court abbreviation›] [‹English translation of court name›], ‹date of decision in Spanish, in day month year format›, "‹case name›," Rol de la causa: ‹case number›, ‹case type›, ‹publication name› [‹publication abbreviation›] ‹publication volume and/or number› p.‹first page› (‹country abbreviation if not evident from context›). Note that many reporters depart from this format, as detailed below.

In the case name, use "c." between the party names, which refers to "contra," Spanish for "versus."

  ▶ Corte Suprema de Justicia [C.S.J.] [Supreme Court], 15 noviembre 1954, "Suárez, Alfredo c. Perez, Estela," Rol de la causa: 124-2008 s., divorcio, Revista Gaceta Jurídica [R.G.J.] No. 190 p.145 (Chile).

National jurisdiction

Corte Suprema de Justicia (C.S.J.) (Supreme Court) and **Tribunal Constitucional** (T.C.) (Constitutional Court) (highest court on constitutional matters).

Appellate courts

Corte de Apelaciones (C. Apel.) (courts of appeals): Cite to R.D.J., G.T., or F. del M.

Lower courts

Tribunales de Juicio Oral en lo Penal (T.J.O.P.) (criminal trial courts), **Juzgados de Garantía** (J.G.) (criminal courts), **Juzgados de Familia** (J.F.) (family courts), **Juzgados de Cobranza Laboral y Previsional** (J.C.L.P.) (labor and social security courts), **Juzgados Civiles** (J. Civ.) (civil courts), **Juzgados del Crimen** (J. Cri.) (criminal courts), **Juzgados de Menores** (J. Men.) (juvenile courts), **Juzgados del Trabajo** (J.T.) (labor courts), **Juzgados Mixtos** (J. Mix.), and **Juzgados de Letras** (J.L.) (small claims courts).

Reporters

Generally follow the examples below when citing to the volumes and/or numbers of these reporters. Note that "t." refers to "tomo," Spanish for "volume."

▶ Fallos del Mes	1958–date	e.g., F. del M. vol. 37 No. Sentencia 436 (1995)
▶ Gaceta Jurídica	1974–date	e.g., G.J. t. 33, p.438 (1936)
▶ Gaceta de los Tribunales	1962–date	e.g., G.T. vol. 13, p.349 (1978)
▶ Revista de Derecho y Jurisprudencia	1904–date	e.g., R.D.J. t. 22, sec. 2a, p.45 (1990)

Constitution

  ▶ Constitución Política de la República de Chile   C.P.

  ▶ Constitución Política de la República de Chile [C.P.] art. 3.

Codes

  ▶ Código Civil (Civil Code)   Cód. Civ.
  ▶ Código de Comercio (Commercial Code)   Cód. Com.
  ▶ Código Penal (Criminal Code)   Cód. Pen.

- Código De Procedimiento Civil (Civil Procedure Code) Cód. Proc. Civ.
- Código Procesal Penal (Criminal Procedure Code) Cód. Proc. Pen.
- Código Orgánico de Tribunales (Judiciary Code) Cód. Org. Trib.
- Código de Justicia Militar (Military Justice Code) Cód. Jus. Mil.
- Código del Trabajo (Labor Code) Cód. Trab.
- Código Tributario (Revenue and Taxation Code) Cód. Trib.
- Código de Aguas (Water Code) Cód. Aguas
- Código Sanitario (Health Code) Cód. Sanit.
- Código de Minería (Mining Code) Cód. Min.
- Código Aeronáutico (Aeronautics Code) Cód. Aer.
- Código de Derecho Internacional Privado/Código Cód. Der. Int. Priv.
  Bustamante (Conflict of Laws Code)

Statutes and decrees

Citation format: **Law No.** ‹number of law›, ‹promulgation date in Spanish in month day, year format›, ‹reporter name› [‹reporter abbreviation›] (‹country abbreviation if not evident from context›).

- **Law No.** 19496, Marzo 7, 1997, Diario Oficial [D.O.] (Chile).
- Diario Oficial D.O.
- Gaceta Jurídica G.J.
- Repertorio de Legislación y Jurisprudencia Chilenas Rep. Leg. Jurisp.

Periodicals

- Jurisprudencia al Día J.D.
- Revista de Derecho y Jurisprudencia y Gaceta de los Tribunales R.D. y J. y G.T.

Internet sources

http://www.legalpublishing.cl (legal publishing company offering jurisprudence, doctrine, and legislation online; paid subscription)

http://www.diariodigital.cl (official digest, paid subscription for full text, free summaries)

http://www.editorialjuridica.cl (provides free access to some recent issues of Informativo Jurídico and Informativo Semanal)

http://www.bcn.cl (database of the Library of the National Congress, free access)

http://www.lexadin.nl/wlg/legis/nofr/oeur/lxwechl.htm (unofficial source for legislation, free access)

http://glin.gov (Global Legal Information Network, a database of laws, regulations, and other complementary legal sources)

http://www.tribunalconstitucional.cl (the official website of the Constitutional Court; complete free access to its decisions)

http://www.scielo.cl (free access to the law journals *Ius et Praxis* (Universidad de Talca), *Revista Chilena de Derecho* (Universidad Católica de Chile), *Revista de Derecho* (Universidad Austral de Chile), and *Revista de Derecho* (Universidad Católica de Valparaíso))

http://www.loc.gov/law/help/guide/nations/chile.html (Library of Congress Guide to Law Online: Chile)

T2.9   China, People's Republic of

(Civil Law)

Jurisdictional note

Apply these guidelines to sources relating to the People's Republic of China (after 1949). When citing sources related to the Republic of China between 1912 and 1949, see the guidelines for **table T2.41 Taiwan, Republic of China**. For sources prior to the founding of the Republic of China in 1912, adapt these guidelines as necessary.

Romanization

For romanization of Chinese language citations, follow the instructions in **rule 20.2.4**.

Translated sources

For citations to translated or bilingual sources, choose one of the following options:

1) Follow **rule 20.2.5**, giving parallel citations to the original language source and a translated version;

2) Where the original is difficult or impossible to verify, cite to the translated source without reference to the original language version. In this case, it is not necessary to preface the source with "*translated in.*"

> ▶ Foreign Economic Contract Law (promulgated by the Standing Comm. Nat'l People's Cong., Mar. 21, 1985, effective July 1, 1985), art. 7, 24 I.L.M. 799, 802 (1985) (China).

Abbreviations

Regardless of the language of the document being cited, cite to official or well-known English equivalents where possible and abbreviate according to **tables T6, T7, T10,** and **T13**. If no such abbreviation is available, use any abbreviated Chinese form in common use, or use the full form the first time and use an appropriate "**hereinafter**" reference for subsequent citations. For example:

▶ Zuigao Renmin Fayuan	Sup. People's Ct.
▶ Shanghai Zhongji Renmin Fayuan	Shanghai Interm. People's Ct.
▶ Guowuyuan	St. Council
▶ Quanguo Renmin Daibiao Dahui Changwu Weiyuanhui	Standing Comm. Nat'l People's Cong.
▶ Zhongguo Falü Nianjian	Law Y.B. China

Choice of authorities

Chinese laws are not codified (although some publications call themselves "codes"), case reports are not systematically published, and few sources are explicitly called "official." Where not specified otherwise herein, prefer sources published by or with the cooperation of a court or government agency (including agency websites) over other sources. Chinese sources are always more authoritative than translations, but sometimes it may be appropriate to cite to a translation where available.

Cases

Citation format: ‹romanized Chinese case name› (‹Chinese case name›) [‹English translation of case name›], ‹source› (‹court abbreviation› ‹date of decision, following rule 10.5›) (‹country abbreviation if not evident from context›).

Cite to sources named below, if therein and available. Otherwise, cite to a source published by or with the cooperation of a court or government agency (including agency or court websites), if therein and available, then any source.

▸ Zuigao Renmin Fayuan Gongbao   SUP. PEOPLE'S CT. GAZ.
   (Supreme People's Court Gazette)

▸ Zuigao Renmin Jianchayuan Gongbao   SUP. PEOPLE'S PROC. COMMUNIQUE
   (Supreme People's Procuratorate
   Communique)

▸ Renmin Fayuan Anli Xuan (Selected   RENMIN FAYUAN ANLI XUAN
   Cases from the People's Courts)

▸ Wei Qinjian Su Zhongbao Caichan Baoxian Youxian Gongsi Taishan Shi Zhigongsi, Zhongguo Nongye Yinhang Taishan Shi Zhihang Xiachuan Yingyesuo (卫勤俭诉中保财产保险有限公司台山市支公司，中国农业银行台山市支行下川营业所) [Wei Qinjian v. PICC P&C Ltd., Taishan Branch & China Agric. Bank, Taishan Branch, Xiachuan Operation Office], 1991 SUP. PEOPLE'S CT. GAZ. 101 (Sup. People's Ct. 2001) (China).

▸ China Nat'l Technical Imp./Exp. Corp. v. Indus. Res. Co., CHINA L. & PRAC., Aug. 22, 1988, at 26 (Shanghai Interm. People's Ct. May 11, 1988).

▸ Xu Moumou Feifa Chiyou Dupin An (徐某某非法持有毒品案) [In re Xu Moumou Unlawful Possession of Drugs] (Shanghai Putuo Dist. People's Ct. Aug. 22, 2008) (Westlaw China).

Constitutions

Citation format: XIANFA ‹article›, ‹section› (‹year›) (‹country abbreviation if not evident from context›).

Give the promulgation year of the version cited. Abbreviate the subdivisions of constitutions, such as article and clause, using English abbreviations, according to table T16.

▸ Zhonghua Renmin Gongheguo Xianfa   XIANFA

  ▸ XIANFA art. 35, § 1 (1982) (China).

Laws

Citation format: ‹romanized Chinese law name› (‹Chinese law name›) [‹English translation of law name or shortened name›] (promulgated by ‹enacting/adopting authority›, ‹promulgation date›, effective ‹effective date›) ‹volume number› ‹source› ‹first page›, ‹page(s) of specific material, if desired› (‹country abbreviation if not evident from context›).

Cite to sources named below, if therein and available. Otherwise, cite to a source published by or with the cooperation of a court or government agency (including agency or court websites), if therein and available, then any source.

► Quanguo Renmin Daibiao Dahui Changwu
  Weiyuanhui Gongbao

STANDING COMM. NAT'L
  PEOPLE'S CONG. GAZ.

► Zhonghua Renmin Gongheguo Fadian

FADIAN

► Zhonghua Renmin Gongheguo Falü Quanshu

FALÜ QUANSHU

► Zhonghua Renmin Gongheguo Fagui Huibian

FAGUI HUIBIAN

► Zhonghua Renmin Gongheguo Xin Fagui Huibian

XIN FAGUI HUIBIAN

► Laws of the People's Republic of China

P.R.C. LAWS

► Laws and Regulations of the People's Republic
  of China

P.R.C. LAWS & REGS

► Lifa Fa (立法法) [Law on Legislation] (promulgated by the Standing
  Comm. Nat'l People's Cong., Mar. 15, 2000, effective July 1, 2000)
  2000 STANDING COMM. NAT'L PEOPLE'S CONG. GAZ. 112 (China).

► Canjiren Baozhang Fa (残疾人保障法) [Law on the Protection of
  Disabled Persons] (promulgated by the Standing Comm. Nat'l
  People's Cong., Dec. 28, 1990, effective May 15, 1991) 1990–1992
  FALÜ QUANSHU 1268 (China), *translated in* 14 P.R.C. LAWS & REGS V-
  03-00-101.

► Provisions on Labor Administration in Enterprises with Foreign
  Investment (promulgated by the Ministry of Labor & the Ministry of
  Foreign Trade & Econ. Cooperation, Aug. 11, 1994, effective Aug. 11,
  1994) 14 P.R.C. LAWS & REGS V-05-00-303 (China).

....

Rules and regulations

(Including xingzheng fagui 行政法规, and bumen guizhang 部门规章.)

Citation format: ‹romanized Chinese regulation or rule name› (‹Chinese
regulation or rule name›) [‹English translation of regulation or rule name
or shortened name›] (promulgated by ‹enacting/adopting authority›,
‹promulgation date›, effective ‹effective date›) ‹source›, ‹publication
date›, at ‹first page›, ‹page(s) of specific material, if desired› (‹country
abbreviation if not evident from context›).

Cite to the source below, if therein. Otherwise, cite to a source published by or
with the cooperation of a court or government agency (including agency or court
websites), if available, then any source.

► Guowuyuan Gongbao

St. Council Gaz.

► Yaopin Jiandu Xingzheng Chufa Chengxu Guiding
  (药品监督行政处罚程序规定) [Provisions on Procedures for
  Administrative Penalties of Drug Supervision] (promulgated by the
  St. Food & Drug Admin., Mar. 28, 2003, effective July 2, 2003) ST.
  COUNCIL GAZ., Oct. 20, 2003, at 29 (China).

Note that many Chinese databases do not provide searchable codes or numbers
uniquely identifying a case, regulation, etc. Many also do not provide the information regarding the currency of the database that **rule 18.3.2** requires to be
included in the citation.

► Regulation on the Administration of Tourism in Beijing Municipality
  (promulgated by the Standing Comm. People's Cong. Beijing
  Municipality, Sept. 10, 2004, effective Dec. 1, 2004) (Lawinfochina)
  (China).

▶ Jumin Shenfenzheng Fa (居民身份证法) [Resident Identification Card Law] (promulgated by the Standing Comm. Nat'l People's Cong., June 28, 2003, effective Jan. 1, 2004), http://www.china.com.cn/chinese/law/356043.htm (China).

Local regulations, regulations of autonomous regions, and special rules

(Including difangxing fagui 地方性法规, zizhiqu zizhi tiaoli 自治区自治条例, and danxing tiaoli 单行条例.)

Cite to the gazette of the standing committee of the corresponding local or regional government, if therein and available, then any source.

....

Treaties and conventions

Citation of a bilateral treaty, convention, or international agreement: ‹treaty name›, ‹date of signing›, ‹subdivision›, ‹abbreviated names of parties to agreement›, ‹treaty source› (‹country abbreviation if not evident from context›).

Citation of a multilateral treaty, convention, or international agreement: ‹treaty name›, ‹date of signing›, ‹subdivision›, ‹one Chinese treaty source›, ‹one international treaty source, if applicable› (‹country abbreviation if not evident from context›).

Cite to one of the sources below, if therein. Otherwise, cite to a source published by or with the cooperation of a court or government agency (including agency or court websites), then any source.

▶ Guowuyuan Gongbao	ST. COUNCIL GAZ.
▶ Zhonghua Renmin Gongheguo Tiaoyue Ji	TIAOYUE JI
▶ Zhonghua Renmin Gongheguo Duobian Tiaoyue Ji	DUOBIAN TIAOYUE JI

....

Sources

▶ China Law and Practice	CHINA L. & PRAC.
▶ China Patents & Trademarks (中國專利與商標)	CHINA PAT. & TRADEMARKS
▶ Code of the People's Republic of China (中华人民共和国法典)	FADIAN
▶ Duobian Tiaoyue Ji (多边条约集)	DUOBIAN TIAOYUE JI
▶ Fagui Huibian (法规汇编)	FAGUI HUIBIAN
▶ Falü Quanshu (法律全书)	FALÜ QUANSHU
▶ Guowuyuan Gongbao (国务院公报)	ST. COUNCIL GAZ.
▶ Law Year Book of China (中国法律年鉴)	LAW Y.B. CHINA
▶ Laws and Regulations of the People's Republic of China	P.R.C. LAWS & REGS
▶ Laws of the People's Republic of China	P.R.C. LAWS
▶ Quanguo Renmin Daibiao Dahui Changwu Weiyuanhui Gongbao (全国人民代表大会常务委员会公报)	STANDING COMM. NAT'L PEOPLE'S CONG. GAZ.
▶ Renmin Fayuan Anli Xuan (人民法院案例选)	RENMIN FAYUAN ANLI XUAN
▶ Xin Fagui Huibian (新法规汇编)	XIN FAGUI HUIBIAN

- Zhonghua Renmin Gongheguo Tiaoyue Ji   TIAOYUE JI
  (中华人民共和国条约集)
- Zhonghua Renmin Gongheguo Xianfa   XIANFA
  (中华人民共和国宪法)
- Zuigao Renmin Fayuan Gongbao   SUP. PEOPLE'S CT. GAZ.
  (中华人民共和国最高人民法院公报)
- Zuigao Renmin Jianchayuan Gongbao   SUP. PEOPLE'S PROC.
  (最高人民检察院公报)   COMMUNIQUE

Internet sources

http://china.eastview.com (China Academic Journals 中国期刊全文数据库 (CAJ))

http://open.oriprobe.com/laws_index.aspx (China Legal Access (CLASS))

http://www.wanfangdata.com/COJ/intr.asp (China Online Journals 数字化期刊全文数据库 (COJ))

http://journal.chinalawinfo.com (Chinalaw Journals 法学期刊) (Chinal. J.))

http://chinalawinfo.com (Chinalawinfo 北大法律信息网)

http://www.isinolaw.com (Isinolaw 中华法律网)

http://www.lawinfochina.com (Lawinfochina 北大法律英文网)

http://www.lawyee.net (Lawyee 北大法意)

http://www.lexiscn.com (Lexis China Online 律商网(LEXIS China Online))

http://www.wanfangdata.com/ploc/intr.asp (Policies & Laws of China (PLOC))

http://westlawchina.com (Westlaw China 万律 (Westlaw China))

T2.10   Colombia, Republic of

(Civil Law)

Cases

Citation format: ‹court name› [‹court abbreviation›][‹English translation of court name›], ‹chamber, if applicable› ‹date of decision in Spanish›, ‹writer of ruling if applicable›, ‹decision number›, ‹publication name› [‹publication abbreviation›] (‹publication volume and/or number›, **p.** ‹page number›) (‹country abbreviation if not evident from context›).

- Corte Suprema de Justicia [C.S.J.] [Supreme Court], Sala. Lab. febrero 9, 1994, M.P: E. Ramirez, Expediente 1994-0002346, Gaceta Judicial [G.J.] (No. 10, p. 120) (Colom.).

- Corte Constitucional [C.C.] [Constitutional Court], noviembre 15, 1995, Sentencia C-225/95, Gaceta de la Corte Constitucional [G.C.C.] (vol. 4, p. 39) (Colom.).

Ordinary jurisdiction (particular disputes and crime, including family law, civil law, commercial law, and labor law)

Corte Suprema de Justicia (C.S.J.) (Supreme Court of Justice: divided into three chambers: Civil, Criminal and Labor), **Tribunales Superiores** (T. Sup.)

(appellate courts: divided into three chambers: Civil, Criminal and Labor), **Juzgados de Circuito** (Juzg. Circ.) (circuit courts: labor, civil and criminal jurisdiction), and **Juzgados Municipales** (Juz. Mun.) (lower courts: civil and criminal jurisdiction).

Constitutional jurisdiction (all Colombian Courts have jurisdiction to rule on constitutional matters through *Acciones de Tutela* (actions in defense of constitutional rights))

Corte Constitucional (C.C.) (Highest Court on Constitutional Matters: rules on the constitutionality of laws, codes, and decrees with force of law and is the highest court of review on *Acciones de Tutela*) and **Consejo de Estado** (C.E.) (Highest Court on Administrative Law: rules on the constitutionality of decrees).

Administrative jurisdiction

Consejo de Estado (C.E.) (Highest Court on Administrative Law: divided into five chambers: General Matters; Labor; Public Contracts, Arbitration Control & Torts; Taxes; and Electoral), **Tribunales Administrativos** (T. Admtivos.) (administrative superior courts: divided into four chambers: General Matters; Labor; Public Contracts, Arbitration Control & Torts; and Taxes), and **Juzgados Administrativos** (J. Admtivos.) (administrative circuit courts).

Reporters

Generally follow the examples below when citing to the volumes and/or numbers of these reporters. Where appropriate, use "t." to refer to "tomo," the Spanish word for "volume."

- GACETA DE LA CORTE CONSTITUCIONAL   1992-date   e.g., G.C. t. 1, p. 104
- GACETA JUDICIAL   1887-date   e.g., G.J. vol. 10, p. 74
- ANALES DEL CONSEJO DE ESTADO   1915-date   e.g., An.C.E. t. 10, p. 13

There is no comprehensive official or unofficial regular publication of appellate or lower court opinions. Some of the lower courts have their own journals:

- AUTOS Y SENTENCIAS   A.S.
- TRIBUNAL SUPERIOR DE MEDELLIN   T.S.M.
- CASOS CIVILES JURISPRUDENCIA (civil cases)   C.C.J.
- GACETA ADMINISTRATIVA (administrative cases)   G.A.

Constitution

- CONSTITUCIÓN POLÍTICA DE COLOMBIA   C.P.
  - CONSTITUCIÓN POLÍTICA DE COLOMBIA [C.P.] art. 3.

Codes

- CÓDIGO CIVIL (Civil Code)   C.C.
- CÓDIGO DE COMERCIO (Commercial Code)   C. COM.
- CÓDIGO PENAL (Criminal Code)   C. PEN.
- CÓDIGO DE PROCEDIMIENTO CIVIL (Civil Procedure Code)   C.P.C.
- CÓDIGO DE PROCEDIMIENTO PENAL (Criminal Procedure Code)   C.P.P.
- CÓDIGO CONTENCIOSO ADMINISTRATIVO (Administrative Litigation Code)   C.C.A.
- CÓDIGO DE LA INFANCIA Y LA ADOLESCENCIA (Childhood and Adolescence Code)   COD. INF. ADOL.
- CÓDIGO SUSTANTIVO DEL TRABAJO (Labor Code)   C.S.T.
- CÓDIGO PROCESAL DEL TRABAJO (Labor Procedure Code)   C.P.T.

▸ Código Nacional de los Recursos Naturales Renovables y de Proteccion al Medio Ambiente (Natural Resources and Environmental Protection Code) — Cód. Nac. Rec. Nat. y Prot. Med. Amb.

▸ Código Sanitario (Health Code) — Cód. Sanit.

▸ Código de Minas (Mining Code) — Cód. Min.

Statutes and decrees

Citation format: L. ‹law number›, ‹promulgation date in Spanish›, [‹volume number, if applicable›] ‹reporter name› [‹reporter abbreviation›] ‹page, if desired› (‹country abbreviation if not evident from context›).

▸ L. 50/90, marzo 7, 1990, Diario Oficial [D.O.] (Colom.).

▸ Diario Oficial — 1864–date — D.O.

Periodicals

▸ Jurisprudencia al Dia — J.D.

▸ Revista Legislacion — R. Leg.

▸ Revista Jurisprudencia y Doctrina — R.J. y D.

▸ Revista Colombiana de Derecho Constitucional — R.C.D.C.

▸ Revista de Derecho Civil — R.D.C.

▸ Revista de Derecho Penal — R.D.P.

▸ Revista de la Facultad de Derecho y Ciencias Politicas (Universidad Pontificia Bolivariana, Medellín) — R.F.D.C.P.

▸ Jurisprudencia Penal — J.P.

Internet sources

http://www.ramajudicial.gov.co (official site of the judiciary; free access to court decisions)

http://www.secretariasenado.gov.co (official site of the Colombian Congress; free access to legislation)

http://www.lexadin.nl/wlg/legis/nofr/oeur/lxwecol.htm (unofficial site; free access to legislation)

http://banrep.gov.co/juriscol (official site of the Banco de la Republica; free access to legislation and court decisions)

http://www.todoelderecho.com/Colombia (unofficial site for legal information; partially paid subscription)

http://www.javeriana.edu.co/juridicas/dep2.html (free access to the law journal of the Pontificia Universidad Javeriana in Bogotá)

http://www.gacetaconstitucional.com.pe/gconstitucional/gaceta-consti.php (free access to the Gaceta Constitucional)

http://www.legismovil.com (legal information online; private publishing company; paid subscription)

http://www.imprenta.gov.co (provides the Diario Oficial; paid subscription)

http://www.mij.gov.co/biblioteca/consulta.htm (official database of the Ministry of the Interior and Justice; free access to legislation and court decisions)

http://www.coljuristas.org (official site of the Colombian Commission of Jurists; free access to legal information on human rights)

http://glin.gov (Global Legal Information Network; a database of laws, regulations, and other complementary legal sources)

http://www.loc.gov/law/help/guide/nations/colombia.html (Library of Congress Guide to Law Online: Colombia)

T2.11   Czech Republic

(Civil Law)

Cases

Citation format: ‹court› ‹date of adoption of decision in day.month.year format› (‹court abbreviation, if available›) [‹English translation›], ‹docket identification and number› **publ. in:** ‹reporter name, if the decision is reported›, ‹subdivisions, if desired› (‹country abbreviation if not evident from context›).

▸ Rozsudek Krajského soudu v Plzni ze dne 14.11.2006 (KS) [Decision of the Circuit Court in Plzeň of Nov. 14, 2006], sp.zn. 31 Odo 50/2004 (Czech).

▸ Rozsudek Nejvyššího soudu ze dne 30.11.1999 (NS) [Decision of the Supreme Court of Nov. 30, 1999], sp.zn. 20 Cdo 1601/1998 (Czech).

▸ Rozsudek Nejvyššího správního soudu ze dne 27.9.2007 (NSS) [Decision of the Supreme Administrative Court of Sept. 27, 2007], čj. 4 Azs 31/2007-58 (Czech).

▸ Nález Ústavního soudu ze dne 29.05.1997 (ÚS) [Decision of the Constitutional Court of May 29, 1997], sp.zn. III. ÚS 31/97 publ. in: Sbírka nálezů a usnesení ÚS, sv. 8, č. 66 (Czech).

When citing to a reporter, cite to *Sbírka rozhodnutí Nejvyššího správního soudu* (Collection of Court Decisions of the Supreme Administrative Court), in which selected decisions of Nejvyšší správní soud České republiky (NSS) and lower courts are reported. Note, however, that apart from decisions of the Constitutional Court (ÚS), court decisions are not systematically reported by any published court reporter. All decisions of the NS (Supreme Court), NSS (Supreme Administrative Court), and ÚS (Constitutional Court) are systematically published in Czech on the courts' respective websites.

Ordinary jurisdiction

Nejvyšší soud Ceské republiky (NS) (Supreme Court), **Vrchní soud** (VS) (high courts), **Krajský soud** (KS) (circuit courts), **Městský soud** (MS) (Circuit Court in the City of Prague and District Court in the City of Brno), **Okresní soud** (district courts), and **Obvodní soud** (District Court in the City of Prague): Cite using the docket identification "sp.zn."

Administrative jurisdiction

Krajský soud (KS) (Circuit Court), **Městský soud v Praze** (MS) (Circuit Court in the City of Prague), **Nejvyšší správní soud České republiky** (NSS) (Supreme Administrative Court: cite using the docket identification "čj.").

Constitutional jurisdiction

Ústavní soud České republiky (ÚS) (Constitutional Court): Cite by identifying the court, the date on which the decision was adopted, the docket identification "sp.zn.," and optionally, the court reporter *Sbírka nálezů a usnesení Ústavního soudu* (Collection of Court Decisions of the Constitutional Court).

Constitution

There are several laws which are considered to be of constitutional importance in Czech. Cite according to the format for statutes, appending the description of the law if desired:

> ▸ Ústavní zákon č. 1/1993 Sb., Ústava České Republiky [Constitution of the Czech Republic].

Statutes and regulations

Cite a **zákon** (statute), **ústavní zákon** (constitutional statute), or **vyhláška** (regulation) to *Sbírka zákonů* (**Sb.**) (Collection of Laws (**Coll.**)).

> ▸ Zákon č. 1/1995 Sb. (Czech).

Relevant codes include: **občanský zákoník** (Civil Code), **obchodní zákoník** (Commercial Code), **občanský soudní řád** (Civil Procedure Code), **trestní zákon** (Criminal Code), **trestní řád** (Criminal Procedure Code), and **správní řád** (Administrative Procedure Code).

There are two types of administrative rules: **nařízení** (decree issued by the **vláda České republiky** (cabinet)) and **vyhláška** (regulation issued either by a **ministerstvo** (ministry) or another **ústřední orgán státní správy** (central administrative agency)).

> ▸ Nařízení č. 303/1995 Sb. (Czech).

Treaties

Cite international treaties promulgated through 1999 to *Sbírka zákonů* (**Sb.**) (Collection of Laws (**Coll.**)). Cite international treaties promulgated since 2000 to *Sbírka mezinárodních smluv* (**Sb.m.s.**) (Collection of International Treaties).

Internet sources

http://www.nsoud.cz (Supreme Court of the Czech Republic)

http://www.nssoud.cz (Supreme Administrative Court of the Czech Republic)

http://www.concourt.cz (Constitutional Court of the Czech Republic)

http://www.senat.cz (Parliament of the Czech Republic)

http://www.mvcr.cz/clanek/sbirka-zakonu.aspx (Ministry of the Interior: provides access to archived issues of the Collection of Laws (Coll.) from 1945, but not updated frequently)

http://www.sagit.cz/pages/zakony.asp (free access to legislation and treaties published in the Collection of Laws (Coll.) from 1993 to date)

http://www.lexdata.cz (searchable database of case law and legislation available upon subscription)

http://www.lexgalaxy.cz (searchable database of case law and legislation available upon subscription)

T2.12   Egypt, Arab Republic of

(Civil Law)

The Egyptian legal system is built on the combination of Islamic law (*Shariah*) and the Napoleonic Code, which was first introduced during Napoleon Bonaparte's occupation of Egypt. As a civil law system, the codified laws are well established and extensive.

Romanization

Use the *ALA-LC Romanization Tables: Transliteration Schemes for Non-Roman Scripts*, approved by the Library of Congress and the American Library Association, available at **http://www.loc.gov/catdir/cpso/romanization/arabic.pdf**.

Cases

No established system of legally (de jure) binding precedents exists, but previous judicial decisions have persuasive authority. Courts are morally and practically bound (de facto binding effect) by the principles and precedents of the **Court of Cassation** (appeals from civil, including the Family Court, and criminal matters), sometimes referred to as the Supreme Court before the establishment of the Supreme Constitutional Court in 1971 (sometimes referred to as 1979), and the **Supreme Administrative Court** (for administrative and other public law matters). **Court of Cassation** judgments, **State Council** judgments, and **Constitutional Court** judgments are organized in book format in the *Collection of Awards*. These are organized in chronological order by judicial years. Two subscription-only databases also contain court rulings: Tashreaat, available at **http://www.tashreaat.com**, and East Laws, available at **http://www.eastlaws.com**.

Citation format: Case no. ‹number›/‹year›/‹court name›, (‹court division, if desired›, ‹geographical indicator, if desired›) (‹country abbreviation if not evident from context›).

Constitutions

▶ CONSTITUTION OF THE ARAB REPUBLIC OF EGYPT, 11 Sept. 1971, *as amended*, May 22, 1980, May 25, 2005, March 26, 2007.

Egypt has had a series of written constitutional documents, beginning with the 1923 foundational instrument. The Constitution of 1971 must be cited to a consolidated text incorporating the revisions and substantial reforms adopted in 2007. The consolidated text can be found on the Egyptian Shura Council (the upper legislative house in Egypt) website at **http://www.egypt.gov.eg/english/laws/Constitution**.

Codes, statutes, and decrees

Citation format: ‹Law, Act, or Decision number› of ‹year of enactment› (‹subject matter of code, statute, or decree, if available›), ‹name of publication in italics›, ‹date of enactment in day month year format›, ‹page(s) or section(s) of specific material, if desired› (‹country abbreviation if not evident from context›).

- ► Law No. 88 of 2003 (Law of the Central Bank, the Banking Sector, and Monetary Policy), *Al-Jarida Al-Rasmiyya*, 15 June 2003 (Egypt).

- ► Law No. 117 of 1983 (Law on the Protection of Antiquities), *Al-Jarida Al-Rasmiyya*, 11 Aug. 1983 (Egypt).

- ► Law No. 131 of 1948 (Civil Code), *Al-Jarida Al-Rasmiyya*, 29 July 1948, §§ 418–81 (sales) (Egypt).

- ► Law No. 58 of 1937 (Criminal Code of 1937, reformed in 1952), *Al-Jarida Al-Rasmiyya* (Egypt).

- ► Act No. 81 of 1996 (To Amend Provisions of the Code of Civil and Commercial Procedure, Law No. 13 of 1968), *Al-Jarida Al-Rasmiyya*, 22 May 1996, vol. 39, No. 19 bis, pp. 2-3 (Egypt).

- ► President of the Republic of Egypt Decision No. 32 of 2001 (Ratification of the African Charter on the Rights and Welfare of the Child), *Al-Jarida Al-Rasmiyya*, 28 Oct. 2004, No. 44, pp. 2447-71 (Egypt).

The Official Gazette (*Al-Jarida Al-Rasmiyya*) is the authoritative source for the promulgation of presidential and ministerial decrees and Egyptian laws.

With respect to transactions between natural persons or legal entities, the most important legislation is the Egyptian Civil Code of 1948, which remains the main source of legal rules applicable to contracts. Much of the Egyptian Civil Code is based upon the French Civil Code and, to a lesser extent, various other European codes as well as Islamic law (*Shariah*) (especially in the context of personal status).

► *Al-Waqa'i' al-Misriyah*	Dec. 5, 1828–Feb. 22, 1958
► *Journal officiel du gouvernement égyptien* (French-language edition of *Al-Waqa'i' al-Misriyah*)	1873–1958
► [*United Arab Republic*] *Al-Jaridah al-rasmiyah/ al-Jumhuriyah al-Arabiyah al-Muttahidah*	Mar. 1958–Aug. 1971
► *Al-Jaridah al-rasmiyah-Jumhuriat Misr al-Arabiyah, Riyasat al-Jumhuriyah*	Sept. 9, 1971–date

....

Internet sources

http://www.tashreaat.com (text of the Official Gazette in Arabic)

http://www.tashreaat.com/view_studies2.asp?std_id=82 (English and French translations of laws, including the text of the current Civil Code)

http://www.eastlaws.com (rich collection of Egyptian law resources, including forums and government services)

http://www.ilo.org/dyn/natlex/natlex_browse.country?p_lang=en&p_country=EGY (International Labour Organization; provides access to an updated collection of a wide range of labor, human rights, agriculture, education, and employment laws and decrees, as well as a few references to Egyptian accession to international agreements)

http://www.shoura.gov.eg (Egyptian Shura Council, the upper legislative house in Egypt, provides access to some English language text)

http://www.hccourt.gov.eg (Supreme Constitutional Court; provides access to some useful information and documents, as well as a searchable database of judgments) http://www.egyptlaws.com (Middle East Library for Economic Services; sells printed English translations of laws on specific subjects, such as free zones, mines and quarries, and the environment and pollution)

http://www.parliament.gov.eg/English (parliamentary information available in English)

T2.13   France, Republic of

(Civil Law)

Cases

Citation format: ‹court name› [‹court abbreviation›] [‹English translation of court name›] ‹city, if applicable›, ‹chamber, if applicable›, ‹date of decision in month day, year format›, ‹reporter or journal abbreviation› ‹year of publication›, ‹section of journal if applicable›, ‹page on which decision appears, or decision number›, ‹author of case observation or note› (‹country abbreviation if not evident from context›).

When citing to a reporter or journal, follow the particular formats below where they differ from the general format above.

▶ Tribunal de grande instance [TGI] [ordinary court of original jurisdiction] Nice, May 30, 1990, D. 1991 Somm. 113, obs. F. Derrida (Fr.).

▶ Cour d'appel [CA] [regional court of appeal] Paris, 1e ch., Dec. 20, 1994, JCP 1994, II, 22250, note Neirinck (Fr.).

Ordinary jurisdiction

Cour de cassation (Cass.) (Supreme Court for Judicial Matters (**Tribunal de cassation** prior to 1804)): highest court of ordinary jurisdiction). It ordinarily sits in separate chambers (called "sections" prior to 1826), which are abbreviated as follows:

▶ Assemblée plénière	1978-date	ass. plén.
▶ Chambres réunies	1790-1978	ch. réuns.
▶ Chambre mixte	1976-date	ch. mixte
▶ Première chambre civile	1790-date	1e civ.
▶ Deuxième chambre civile	1952-date	2e civ.
▶ Troisième chambre civile	1967-date	3e civ.
▶ Chambre criminelle	1790-date	crim.
▶ Chambre commerciale et financière	1947-date	com.
▶ Chambre sociale	1938-date	soc.
▶ Chambre des requêtes	1790-1947	req.
▶ Chambres temporaires des expropriations	1964-1967	chs. exprops.

Cour de cassation decisions are published in an official reporter set in two series:

▶ Bulletin des arrêts de la Cour de cassation, chambres civiles	1792-date	Bull. civ.
▶ Bulletin des arrêts de la Cour de cassation, chambre criminelle	1798-date	Bull. crim.

Cite to Bull. civ. or Bull. crim., as appropriate, if therein, indicating part and case number. Otherwise cite to one of the legal reviews listed below. The parts for the five civil chambers are as follows:

- 1e civ.   Bull. civ. I
- 2e civ.   Bull. civ. II
- 3e civ.   Bull. civ. III
- com.   Bull. civ. IV
- soc.   Bull. civ. V

  - Cour de cassation [Cass.] [supreme court for judicial matters] 2e civ., Mar. 16, 2000, Bull. civ. II, No. 46 (Fr.).

  - Cour de cassation [Cass.] [supreme court for judicial matters] soc., July 7, 1983, Bull. civ. V, No. 433 (Fr.).

  - Cour de cassation [Cass.] [supreme court for judicial matters] crim., Jan. 16, 2001, Bull. crim., No. 14 (Fr.).

Cours d'appel (CA) (regional courts of appeal), **Tribunaux de grande instance** (TGI) (ordinary courts of original jurisdiction (**Tribunaux de première instance** (TPI) prior to 1958)), **Cours d'assises** (do not abbreviate) (courts of original jurisdiction for very serious crimes), and **Tribunaux d'instance** (Trib. inst.) (courts of petty jurisdiction (**Juges de paix** (JP) prior to 1958)): All cites should include the city and the chamber, if any.

There are no official reporters for lower judicial court decisions. They are reported in general and specialized commercial legal journals or reviews. The editorial boards of these journals choose what to report and to include either the full text or a summary of a decision. Lower court decisions are also reported in commercial databases or on government websites.

The following legal reviews are among the best known. Some of them have changed name and/or format through the years. They usually contain several parts. The full text of a court decision is generally under the heading "jurisprudence," while summaries are under "sommaires" or "panorama."

- Recueil Dalloz
  - Formerly Dalloz-Sirey   1965–1996
    - *Actualité Jurisprudentielle*   2007–date   e.g., D. ‹year› A.J. ‹page›
    - *Jurisprudence*   1965–2007   e.g., D. ‹year›, ‹page›
    - *Informations Rapides*   1965–2007   e.g., D. ‹year› inf. rap. ‹page›
    - *Sommaires Commentés*   1965–2007   e.g., D. ‹year› Somm. ‹page›
  - Dalloz, *Jurisprudence*   1945–1964   D. Jur.
  - Analytique, *Jurisprudence*   1941–1944   D.A. Jur.
  - Critique, *Jurisprudence*   1941–1944   D.C. Jur.
    Périodique et critique   1825–1940
  - Cour de cassation   D.P. I
    - Cours royales, cours impériales, cours d'appel   D.P. II
    - Conseil d'État   D.P. III
- Recueil Sirey (entitled *Recueil Général des Lois et des Arrêts* until 1950)
  - Sirey, *Jurisprudence*   1956–1964   S. Jur.
                                               1791–1955
    - Cour de cassation   S. Jur. I
    - Other courts   S. Jur. II
    - Jurisprudence administrative   S. Jur. III
- Gazette du Palais   1881–date
  - *Jurisprudence*   e.g., Gaz. Pal. ‹year›, 2, ‹page›
  - *Sommaires des cours et tribunaux*   e.g., Gaz. Pal. ‹year›, Somm. ‹page›

▸ Juris-Classeur Périodique
  ▸ Edition Général (La Semaine   1942-date
    Juridique)
    ▸ *Jurisprudence*   e.g., JCP ‹year› II ‹number›
    ▸ *Panorama de Jurisprudence*   e.g., JCP ‹year› IV ‹number›
  ▸ Bulletin Joly   e.g., Bull. Joly ‹year›, ‹page›
  ▸ Juris-Classeur Périodique
    ▸ Édition Entreprise et Affaires   e.g., JCP E. ‹year›, ‹number›
    ▸ Édition Notariale et Immobilière   e.g., JCP N. ‹year›, ‹number›
    ▸ Édition Sociale   e.g., JCP S. ‹year›, ‹number›
  ▸ JurisData   e.g., JurisData ‹number›

Administrative jurisdiction

Tribunal des conflits (TC) (reconciles disputes between the Conseil d'État and the Cour de Cassation), **Conseil d'État** (CE) (highest administrative court: sits in sub-section (CE), section (CE Sect.), or assembly (CE Ass.)), and **Tribunaux administratifs** (TA) (regional administrative courts of first instance): Cite to Rec. Lebon, if therein; otherwise cite to one of the legal reviews listed above.

▸ Recueil des arrêts du Conseil d'État   1821-date   Rec. Lebon

  ▸ CE Sect., Mar. 5, 1943, Rec. Lebon 62

  ▸ CE Ass., Nov. 8, 1974, Rec. Lebon 541

  ▸ TA Amiens, Apr. 10, 1973, Rec. Lebon 780

Constitutional jurisdiction

Citation format: Conseil constitutionnel [CC] [Constitutional Court] decision No. ‹decision number›‹category of decision›, ‹date of decision in month day, year format›, ‹publication abbreviation› ‹first page›, ‹page(s) of specific material, if desired› (‹country abbreviation if not evident from context›).

  ▸ Conseil constitutionnel [CC] [Constitutional Court] decision No. 82-154DC, Dec. 29, 1982, Rec. 80 (Fr.).

Conseil constitutionnel (CC) (Constitutional Court): Cite to J.O. or Rec., if therein. The Conseil constitutionnel reviews the constitutionality of laws before they are promulgated. When it finds a provision unconstitutional, the provision is not promulgated.

There are several categories of decisions. Déclaration de conformité (DC), which reviews the constitutionality of laws and parliamentary standing orders, is the category cited most often.

▸ Journal Officiel de la République Française (Official Gazette of France)	1871-date	J.O.
▸ Journal Official de l'Empire Français	1852-1870	
▸ Moniteur Universel	1811-1852	
▸ Gazette Nationale	1799-1811	
▸ Bulletin des Lois	1791-1811	
▸ Recueil des décisions du Conseil constitutionnel	1960-date	Rec.

Constitution
  ▸ LA CONSTITUTION   CONST.

Citation format: ‹year› CONST. ‹article› (‹country abbreviation if not evident from context›).

France has had fifteen different constitutions since its first in 1791. The current constitution was adopted in 1958.

Codes

Citation format: ‹code name› [‹code abbreviation›] ‹article› (‹country abbreviation if not evident from context›).

▶ CODE CIVIL [C. CIV.] art. 23 (Fr.).

▶ CODE ADMINISTRATIF	C. ADM.
▶ CODE CIVIL	C. CIV.
▶ CODE DE COMMERCE	C. COM.
▶ CODE PÉNAL	C. PÉN.
▶ CODE DE PROCÉDURE PÉNALE	C. PR. PÉN.
▶ CODE DU TRAVAIL	C. TRAV.
▶ CODE DE PROCÉDURE CIVILE	C.P.C.

Statutes and decrees

Citation format for a French law or decree: Loi ‹law or decree number› du ‹date in French of law or decree› ‹law or decree name› [‹English translation of law or decree number, date, and name›], ‹reporter or journal name› [‹reporter or journal abbreviation›] [‹English translation of reporter or journal›], ‹date of publication›, **p.** ‹page number› (‹country abbreviation if not evident from context›).

▶ Loi 2008-776 du 4 août 2008 de modernisation de l'économie [Law 2008-776 of August 4, 2008 on the Modernization of the Economy], JOURNAL OFFICIEL DE LA RÉPUBLIQUE FRANÇAISE [J.O.] [OFFICIAL GAZETTE OF FRANCE], Aug. 5, 2008, p. 12471.

▶ Loi 85-699 du 11 juillet 1985 tendant à la constitution d'archives audiovisuelles de la justice [Law 85-699 of July 11, 1985 for the Formation of Audiovisual Archives of the Judiciary], LA SEMAINE JURIDIQUE [JCP] [JURIDICAL WEEKLY] III, No. 57447.

Cite to the J.O., if therein; otherwise, cite to one of the following:

▶ JOURNAL OFFICIEL DE LA RÉPUBLIQUE FRANÇAISE		J.O.
▶ RECUEIL DALLOZ		
▶ DALLOZ-SIREY, *LÉGISLATION*	1965–1996	D.S.L.
▶ DALLOZ, *LÉGISLATION*	1945–1964	D.L.
▶ ANALYTIQUE, *LÉGISLATION*	1941–1944	D.A.L.
▶ CRITIQUE, *LÉGISLATION*	1941–1944	D.C.L.
▶ PÉRIODIQUE ET CRITIQUE	1848–1940	D.P. IV
	1825–1847	D.P. III
▶ BULLETIN LÉGISLATIF DALLOZ	1918–1982	B.L.D.
▶ ACTUALITÉ LÉGISLATIVE DALLOZ	1983–1995	A.L.D.
▶ LA SEMAINE JURIDIQUE (JURIS-CLASSEUR PÉRIODIQUE)	1942–2004 1927–date	e.g., JCP III, No. ‹number›
▶ COLLECTION COMPLÈTE, DÉCRETS, ORDONNANCES, RÈGLEMENTS ET AVIS DU CONSEIL D'ÉTAT (DUVERGIER & BOCQUET)	1788–1949	DUV. & BOC.

Treaties and conventions

Citation format: ‹treaty or convention name›, ‹date of signing›, ‹abbreviated names of parties›, JOURNAL OFFICIEL DE LA RÉPUBLIQUE FRANÇAISE

[J.O.] [OFFICIAL GAZETTE OF FRANCE], ‹date of publication›, p. ‹page number› (‹country abbreviation if not evident from context›).

▶ Tourism Accord, Oct. 26, 1979, Fr.-Mex., JOURNAL OFFICIEL DE LA RÉPUBLIQUE FRANÇAISE [J.O.] [OFFICIAL GAZETTE OF FRANCE], June 15, 1980, p. 1478.

Cite to the J.O., if therein; otherwise, cite to one of the following:

▶ RECUEIL DES TRAITÉS ET ACCORDS   1961–date   e.g., ‹year› RECUEIL DES
    DE LA FRANCE   TRAITÉS, No. ‹number›
▶ RECUEIL DES TRAITÉS DE LA FRANCE   1713–1906   e.g., ‹volume› RECUEIL DES
                                            TRAITÉS ‹page›

Internet sources

http://www.legifrance.gouv.fr (government portal to French law; provides access to the constitution; codes (some translated into English); official gazettes since 1990; treaties; recent decisions from the Cour de cassation, Conseil d'État, and Conseil constitutionnel; and links to European laws)

http://www.assemblee-nationale.fr (National Assembly)

http://www.senat.fr (Senate)

http://www.courdecassation.fr (Cour de cassation)

http://www.conseil-etat.fr (Conseil d'État)

http://www.conseil-constitutionnel.fr (Conseil constitutionnel)

http://www.loc.gov/law/help/france.html (Library of Congress Guide to Law Online: France)

T2.14   Germany, Federal Republic of

(Civil Law)

Cases

Citation format: ‹court name› [‹court abbreviation›] [‹English translation of court name›] ‹date of decision›, ‹volume number, if applicable› ‹reporter or periodical name› [‹reporter or periodical abbreviation›] ‹first page› (‹page(s) of specific material, if desired›), ‹for periodicals, year of publication of volume› (‹country abbreviation if not evident from context›).

▶ Bundesgerichtshof [BGH] [Federal Court of Justice] Apr. 16, 2008, NEUE JURISTISCHE WOCHENSCHRIFT [NJW] 2455, 2008 (Ger.).

Format for subsequent citations: ‹volume number, if applicable› ‹reporter or periodical abbreviation› ‹first page› (‹page(s) of specific material, if desired›) (‹country abbreviation if not evident from context›).

▶ 154 BGHZ 370 (371) (Ger.).

Ordinary jurisdiction

Bundesgerichtshof (BGH) (Federal Court of Justice (previously **Reichsgericht** (RG)): court of last resort for civil and criminal matters): Cite civil matters to BGHZ or RGZ, and criminal matters to BGHSt or RGSt, or to a periodical or electronic source.

▶ ENTSCHEIDUNGEN DES BUNDESGERICHTSHOFES IN ZIVILSACHEN   1951–date   BGHZ
▶ ENTSCHEIDUNGEN DES REICHSGERICHTS IN ZIVILSACHEN   1880–1945   RGZ

▸ Entscheidungen des Bundesgerichtshofes in Strafsachen   1951-date   BGHSt
▸ Entscheidungen des Reichsgerichts in Strafsachen   1880-1945   RGSt

Oberlandesgericht (OLG) (in most states, higher regional court): Cite civil matters to OLGZ, and criminal matters to OLGSt, or to a periodical or electronic source; **Bayerisches Oberstes Landesgericht** (BayObLG) (Bavarian Higher Regional Court): Cite civil matters to BayObLGZ and criminal matters to BayObLGSt, or to a periodical or electronic source; **Landgericht** (LG) (regional courts): Cite to periodicals.

▸ Rechtsprechung der Oberlandesgerichte in Zivilsachen	1965-1994	OLGZ
▸ Rechtsprechung der Oberlandesgerichte in Strafsachen	1983-date	OLGSt
▸ Entscheidungen des Bayerischen Obersten Landesgerichts in Zivilsachen	1950-date	BayObLGZ
▸ Entscheidungen des Bayerischen Obersten Landesgerichts in Strafsachen		BayObLGSt

Constitutional jurisdiction

Bundesverfassungsgericht (BVerfG) (Federal Constitutional Court): Cite to BVerfGE, if therein.

▸ Entscheidungen des Bundesverfassungsgerichts	1951-date	BVerfGE

Administrative jurisdiction

Bundesverwaltungsgericht (BVerwG) (Federal Administrative Court): Cite to BVerwGE, if therein; **Oberverwaltungsgericht** (OVG) or **Verwaltungsgerichtshof** (VGH) (higher administrative courts): Cite to the *Entscheidungen* (case reporter) of the court; **Verwaltungsgericht** (VG) (administrative trial courts): Cite to periodicals.

▸ Entscheidungen des Bundesverwaltungsgerichts	1954-date	BVerwGE

Special jurisdiction

Bundesfinanzhof (BFH) (Federal Tax Court): Cite to BFHE, if therein; **Finanzgericht** (FG) (tax courts): Cite to EFG, if therein; **Bundesarbeitsgericht** (BAG) (Federal Labor Court): Cite to BAGE, if therein; **Landesarbeitsgerichte** (LAG) (higher labor courts): Cite to periodicals; **Bundessozialgericht** (BSG) (Federal Social Court): Cite to BSGE, if therein; **Landessozialgericht** (LSG) (higher social courts): Cite to periodicals; **Bundespatentgericht** (BPatG) (Federal Patent Court): Cite to BPatGE, if therein.

▸ Sammlung der Entscheidungen und Gutachten des Bundesfinanzhofs	1952-date	BFHE
▸ Entscheidungen der Finanzgerichte	1953-date	EFG
▸ Entscheidungen des Bundesarbeitsgerichts	1954-date	BAGE
▸ Entscheidungen des Bundessozialgerichts	1955-date	BSGE
▸ Entscheidungen des Bundespatentgerichts	1962-date	BPatGE

....

Constitution

▸ Grundgesetz für die Bundesrepublik Deutschland (Basic Law)	Grundgesetz	GG

The *Basic Law* is subdivided into articles.

When citing the *Basic Law* for the first time within a work, include the date of enactment and gazette of promulgation:

▶ GRUNDGESETZ FÜR DIE BUNDESREPUBLIK DEUTSCHLAND
[GRUNDGESETZ] [GG] [BASIC LAW], May 23, 1949, BGBl. I (Ger.).

Cite amending laws to the *Basic Law* like statutes:

▶ Gesetz zur Änderung des Grundgesetzes [Law Amending Basic
Law], June 28, 1993, BGBl. I at 1002 (Ger.).

Codes

Citation format: ‹code name› [‹code abbreviation›] [‹English translation of
code name›], ‹date of enactment›, ‹name of gazette of promulgation›
[‹gazette abbreviation›] ‹volume number and/or page number›, ‹"as
amended," or amending law with citation, if applicable›, ‹relevant subdivisions, if desired› (‹country abbreviation if not evident from context›).

It is possible to cite to a sentence or clause within the section, paragraph, or
sentence number. Cite the section before paragraphs or sentence numbers.

▶ BÜRGERLICHES GESETZBUCH [BGB] [CIVIL CODE], Aug. 18, 1896,
REICHSGESETZBLATT [RGBL.] 195, as amended, § 793, para. 2,
sentence 2 (Ger.).

▶ BÜRGERLICHES GESETZBUCH (CIVIL CODE)	BGB
▶ HANDELSGESETZBUCH (COMMERCIAL CODE)	HGB
▶ SOZIALGESETZBUCH (SOCIAL CODE)	SGB
▶ STRAFGESETZBUCH (PENAL CODE)	STGB
▶ STRAFPROZESSORDNUNG (CODE OF CRIMINAL PROCEDURE)	STPO
▶ ZIVILPROZESSORDNUNG (CODE OF CIVIL PROCEDURE)	ZPO

The *Sozialgesetzbuch* (SGB) (Social Code) is subdivided into ten titles that are
described by a Roman numeral. For instance, *Sozialgesetzbuch V Gesetzliche
Krankenversicherung* deals with social health insurance.

Statutes and decrees

Citation format: ‹statute or decree full name or, if available and part of the
statutory title, short title› [‹abbreviated statute or decree name, if available›] [‹English translation of short title›], ‹date of enactment›, ‹name of
gazette of promulgation› [‹abbreviation of gazette of promulgation›] at
‹volume, page, and/or sentence number of gazette, if desired›, ‹"as
amended," or amending law with citation, if applicable›, ‹relevant subdivisions, if desired› (‹country abbreviation if not evident from context›).

▶ Finanzmarktstabilisierungsfonds-Verordnung [FMStFV] [Financial
Markets Stabilization Regulation], Oct. 20, 2008, ELEKTRONISCHER
BUNDESANZEIGER [eBANZ.] at 123 2008 VI (Ger.).

Subsequent citation may be made to the abbreviation of the gazette, rather than
the full name of the publication.

▶ Waffengesetz [WaffG] [Weapons Act], Mar. 18, 1938, RGBL. I at 265,
§ 1 (Ger.).

▶ Bundes-Bodenschutz- und Altlastenverordnung [BbodSchV]
[Regulation on Soil Protection and Environmental Burdens], July 7,
1999, BGBL. I at 1554, § 2, no. 6 (Ger.).

> ► Einfuhrliste [List of Import Restrictions], Dec. 15, 2003, BAnz. at
> 26,137 (Beilage no. 243a) (Ger.).

Statutes are often amended by subsequent legislation, and citing the original enactment does not indicate what amendments have since occurred. Add "as amended," or cite a particular amending law. Add a translation of the statute name if helpful, and cite an English translation of the statute if available.

> ► Aktiengesetz [AktG] [Stock Corporation Act], Sept. 6, 1965, BGBL. I
> at 1089, last amended by Gesetz [G], Aug. 24, 2004, BGBL. I at
> 2198, art. 12e, § 1(2) (Ger.), *translated in* Business Transactions
> in Germany app. 7 (Bernd Ruster ed., Matthew Bender 2008).

Many laws are repromulgated years after their enactment to provide an officially updated text. Cite such laws with their latest repromulgation date, or if the former version is also pertinent, cite the first enactment, followed by the date and citation of the pertinent repromulgation.

> ► Bundesnotarordnung [Federal Act on Notaries Public], Feb. 13,
> 1937, RGBL. II at 191, repromulgated Feb. 24, 1961, BGBL. I at 97
> (Ger.).

Cite a **Gesetz** (G) (federal statute) or **Verordnung** (V) (regulation) to the federal law gazette where it was promulgated, either the BGBL. or the RGBL., or, in the case of some regulations, BAnz. or eBAnz. When the BGBL. or RGBL. is divided into Teil I and Teil II, domestic legislation is in the first volume.

► Bundesgesetzblatt, Teil I	1951–date	BGBL. I
► Bundesgesetzblatt, Teil II	1951–date	BGBL. II
► Reichsgesetzblatt	1871–1921	RGBL.
► Reichsgesetzblatt, Teil I	1922–1945	RGBL. I
► Reichsgesetzblatt, Teil II	1922–1945	RGBL. II
► Bundesanzeiger	1949–date	e.g., BAnz. at ‹page number› (Beilage no. ‹number›)
► Elektronischer Bundesanzeiger	2004–date	e.g., eBAnz. at ‹document number›

Legislative materials

There are two federal legislative bodies: the **Deutscher Bundestag** (BT) (Federal Parliament) and the **Bundesrat** (BR) (Federal Council). Cite published **Drucksachen** (legislative materials) by legislative period and number for BT and by number and last two digits of year for BR.

> ► Deutscher Bundestag: Drucksachen und Protokolle [BT] 15/10
> (Ger.).

> ► Bundesrat Drucksachen [BR] 404/01 (Ger.).

If desirable, include type of document (e.g., bill, resolution, inquiry, report) and date.

> ► Gesetzesentwurf, Nov. 7, 2008, BR 830/08 (Ger.).

Treaties and conventions

Cite treaties and conventions to BGBL. II, and use the citation format for statutes.

Internet sources

Commercial services

Germany's comprehensive legal database, JURIS, is an authoritative but not the primary official source. The online, fee-based subscription service offers more than forty online libraries including the text of federal statutes (Bundesrecht), reported cases (Rechtsprechung), the laws of several states, tax regulations and rulings, and bibliographic references to the legal literature. All materials quoted from JURIS should be cited according to the established format for printed materials. In addition, a parallel reference to the JURIS source may be given. For court decisions from an electronic source that may not as yet have been reported elsewhere, also cite the docket number.

▶ Produkthaftungsgesetz [ProdhaftG] [Products Liability Act], Dec. 15, 1989, BGBL. I at 2198 (Ger.), *available at* JURIS.

▶ BverfG, Mar. 17, 2004, docket number 1 BvR 1266/00 (Ger.), *available at* JURIS.

In addition to JURIS, German legal publishers offer numerous electronic products, including commercial CD-ROMs.

▶ Gesetz über Urheberrecht und verwandte Schutzrechte [Urheberrechtsgesetz] [UrhG] [Copyright Act], Sept. 9, 1965, BGBL. I at 1273 (Deutsche Gesetze Schönfelder plus CD-ROM, including 3rd update 2004) (Ger.).

▶ BVerfG, Mar. 30 2004, docket number 2 BvR 1520/01 (JURIS CD-ROM Rechtsprechung des BGH premium (23d ed. 2004)) (Ger.).

Free websites

Reprints of German laws are available on many websites, some published by German agencies and offering reliable up-to-date versions of numerous laws.

Gesetze im Internet, available at **http://www.gesetze-im-internet.de**, published by the Federal Ministry of Justice in partnership with JURIS, provides up-to-date text of most laws and regulations.

▶ Gesetz über Urheberrecht und verwandte Schutzrechte [Urheberrechtsgesetz] [UrhG] [Copyright Act], Sept. 9, 1965, BGBL. I at 1273 (Ger.), *available at* http://www.gesetze-im-internet.de.

Statutes provided on this site are usually updated within one month. Unless indicated by the text, a citation of the amended status is not typically necessary.

Other resources

http://www.cgerli.org/index.php?id=61 (translation of selected laws and court decisions are provided by the Centre for German Legal Information)

http://www.ebundesanzeiger.de/ebanzwww/wexsservlet (regulations published in the electronic Bundesanzeiger (EBANZ.))

The federal courts have websites that make their decisions available:

http://www.bundesverfassungsgericht.de/entscheidungen.html (Bundesverfassungsgericht)

http://www.bundesverwaltungsgericht.ch/index/entscheide.htm (Bundesverwaltungsgericht)

Federal legislative materials:

http://dip.bundestag.de (Bundestag)

http://www.parlamentsspiegel.de (Bundesrat)

___

T2.14.1   German Länder

....

Cases

In the integrated German court system, the trial and appellate courts are state courts, and the courts of last resort are federal courts. Federal courts adjudicate matters of federal and state law.

Constitutional jurisdiction

Staatsgerichtshof (StGH) or **Verfassungsgerichtshof** (e.g., BayVerfGH for Bavaria) (constitutional court that adjudicates matters relating to the state's constitution): Cite to the official reporter, a periodical, or a website.

> ► BayVerfGH July 19, 2007, 60 SAMMLUNG VON ENTSCHEIDUNGEN DES BAYERISCHEN VERWALTUNGSGERICHTSHOFS MIT ENTSCHEIDUNGEN DES BAYERISCHEN VERFASSUNGSGERICHTSHOFS [BAYVGH (N.F.)] 151 (Bavaria) (Ger.).

....

Constitutions

> ► VERFASSUNG BAYERN   VERF BAY

Add the name of the state.

....

Statutes and decrees

Cite a **Landesgesetz** (LG) (state statute) or **Landesverordnung** (LVO) (state administrative regulation) to the law gazette (GVBL.) of the individual state.

> ► Bayerisches Verfassungsschutzgesetz, repromulgated Apr. 10, 1997, BAYERISCHES GESETZ- UND VERORDNUNGSBLATT [BAY GVBL.] 70 (Bavaria) (Ger.).
> ► BAYERISCHES GESETZ- UND VERORDNUNGSBLATT   BAY GVBL.

....

Internet sources

Länder laws and regulations, as well as decisions of the Länder courts, are available on their official websites. For instance, in the Land of North Rhine-Westphalia, the Ministry of Justice provides a legal library that contains the court decisions of North Rhine-Westphalia as well as the most important laws of the Federation and the other Länder. The portal is available in English at **http://www.justiz.nrw.de/WebPortal_en/legal_library**, but the sources are in German.

For additional electronic sources, see table T2.14 Germany, Federal Republic of.

T2.15   Greece

(Civil Law)

Cases

Citation format: ‹court name› [‹court abbreviation›] [‹English translation of
court name›] ‹case number›/‹year›, p. ‹first page›, ‹page(s) of specific
material, if desired› (‹country abbreviation if not evident from context›).

▶ Areios Pagos [A.P.] [Supreme Court] 355/2004, p. 3 (Greece).

▶ Symboulion Epikrateias [S.E.] [Supreme Administrative Court]
1250/1995, p. 8 (Greece).

Areios Pagos (A.P.) (Supreme Court), **Symboulion Epikrateias** (S.E.)
(Supreme Administrative Court), **Erinidokeia** (Erin.) (courts of peace),
Protodikeia (Monomele-Polymele) (Mon. Pr. or Pol. Pr.) (district courts), and
Efeteia (Efet.) (courts of appeals): Cite to various legal journals. There are no offi-
cial reporters for court decisions.

Constitution

Citation format: ‹year› SYNTAGMA [SYN.] [CONSTITUTION] ‹section number›
(‹country abbreviation if not evident from context›).

▶ 1975 SYNTAGMA [SYN.] [CONSTITUTION] 6 (Greece).

Codes

Citation format: ‹code name› [‹code abbreviation›] [‹English translation of
code name›] ‹chapter number›:‹article number› (‹country abbreviation if
not evident from context›).

▶ ASTIKOS KODIKAS [A.K.] [CIVIL CODE] 1:1 (Greece).

▶ ASTIKOS KODIKAS (CIVIL CODE)	A.K.
▶ POINIKOS KODIKAS (CRIMINAL CODE)	P.K.
▶ STRATIOTIKOS POINIKOS KODIKAS (MILITARY CRIMINAL CODE)	STR.P.K.
▶ KODIKAS IDIOTIKOU NAUTIKOU DIKAIOU (CODE OF PRIVATE MARITIME LAW)	KIND
▶ EMPORIKOS KODIKAS (COMMERCIAL CODE)	EK
▶ KODIKAS POLITIKES DIKONOMIAS (CODE OF CIVIL PROCEDURE)	KPOL.D.
▶ KODIKAS POINIKES DIKONOMIAS (CODE OF CRIMINAL PROCEDURE)	KPOI.D.
▶ KODIKAS TON DEMOSION YPALLELON (CODE OF CIVIL SERVANTS)	KDY
▶ KODIKAS ELLENIKES ITHAGENEIAS (CODE OF GREEK CITIZENSHIP)	KEI
▶ DASIKOS KODIKAS (FOREST CODE)	DK
▶ KODIKAS SYMVOLAIOGRAPHON (CODE ON NOTARIES)	KS
▶ KODIKAS DIOIKITIKES DIADIKASIAS (CODE OF ADMINISTRATIVE PROCEDURE)	K.D.DIAD.
▶ KODIKAS DIOIKITIKES DIKONOMIAS (CODE OF ADMINISTRATIVE JUDICIAL PROCEDURE)	K.D.DIK.

Statutes and decrees

Citation format for statutes: Nomos (‹year›:‹law number›) ‹statute name›
[‹English translation of statute name›], ‹publication name› [‹publication
abbreviation›] ‹year›, ‹part›:‹issue number› (‹country abbreviation if not
evident from context›).

> ▶ Nomos (2004:3226) Paroche Nomikes Voetheias se Polites Chamelou Eisodematos kai alles Diatakseis [Legal Aid to Citizens of Low Income and Other Provisions], EPHEMERIS TES KYVERNESEOS TES HELLENIKES DEMOKRATIAS [E.K.E.D.] 2004, A:24 (Greece).

Citation format for decrees: Diatagma ‹year›:‹law number›) ‹decree name› [‹English translation of decree name›], ‹publication name› [‹publication abbreviation›] ‹year›, ‹part›:‹issue number› (‹country abbreviation if not evident from context›).

....

Periodicals

Citation format: ‹author name›, ‹title in transliterated form› [‹English translation of title›] ‹volume number› ‹periodical name› [‹periodical abbreviation›], No. ‹number›, ‹first page›, ‹page(s) of specific material, if desired› (‹year›) (‹country abbreviation if not evident from context›).

> ▶ Kostas Mpeis, *He Anagkastike Ektelese Enantion Allodapou Kratous Kata to Helleniko Dikaio [Enforcement Proceedings Against a Foreign State According to Greek Law]* 52 NOMIKON VEMA [N.V.], No. 4, 558 (2004) (Greece).

The following are the most common journals:

▶ HARMENOPOULOS	HARM.
▶ DIKE (TRIAL)	D.
▶ DELTIO ERGATIKES NOMOTHESIAS (BULLETIN OF LABOR LAW)	D.E.N.
▶ DELTIO PHOROLOGIKES NOMOTHESIAS (BULLETIN OF TAXATION)	D.PH.N.
▶ EPITHEORESES DEMOSIOU KAI DIOIKETIKOU DIKAIOUÝ (JOURNAL OF PUBLIC AND ADMINISTRATIVE LAW)	E.D.D.D.
▶ EPITHEORESES DIKAIOU KOINONIKES ASPHALISEOS (JOURNAL OF SOCIAL INSURANCE LAW)	E.D.K.A.
▶ EPITHEORESES ERGATIKOU DIKAIOU (JOURNAL OF LABOR LAW)	E.ERG.D.
▶ EPHEMERES ELLENON NOMIKON (JOURNAL OF GREEK JURISTS)	E.E.N.
▶ EPITHEORESES EMPORIKOU DIKAIOU (JOURNAL OF COMMERCIAL LAW)	E.EMP.D.
▶ NOMIKON VEMA (LEGAL TRIBUNE)	N.V.
▶ KODIKAS NOMIKOU VEMATOS (CODE OF LEGAL TRIBUNE)	K.N.V.
▶ TO SYNTAGMA (THE CONSTITUTION)	TO S.
▶ DIKAIOMATA TOU ANTRHOPOU (REVIEW OF HUMAN RIGHTS)	D.T.A.

....

Treaties

Cite treaties to the *Official Gazette of Greece*: ‹title›, ‹parties›, ‹date of signature› [EPHEMERIS TES KYVERNESEOS TES HELLENIKES DEMOKRATIAS] [E.K.E.D.], ‹part›:‹issue number›, ‹date of publication› (‹country abbreviation if not evident from context›).

> ▶ Agreement on Double Taxation, Greece-U.S., Oct. 22, 1960 [EPHEMERIS TES KYVERNESEOS TES HELLENIKES DEMOKRATIAS] [E.K.E.D.], A:28, Oct. 28, 1960 (Greece).

....

Internet sources

http://www.et.gr (*Official Gazette of Greece*, by subscription only)

http://www.dsanet.gr (Isokratis (Athens Bar Association))

http://lawdb.intrasoftnet.com (NOMOS)

http://www.loc.gov/law/help/guide/nations/greece.html (Library of Congress Guide to Law Online: Greece)

T2.16   Hong Kong

(Common Law)

Chinese and English language sources

Hong Kong has two official languages: English and Chinese. Where a source is available in both languages, generally cite to the English source, unless there is a specific reason to cite to the Chinese version. When citing an English language primary source, it is not necessary to preface the source with the words "*translated in*."

Romanization

For romanization of Chinese language citations, follow instructions in **rule 20.2.4(b)**.

English abbreviations

Follow abbreviation guidelines for U.S. materials, using **tables T6** and **T10**, unless an exception is provided in **table T2.42 United Kingdom**. Render "Hong Kong Special Administrative Region" or "HKSAR" as "Hong Kong."

....

Cases

Citation format: ‹case name›, [‹year of decision›] ‹volume number or part› ‹reporter abbreviation› ‹first page›, ‹page(s) of specific material, if desired› (‹court abbreviation›) (‹country abbreviation if not evident from context›).

- ► Law Soc'y of H.K. v. Brook, [1997–1998] 1 H.K.C.F.A.R. 228, 231D (C.F.I.).

- ► Hong Kong v. Chan Hing Hung, [1998] 4 H.K.C. 487, 488C (C.F.I.).

- ► Tong Ping-chuen v. AG, [1990] 1 H.K.L.R. 551, 559E (H.C.).

Privy Council (P.C.) (all criminal and civil final appeals until July 1, 1997): Cite to reports listed under **table T2.42 United Kingdom**.

Court of Final Appeal (C.F.A.) (all criminal and civil final appeals after July 1, 1997): Cite to H.K.C.F.A.R., H.K.C., or Legal Reference System, if therein.

► Hong Kong Court of Final Appeal Reports	1997/1998–date	H.K.C.F.A.R.
► Hong Kong Cases	1946–date	H.K.C.
► Legal Reference System	1997–date	Legal Reference System

Court of Appeal of the High Court (C.A.): Cite to H.K.L.R.D., H.K.L.R., H.K.C., or Legal Reference System, in that order of preference.

► The Authorized Hong Kong Law Reports and Digest	1997–date	H.K.L.R.D.
► Hong Kong Law Reports	1905/1906–1996	H.K.L.R.
► Hong Kong Cases	1946–date	H.K.C.
► Legal Reference System	1946–date	Legal Reference System

Court of First Instance of the High Court (C.F.I.) (**High Court of Justice** (H.C.) from 1975 to 1998): Cite to H.K.L.R.D., H.K.L.R., H.K.C., or Legal Reference System, if therein.

District Court (D.C.): For an online source, cite using application number, abbreviation, and date as provided in the judgment. Cite to D.C.L.R. or Legal Reference System, if therein. Provide a parallel print source citation where available.

- District Court Law Reports   1953-1996   D.C.L.R.
  (Supplement to Hong Kong Law Reports)
- Legal Reference System   1968-date   Legal Reference System

  - Ward v. Harting (HK) Ltd., DCCJ 2744/2004 (D.C. Dec. 14, 2005) (Legal Reference System) (H.K.).

Family Court (F.C.): Cite using application number, abbreviation, and date as provided in the judgment. Cite to Legal Reference System. Provide a parallel print source citation where available.

- Legal Reference System   1972-date   Legal Reference System

  - C v. L, [2004] 2 H.K.L.R.D. 1, FCMC 7268/2000 (F.C. Jan. 18, 2002) (Legal Reference System) (H.K.).

Lands Tribunal (L.D.): Cite using application number, abbreviation, and year as provided in the judgment. Cite to Legal Reference System.

- Legal Reference System   1970-date   Legal Reference System

  - Naylor v. Konmill Ltd., LDNT 61/2004 (L.D. July 27, 2004) (Legal Reference System) (H.K.).

Constitution

See also listing under table T2.9 China, People's Republic of.

- The Basic Law of the Hong Kong Special Administrative   XIANGGANG JIBEN FA
  Region of the People's Republic of China

  - XIANGGANG JIBEN FA art. 24, § 1 (H.K.).

Laws and ordinances

Cite to one or more of the following sources, if therein and available. Provide a parallel citation where available.

- The Laws of Hong Kong (香港法例)
- Ordinances of the Hong Kong Special Administrative   1855-date   O.H.K.
  Region for the year ‹year› (Legal Supplement No. 1 to
  The Government of the Hong Kong Special Administrative
  Region Gazette)
- Bilingual Laws Information System   BLIS

Citation format for *The Laws of Hong Kong*: ‹statute or ordinance name›, (‹edition year›) Cap. ‹chapter number›, ‹page number›, § ‹section› (‹country abbreviation if not evident from context›).

- Matrimonial Proceedings and Property Ordinance, (1990) Cap. 192, 1, § 1(1) (H.K.).

Citation format for the *Ordinances of the Hong Kong Special Administrative Region*: ‹statute or ordinance name›, No. ‹ordinance number›, (‹year of publication›) ‹volume› O.H.K., § ‹section› (‹country abbreviation if not evident from context›).

- Hong Kong Reunification Ordinance, No. 110, (1997) 3 O.H.K., § 29(1).

Regulations

Cite to *The Laws of Hong Kong*, if therein; otherwise, cite to **R.H.K.**

▸ Regulations of the Hong Kong Special Administrative   1948-date   **R.H.K.**
Region for the year ‹year› (Legal Supplement No. 2 to
The Government of the Hong Kong Special Administrative
Region Gazette)

Internet sources

http://www.legislation.gov.hk/eng/index.htm (Bilingual Laws Information System (BLIS))

http://www.gld.gov.hk/cgi-bin/gld/egazette/index.cgi?lang=e (The Government of the Hong Kong Special Administrative Region Gazette (Hong Kong Gaz.))

http://www.hklii.org (Hong Kong Legal Information Institute (HKLII))

http://legalref.judiciary.gov.hk/lrs/common/ju/judgment.jsp (Legal Reference System)

http://www.legislation.gov.hk/choice.htm (Treaties and International Agreements (In Force and Applicable to the Hong Kong SAR) (HK TIA))

http://www.hku.hk/ccpl/hktreaty/database.html (Hong Kong Treaty Database)

T2.17   Hungary, Republic of

(Civil Law)

Cases

Citation format: ‹court name› (‹court abbreviation, if applicable›) [‹English translation of court name›] ‹full date of judgment, if available›, ‹gazette abbreviation, if citing to a gazette›. ‹case number, or if none available, docket number› (‹country abbreviation if not evident from context›).

▸ Legfelsőbb Bíróság (LB) [Supreme Court] BH.1993.11.35 (Hung.).

▸ Fővárosi Ítélőtábla [Metropolitan Court of Appeal] June 11, 2008, 2.Kf.27.052/2007, http://www.gvh.hu/domain2/files/modules/module25/5021847AD6ACD66A.pdf (Hung.).

Constitutional and civil law courts

Alkotmánybíróság (AB) (Constitutional Court): Cite to **MK** or **AK**, if therein; **Legfelsőbb Bíróság** (LB) (Supreme Court): Cite to **BH**, if therein; **Szegedi Ítélőtábla**, **Pécsi Ítélőtábla**, **Győri Ítélőtábla**, **Debreceni Ítélőtábla**, and **Fővárosi Ítélőtábla** (regional court of appeal; adjudicates civil and criminal matters of major importance and commercial matters as a second-instance forum); **Megyei bíróság** and **Fővárosi Bíróság** (county court and the Metropolitan Court) and **Helyi**, **városi**, or **kerületi bíróság** (local, town, or district court): Cite to **BH**, if therein; **Munkaügyi bíróság** (labor court).

Major gazettes

▸ Magyar Közlöny (Hungarian Gazette)   **MK**
▸ Alkotmánybírósági Közlöny (Gazette of the Constitutional Court)   **AK**
▸ Bírósági Határozatok (Supreme Court Cases)   **BH**

- ▸ Határozatok Tára (Inventory of Resolutions)   HT
- ▸ Igazságügyi Közlöny (Judicial Gazette)   IK
- ▸ Ítélőtáblai Határozatok (Cases of the Courts of Appeal)   ÍH

Law journals
- ▸ Magyar Jog (Hungarian Law)   MJ
- ▸ Jogtudományi Közlöny (Gazette of Legal Science)   JK
- ▸ Gazdaság és Jog (Economy and Law)
- ▸ Polgári Jogi Kodifikáció (Civil Law Codification)
- ▸ Európai Jog (European Law)

Constitution

- ▸ A Magyar Köztársaság Alkotmánya [Constitution of the Republic of Hungary].

Statutes and decrees

Where available, cite statutes to *Magyar Közlöny* (MK) (Hungarian Gazette) and decrees to the specific ministerial gazette, e.g., *Igazságügyi Közlöny* (IK) (Judicial Gazette).

Citation format for **törvény(ek)** (act(s)): ‹year of issuance›. ‹number of the act within that year›. ‹scope of regulation› (‹English translation of the name of the act›) (‹country abbreviation if not evident from context›).

- ▸ 1959. évi IV. törvény a Polgári Törvénykönyvről (Act IV of 1959 on the Civil Code) (Hung.).

Citation format for decrees: ‹decree number›/‹year of issuance›. (‹month of issuance, in roman numerals›.‹day›.) ‹abbreviation of issuer› ‹abbreviation of type of decree› ‹scope of regulation› (‹English translation of the name of the decree›) (‹country abbreviation if not evident from context›).

When following the format above, use "**Korm.**" (Government), "**FVM**" (Minister of Agriculture), "**EüM**" (Minister of Health), and so on. For governmental and ministerial decrees, use "**r.**" for "rendelet" (decree); for municipal decrees, use "**ör.**" for "önkormányzati rendelet."

- ▸ 31/2008. (XII.31.) Korm. r. az igazságügyi szakértői működésről (Governmental Decree No. 31/2008 (XII.31.) on the Operation of Forensic Experts) (Hung.).

- ▸ 52/2005. (XI.18.) EüM. r. az emberi alkalmazásra kerülő gyógyszerek forgalomba hozataláról (Decree of the Minister of Health No. 52/2005 (XI.18.) on the Marketing of Medicinal Products for Human Use) (Hung.).

Codes

- ▸ Polgári Törvénykönyv (Civil Code)   Ptk.
- ▸ Büntető Törvénykönyv (Criminal Code)   Btk.
- ▸ Polgári perrendtartás (Civil Procedure Code)   Pp.
- ▸ Büntetőeljárási törvény (Criminal Procedure Code)   Be.
- ▸ Közigazgatási eljárásról szóló törvény (Administrative Procedure Act)   Ket.
- ▸ Gazdasági társaságokról szóló törvény (Company Law)   Gt.
- ▸ Cégtörvény (Act on Company Registration Procedure)   Ctv.

▸ Törvény a külföldiek magyarországi beruházásáról
  (Law on Investments of Foreigners in Hungary)

▸ Bírósági Törvény (Law on the Organization of the Courts)   Bszi.

T2.18   India

(Common Law)

English is the primary language of the legal system of India. Publication of cases, laws, regulations, and reporting systems are all in English.

Cases

Citation format: ‹case name›, (‹year of reporter›) ‹volume number› ‹reporter abbreviation› ‹first page› (‹year of decision if different from the year of reporter›) (‹country abbreviation if not evident from context›). Note that many reporters depart from this format, as detailed below.

▸ Charan Lal Sahu v. Union Carbide, (1989) 1 S.C.C. 674 (India).

▸ Singh v. Punjab, (1980) 2 S.C.J. 475, 524 (India).

▸ Jabalpur v. Shukla, A.I.R. 1976 S.C. 1207 (India).

Cite to *Privy Council Reports* (I. App.), *Indian Appeals* (I.A.), *Supreme Court Reports* (S.C.R.) or *Supreme Court Journal* (S.C.J.), or *All India Reporter* (A.I.R.). *Indian Law Reports* is the official law reporter for each High Court. Preference should be given to this reporter for High Court decisions.

Privy Council (P.C.) (appeals until 1949): Cite to I.A., Ind. App. or I. App., or to A.I.R. or Ind. Cas., in that order of preference.

▸ Indian Appeals	1873-1950	I.A.
▸ Law Reports, Privy Council	1836-1872	I. App.
▸ All India Reporter	1914-date	e.g., (‹year›) A.I.R. ‹volume› P.C. ‹page›
▸ Indian Cases	1909-1947	Ind. Cas.

Supreme Court (India) (**Federal Court** (India Fed.) from 1937 to 1950): Cite to S.C.R. if therein; otherwise cite to one of the reporters below in the following order of preference:

▸ Supreme Court Reports	1950-date	e.g., (‹year›) ‹volume› S.C.R. ‹page›
▸ All India Reporter	1914-date	e.g., federal courts: A.I.R. ‹year› S.C. ‹page› state courts: A.I.R. ‹year› ‹state› ‹page›
▸ Supreme Court Journal	1936-date	S.C.J.
▸ Supreme Court Cases	1969-date	e.g., (‹year›) ‹volume› S.C.C. ‹page›
▸ Unreported Judgments	1969-date	e.g., Unreported Judgments ‹year›, ‹page›
▸ Supreme Court Almanac	1979-date	e.g., ‹year› S.C.A.L.E. ‹page›
▸ Federal Court Reports	1939-1950	F.C.R.
▸ Federal Law Journal	1937-1949	F.L.J.
▸ Indian Cases	1909-1947	Ind. Cas.
▸ Accidents Claims Journal	1966-date	e.g., (‹year›) ‹volume› A.C.J. ‹page› (‹year of decision›)

► Criminal Law Journal	1904-date	e.g., ⟨year⟩ ⟨volume⟩ **Crim.L.J.** (⟨"S.C." or "H.C."⟩) ⟨page⟩ (⟨date of decision⟩)
► All India Criminal Law	1983-date	e.g., ⟨year⟩ ⟨volume⟩ **Crim.L.Rptr.** (⟨"S.C." or "H.C."⟩) ⟨page⟩ (⟨date of decision⟩)
► Election Law Reports	1945-date	e.g., ⟨year⟩ ⟨volume⟩ **E.L.R.** (⟨"S.C." or "H.C."⟩) ⟨page⟩ (⟨date of decision⟩)
► Indian Factories & Labor Reports	1960-date	e.g., ⟨year⟩ ⟨volume⟩ **F.L.R.** (⟨"S.C." or "H.C."⟩) ⟨page⟩ (⟨date of decision⟩)
► Labor & Industrial Cases	1968-date	e.g., ⟨year⟩ ⟨volume⟩ **L.I.C.** (⟨"S.C." or "H.C."⟩) ⟨page⟩ (⟨date of decision⟩)
► Labor Law Journal	1957-date	e.g., ⟨year⟩ ⟨volume⟩ **L.L.J.** (⟨"S.C." or "H.C."⟩) ⟨page⟩ (⟨date of decision⟩)
► Sales Tax Cases	1970-date	e.g., ⟨year⟩ ⟨volume⟩ **S.T.C.** (⟨"S.C." or "H.C."⟩) ⟨page⟩ (⟨date of decision⟩)

High Courts (e.g., Madras H.C.) (highest state courts (**Supreme Courts** (e.g., Calcutta S.C.) prior to 1860)) and **Courts of the Judicial Commissioner** (e.g., C.J.C. Manipur) (**Sadar Dewani Adalats** (e.g., S.D.A. Agra) prior to 1860): Cite to A.I.R., Indian Dec., or I.L.R., in that order of preference. When citing to A.I.R. or to I.L.R., give the state or regional jurisdiction parenthetically.

> ► 1954 A.I.R. 74 (Del.) 45

> ► I.L.R. 53 (Cal.) 182

► All India Reporter (different series for each state)	1914-date	A.I.R.
► Indian Decisions	1774-date	Indian Dec.
► Indian Law Reports (different series for each region)	1876-date	I.L.R.

Constitution

India's constitution took effect fully in 1950. Since its adoption, the constitution has undergone a large number of amendments without changing its basic structure. Thus, in citing the constitution and its amendments the following form may be used.

> ► INDIA CONST. art. 1, § 9, cl. 2.

> ► INDIA CONST. art. 269, *amended by* The Constitution (Eightieth Amendment) Act, 2000.

Statutes

Codes

A government publication is preferred over other sources. India Code, a statutory compilation of all laws of India, must be the primary source of citation. Absent an update, cite to the *All India Reporter Manual, 6th Edition* and then update by a session law volume and the individual amending act for a subsequent amendment.

> ► The Banking Regulation Act, No. 10 of 1949, INDIA CODE (1993), vol. 15.

> ► The Industrial Disputes Act, No. 14 of 1947, INDIA CODE (1993), vol. 13.

► India Code	INDIA CODE
► Code of Civil Procedure	CODE CIV. PROC.
► Code of Criminal Procedure	CODE CRIM. PROC.
► Hindu Code	HINDU CODE
► Indian Penal Code	PEN. CODE
► General Statutory Rules and Orders	GEN. S. R. & O.
► A.I.R. Manual: Unrepealed Central Acts (5th ed.)	A.I.R. MANUAL

Session laws

Session laws of India are published annually in a consolidated form under the title *Acts of Parliament*. Citation format: ‹act name›, **No.** ‹act number›, **Acts of Parliament,** ‹year of volume› (‹country abbreviation if not evident from context›).

> ► The Copyright (Amendment) Act, 1992, No. 13, Acts of Parliament, 1992 (India).

At times, year-end enactments are published in the subsequent year.

> ► The Taxation Laws (Amendment) Act, 2000, No. 1, Acts of Parliament, 2001 (India).

Alternative Statutory Sources:

► Subsidiary Legislation	India Subs. Leg.
► Current Indian Statutes	C.I.S.
► Current Central Legislation	Indian Curr. Cen. Leg.

Regulations

General Statutory Rules and Orders (**Gen. S. R. & O.**) is the official publication for rules and orders issued under acts, but the compilation is not very current. When the government publication does not include a rule or order, a reference may be made to any commercial publication, for example, *Current Indian Statutes* (**C.I.S.**), which is generally more up to date. In addition, regulations are also published in the government gazettes on a weekly basis. Rules may be found in the *Gazette of India*, subsection II(3)(i).

Citation format: ‹regulation name›, ‹year of enactment›, ‹volume number› ‹publication abbreviation› ‹page(s) of specific material› (‹country abbreviation if not evident from context›).

> ► The Beedi Workers Welfare Cess Rules, 1977, 22 Gen. S. R. & O. 719 (India).

> ► Indian Post Office (1st Amendment) Rules, 1996, 1997 C.I.S. 135 (India).

> ► Indian Medical Council (Profession Conduct, Etiquette and Ethics) Regulations, 2002, Gazette of India, section III(4) (Apr. 6, 2002).

Internet sources

Parliamentary bills, including texts, and other enactments may also be searched and located on the website of the Government of India at **http://indiacode .nic.in**. The site provides information from the *India Code*, an official publication, and provides a wide variety of other information.

> ► The Indian Majority Act, No. 9 of 1875, INDIA CODE (1993), vol. 2, *available at* http://indiacode.nic.in.

Other resources

http://www.loc.gov/law/help/guide/nations/india.html (Library of
Congress Guide to Law Online: India)

http://judis.nic.in/supremecourt/chejudis.asp (Judgment Information
System of the Supreme Court of India: free access to all the judgments of the
Supreme Court and certain High Courts, as well as the SCR journal from 1950
to present)

http://www.manupatra.com (subscription database that includes the latest
acts, regulations, rules and amendments made by the Parliament and the state
legislatures, as well as judgments of the Supreme Court and the High Courts
from 1950 to present)

T2.19   Iran, Islamic Republic of
(Civil Law)

Cases

Since the 1979 revolution, lower court cases are not reported and the only
Supreme Court cases reported are unification cases (cases taken to resolve split
decisions by the different branches of the Supreme Court or by lower courts).
Such cases from 1944 to 2002 are contained in a one-volume reporter, issued by
the Law Research Directorate of the President's Office in 2003. It organizes the
cases chronologically by subject. The title of this volume is as follows:

▶ MAJMUAHI ARAI VAHDATI RAVIIAHI DIVANI AALII KISHVAR
[COMPILATION OF THE UNIFICATION DECISIONS OF THE SUPREME
COURT]

Citation format: ‹serial number› ‹case name› [‹English translation of the
case name›] ‹case number›–‹date on Iranian calendar in month/day/year
format› [‹date on Gregorian calendar in month/day/year format›] ‹first
page›, ‹page(s) of specific material, if desired› (‹country abbreviation if not
evident from context›).

▶ 17 Marjai Rasidegui Be Amri Taabeiat [The Court Having Jurisdiction
To Hear a Citizenship Case] 701–01/20/1381 [1/20/2003] 1372
(Iran).

Historically, following the dissolution of the Islamic religious courts, introduction of the European legal system, and formation of what was then called *Adliehe
Jadid* (New Justice) in Iran in 1927, reporting of court decisions was not a practice. In 1954, the decisions of the then eight chambers of the Supreme Court, as
well as the decisions taken at the general meetings (the court sitting en banc) of
the Supreme Court from 1932 to 1954, were published. This serial collection
continued its publication annually, with a change of publisher and format in 1964,
until the 1979 revolution.

▶ MAJMUAHI RAWAYIHI QAZAI [COMPILATION OF JURISPRUDENCE]

Tribunal of Administrative Justice: Article 173 of the 1979 constitution established the Tribunal of Administrative Justice in order to investigate complaints and
grievances concerning civil servants, organs, or state agencies and regulations.
Currently, the Tribunal has ten chambers but may have more chambers in Tehran

and other places as approved by the High Judicial Council. The Official Gazette regularly carries the decisions of the Tribunal.

Citation format: ‹date on Iranian calendar in year/month/day format› [‹date on Gregorian calendar›], File. No. ‹file number›, ‹case name› [‹English translation of the case name›] (‹country abbreviation if not evident from context›).

▶ 1382/9/23 [Dec. 9, 2004], File No. 446/79, Raye Heyati Umoomii Divani Idaalati Idari [Ruling of the General Meeting of the Administrative Justice Tribunal] (Iran).

Constitutions

Iran has had two constitutions, as indicated below. Cite by the name of the constitution or amendment, followed by an English translation in brackets, and the year of the constitution or amendment (either in the Iranian calendar with the Gregorian equivalent in brackets, or in the Gregorian calendar without brackets). To refer to a particular passage, include the article number.

▶ QANUNI ASSASSI JUMHURII ISLAMAI IRAN [THE CONSTITUTION OF THE ISLAMIC REPUBLIC OF IRAN] 1358 [1980].

▶ ISLAHAT VA TAQYYRATI VA TATMIMAH QANUNI ASSASSI [AMENDMENT TO THE CONSTITUTION] 1368 [1989] (Iran).

▶ QANUNI ASSAASSI IRAN [IRANIAN CONSTITUTION] 1906.

According to the Constitution of 1980, the Guardian Council ensures that the House of Representatives passes no law inconsistent with Islamic law or the constitution. The decisions of the Guardian Council are published under the following title:

▶ Majmuahi Nazariati Shurai Nigahban [Compilation of the Opinions of the Guardian Council] Tehran 1992

Codes

Citation format: ‹name of the code› [‹English translation of the name of the code›] [‹abbreviation for the code, if applicable›] ‹year of publication› [‹if the year has been given in the Iranian calendar, then append the date from the Gregorian calendar in brackets›], ‹article number(s)› (‹country abbreviation if not evident from context›).

▶ QANUNI MADANI [CIVIL CODE] Tehran 1314 [1935], arts. 656–83 (Iran).

▶ AINI DADRASSII MADANI [CIVIL PROCEDURE CODE] Tehran 1379 [2000] (Iran).

▶ MAJMUAHI KAMILI QAVANINI VA MUQARRATI BAZERGANI VA TIJARI [CODE OF THE COMMERCIAL LAWS AND REGULATIONS] Tehran 1370 [1990] (Iran).

▶ MAJMUAHI QAVANINI JAZAI [CODE OF CRIMINAL LAWS] Tehran 1381 [2002] (Iran).

▶ MAJMUAHI QAVANINI NIRUHAI MUSSALAHI JUMHURII ISLAMII IRAN [COMPILATION OF THE LAWS OF THE ARMED FORCES OF THE ISLAMIC REPUBLIC OF IRAN] Tehran 1364 [1985].

▶ MAJMUAHI QAVANINI SABTI [LAND REGISTRATION LAWS] Tehran 1382 [2003] (Iran).

Statutes and regulations

Citation format: ‹statute or regulation name› **of** ‹date of enactment in day month year format› (‹country abbreviation if not evident from context›).

Or: ‹type of law› **of** ‹date of enactment in day month year format› (‹subject of law›) (‹country abbreviation if not evident from context›).

- ▶ State Monetary and Banking Law of 9 July 1972, amended 1975 (Iran).
- ▶ Law of 12/13 May 1982 (Nationalization of Foreign Trade) (Iran).
- ▶ Act of 19 Feb. 1988 (Direct Taxation) (Iran).
- ▶ Regulations of 2 June 1984 (Establishment, Operation, and Dissolution of Representative Offices of Foreign Banks) (Iran).

Official Gazette

The *Official Gazette* is published daily. Its supplement is nominally published on a weekly basis, but in reality publications are irregular. The Iranian Ministry of Justice publishes these publications and the annual compilation.

Citation format for an Iranian gazette: RUZNAMEHI RASMI JUMHURI ISLAMI IRAN [THE OFFICIAL GAZETTE OF THE ISLAMIC REPUBLIC OF IRAN], ‹statute or regulation citation›, ‹serial number› ‹first page›, ‹page(s) of specific material, if desired› (‹country abbreviation if not evident from context›).

Or: ZAMIMAHI RUZNAMEHI RASMI [SUPPLEMENT TO THE OFFICIAL GAZETTE OF THE ISLAMIC REPUBLIC OF IRAN], ‹statute or regulation citation›, ‹serial number› ‹first page›, ‹page(s) of specific material, if desired› (‹country abbreviation if not evident from context›).

Or: MAJMUAHI QAVANIN SALANEH [ANNUAL COMPILATION OF LAWS], ‹statute or regulation citation›, ‹first page›, ‹page(s) of specific material, if desired› (‹country abbreviation if not evident from context›).

Citation for the 1945–1979 *Official Gazette*: RUZNAMEHI RASMI KISHVARI SHAHANSHAHI [THE IMPERIAL IRANIAN OFFICIAL GAZETTE], ‹statute or regulation citation›, ‹serial number› ‹first page›, ‹page(s) of specific material, if desired› (‹country abbreviation if not evident from context›).

Internet sources

http://www.justice.ir/Portal/Home (Ministry of Justice)

http://www.rooznamehrasmi.ir/Contact.asp (Ruznamahi Rasmi (Iranian Official Journal))

http://www.elaw.ir/about/staff.php (the Iranian Cyber Department for Strategic Researches: links to most Iranian law centers)

http://www.loc.gov/law/help/guide/nations/iran.html (Library of Congress Guide to Law Online: Iran)

T2.20   Iraq, Republic of

(Civil Law)

....

Cases

Citation format: ‹name of court› [‹short name of court›] [‹name of court and/or chamber in English›] [‹short name of court in English›], ‹region if applicable›, ‹decision number, if available› **of** ‹date of decision, spelled out›, ‹reporter or journal›, ‹volume of journal, if applicable›, ‹year of publication›, ‹first page› (‹country abbreviation if not evident from context›).

> ▶ Mahkamat al-Tamiez [Tamiez] [Court of Cassation] [Cassation], decision No. 1428 of March 6, 1974, Al-Nashra al-Qadaiah, vol. 1, year 5, p. 161 (Iraq).

Courts

Mahkamat al-Tamiez (Tamiez) (Court of Cassation: highest court of ordinary jurisdiction, sits only in the capital and has several chambers): Citation is sufficiently recognized by referring to this court as "Mahkamat al-Tamiez" or simply "Tamiez."

> ▶ Tamiez [Cassation, civil chamber], decision No. 1509 of March 18, 1974, Al-Nashra al-Qadaiah, vol. 1, year 5, p. 11 (Iraq).

Mahkamat al-Isteinaf (Isteinaf) (courts of appeals: general courts of second instance): Cite with the name followed by the geographic area.

> ▶ Isteinaf Baghdad [Court of Appeals, Baghdad], decision No. 48 of September 1985, Majmouat al-Ahkam al-Adliah, issues 3 and 4 of 1985, p. 141 (Iraq).

Sources

Cite to the following publications of the Iraqi Government:

▶ Al-Nashra al-Qadaiah

> ▶ Tamiez [Cassation], decision No. 901 of 1973, Al-Nashra al-Qadaiah, vol. 1, year 5, p. 247 (Iraq).

▶ Majmouat al-Ahkam al-Adliah

> ▶ Isteinaf Baghdad [Court of Appeals, Baghdad], decision No. 1872 of 1979, Majmouat al-Ahkam al-Adliah, vol. 4, year 5, p. 112 (Iraq).

....

Official Gazette

The Official Gazette of Iraq is called *Al-Waqaeh al-Iraqia* and is published periodically by the Iraqi Government. Cite by the issue number and date of publication.

Citation format: ‹title of the law›, Al-Waqaeh al-Iraqia [Iraqi Official Gazette] ‹issue number› of ‹date of issue› ‹page number, if desired› (‹country abbreviation if not evident from context›).

....

Statutes, codes, and decrees

Citation format: ‹name and number of the law› of ‹year› (‹country abbreviation if not evident from context›).

Or: ‹subject of the law› **Law of** ‹year› (‹country abbreviation if not evident from context›).

Or: ‹name or subject of the law› (‹country abbreviation if not evident from context›).

- ▶ Residency of Foreigners Law No. 118 of 1987 (Iraq).
- ▶ Weapons Law of 1992 (Iraq).
- ▶ Civil Procedures Law (Iraq).

Constitutions

Iraq has had several constitutions since its creation after World War I. If referring to a particular provision, provide the article and section number before the name.

- ▶ Article 12, Al-Qanoun al-Assasi al-Iraqi [The Organic Law] of 1924 (Iraq).
- ▶ Al-Doustour al-Iraqi al-Mouakkat [The Interim Iraqi Constitution] of 1958.
- ▶ Al-Doustour al-Iraqi al-Mouakkat [The Interim Iraqi Constitution] of 1964.
- ▶ Al-Doustour al-Iraqi al-Mouakkat [The Interim Iraqi Constitution] of 1968.
- ▶ Al-Doustour al-Iraqi al Mouakkat [The Interim Iraqi Constitution] of 1970.
- ▶ Article 4, Section 2, Doustour Joumhouriat al-Iraq [The Constitution of the Republic of Iraq] of 2005.

Internet sources

http://www.arablegalportal.org (database of Iraqi laws maintained by the United Nations Development Programme)

http://www.parliament.iq (official site of the Iraqi Parliament with a number of laws and proposed draft laws)

T2.21   Ireland (Éire), Republic of

(Common Law)

Cases

Citation format: ‹case name›, [‹year›] ‹volume number, if one exists› ‹reporter/publication abbreviation, or court abbreviation for neutral citations and unreported cases› ‹first page of case, or opinion number in that calendar year for neutral citations and unreported cases› (‹court abbreviation, unless citing to the highest court›, ‹year of decision if not already provided›) ‹additional identifying information if commonly used› (‹country abbreviation if not evident from context›).

- ▶ Ryan v. Att'y Gen., [1965] I.R. 294 (Ir.).
- ▶ KSK Enters. Ltd. v. An Bord Pleanála, [1994] 2 I.R. 128, 135 (Ir.).
- ▶ Dir. of Pub. Prosecutions v. Carolan, [1998] 2 I.L.R.M. 212 (H. Ct.) (Ir.).

Supreme Court of Éire (S.C.), **High Court** (H. Ct.), and **Court of Criminal Appeal** (C.C.A.): Cite to I.R., if therein; otherwise, cite to one of the reporters below:

► Employment Law Reports	1990–date	E.L.R.
► Irish Company Law Reports	1963–1993	I.C.L.R.
► Irish Reports	1868–date	I.R.
► Irish Law Times Reports	1866–1980	I.L.T.R.
► Irish Law Reports Monthly	1976–date	I.L.R.M.
► Irish Law Reports	1838–1912	I.L.R.
► Irish Jurist Reports	1935–1966 1849–1866	Ir. Jur. Rep.
► Irish Tax Reports	1922–1927	I.T.R.
► Frewen	1924–1989	Frewen

Constitution

Citation format: IR. CONST., ‹year›, art. ‹article number›.

- ► IR. CONST., 1937, art. 2, *available at* http://www.taoiseach.gov.ie/upload/static/256.htm.

- ► IR. CONST., 1922, art. 5.

► IRISH CONSTITUTION (BUNREACHT NA HÉIREANN)	IR. CONST., 1937.
► CONSTITUTION OF THE IRISH FREE STATE (SAORSTÁT ÉIREANN)	IR. CONST., 1922.

Statutory compilations and session laws

Citation format: ‹short title, including year if in title› (‹Act No., or if before 1938, Pub. Stat. No.›/‹year›) (‹country abbreviation if not evident from context›).

- ► Control of Exports Act 2008 (Act No. 1/2008) (Ir.), *available at* http://www.irishstatutebook.ie/2008/acts.html.

- ► Dublin Transport Authority Act 2008 (Act No. 15/2008) (Ir.), *available at* http://www.bailii.org/ie/legis/num_act/2008/a1508.html.

► ACTS OF THE OIREACHTAS	1937–date
► ACTS OF THE OIREACHTAS (SAORSTÁT ÉIREANN)	1922–1937

Administrative materials

Citation format: ‹short name of instrument or order› (S.I. No. ‹number›/‹year›) (‹country abbreviation if not evident from context›).

Or: ‹short name of instrument or order› (S.R. & O. No. ‹number› of ‹year›) (‹country abbreviation if not evident from context›).

- ► Control of Fishing for Salmon Order 2008 (S.I. No. 98/2008) (Ir.), *available at* http://www.attorneygeneral.ie/esi/2008/B26061.pdf.

- ► Irish Nationality and Citizenship Regulations 2005 (S.I. No. 1/2005) (Ir.), *available at* http://www.irishstatutebook.ie/2005/en/si/0001.html.

► Eggs (Regulation of Export to Germany) Order 1936 (S.R. & O. No. 89 of 1936) (Ir.), *available at* http://www.irishstatutebook.ie/ ZZSI89Y1936.html.

► District Court (Districts) Order 2008 (S.I. No. 461/2008) (Ir.), *available at* http://www.irishstatutebook.ie/2008/en/si/ 0461.html.

► STATUTORY INSTRUMENTS	1947–date	S.I.
► STATUTORY RULES AND ORDERS	1922–1947	S.R. & O.

Parliamentary debates

Citation format: ‹volume number› ‹publication abbreviation› col. ‹column number› (‹date›) (‹country abbreviation if not evident from context›).

► 83 DÁIL DEB. col. 556 (Feb. 17, 1979) (Ir.).

► 87 SEANAD DEB. col. 970 (Mar. 21, 1977) (Ir.).

► PARLIAMENTARY DEBATES, DÁIL DEBATES	1922–date	DÁIL DEB.
► PARLIAMENTARY DEBATES, SEANAD DEBATES	1922–date	SEANAD DEB.

Citation format for debates that occurred prior to the availability of the print version: ‹volume and number as given by the online source›, ‹printed publication abbreviation›, ‹section of the debate being cited› (‹date›) (‹country abbreviation if not evident from context›), ‹URL›.

► 188 NO. 7, SEANAD DEB., Business of Seanad (Jan. 30, 2008), http:// debates.oireachtas.ie/Ddebate.aspx?F=SEN20080130.XML (Ir.).

Committee or commission reports

Citation format: ‹author name›, ‹title› (‹Parliament number if available›, ‹year of publication if available›) (‹country abbreviation if not evident from context›).

► GOV'T OF IR., INTER-DEPARTMENTAL WORKING GROUP ON ABORTION, GREEN PAPER ON ABORTION (1999), *available at* http://www.taoiseach .gov.ie/eng/Publications/Publications_Archive/Publications_2006/ Publications_for_1999/GreenPaperOnAbortion.pdf.

Treaties

Citation format: ‹treaty name›, I.T.S. No. ‹treaty number›/‹year› (‹country abbreviation if not evident from context›).

► Agreement Between the Government of Ireland and the Government of the United Kingdom of Great Britain and Northern Ireland, I.T.S. No. 1/2008 (Ir.), *available at* http://www.dfa.ie/ home/index.aspx?id=42915&yr=2008.

► IRELAND TREATY SERIES	1930–date	I.T.S.

Internet sources

http://www.bailii.org (British and Irish Legal Information Institute)

http://www.irishstatutebook.ie (Irish Statute Book)

http://www.irishlaw.org, **http://www.ucc.ie/law/irishlaw** (Irish Law Site at the University College Cork (hosted by the University College Cork law faculty))

http://www.attorneygeneral.ie/index_en.html (Office of the Attorney General)

http://www.loc.gov/law/help/guide/nations/ireland.html (Library of Congress Guide to Law Online: Ireland)

T2.22   Israel

(Mixed Jurisdiction)

....

Cases

Supreme Court (functions both as a **Court of Appeals**, hearing civil appeals (CA), administrative appeals (AdminA), and criminal appeals (CrimA) from the district courts, and as a **High Court of Justice** (HCJ), sitting as a court of first instance in constitutional and some administrative cases): Cite to *Piske Din* (PD, sometimes referred to as IsrSC), which contains reports of decisions of the Supreme Court of Israel, from 1948 to date.

Citation format: ‹court abbreviation› ‹case number› ‹case name› ‹volume number›(‹part number›) ‹reporter abbreviation› ‹first page›, ‹page(s) of specific material, if desired› [‹year of decision›] (‹country abbreviation if not evident from context›).

> ► CA 1482/92 Hager v. Hager 47(2) PD 793 [1993] (Isr.).

> ► HCJ 852/86 Aloni v. Minister of Justice 41(2) PD 1, 5 [1987] (Isr.).

District courts (DC) (hear civil appeals (CA) and criminal appeals (CrimA) from the magistrate courts, and original matters in civil cases (CC), some administrative cases (AdminC), and severe criminal cases (CrimC), in six judicial districts, Jerusalem (Jer), Tel-Aviv-Jaffa (TA), Haifa (Hi), Be'er-Sheva (BS), Nazareth (Nz), and Central District (CT)): Cite to *Psakim Mehoziim* (PM), which contains reports of decisions of the district courts of Israel, from 1949 to date.

Citation format: ‹court abbreviation› (‹location›) ‹case number› ‹case name›, ‹reporter abbreviation› ‹Hebrew calendar year of volume› (‹part number›) ‹first page›, ‹page(s) of specific material, if desired› (‹Gregorian calendar year of decision›) (‹country abbreviation if not evident from context›).

> ► CrimC (TA) 521/91 Ben Moshe Kokhavi v. State of Israel, PM 5753(2) 267 (1993) (Isr.).

Religious courts

For recognized communities, religious courts generally have jurisdiction in matters of marriage and divorce, with the *Shariah* courts having jurisdiction in all personal status matters. Some decisions of the rabbinical courts are periodically published in *Piske din shel batei ha-din ha-rabaniyim be-Yisrael* (PDR). To distinguish between first instance cases and cases on appeal, note the location of the first instance courts in order to be consistent with citation of the decisions of the district court.

Citation format: File No. ‹file number› ‹court name/details› (‹location›), ‹case name›, ‹volume number› ‹reporter abbreviation› ‹first page›, ‹page(s) of specific material, if desired› (‹country abbreviation if not evident from context›).

▶ File No. 656/35 Rabbinical Court (PT), A v. The Electing Body for Principal Ashkenazi City Rabbi, 11 PDR 97 (Isr.).

Electronic databases

Many unreported decisions—particularly of special courts such as the rabbinical courts and the military courts, but also of the general courts—are available on widely used electronic databases such as the Nevo Legal Database at **http://www.nevo.co.il**.

Citation format: File No. ‹file number› ‹court name› (‹location›), ‹case name› (‹date of decision›), ‹database name› (by subscription) (‹country abbreviation if not evident from context›).

Or: Mil. Appeal ‹military appeal number› ‹court name› (‹location›), ‹case name› (‹date of decision›), ‹database name› (by subscription) (‹country abbreviation if not evident from context›).

▶ File No. 3437-21-1 Rabbinical Court (Netanya), Anonymous v. Anonymous (Oct. 26, 2008), Nevo Legal Database (by subscription) (Isr.).

▶ Mil. Appeal 4987/08 Military Court of Appeals (Judea & Samaria), Hasin Nafa v. Military Prosecution (Nov. 13, 2008), Nevo Legal Database (by subscription) (Isr.).

Statutes

Cite to *Laws of the State of Israel* (LSI), which contains the authorized English translation of legislative enactments, from 1949 to date.

Citation format: ‹statute name›, ‹Hebrew calendar year of enactment›– ‹Gregorian calendar year of enactment (except for Basic Laws)›, ‹volume number› ‹compilation abbreviation› ‹first page›, ‹section, if desired› (‹coverage date range of volume›) (‹country abbreviation if not evident from context›).

▶ Extradition Law, 5714–1954, 8 LSI 144 (1953–1954) (Isr.).

If citation to the LSI is impossible (for example, if the translation is partial or is not available), cite to *Sefer HaHukim* (SH), which contains the legislative enactments of the Knesset (the Israel parliament), from 1949 to date.

Citation format: ‹statute name›, ‹Hebrew calendar year›–‹Gregorian calendar year›, ‹publication abbreviation› ‹issue number› p. ‹page(s) of specific material, if desired› (‹country abbreviation if not evident from context›).

▶ Protection of Witnesses Law, 5769-2008, SH No. 2192 p. 98 (Isr.).

Legislative history

For draft bills, cite to *Hatza'ot Hok* (HH), from 1949 to date.

Citation format: ‹proposed statute name› (No. ‹number›), ‹Gregorian calendar year of submission›, ‹publication abbreviation› ‹first page›, ‹page(s) of specific material, if desired› (‹country abbreviation if not evident from context›).

▶ Draft Bill Amending the Income Tax Order (No. 21), 1974, HH 142 (Isr.).

For protocols of Knesset proceedings, cite to *Divrei HaKnesset* (DK), from 1949 to date.

Citation format: ‹series abbreviation› (‹Gregorian calendar year of proceedings›) ‹first page›, ‹page(s) of specific material, if desired› (‹country abbreviation if not evident from context›).

▶ DK (1966) 2085 (Isr.).

Regulations

Cite to *Kovetz HaTakanot* (KT), which contains regulations of the State of Israel, from 1949 to date.

Citation format: ‹subsidiary legislation name›, ‹Gregorian calendar year of enactment›, ‹publication abbreviation› ‹issue number›, ‹first page›, ‹page(s) of specific material, if desired› (‹country abbreviation if not evident from context›).

▶ Knesset Election Ordinances, 1970, KT 2454, 42 (Isr.).

Treaties

Cite to *Kitvei Amana* (KA), which contains treaties and conventions signed by Israel.

Citation format: ‹treaty name›, ‹volume number› ‹series abbreviation› ‹issue number› p. ‹first page›, ‹page(s) of specific material, if desired› (‹Gregorian calendar year of publication›) (‹country abbreviation if not evident from context›).

▶ Convention for the Suppression of the Financing of Terrorism, 50 KA 1401 p. 1 (2004) (Isr.).

Internet sources

http://www.gov.il/firstgov/english (main government portal)

http://www.knesset.gov.il (The Knesset (parliament))

http://www.court.gov.il (Israeli courts)

http://www.pmo.gov.il/PMOEng (The Prime Minister's Office)

http://www.mfa.gov.il/MFA (Ministry of Foreign Affairs)

http://www.rbc.gov.il/index.asp (Rabbinical courts)

http://www.loc.gov/law/help/israel.html (Library of Congress Guide to Law Online: Israel)

http://www.llrx.com/features/israel3.htm (Israeli Law Guide)

T2.23   Italy, Republic of

(Civil Law)

....

Cases

Citation format: ‹court name›, ‹court session, for the Supreme Court only›, ‹date of decision in Italian, in day month year format›, **n.** ‹case number, for the Supreme Court only›, ‹reporter or journal abbreviation› ‹year of publication of decision›, ‹part of reporter›, ‹session number›, ‹page or column number› (‹country abbreviation if not evident from context›).

> ► Cass., sez. un., 17 novembre 1975, n. 3852, Giur. it. 1977, I, 1, 132 (It.).

Ordinary jurisdiction

Corte Costituzionale (Corte Cost.) (Constitutional Court): Cite to Racc. uff. corte cost., Foro it., or Giur. it., if therein.

► Raccolta Ufficiale delle Sentenze e Ordinanze delle Corte Costituzionale	1956-date	Racc. uff. corte cost.
► Foro Italiano (indicate section)	1876-date	e.g., Foro it. I
► Giurisprudenza Italiana (indicate section)	1849-date	e.g., Giur. it. II

Corte di cassazione (Cass.) (court of last appeal on issues of law in civil (as **Cassazione Sezione Civile** (Cass.)) and criminal (as **Cassazione Sezione Penale** (Cass. Pen.)) matters): Cite to Foro it. or Giur. it., if therein; **Corte di Appello** (App.) (ordinary courts of appeal): Cite to Foro it. or Giur. it., if therein, followed by the location of the court; **Corte di Assise di Appello** (Ass. App.) (extraordinary court of appeal): Cite to Foro it. or Giur. it., if therein; **Tribunale** (Trib.) (ordinary courts of first instance): Cite to Foro it. or Giur. it., if therein, followed by the location of the court and the date; **Corte di Assise** (Corte d'Ass.) (court of original jurisdiction for very serious crimes): Cite to Foro it. or Giur. it., if therein; **Pretore** (Pret.) (abolished after 1999), **Giudice Concilia-tore** (Concil.) (abolished after 1995) (courts of petty jurisdiction), and **Giudice di Pace** (Giud. Pace): Cite to Foro it. or Giur. it., if therein.

► Foro Italiano	1876-date	
► Corte Cost., Cass.		Foro it. I
► Criminal cases		Foro it. II
► Administrative cases		Foro it. III
► EEC and foreign cases		Foro it. IV
► Miscellaneous		Foro it. V
► Giurisprudenza Italiana (indicate section)	1849-date	e.g., Giur. it. II
► Giurisprudenza completa della Suprema Corte di Cassazione	1944-1955	Giur. compl. Cass. civ. or Giur. compl. Cass. pen.
► Giurisprudenza delle imposte Dirette di registro e di negoziazione	1928-date	Giur. imp. reg. negoz.
► Giustizia civile (indicate section)	1951-date	e.g., Giust. Civ. II
► Giustizia penale (indicate section)	1895-date	e.g., Giust. Pen. I

Administrative jurisdiction

Consiglio di Stato (Cons. Stato) (court of last appeal in administrative matters), **Tribunale amministrativo regionale** (TAR) (regional administrative court of first instance), **Corte dei conti** (Corte conti) (high court for fiscal matters), **Giunta provinciale amministrativa** (Giun. pro. ammin.) (formerly the administrative court of first instance), and **Consiglio di giustizia amministrativa per la Regione siciliana** (Cons. gius. ammin. reg. sic.) (administrative judicial body for the region of Sicily): Cite to Foro amm. or Giur. it., if therein.

▸ Foro Amministrativo (indicate section) 1925–date e.g., Foro amm. III
▸ Giurisprudenza Italiana (indicate section) 1849–date e.g., Giur. it. II

Constitution
▸ Costituzione   Cost.

  ▸ Art. 2 Costituzione [Cost.] (It.).

Codes
▸ Codice civile   C.c.
▸ Codice di commercio (merged with Codice civile in 1942)   C. comm.
▸ Codice della navigazione   C. nav.
▸ Codice penale   C.p.
▸ Codice di procedura civile   C.p.c.
▸ Codice di procedura penale   C.p.p.

Statutes and decrees

Citation format: ‹type of law› ‹date in Italian, in day month year format›, n. ‹law number›, in ‹publication abbreviation› ‹publication date›, n. ‹publication number› (‹country abbreviation if not evident from context›).

  ▸ Legge 21 novembre 1991, n. 374 (It.).

Short form citation format: ‹abbreviation of type of law› n. ‹law number›/‹year› (‹country abbreviation if not evident from context›).

  ▸ L. n. 374/1991 (It.).

Types of laws and abbreviations:
▸ Legge   L.
▸ Decreto Legge   D.L.
▸ Decreto Legislativo   D.Lgs.
▸ Decreto Ministeriale   D.M.
▸ Decreto Presidente della Repubblica   D.P.R.
▸ Decreto Presidente del Consiglio dei Ministri   D.P.C.M.
▸ Legge regionale   L. Reg. ‹region›
▸ Decreto Luogotenenziale (prior to 1942 only)   D.Lgt.
▸ Regio Decreto (prior to 1942 only)   R.D.

Cite to Racc. Uff. or G.U., or, if appropriate, to the official reporter for an autonomous region; if available, give a parallel citation to Lex, Leggi, or Legisl. ital.

▸ Gazzetta Ufficiale della Repubblica Italiana   G.U.
▸ Raccolta Ufficiale degli Atti Normativi della Repubblica Italiana   1987–date   Racc. Uff. or R.U.
▸ Raccolta Ufficiale delle Leggi e dei Decreti della Repubblica Italiana   1946–1987   Racc. Uff. or R.U.

▶ Bollettino Ufficiale della Sardegna	Boll. Uff. Reg. Sardegna
▶ Gazzetta Ufficiale della Sicilia	G.U. Reg. Sic.
▶ Lex: Legislazione Italiana (Utet) (indicate section)	Lex
▶ Le Leggi (Sefi)	Leggi
▶ La Legislazione Italiana (Giuffrè) (indicate section)	Legisl. ital.
▶ National legislation	Legisl. ital. I
▶ Parliamentary reports	Legisl. ital. II
▶ Regional legislation	Legisl. ital. III

Treaties and conventions

Current treaties are printed in *Gazzeta Ufficiale* and *Raccolta Ufficiale* when they are promulgated in the form of a law incorporating the text of the treaty. Cite older treaties according to **rule 21.4**, followed by a cite to either **G.U.** or **Racc. Uff.**, using the format below:

▶ Trattati e Convenzioni fra L'Italia e gli Altri Stati	1861–1945	‹volume› Trattati e Convenzioni ‹first page›

Internet sources

http://www.loc.gov/law/help/guide/nations/italy.html (Library of Congress Guide to Law Online: Italy)

T2.24   Japan

(Civil Law)

Romanization

For romanization, word division, and capitalization of Japanese words, apply the rules of the American Library Association and the Library of Congress: Use the modified Hepburn romanization system adopted by Japanese-English dictionaries, such as KENKYŪSHA SHIN WA-EI DAIJITEN (KENKYŪSHA'S NEW JAPANESE-ENGLISH DICTIONARY). Indicate long vowels with a macron as in "hōrei" or "hanreishū." Add an alif, or an apostrophe as a substitute, to clarify word division between 'n' and a vowel, and 'n' and 'y' as in "gen'in," or "kin'yū." For details, see the Library of Congress ALA-LC Romanization Tables at **http://www.loc.gov/catdir/cpso/roman.html**.

Cases

Citation format: ‹court name› [‹English abbreviated translation of court name›] ‹date of decision›, ‹case number, if desired›, ‹volume number› ‹reporter or periodical name› [‹reporter or periodical abbreviation›] ‹first page›, ‹page(s) of specific material, if desired› (‹country abbreviation if not evident from context›).

- ▶ Saikō Saibansho [Sup. Ct.] Dec. 4, 2007, Hei 18 (kyo) no. 45, 61 SAIKŌ SAIBANSHO MINJI HANREISHŪ [MINSHŪ] 3245, 3252 (Japan).

- ▶ Tōkyō Chihō Saibansho [Tōkyō Dist. Ct.] June 8, 2006, Hei 15 (wa) no. 29850, 1271 HANREI TAIMUZU [HANTA] 183, 201 (Japan).

Electronic resources

Citation format: ‹court name› [‹English abbreviated translation of court name›] ‹date of decision›, ‹case number›, ‹database name› [‹database abbreviation›] ‹first page›, ‹page(s) of specific material, if desired›, ‹URL› (‹country abbreviation if not evident from context›).

▶ Chiteki Zaisan Kōtō Saibansho [Intellectual Prop. High Ct.] Nov. 13, 2008, Hei 20 (gyō ke) no. 10112, SAIKŌ SAIBANSHO SAIBANREI JŌHŌ [SAIBANREI JŌHŌ] 1, 8, http://www.courts.go.jp (Japan).

Cases under the constitution of 1946

Saikō Saibansho (Supreme Court: court of last appeal in all matters): Cite to reporters below, if therein; otherwise, cite to topical reporters or periodicals.

▶ SAIKŌ SAIBANSHO MINJI HANREISHŪ 最高裁判所民事判例集	1947–date	MINSHŪ
▶ SAIKŌ SAIBANSHO KEIJI HANREISHŪ 最高裁判所刑事判例集	1947–date	KEISHŪ
▶ SAIKŌ SAIBANSHO SAIBANSHŪ MINJI 最高裁判所裁判集民事	1947–date	SAIBANSHŪ MINJI
▶ SAIKŌ SAIBANSHO SAIBANSHŪ KEIJI 最高裁判所裁判集刑事	1947–date	SAIBANSHŪ KEIJI
▶ SAIBANSHO JIHŌ 裁判所時報	1948–date	SAIBANSHO JIHŌ
▶ SAIKŌ SAIBANSHO MINJI HANREI TOKUHŌ 最高裁判所民事判例特報	1947–1950	SAIMIN HANTOKU
▶ SAIKŌ SAIBANSHO KEIJI HANKETSU TOKUHŌ 最高裁判所刑事判決特報	1947–1950	SAIKEI HANTOKU
▶ SAIKŌ SAIBANSHO SAIBANREI JŌHŌ HANREI KENSAKU SHISUTEMU 最高裁判所裁判例情報判例検索システム (available at **http://www.courts.go.jp**)	1947–date	SAIBANREI JŌHŌ
▶ SAIKŌ SAIBANSHO HANREISHŪ 最高裁判所判例集 (available at **http://www.courts.go.jp**)	1947–date	SAIBANREI JŌHŌ

Kōtō Saibansho (high courts: regional courts of appeal for appeals from district, family, and summary courts), **Chihō Saibansho** (district courts: courts of original jurisdiction in general civil and criminal cases, which hear appeals from summary courts), **Katei Saibansho** (family courts: courts of original jurisdiction in domestic relations and juvenile delinquency cases), **Kan'i Saibansho** (summary courts: courts of petty jurisdiction in minor civil and criminal cases), and **Chiteki Zaisan Kōtō Saibansho** (Intellectual Property High Court: hears suits against appeal/trial decisions made by the Japan Patent Office and against civil cases pertaining to intellectual property): Cite to reporters below, if therein; otherwise, cite to topical reporters or periodicals.

▶ DAIISSHIN KEIJI SAIBAN REISHŪ 第一審刑事裁判例集	1958	ISSHIN KEISHŪ
▶ KAKYŪ SAIBANSHO KEIJI SAIBAN REISHŪ 下級裁判所刑事裁判例集	1959–1968	KAKEISHŪ
▶ KAKYŪ SAIBANSHO MINJI SAIBAN REISHŪ 下級裁判所民事裁判例集	1950–1984	KAMINSHŪ
▶ KAKYŪ SAIBANSHO HANREISHŪ 下級裁判所判例集 (available at **http://www.courts.go.jp**)	2002–date	SAIBANREI JŌHŌ

▸ KEIJI SAIBAN GEPPŌ 刑事裁判月報	1969-1986	KEISAI GEPPŌ
▸ KŌTŌ SAIBANSHO HANREISHŪ 高等裁判所判例集 (available at **http://www.courts.go.jp**)	1947-date	SAIBANREI JŌHŌ
▸ KŌTŌ SAIBANSHO KEIJI HANKETSU TOKUHŌ 高等裁判所刑事判決特報	1950-1956	KŌKEI HANTOKU
▸ KŌTŌ SAIBANSHO KEIJI HANREISHŪ 高等裁判所刑事判例集	1947-date	KŌKEISH
▸ KŌTŌ SAIBANSHO KEIJI SAIBAN SOKUH SHŪ 高等裁判所刑事裁判速報集	1981-date	KŌKEI SAISOKUSH
▸ KŌTŌ SAIBANSHO KEIJI SAIBAN TOKUHŌ 高等裁判所刑事裁判特報	1954-1958	KŌKEI SAITOKU
▸ KŌTŌ SAIBANSHO MINJI HANREISHŪ 高等裁判所民事判例集	1947-date	KŌMINSHŪ
▸ SAIKŌ SAIBANSHO SAIBANREI JŌHŌ HANREI KENSAKU SHISUTEMU 最高裁判所裁判例情報判例検索システム (available at **http://www.courts.go.jp**)	1947-date	SAIBANREI JŌHŌ
▸ TŌKYŌ KŌTŌ SAIBANSHO HANKETSU JIHŌ (KEIJI) 東京高等裁判所判決時報（刑事）	1953-date	TŌKŌ JIHŌ KEIJI
▸ TŌKYŌ KŌTŌ SAIBANSHO HANKETSU JIHŌ (MINJI) 東京高等裁判所判決時報（民事）	1953-date	TŌKŌ JIHŌ MINJI
▸ TŌKYŌ KŌTŌ SAIBANSHO KEIJI HANKETSU JIHŌ 東京高等裁判所刑事判決時報	1951-1953	TŌKŌKEI JIHŌ

Topical reporters

▸ CHITEKI ZAISAN KŌTŌ SAIBANSHO HANKETSU SHŌKAI HANREI KENSAKU SHISUTEMU 知的財産高等裁判所判決紹介判例検索 システム (available at **http://www.ip .courts.go.jp/search/jihp0010**)	2004-date	CHIZAI KŌSAI WEB
▸ CHITEKI ZAISAN SAIBAN REISHŪ 知的財産裁判例集 (available at **http:// www.courts.go.jp**)	1969-date	SAIBANREI JŌHŌ
▸ CHITEKI ZAISANKEN KANKEI MINJI GYŌSEI SAIBAN REISHŪ 知的財産権関係民事　行政裁判例集	1991-1998	CHITEKI SAISHŪ
▸ GYŌSEI JIKEN SAIBAN REISHŪ 行政事件裁判例集	1950-1997	GYŌSAI REISHŪ
▸ GYŌSEI JIKEN SAIBAN REISHŪ 行政事件裁判例集 (available at **http://www.courts.go.jp**)	1969-date	SAIBANREI JŌHŌ
▸ GYŌSEI SAIBAN GEPPŌ 行政裁判月報	1948-1950	GYŌSAI GEPPŌ
▸ KATEI SAIBAN GEPPŌ 家庭裁判月報	1949-date	KASAI GEPPŌ
▸ MUTAI ZAISANKEN KANKEI MINJI GYŌSEI SAIBAN REISHŪ 無体財産権関係民事 行政裁判例集	1969-1990	MUTAI REISHŪ
▸ RŌDŌ JIKEN SAIBAN REISHŪ 労働事件裁判例集 (available at **http://www.courts.go.jp**)	1969-date	SAIBANREI JŌHŌ
▸ RŌDŌ KANKEI MINJI SAIBAN REISHŪ 労働関係民事裁判例集	1950-1997	RŌMINSHŪ
▸ SHŌMU GEPPŌ 訟務月報	1955-date	SHŌMU GEPPŌ

Periodicals

▸ HANREI CHIHŌ JICHI 判例地方自治	1984-date	HANREI JICHI	
▸ HANREI JIHŌ 判例時報	1953-date	HANJI	
▸ HANREI TAIMUZU 判例タイムズ	1948-date	HANTA	
▸ HŌSŌ SHINBUN 法曹新聞	1946-1964	HŌSŌ SHINBUN	
▸ JUNKAN KIN'YŪ HŌMU JIJŌ 旬刊金融法務事情	1953-date	KIN'YŪ HŌMU	
▸ JUNKAN SHŌJI HŌMU 旬刊商事法務	1972-date	SHŌJI HŌMU	
▸ JURISUTO ジュリスト	1952-date	JURISUTO	
▸ KIN'YŪ SHŌJI HANREI 金融　商事判例	1976-date	KINYŪ HANREI	
▸ KŌTSŪ JIKO MINJI SAIBAN REISHŪ 交通事故民事裁判例集	1968-date	KŌTSŪ MINSH	
▸ RŌDŌ HANREI 労働判例	1969-date	RŌDŌ HANREI	
▸ RŌDŌ HŌRITSU JUNPŌ 労働法律旬報	1949-date	RŌDŌ JUNPŌ	
▸ RŌDŌ KEIZAI HANREI SOKUHŌ 労働経済判例速報	1950-date	RŌKEISOKU	
▸ SHIRYŌBAN SHŌJI HŌMU 資料版商事法務	1984-date	SHIRYŌBAN SHŌJI	
▸ SHUTOIERU シュトイエル	1962-1995	SHUTOIERU	

Kōsei Torihiki Iinkai (Fair Trade Commission; administers the enforcement of antitrust laws): Cite to one of the following sources:

▸ KŌSEI TORIHIKI IINKAI SHINKETSUSHŪ 公正取引委員会審決集	1947-date	SHINKETSUSHŪ
▸ KŌSEI TORIHIKI IINKAI SHINKETSUSHŪ 公正取引委員会審決集 (available at **http://snk.jftc.go.jp**)	1962-date	KŌTORII DB
▸ KŌSEI TORIHIKI IINKAI HAIJO MEIREISHŪ 公正取引委員会排除命令集	1962-date	HAIMEISH
▸ KŌSEI TORIHIKI IINKAI HAIJO MEIREISHŪ 公正取引委員会排除命令集 (available at **http://snk.jftc.go.jp**)	1962-date	KŌTORII DB
▸ KŌSEI TORIHIKI IINKAI SHINKETSU TŌ DĒTABĒSU 公正取引委員会審決等データベース (available at **http://snk.jftc.go.jp**)	1962-date	KŌTORII DB

Chuō Rōdō Iinkai (Central Labor Relations Commission; administers labor relations disputes): Cite to one of the following sources:

▸ BESSATSU CHŪŌ RŌDŌ JIHŌ 別冊中央労働時報	1968-date	CHŪRŌI JIHŌ
▸ FUTŌ RŌDŌ KŌI JIKEN MEIREISHŪ 不当労働行為事件命令集	1967-date	CHURŌI MEIREI
▸ FUTŌ RŌDŌ KŌI JIKEN MEIREISHŪ 不当労働行為事件命令集 (available at **http://www.churoi.go.jp**)	1970-date	CHURŌI DB
▸ RŌDŌ IINKAI MEIREI KANKEI SAIBANREI DĒTABĒSU KENSAKU 労働委員会命令　関係 裁判例データベース検索 (available at **http://www.churoi.go.jp**)	1970-date	CHURŌI DB

Cases under the constitution of 1889

Daishin'in or **Taishin'in** (Great Court of Judicature; court of last appeal for civil and criminal matters, and the only court concerning matters of the imperial household and insurrection against the state): Cite to reporters below, if therein; otherwise, cite to newspapers or periodicals. Append the version or publisher, such as Shihōshō or Hōsōkai.

▶ DAISHIN'IN MINJI HANKETSUROKU [DAIHAN MINROKU] (Shihōshō)

▶ Meiji zenki Daishin'in minji hanketsuroku 明治前期大審院民事判決録	1875–1887	Meiji Daihan minroku
▶ Daishin'in minji hanketsuroku 大審院民事判決録	1875–1921	Daihan minroku
▶ Daishin'in keiji hanketsuroku 大審院刑事判決録	1875–1921	Daihan keiroku
▶ Daishin'in minji hanketsu shōroku 大審院民事判決抄録	1898–1921	Minshōroku
▶ Daishin'in keiji hanketsu shōroku 大審院刑事判決抄録	1891–1921	Keishōroku
▶ Daishin'in minji hanreishū 大審院民事判例集	1922–1946	Daihan minshū
▶ Daishin'in keiji hanreishū 大審院刑事判例集	1922–1947	Daihan keishū

Gyōsei Saibansho (Administrative Court, court for all administrative cases): Cite to the following source:

▶ Gyōsei Saibansho hanketsuroku 行政裁判所判決録	1890–1947	Gyōroku

Newspapers and periodicals

Daishin'in or **Taishin'in** (Great Court of Judicature), **Kōsoin** (Court of Appeal), **Chihō Saibansho** (District Court), and **Ku Saibansho** (Ward Court): Cite to one of the sources below, if therein.

▶ Daishin'in hanketsu zenshū 大審院判決全集	1934–1944	Hanketsu zenshū
▶ Daishin'in hanrei shūi 大審院判例拾遺	1925–1927	Hanrei shūi
▶ Daishin'in saibanrei 大審院裁判例	1927–1938	Saibanrei
▶ Hōgaku 法学 (東北大学法学会)	1931–1944	Hōgaku
▶ Hōritsu shinbun 法律新聞	1900–1944	Shinbun
▶ Hōsō kiji 法曹記事	1891–1923	Hōsō kiji
▶ Hōsōkai zasshi 法曹会雑誌	1923–1944	Hōsōkai zasshi

Legislative materials

Cite from authoritative sources, such as *Kanpō* 官報, *Hōrei zensho* 法令全書, *Genkō hōki sōran* 現行法規総覧 (Daiichi Hōki), *Genkō Nihon hōki* 現行日本法規 (Gyōsei), *Roppō zensho* 六法全書 (Yūhikaku), and various tsūtatsushū 通達集, if therein. When citing to Internet sources, follow **rule 18**.

Constitutions

Citation format: ‹Constitution name› [‹Constitution abbreviation›] [Consti-tution], art. ‹article›, para. ‹paragraph› (‹country abbreviation if not evident from context›).

▶ Nihonkoku Kenpō [Kenpō] [Constitution], art. 9, para. 2 (Japan).

▶ Nihonkoku Kenpō (1946)   日本国憲法   Kenpō
▶ Dai Nihon Teikoku Kenpō (1889)   大日本帝国憲法   Meiji Kenpō

Codes

Citation format: ‹code name› [‹code abbreviation›] [‹English translation of code abbreviation or name›] ‹year of enactment, if not evident›, ‹article, paragraph, number, if applicable› (‹country abbreviation if not evident from context›).

▶ Minpō [Minpō] [Civ. C.] art. 398-20, para. 1, no. 1 (Japan).

▶ Minji soshōhō [Minsohō] [C. Civ. Pro.] 1996, art. 4, para. 6 (Japan).

▶ Minpō (Civil Code)   Minpō (Civ. C.)
　 民法
▶ Shōhō (Commercial Code)   Shōhō (Comm. C.)
　 商法
▶ Minji soshōhō (Code of Civil Procedure)   Minsohō (C. Civ. Pro.)
　 民事訴訟法
▶ Keihō (Penal Code)   Keihō (Pen. C.)
　 刑法
▶ Keiji soshōhō (Code of Criminal Procedure)   Keisohō (C. Crim. Pro.)
　 刑事訴訟法

Statutes, regulations, and orders

The following citation format applies to **hōritsu** (statutes), **kisoku** (rules and regulations), **chokurei** (imperial orders), **seirei** (cabinet orders), **furei** (Prime Minister's Office orders), **shōrei** (ministry ordinances), **kunrei** (instructions), **kokuji** (notifications), and **tsūtatsu** (circulars).

Citation format: ‹law name› [‹law abbreviation, if available›] [‹English trans-lation of law abbreviation or name›], ‹number› of ‹year›, ‹article, para-graph, number, if applicable› (‹country abbreviation if not evident from context›).

▶ Hakai katsudō bōshihō [Habōhō] [Subversive Activities Prevention Act], Law No. 240 of 1952, art. 4, para. 1 (Japan).

▶ Shōnen shinpan kisoku [Rules of Juvenile Proceedings], Sup. Ct. Rule No. 33 of 1948, art. 26 (Japan).

When citing a translation, include the translation source in addition to the original version, following **rule 20.2.5**:

▶ Kankyō kihonhō [Basic Environmental Act], Law No. 91 of 1993, art. 37 (Japan), *translated in* 7 EHS Law Bull. Ser. no. 7800 (1996).

Citation format for statutes published in electronic sources: ‹statute name› [‹statute abbreviation, if different from full name›] [‹English translation of statute abbreviation or name›], ‹number and year›, ‹article, paragraph, number, if applicable› (‹database name›[‹database abbreviation›]), ‹URL› (‹country abbreviation if not evident from context›).

▶ Hōjinzeihō [Corporate Taxation Act], Law No. 34 of 1965, art. 6-2 (Hōrei teikyō dēta shisutemu [Hōrei DB]), http://law.e-gov.go.jp/ cgi-bin/idxsearch.cgi (Japan).

Treaties and conventions

For citation of treaties and other international agreements, follow **rule 21.4**. Cite to treaty sets published by the Ministry of Foreign Affairs, Treaties Bureau, if therein; otherwise, cite to other authoritative sources such as *Hōrei zensho* or *Kanpō* (see the **Legislative Materials** section above).

▶ Jōyakushū 条約集	1922–1964	JŌYAKUSHŪ
▶ Jōyakushū: nikokukan jōyaku 条約集二国間条約	1964–date	NIKOKUKAN JŌYAKU
▶ Jōyakushū: tasūkokukan jōyaku 条約集多数国間条約	1964–date	TAKOKUKAN JŌYAKU
▶ Gaimushō Jōyaku 外務省条約 (available at **http://www.mofa.go .jp/mofaj/gaiko/treaty**)	2002–date	JŌYAKU WEB

▶ Nihonkoku to Chūka Jinmin Kyōwakoku to no aida no heiwa yūkō jōyaku [Heiwa yūkō jōyaku] [Treaty of Peace and Friendship Between Japan and the People's Republic of China], Japan-China, Aug. 12, 1978, Treaty No. 19, 1978 NIKOKUKAN JŌYAKU, 323, 327 (Japan).

Internet sources

Governmental

http://law.e-gov.go.jp (Hōrei teiky dēta shisutemu 法令提供データシステム (HŌREI DB) (Ministry of Internal Affairs and Communications Administrative Management Bureau: constitutions, statutes, orders, rules, regulations, and ordinances))

http://www.kantei.go.jp/jp/kanpo/digest.html (Shushō Kantei kanpō daijesuto 首相官邸官報ダイジェスト (KANPŌ WEB) (Official Residence of the Prime Minister: Official gazette))

http://www.shugiin.go.jp/index.nsf/html/index_houritsu.htm (Shōgiin seitei hōritsu 衆議院制定法律 (SEITEI HŌRITSU) (House of Representatives: Session laws))

http://www.courts.go.jp/kisokusyu (Courts in Japan, Saibansho kisokush 裁判所規則集 (SAIBANSHO KISOKU WEB) (Supreme Court of Japan: Supreme Court rules))

http://www.mofa.go.jp/mofaj/gaiko/treaty (Gaimushō Jōyaku 外務省条約 (JŌYAKU WEB) (Ministry of Foreign Affairs: Treaties and other international agreements))

http://www.cas.go.jp/jp/seisaku/hourei/data1.html (Translations of Japanese Laws and Regulations (Hōrei hon'yaku dētashū) (HON'YAKU DB) (Cabinet Secretariat))

Commercial (paid subscription)

http://www.d1-law.com (D1-law.com: Hanrei taikei/Genkō hōki (Daiichi Hōki); cases and legislative materials)

http://www.gyosei.co.jp/horei_data (Gyōsei genkō hōki, hanrei kensaku (Gyōsei); cases and legislative materials)

http://isho.hanrei.jp (Ishō hanrei dētabēsu (Patent Bureau); cases only)

http://jlic.softhouse-ilu.com (LEGALBase (Japan Legal Information Center); cases and legislative materials)

http://www.tkclex.ne.jp (LEX/DB (TKC); cases only)

http://www.hanreihisho.jp (LLI/DB Hanrei Hisho (Legal Information Center); cases and legislative materials)

http://legal.lexisnexis.jp (LexisNexisJP; cases and legislative materials)

http://www.westlawjapan.com (Westlaw Japan; cases and legislative materials)

T2.25   Kenya

(Common Law)

....

Cases

Citation format: ‹case name›, (‹year decision reported›) ‹volume number› ‹reporter abbreviation› ‹first page›, ‹page(s) of specific material, if desired› (‹court name, if in reporter›) (‹country abbreviation if not evident from context›).

▶ Alla Rakha v. Mohamed Ahmed, (1956) 29 L.R.K. 6 (Kenya).

▶ E. N. Wainaina v. Franz Haas, (1986) 2 K.A.R. 79 (C.A.K.) (Kenya).

Privy Council (P.C.) (all final appeals until 1964): Cite to reports listed under table T2.42 United Kingdom, or cite to L.R.K. or E.A.L.R.

▶ Law Reports of Kenya	1897–1956	L.R.K.
▶ East African Law Reports	2001–date 1957–1975	E.A.L.R.

Court of Appeal for Kenya (C.A.K.) (highest appeals court, formerly the East African Court of Appeal from 1897 to 1979); **High Court of Kenya** (H.C.K.): Cite to a reporter listed below.

(* denotes an official reporter)

▶ Law Reports of Kenya*	1897–1956	L.R.K.
▶ East African Law Reports	1957–1975	E.A.L.R.
▶ Kenya Law Reports*	2001–2005 1976–1991	K.L.R.
▶ Kenyan Appeal Reports	1982–1992	K.A.R.
▶ LawAfrica Law Reports (online)	1999–date	L.L.R.

High Court-Milimani Commercial Courts of Kenya (C.C.K.): Cite to a reporter listed below.

▶ LawAfrica Law Reports (online)	1999–date	L.L.R.
▶ East African Law Reports	1957–1975	E.A.L.R.
▶ Law Reports of Kenya*	1897–1956	L.R.K.

Industrial Court of Kenya (I.C.K.): Cite to L.L.R., if therein.

Constitution

Give the article number, section (if applicable), and promulgation year of the version cited.

▶ CONSTITUTION, art. 12 (1992) (Kenya).

Legislation

Citation format: ‹title›, (‹revised edition year›) Cap. ‹number› ‹section› (‹country abbreviation if not evident from context›).

Or: ‹title›, No. ‹number› (‹year›), ‹KENYA GAZETTE/KENYA GAZETTE SUPPLEMENT› No. ‹supplement number› ‹section› (‹country abbreviation if not evident from context›).

▶ The Advocates Act, (1992) Cap. 16 § 14 (Kenya).

▶ The Finance Act, No. 8 (1991), KENYA GAZETTE SUPPLEMENT No. 73 § 4.

For legislation, cite to *The Laws of Kenya* and provide the date of the revised edition, or cite to the *Official Gazette*. The reference to laws as chapters (Caps.) and to the dates of revised editions is only for those laws that make up part of the consolidated materials.

▶ THE LAWS OF KENYA, REVISED EDITION	1962-date	
▶ THE OFFICIAL GAZETTE OF THE EAST AFRICA AND UGANDA PROTECTORATES	1899-1908	Vols. 1–10
▶ THE OFFICIAL GAZETTE OF THE EAST AFRICA PROTECTORATE	1908-1920	Vols. 11–22
▶ OFFICIAL GAZETTE OF THE COLONY OF KENYA AND EAST AFRICA PROTECTORATE	1921-1956	Vols. 23–58
▶ KENYA GAZETTE	1957-1963	Vols. 59–65
▶ THE KENYA GAZETTE [REPUBLIC OF KENYA]	1964-date	Vols. 66–current
▶ KENYA GAZETTE SUPPLEMENT	1931-date	

Internet sources

http://www.kenyalaw.org (official source on judgments, rulings, and opinions of the superior courts of record and/or acts, legal notices, bills, and parliamentary proceedings)

http://www.loc.gov/law/help/guide/nations/kenya.html (Library of Congress Guide to Law Online: Kenya)

T2.26   Lebanon, Republic of

(Civil Law)

Cases

Citation format: ‹court name› [‹court abbreviation›] [‹English translation of court name›], ‹region if applicable›, ‹number and/or date of decision in day month year format›, ‹reporter or journal name› [‹reporter or journal abbreviation›], ‹section of journal if applicable›, ‹year of publication›, **p.** ‹first page› (‹country abbreviation if not evident from context›).

► Mahkamat al-Tamiez [Tamiez] [Court of Cassation], 10 Dec. 1962, MAJMOUAT BAZ [BAZ], 1962, p. 73 (Leb.).

Courts

Lebanon has different categories of courts, including religious courts dealing mainly with family law matters. The most commonly cited courts are as follows:

Mahkamat al-Tamiez (Tamiez) (Court of Cassation: highest court of ordinary jurisdiction). This court sits only in the capital and has several chambers referred to generally by numbers (Chamber 1, 2, and so forth). Citation is sufficiently recognized by referring to this court only as "Tamiez" or "Qarar (decision) Tamiez."

Mahkamat al-Isteinaf (Isteinaf) (courts of appeals: general courts of second instance). Lebanon is divided into a number of appellate jurisdictions. Citation is sufficiently recognized by referring to this court as "Isteinaf" or "Qarar Isteinaf," followed by the name of its geographic jurisdiction.

Mahkamat al-Darajat al-Ula (courts of first instance). These courts are composed of two sections, the section of the "Qadi Munfared" (Judge of First Instance), and the "Gurfat Mahkamat al-Darajat al-Ula" (Chamber of First Instance). Lebanon is divided into a large number of first instance jurisdictions. Decisions of judges of first instances are seldom published or cited. Citations are sufficiently recognized by referring to the section (judge or chamber of first instance) or to the "hukm" (judgment) of such sections followed by the name of its geographic jurisdiction.

Sources for cases

Case citations can be made to the following publications:

Al-Nashra al-Qadaiah (Al-Nashra), an official publication of the Lebanese Ministry of Justice containing full texts of court decisions.

Majmouat Baz (Baz), a private publication issued on a yearly basis containing the legal reasoning of the Court of Cassation decisions.

Majmouat Hatem (Hatem), a private publication identified by its consecutive issue numbers containing selected portions of court decisions.

Majallat al-Adl (Adl or Al-Adl), an official publication of the Beirut Bar. It is published quarterly and has a section for court cases.

....

Statutes and decrees

Citation format: ‹statute or decree name or number› of ‹date in day month year format› (‹translation of subject matter of the law, if desired›) (‹country abbreviation if not evident from context›).

► Legislative Decree 138 of 7 Sept. 1983 (Leb.).

► Decree Law 144 of 12 June 1959 (Taxation on Natural and Juridical Persons) (Leb.).

► Decree 2,385 of the French High Commissioner of 17 Jan. 1924 (Leb.).

► Law of 17 Sept. 1962 (Taxation on Structures Built on Land) (Leb.).

Two compilations of Lebanese legislation currently in force (in Arabic), published in Beirut are:

> MAJMU'AT AL-TASHRI AL-LUBNANI   1961–date
> QAWANIN LUBNAN: MAJMU'AT AL-NUSUS ALTASHRIIYAH WA-AL-TANZIMIYAH   1968–date

Official Gazette

The Official Gazette, *al-Jaridah al-Rasmiyah*, is published weekly and divided into two parts. The first contains laws, decree-laws, and decrees and decisions by ministries. The second part contains official notices and announcements.

Internet sources

http://www.lp.gov.lb (Lebanese constitution and electoral law)

http://www.loc.gov/law/help/lebanon.html (Library of Congress Guide to Law Online: Lebanon)

http://www.law.cornell.edu/world/mideast.html#lebanon (online guide to legal material and other information about Lebanon)

T2.27   Mexico

(Civil Law)

Cases

Mexico does not have an official system of citation for cases decided by courts at the federal level. It is customary to cite federal cases in the following format:

Citation format for cases decided by the Mexican Supreme Court and the Tribunales Colegiados de Circuito: ‹rubro›, ‹court name› [‹court abbreviation›] [‹English translation of court name›], ‹reporter name›, ‹época (time period)›, **tomo** ‹volume number›, ‹month and year of reporter›, ‹number of decision in reporter›, ‹case number›, **Página** ‹first page› (‹country abbreviation if not evident from context›).

> Personalidad. En contra de la resolución que dirime esta cuestión, previamente al fondo, procede el amparo indirecto, Pleno de la Suprema Corte de Justicia [SCJN] [Supreme Court], Semanario Judicial de la Federación y su Gaceta, Novena Época, tomo XIII, Enero de 2001, Tesis P./J. 4/2001, Página 11 (Mex.).

The "rubro," or "case title" in English, is a short statement prepared by a court on the topic and issue discussed in the case. "Épocas," or "time periods" in English, are periods of time determined by the Supreme Court of Mexico in order to organize cases by chronological order. As of 2008, the Supreme Court was in the ninth época. The first four are no longer in force. The last five épocas (from the fifth through the ninth) include cases that are currently in force. All cases decided by federal courts indicate the época in which the case was decided.

Federal Courts

Suprema Corte de Justicia de la Nación (SCJN) (Supreme Court: the highest court of constitutional and federal jurisdiction, which sits as a full court (*pleno*) and in chambers) and **Tribunales Colegiados de Circuito** (TCC) (Collegiate Circuit Courts: equivalents, to some extent, to the U.S. federal courts of appeals).

Cases decided by federal courts in Mexico are currently published in the *Semanario Judicial de la Federación y su Gaceta* (SJFG) (Federal Judicial Reports). Only cases decided by the SCJN and the TCC are published in the SJFG. The SJFG volumes are published on a monthly basis.

▸ Anales de Jurisprudencia (Annals of Jurisprudence)	1933-1944	AJ
▸ Apéndice al Semanario Judicial de la Federación (Appendix to the Federal Judicial Weekly Report)	1917-1995 1954-1988	ASJF
▸ Boletín Judicial (Judicial Bulletin)	1954-date	BJ
▸ Boletín de Información Judicial (Bulletin of Judicial Information)	1945-1953	BIJ
▸ Boletín del Semanario Judicial de la Federación (Bulletin of the Federal Judicial Weekly Report)		BSJF
▸ Informe de la Suprema Corte de Justicia (Report of the Supreme Court of Justice)	1850-date	Info.
▸ Jurisprudencia por Contradicción de Tesis (Jurisprudence by Contradiction)	1988-date	JCT
▸ Juzgados de Distrito (District Courts)	1917-date	JD
▸ Precedentes Relevantes (Relevant Precedents)	1917-date	PR
▸ Semanario Judicial de la Federación (Federal Judicial Weekly Report)	1870-1995	SJF
▸ Semanario Judicial de la Federación y su Gaceta (Federal Judicial Weekly Report and Its Gazette); or Gaceta del Semanario Judicial de la Federación (Gazette of the Federal Judicial Weekly Report)	1995-date or GSJF	SJFG
▸ Tribunal Federal Electoral (Federal Electoral Court)		TFE
▸ Tribunal Federal de Justicia Fiscal y Administrativa (Federal Court of Fiscal and Administrative Justice)		TFJFyA

Cases decided by federal courts since 1917 are available in Spanish at the official website of the Supreme Court of Mexico, **http://www.scjn.gob.mx**.

A number of state courts publish their cases as well. There is no uniform system of citations at the state level, however, probably because publications of cases decided by state courts are not as consistent or as well organized as the SJFG. Cite state court cases analogously to federal cases.

....

Constitution

▸ Constitución Política de los Estados Unidos Mexicanos (Political Constitution of the United Mexican States)	C.P.

Citation format: ‹constitution name› [‹constitution abbreviation›], ‹"*as amended*," if applicable›, ‹specific provision(s) cited, if applicable›, **Diario Oficial de la Federación [DO]**, ‹date of publication in Spanish› (‹country abbreviation if not evident from context›).

> ▸ Constitución Política de los Estados Unidos Mexicanos [C.P.], *as amended*, Diario Oficial de la Federación [DO], 5 de Febrero de 1917 (Mex.).

....

Codes

Citation format: ‹code name› [‹code abbreviation›] [‹English translation of code name›], ‹"*as amended*," if applicable›, **Diario Oficial de la Federación [DO]**, ‹date of publication in Spanish› (‹country abbreviation if not evident from context›).

▶ **Código Penal Federal [CPF] [Federal Criminal Code]**, *as amended*, Diario Oficial de la Federación [DO], 14 de Agosto de 1931 (Mex.).

▶ Código Civil Federal (Federal Civil Code)	CC
▶ Código Agrario (Agrarian Code)	CA
▶ Código Contencioso Administrativo (Administrative Action Code)	CCA
▶ Código de Procedimientos Civiles (Civil Procedure Code)	CPC
▶ Código de Comercio (Commercial Code)	CCo.
▶ Código Financiero del Distrito Federal (Financial Code for the Federal District)	CFDF
▶ Código Federal Electoral (Federal Elections Code)	CFE
▶ Código Fiscal de la Federación (Federal Tax Code)	CFF
▶ Código Federal de Procedimientos Civiles (Federal Civil Procedure Code)	CFPC
▶ Código Federal de Procedimientos Penales (Federal Criminal Procedure Code)	CFPP
▶ Código de Justicia Militar (Military Justice Code)	CJM
▶ Código Federal de Instituciones y Procedimientos Electorales (Federal Code for Electoral Institutions and Procedures)	COFIPE
▶ Código Penal (Criminal Code)	CP
▶ Código Penal Federal (Federal Criminal Code)	CPF
▶ Código Sanitario (Health Code)	CS

The Mexican government publishes legislative and executive materials in the *Diario Oficial de la Federación* (DO), which is the official gazette of the federal government in Mexico. The DO informs citizens of their rights and obligations by providing ready access to the official text of federal laws, presidential documents, administrative regulations and notices, treaties, and descriptions of federal organizations, programs and activities. Some administrative orders issued by the Supreme Court are published in the DO as well. Cite to DO for all federal legislation.

▶ Diario Oficial de la Federación	DO

Subdivisions

▶ artículo[s] (article[s])	art., arts.
▶ edición (edition)	ed.
▶ fracción[es] (section[s])	frac., fracc.
▶ página[s] (page[s])	p., pp.
▶ párrafo[s] (paragraph[s])	pfo., pfos.
▶ reglamento[s] (regulation[s])	reg., regs.

Statutes

Citation format: ‹statute name› [‹statute abbreviation›] [‹English translation of statute name›], ‹"*as amended*," if applicable›, ‹specific provision(s) cited, if applicable›, **Diario Oficial de la Federación [DO]**, ‹date of publication in Spanish› (‹country abbreviation if not evident from context›).

▶ **Ley Federal de Competencia Económica [LFCE] [Antitrust Law]**, *as amended*, Diario Oficial de la Federación [DO], 24 de Diciembre de 1992 (Mex.).

‣ Ley de Amparo (Legal Protection Law)	LA
‣ Ley de Aviación Civil (Civil Aviation Law)	LAC
‣ Ley Aduanera (Customs Law)	LAD
‣ Ley de Adquisiciones para el Distrito Federal (Acquisitions Law for the Federal District)	LADF
‣ Ley Agraria (Agrarian Law)	LAG
‣ Ley General de Asentamientos Humanos (General Law on Population Centers)	LAH
‣ Ley de Amnistía (Amnesty Law)	LAM
‣ Ley de Adquisiciones y Obras Públicas (Acquisitions and Public Works Law)	LAOP
‣ Ley del Banco de México (Mexican Bank Law)	LBM
‣ Ley de Comercio Exterior (Foreign Commerce Law)	LCE
‣ Ley de Concursos Mercantiles (Bankruptcy Law)	LCM
‣ Ley de Contrato de Seguros (Insurance Contracts Law)	LCS
‣ Ley de Desarrollo Urbano (Urban Development Law)	LDU
‣ Ley de Expropiación (Expropriation Law)	LE
‣ Ley Federal de Competencia Económica (Federal Antitrust Law)	LFCE
‣ Ley Federal de Derechos (Federal Fiscal Rights Law)	LFD
‣ Ley Federal de Derechos de Autor (Authors' Rights Law)	LFDA
‣ Ley Federal de Procedimientos Administrativos (Administrative Procedures Law)	LFPA
‣ Ley Federal de Protección al Consumidor (Federal Consumer Protection Law)	LFPC
‣ Ley Federal de Reforma Agraria (Federal Agrarian Reform Law)	LFRA
‣ Ley Federal del Trabajo (Federal Labor Law)	LFT
‣ Ley Federal de los Trabajadores al Servicio del Estado (Federal Civil Servant Law)	LFTSE
‣ Ley General de Educación (General Education Law)	LGE
‣ Ley General de Equilibrio Ecológico y Protección al Ambiente (General Environmental Law)	LGEEPA
‣ Ley General de Organizaciones y Actividades Auxiliares de Crédito (General Law of Organizations and Activities Related to Credit)	LGOC
‣ Ley General de Población (General Population Law)	LGP
‣ Ley General de Sociedades Cooperativas (General Law for Cooperative Associations)	LGSC
‣ Ley General de Sociedades Mercantiles (General Law for Commercial Corporations)	LGSM
‣ Ley General de Títulos y Operaciones de Crédito (General Law for Securities and Credit Operations)	LGTOC
‣ Ley de Instituciones de Crédito (Credit Institutions Law)	LIC
‣ Ley de Inspección de Contratos y Obras Públicas (Contract Inspection and Public Works Law)	LICOP
‣ Ley para Promover la Inversión Mexicana y Vigilar la Inversión Extranjera (Law to Promote Mexican Investments and Monitor Foreign Investments)	LIE
‣ Ley Federal de Instituciones de Fianza (Federal Law for Bond Institutions)	LIF
‣ Ley de Invenciones y Marcas (Law on Inventions and Trademarks)	LIM
‣ Ley del Impuesto Sobre la Renta (Income Tax Law)	LIR

- Ley General de Instituciones de Seguros (General Law for Insurance Institutions) — LIS
- Ley de Impuestos sobre Ingresos Mercantiles (Tax Law on Commercial Income) — LISIM
- Ley del Instituto de Seguridad y Servicios Sociales para los Trabajadores del Estado (Law of the Social Security Institute for Civil Servants) — LISSSTE
- Ley del Impuesto al Valor Agregado (Added Value Tax Law) — LIVA
- Ley de Inversión Extranjera (Foreign Investment Law) — LIEX
- Ley Monetaria de los Estados Unidos Mexicanos (Monetary Law of the United Mexican States) — LM
- Ley del Mercado de Valores (Stock Market Law) — LMV
- Ley Federal Sobre Monumentos y Zonas Arqueológicas (Federal Law for Monuments and Archaeological Areas) — LMZAA
- Ley de Nacionalidad (Nationality Law) — LN
- Ley de Navegación (Navigation Law) — LNAV
- Ley de Navegación y Comercio Marítimos (Navigation Law and Maritime Commerce) — LNCM
- Ley de Nacionalidad y Naturalizacion (Nationality and Naturalization Law) — LNN
- Ley del Notariado (Notaries Law) — LNO
- Ley Orgánica de la Administración Pública Federal (Enabling Law for Federal Public Administration) — LOAPF
- Ley de Comercio Exterior (Foreign Commerce Law) — LOCE
- Ley Orgánica de Nacional Financiera (Enabling Law for National Financial Assistance) — LONF
- Ley Orgánica del Tribunal de los Contencioso Administrativo (Enabling Law for the Administrative Courts of the Federal District) — LOTCADE
- Ley Orgánica del Poder Judicial de la Federación (Enabling Law for the Federal Judiciary) — LOPJF
- Ley Federal de Organizaciones Políticas y Procesos Electorales (Federal Code for Electoral Institutions and Procedures) — LOPPE
- Ley Orgánica del Tribunal de los Contencio Administrativo (Enabling Law for the Administrative Disputes Court) — LOTCA
- Ley Orgánica del Tribunal Fiscal de la Federación (Enabling Law for the Federal Fiscal Court) — LOTFF
- Ley Orgánica de los Tribunales de Justicia del Fuero Comun del Distrito Federal (Enabling Law for the Justice Court of the Federal District) — LOTJFC
- Ley Federal de Protección al Consumidor (Federal Consumer Protection Law) — LPC
- Ley de Protección a la Propiedad Industrial (Industrial Property Protection Law) — LPPI
- Ley de Quiebras y Suspension de Pagos (Bankruptcy and Suspension of Payments Law) — LQ
- Ley de Responsabilidades (Public Service Accountability Law) — LR
- Ley para Regular las Agrupaciones Finacieras (Law To Regulate Financial Groups) — LRAF
- Ley del Régimen Patrimonial y del Servicio Público (Patrimonial Property and Public Service Law) — LRPSP
- Ley Reglamentaria del Servicio Público de Banca y Crédito (Regulatory Law of Public Banking Services and Credit Services) — LRSPB

- ▸ Ley de Sociedades de Inversion (Investment Corporations Law) **LSI**
- ▸ Ley del Servicio Militar (Military Service Law) **LSM**
- ▸ Ley de Seguridad Pública (Public Security Law) **LSP**
- ▸ Ley del Seguro Social (Social Security Law) **LSS**
- ▸ Ley de Transparencia y Acceso a la Información Pública del Distrito Federal (Transparency and Access to Public Information Law for the Federal District) **LTAIPDF**
- ▸ Ley de Títulos y Operaciones de Crédito (General Law of Securities and Credit Operations) **LTOC**
- ▸ Ley de Vías Generales de Comunicación (Law of General Venues of Communication) **LVGC**

Administrative and executive materials

Citation format: ‹document title› [‹English translation of title›], ‹"*as amended*," if applicable›, ‹specific provision(s) cited, if applicable›, Diario Oficial de la Federación [DO], ‹date of publication in Spanish› (‹country abbreviation if not evident from context›).

- ▸ Decreto de Promulgación de la Convención de Viena, sobre el Derecho de los Tratados entre Estados y Organización Internacionales [Decree To Enact the Vienna Convention on Treaties], Diario Oficial de la Federación [DO], 24 de Diciembre de 1992 (Mex.).

State materials

It is common to cite local materials analogously to the federal examples given in the above table.

State governments have websites where local statutes and codes are often available. A comprehensive list of state government official websites is provided in the federal government's online legal repository, which is maintained by the Mexican Department of the Interior, at **http://www.ordenjuridico.gob.mx**.

Links to state materials can also be found at **http://www.mexlaw.com/best _websites/appendix3.html**.

Periodicals

▸ Boletín del Instituto de Derecho Comparado (Bulletin of the Institute of Comparative Studies)	1948-1967	BIDC
▸ Boletín Mexicano de Derecho Comparado (Mexican Bulletin of Comparative Law)	1968-date	BMDC
▸ Boletín Oficial (Official Bulletin)		BO
▸ Diario Oficial de la Federación (Official Federal Daily Gazette)	1916-date	DO
▸ Gaceta Oficial del Distrito Federal (Official Gazette for the Federal District)	1946-date	GODF
▸ Revista Critica de Derecho Inmobiliario (Critical Journal of Real Estate Law)	1861-date	RCDI
▸ Revista de Derecho Administrativo (Journal of Administrative Law)	1989-date	RDA
▸ Revista de Derecho Mercantil (Journal of Commercial Law)		RM

- Revista de Derecho Mexicano (Journal of Mexican Law)   RDM
- Revista de Derecho Notarios (Journal of Notary Law)   1956-1968   RDN
- Revista de Derecho Privado (Journal of Private Law)   1990-date   RDP
- Revista de Derecho Público (Journal of Public Law)   1946-date   RDPP
- Revista de la Facultad de Derecho de Mexico (Journal   1951-2005   RFDM
  of the Law Faculty of Mexico)
- Revista General de Legislación y Jurisprudencia   1926-1930   RGLJ
  (Journal of Legislation and Jurisprudence)
- Revista Mexicana de la Propiedad Industrial y Artística   RMPIA
  (Mexican Journal of Industrial and Artistic Property)
- Revista del Tribunal Fiscal de la Federación   RTFF
  (Journal of the Federal Tax Court)

Internet sources

Official government websites:
http://www.diputados.gob.mx
http://www.senado.gob.mx
http://www.presidencia.gob.mx
http://www.juridicas.unam.mx

The following websites provide links to the law and codes of Mexico:

http://www.loc.gov/law/help/guide/nations/mexico.html
http://www.washlaw.edu/forint/america/mexico.html
http://www.mexlaw.com
http://www.llrx.com/features/mexican.htm
http://tarlton.law.utexas.edu/vlibrary/outlines/mexico.html
http://www.mexicanlaws.com
http://www.diputados.gob.mx

The Mexican government has a website where several federal statutes and regulations are available in Spanish at **http://www.ordenjuridico.gob.mx**.

Global Legal Information Network, a database of laws, regulations, and other complementary legal sources, is available at **http://www.glin.gov**.

The official website for the Diario Oficial de la Federación is available at **http://www.diariooficialdigital.com**.

T2.28   Netherlands, Kingdom of the

(Civil Law)

Cases

Citation format: ‹court abbreviation› ‹city (except when citing HR)› ‹date of decision in Dutch›, ‹reporter abbreviation› ‹publication year›, ‹publication number› **m.nt.** ‹initials or name of annotator› (‹plaintiff name›/ ‹defendant name›) (‹country abbreviation if not evident from context›).

- HR 30 januari 1959, NJ 1959, 548 m.nt. DJV (Quint/Te Poel) (Neth.).

> ▶ Hof 's-Gravenhage 27 mei 2004, JOR 2004, 206 m.nt. Van Ravels en Van Andel (Vie d'Or/Stichting Pensioen- en Verzekeringskamer en Staat) (Neth.).

Ordinary jurisdiction

Hoge Raad der Nederlanden (HR) (Supreme Court of the Netherlands), **Gerechtshof** (Hof) (ordinary courts of appeals), **Hoog Militair Gerechtshof** (HMG) (Military Court of Appeals) (abolished in 1991), and **Krijgsraad** (Kr.) (Court Martial) (no longer in existence): Cite to NJ or W, if therein.

Prior to 2002, there were two courts of first instance: **Arrondissementsrecht-bank** (Rb.) (ordinary court of first instance and court of appeals to the Kanton-gerecht) and **Kantongerecht** (Ktg.) (court of first instance for labor, rent, and misdemeanor cases). In 2002, these two courts merged, eliminating the latter court as a separate court (instead, it is now a subdivision of the former court). Currently, labor, rent, and small claim (rather than misdemeanor) cases are still decided by a different kind of judge—the **Kantonrechter** (Ktr.)—than are other civil cases. Because of the merger, the **Arrondissementsrechtbank** (Rb.) is no longer a court of appeals to the **Kantongerecht** (Ktg.). After the merger, those specific types of cases should be cited to the **Kantonrechter** (Ktr.) instead of the **Kantongerecht** (Ktg.), following the form mentioned above. Cite to Prg. or NJF, if therein.

Reporters

▶ Nederlandse Jurisprudentie		1913-date	NJ
▶ Weekblad van het Recht (by issue number)		1839-1943	W
▶ Kort Geding		1981-2003	KG
▶ Kort Geding Kort		1981-2003	KGK
▶ Rechtspraak van de Week		1939-date	RvdW
▶ Administratiefrechtelijke beslissingen		1985-date	AB
▶ Beslissingen in belastingzaken		1910-1953	B.
▶ Beslissingen in belastingzaken / Nederlandse Belastingrechtspraak		1953-date	BNB
▶ Delikt en Delinkwent		1970-date	DD
▶ Practijkgids		1963-date	Prg.
▶ Nederlandse jurisprudentie Feitenrechtspraak		2003-date	NJF
▶ Jurisprudentie bestuursrecht		1994-date	JB
▶ Belastingblad		1982-date	BB
▶ Jurisprudentie Onderneming en Recht		1996-date	JOR

Special jurisdiction

Afdeling Bestuursrechtspraak van de Raad van State (ABRvS) (Administrative Court of Highest Instance (**Afdeling Rechtspraak van de Raad van State** (ARRvS) prior to 1994)), **Centrale Raad van Beroep** (CRvB) (Central Council of Appeal), and **College van Beroep voor het Bedrijfsleven** (CBB) (Administrative Court for Trade and Industry): Cite to AB, if therein.

....

Constitutions

▶ BelastingrechtspraakStatuut voor het Koninkrijk der Nederlanden (Charter of the Kingdom of the Netherlands)	STATUUT NED	
▶ Grondwet voor het Koninkrijk der Nederlanden (Constitution of the Kingdom of the Netherlands)	Gw.	

Codes

▸ Burgerlijk Wetboek (Civil Code) (established in 1992)   BW

▸ Wetboek van Burgerlijke Rechtsvordering (Code of Civil   Rv
   Procedure)

▸ Wetboek van Koophandel (Commercial Code)   WvK

▸ Wetboek van Strafrecht (Criminal Code)   SR

▸ Wetboek van Strafvordering (Code of Criminal Procedure)   Sv

▸ Faillisementswet (Bankruptcy Code)   Fw

▸ Wet op de Rechterlijke Organisatie (Law on Judicial Organization)   WET RO

▸ Burgerlijk Wetboek van 1838 (Civil Code of 1838)   BW (OUD)
   (in force until 1992)

The **Algemene Wet Bestuursrecht (Awb.)** (General Administrative Law Act), enacted in 1992, is not technically a code, but it provides a general foundational framework for Dutch administrative law.

Statutes and decrees

The *Staatsblad van het Koninkrijk der Nederlanden* (**Stb.**, sometimes cited as **S.**) is the official gazette of the Kingdom of the Netherlands. It is the official source for finding and citing the authoritative text of all codes, laws, general administrative measures, and royal decrees.

The *Nederlandse Staatscourant* (**Stcrt.**) is an official daily journal used for the publication of some royal decrees, ministerial decrees, ministerial circulars, and other official statements.

A parallel citation to *Nedersandse Staatswetten* (**Schuurman & Jordens**) or *Nederlandse Wetgeving* (**Cremers**) may be given.

▸ Staatsblad van het Koninkrijk der Nederlanden   Stb./S.

▸ Staatscourant   Stcrt.

▸ Nederlandse Staatswetten (edited by L.N.   Schuurman & Jordens
   Schuurman and P.H. Jordens)

▸ Nederlandse Wetgeving (edited by Cremers)   Cremers

The year and page number follow after the abbreviation:

▸ Stb. 1996, p. 204

▸ Stcrt. 1918, p. 7

Periodicals

▸ Nederlands Juristenblad	1925–date	NJB
▸ Ars Aequi	1951–date	AA
▸ Weekblad voor Privaatrecht, Notariaat en Registratie	1870–date	WPNR
▸ Advocatenblad	1918–date	Adv.bl.
▸ Rechtsgeleerd Magazijn Themis	1839–date	RM Themis
▸ Nederlands Tijdschrift voor Burgerlijk Recht		NTBR
▸ Ondernemingsrecht	1999–date	
▸ Weekblad voor Fiscaal Recht	1955–date	WFR
▸ Maandblad Belastingbeschouwingen	1958–date	BB
▸ Tijdschrift voor Criminologie	1977–date	TvCr

| ▸ Tijdschrift voor Civiele Rechtspleging | 1993-date | TCR |
| ▸ Nederlands Tijdschrift voor Bestuursrecht | 1987-date | NTB |

Treaties and conventions

| ▸ Tractatenblad van het Koninkrijk der Nederlanden | 1950-date | Trb. |

Internet sources

Legislation passed since January 1, 1995, which has been published in the *Staatblad* or the *Staatscourant*, is available on the government's website at **http://www.overheid.nl**. Treaties and Parliamentary Papers are also available from this site. This site gives further access to all Ministries and other government organizations.

The de Rechtspraak website, available at **http://www.rechtspraak.nl**, provides free access to cases.

Comprehensive online access to legislation may be obtained through a paid subscription to the SDU online database, **http://www.sdu.nl**.

T2.29   New Zealand

(Common Law)

Cases

Reported decisions

Citation format: ‹case name› ‹year of decision in parentheses or brackets› ‹volume number› ‹reporter abbreviation› ‹first page› (‹court abbreviation›) ‹page(s) of specific material, if desired› (‹country abbreviation if not evident from context›).

Note that all case names are in italics, and the abbreviation "v" for "versus" is not followed by a period. Case names may be abbreviated according to tables T6 and T10.

Year of decision:

1) If the reports are in a consecutively numbered series from the first volume, use parentheses around the year, which references the year of the decision.

▸ *R v Noble* (2006) 22 CRNZ 422 (HC).

2) If the report series consists of one or more volumes per year with no consecutive number sequence, use square brackets.

In some reports, the year acts as the volume number and therefore there is no separate volume number. In such cases, square brackets are used instead of parentheses around the year. Particular attention should be paid to reports that have changed titles (see below).

▸ *Kerridge v Kerridge* [2008] NZFLR 30 (HC).

▸ *Kain v Hutton* [2008] 3 NZLR 589 (SC).

▸ *Zaoui v Att'y Gen.* [2006] 1 NZLR 289 (SC) 300.

3) All pre-1900 reports use parentheses and the year reference is to the year of the decision.

▶ *Wellington Gas Co. v Patten* (1881) NZLR 3 CA 205.

If available, the official report (NZLR) should be cited. Cite the official report first when including more than one citation. The correct citation form with abbreviation is indicated in the front of the reports.

Where the court of decision is not obvious from the title of the report, the name of the court (abbreviated) should be included at the end of the citation. Common abbreviations are **High Court** (HC), **Court of Appeal** (CA), **Supreme Court** (SC), and **Judicial Committee of the Privy Council** (P.C.).

Official reports

▶ New Zealand Law Reports	1881-1887	NZLR

These volumes contain separately numbered and paginated parts for Court of Appeal cases and Supreme Court cases. Citation format: ‹case name› (‹year of publication›) NZLR ‹volume number› ‹court abbreviation› ‹first page›, ‹page(s) of specific material, if desired› (‹country abbreviation if not evident from context›).

▶ *Wellington Gas Co. v Patten* (1881) NZLR 3 CA 205.

▶ New Zealand Law Reports (vols. 6-34)	1888-1915	NZLR

In these volumes, Court of Appeal and Supreme Court decisions are mixed. Citation format: ‹case name› (‹year of publication›) ‹volume number› NZLR ‹first page›, ‹page(s) of specific material, if desired› (‹court abbreviation›) (‹country abbreviation if not evident from context›).

▶ *Cleland v S. British Ins. Co.* (1890) 9 NZLR 177 (CA).

▶ New Zealand Law Reports (volume numbers discontinued)	1916-date	NZLR

Since 1973, more than one volume has been published each year and they are consecutively numbered only within each year. Citation format: ‹case name› [‹year of publication›] ‹volume number, if applicable› NZLR ‹first page›, ‹page(s) of specific material, if desired› (‹year of decision, if applicable›, ‹court abbreviation›) (‹country abbreviation if not evident from context›).

▶ *Moreton v Montrose Ltd.* [1986] 2 NZLR 496 (CA).

Other reports

▶ Magistrates' Court Decisions (continued as *District Court Reports*)	1939-1980	MCD
▶ Magistrates' Court Reports (continued as *Magistrates' Court Decisions*)	1906-1952	MCR

Each volume contains multiple years and therefore the year and volume must be cited. Citation format: ‹case name› (‹year of decision›) ‹volume number› ‹reporter abbreviation› ‹first page› (‹country abbreviation if not evident from context›).

▶ *Christchurch City Council v McCleary* (1966) 11 MCD 465 (N.Z.).

▶ *Police v Martin* (1931) 26 MCR 75 (N.Z.).

▶ District Court Reports	1980-1988	DCR

These volumes contain multiple years. Citation format: ‹case name› (‹year of decision›) ‹volume number› ‹reporter abbreviation› ‹first page›, ‹page(s) of specific material, if desired› (‹country abbreviation if not evident from context›).

▶ *Tipple v Att' y Gen.* (1982) 1 DCR 358 (N.Z.).

▶ District Court Reports   1989–date   **DCR**

In these volumes, the year of the volume is the same as the year of decision. Citation format: ‹case name› [‹year of volume›] **DCR** ‹first page› (‹court abbreviation, if necessary›) (‹country abbreviation if not evident from context›).

▶ *MK v Police* [2007] DCR 770 (N.Z.).

Specialist series reports should be cited as directed within the report:

▶ Book of Awards   1894–date   **BA**
▶ Gazette Law Reports   1898-1953   **GLR**

Judicial Committee of the Privy Council (P.C.)

Until 2004, the Privy Council was New Zealand's highest court of appeal. When reported in *New Zealand Law Reports* (NZLR) (since 1932), cite according to the NZLR citation format above, with the court abbreviation following the citation.

▶ *O'Connor v Hart* [1985] 1 NZLR 159 (P.C.).

▶ New Zealand Privy Council Cases   1840-1932   **NZPCC**

Citation format: ‹case name› (‹year of decision›) **NZPCC** ‹first page›, ‹page(s) of specific material, if desired› (‹country abbreviation if not evident from context›).

▶ *Barker v Edger* (1898) NZPCC 422 (N.Z.).

Unreported decisions

In 2005, the Supreme Court of New Zealand and the Court of Appeal adopted a medium-neutral citation format for unreported decisions. Citation format: ‹case name› [‹year›] ‹medium-neutral court abbreviation› ‹case reference number› ‹"at para" and paragraph number in brackets, if desired› ‹judge identifier, if applicable› (‹country abbreviation if not evident from context›).

▶ *Aylwin v N.Z. Police* [2008] NZSC 113 at para [12] Wilson J for the Court (N.Z.).

When citing to an unreported decision for which a medium-neutral citation format has not been adopted, the format is: ‹case name› **(unreported)** ‹court abbreviation ("SC" or "CA")› ‹file number›, ‹date in day month year format›, ‹judge identifier, if applicable› (‹country abbreviation if not evident from context›).

▶ *Waitikiri Links Ltd. v Windsor Golf Club Inc.* (unreported) CA 132/95, 25 June 1998 (N.Z.).

When citing any court other than the Supreme Court or the Court of Appeal, spell out the court name rather than using the abbreviation. Also, include the place of registry:

▶ *Gitmans v Alexander* (unreported) High Court, Auckland, CIV 2001-404-1937, 9 December 2003, Chambers J, at paras 16–18 (N.Z.).

Statutes, session laws, and regulations

Citation format for statutes: ‹act short name› ‹year of passage› (‹country abbreviation if not evident from context›).

▶ Children's Commissioner Act 2003 (N.Z.).

Amendments to statutes should be cited as the amending law unless the amended statute has been consolidated. For example, if section 5(a) of the Adoption Act of 1955 has been amended by section 10 of the Child Rights Act of 1956, cite as follows:

▶ Section 5(a) of the Adoption Act 1955, as substituted by section 10 of the Child Rights Act 1956 (N.Z.).

However, where the Adoption Act of 1955 has been consolidated, the reference may be directly to section 5 of the Adoption Act.

Subdivisions of schedules within a statute are cited as clauses:

▶ Adoption Act 1955, First Schedule, cl 4(1) (N.Z.).

Cite delegated legislation (regulations) to the *Statutory Regulations Series* (SR). Provisions within a regulation are referred to as regulations and abbreviated as "reg" or "regs" in a citation.

Citation format for regulations: ‹regulation name› ‹year of regulation›, SR ‹SR number›, reg ‹section› (‹country abbreviation if not evident from context›).

▶ Adoption Regulations 1976, SR 1976/22, reg 4(a) (N.Z.).

Citation format for bills: ‹bill name› ‹year› ‹number›-‹version› cl ‹clause number(s)› (‹country abbreviation if not evident from context›).

▶ Adoption Reform Bill 1985 25-1 cl 3 (N.Z.).

Treaties

▶ New Zealand Treaty Series   1950–date   NZTS

Citation format: ‹treaty name› ‹date signed, if appropriate› [‹year›] NZTS ‹number› (‹country abbreviation if not evident from context›).

▶ Treaty Between New Zealand and the United States of America on the Delimitation of the Maritime Boundary Between Tokelau and the United States of America [1983] NZTS 17 (N.Z.).

Parliamentary debates

Citation format (Hansard): [‹year›] ‹volume› NZPD ‹page number› (‹country abbreviation if not evident from context›).

▶ [1995] 575 NZPD 15484 (N.Z.).

Internet sources

http://www.parliament.nz (provides access to Hansard transcripts and other parliamentary materials, as well as up-to-date information on the progress of bills currently before the House)

http://www.nzlii.org (New Zealand Legal Information Institute (NZLII) website: unofficial reports with some case law and statutes; also publishes NZTS)

http://www.justice.govt.nz (New Zealand Ministry of Justice website: publishes all Supreme Court cases, Court of Appeal decisions after January 2003, and High Court decisions after August 2005)

http://www.courtsofnz.govt.nz (court-issued PDF copies of all Supreme Court decisions and a few high-profile Court of Appeal decisions)

http://www.thomsonreuters.co.nz (Thomson Reuters (commercial source))

http://www.cch.co.nz (CCH New Zealand Ltd. (commercial source))

http://www.legislationdirect.co.nz (Legislation Direct (contracted with the Parliamentary Counsel office for print and distribution of legislation) (commercial source))

http://www.lexisnexis.co.nz (LexisNexis New Zealand (commercial source))

T2.30   Nicaragua

(Civil Law)

....

Cases

Citation of a Nicaraguan Supreme Court of Justice case: Sentencia [S.] No. ‹judgment number›, ‹time of judgment, in Spanish›, ‹date of judgment in day month year format›, ‹publication name› [‹publication abbreviation›] [‹English translation of court name›] p. ‹first page›, ‹page(s) of specific material, if desired›, Cons. ‹paragraph number(s)› (‹country abbreviation if not evident from context›).

> ► Sentencia [S.] No. 77, de las 10:45 a.m., 26 May 1992, BOLETÍN JUDICIAL [B.J.] [Supreme Court of Justice] p. 102, Cons. I (Nicar.).

Because the *Boletín Judicial* (B.J.) is published only at the end of each year, the Supreme Court also publishes its most important cases in its quarterly magazine, *Justicia*.

Citation of a case published in the magazine *Justicia*: Sentencia [S.] No. ‹judgment number›, ‹time of judgment, in Spanish›, ‹date of judgment in day month year format›, REVISTA JUSTICIA [‹English translation of court name›] No. ‹volume number› ‹month and year of publication› p. ‹page number(s)›, Cons. ‹paragraph number(s) of opinion› (‹country abbreviation if not evident from context›).

> ► Sentencia [S.] No. 2, de las 12:00 p.m., 15 July 1997, REVISTA JUSTICIA [Supreme Court of Justice] No. 11 Jan. 1998 p. 35, Cons. II (Nicar.).

The cases of the nine Nicaraguan Tribunals of Appeals and other lower courts are published in *Boletín Informativo* (B.I.), which is published by the Center of Judicial Documents (Centro de Documentación Judicial) of the Judicial Branch.

Citation of a Nicaraguan Tribunal of Appeals case: Sentencia [S.] No. ‹judgment number›, ‹time of judgment, in Spanish›, ‹date of judgment in day month year format›, ‹court name› [‹court abbreviation›] [‹English translation of court name›], ‹chamber›, ‹city›, ‹publication name› [‹publication abbreviation›] No. ‹volume number›, ‹month and year of publication›, p. ‹page number(s)› (‹country abbreviation if not evident from context›).

▶ Sentencia [S.] No. 27, de las 10:00 a.m., 1 March 2000, Tribunal de Apelación, Circumscripción Norte [TACN] [Appellate Tribunal of the North Region], Sala de lo Penal, Matagalpa, BOLETÍN INFORMATIVO [B.I.] No. 4, July 2002, p. 266 (Nicar.).

Courts: **Corte Suprema de Justicia** (CSJ) (Supreme Court of Justice): Cite to B.J., if therein; **Tribunales de Apelación** (TA) (tribunals of appeals: one for each judicial region of the country), **Juzgados de Distrito** (district courts), and **Juzgados Locales** (local courts).

Tribunals of Appeals

▶ Tribunal de Apelación, Circumscripción Las Segovias	TACLS
▶ Tribunal de Apelación, Circumscripción Norte	TACN
▶ Tribunal de Apelación, Circumscripción Occidental	TACO
▶ Tribunal de Apelación, Circumscripción Managua	TACM
▶ Tribunal de Apelación, Circumscripción Sur	TACS
▶ Tribunal de Apelación, Circumscripción Oriental	TACOr.
▶ Tribunal de Apelación, Circumscripción Central	TACC
▶ Tribunal de Apelación, Circumscripción Atlántico Norte	TACAN
▶ Tribunal de Apelación, Circumscripción Atlántico Sur	TACAS

Constitution

Citation format for the Nicaraguan constitution published in the official gazette: ‹constitution name› [‹constitution abbreviation›] ‹relevant subdivisions, if desired›, LA GACETA, DIARIO OFICIAL [L.G.] ‹date of publication in day month year format›, **as amended by** ‹citation of amending act, if necessary›, **L.G.** ‹date of publication of amending act› (‹country abbreviation if not evident from context›).

▶ CONSTITUCIÓN POLÍTICA DE LA REPÚBLICA DE NICARAGUA [CN.] tit. VIII, ch. III, LA GACETA, DIARIO OFICIAL [L.G.] 9 January 1987, as amended by Ley No. 330, Reforma Parcial a la Constitución Política de la República de Nicaragua, Jan. 18, 2000, L.G. Jan. 19, 2000.

Statutes

There are three types of legislative enactments: **ley** (statutes promulgated by the National Assembly), **decreto A.N.** (decrees promulgated by the National Assembly), and **decreto** (decrees promulgated by the President of the Republic).

Citation format: ‹type of legislative enactment› **No.** ‹enactment number›, ‹date of enactment in day month year format›, ‹full law or decree name› [‹law or decree abbreviation, if available›] [‹English translation of law or decree name›] ‹title(s), chapter(s), and section(s), if any; or article(s) and clause(s) or paragraph(s), if any› LA GACETA, DIARIO OFICIAL [L.G.], ‹date of publication in day month year format› (‹country abbreviation if not evident from context›).

▶ Ley No. 217, 2 May 1996, Ley General del Medio Ambiente y los Recursos Naturales [Ley del Medio Ambiente] [Environmental and Natural Resources Law] tit. III, ch. II, sec. I, LA GACETA, DIARIO OFICIAL [L.G.], 6 June 1996 (Nicar.).

Citations to a law subsequent to the first citation to that law may include only the abbreviated law or decree name and the abbreviation of the official gazette instead of the full law or decree name and full name of the official gazette.

Official Gazette

The official publication of all legislation, including the constitution and international treaties ratified by Nicaragua, is the Official Gazette, *La Gaceta, Diario Oficial* (**L.G.**). The legislation becomes binding after it has been published in *La Gaceta*.

Internet sources

http://www.asamblea.gob.ni (Asamblea Nacional (National Assembly))

http://www.csj.gob.ni (Corte Suprema de Justicia (Supreme Court of Justice))

http://www.loc.gov/law/help/guide/nations/nicaragua.html (Library of Congress Guide to Law Online: Nicaragua)

T2.31 Nigeria

(Common Law)

Cases

Citation format: ‹case name›, [‹year of decision›] ‹volume number› ‹reporter abbreviation› ‹first page›, ‹page(s) of specific material, if desired› (‹country abbreviation if not evident from context›).

> ► Oladele v. State, [1993] 1 NSCC 12 (Nigeria).
> ► Mohammadu Labaran v. Nigeria Custom Serv., [1999] 1 FHCNLR 648 (Nigeria).

Privy Council (**P.C.**) (highest appeals court until 1960): Cite to **NLR** or **WALR**, if therein.

► Law Reports	1881–1955	**NLR**
► West African Law Reports	1956–1958	**WALR**

West African Court of Appeal (**WACA**): Cite to **SJWACA** or **WALR**, if therein.

► Selected Judgments of the West African Court of Appeal	1930–1960	**SJWACA**
► West African Law Reports	1956–1958	**WALR**

Supreme Court (**S.C.**) (highest appeals court after 1960): Cite to a reporter in the following order of preference.

► Law Reports	1881–1955	**NLR**
► Nigerian Supreme Court Cases	1956–date	**NSCC**
► Federal Supreme Court Selected Judgments	1956–date	**FSC**
► Supreme Court of Nigeria Judgments	1987–date	**SCNJ**
► Nigeria Weekly Law Report	1985–date	**NWLR**

Court of Appeal (**C.A.**): Cite to a reporter below.

► Federal Court of Appeal Reserved Judgments	1977–1978	**FCA**
► Nigeria Court of Appeal Reports	1978	**NCAR**

| ▸ Nigerian Appeal Cases Report | 1994 | **NACR** |
| ▸ Nigeria Weekly Law Reports | 1985–date | **NWLR** |

Note that these reporters provide only intermittent reporting.

Federal High Court (F.H.C.): Cite to a reporter below.

| ▸ Law Reports | 1881–1955 | **NLR** |
| ▸ Federal High Court of Nigeria Law Reports | 1973–date | **FHCNLR** |

Constitution

Citation format: ‹constitution name› (**year of the version cited**), ‹section, if desired› (‹country abbreviation if not evident from context›).

▸ CONSTITUTION OF NIGERIA (1999), § 22.

Statutes

Citation format: ‹statute name› (‹revised edition year›) **Cap.** (‹number›), ‹section, if desired› (‹country abbreviation if not evident from context›).

Or: ‹decree name› **No.** (‹number›) (‹year›) ‹volume number›:‹issue number, if applicable› ‹"O.G." or "S.O.G."›, ‹page(s) of specific material, if desired› ‹section, if desired› (‹country abbreviation if not evident from context›).

▸ Arbitration and Conciliation Act (1990) Cap. (19), § 17 (Nigeria).

▸ Civil Aviation (Amendment) Decree No. (51) (1999) 86:35 O.G., A1895 § 1 (Nigeria).

▸ Electoral Act No. (1) (1965) 52 S.O.G., A1 (Nigeria).

For legislation, either cite to the Laws of Nigeria and provide the date of the revised edition, or cite to the Official Gazette.

▸ Laws of the Federation of Nigeria, Revised Edition (available at **http://www.nigeria-law.org**)	1990–date	
▸ The Nigeria Gazette	1914–1954	
▸ Federation of Nigeria Gazette	1954–1963	
▸ Official Gazette—Federal Republic of Nigeria	1963–date	**O.G.**
▸ Supplement to the Official Gazette	1916–1968	**S.O.G.**

Internet sources

The International Center for Nigerian Law provides access to the constitution, cases from the Court of Appeal and the Supreme Court, and legislation at its website, **http://www.nigeria-law.org/LawLibrary.htm**.

▸ Acts Authentication Act (1990) Cap. (4), § 1 (Nigeria), *available at* http://www.nigeria-law.org/Acts Authentication Act.htm.

▸ Adiatu Ladunni v. Oludoyin Adekunle Kukoyi & Ors, [1972] 3 NLR 3 (Nigeria), *available at* http://www.nigeria-law.org/LawReporting Before2000.htm.

http://www.loc.gov/law/help/guide/nations/nigeria.html (Library of Congress Guide to Law Online: Nigeria)

T2.32   Pakistan, Islamic Republic of

(Common Law)

The legal system of Pakistan is based on the common law system of England and the United States. The publication of laws, regulations, and reporting systems is in English.

Cases

Citation format: ‹case name›, (‹year of reporter›) ‹volume number› ‹reporter abbreviation› (‹court abbreviation or province, if applicable›) ‹first page›, ‹page(s) of specific material, if desired› (‹year of decision if different from year of reporter›) (‹country abbreviation if not evident from context›).

Province names are not abbreviated, with the exception of North-West Frontier Province (N-W.F.P.).

- ▶ Muhammad v. State, (1986) 38 PLD (SC) 13 (Pak.).
- ▶ Nayak v. Goa University, (2002) 30 PLJ (SC India) 133 (Pak.).
- ▶ Abdulla v. Government of Punjab, (2004) 27 NLR Civil 85 (Pak.).

For decisions relating to Islamic law, Pakistan has established a separate **Federal Shariat Court** (FSC) whose decisions are subject to review by the **Supreme Court of Pakistan** (SC). The Federal Shariat Court may call for and examine the record of any case decided by any criminal court under any law relating to the enforcement of Islamic law.

- ▶ Sharman v. State, (2002) 30 PLJ (FSC) 33 (Pak.).

Reporters

▶ All-Pakistan Legal Decisions	1949–date	PLD
▶ Pakistan Law Journal	1973–date	PLJ
▶ National Law Reporter	1981–date	NLR
◂ Karachi Law Reports	1982–date	KLR

Constitution

Since 1947, when Pakistan was created, the country has adopted three constitutions: one in 1956, another in 1962, and the last one, which is still effective, in 1973. The latest constitution took effect on August 14, 1973. Since its adoption, it has undergone a number of amendments. In citing the constitution and its amendments, the following forms may be used:

- ▶ PAKISTAN CONST. art. 4, § 2, cl. a.
- ▶ PAKISTAN CONST. art. 63(1)(h), *substituted by* The Legal Framework Order, 2002, C.E.'s Order No. 24 of 2002 (Pak.).

Statutes

Government publications are preferred sources. The Pakistan Code (PAK. CODE), an official publication of the compilation of all laws of Pakistan, is the primary source of citation. The Code, however, is not regularly updated to reflect enactments amending the statutes. Otherwise, citation to a commercial law publisher is appropriate. The most commonly cited commercial law publications for statutes are *All-Pakistan Legal Decisions*, *National Law Reporter*, *Key Law Reports*, and *Pakistan Law Journal*. These reporters publish statutes, regulations, and decisions of the superior courts of Pakistan.

> ► The Political Parties Act, No. 5 of 1962, PAK. CODE (2d ed. 1967), v. 14, *amended by* The Political Parties (Amendment) Act, No. 22 of 1985, 1985 PLD (Statutes) 18 (Pak.).

Other codes may be cited as follows:

► Pakistan Code	PAK. CODE
► Code of Civil Procedure	PAK. CODE CIV. PROC.
► Code of Criminal Procedure	PAK. CODE CRIM. PROC.
► Pakistan Penal Code	PAK. PENAL CODE

Session laws

> ► The National Command Authority Ordinance, No. 70 of 2007, THE GAZETTE OF PAKISTAN EXTRAORDINARY, Dec. 13, 2007.

> ► The National Vocational and Technical Education Commission Ordinance, No. 5 of 2008, THE GAZETTE OF PAKISTAN EXTRAORDINARY, May 31, 2008.

Session laws of Pakistan, including amendments of former acts, are published in the official gazettes of Pakistan. The gazettes are difficult to obtain, however, and receipt is often delayed. Furthermore, the government printer does not bind the looseleaf form gazettes individually or annually. Private commercial law publishers print them in bound volumes annually, and session laws may be cited to such commercial publications as those listed previously. The official gazettes should be cited as sources for the most recent laws if a commercial publication has not yet reported them.

Regulations

Statutory Rules and Orders (S.R. & O.) is the primary official source for regulations issued under Central Acts and should be preferred to other sources. For rules after 1970, commercial publications should be cited as: ‹regulation name› (‹year›), ‹volume number› ‹reporter abbreviation› ‹first page›, ‹page(s) of specific material, if desired› (‹country abbreviation if not evident from context›).

> ► The Cost and Industrial Accountants Regulations (1966), 5 S.R. & O. 134 (Pak.).

> ► The Pakistan Legal Practitioners and Bar Council Rules (1985), 38 PLD (Statutes) 37 (Pak.).

Internet sources

http://pakistan.gov.pk (official site of the government of Pakistan)

http://www.supremecourt.gov.pk (Supreme Court of Pakistan)

http://pakistani.org/pakistan/legislation (legislation available online from selected dates)

http://www.pakistanlawsite.com (online access to Pakistani legal materials, available by subscription)

http://www.loc.gov/law/help/guide/nations/pakistan.html (Library of Congress Guide to Law Online: Pakistan)

T2.33 Philippines

(Mixed Jurisdiction)

Cases

Citation format: ‹case name›, ‹volume number›:‹docket number where applicable› ‹reporter abbreviation› ‹first page›, ‹page(s) of specific material, if desired› (‹court abbreviation›, ‹date of decision›) (‹country abbreviation if not evident from context›).

Or: ‹case name›, ‹volume number›:‹number› **O.G.** ‹first page›, ‹page(s) of specific material, if desired› (‹court abbreviation›, ‹date of decision›) (‹country abbreviation if not evident from context›).

Or: ‹case name›, **G.R. No.** ‹docket number›, ‹parallel citation, if desired› (‹court abbreviation if not evident from context›, ‹date of decision›) (‹country abbreviation if not evident from context›), *available at* ‹URL, if no parallel citation to a print source provided›.

- ► People v. Quimson, 419 PHIL. REP. 28, 33–43 (S.C., Oct. 5, 2001).
- ► Banez v. Banez, 99:30 O.G. 4775 (S.C., July 28, 2003) (Phil.).
- ► Gonzalez v. Katigbak, G.R. No. L-69500, 37 S.C.R.A. 717, 728 (July 22, 1985) (Phil.).
- ► People v. Diaz, G.R. No. 133737 (S.C., Jan. 13, 2003) (Phil.), *available at* http://sc.judiciary.gov.ph/jurisprudence/2003/ jan2003/133737.htm.

Supreme Court of the Philippines (S.C.) (highest appeals court and the only court that can produce binding precedents): Cite to an official reporter or to an unofficial reporter in the following order of preference:

► OFFICIAL GAZETTE	1902–date	O.G.
► SUPREME COURT REPORTS, ANNOTATED	1961–date	S.C.R.A.
► PHILIPPINE REPORTS	1901–date	PHIL. REP.
► The Supreme Court (available at **http://sc.judiciary.gov.ph**)	1901–date	

Constitution

Citation format: CONST. (‹promulgation year, if citing a previous constitution›), ‹article›, ‹section› (‹country abbreviation if not evident from context›).

- ► CONST. (1987), art. VI (Phil.).
- ► CONST. (1973), art. VII, sec. 1 (Phil.).
- ► CONST. (1935), art. VII, sec. 1 (Phil.).

Codes

Give the code name, subdivision if relevant, legislation type and number, and amendment information if applicable.

- ▶ ADMINISTRATIVE CODE, § 1, Exec. Ord. No. 292, as amended by Rep. Act 6682 (Phil.).
- ▶ CIVIL CODE, § 10, Rep. Act 386, as amended (Phil.).
- ▶ CORPORATION CODE, B.P.Blg 68 (Phil.).
- ▶ FAMILY CODE, Exec. Ord. 209, as amended (Phil.).
- ▶ REVISED PENAL CODE, Act No. 3815, as amended (Phil.).

Legislation

Citation format: ‹statute name›, ‹legislation type› No. ‹number›, ‹section(s) of specific material, if desired› (‹year of promulgation›), ‹reporter abbreviation› (‹series›), **Book** ‹book number›, p. ‹first page›, ‹page(s) of specific material, if desired› (‹country abbreviation if not evident from context›).

Or: ‹statute name›, **Rep. Act No.** ‹number›, ‹section(s) of specific material, if desired›, ‹volume number›:‹number› **O.G.** ‹first page›, ‹page(s) of specific material, if desired› (‹date of enactment›) (‹country abbreviation if not evident from context›).

- ▶ An Act Converting the Municipality of Sipalay, Province of Negros Occidental into a Component City To Be Known as the City of Sipalay, Rep. Act No. 9027, § 30 (1 A) (2001), V.L.Doc. (2d), Book 15, p. 138 (Phil.).
- ▶ An Act Providing for a System of Overseas Absentee Voting by Qualified Citizens of the Philippines Abroad, Appropriating Funds Therefor, and for Other Purposes, Rep. Act No. 9189, § 5(a), 99:19 O.G. 2997 (May 12, 2003) (Phil.).

Cite to a source in the following order of preference.

▶ OFFICIAL GAZETTE	1902-date	O.G.
▶ PUBLIC LAWS	1903-1937	P.L.
▶ LAWS AND RESOLUTIONS	1946-1972	LAWS & RES.
▶ VITAL LEGAL DOCUMENTS	1971-date	V.L.DOC.

Types of legislation:

▶ Acts (Nos. 1-4275)	1900-1934	Act
▶ Commonwealth Acts (Nos. 1-733)	1935-1945	Comm. Act
▶ Republic Acts (Nos. 1-6635)	1946-1972	Rep. Act
▶ Presidential Decrees (Nos. 1-2027)	1972-1982	Pres. Dec.
▶ Batas Pambansa (Nos. 1-884)	1978-1986	B.P.Blg.
▶ Republic Acts (Nos. 6636-current)	1987-date	Rep. Act

Cite to the *Official Gazette*:

▶ Executive Order	Exec. Ord.
▶ Proclamation	Proc.
▶ Memorandum Order	Mem.

Treaties

Cite the title, the date of signature or accession by the Philippines, and the date of entry into force. Cite at least one Philippine source and one other source listed in table T4, if available, or two sources listed in table T4.

► Treaty of Friendship with India, July 11, 1952 (1953), II-2 D.F.A.T.S. 1, 2 P.T.S. 797, 203 U.N.T.S. 73 (Phil.).

► Department of Foreign Affairs Treaty Series   D.F.A.T.S.
► Philippine Treaty Series   P.T.S.

Internet sources

http://www.gov.ph (Government of the Philippines)

http://elibrary.judiciary.gov.ph (The Philippine Supreme Court e-library, an online legal repository maintained by the Philippines Supreme Court)

http://www.congress.gov.ph (House of Representatives of the Philippines)

http://www.senate.gov.ph (Senate of the Philippines)

http://www.chanrobles.com/index1.htm (The Chan Robles Virtual Law Library, a website maintained by the Chan Robles Law Firm, a Philippine legal services company)

http://www.lawphil.net (The Lawphil Project, a legal website maintained by the Arellano Law Foundation, a Philippine nonprofit institution specializing in legal education)

http://www.loc.gov/law/help/guide/nations/philippines.html (Library of Congress Guide to Law Online: Philippines)

T2.34   Roman Law

(Civil Law)

Cite all Roman legal materials by the name of the individual document or fragment, as in the examples below, not by the title of a collection that includes the material. "Pr." may be used for *principio*, which refers to the first paragraph or the fragment of a title of any of the sources below. Citations to a particular English translation may be included parenthetically.

► Nov. 15.pr. (535).
► G. Inst. 1.144 (F. de Zulota trans., 1946).

Institutes of Justinian. Citation format: ‹work abbreviation› ‹book number›. ‹title number›.‹section number(s)›.

► J. Inst. 2.23.1.

Digest of Justinian. Citation format: ‹work abbreviation› ‹book number›. ‹section number›.‹item number› (‹name of author›, ‹title of work of author› ‹book number of work of author›).

► Dig. 9.2.23 (Ulpian, Ad Edictum 18).

Code of Justinian. Citation format: ‹work abbreviation› ‹book number›.‹title number›.‹section number(s)› (‹relevant emperor name(s)› ‹year(s)›).

► Code Just. 2.45.3 (Diocletian & Maximian 290/293).

Novels of Justinian. Citation format: ‹work abbreviation› ‹number of novella›. ‹section number› (‹year›).

▶ Nov. 15.1 (535).

Institutes of Gaius. Citation format: ‹work abbreviation› ‹book number›. ‹section number›.

▶ G. Inst. 1.144.

Code of Theodosius. Citation format: ‹work abbreviation› ‹book number›. ‹title›.‹section number(s)›.

▶ Code Theod. 8.4.14.

T2.35   Russian Federation

(Civil Law)

Romanization

Use the *ALA-LC Romanization Tables: Transliteration Schemes for Non-Roman Scripts*, approved by the Library of Congress and the American Library Association, available at **http://www.lcweb.loc.gov/catdir/cpso/roman.html**.

....

Cases

Citation of a ruling or explanation of the **Verkhovnyi Sud Rossiiskoi Federatsii** (Verkh. Sud RF) (Russian Federation Supreme Court): ‹ruling or decision name, with subdivisions if desired› [‹English translation of ruling or decision name, with subdivisions if desired›], ‹publication name› [‹publication abbreviation›] [‹English translation of publication name›] ‹year of publication, or full date of publication if citation is made to a newspaper›, No. ‹issue number›, p(p). ‹page(s) of specific material› (‹country abbreviation if not evident from context›).

▶ Postanovlenie Plenuma Verkhovnogo Suda RF "Nekotorye Voprosy Vozmescheniia Vreda" ot 1 noiabria 2008 g., abz. 4 p. 3. [Part 3, Section 4 of the Russian Federation Supreme Court Plenary Ruling on Selected Issues of Damage Compensation of Nov. 1, 2008], Biulleten' Verkhovnogo Suda RF [BVS] [Bulletin of the Supreme Court of the Russian Federation] 2008, No. 12, p. 17.

▶ Postanovlenie Plenuma Verkhovnogo Suda RF "Nekotorye Voprosy Vozmescheniia Vreda" ot 1 noiabria 2008 g., abz. 4 p. 3 st. 89 [Article 89, Part 3, Section 4 of the Russian Federation Supreme Court Plenary Ruling on Selected Issues of Damage Compensation of Nov. 1, 2008], Rossiiskaia Gazeta [Ros. Gaz.] Dec. 1, 2008.

For individual cases and rulings of other courts of general jurisdiction, cite to a description of the case in a Russian publication.

Konstitutsionnyi Sud Rossiiskoi Federatsii (Konst. Sud RF) (Russian Federation Constitutional Court): Cite to the Russian official gazettes *Sobranie Zakonodatel'stva Rossiiskoi Federatsii* or *Rossiiskaia Gazeta*.

Citation format: ‹ruling or decision name, with subdivisions if desired› [‹English translation of ruling or decision name, with subdivisions if desired›], Sobranie Zakonodatel'stva Rossiiskoi Federatsii [SZ RF]

[Russian Federation Collection of Legislation] ‹year of publication›, No. ‹issue number›, Item ‹item number› (‹country abbreviation if not evident from context›).

Or: ‹document name› [‹English translation of document name, with subdivisions if desired›], ROSSIISKAIA GAZETA [ROS. GAZ.] ‹date of publication› (‹country abbreviation if not evident from context›).

▸ Postanovlenie Konstitutsionnogo Suda RF ot 1 dekabria 2008 g. [Ruling of the Russian Federation Constitutional Court of Dec. 1, 2008], SOBRANIE ZAKONODATEL'STVA ROSSIISKOI FEDERATSII [SZ RF] [Russian Federation Collection of Legislation] 2008, No. 37, Item 3451.

▸ Postanovlenie Konstitutsionnogo Suda RF ot 1 dekabria 2008 g. [Ruling of the Russian Federation Constitutional Court of Dec. 1, 2008], ROSSIISKAIA GAZETA [ROS. GAZ.] Sept. 17, 2003.

Vysshii Arbitrazhnyi Sud RF (Highest Arbitration Court of the Russian Federation: hears commercial disputes between juridical persons, and reviews decisions of federal circuit arbitration courts): Cite to *Vestnik Vysshego Arbitrazhnogo Suda RF* (Vestn. VAS).

▸ VESTNIK VYSSHEGO ARBITRAZHNOGO SUDA RF [VESTN. VAS] [The Highest Arbitration Court of the RF Reporter] 2004, No. 3, p. 5

Constitutions

Citation format of the current Russian constitution: ‹name of constitution› [‹abbreviation of constitution›] [CONSTITUTION] ‹section› (‹country abbreviation if not evident from context›).

▸ KONSTITUTSIIA ROSSIISKOI FEDERATSII [KONST. RF] [CONSTITUTION] art. 27 (Russ.).

For constitutions in force before 1993, indicate the jurisdiction and the date of adoption:

▸ KONSTITUTSIIA RSFSR (1978) [KONST. RSFSR] [RSFSR CONSTITUTION].

▸ KONSTITUTSIIA SSSR (1977) [KONST. SSSR] [USSR CONSTITUTION].

Codes

Codes can be cited to their publication in Russia's official gazette or as individual documents.

Citation format: ‹code name› [‹code abbreviation›] [‹English translation of code name›] ‹article› (‹country abbreviation if not evident from context›).

▸ GRAZHDANSKII KODEKS ROSSIISKOI FEDERATSII [GK RF] [Civil Code] art. 123 (Russ.).

Russian Codes presently in force:

▸ GRAZHDANSKII KODEKS ROSSIISKOI FEDERATSII (Civil Code)	GK RF
▸ GRAZHDANSKII PROTSESSUAL'NYI KODEKS ROSSIISKOI FEDERATSII (Civil Procedural Code)	GPK RF
▸ UGOLOVNYI KODEKS ROSSIISKOI FEDERATSII (Criminal Code)	UK RF

- UGOLOVNO-PROTSESSUAL'NYI KODEKS ROSSIISKOI FEDERATSII (Criminal Procedural Code) — **UPK RF**
- NALOGOVYI KODEKS ROSSIISKOI FEDERATSII (Tax Code) — **NK RF**
- BIUDZHETNYI KODEKS ROSSIISKOI FEDERATSII (Budget Code) — **BK RF**
- KODEKS ROSSIISKOI FEDERATSII RF OB ADMINISTRATIVNYKH PRAVONARUSHENIIAKH (Code of Administrative Violations) — **KOAP RF**
- UGOLOVNO-ISPOLNITELNYI KODEKS ROSSIISKOI FEDERATSII (Correctional Code) — **UIK RF**
- ARBITRAZHNO-PROTSESSUALNYI KODEKS ROSSIISKOI FEDERATSII (Code of Arbitration Procedure) — **APK RF**
- TAMOZHENNYI KODEKS ROSSIISKOI FEDERATSII (Customs Code) — **TAK RF**
- TRUDOVOI KODEKS ROSSIISKOI FEDERATSII (Labor Code) — **TK RF**
- SEMEINYI KODEKS ROSSIISKOI FEDERATSII (Family Code) — **SK RF**
- ZHILISCHNYI KODEKS ROSSIISKOI FEDERATSII (Residential Code) — **ZHK RF**
- GRADOSTROITELNYI KODEKS ROSSIISKOI FEDERATSII (Code of Urban Architecture) — **GRAK RF**
- LESNOI KODEKS ROSSIISKOI FEDERATSII (Forestry Code) — **LK RF**
- VODNYI KODEKS ROSSIISKOI FEDERATSII (Water Code) — **VK RF**
- ZEMELNYI KODEKS ROSSIISKOI FEDERATSII (Land Code) — **ZK RF**
- VOZDUSHNYI KODEKS ROSSIISKOI FEDERATSII (Air Code) — **VOK RF**
- KODEKS TORGOVOGO MOREPLAVANIIA ROSSIISKOI FEDERATSII (Code of Merchant Shipping) — **KTM RF**

Statutes and decrees

Citation format: ‹name of law› [‹English translation of law›], ‹name of publication› [‹abbreviation of publication›] [‹name of publication in English, unless citing to Ros. Gaz.›] ‹year of publication, or full date of publication if citation is made to a newspaper›, ‹issue number›, ‹item number› (‹country abbreviation if not evident from context›).

Cite **federal'nyi konstitutsionnyi zakon** (federal constitutional laws), **federal'nyi zakon** (federal laws), **postanovleniia palat Federal'nogo Sobraniia** (resolutions of the **duma** (state legislature) and Federation Council of the Federal Assembly), **ukazy** (decrees) and **rasporiazheniia** (resolutions) of the RF President, **postanovleniia** (regulations) and **rasporiazheniia** (resolutions) of the RF Government, and rulings of the RF Constitutional Court to the official gazette where the document was published.

- Federal'nyi Zakon RF o Grazhdanstve Rossiiskoi Federatsii [Federal Law of the Russian Federation on Citizenship of the Russian Federation], SOBRANIE ZAKONODATEL'STVA ROSSIISKOI FEDERATSII [SZ RF] [Russian Federation Collection of Legislation] 2004, No. 12, Item 1151.

- Federal'nyi Zakon RF o Grazhdanstve Rossiiskoi Federatsii [Federal Law of the Russian Federation on Citizenship of the Russian Federation], ROSSIISKAIA GAZETA [ROS. GAZ.] Apr. 23, 2004.

- SOBRANIE ZAKONODATEL'STVA ROSSIISKOI FEDERATSII (Russian Federation Collection of Legislation) — 1994–date — **SZ RF**
- SOBRANIE AKTOV PRESIDENTA I PRAVITELSTVA ROSSIISKOI FEDERATSII (Collection of Acts of the President and Government of the Russian Federation) — June 1992–Apr. 1994 — **SAPP**

▸ Vedomosti S"ezda Narodnykh Deputatov Rossiiskoi Federatsii i Verkhovnogo Soveta Rossiiskoi Federatsii (Bulletin of the Congress of People's Deputies of the Russian Federation and Supreme Council of the Russian Federation)	Feb. 1992–Sept. 1993	Ved. RF
▸ Vedomosti S"ezda Narodnykh Deputatov RSFSR i Verkhovnogo Soveta RSFSR (Bulletin of the Congress of People's Deputies of the Russian Soviet Federal Socialist Republic and Supreme Council of the RSFSR)	June 1990–Jan. 1992	Ved. RSFSR
▸ Vedomosti S"ezda Narodnykh Deputatov SSSR i Verkhovnogo Soveta SSSR (Bulletin of the Congress of People's Deputies of the USSR and Supreme Council of the USSR)	June 1989–Dec. 1991	Ved. SSSR
▸ Vedomosti Verkhovnogo Soveta SSSR (Bulletin of the USSR Supreme Council)	1937–June 1989	VVS SSSR
▸ Vedomosti Verkhovnogo Soveta RSFSR (Bulletin of the USSR Supreme Council)	1938–May 1990	VVS RSFSR

Cite executive regulations for the period before 1991 to the following publications:

▸ Sobranie Postanovlenii Soveta Ministrov (Pravitel'stva) SSSR [SPP SSSR] [Collection of USSR Government Regulations]

▸ Sobranie Postanovlenii Soveta Ministrov (Pravitel'stva) RSFSR [SPP RSFSR] [Collection of RSFSR Government Regulations]

Publication of legal acts in the following government-published newspapers is recognized as official:

▸ Rossiiskaia Gazeta (Russian Newspaper)	1991–date	Ros. Gaz.
▸ Parlamentskaia Gazeta (Parliamentary Newspaper)	1998–date	Parl. Gaz.
▸ Izvestiia (News, daily newspaper)	1918–1991	Izvestiia

Citation format for acts published in a newspaper: ‹name of act› [‹name of act in English›], ‹name of publication›, ‹date of publication›, ‹page number› (‹country abbreviation if not evident from context›).

▸ Zakon SSSR o Grazhdanstve SSSR [USSR Law on Citizenship of the USSR], Izvestiia, Dec. 12, 1988, p. 3.

Cite legislative acts for the period of 1917-1937 to *Soviet Acts* or *Russian Acts*:

▸ Izvestiia Tsentral'nogo Ispolnitel'nogo Komiteta Sovetov Rabochikh i Krestianskikh Deputatov SSSR [Izv. TsIK] [Bulletin of the USSR Central Executive Committee of the Councils of Workers' and Peasants' Deputies]

▸ Izvestiia Vserossiiskogo Tsentralnogo Ispolnitel'nogo Komiteta Sovetov Rabochikh, Soldatskikh i Krestianskikh Deputatov [Izv. VTsIK] [Bulletin of the All-Russian Central Executive Committee of the Councils of Workers', Soldiers', and Peasants' Deputies]

Citation format for laws of the Russian Empire: ‹name of law› [‹English translation of law›] ‹name of publication› [‹abbreviation of publication›] [‹name of publication in English›], ‹volume number›, ‹year of publication›, ‹item number› (‹country abbreviation if not evident from context›).

> ▶ Zakon o Poseleniiakh na Kitaiskoi Granitse [Law on the Chinese Border Settlements] Polnoe Sobranie Zakonov Rossiiskoi Imperii [PSZ] [Complete Collection of Laws of the Russian Empire] II, v. XXXXIX, 1874, No. 53418.

Administrative regulations

For the **postanovlenie** (regulations), **instruktsiia** (instructions), **raz'iasneniia** (clarifications), **pis'mo** (letters), **ukazanie** (directives), and other legal acts of ministries, state committees, and other government agencies, follow the citation format used for official gazettes. Cite to:

> ▶ Biulleten' Normativnykh Aktov Ministerstv i Vedomstv Rossiiskoi Federatsii [BNA] [Bulletin of Legal Acts of Ministries and Agencies of the Russian Federation]

> ▶ Biulleten' Normativnykh Aktov Federal'nykh Organov Ispolnitel'noi Vlasti [BNA] [Bulletin of Legal Acts of Federal Executive Authorities]

Acts of executive agencies, which were not officially published, are cited by their name, date of issuance, and Ministry of Justice registration number:

> ▶ Sanitary Zones and Sanitary Certification of Enterprises, Instruction 2.2.1/2.11-03, approved by the Chief Sanitary Physician of the Russian Federation, Mar. 20, 2008, registered by the Ministry of Justice, Apr. 29, 2008, No. 4459 (Russ.).

Legislative hearings

Citation format for parliamentary hearings conducted by the State Duma: ‹hearing title› [‹English translation of hearing title›] ‹publication name› [‹publication abbreviation›] [‹English translation of publication name›] Issue ‹issue number›, ‹period of coverage›, p(p). ‹page(s) of specific material› (‹country abbreviation if not evident from context›).

> ▶ O Razvitii Sporta v Rossiiskoi Federatsii [On Sport Development in the Russian Federation] Parlamentskie Slushaniia v Gosudarstvennoi Dume [Parl. Slush.] [Parliamentary Hearings in the State Duma] Issue XI, Jan.–June 2003, p. 17 (Russ.).

Citation format for hearings conducted by the Council of Federation, the upper chamber of the Russian legislature, are cited to the particular publication that reported the hearings or to the Council's official website:

> ▶ Sostoianie Zakonodatelnoi Bazy Okhrany Zdorov'ia, Slushaniia v Sovete Federatsii RF [State of Legislation on Health Care, Hearings in the RF Federation Council], Mar. 25, 2004 (Russ.), *available at* http://council.gov.ru/lawmaking/parliament/item/5.

Periodicals

Government publications

▶ Vestnik Konstitutsionnogo Suda RF	VKS
▶ Vestnik Tsentralnoi Izbiratelnoi Komissii RF	Vestn. TsIK
▶ Biulleten' Schetnoi Palaty RF	BSP

Newspapers

► Rossiiskaia Gazeta	Ros. Gaz.
► Rossiiskie Vesti	Ros. Vesti
► Ekonomika i Zhizn	Ekon. i Zh.
► Finansovye Izvestiia	Fin. Izv.
► Kommersant	Kommers.
► Parlamentskaia Gazeta	Parl. Gaz.

Magazines

► Gosudarstvo i Pravo	Gos. i Pravo
► Pravovedenie	Prav.
► Zhurnal Rossiiskogo Prava	Zh. R. P.
► Zakonnost	Zakonnost
► Vestnik Moskovskogo Universiteta	Vestn. MGU
► Khoziaistvo i Pravo	Khoz. i Pravo

Treaties

► Biulleten' Mezhdunarodnykh Dogovorov (Bulletin of International Treaties)	Mar. 1993–date	BMD
► Sbornik Mezhdunarodnykh Dogovorov (Collection of International Treaties)	1980–Feb. 1993	SMD
► Sbornik Deistvuiuschikh Dogovorov	1924–1979	SDD
► Soglashenii i Konventsii, Zakliuchennykh s Inostrannymi Gosudarstvami (Collection of Treaties, Agreements, and Conventions Concluded with Foreign States)		SKZIG

Internet sources

http://www.systema.ru (official online versions of legislation)

http://www.kremlin.ru/eng (official translations of presidential acts into English on the president's website)

http://www.loc.gov/law/help/russia.html (Library of Congress Guide to Law Online: Russia)

T2.36   South Africa

(Mixed Jurisdiction)

Cases

Citation format: ‹case name, in italics› ‹year of publication› (‹volume number›) ‹reporter abbreviation› ‹first page› (‹court abbreviation›) at ‹page(s) of specific material, if desired› ‹paragraph, if desired› (‹country abbreviation if not evident from context›).

► *Fraser v. Naude* 1999 (1) SA 1 (CC) at 78 H (S. Afr.).

When citing to a case in which the court numbers the paragraphs, which is a style that courts are increasingly adopting, cite to the paragraph number.

► *Fraser v. Naude* 1999 (1) SA 1 (CC) at 78 para. 10 (S. Afr.).

1994–date:

Constitutional Court (CC) (highest appellate court and occasionally court of first instance for all constitutional questions), **Appellate Division** (A) (highest appellate court for nonconstitutional matters, especially for decisions after 1994), and **Provincial & Local Divisions of Supreme Court** (original and appellate jurisdiction for all matters): Cite to SA or BCLR, if therein.

▸ South African Law Reports	1947–date	SA
▸ Butterworths Constitutional Law Reports	1994–date	BCLR
▸ South African Criminal Law Reports	1990–date	SACR
▸ All South African Law Reports	1996–date	All SA

1910–1994:

Judicial Committee of Privy Council (P.C.) (until 1950): Cite to Eng. Rep., if therein (see table T2.42 United Kingdom). **Appellate Division** (A) (highest appellate court from Provincial & Local Divisions in all matters since 1950; highest domestic appellate court in all matters prior to 1950): Cite to AD, if therein.

Provincial and Local Divisions of the Supreme Court: Supreme Court (Appellate Division & Supreme Court) of Transkei (1976–1994), **Supreme Court (Appellate Division & General Division) of Bophuthatswana** (1977–1994), **Supreme Court of Venda** (1979–1994), and **Supreme Court (Appellate Division & General Division) of Ciskei** (1981–1994): Cite to SA, if therein.

▸ South African Law Reports	1947–date	SA
▸ South African Criminal Law Reports	1990–date	SACR
▸ Prentice-Hall Weekly Legal Series	1923–date	PH
▸ Bophuthatswana Law Reports (six volumes)	1977–1990	BSC
▸ Appellate Division Reports	1910–1946	AD
▸ Cape Provincial Division Reports	1910–1946	CPD
▸ Eastern Districts Local Division Reports	1910–1946	EPD
▸ Griqualand West Local Division Reports/Griqualand High Court Reports	1882–1945	GWL
▸ Orange Free State Provincial Division Reports	1910–1946	OPD
▸ Transvaal Provincial Division Reports	1910–1946	TPD
▸ Witwatersrand Local Division Reports	1910–1946	WLD
▸ Natal Provincial Division Reports	1933–1946	NPD
▸ Natal Law Reports (New Series)	1879–1932	NLR
▸ Industrial Law Reports	1980–date	ILJ
▸ South African Tax Cases	1926–date	SATC
▸ Bantu Appeal Court Reports	1961–date	BAC
▸ Native Appeal Court Reports	1952–1961	NAC

Prior to 1910:

▸ Cape Supreme Court Reports	1828–1910	SC
▸ Reports of the Eastern Districts of the Cape of Good Hope	1891–1909	EDC
▸ Orange River Colony Reports	1903–1909	ORC
▸ Transvaal Supreme Court Reports	1902–1909	TS
▸ Witwatersrand High Court Reports	1902–1909	TH

Constitution

Unlike citations to statutes, citations to the constitution and its amending laws do not include act numbers. Titles of laws amending the constitution reflect their chronological order.

Constitution of the Republic of South Africa Act, 1996:

▶ S. AFR. CONST., 1996.

Constitution of the Republic of South Africa First Amendment Act of 1997:

▶ S. AFR. CONST., First Amendment Act of 1997.

Constitution of the Republic of South Africa Act 200 of 1993 (Interim Constitution):

▶ S. AFR. (INTERIM) CONST., 1993.

Statutes

Citation format: ‹Act name› ‹Act number› of ‹year of passage› ‹section(s), if applicable› (‹country abbreviation if not evident from context›).

▶ Interpretation Act 33 of 1957 § 1 (S. Afr.).

Statutory compilations

▶ Butterworths Statutes of the Republic of South Africa	1910–date	BSRSA
▶ Jutas Statutes of the Republic of South Africa	1991–date	JSRSA

Other legislation

Provincial ordinances (collected by province by year) (1910–1994):

▶ Road Traffic Ordinance 21 of 1966 (Cape Province) (S. Afr.).

Laws of provincial legislatures (1994–date):

▶ Western Cape Colleges Law 12 of 1994 (S. Afr.).

Bills, proclamations, regulations, and other government notices are collected in *Government Gazettes* (GG).

Bills:

▶ Prevention of Family Violence Bill, 1993, Bill 144-93 (GN) (S. Afr.).

Regulations:

▶ Government Notice (GN) R3/1981 (S. Afr.).
▶ GN R3 of 2 Jan. 1981 (S. Afr.).

Proclamations:

▶ Proc R255/1977 (S. Afr.).
▶ Proc R255 in GG5766 of 7 Oct. 1971 (S. Afr.).

Parliamentary debates

Cite to *Hansard's Parliamentary Reports*:

▶ House of Assembly *Hansard* 9 Dec. 1993 Col 14768 (S. Afr.).

Law Commission Papers

- ▶ SA Law Commission Issue Paper 3 Customary Marriages (Aug. 1996) (S. Afr.).

- ▶ SA Law Commission Discussion Paper 76 Conflicts of Law (Apr. 1998) (S. Afr.).

Periodicals

▶ South African Law Journal (continues Cape Law Journal)	1900-date	SALJ
▶ Cape Law Journal	1884-1900	
▶ Acta Juridica, Comparative and International Law Journal of South Africa		CILSA
▶ De Jure		
▶ Industrial Law Journal (available by subscription at **http://www.jutalaw.co.za**)		ILJ
▶ South African Journal on Human Rights (available by subscription at **http://www.jutalaw.co.za**)		SAJHR
▶ South African Mercantile Law Journal		SAMLJ
▶ South African Yearbook of International Law		SAYIL

Internet sources

http://www.lexis.com (direct access by subscription to the digital version of *Butterworth Statutes of South Africa*, *Butterworth South African Constitutional Law Reports*, and *South Africa Tax Cases*)

http://www.polity.org.za (full text of acts (1993-date), bills and draft bills (1995-date), and more)

http://www.parliament.gov.za (South African Parliament official website)

http://www.info.gov.za/documents/constitution (Constitution of the Republic of South Africa, 1996)

http://www.constitutionalcourt.org.za (South African Constitutional Court (1995-date))

http://www.supremecourtofappeal.gov.za (Supreme Court of Appeal (1999-date))

http://www.saflii.org/za/cases/ZALCC (Land Claims Court (1996-date))

http://www.saflii.org/za/cases/ZALAC (Labour Appeal Court (1997-date))

http://www.dfa.gov.za/foreign (list of treaties to which South Africa is a party provided by the Department of International Relations and Cooperation)

http://www.satreatyseries.net/trindex.htm (treaties to which South Africa is a party and ratification information provided by a private website, the South African Cyber Treaty Series)

http://www.loc.gov/law/help/guide/nations/southafrica.html (Library of Congress Guide to Law Online: South Africa)

T2.37 South Korea

(Civil Law)

Romanization

For romanization of Korean sources, use the official romanization system released by the Korean government in 2000, available at **http://www.korean.go. kr/eng/roman/roman.jsp**. Available but not used here are the *ALA-LC Romanization Tables: Transliteration Schemes for Non-Roman Scripts* that were approved by the Library of Congress and the American Library Association, which continue to follow the McCune-Reischauer system as of 2008, available at **http://www.loc.gov/catdir/cpso/romanization/korean.pdf**.

Cases

Citation format: ‹English translation of court name› [‹English court abbreviation›], ‹case number›, ‹date of decision›, (‹volume number› ‹reporter abbreviation›, ‹first page›, ‹page(s) of specific material, if desired›) (‹country abbreviation if not evident from context›).

Reporter abbreviation, volume number, and page numbers are not common in Korean citation practice, but if available, add such information.

- ▶ Supreme Court [S. Ct.], 96Da47517, Sept. 9, 1997 (S. Kor.).
- ▶ Constitutional Court [Const. Ct.], 2004Hun-Ma554 & 556 (consol.), Oct. 21, 2004, (2004 DKCC, 11) (S. Kor.).
- ▶ Seoul High Court [Seoul High Ct.], 95Na14840, Sept. 18, 1966 (S. Kor.).
- ▶ Incheon District Court [Dist. Ct.], 2004Ga-Hap8803, Dec. 14, 2004 (S. Kor.).

Daebeobwon (S. Ct.) (Supreme Court): Cite to JIP, GONG, or SCD, if therein; **Hunbeob jaepanso** (Const. Ct.) (Constitutional Court: court of original and final jurisdiction to determine the constitutionality of laws): Cite to KCCR, KCCG, or DKCC, if therein; **Godeung beobwon** (High Ct.) (high courts) and **Jibang beobwon** (Dist. Ct.) (district courts): Cite to GODEUNG JIP, GAKGONG, or HAJIP, if therein, adding the location of the court before the name.

Specialized jurisdiction: **Teukheo beobwon** (Pat. Ct.) (Patent Court), **Haengjeong beobwon** (Admin. Ct.) (administrative courts), and **Gajeong beobwon** (Fam. Ct.) (family courts).

Sources

Cases are available on the supreme court's website at **http://eng.scourt.go.kr**.

Print reporters published by the Court Administration:

▶ Daebeobwon palyejip	1980–date	JIP
▶ Daebeobwon pangyuljip	1957–1980	JIP
▶ Panrye gongbo	1996–date	GONG
▶ Supreme Court Decisions	2004–date	SCD
▶ Gagkeup beobwon pangyul gongbo	2003–date	GAKGONG
▶ Godeung beobwon palyejip	1960–2003	GODEUNG JIP
▶ Hageupsim pangyuljip	1984–2004	HAJIP

► Hunbeob jaepanso palyejip	1989–date	KCCR
► Hunbeob jaepanso gongbo	1993–date	KCCG
► Decisions of the Korean Constitutional Court	2000–date	DKCC

Constitution

Current constitution

► Daehanminkuk Hunbeob	1987	Hunbeob

> ► Daehanminkuk Hunbeob [Hunbeob] [Constitution] art. 4 (S. Kor.).

Previous constitutions

The constitution was amended nine times as of 1987. Among them, five amendments were total amendments. Cite previous constitutions by year.

Citation format for previous constitutions: ‹"Amended" if applicable› ‹year› Daehan minkuk hunbeob [Hunbeob] [Constitution] ‹article› (‹date of amendment if applicable›) (‹country abbreviation if not evident from context›).

> ► 1948 Daehan minkuk hunbeob [Hunbeob] [Constitution] (July 17, 1948) (S. Kor.).

> ► 1960 Daehan minkuk hunbeob [Hunbeob] [Constitution] (June 15, 1960) (S. Kor.).

> ► 1962 Daehan minkuk hunbeob [Hunbeob] [Constitution] (Dec. 26, 1962) (S. Kor.).

> ► 1972 Daehan minkuk hunbeob [Hunbeob] [Constitution] (Dec. 27, 1972) (S. Kor.).

> ► 1980 Daehan minkuk hunbeob [Hunbeob] [Constitution] (Oct. 27, 1980) (S. Kor.).

> ► 1962 Daehan minkuk hunbeob [Hunbeob] [Constitution] art. 3 (S. Kor.).

> ► Amended 1948 Daehan minkuk Hunbeob [Hunbeob] [Constitution] (July 7, 1952) (S. Kor.).

Statutes and decrees

Citation format for **beobyul/beob** (statutes): ‹romanized Korean statute name› [‹English translation of statute name›], **Act No.** ‹statute number›, ‹date of promulgation›, ‹article› (‹country abbreviation if not evident from context›).

> ► Minbeob [Civil Act], Act. No. 471, Feb. 22, 1958, art. 844 (S. Kor.).

> ► Sangbeob [Commercial Act], Act. No. 1000, Jan. 20, 1962, art. 174 (S. Kor.), *translated in* Statutes of the Republic of Korea 4, 35 (Korea Legislation Res. Inst. 1997 & Supp. 34).

> ► Hyongsa sosong beob [Criminal Procedure Act], Act No. 341, Sept. 23, 1954, *amended by* Act. No. 7965, July 19, 2006 (S. Kor.).

> ► Dokjeom gyuje mit gongjeong geooraeae gwanhan beobyul [Monopoly Regulation and Fair Trade Act], Act. No. 8666, Oct. 17, 2007, art. 1 (S. Kor.).

If only a translation of a law was consulted, the romanized Korean name of the law can be omitted.

▶ Management of Drinking Water Act, Act. No. 8368, Apr. 11, 2007, art. 3, *amended by* Act. No. 8629, Aug. 3, 2007 (S. Kor.), *translated in* 18 STATUTES OF THE REPUBLIC OF KOREA 451–52 (Korea Legislation Research Inst. 1997 & Supp. 40).

Myungryung/ryung (decrees) include **daetongryung ryung** (presidential decrees), **chongri ryung** (Prime Minister decrees), and **coo ryung** (Ministry decrees).

Citation format: ‹romanized Korean decree name› [‹English translation of decree name›], ‹type of decree› No. ‹decree number›, ‹date of promulgation› (‹country abbreviation if not evident from context›).

▶ Dokjeom gyuje mit gongjeong geooraeae gwanhan beobyul sihaengryung [Enforcement Decree of the Monopoly Regulation and Fair Trade Act], Presidential Decree No. 12979, Apr. 14, 1990, *as amended* (S. Kor.).

▶ Bohumup beob sihaeng gyuchik [Enforcement Rules on the Insurance Business Act], Prime Minister Decree No. 885, Aug. 4, 2008, *as amended* (S. Kor.).

▶ Geonchook beob sihaeng gyuchik [Enforcement Rules on the Building Act], Ministry Decree No. 594, Dec. 13, 2007, *as amended* (S. Kor.).

If only a translation of a decree was consulted, the romanized Korean name of the decree can be omitted.

▶ Enforcement Decree of the Labor Standards Act, Presidential Decree No. 20142, June 29, 2007, art. 2 (S. Kor.), *translated in* 18 STATUTES OF THE REPUBLIC OF KOREA 40 (Korea Legislation Research Inst. 1997 & Supp. 39).

Internet sources

http://www.moj.go.kr (homepage of the Ministry of Justice, with English pages)

http://glaw.scourt.go.kr/jbsonw/jbson.do (the Korean Supreme Court's comprehensive database of cases, laws, and articles in Korean)

http://english.ccourt.go.kr (English summaries of recent decisions and major decisions by the Constitutional Court of Korea)

http://eng.scourt.go.kr/eng/decisions/guide.jsp (English summaries of selected decisions of the Supreme Court of Korea)

http://korea.na.go.kr (the Korean National Assembly's website with English summaries of recently enacted laws)

http://elaw.klri.re.kr/indexE.jsp (English translations of Korean laws published by the Korea Legislation Research Institute, available by subscription)

http://english.president.go.kr/government/branch/branch.php (the Korean Office of the President's website with links to the executive branch's English websites)

http://www.loc.gov/law/help/guide/nations/southkorea.html (Library of Congress Guide to Law Online: South Korea)

T2.38   Spain

(Civil Law)

. . . .

Cases

Citation format: ‹court decision abbreviation›, ‹date of decision› (‹reporter abbreviation›, **No.** ‹decision number›, **p.** ‹first page, if desired›) (‹country abbreviation if not evident from context›).

For the court decision abbreviation, use "**S.**" for sentencia (decision), followed by the court abbreviation.

▶ S.T.S., Feb. 5, 1993 (R.A.J., No. 876, p. 1135) (Spain).

Constitutional court: Tribunal Constitucional (T.C.) (highest court on constitutional matters; separate from the judiciary): Cite to **B.J.C.** or **R.T.C.**, if therein; otherwise, cite to **S.T.C.**

▶ Boletín de Jurisprudencia Constitucional	B.J.C.
▶ Repertorio Aranzadi del Tribunal Constitucional	R.T.C.
▶ Sentencias del Tribunal Constitucional Sistematizadas y Comentadas	S.T.C.

Ordinary courts: Tribunal Supremo (T.S.) (highest court of ordinary jurisdiction: divided into five chambers: civil, criminal, administrative, military, and labor), **Audiencia Nacional** (A.N.) (national appellate courts of ordinary jurisdiction: divided into three chambers), **Audiencia Provincial** (A.P.) (provincial appellate courts in criminal and civil matters sitting in the capital of each province), **Tribunal Superior de Justicia** (T.S.J.) (highest court in the autonomous regions: divided into four chambers with jurisdiction over cases arising from regional law), **Juzgado de Primera Instancia** (Juz. Prim.) (trial courts for both civil and criminal matters sitting in the major town of each judicial district), **Juzgado de lo Contencioso Administrativo** (Juz. Cont. Adm.) (administrative courts), **Juzgado de lo Social** (Juz. Soc.) (labor courts), **Juzgado de Menores** (Juz. Men.) (juvenile courts), **Juzgado de Vigilancia** (Juz. Vig.) (prison administration courts), **Juzgado de Paz** (Juz. Paz) (justices of the peace with jurisdiction over minor civil and criminal matters), and **Tribunal Militar** (military courts: sentences subject to appeal to the **Tribunal Supremo** and the **Tribunal Constitucional**): Cite to **J.T.S.** or **R.J.**, if therein; otherwise, cite to **R.G.D.**

▶ Jurisprudencia del Tribunal Supremo	J.T.S.
▶ Repertorio Aranzadi de Jurisprudencia	R.J.
▶ Revista General de Derecho	R.G.D.

. . . .

Constitution

▶ Constitución Española	C.E.

Cite to the *Boletín Oficial del Estado* (B.O.E.).

Citation format: ‹constitution name or, for short form, abbreviation›, **B.O.E. n.** ‹number›, ‹date› (‹country abbreviation if not evident from context›).

▶ C.E., B.O.E. n. 311, Dec. 29, 1978 (Spain).

Codes

► Código Civil (Civil Code)	C.C.
► Código de Comercio (Commercial Code)	C. Com.
► Código Penal (Criminal Code)	C.P.
► Ley de Enjuiciamiento Civil (Code of Civil Procedure)	L.E. Civ.
► Ley de Enjuiciamiento Criminal (Code of Criminal Procedure)	L.E. Crim.
► Ley de Procedimiento Administrativo (Administrative Procedure Act)	L.P.A.
► Ley de Procedimiento Laboral (Labor Procedure Code)	L.P.L.
► Ley Orgánica del Poder Judicial (Law on the Judiciary)	L.O.P.J.
► Ley de la Jurisdicción Contencioso-Administrativa (Law on Administrative Jurisdiction)	L.J.C.A.
► Ley Orgánica del Régimen Electoral General (Electoral Organization Act)	L.O.R.E.G.
► Ley Orgánica del Tribunal Constitucional (Constitutional Court Organization Act)	L.O.T.C.

Statutes and decrees

Citation format: ‹statute name› ‹subdivision, if desired› (‹compilation abbreviation› ‹year of enactment›, ‹number assigned to statute›) (‹country abbreviation if not evident from context›).

The rank of the statute (e.g., **L.O.**, **R.D.**, **R.D.L.**, **R.D.-Ley**) is not included in the citation.

> ► Labor Procedure Law art. X (R.C.L. 1990, 922) (Spain).

Cite a **Ley Ordinaria** (L.O.), **Real Decreto** (R.D.), **Real Decreto Legislativo** (R.D.L.), or **Real Decreto Ley** (R.D.-Ley) to B.O.E. or R.C.L., if therein.

► Boletín Oficial del Estado (Official Gazette)	B.O.E.
► Repertorio Aranzadi Cronológico de Legislación	R.C.L.

> ► B.O.E. 1985, 166

> ► R.C.L. 1985, 1463

Internet sources

http://www.boe.es (the Official Gazette; free access to legislation)

http://www.tribunalconstitucional.es (official site of the Constitutional Court; free access to court decisions)

http://www.poderjudicial.es (official site of Tribunal Supremo; free access to court decisions)

http://www.aranzadi.es (private legal publisher of legislation, court decisions, and journals; paid subscription and free access to latest information)

http://www.elderecho.com (database of legal information; paid subscription)

http://laleydigital.laley.es (database of legal information; paid subscription)

http://www.tirant.com (database of legal information; paid subscription)

http://www.unirioja.es (Revista Electrónica de Derecho de la Universidad de la Rioja (University of Rioja Electronic Law Review); free access)

http://criminet.ugr.es/recpc (Revista Electrónica de Ciencia Penal y Criminología (Electronic Law Review of Criminal Science and Criminology); free access)

http://www.cica.es/aliens/gimadus (Revista Electrónica de Derecho Ambiental (Electronic Law Review of Environmental Law); free access)

http://vlex.com/jurisdictions/ES (database of legal information; paid subscription)

http://www.jurisweb.com (legal portal; paid subscription)

http://constitucion.rediris.es/principal/RevistasElectronicasJuridicas-Espannolas.html (revistas electrónicas de derecho constitucional (constitutional law journals); free access)

http://www.loc.gov/law/help/guide/nations/spain.html (Library of Congress Guide to Law Online: Spain)

T2.39   Sweden
(Civil Law)

Swedish constitutions, codes, and statutes are usually divided into chapters, and are always organized by sections (§). Note that a section in Swedish is called *paragraf*, which may cause some confusion.

Cases

Ordinary jurisdiction

Citation format for a supreme court case: ‹publication name› [‹publication abbreviation›] [‹English translation of court name›] ‹date of decision in year-month-day format› p. ‹first page› ‹case number› (‹country abbreviation if not evident from context›).

► Nytt Juridiskt Arkiv [NJA] [Supreme Court] 2004-01-28 p. 19 T4320-02 (Swed.).

► Nytt Juridiskt Arkiv [NJA] [Supreme Court] 2004-01-28 T4320-02 (Swed.), *available at* http://www.domstol.se/Domstolar/hogstadomstolen/Avgoranden/2004/2004-01-28_T_4320-02_dom.pdf.

Högsta Domstolen (HD) (Supreme Court): Cite to NJA; **Hovrätt** (HovR) (Court of Appeals) and **Tingsrätt** (TR) (district courts: courts of first instance in civil and criminal matters).

► Nytt Juridiskt Arkiv (Supreme Court Reports)   NJA

Administrative jurisdiction

Citation format for a Supreme Administrative Court case: ‹publication name› [‹publication abbreviation›] [‹English translation of court name›] ‹date of decision in year-month-day format› ref ‹report number› (‹country abbreviation if not evident from context›).

► Regeringsrättens årsbok [RÅ] [Supreme Administrative Court] 2004-05-06 ref 34 (Swed.).

Regeringsrätten (RegR) (Supreme Administrative Court): Cite to RÅ; **Fastighetsdomstolar** (VD) (land courts), **Vattendomstolar** (VD) (water courts), **Arbetsdomstolen** (AD) (labor courts), **Marknadsdomstolen** (MD) (Market Court), **Länsrätten** (LR) (county administrative courts), and **Kammarrätten** (KR) (administrative courts of appeal).

▸ Regeringsrättens årsbok   RÅ

Constitutions

Citation format: ‹name of constitution› [‹abbreviation of constitution›] [CONSTITUTION] ‹chapter number›:‹section number› (‹country abbreviation if not evident from context›).

▸ REGERINGSFORMEN [RF] [CONSTITUTION] 5:1 (Swed.).

▸ REGERINGSFORMEN (Instrument of Government)   RF
▸ SUCCESSIONSORDNINGEN (Act of Succession)   SO
▸ TRYCKFRIHETSFÖRORDNINGEN (Freedom of the Press Act)   TF
▸ YTTRANDEFRIHETSGRUNDLAGEN (Freedom of Expression Act)   YGL

Codes

The National Code of Sweden of 1734 is still formally in use but is not a systematic codification as is, for example, the Civil Code of France. The National Code serves to collect and organize laws on the same legal topic, but many statutes fall outside the scope of the National Code.

Citation format: ‹code name› [‹code abbreviation›] [‹English translation of code name›] ‹chapter number›:‹section number› (‹country abbreviation if not evident from context›).

▸ ÄKTENSKAPSBALK [ÄKTB] [MARRIAGE CODE] 1:1 (Swed.).

▸ ÄKTENSKAPSBALK (Marriage Code)   ÄktB
▸ FÖRÄLDRABALK (Code Relating to Parents, Guardians, and Children)   FB
▸ ÄRVDABALK (Inheritance Code)   ÄB
▸ JORDABALK (Land Law Code)   JB
▸ MILJÖBALK (Environmental Code)   MB
▸ FASTIGHETSBILDNINGSLAG (Real Property Formation Act)   FBL
▸ BYGGNINGABALK (Book on Building)   BB
▸ HANDELSBALK (Book on Commerce)   HB
▸ SKADESTÅNDSLAG (Tort Liability Act)   SkadesL
▸ KONKURSLAG (Bankruptcy Code)   KonkL
▸ RÄTTEGÅNGSBALKEN (Code of Civil Procedure)   RB
▸ BROTTSBALKEN (Criminal Code)   BrB
▸ UTSÖKNINGSBALK (Enforcement Code)   UB

Statutes

Citation format: ‹chapter number› ch. ‹section number› § ‹statute name› (‹publication name› [‹publication abbreviation›] ‹year›:‹law number›) (‹country abbreviation if not evident from context›).

▸ LAG OM UTGIVNING AV ELEKTRONISKA PENGAR (Svensk författningssamling [SFS] 2002:149) (Swed.).

Note that to cite a specific subdivision from a statute, the subdivision (section and/or chapter number) comes before the statute name.

For short forms, give only the publication abbreviation:

- ► 2 ch. 3 § VAPENLAG (SFS 1996:1830) (Swed.).
- ► 1 § LIVSMEDELSLAG (SFS 2006:804) (Swed.).

Legislative history

Government bills, government report series, and parliamentary committee reports are part of the legislative history of an enactment.

Citation format for a government bill: Proposition [Prop.] ‹Parliament session years›:‹bill number› ‹government bill name› [government bill] (‹country abbreviation if not evident from context›).

- ► Proposition [Prop.] 2004/2005:19 Beskattning av utomlands bosatta [government bill] (Swed.).

Citation format for government report series: Statens Offentliga Utredningar [SOU] ‹year›:‹number› ‹government report name› [government report series] (‹country abbreviation if not evident from context›).

- ► Statens Offentliga Utredningar [SOU] 2004:95 Nya regler om prospekt m.m. [government report series] (Swed.).

Citation format for parliamentary committee reports: ‹name of the parliamentary committee› ‹parliament session years›:‹committee and report acronym› [parliamentary committee report] (‹country abbreviation if not evident from context›).

- ► Sammansatta konstitutions- och utrikesutskottets betänkande 2006/2007:KUU1 [parliamentary committee report] (Swed.).

Periodicals

- ► Svensk Juristtidning　　　　　　　SvJT

Internet sources

http://www.riksdagen.se (Riksdagen (Swedish Parliament))

http://www.regeringen.se (Regeringen (Swedish Government))

http://www.domstol.se (Sveriges Domstolar (Swedish courts))

http://www.lagrummet.se (Offentliga förvaltningens webplats för rättslig information (Public Administration's website for legal information))

http://www.hogstadomstolen.se (Högsta Domstolen (Swedish Supreme Court))

http://www.advokatsamfundet.se (Sveriges Advokatsamfund (Swedish Bar Association))

http://www.loc.gov/law/help/sweden.html (Library of Congress Guide to Law Online: Sweden)

T2.40   Switzerland

(Civil Law)

For federal statutes and legislative materials, parallel German and French citations may be used, and, if available and pertinent, Italian citations. Alternatively, give all citations in the language most relevant to the discussion in which the materials are cited. Cite cases in the language in which the decision is issued.

....

Cases

Bundesgericht (BGer)/**Tribunal fédéral** (TF)/**Tribunale federale** (TF) (Federal Supreme Court): Cite to BGE/ATF/DTF, or SJ, if therein; otherwise, cite to PRA. or JDT.

Citation format: ‹court name› [‹court abbreviation›] [‹English translation of court name›] ‹date of decision›, ‹volume number› ‹reporter or periodical name› [‹reporter or periodical abbreviation›] ‹part number› ‹page number› (‹country abbreviation if not evident from context›).

In subsequent citations in short form, use only the court and reporter abbreviations rather than their full names and English translations.

▶ Bundesgericht [BGer] [Federal Supreme Court] Jan. 28, 1999, 125 ENTSCHEIDUNGEN DES SCHWEIZERISCHEN BUNDESGERICHTS [BGE] I 96 (Switz.).

The following official publication is the same source, and may be cited according to the language in which the court has written the particular decision:

▶ ENTSCHEIDUNGEN DES SCHWEIZERISCHEN BUNDESGERICHTS (AMTLICHE SAMMLUNG)	1875-date	BGE
▶ ARRÊTS DU TRIBUNAL FÉDÉRAL SUISSE (RECUEIL OFFICIEL)	1875-date	ATF
▶ DECISIONI DEL TRIBUNALE FEDERALE SVIZZERO (RACCOLTA UFFICIALE)	1875-date	DTF

Volumes by subject matter since 1995:

▶ Constitutional Cases	BGE/ATF/DTF I
▶ Administrative and international law cases	BGE/ATF/DTF II
▶ Civil and bankruptcy cases	BGE/ATF/DTF III
▶ Criminal cases	BGE/ATF/DTF IV
▶ Social security cases	BGE/ATF/DTF V

The following publications may also be useful.

▶ DIE PRAXIS DES BUNDESGERICHTS (BASEL)	1912-date	PRA.
▶ JOURNAL DES TRIBUNAUX	1854-date	JDT
▶ LA SEMAINE JUDICIAIRE	1879-date	SJ

Bundesstrafgericht (BStR)/**Tribunal pénal fédéral** (TPF)/**Tribunale penale federale** (TPF) (Federal Criminal Court, since April 1, 2004): Cite to TPF, if therein.

Citation format: ‹court name› [‹court abbreviation›] [‹English translation of court name›] ‹date of decision›, ‹reporter name› [‹reporter abbreviation›] ‹year of reporter volume›, ‹page number› (‹country abbreviation if not evident from context›).

> ► Bundesstrafgericht [BStR] [Federal Criminal Court] Jan. 9, 2006,
> ENTSCHEIDUNGEN DES SCHWEIZERISCHEN BUNDESSTRAFGERICHTS
> [TPF] 2006, 217 (Switz.).

Cite to the following publication, according to the language of the court decision:

► ENTSCHEIDE DES SCHWEIZERISCHEN BUNDESSTRAFGERICHTS	**TPF**
► ARRÊTS DU TRIBUNAL FÉDÉRAL PÉNAL SUISSE	**TPF**
► DECISIONI DEL TRIBUNALE FEDERALE PENALE SVIZZERO	**TPF**

Bundesverwaltungsgericht (BVGE)/**Tribunal administratif fédéral** (TAF)/**Tribunale amministrativo federale** (TAF) (Federal Administrative Court, since January 1, 2007): Cite to **BVGE/ATAF/DTAF**, if therein.

► Amtliche Sammlung der Entscheide des schweizerischen Bundesverwaltungsgerichts	BVGE
► Recueil officiel des Arrêts du Tribunal fédéral administratif suisse	ATAF
► Decisioni del Tribunale amministrativo federale svizzero	DTAF

Federal administrative agencies: Cite decisions to **VPB/JAAC/GAAC**, if therein, using the citation format for periodicals.

► VERWALTUNGSPRAXIS DER BUNDESBEHÖRDEN	**VPB**
► JURISPRUDENCE DES AUTORITÉS ADMINISTRATIVES DE LA CONFÉDÉRATION	**JAAC**
► GIURISPRUDENZA DELLE AUTORITÀ AMMINISTRATIVE DELLA CONFEDERAZIONE	**GAAC**

From 1987 until 2006, VPB was published in hard copy. From 2007 onward, it has been published only electronically. The VPB reporter is available at **http://www .bk.admin.ch/dokumentation/02574** (click on "VPB: 1987-2006" for decisions issued between 1987 and 2006).

Cite decisions of federal administrative agencies by number of the decision and volume:

> ► Consiglio federale, Sept. 25, 1989, 54 GIURISPRUDENZA DELLE
> AUTORITÀ AMMINISTRATIVE DELLA CONFEDERAZIONE [GAAC] no. 34
> (Switz.).

Electronic sources

Citation format: ‹court abbreviation›, ‹date of decision›, ‹docket number›, ‹official reporter citation if available› (‹country abbreviation if not evident from context›), ‹direct or parallel Internet citation›.

The docket number is optional, except for decisions that are not or not as yet reported in the official reporter.

> ► BGer, Mar. 12, 2003, docket no. B 8/03 (Switz.), *available at*
> http://www.bger.ch.

> ► TF, Jan. 14, 2003, docket no. B 76/02, 129 ATF V 145 (Switz.),
> *available at* http://www.bger.ch.

> ► Conseil fédéral, May 12, 2004, 68 JURISPRUDENCE DES AUTORITÉS
> ADMINISTRATIVES DE LA CONFÉDÉRATION [JAAC] No. 95 (2004)
> (Switz.), *available at* http://www.vpb.admin.ch.

To cite a decision which is only electronically published: ‹court name› [‹court abbreviation›] [‹English translation of court name›] ‹date of decision›, ‹docket number› (‹country abbreviation if not evident from context›).

▶ Bundesgericht [BGer] [Federal Supreme Court] Sept. 23, 2008, 2C.268/2008 (Switz.).

Constitution

Citation format for the current constitution: ‹constitution name in German or French› [‹constitution abbreviation in German or French›] [CONSTITUTION] ‹date of enactment›, ‹abbreviation or full title of systematic collection of laws› ‹number of law›, ‹article›, ‹paragraph, if applicable› (‹country abbreviation if not evident from context›).

In German:

▶ BUNDESVERFASSUNG [BV] [CONSTITUTION] Apr. 18, 1999, SR 101, art. 29, para. 1 (Switz.).

In French:

▶ CONSTITUTION FÉDÉRALE [CST] [CONSTITUTION] Apr. 18, 1999, RO 101, art. 29, para. 1 (Switz.).

Citation format for the former constitution: ‹title in German and/or French›, ‹date›, ‹abbreviation or full title of chronological collection of laws in German and/or French› [‹abbreviation of former constitution in German and/or French›] ‹article› ‹paragraph, if applicable› (‹country abbreviation if not evident from context›).

▶ Bundesverfassung, Constitution fédérale, May 29, 1874, AS 1, RO 1 [BV 1874, Cst 1874] art. 4 (Switz.).

Codes

Citation format: ‹code name in German, French, and/or Italian› [‹code abbreviation in German, French, and/or Italian›] [‹English translation of code name›] ‹date of enactment›, ‹compilation of laws› ‹number of law›, ‹article›, ‹paragraph, if applicable› (‹country abbreviation if not evident from context›).

▶ SCHWEIZERISCHES ZIVILGESETZBUCH [ZGB], CODE CIVIL [CC], CODICE CIVILE [CC] [CIVIL CODE] Dec. 10, 1907, SR 210, RS 210, art. 3 (Switz.).

To cite a former version of a code that was in effect at an earlier date, rather than citing to the updated and systematic compilation of laws, which is maintained as a loose-leaf system and available online, it is preferable to cite to the chronological collection of laws and to mention the operative date or the last amending law:

▶ SCHWEIZERISCHES STRAFGESETZBUCH [STGB] [CRIMINAL CODE] Dec. 21, 1937, SR 757 (1938), *as amended by* Gesetz, Oct. 4, 1991, AS 2465 (1992), art. 37, para. 1 (Switz.).

Swiss codes and statutes are subdivided into articles (not sections) and thereafter into paragraphs and/or numbers. When new articles are inserted into an act, they are often numbered as follows: art. 264, art. 264a, art. 264b, etc. Until recently, this numbering looked like this: art. 179, 179bis, 179ter, up to art. 179novies. In some English translations, this numbering has been replaced by art. 179, art. 179a, etc. This substitution appears permissible; it may be preferable, however, to give both versions:

▶ STGB art. 179bis (STGB art. 179a)

- SCHWEIZERISCHES ZIVILGESETZBUCH, CODE CIVIL, CODICE CIVILE (Civil Code)   ZGB, CC, CC
- OBLIGATIONENRECHT, CODE DES OBLIGATIONS, CODICE DELLE OBLIGAZIONI (Code of Obligations)   OR, CO, CO
- SCHWEIZERISCHES STRAFGESETZBUCH, CODE PÉNAL SUISSE, CODICE PENALE SVIZZERO (Criminal Code)   StGB, CP, CP

Statutes and decrees

The citation format for laws and regulations is the same as for the codes. Cite codes, statutes, and decrees to the updated and systematic compilation of federal law and/or to the chronological collection of federal law.

Updated compilation (cite by law number):

► SYSTEMATISCHE SAMMLUNG DES BUNDESRECHTS	1987–date	SR e.g., SR 210
► RECUEIL SYSTÉMATIQUE DU DROIT FÉDÉRAL	1987–date	RS
► RACCOLTA SISTEMATICA DEL DIRITTO FEDERALE	1987–date	RS

Chronological collection (cite by page and year):

► AMTLICHE SAMMLUNG DES BUNDESRECHTS	1848–date	AS e.g., AS 90 (1995)
► RECUEIL OFFICIEL DU DROIT FÉDÉRAL	1848–date	RO
► RACCOLTA UFFICIALE DELLE LEGGI FEDERALI	1848–date	RU

Legislative materials

Draft laws and decrees can be found in the following sources:

► BUNDESBLATT	1848–date	BBL
► FEUILLE FÉDÉRALE SUISSE	1848–date	FF
► FOGLIO FEDERALE SVIZZERO	1848–date	FF

Until 1997, cite by volume, page, and year; since 1998, cite by page and then year.

- ► BBL I 1493 (1978)
- ► FF 6051 (2001)

Internet sources

The most comprehensive electronic source is the Federal Authorities of the Swiss Confederation website at **http://www.admin.ch**. This site has a portal in English that links to the Parliament, the Executive Branch of Government, and to the three federal courts. Legislation, legislative materials, and cases are available in the three or four national languages (some documentation is also in Rumantsch).

http://www.bger.ch (Federal Court)

http://www.bger.ch/index/juridiction/jurisdiction-inherit-template/jurisdiction-recht.htm (decisions in German)

http://www.bstger.ch (Federal Criminal Court)

http://bstger.weblaw.ch/?method=tpf&ul=fr (decisions in French)

http://www.bundesverwaltungsgericht.ch (Federal Administrative Court)

http://www.bundesverwaltungsgericht.ch/it/index/entscheide.htm (decisions in Italian)

http://www.admin.ch/ch/d/sr/sr.html (Updated and Systematic Compilation of Federal Law (in German))

http://www.admin.ch/ch/f/as (Chronological Collection of Laws (in French))

T2.40.1   Swiss Cantons

Cases

Cite cantonal material and give court names in the official language or languages of the Canton.

Ordinary jurisdiction

The names of courts vary among the cantons. Common names are: **Obergericht/Cour d'Appel/Corte d'Appello** (cantonal court of appeal), **Bezirksgericht/Tribunal de district/Tribunale di Prima Istanza** (ordinary court of first instance), and **Friedensrichter/Justice de Paix/Giudice di Pace** (court of petty jurisdiction). Cite to the official publication, if any, of the courts of that Canton, if therein; otherwise, cite to periodicals or reporters.

► AKTUELLE JURISTISCHE PRAXIS	1992–date	AJP
► BASLER JURISTISCHE MITTEILUNGEN	1954–date	BJM
► BLÄTTER FÜR ZÜRCHERISCHE RECHTSPRECHUNG	1902–date	ZR
► JOURNAL DES TRIBUNAUX, III, DROIT CANTONAL	1846–date	JDT III
► SCHWEIZERISCHE JURISTENZEITUNG	1904–date	SJZ
► LA SEMAINE JUDICAIRE	1879–date	SJ
► ZEITSCHRIFT DES BERNISCHEN JURISTENVEREINS	1864–date	ZBJV
► ZEITSCHRIFT FÜR SCHWEIZERISCHES RECHT	1852–date	ZSR
► REPERTORIO DI GIURISPRUDENZA PATRIA	1881–date	REP.
► ZENTRALBLATT FÜR STAATS–UND GEMEINDEVERWALTUNG	1888–date	ZBI

Administrative jurisdiction

Verwaltungsgericht/Tribunal administratif/Tribunale amministrativo (administrative court): Cite to one of the sources listed above, if therein.

Statutes and decrees

Use the citation format for federal statutes and decrees. Cite to the official compilation of the canton or to its official gazette, according to the organization of the publication being cited. For example:

► SYSTEMATISCHE SAMMLUNG DES AARGAUISCHEN RECHTS	SAR
► RECUEIL SYSTÉMATIQUE DE LA LÉGISLATION GENEVOISE	RSG
► BERNISCHE SYSTEMATISCHE GESETZESSAMMLUNG	RSB

Internet sources

The websites of the Cantons are accessible from the Federal Authorities of the Swiss Confederation website at **http://www.admin.ch**. The link labeled "The Cantons online" takes you to a drop-down menu from which you can select a specific Canton's website. The cantonal websites are in the language(s) spoken in the Canton. For instance, the website of the Canton of Aargau, at **http://www.ag.ch**, is in German. From there, click on "Gesetzes- & Entscheidsammlungen" to access the systematic compilation of Aargau legislation in German. The cantonal pages differ slightly, so an understanding of the language is necessary to navigate and link to the appropriate files.

T2.41   Taiwan, Republic of China

(Civil Law)

Jurisdictional note

Apply these guidelines to sources relating to the Republic of China on Taiwan (1949-date) and to the Republic of China during its Mainland period (1912-1949). For sources relating to Taiwan under Japanese occupation (1895-1945), adapt the guidelines for **table T2.24 Japan** as needed. For sources related to the People's Republic of China (1949-date), see the guidelines for **table T2.9 China, People's Republic of**. For sources related to China prior to the founding of the Republic of China in 1912, adapt these guidelines as necessary. When a geographical qualifier is needed for Taiwan, use "(Taiwan)." For Mainland China before the declaration of the People's Republic of China in 1949, use "(China)."

Romanization and capitalization

For romanization and capitalization of Chinese language citations, follow instructions in **rule 20.2.4**.

Translated sources

For citations to translated or bilingual sources, choose one of the following options:

1) Follow **rule 20.2.5**, giving parallel citations to the original language source and a translated version;

2) Where the original is difficult or impossible to verify, cite to the translated source without reference to the original language version. In this case, it is not necessary to preface the source with "*translated in*."

Choice of authorities

Where not specified otherwise herein, prefer any source published by or with the cooperation of a court or government agency (including agency websites). Chinese language sources are always more authoritative than translations, but it may be more appropriate to cite to a translation where available.

Cases

Citation format: ‹case name›, ‹year of publication› ‹source› ‹first page›, ‹page(s) of specific material, if desired› (‹court abbreviation› ‹date of decision›) (‹country abbreviation if not evident from context›).

Abbreviate English court names according to **table T7**.

> ▶ Chen Hsiao v. Ministry of Foreign Affairs, 2002 CHINESE (TAIWAN) Y.B. INT'L L. & AFF. 129 (Taipei Admin. High Ct. May 15, 2002).

Sifayuan Dafaguan Huiyi (Council of Grand Justices: constitutional court), **Zuigao Fayuan** (Supreme Court), **Gaodeng Fayuan** (High Court), **Difang Fayuan** (district courts): Cite to one of the following sources, if therein.

> ▶ Dafaguan Huiyi Jieshi Huibian (Collection of Grand Justices   SHIZI Council Interpretations) (title varies slightly by edition)

- ▸ Dafaguan Jieshi (Grand Justices Interpretations)   JIESHI
- ▸ Zuigao Fayuan Minshi Caipanshu Huibian (Supreme Court Civil Judgments Collection)   MINSHI HUIBIAN
- ▸ Zuigao Fayuan Xingshi Caipanshu Huibian (Supreme Court Criminal Judgments Collection)   XINGSHI HUIBIAN

Constitution

Give the promulgation year of the version or revision cited.

- ▸ Zhonghua Minguo Xianfa (Constitution of the Republic of China)   MINGUO XIANFA

  - ▸ MINGUO XIANFA art. 1 (1947) (Taiwan).

Statutes, regulations, and decrees

For laws, regulations, and official decrees of the Republic of China, cite to the source named below, if therein. Otherwise, cite to any source published by or with the cooperation of a court or government agency (including agency or court websites), if therein, then any source.

Zhonghua Minguo Xianxing Fagui Huibian   1994-date   XIANXING FAGUI HUIBIAN

Treaties and conventions

Citation of a bilateral treaty, convention or international agreement: ‹name of agreement›, ‹date of signing›, ‹subdivision, if desired›, ‹abbreviated names of parties to agreement›, ‹source› (‹country abbreviation if not evident from context›).

Citation of a multilateral treaty, convention or international agreement: ‹name of agreement›, ‹date of signing›, ‹subdivision, if desired›, ‹one Taiwan treaty source›, ‹one international treaty source, if applicable› (‹country abbreviation if not evident from context›).

Cite to one of the sources named below, if therein and available. Otherwise cite to any source published by or with the cooperation of a court or government agency (including agency or court websites), if therein.

- ▸ Zhongwai Tiaoyue Jibian (Treaties Between the Republic of China and Foreign States)   1927-1998   ZHONGWAI TIAOYUE JIBIAN
- ▸ Waijiaobu Gongbao   1999-date   WAIJIAOBU GONGBAO

Sources

- ▸ Dafaguan Huiyi Jieshi Huibian
  大法官會議解釋彙編   SHIZI
- ▸ The Republic of China Constitutional Court (Grand Justices Council) Reporter: Interpretations   CONST. CT. INTERP.
- ▸ Waijiaobu Gongbao
  外交部公報   WAIJIAOBU GONGBAO
- ▸ Zhonghua Minguo Xianfa
  中華民國憲法   MINGUO XIANFA
- ▸ Zhonghua Minguo Xianxing Fagui Huibian
  中華民國現行法規彙編   XIANXING FAGUI HUIBIAN

► Zhongwai Tiaoyue Jibian 中外條約輯編	ᴢʜᴏɴɢᴡᴀɪ Tɪᴀᴏʏᴜᴇ Jɪʙɪᴀɴ
► Zuigao Fayuan Minshi Caipanshu Huibian 最高法院民事裁判書彙編	Mɪɴsʜɪ Hᴜɪʙɪᴀɴ
► Zuigao Fayuan Xingshi Caipanshu Huibian 最高法院刑事裁判書彙編	Xɪɴɢsʜɪ Hᴜɪʙɪᴀɴ

T2.42   United Kingdom

(Common Law and Mixed Jurisdiction (Scotland))

► England	pre-1215–1536
► England and Wales	1536–1707
► Great Britain (England, Wales, and Scotland)	1707–1800
► United Kingdom of Great Britain and Ireland (England, Wales, Scotland, and Ireland)	1800–1921

United Kingdom of Great Britain and Northern Ireland (England, Wales, Scotland, and Northern Ireland)	1921–date

The United Kingdom of Great Britain and Northern Ireland is the collective name of four countries: England, Wales, Scotland, and Northern Ireland. The four separate countries were united under a single parliament in London, known as the United Kingdom Parliament at Westminster, through a series of Acts of Union. The United Kingdom has recently undergone a period of devolution with the creation of a Scottish Parliament, Welsh Assembly, and Northern Ireland Assembly that may pass legislation in certain areas. As such, it is necessary to establish whether an Act of Parliament applies to the entire United Kingdom; to England; to England and Wales; to England, Wales, and Northern Ireland; or to Great Britain (England, Wales, and Scotland); and refer to the countries appropriately. This information can be found at the end of Acts of Parliament in the section entitled "extent."

Cases

Jurisdiction, if not evident from context

Following rule 20.1, if the jurisdiction is not clear from the context or citation, it should be indicated in parentheses at the position noted in the citation formats below.

Jurisdictions for the United Kingdom:

► United Kingdom (England, Wales, Scotland and Northern Ireland)	U.K.
► Great Britain (England, Wales, and Scotland)	Gr. Brit.
► England	Eng.
► Wales	Wales
► Scotland	Scot.
► Northern Ireland	N. Ir.

Courts

Judicial Committee of the Privy Council (P.C.) (hears matters referred by the Crown; appeals from certain superior courts of England, Wales, Scotland, and Northern Ireland; matters concerning issues of devolution in Northern Ireland,

Scotland, and Wales; appeals from the English Ecclesiastical Courts on certain matters, from the Court of Admiralty, the Prize Courts, and the courts of the Crown Dependencies, Overseas Territories and Commonwealth countries that have retained the right of appeal to Her Majesty's Council or Judicial Committee): Cite to the *Law Reports* or to **Eng. Rep.**

When citing decisions of the Privy Council or another court that hears appeals from more than one jurisdiction, indicate parenthetically the jurisdiction from which the appeal was taken.

Citation format: ‹case name›, (‹year of publication›) ‹volume, if any› ‹reporter abbreviation› ‹first page› (‹court abbreviation if not clearly indicated by reporter›) ‹page(s) of specific material, or paragraph number(s) of specific material in brackets, if desired› **(appeal taken from ‹relevant abbreviation›) (‹jurisdiction abbreviation if not evident from context›).**

> ► B.C. Elec. Ry. v. Loach, [1916] 1 A.C. 719 (P.C.) (appeal taken from B.C.).

► Appeal Cases (3rd Series)	1891–date	A.C.
► Appeal Cases (2nd Series)	1876–1890	App. Cas.
► Privy Council Appeal Cases (continued by Appeal Cases, 2nd Series)	1866–1875	L.R.P.C.
► English Reports—Full Reprint	1094–1873	Eng. Rep.

House of Lords (H.L.) (final court of appeal for civil cases in the United Kingdom and for criminal cases in England, Wales, and Northern Ireland): Cite to the *Law Reports*, to **Eng. Rep.**, or in Scottish civil cases to the House of Lords section of Session Cases, listed under **table T2.42.3 Scotland**, in that order of preference. The **Supreme Court of the United Kingdom** (S.C.) took over the appellate jurisdiction of the House of Lords and the devolution jurisdiction of the Judicial Committee of the Privy Council on October 1, 2009.

When citing decisions of the House of Lords, or another court that hears appeals from more than one jurisdiction, indicate parenthetically the jurisdiction from which the appeal was taken.

Citation format: ‹case name›, ‹year of publication in parentheses or in brackets, depending on the reporter› ‹volume number, if any› ‹reporter abbreviation› ‹first page› (‹court abbreviation, if not clearly indicated by reporter›) ‹page(s) of specific material, or paragraph number(s) of specific material in brackets, if desired› **(appeal taken from ‹relevant abbreviation›) (‹jurisdiction abbreviation if not evident from context›).**

> ► Donoghue v. Stevenson, [1932] A.C. 562 (H.L.) 564 (appeal taken from Scot.).

> ► R v. Shayler, [2002] UKHL 11, [2003] 1 A.C. (H.L.) [35] (appeal taken from Eng.).

► Appeal Cases (3rd Series)	1891–date	A.C.
► Appeal Cases (2nd Series)	1875–1890	App. Cas.
► English and Irish Appeals (continued by Appeal Cases, 2nd Series)	1866–1875	L.R.E. & I. App.
► Scotch and Divorce Appeals (continued by Appeal Cases, 2nd Series)	1866–1875	L.R.S. & D. App.

Neutral citation

All judgments after 2001 have a neutral citation, a format independent of the publishing source that allows for immediate online publishing.

Citation format: ‹case name›, [‹year of publication›] ‹neutral citation abbreviation› ‹neutral citation court abbreviation, if necessary› ‹case reference number›, [‹paragraph(s) of specific material, if desired›] (appeal taken from ‹relevant abbreviation›) (‹jurisdiction abbreviation if not evident from context›).

 ► Archbold v. Royal Coll. of Veterinary Surgeons, [2004] UKPC 1, [2]–[3] (appeal taken from Eng.).

Cases that are also reported in the official *Law Reports* should first list the neutral citation and then the citation of the official reporter: ‹case name›, ‹neutral citation›, ‹citation to official reporter› (‹jurisdiction abbreviation if not evident from context›).

 ► R v. Pyrah, [2002] UKHL 47, [2003] 1 A.C. 903 (appeal taken from Eng.).
 ► Privy Council   UKPC
 ► House of Lords   UKHL
 ► Supreme Court   UKSC

See **table T2.42.1 England and Wales** for a list of more neutral citation abbreviations, along with appropriate court abbreviations.

Parentheses and square brackets

For England, Wales, and Northern Ireland, the year should be in parentheses in citations when the reporter can be found without reference to the year. If the year is an integral part of the citation and necessary to locate the correct volume of the reporter, it should be in square brackets. An easy way to determine whether square brackets or parentheses are needed is to look at the citation. If you need the year to locate the case, it should be in square brackets:

 ► Donoghue v. Stevenson, [1932] A.C. 562 (H.L.) (appeal taken from Scot.).
 ► R v. Lockwood, (1782) 99 Eng. Rep. 379 (K.B.).

Scotland only uses square brackets for neutral citations.

Internet sources for cases

For citations to an Internet source, follow **rule 18.2.3**:

 ► R v. Shayler, [2002] UKHL 11, [2003] 1 A.C. (H.L.) [35] (appeal taken from Eng.), *available at* http://www.publications.parliament.uk/pa/ld200102/ldjudgmt/jd020321/shayle-1.htm.

Electronic subscription databases

 ► Lawtel Transcripts (available at   1984–date   L.T.L.
   http://www.lawtel.com)
 ► Westlaw Transcripts (available at   1999–date   W.L.
   http://www.westlaw.co.uk)
 ► Casetrack Transcripts (available at   1996–date
   http://www.casetrack.com)

Statutes

Citation format: ‹statute short title, where available›, ‹year(s)›, ‹regnal year(s) for statutes enacted prior to 1963›, c. ‹chapter number(s)›, §(§) ‹section number(s)›, sch(s). ‹schedule(s), if any› (‹jurisdiction abbreviation if not evident from context›).

▶ Supreme Court of Judicature Act, 1925, 15 & 16 Geo. 5, c. 49, § 226, sch. 6 (Eng.).

Indicate regnal years by the following format: ‹year(s) of reign› ‹abbreviated name of the monarch› ‹numeric designation of the monarch in Arabic numerals›. If the monarch was the first of that name, omit the numeric designation.

▶ 11 Hen. 7

▶ 15 & 16 Geo. 5

▶ 13 Eliz.

If a short title has been established by the Short Titles Act or the Statute Law Revision Act, it should be used:

▶ Fatal Accidents Act, 1846, 9 & 10 Vict., c. 93 (Eng.).

If the name is omitted or does not include the date or year, use the citation format: ‹statute short title, where available›, ‹regnal year(s) for statutes enacted prior to 1963›, c. ‹chapter number(s)›, §(§) ‹section number(s)›, sch(s). ‹schedule(s), if any› (‹year if not included in the title of the act›) (‹jurisdiction abbreviation if not evident from context›).

▶ Hypnotism Act, 15 & 16 Geo. 6 & 1 Eliz. 2, c. 44, § 117 (1952) (U.K.).

For statutes enacted since 1963, omit the regnal year:

▶ Airports Authority Act, 1965, c. 16 (U.K.).

Abbreviate monarchs' names as follows:

▶ Anne	Ann.
▶ Charles	Car.
▶ Edward	Edw.
▶ Elizabeth	Eliz.
▶ George	Geo.
▶ Henry	Hen.
▶ James	Jac.
▶ Philip & Mary	Phil. & M.
▶ Richard	Rich.
▶ Victoria	Vict.
▶ William	Will.
▶ William & Mary	W. & M.

Regnal years

Regnal years can be determined from calendar years by reference to *A Handbook of Dates for Students of English History* or *Sweet & Maxwell's Guide to Law Reports and Statutes*, among other sources.

Statutory compilations

Preferably, official sources should be used when citing to legislation. If a statutory compilation is used, follow the citation format: ‹statute title›, (‹year of enactment›) ‹section or article number(s), if any›, ‹volume number› ‹compilation name› (‹edition of compilation, if appropriate›) ‹first page›, ‹page(s) of specific material, if desired› (‹jurisdiction abbreviation if not evident from context›).

> ► An Ordinance of the Lords and Commons in Parliament for the Safety and Defence of the Kingdom of England and Dominion of Wales, (1642) I Acts & Ords. Interregnum 1 (Eng.).

> ► Christmas Day (Trading) Act, (2004) § 2, 2 Current Law 234, 236.

> ► Law of Property Act, (1925) § 44, 37 Hals. Stat. (4th ed.) 139.

► Acts and Ordinances of the Interregnum	1642–1660	Acts & Ords. Interregnum
► Current Law Statutes	1986–date	Current Law
► Halsbury's Statutes of England	1929–date	Hals. Stat.

Regulations

Citation format: ‹regulation name›, ‹year of enactment›, ‹publication abbreviation› ‹instrument number›, ‹article›, ‹paragraph› (‹jurisdiction abbreviation if not evident from context›).

> ► Patent Rules, 1958, S.I. 1958/73, art. 3, ¶ 3 (U.K.).

► Statutory Instruments	1947–date	S.I.
► Statutory Rules and Orders	1890–1947	Stat. R. & O.

....

Parliamentary materials

Bills

Citation format: ‹bill name›, ‹session year›, ‹abbreviation of applicable House of Parliament› Bill [‹bill number›] cl. ‹clause› (‹jurisdiction abbreviation if not evident from context›).

> ► Assisted Dying for the Terminally Ill Bill, 2004-5, H.L. Bill [17] cl. 2 (Gr. Brit.).

> ► Criminal Justice (Justifiable Conduct) Bill, 2004-5, H.C. Bill [36] cl. 2 (Eng.).

Parliamentary debates

Parliamentary Debates contains the official verbatim reports of debates, speeches, answers to written and oral questions, and records of divisions.

Citation format: ‹volume number› Parl. Deb., ‹abbreviation of applicable House of Parliament› (‹series›) (‹year of debate›) ‹column number› (‹jurisdiction abbreviation if not evident from context›).

> ► 405 Parl. Deb., H.C. (6th ser.) (2003) 23 (U.K.).

Due to publication of the *Parliamentary Debates* online, recent debates may be available but may not yet have a volume number. In these instances, it is permissible to include the exact date of the debate, following the citation format:

‹date›, PARL. DEB., ‹abbreviation of applicable House of Parliament› (‹year of debate›) ‹column number› (‹jurisdiction abbreviation if not evident from context›).

▶ 26 NOV. 2008, PARL. DEB., H.C. (2008) 707 (U.K.).

▶ House of Lords, 5th series	1909–date	PARL. DEB., H.L. (5th ser.)
▶ House of Commons, 6th series	1981–date	PARL. DEB., H.C. (6th ser.)
▶ House of Commons, 5th series	1909–1981	PARL. DEB., H.C. (5th ser.)

Prior to 1909, the proceedings of the House of Lords and House of Commons were produced together in the same volumes:

▶ HOUSE OF LORDS AND HOUSE OF COMMONS, 4th series	1892–1908	PARL. DEB., H.C. (4th ser.)
▶ HOUSE OF LORDS AND HOUSE OF COMMONS, 3rd series	1830–1891	PARL. DEB., H.C. (3d ser.)
▶ HOUSE OF LORDS AND HOUSE OF COMMONS, 2nd series	1820–1830	PARL. DEB., H.C. (2d ser.)
▶ HOUSE OF LORDS AND HOUSE OF COMMONS, 1st series	1803–1820	PARL. DEB., H.C. (1st ser.)
▶ PARLIAMENTARY HISTORY	1066–1803	PARL. HIST. ENG.
▶ JOURNAL		H.L. JOUR., H.C. JOUR.

Official government reports

Citation format: ‹government department or committee name›, ‹report title›, ‹session year›, ‹abbreviation of applicable House of Parliament where report was issued› ‹paper number›, ‹paragraph symbol and number, or "at" page number of specific material› (‹jurisdiction abbreviation if not evident from context›).

▶ CONSTITUTIONAL AFFAIRS COMMITTEE, JUDICIAL APPOINTMENTS AND A SUPREME COURT (COURT OF FINAL APPEAL), 2003-4, H.C. 48-I, at 12 (U.K.).

▶ SELECT COMMITTEE ON ANIMALS IN SCIENTIFIC PROCEDURES, REPORT, 2001-2, H.L. 150-I, ¶ 5(2) (U.K.).

Command Papers

Citation format: ‹government department or committee name›, ‹report title›, ‹year›, ‹relevant abbreviation› ‹Command Paper number›, ‹paragraph symbol and number, or "at" page number of specific material› (‹jurisdiction abbreviation if not evident from context›).

▶ DEPARTMENT FOR ENVIRONMENT, FOOD AND RURAL AFFAIRS, LAUNCH OF THE DRAFT ANIMAL WELFARE BILL, 2004, Cm. 6252, at 5 (U.K.).

Relevant abbreviations are as follows:

▶ 1st series	1833–1869	[C. (1st series)]
▶ 2nd series	1870–1899	[C. (2d series)]
▶ 3rd series	1900–1918	[Cd.]
▶ 4th series	1919–1956	[Cmd.]
▶ 5th series	1957–1986	Cmnd.
▶ 6th series	1986–date	Cm.

Treaties

Citation format: ‹treaty name›, ‹date of signing›, ‹abbreviated names of parties to agreement›, ‹article, if desirable›, ‹treaty source› (‹year of treaty source volume›) (‹relevant abbreviation› ‹Command Paper number, for the *British Treaty Series*›).

> ▶ Declaration Between the United Kingdom and France and Russia Engaging Not To Conclude Peace Separately During the Present European War, Sept. 5, 1914, Gr. Brit.-Fr.-Russ., GR. BRIT. T.S. No. 1 (1915) (Cd. 7737).

▶ BRITISH TREATY SERIES	1892–date	GR. BRIT. T.S. No. ‹treaty number› (‹year›), (‹relevant abbreviation› ‹Command Paper number›).
▶ BRITISH FOREIGN AND STATE PAPERS	1812–1968	‹volume number› B.S.P. ‹first page›.
▶ HERTSLET'S COMMERCIAL TREATIES	1820–1891	‹volume number› H.C.T. ‹first page›.

Common abbreviations

These abbreviations should be used in case names, in addition to those found in tables **T6** and **T10**, or other citation formats where appropriate.

▶ Attorney-General	A-G or AG
▶ Borough Council	BC
▶ County Council	CC
▶ Civil Procedure Rules	CPR
▶ Crown Prosecution Service	CPS
▶ District Council	DC
▶ Director of Public Prosecutions	DPP
▶ His/Her Majesty	HM
▶ Inland Revenue Commission	IRC
▶ London Borough Council	LBC
▶ Practice Direction	PD
▶ Rex (the King) and Regina (the Queen) unless the King or Queen is the respondent	R
▶ Rules of the Supreme Court	RSC

Journals

▶ BRITISH TAX REVIEW	1956–date	B.T.R.
▶ CONTEMPORARY ISSUES IN LAW	1995–date	C.I.L.
▶ CURRENT LEGAL PROBLEMS	1948–date	C.L.P.
▶ DENNING LAW JOURNAL	1986–date	DENNING L.J.
▶ ENTERTAINMENT LAW REVIEW	1990–date	ENT. L.R.
▶ INDUSTRIAL LAW JOURNAL	1972–date	IND. LAW. J.
▶ INDUSTRIAL RELATIONS LAW REVIEW	1972–date	I.R.L.R.
▶ INTERNATIONAL AND COMPARATIVE LAW QUARTERLY	1951–date	INT. COMP. LAW. Q.
▶ JOURNAL OF LAW AND SOCIETY	1982–date	J.L.S.
▶ JOURNAL OF LEGAL HISTORY	1979–date	J. LEGAL HIST.

▸ King's College Law Journal	1990–2006	K.C.L.J.
▸ King's Law Journal	2006–date	K.L.J.
▸ Law Quarterly Review	1885–date	L.Q.R.
▸ Lloyd's Maritime & Commercial Law Quarterly	1974–date	L.M.C.L.Q.
▸ Medical Law Review	1993–date	Med. L. Rev.
▸ Modern Law Review	1937–date	M.L.R.
▸ New Law Journal	1965–date	N.L.J.
▸ Report of Patent, Design and Trademark Cases	1884–date	R.P.C.
▸ Social & Legal Studies	1992–date	Soc. & Leg. S.
▸ Trust & Trustees	1996–date	T. & T.

Internet sources

http://www.parliament.uk (Parliament of the United Kingdom of Great Britain and Northern Ireland)

http://www.opsi.gov.uk (Office of Public Sector Information (OPSI) (official legislative site))

http://www.justice.gov.uk (Ministry of Justice)

http://www.official-documents.gov.uk (Official Documents of the United Kingdom)

http://www.lawcom.gov.uk (Law Commission)

http://www.direct.gov.uk (Information Site for Central Government)

http://www.statutelaw.gov.uk (The U.K. Statute Law Database (official revised edition of the primary legislation of the United Kingdom))

http://www.privy-council.org.uk (Privy Council Office)

http://bills.ais.co.uk (Index to Bills)

http://www.legalabbrevs.cardiff.ac.uk (Cardiff Index to Legal Abbreviations)

http://www.publications.parliament.uk/pa/ld/ldjudgmt.htm (House of Lords Judgments from 1996)

http://www.gazettes-online.co.uk (Gazettes)

http://www.bailii.org (British and Irish Legal Information Institute)

http://www.british-history.ac.uk (British History Online (contains historical Parliamentary Debates))

http://www.loc.gov/law/help/guide/nations/uk.html (Law Library of Congress Legal Research Guide: United Kingdom)

http://www.number10.gov.uk/news/latest-news (Latest News (Prime Minister's press releases))

T2.42.1   England and Wales

Cases

Prior to 1865

Prior to 1865, there was no official series of law reports. Cases were reported in numerous commercial reporters, commonly referred to as the nominate reporters. Subsequently, most of the nominate reporters were reprinted in a series referred to as the *English Reports* (Eng. Rep.). The *English Reports* should be cited if the case is available therein, and a parallel citation to the original nominate reporter should also be given.

Citation format: ‹case name›, (‹year of publication›) ‹volume number, if any› Eng. Rep. ‹first page› (‹court abbreviation if not clearly indicated by reporter›) ‹page(s) of specific material, if desired›; ‹volume number, if any› ‹nominate reporter abbreviation› ‹first page›, ‹page(s) of specific material, if desired› (‹jurisdiction abbreviation if not evident from context›).

> ▶ Semayne's Case, (1604) 77 Eng. Rep. 194 (K.B.) 195; 5 Co. Rep. 91 a, 93 b.

English Reports

▶ English Reports—Full Reprint	1220-1867	Eng. Rep.
▶ Revised Reports	1785-1866	Rev. Rep.
▶ Year Books		Y.B.

In citing the Year Books, include the regnal year, folio, term in which the plea was heard, and plea number; include a parallel citation to a nineteenth- or twentieth-century reprint if possible.

> ▶ Y.B. 17 Edw. 4, fol. 2a, Pasch, pl. 3 (1477) (Eng.).

> ▶ Y.B. 10 Edw. 2, Hil. 20 (1317) (Eng.), *reprinted in* 54 SELDEN SOCIETY 53 (1935).

After 1865

Cite to the official *Law Reports*, if therein. The *Law Reports* consist of the House of Lords cases (H.L.), Privy Council cases (P.C.), Appeal Courts (Criminal and Civil) (A.C.), Queen's Bench (Q.B.), Chancery (Ch.), Family (Fam.), Probate (P.), Employment Appeal Tribunal (E.A.T.), and relevant cases from the European Court of Justice (E.C.J.). Other reporters should only be used if a case has not been reported in the *Law Reports*, in the following order of preference: *Weekly Law Reports* (W.L.R.), *All England Law Reports* (All E.R.), or other reporters.

Citation format: ‹case name›, ‹year of publication in parentheses or in brackets, depending on the reporter› ‹volume number, if any› ‹reporter abbreviation› ‹first page› (‹court abbreviation if not clearly indicated by reporter›) ‹"at" page(s) of specific material, or paragraph number(s) of specific material in brackets, if desired› (‹jurisdiction abbreviation if not evident from context›).

> ▶ R v. Kelly, [1999] Q.B. 621 at 625 (Eng.).

Neutral citation

All judgments after 2001 have a neutral citation. For these cases, cite first to the neutral citation and then to the official *Law Reports*, if therein. Note that not all cases are published in the *Law Reports*. Follow the order of preference of the *Law Reports* as noted above.

Cases that are also reported in the official *Law Reports* should first list the neutral citation and then the citation of the official reporter following the citation format: ‹case name›, [‹year of publication›] ‹neutral citation court abbreviation› (‹court abbreviation if not evident from citation›) ‹case reference number›, [‹paragraph(s) of specific material, if desired›], ‹citation to official reporter› (‹jurisdiction abbreviation if not evident from context›).

- ▶ Quinland v. Governor of Swaleside Prison, [2002] EWCA (Civ) 174, [178], [2003] Q.B. 306 [317] (Eng.).
- ▶ Michael Charman v. Orion Publishing, [2007] EWCA (Civ) 972, [43], [50], [52]–[55] (Eng.).

Neutral citation abbreviations

▶ Court of Appeal (Civil)	EWCA (Civ)
▶ Court of Appeal (Criminal)	EWCA (Crim)
▶ High Court (Chancery)	EWHC (Ch)
▶ High Court (Queen's Bench)	EWHC (QB)
▶ High Court (Administrative Court)	EWHC (Admin)
▶ High Court (Family)	EWHC (Fam)
▶ High Court (Admiralty)	EWHC (Admlty)
▶ High Court (Technology & Construction)	EWHC (TCC)
▶ Patents Court	EWHC (Pat)
▶ Commercial Court	EWHC (Comm)

The rules for the use of these citations are set out in Practice Directions issued by the Lord Chief Justice of England and Wales:

- ▶ Practice Direction (Court of Appeal: Citation of Authority), [1995] 1 W.L.R. 1096 (Eng.).
- ▶ Practice Direction (Form of Judgments, Paragraph Marking and Neutral Citation), (2001) 1 W.L.R. 194 (Eng.).
- ▶ Practice Direction (Judgments: Form Citation) (Supreme Court), [2001] 1 W.L.R. 194 (Eng.).
- ▶ Practice Direction (Neutral Citations), (2002) 1 W.L.R. 346 (Eng.).

Attributions to judges

When attributing an opinion to a judge, use the following citation format: ‹case name›, ‹year of publication in parentheses or brackets, depending on the reporter› ‹volume number, if any› ‹reporter abbreviation› ‹first page› (‹court if not clearly indicated by reporter›) ‹page(s) of specific material, or paragraph number(s) of specific material in brackets, if desired› (‹judge name›) (appeal taken from ‹court abbreviation, if applicable›) (‹jurisdiction abbreviation if not evident from context›).

- ▶ R v. Martin, [1998] A.C. 917 (H.L.) 948 (Lord Hope of Craighead) (appeal taken from H.M. Court-Martial App. Ct.) (U.K.).

For Law Lords of Appeal in the Ordinary, territorial qualifications may be used the first time they are mentioned, then subsequently omitted (e.g., "Lord Hope of Craighead," then "Lord Hope").

Abbreviations of judges

▶ Law Lord of Appeal in Ordinary	no abbreviation	E.g., Lord Hope of Craighead E.g., Baroness Hale
▶ Lord Chief Justice	‹title› ‹last name› C.J.	E.g., Lord Woolf C.J.

▸ Master of the Rolls	‹title› ‹last name› M.R.	E.g., Lord Woolf M.R.	
▸ Lord Chancellor	‹title› ‹last name› L.C.	E.g., Lord Irvine of Lairg L.C.	
▸ Justice of the Court of Appeal	‹title, if the Justice is a peer› ‹last name› L.J.	E.g., Smith L.J. or Lord Smith L.J.	
▸ Justices of the High Court	‹last name› J.	E.g., Smith J.	

Official law reports

▸ Appeal Cases (3d Series)	1891–date	A.C.
▸ Appeal Cases (2d Series)	1875–1890	App. Cas.
▸ Chancery Division	1891–date	Ch.
▸ Queen's Bench	1952–date	Q.B.
▸ Family Division	1972–date	Fam.
▸ Admiralty & Ecclesiastical Cases	1865–1875	L.R.A. & E.
▸ Chancery Appeal	1865–1874	Ch.App.
▸ Chancery Division	1875–1890	Ch.D.
▸ Chancery Division	1866–1875	L.R.Ch.
▸ Common Pleas	1875–1880	C.P.D.
▸ Common Pleas	1865–1875	L.R.C.P.
▸ Criminal Appeal Reports	1908–date	Crim. App.
▸ Crown Cases Reserved	1865–1875	L.R.C.C.R.
▸ English and Irish Appeals (continued by Appeal Cases, 2nd Series)	1866–1875	L.R.E. & I. App.
▸ Equity Cases	1865–1875	L.R.Eq.
▸ Exchequer Cases	1865–1875	L.R. Exch.
▸ Exchequer Division (merged with Queen's Bench)	1875–1880	Exch. Div.
▸ House of Lords, Scotch & Divorce Appeals	1866–1875	L.R.H.L.Sc.
▸ King's Bench	1901–1951	K.B.
▸ Privy Council Appeal Cases (continued by Appeal Cases, 2nd Series)	1865–1875	L.R.P.C.
▸ Probate (continued by Family Division)	1891–1970	P.
▸ Probate, Divorce & Admiralty Division	1875–1890	P.D.
▸ Probate & Divorce Cases	1865–1875	L.R.P. & D.
▸ Queen's Bench	1891–1900	Q.B.
▸ Queen's Bench	1865–1875	L.R.Q.B.
▸ Queen's Bench Division	1875–1890	Q.B.D.
▸ Scotch and Divorce Appeals (continued by Appeal Cases, 2nd Series)	1866–1875	L.R.S. & D. App.

Law reports and journals

▸ All England Law Reports	1936–date	All E.R.
▸ All England Law Reports (Commercial Cases)	1998–date	All E.R. (Comm.)
▸ All England Law Reports (European Cases)	1995–date	All E.R. (EC)
▸ All England Law Reports Annual Review	1982–date	All E.R. Rev.
▸ Annotated Tax Cases	1922–1976	A.T.C.

▶ Banking Law Reports	1992–1997	Bank. L.R.
▶ Butterworth's Company Law Cases	1983–date	B.C.L.C.
▶ Butterworth's Medico-Legal Reports	1992–date	B.M.L.R.
▶ Commercial Cases	1896–1941	Com. Cas.
▶ Criminal Appeal Reports (Sentencing)	1979–date	Cr. App. R.(S).
▶ De-Rating Appeals	1930–1961	D.R.A.
▶ Financial Times Law Reports	1981–date	F.T.L.R.
▶ Industrial Cases Reports (formerly Industrial Court Reports)	1975–date	I.C.R.
▶ Information Technology Law Reports	1997–date	Info. T.L.R.
▶ Justice of the Peace and Local Government Review Reports	1837–date	J.P.R.
▶ Justice of the Peace Reports	1983–date	J.P.
▶ Knight's Local Government Reports	1903–1998	L.G.R.
▶ L.J.R., King's Bench, New Series	1831–1946	L.J.K.B.
▶ L.J.R., King's Bench, Old Series	1822–1831	L.J.K.B.O.S.
▶ Law Journal Reports	1822–1949	L.J.R.
▶ Law Times Reports	1859–1947	L.T.
▶ Law Times Reports, Old Series	1843–1859	L.T.O.S.
▶ Lloyd's Law Reports	1968–date	Lloyd's Rep.
▶ Lloyd's Law Reports Banking	1999–date	Lloyd's Rep. Bank.
▶ Lloyd's List Law Reports	1919–1967	Lloyd's List L.R.
▶ Magisterial Cases	1896–1946	Mag. Cas.
▶ Professional Negligence and Liability Reports	1996–date	P.N.L.R.
▶ Property and Compensation Reports (formerly Planning and Compensation Reports)	1949–1985	P. & C.R.
▶ Property Planning and Compensation Reports	1986–date	P.P. & C.R.
▶ Rating and Valuation Reporter	1960–date	R. & V.R.
▶ Rating Appeals	1962–date	R.A.
▶ Reports of Patent Cases	1884–1885	R.P.C.
▶ Reports of Patent, Design, and Trade Mark Cases	1884–date	R.P.D.T.M.C./ R.P.C.
▶ Reports of Tax Cases	1875–date	T.C.
▶ Road Haulage Cases	1950–1953	R.H.C.
▶ Road Traffic Reports	1970–date	R.T.R.
▶ Simon's Tax Cases	1973–date	S.T.C.
▶ Solicitors' Journal	1857–date	S.J.
▶ Taxation Reports	1939–1981	T.R.
▶ Times Law Reports	1884–1952	T.L.R.
▶ Times Newspaper Law Reports	1953–date	The Times
▶ Weekly Law Reports	1953–date	W.L.R.
▶ Weekly Notes	1866–1952	W.N.

Welsh statutory instruments

Citation format: ‹statute name›, ‹year of enactment›, **W.S.I.** ‹instrument number› **(W.** ‹number›**)** ‹article›, ‹paragraph› (‹jurisdiction abbreviation if not evident from context›).

> ► The Food (Hot Chilli and Hot Chilli Products) (Emergency Control) (Amendment) (Wales) Regulations, 2004, W.S.I. 2004/392 (W. 40) art. 2, ¶ 3 (Wales).

Journals

► Cambridge Law Journal	1921–date	C.L.J.
► Charity Law & Practice Review	1992–date	C.L. & P.R.
► Child & Family Law Quarterly	1989–date	C.F.L.Q.
► Civil Justice Quarterly	1982–date	C.J.Q.
► Counsel: Journal of the Bar of England and Wales	1985–date	Counsel
► Criminal Law Review	1954–date	Crim. L.R.
► Family Law	1971–date	Fam. Law
► Journal of Criminal Law	1936–date	J.C.L.
► Law Society's Gazette	1903–date	Law Soc. Gaz.
► Magistrate	1921–date	Mag.
► Oxford Journal of Legal Studies	1981–date	O.J.L.S.
► Public Law	1956–date	P.L.
► Solicitors' Journal	1857–date	S.J.
► Wales Journal of Law and Policy	2003–date	W.J.L.P.
► Wales Law Journal (Cylchgrawn Cyfraith Cymru)	2001–date	Wales L.J.

Internet sources

http://www.opsi.gov.uk/legislation/uk (Office of Public Sector Information (U.K.))

http://www.opsi.gov.uk/legislation/wales/wales_legislation (Office of Public Sector Information (Wales))

http://wales.gov.uk (Welsh Assembly Government)

http://www.hmcourts-service.gov.uk (Her Majesty's Courts Service)

http://www.bailii.org/databases.html (British and Irish Legal Information Institute (English and Welsh case law))

http://www.oldbaileyonline.org (Proceedings of the Old Bailey—Cases from 1674-1913)

http://www.cps.gov.uk (Crown Prosecution Service)

http://www.lawsociety.org.uk (Law Society)

http://www.loc.gov/law/help/guide/nations/uk.html (Library of Congress Guide to Law Online: United Kingdom)

T2.42.2   Northern Ireland (and Ireland Until 1924)

The Northern Ireland Assembly was established in 1998 (and came into effect in December 1999) as part of the Belfast Agreement that devolved legislative powers in certain areas to Northern Ireland.

Cases

All courts: Cite to N.I. or Ir. R., if therein. The court structure is similar to the English court system.

Citation format: ‹case name›, ‹year of publication in parentheses or brackets, depending on reporter› ‹volume number, if any› ‹reporter abbreviation› ‹first page› (‹court abbreviation, if not clearly indicated by reporter›) (‹jurisdiction abbreviation if not evident from context›).

▸ Re Taylor, [1973] N.I. 159 (Q.B.) [18].

Law reports

▸ Northern Ireland Law Reports	1925–date	N.I.
▸ Irish Reports	1894–date	Ir. R.
▸ Law Reports, Ireland (4th series) (continued by Irish Reports)	1878–1893	L.R. Ir.
▸ Irish Reports, Common Law Series (2nd series)	1867–1878	Ir. R.-C.L.
▸ Irish Common Law Reports (2nd series) (continued by Irish Reports, Common Law Series)	1850–1866	Ir. C.L.
▸ Irish Law Reports (1st series) (continued by Irish Common Law Reports)	1838–1850	Ir. L.R.
▸ Irish Law Times Reports	1867–date	Ir. L.T.R.
▸ Irish Jurist Reports	1849–1867	Ir. Jur.

Neutral citation

All judgments after 2001 have a neutral citation. Cases that are also reported in the official *Law Reports* should first list the neutral citation and then the citation of the official reporter.

Citation format: ‹case name›, [‹year of publication›] ‹neutral citation› (‹court abbreviation if not evident from citation›) ‹case reference number›, [‹paragraph number(s) of specific material, if desired›]; ‹year in parentheses or brackets, depending on reporter› ‹reporter abbreviation› ‹first page›, ‹court, if not clearly indicated by reporter› (‹jurisdiction abbreviation if not evident from context›).

▸ R v. Singleton, [2003] NICA (Civ) 29, [2]; [2004] N.I. 71, CA.

▸ R v. Pollock, [2004] NICA (Crim) 34, [38] (N. Ir.).

Neutral citation court abbreviations

▸ Court of Appeal (Civil)	NICA (Civ)
▸ Court of Appeal (Criminal)	NICA (Crim)
▸ High Court (Chancery)	NICh
▸ High Court (Queen's Bench)	NIQB
▸ High Court (Family)	NIFam
▸ Crown Court	NICC

Neutral citation tribunal abbreviations

▸ Northern Ireland Fair Employment Tribunal	NIFET
▸ Northern Ireland Industrial Tribunals	NIIT

Statutes

The citation format of statutes applicable to Northern Ireland always includes, in parentheses, "(Northern Ireland)," either before or after the word "Act," as part of the title. The location of the words "(Northern Ireland)" is dependent upon whether the act was passed in the Westminster Parliament, Northern Ireland, or Ireland. For acts passed by the United Kingdom Parliament (1226–date), "(Northern Ireland)," or "(Ireland)," whichever is appropriate, is located before the word "Act."

Citation format: ‹statute short title, if available›, ‹year(s) of enactment›, ‹regnal year(s) for statutes prior to 1963›, ‹chapter›, ‹section›, ‹schedule, if any›.

> ▶ Commission for Victims and Survivors Act (Northern Ireland), 2008, c. 6, § 1, sch. 1.

> ▶ Public Processions (Northern Ireland) Act, 1998, c. 2.

For acts passed in Ireland by the Irish Parliament in Dublin (1310–1800) and in Northern Ireland by the Parliament in Northern Ireland (1921–1977) and the Northern Ireland Assembly (2000–date), "(Ireland)" or "(Northern Ireland)," whichever is appropriate, is located after the word "Act" and before the year.

> ▶ Electronic Communications Act (Northern Ireland), 2001, c. 9.

Statutory compilations and session laws

▶ Northern Ireland Statutes	1972–date	N. Ir. Stat.
▶ Northern Ireland Public General Acts	1947–1971	N. Ir. Pub. Gen. Acts
▶ Northern Ireland Public General Statutes	1921–1946	N. Ir. Pub. Gen. Stat.
▶ Statutes Revised, Northern Ireland, Cumulative Supplement	1981–date	N. Ir. Rev. Stat. Cm. Sup.
▶ Statutes Revised, Northern Ireland	1226–1981	N. Ir. Rev. Stat.

Regulations

The rule above concerning the location of "(Northern Ireland)" should be followed in the citation of Orders in Council and other regulations.

Citation format for Orders in Council (treated as primary legislation in Northern Ireland): ‹order title›, ‹year of enactment›, SI ‹year of enactment›/‹Statutory Instrument number› (N. Ir. ‹number›), ‹article›, ‹paragraph› (‹jurisdiction abbreviation if not evident from context›).

> ▶ The Energy (Northern Ireland) Order, 2003, SI 2003/419 (N. Ir. 6), art. 5, ¶ 2.

Citation format for Northern Ireland Statutory Rules: ‹rule title› ‹year of enactment› S.R. ‹year of enactment›/‹Statutory Rule number›, ‹article›, ‹paragraph› (‹jurisdiction abbreviation if not evident from context›).

> ▶ Identification and Notification of Cattle Regulations (Northern Ireland) 2004 S.R. 2004/420, art. 2, ¶ 1.

> ▶ Statutory Rules and Orders of Northern Ireland   1922–1973   S.R. & O. (N. Ir.).

Journals

► Northern Ireland Judgments Bulletin	1970–date	N.I.J.B.
► Northern Ireland Legal Quarterly	1936–date	N.I.L.Q.
► Bulletin of Northern Ireland Law	1981–date	B.N.I.L.
► Irish Law Times & Solicitors' Journal (continued by Irish Law Times (New Series))	1867–1980	Ir. L.T.

Internet sources

http://www.niassembly.gov.uk (Northern Ireland Assembly)

http://www.niassembly.gov.uk/record/hansard.htm (Official Report of the Northern Ireland Assembly (Hansard))

http://www.opsi.gov.uk/legislation/northernireland/ni_legislation (Office of Public Sector Information (OPSI), Northern Ireland Legislation)

http://www.opsi.gov.uk/revisedstatutes/northernireland (Revised Northern Ireland Legislation)

http://www.opsi.gov.uk/legislation/northernireland/ni-srni.htm (Statutory Rules of Northern Ireland (1998-date))

http://www.bailii.org/nie/legis/num_act (Statutes Revised, Northern Ireland, 2nd ed. (1495-date))

http://www.statutelaw.gov.uk (Statute Law Database)

http://www.nio.gov.uk (Northern Ireland Office)

http://www.courtsni.gov.uk (Northern Ireland Court Service)

http://www.olrni.gov.uk (Official Law Reform of Northern Ireland)

http://www.lawsoc-ni.org (Law Society of Northern Ireland)

http://www.loc.gov/law/help/uk.html (Library of Congress Guide to Law Online: United Kingdom)

T2.42.3   Scotland

A Scottish Parliament was created by an Act of Parliament in 1998 that devolved certain legislative powers to Scotland. The Scottish Parliament opened in 1999 and has authority to pass primary legislation in areas such as health, education, agriculture, and justice in the form of Acts of Scottish Parliament and Scottish Statutory Instruments.

Cases

The Supreme Courts of Scotland consist of the **Court of Session**, which hears civil cases, and the **High Court of Justiciary**, which hears criminal cases. The **Sheriff Courts** are lower courts that hear civil and criminal cases, as well as fatal accident inquiries.

Citation format: ‹case name›, (‹year of publication›) ‹reporter abbreviation› ‹first page›, ‹page(s) of specific material, or paragraph number(s) of specific material in brackets, if desired› (‹jurisdiction abbreviation if not evident from context›).

   ► Allison v. Orr, (2004) S.C.L.R. 767, 768 (Scot.).

All judgments after 2001 have a neutral citation. For cases that are also reported in the official *Law Reports*, a parallel citation should be included after the neutral citation.

Citation format: ‹case name›, [‹year of publication›] ‹neutral citation› ‹court abbreviation if not evident from citation› ‹case reference number› [‹paragraph(s) of specific material, if desired›]; ‹year in parentheses or brackets, depending on the reporter›) ‹reporter abbreviation› ‹first page›, ‹page(s) of specific material, or paragraph number(s) of specific material in brackets, if desired› (‹jurisdiction abbreviation if not evident from context›).

▶ Smith v. Jones, [2006] CSIH 34 [45]; (2006) S.C. 236, 239 (Scot.).

Court of Session (Sess.) (general original and appellate jurisdiction of civil cases): Cite to S.C., if therein. Citations to S.C. should include the year as above; citations to the older series are to the volume in place of the year.

▶ Dalgleish v. Assessor for Strathclyde Region, (1986) S.C. 23 (Scot.).

▶ Crichton v. Henderson's Trs., 1 F. 24 (Scot.).

▶ Session Cases	1907–date	S.C.
▶ Fifth Series (edited by Fraser)	1898–1906	F.
▶ Fourth Series (edited by Rettie)	1873–1898	R.
▶ Third Series (edited by Macpherson)	1862–1873	M.
▶ Second Series (edited by Dunlop)	1838–1862	D.
▶ First Series (edited by Shaw)	1821–1838	S.
▶ Scottish Civil Law Reports	1987–date	S.C.L.R.
▶ Session Cases (House of Lords) Session Section	1850–date	S.C.(H.L.)

High Court of Justiciary (H.C.J.) (criminal appeals and trials of the most serious crimes): Cite to J.C. or S.C.(J.), if therein.

▶ Lloyd v. H. M. Advocate, 1 F.(J.) 31 (Scot.).

▶ Scott v. Smith, (1981) J.C. 46 (Scot.).

▶ Justiciary Cases (sometimes bound with Session Cases)	1917–date	J.C.
▶ Session Cases, High Court of Justiciary section	1906–1916	S.C.(J.)
▶ Fifth Series (edited by Fraser)	1898–1906	F.(J.)
▶ Fourth Series (edited by Rettie)	1873–1898	R.(J.)

Neutral citations before 2005

▶ Scottish Court of Session Decisions	ScotCS
▶ Scottish High Court Decisions	ScotHC
▶ Scottish Sheriff Court Decisions	ScotSC

Neutral citations after 2005

▶ Scottish Court of Session, Inner House	CSIH
▶ Scottish Court of Session, Outer House	CSOH
▶ Scottish High Court of Justiciary	HCJT
▶ Scottish Court of Criminal Appeal	HCJAC

Statutes

Acts of the Scottish Parliament since 1999:

Citation format: ‹statute short title, if available›, ‹year of enactment›, (A.S.P. ‹Act of Scottish Parliament number›), ‹section›, ‹schedule, if any›, ‹paragraph› (‹jurisdiction abbreviation if not evident from context›).

▶ Vulnerable Witnesses (Scotland) Act, 2004, (A.S.P. 3), § 3, sch. 2, ¶ 3.

The acts of the Scottish Parliament that existed from 1235 to 1707 may be cited to the following compilations:

▶ The Acts of the Parliaments of Scotland	1814-1875	A.P.S.
▶ Records of the Parliaments of Scotland to 1707 (available at **http://www.rps.ac.uk**)		R.P.S.

Journals

▶ Scots Law Times	1893-date	S.L.T.
▶ Juridical Review (Scotland)	1889-date	Jur. Rev.
▶ The Edinburgh Law Review	1992-date	Edin. L.R.
▶ Scottish Law Review	1885-1963	Sc. L.R.
▶ Scottish Law Reporter	1865-1925	S.L.R.
▶ Journal of the Law Society of Scotland	1956-date	J. Law. Soc. Sc.
▶ Scottish Law Gazette	1933-date	S.L.G.

Internet sources

http://www.scottish.parliament.uk (Scottish Parliament)

http://www.scotcourts.gov.uk (Scottish Court Services)

http://www.opsi.gov.uk/revisedstatutes/scotland (Office of Public Sector Information (OPSI), Scottish Legislation)

http://www.statutelaw.gov.uk (U.K. Statute Law Database)

http://www.scottish.parliament.uk/business/bills/billsInProgress (Current Scottish Bills)

http://www.bailii.org/databases.html#scot (British and Irish Legal Information Institute, Scottish Legislation and Cases)

http://www.scottishlaw.org.uk/scotlaw/scotorgsgov.html (Scottish Government links)

http://www.lawscot.org.uk (Law Society of Scotland)

http://www.journalonline.co.uk (Online Journal of the Law Society of Scotland)

http://www.scotlawcom.gov.uk (Scottish Law Commission)

http://www.loc.gov/law/help/uk.html (Library of Congress Guide to Law Online: United Kingdom)

T2.43   Zambia, Republic of
(Common Law)

....

Cases

Supreme Court of Zambia (SC) (highest court of the country with appellate jurisdiction in both civil and criminal matters) and **High Court of Zambia** (HC) (superior court of record with general original civil and criminal jurisdiction): Cite to ZLR, if therein; **Magistrate's Courts** (limited original civil and criminal jurisdiction, divided into four classes), **Industrial Relations Court** (original and exclusive jurisdiction to hear and determine any industrial relations matters and any proceedings under the Industrial and Labor Relations Act), and **Land Tribunal** (deals with land disputes and other matters affecting land rights and obligations).

Current law reports

Zambia Law Reports is the only law reporter in Zambia. It publishes the decisions of the Supreme Court and selected decisions of the High Court.

▹ Zambia Law Reports   1964–date   ZLR

Citation format: ‹case name›, (‹reporter year›) ZLR ‹first page› [‹court abbreviation›] (‹country abbreviation if not evident from context›).

▸ Att'y Gen. v. Valentine Shula Musakanya, (1981) ZLR 1 [SC] (Zam.).

Reports prior to 1964

Cases prior to Zambia's independence in 1964 were published in the *Northern Rhodesia Law Reports*, which reported cases from the High Court of Northern Rhodesia, and the *Rhodesia and Nyasaland Law Reports*, which reported decisions of the Supreme Court, the High Court, and other territorial courts.

▹ Northern Rhodesia Law Reports   1911–1954   NRLR

Citation format: ‹case name›, ‹volume number› NRLR ‹first page› (‹year(s) of decision›) (‹country abbreviation if not evident from context›).

▸ Susman Bros. & Wulfsohn Ltd. v. The King, 5 NRLR 2 (1949–1954) (N. Rhodesia).

▹ Rhodesia and Nyasaland Law Reports   1954–1963   R&N

Citation format: ‹case name› (‹year of decision› R&N ‹first page›) (‹country abbreviation if not evident from context›).

▸ Shingadia Bros. v. Karson Jadavjee Shingadia (1958 R&N 1) (Rhodesia & Nyasaland).

....

Constitutions

The Zambian Constitution of 1991 (as amended in 1995) is Chapter 1 of the Laws of the Republic of Zambia, a compilation of Zambian laws in 26 volumes published by the Zambian government.

Cite to the constitution as part of the consolidated laws of Zambia, or directly.

Citation format: Const. of Zambia of ‹commencement year›, Cap. ‹number›, ‹volume number› Laws of Rep. of Zambia (‹revised edition year›) ‹section(s), if desired› (‹country abbreviation if not evident from context›).

Or: CONST. OF ZAMBIA of ‹commencement year› (as amended by Act. No. ‹act number› of ‹act year›) (‹country abbreviation if not evident from context›).

- ► CONST. OF ZAMBIA of 1991, Cap. 1, 1 LAWS OF REP. OF ZAMBIA (1995) § 4.
- ► CONST. OF ZAMBIA of 1991 (as amended by Act No. 18 of 1996).

Previous constitutions are cited as follows:

- ► CONST. OF ZAMBIA (Act No. 27 of 1973).
- ► CONST. OF ZAMBIA (1964).

Cite the Constitution of the Federation of Rhodesia and Nyasaland of 1953 as follows:

- ► FED. R. & N. CONST. (S.I. No. 1199 of 1953) STAT. L. FED. R. & N. (1954) (Rhodesia & Nyasaland).

....

Statutes

Citation format: ‹statute name› of ‹year of entry into force›, Cap. ‹chapter number›, ‹volume number› LAWS OF REP. OF ZAMBIA (‹revised edition year›) ‹section(s), if applicable› (‹country abbreviation if not evident from context›).

Or: ‹statute name› No. ‹statute number› (‹year of last statutory revision›) GOVT. GAZETTE (‹"Acts," "Bills," or "S.I."›), at ‹page(s)›, ‹section(s), if desired› (‹country abbreviation if not evident from context›).

- ► Electoral Act of 1991, Cap. 13, 2 LAWS OF REP. OF ZAMBIA (1995) § 45.
- ► Electoral Act No. 2 (1991) GOVT. GAZETTE (Acts), at 20–40, § 45 (Zam.).

....

Internet sources

http://www.parliament.gov.zm (official site of the Zambian Parliament; provides access to the 1996 revised edition of *Laws of Zambia*)

http://www.unza.zm/zamlii (site of the Zambian Legal Information Institute (ZAMLII), established by the University of Zambia Law School; provides access to the constitution, rules, and selected court decisions, acts, and legal commentary)

http://www.laz.org.zm (Law Association of Zambia)

http://www.loc.gov/law/help/guide/nations/zambia.html (Library of Congress Guide to Law Online: Republic of Zambia)

T3   INTERGOVERNMENTAL ORGANIZATIONS

T3.1   United Nations

Principal Organs: In citations to official records, abbreviate the records of the principal organs of the United Nations as follows:

► General Assembly	GAOR
► Security Council	SCOR
► Economic and Social Council	ESCOR
► Trusteeship Council	TCOR
► Trade and Development Board of the Conference on Trade and Development	TDBOR

Courts: International Court of Justice (I.C.J.): Cite decisions to I.C.J.; cite separately published pleadings to I.C.J. Pleadings; cite rules and acts to I.C.J. Acts & Docs.

► Report of Judgments, Advisory Opinions, and Orders	1946-date	‹year› I.C.J. xx
► Pleadings, Oral Arguments, and Documents	1946-date	‹year› I.C.J. Pleadings xx
► Acts and Documents	1946-date	‹year› I.C.J. Acts & Docs. xx

Treaties and international agreements: Cite to U.N.T.S.

► United Nations Treaty Series	1946-date	‹volume› U.N.T.S. xxx

T3.2   League of Nations

Courts: Permanent Court of International Justice (P.C.I.J.): Cite decisions, separately published pleadings, and rules and acts to P.C.I.J., indicating the series and the case or document number:

► Reports of Judgments, Advisory Opinions, and Orders	1920-1945	‹year› P.C.I.J. (ser. x) No. x

Treaties and international agreements: Cite to L.N.T.S.

► Opinions and Orders, League of Nations Treaty Series	1920-1945	<volume> L.N.T.S. xxx (‹year›)

T3.3   European Communities

Courts: Cite cases before the **Court of Justice of the European Union** (E.C.J.) and the **General Court** (Gen. Ct.) to E.C.R., if therein. If not, cite to C.M.L.R., or to **Common Mkt. Rep. (CCH)** or CEC (CCH), if therein, in that order of preference. Always provide a parallel citation to C.M.L.R., if possible; otherwise provide a parallel citation to Common Mkt. Rep. (CCH), or CEC (CCH), if possible.

► Report of Cases Before the Court of Justice of the European Communities	1973-date	‹year› E.C.R. xxx
► Common Market Law Reports	1962-date	‹year› C.M.L.R. xxx
► Common Market Reports	1962-1988	‹year› Common Mkt. Rep. (CCH) xxx
► European Community Cases	1989-date	‹year› CEC (CCH) xxx

Legislative acts: Cite acts of the Council and Commission to O.J., (the Official Journal of the European Union, formerly the Official Journal of the European Communities), if therein; otherwise cite to O.J. SPEC. ED., if therein; otherwise cite to J.O. For issues of J.O. before 1967, always indicate the issue number. For issues of O.J. and J.O. dating from 1967 and later, always indicate the series and issue number.

- Official Journal of the European Union   1973-date   ⟨year⟩ O.J. (L ⟨act number⟩) xxx
- Official Journal of the European Community, Special Edition   1952-1972   ⟨year⟩ O.J. SPEC. ED. xxx
- Journal Officiel des Communautés Européennes   1958-date   ⟨year⟩ J.O. (L ⟨act number⟩) xxx

Parliamentary documents: Cite as follows:

- European Parliamentary Debates   EUR. PARL. DEB. (⟨debate number⟩) x
- European Parliament Working Session or Session Documents   EUR. PARL. DOC. (COM ⟨document number⟩) x
- Parlement Européen Documents de Séance   PARL. EUR. DOC. (SEC ⟨document number⟩) x

T3.4 European Court and Commission of Human Rights

European Court of Human Rights: Cite to Eur. Ct. H.R. or to Y.B. Eur. Conv. on H.R.:

- European Court of Human Rights   xx Eur. Ct. H.R. (⟨year⟩)
- Yearbook of the European Convention on Human Rights   Y.B. Eur. Conv. on H.R.

European Commission of Human Rights: Cite to Eur. Comm'n H.R. Dec. & Rep., Y.B. Eur. Conv. on H.R., or Eur. H.R. Rep., in that order of preference:

- Collections of Decisions of the European Commission of Human Rights   ⟨volume⟩ Eur. Comm'n H.R. Dec. & Rep. xxx
- European Human Rights Reports   ⟨volume⟩ Eur. H.R. Rep. xxx

T3.5 Inter-American Commission on Human Rights

Cite to Inter-Am. Comm'n H.R.:

- Annual Report of the Inter-American Commission on Human Rights   Inter-Am. Comm'n H.R.

T3.6 Inter-American Court of Human Rights

Cite to Series, to Rep. Inter-Am. Ct. H.R., or to official online sources:

Series:

- A - Advisory Opinions and others   Inter-Am. Ct. H.R. (ser. A) No. xx
- B - Pleadings, Oral Arguments and Documents related to Series A   Inter-Am. Ct. H.R. (ser. B) No. xx, xxx
- C - Decisions and Judgments   Inter-Am. Ct. H.R. (ser. C) No. xx
- D - Pleadings, Oral Arguments and Documents related to Series C   Inter-Am. Ct. H.R. (ser. D) No. xx, xxx
- E - Provisional Measures compendium   Inter-Am. Ct. H.R. (ser. E) No. xx, xxx
- F - Procedural Decisions compendium   Inter-Am. Ct. H.R. (ser. F) No. xx, xxx

Annual Reports of the Inter-American Court of Human Rights:

- ▸ Complete Opinions: 1980-2003   Rep. Inter-Am. Ct. H.R. xxx
  Abstracts: 2004-date

Official Online Sources:

- ▸ Advisory Opinions (Series A)   http://www.corteidh.or.cr/opiniones.cfm
- ▸ Decisions and Judgments   http://www.corteidh.or.cr/casos.cfm
  (Series C)
- ▸ Provisional Measures (Series E)   http://www.corteidh.or.cr/medidas.cfm
- ▸ Compliance with Judgment   http://www.corteidh.or.cr/supervision.cfm
- ▸ Jurisprudence by Country   http://www.corteidh.or.cr/porpais.cfm

---

T3.7   International Tribunal for the Law of the Sea

Cite to ITLOS Rep.:

- ▸ International Tribunal for the Law of the Sea   1956-date   ITLOS Rep.
  Reports of Judgments, Advisory Opinions and Orders

T3.8   Other Intergovernmental Organizations

▸ General Agreement on Tariffs and Trade	GATT
▸ Global Legal Information Network	GLIN
▸ International Atomic Energy Agency	IAEA
▸ International Civil Aviation Organization	ICAO
▸ International Labour Organisation	ILO
▸ International Maritime Organization (until May 1982 known as the Intergovernmental Maritime Consultative Organization)	IMO
▸ International Telecommunication Union	ITU
▸ World Health Organization	WHO
▸ World Meteorological Organization	WMO
▸ World Trade Organization	WTO

Names of other organizations should be written out the first time they are used, and the abbreviation to be used in subsequent citations should be indicated in brackets.

T4   TREATY SOURCES

Dates in the center column below refer to the years of the treaties contained in the source, not to the years in which the source was published.

T4.1   Official U.S. sources

▸ United States Treaties and Other International Agreements	1950-date	‹volume› U.S.T. xxx
▸ Statutes at Large (indexed at 64 Stat. B1107)	1778-1949	‹volume› Stat. xxx
▸ Treaties and Other International Acts Series	1945-date	T.I.A.S. No. x
▸ Treaty Series	1778-1945	T.S. No. x

▸ Executive Agreement Series	1922–1945	E.A.S. No. x
▸ Senate Treaty Documents	1981–date	S. TREATY DOC. NO. x
▸ Senate Executive Documents	1778–1980	S. EXEC. DOC. x

T4.2   Intergovernmental treaty sources

▸ United Nations Treaty Series	1946–date	‹volume› U.N.T.S. xxx
▸ League of Nations Treaty Series	1920–1945	‹volume› L.N.T.S. xxx
▸ Pan-American Treaty Series	1949–date	‹volume› Pan-Am. T.S. xxx
▸ European Treaty Series	1948–2003	E.T.S. No. xxx
▸ Organization of American States Treaty Series	1970–date	O.A.S.T.S. No. xxx
▸ Council of Europe Treaty Series	2004–date	C.E.T.S. No. xxx

T4.3   Unofficial treaty sources

▸ International Legal Materials	1962–date	‹volume› I.L.M. xxx
▸ Nouveau Recueil Général des Traités	1494–1943	‹volume› Martens Nouveau Recueil (ser. ‹series number›) xxx
▸ Parry's Consolidated Treaty Series	1648–1919	‹volume› Consol. T.S. xxx
▸ Hein's United States Treaties and Other International Agreements	1984–date	Hein's No. KAV xxxx
▸ Bevans	1776–1949	‹volume› Bevans xxx

T5   ARBITRAL REPORTERS

The following list gives abbreviations for frequently cited arbitration reporters. See rule 21.6 for guidance on citing international arbitrations.

▸ Arbitration Materials	Arb. Mat'l
▸ Hague Court Reports, First Series	Hague Ct. Rep. (Scott)
▸ Hague Court Reports, Second Series	Hague Ct. Rep. 2d (Scott)
▸ International Centre for Settlement of Investment Disputes (ICSID) Reports	ICSID Rep.
▸ International Centre for Settlement of Investment Disputes (ICSID) Review	ICSID Rev.
▸ International Chamber of Commerce Arbitration	Int'l Comm. Arb.
▸ International Tribunal for the Law of the Sea Reports of Judgments, Advisory Opinions and Orders	ITLOS Rep.
▸ Iran-United States Claims Tribunal Reports	Iran-U.S. Cl. Trib. Rep.
▸ Tribunaux Arbitraux Mixtes	Trib. Arb. Mixtes
▸ United Nations Reports of International Arbitral Awards	R.I.A.A.
▸ World Arbitration Reporter	World Arb. Rep. (‹issue number›)

T6 CASE NAMES AND INSTITUTIONAL AUTHORS IN CITATIONS

Abbreviate case names in citations by abbreviating any word listed below (rule 10.2.2). It is permissible to abbreviate other words of eight letters or more if *substantial* space is thereby saved and the result is unambiguous in context. (Thus, it would be permissible to abbreviate "Encyclopaedia Britannica" to "Encyc. Britannica," "Attorney" to "Att'y," or "Petroleum" to "Petrol.") Unless otherwise indicated, plurals are formed by adding the letter "s."

Academy	Acad.	Cooperative	Coop.
Administrat[ive, ion]	Admin.	Corporation	Corp.
Administrat[or, rix]	Adm'[r, x]	Correction[s, al]	Corr.
Advertising	Adver.	County	Cnty.
Agricultur[e, al]	Agric.	Defense	Def.
Alternative	Alt.	Department	Dep't
America[n]	Am.	Detention	Det.
and	&	Development	Dev.
Associate	Assoc.	Director	Dir.
Association	Ass'n	Discount	Disc.
Atlantic	Atl.	Distribut[or, ing]	Distrib.
Authority	Auth.	District	Dist.
Automo[bile, tive]	Auto.	Division	Div.
Avenue	Ave.	East[ern]	E.
Bankruptcy	Bankr.	Econom[ic, ics, ical, y]	Econ.
Board	Bd.	Education[al]	Educ.
Broadcast[ing]	Broad.	Electr[ic, ical, icity, onic]	Elec.
Brotherhood	Bhd.	Employee	Emp.
Brothers	Bros.	Employ[er, ment]	Emp'[r, t]
Building	Bldg.	Engineer	Eng'r
Business	Bus.	Engineering	Eng'g
Casualty	Cas.	Enterprise	Enter.
Cent[er, re]	Ctr.	Entertainment	Entm't
Central	Cent.	Environment	Env't
Chemical	Chem.	Environmental	Envtl.
Coalition	Coal.	Equality	Equal.
College	Coll.	Equipment	Equip.
Commission	Comm'n	Examiner	Exam'r
Commissioner	Comm'r	Exchange	Exch.
Committee	Comm.	Executive	Exec.
Communication	Commc'n	Execut[or, rix]	Ex'[r, x]
Community	Cmty.	Export[er, ation]	Exp.
Company	Co.	Federal	Fed.
Compensation	Comp.	Federation	Fed'n
Condominium	Condo.	Fidelity	Fid.
Congress[ional]	Cong.	Financ[e, ial, ing]	Fin.
Consolidated	Consol.	Foundation	Found.
Construction	Constr.	General	Gen.
Continental	Cont'l	Gender	Gend.

▶ Government	Gov't	▶ Product[ion]	Prod.
▶ Group	Grp.	▶ Professional	Prof'l
▶ Guaranty	Guar.	▶ Property	Prop.
▶ Hospital	Hosp.	▶ Protection	Prot.
▶ Housing	Hous.	▶ Public	Pub.
▶ Import[er, ation]	Imp.	▶ Publication	Publ'n
▶ Incorporated	Inc.	▶ Publishing	Publ'g
▶ Indemnity	Indem.	▶ Railroad	R.R.
▶ Independent	Indep.	▶ Railway	Ry.
▶ Industr[y, ies, ial]	Indus.	▶ Refining	Ref.
▶ Information	Info.	▶ Regional	Reg'l
▶ Institut[e, ion]	Inst.	▶ Rehabilitation	Rehab.
▶ Insurance	Ins.	▶ Reproduct[ion, ive]	Reprod.
▶ International	Int'l	▶ Resource[s]	Res.
▶ Investment	Inv.	▶ Restaurant	Rest.
▶ Laboratory	Lab.	▶ Retirement	Ret.
▶ Liability	Liab.	▶ Road	Rd.
▶ Limited	Ltd.	▶ Savings	Sav.
▶ Litigation	Litig.	▶ School[s]	Sch.
▶ Machine[ry]	Mach.	▶ Science	Sci.
▶ Maintenance	Maint.	▶ Secretary	Sec'y
▶ Management	Mgmt.	▶ Securit[y, ies]	Sec.
▶ Manufacturer	Mfr.	▶ Service	Serv.
▶ Manufacturing	Mfg.	▶ Shareholder	S'holder
▶ Maritime	Mar.	▶ Social	Soc.
▶ Market	Mkt.	▶ Society	Soc'y
▶ Marketing	Mktg.	▶ South[ern]	S.
▶ Mechanic[al]	Mech.	▶ Southeast[ern]	Se.
▶ Medic[al, ine]	Med.	▶ Southwest[ern]	Sw.
▶ Memorial	Mem'l	▶ Steamship[s]	S.S.
▶ Merchan[t, dise, dising]	Merch.	▶ Street	St.
▶ Metropolitan	Metro.	▶ Subcommittee	Subcomm.
▶ Mortgage	Mortg.	▶ Surety	Sur.
▶ Municipal	Mun.	▶ System[s]	Sys.
▶ Mutual	Mut.	▶ Technology	Tech.
▶ National	Nat'l	▶ Telecommunication	Telecomm
▶ North[ern]	N.	▶ Tele[phone, graph]	Tel.
▶ Northeast[ern]	Ne.	▶ Temporary	Temp.
▶ Northwest[ern]	Nw.	▶ Township	Twp.
▶ Number	No.	▶ Transcontinental	Transcon.
▶ Opinion	Op.	▶ Transport[ation]	Transp.
▶ Organiz[ation, ing]	Org.	▶ Trustee	Tr.
▶ Pacific	Pac.	▶ Turnpike	Tpk.
▶ Partnership	P'ship	▶ Uniform	Unif.
▶ Person[al, nel]	Pers.	▶ University	Univ.
▶ Pharmaceutic[s, al, als]	Pharm.	▶ Utility	Util.
▶ Preserv[e, ation]	Pres.	▶ Village	Vill.
▶ Probation	Prob.	▶ West[ern]	W.

T7   COURT NAMES

The following alphabetical list provides abbreviations for court names to be used in citing cases according to **rule 10.4**. If the abbreviation for the full name of the court is not listed below, a composite abbreviation may be assembled using the words listed in this table.

▸ Administrative Court	Admin. Ct.
▸ Admiralty [Court, Division]	Adm.
▸ Aldermen's Court	Alder. Ct.
▸ Appeals Court	App. Ct.
▸ Appellate Court	App. Ct.
▸ Appellate Department	App. Dep't
▸ Appellate Division	App. Div.
▸ Armed Services Board of Contract Appeals	ASBCA
▸ Bankruptcy Appellate Panel	B.A.P.
▸ Bankruptcy [Court, Judge]	Bankr.
▸ Board of Contract Appeals	B.C.A.
▸ Board of Immigration Appeals	B.I.A.
▸ Board of Patent Appeals and Interferences	B.P.A.I.
▸ Board of Tax Appeals	B.T.A.
▸ Borough Court	‹Name› Bor. Ct.
▸ Central District	C.D.
▸ Chancery [Court, Division]	Ch.
▸ Children's Court	Child. Ct.
▸ Circuit Court (old federal)	C.C.
▸ Circuit Court (state)	Cir. Ct.
▸ Circuit Court of Appeals (federal)	Cir.
▸ Circuit Court of Appeals (state)	Cir. Ct. App.
▸ City Court	‹Name› City Ct.
▸ Civil Appeals	Civ. App.
▸ Civil Court of Record	Civ. Ct. Rec.
▸ Civil District Court	Civ. Dist. Ct.
▸ Claims Court	Cl. Ct.
▸ Commerce Court	Comm. Ct.
▸ Commission	Comm'n
▸ Common Pleas	C.P. ‹when appropriate, name county or similar subdivision›
▸ Commonwealth Court	Commw. Ct.
▸ Conciliation Court	Concil. Ct.
▸ County Court	‹Name› Cnty. Ct.
▸ County Judge's Court	Cnty. J. Ct.
▸ Court	Ct.
▸ Court of Appeal (English)	C.A.
▸ Court of Appeals (federal)	Cir.
▸ Court of Appeal[s] (state)	Ct. App.
▸ Court of Appeals for the Armed Forces	C.A.A.F.

► Court of Civil Appeals	Civ. App.
► Court of Claims	Ct. Cl.
► Court of Common Pleas	Ct. Com. Pl.
► Court of Criminal Appeals	Crim. App.
► Court of Customs and Patent Appeals	C.C.P.A.
► Court of Customs Appeals	Ct. Cust. App.
► Court of Errors	Ct. Err.
► Court of Errors and Appeals	Ct. Err. & App.
► Court of Federal Claims	Fed. Cl.
► Court of [General, Special] Sessions	Ct. ‹Gen. or Spec.› Sess.
► Court of International Trade	Ct. Int'l Trade
► Court of Military Appeals	C.M.A.
► Court of Military Review	C.M.R.
► Court of Special Appeals	Ct. Spec. App.
► Court of Veterans Appeals	Ct. Vet. App.
► Criminal Appeals	Crim. App.
► Criminal District Court	Crim. Dist. Ct.
► Customs Court	Cust. Ct.
► District Court (federal)	D.
► District Court (state)	Dist. Ct.
► District Court of Appeal[s]	Dist. Ct. App.
► Division	Div.
► Domestic Relations Court	Dom. Rel. Ct.
► Eastern District	E.D.
► Emergency Court of Appeals	Emer. Ct. App.
► Equity [Court, Division]	Eq.
► Family Court	Fam. Ct.
► High Court	High Ct.
► Judicial District	Jud. Dist.
► Judicial Division	Jud. Div.
► Judicial Panel on Multidistrict Litigation	J.P.M.L.
► Justice of the Peace's Court	J.P. Ct.
► Juvenile Court	Juv. Ct.
► Land Court	Land Ct.
► Law Court	Law Ct.
► Law Division	Law Div.
► Magistrate Division	Magis. Div.
► Magistrate's Court	Magis. Ct.
► Middle District	M.D.
► Municipal Court	‹Name› Mun. Ct.
► Northern District	N.D.
► Orphans' Court	Orphans' Ct.
► Parish Court	‹Name› Parish Ct.
► Police Justice's Court	Police J. Ct.
► Prerogative Court	Prerog. Ct.
► Probate Court	Prob. Ct.

▸ Public Utilities Commission	P.U.C.
▸ Real Estate Commission	Real Est. Comm'n
▸ Recorder's Court	Rec's Ct.
▸ Southern District	S.D.
▸ Special Court Regional Rail Reorganization Act	Reg'l Rail Reorg. Ct.
▸ Superior Court	Super. Ct.
▸ Supreme Court (federal)	U.S.
▸ Supreme Court (other)	Sup. Ct.
▸ Supreme Court, Appellate Division	App. Div.
▸ Supreme Court, Appellate Term	App. Term
▸ Supreme Court of Errors	Sup. Ct. Err.
▸ Supreme Judicial Court	Sup. Jud. Ct.
▸ Surrogate's Court	Sur. Ct.
▸ Tax Appeal Court	Tax App. Ct.
▸ Tax Court	T.C.
▸ Teen Court	Teen Ct.
▸ Temporary Emergency Court of Appeals	Temp. Emer. Ct. App.
▸ Territor[ial,y]	Terr.
▸ Trademark Trial and Appeal Board	T.T.A.B.
▸ Traffic Court	Traffic Ct.
▸ Tribal Court	‹Name› Tribal Ct.
▸ Tribunal	Trib.
▸ Water Court	Water Ct.
▸ Western District	W.D.
▸ Workmen's Compensation Division	Workmen's Comp. Div.
▸ Youth Court	Youth Ct.

T8   EXPLANATORY PHRASES

The following table lists a number of explanatory phrases (some of which contain abbreviations) commonly used to indicate prior or subsequent history and weight of authority of judicial decisions. As indicated below, phrases that are followed by a case citation as their direct object (such as "*aff'g*" or "*overruled by*") are *not* followed by commas. Phrases introducing a case citation for the action indicated by the explanatory phrase (such as "*cert. denied,*") *are* followed by commas, which are *not* italicized (see rule 2.1(f)). See rule 10.7 for guidance in using explanatory phrases.

▸ *acq.*
▸ *acq. in result*
▸ *aff'd,*
▸ *aff'd by an equally divided court,*
▸ *aff'd mem.,*
▸ *aff'd on other grounds,*
▸ *aff'd on reb'g,*
▸ *aff'g*
▸ *amended by*

- *appeal denied,*
- *appeal dismissed,*
- *appeal docketed,*
- *appeal filed,*
- *argued,*
- *cert. denied,*
- *cert. dismissed,*
- *cert. granted,*
- *certifying questions to*
- *denying cert. to*
- *dismissing appeal from*
- *enforced,*
- *enforcing*
- *invalidated by*
- *mandamus denied,*
- *modified,*
- *modifying*
- *nonacq.*
- *overruled by*
- *perm. app. denied,*
- *perm. app. granted,*
- *petition for cert. filed,*
- *prob. juris. noted,*
- *reh'g granted [denied],*
- *rev'd,*
- *rev'd on other grounds,*
- *rev'd per curiam,*
- *rev'g*
- *vacated,*
- *vacating as moot*
- *withdrawn,*

T9   LEGISLATIVE DOCUMENTS

This table gives suggested abbreviations for citation of the words most commonly found in legislative documents. In some cases, it indicates that a word should not be abbreviated. Words of more than six letters not appearing on the list may also be abbreviated if the abbreviation selected is unambiguous. Omit all articles and prepositions from any abbreviated title if the document can be identified unambiguously without them.

Annals	Annals
Annual	Ann.
Assembly[man, woman, member]	Assemb.
Bill	B.
Committee	Comm.

▸ Concurrent	Con.	
▸ Conference	Conf.	
▸ Congress[ional]	Cong.	
▸ Debate	Deb.	
▸ Delegate	Del.	
▸ Document[s]	Doc.	
▸ Executive	Exec.	
▸ Federal	Fed.	
▸ House	H.	
▸ House of Delegates	H.D.	
▸ House of Representatives	H.R.	
▸ Joint	J.	
▸ Legislat[ion, ive]	Legis.	
▸ Legislature	Leg.	
▸ Miscellaneous	Misc.	
▸ Number	No.	
▸ Order	Order	
▸ Record	Rec.	
▸ Register	Reg.	
▸ Regular	Reg.	
▸ Report	Rep.	
▸ Representative	Rep.	
▸ Resolution	Res.	
▸ Senate	S.	
▸ Senator	Sen.	
▸ Service	Serv.	
▸ Session	Sess.	
▸ Special	Spec.	
▸ Subcommittee	Subcomm.	

T10   GEOGRAPHICAL TERMS

The following list provides abbreviations for geographical locations for use in case citations (**rules 10.2.2** and **10.4**), names of institutional authors (**rule 15.1(c)**), periodical abbreviations (**rule 16** and **table T13**), foreign materials (**rule 20.1**), and treaty citations (**rule 21.4.2**).

T10.1   U.S. states, cities, and territories

States

▸ Alabama	Ala.	▸ Colorado	Colo.
▸ Alaska	Alaska	▸ Connecticut	Conn.
▸ Arizona	Ariz.	▸ Delaware	Del.
▸ Arkansas	Ark.	▸ Florida	Fla.
▸ California	Cal.	▸ Georgia	Ga.

▸ Hawaii	Haw.	▸ New Mexico	N.M.
▸ Idaho	Idaho	▸ New York	N.Y.
▸ Illinois	Ill.	▸ North Carolina	N.C.
▸ Indiana	Ind.	▸ North Dakota	N.D.
▸ Iowa	Iowa	▸ Ohio	Ohio
▸ Kansas	Kan.	▸ Oklahoma	Okla.
▸ Kentucky	Ky.	▸ Oregon	Or.
▸ Louisiana	La.	▸ Pennsylvania	Pa.
▸ Maine	Me.	▸ Rhode Island	R.I.
▸ Maryland	Md.	▸ South Carolina	S.C.
▸ Massachusetts	Mass.	▸ South Dakota	S.D.
▸ Michigan	Mich.	▸ Tennessee	Tenn.
▸ Minnesota	Minn.	▸ Texas	Tex.
▸ Mississippi	Miss.	▸ Utah	Utah
▸ Missouri	Mo.	▸ Vermont	Vt.
▸ Montana	Mont.	▸ Virginia	Va.
▸ Nebraska	Neb.	▸ Washington	Wash.
▸ Nevada	Nev.	▸ West Virginia	W. Va.
▸ New Hampshire	N.H.	▸ Wisconsin	Wis.
▸ New Jersey	N.J.	▸ Wyoming	Wyo.

Cities

Abbreviations for city names may also be composed from state name abbreviations above. For example, "Oklahoma City" should be shortened to "Okla. City."

▸ Atlanta	Atl.	▸ Houston	Hous.
▸ Baltimore	Balt.	▸ Los Angeles	L.A.
▸ Boston	Bos.	▸ New York	N.Y.C.
▸ Chicago	Chi.	▸ Philadelphia	Phila.
▸ Dallas	Dall.	▸ Phoenix	Phx.
▸ District of Columbia	D.C.	▸ San Francisco	S.F.

Territories

▸ American Samoa	Am. Sam.
▸ Guam	Guam
▸ Northern Mariana Islands	N. Mar. I.
▸ Puerto Rico	P.R.
▸ Virgin Islands	V.I.

T10.2 Australian states and Canadian provinces and territories

Australia
▸ Australian Capital Territory	Austl. Cap. Terr.
▸ New South Wales	N.S.W.
▸ Northern Territory	N. Terr.
▸ Queensland	Queensl.
▸ South Australia	S. Austl.
▸ Tasmania	Tas.
▸ Victoria	Vict.
▸ Western Australia	W. Austl.

Canada
▸ Alberta	Alta.
▸ British Columbia	B.C.
▸ Manitoba	Man.
▸ New Brunswick	N.B.
▸ Newfoundland & Labrador	Nfld.
▸ Northwest Territories	N.W.T.
▸ Nova Scotia	N.S.
▸ Nunavut	Nun.
▸ Ontario	Ont.
▸ Prince Edward Island	P.E.I.
▸ Québec	Que.
▸ Saskatchewan	Sask.
▸ Yukon	Yukon

T10.3 Foreign countries and regions
▸ Afghanistan	Afg.
▸ Africa	Afr.
▸ Albania	Alb.
▸ Algeria	Alg.
▸ Andorra	Andorra
▸ Angola	Angl.
▸ Anguilla	Anguilla
▸ Antarctica	Antarctica
▸ Antigua & Barbuda	Ant. & Barb.
▸ Argentina	Arg.
▸ Armenia	Arm.
▸ Asia	Asia
▸ Australia	Austl.
▸ Austria	Austria
▸ Azerbaijan	Azer.
▸ Bahamas	Bah.

▶ Bahrain	Bahr.
▶ Bangladesh	Bangl.
▶ Barbados	Barb.
▶ Belarus	Belr.
▶ Belgium	Belg.
▶ Belize	Belize
▶ Benin	Benin
▶ Bermuda	Berm.
▶ Bhutan	Bhutan
▶ Bolivia	Bol.
▶ Bosnia & Herzegovina	Bosn. & Herz.
▶ Botswana	Bots.
▶ Brazil	Braz.
▶ Brunei	Brunei
▶ Bulgaria	Bulg.
▶ Burkina Faso	Burk. Faso
▶ Burundi	Burundi
▶ Cambodia	Cambodia
▶ Cameroon	Cameroon
▶ Canada	Can.
▶ Cape Verde	Cape Verde
▶ Cayman Islands	Cayman Is.
▶ Central African Republic	Cent. Afr. Rep.
▶ Chad	Chad
▶ Chile	Chile
▶ China, People's Republic of	China
▶ Colombia	Colom.
▶ Comoros	Comoros
▶ Congo, Democratic Republic of the	Dem. Rep. Congo
▶ Congo, Republic of the	Congo
▶ Costa Rica	Costa Rica
▶ Côte d'Ivoire	Côte d'Ivoire
▶ Croatia	Croat.
▶ Cuba	Cuba
▶ Cyprus	Cyprus
▶ Czech Republic	Czech
▶ Denmark	Den.
▶ Djibouti	Djib.
▶ Dominica	Dominica
▶ Dominican Republic	Dom. Rep.
▶ Ecuador	Ecuador
▶ Egypt	Egypt
▶ El Salvador	El Sal.
▶ England	Eng.
▶ Equatorial Guinea	Eq. Guinea
▶ Eritrea	Eri.
▶ Estonia	Est.

▸ Ethiopia	Eth.
▸ Europe	Eur.
▸ Falkland Islands	Falkland Is.
▸ Fiji	Fiji
▸ Finland	Fin.
▸ France	Fr.
▸ Gabon	Gabon
▸ Gambia	Gam.
▸ Georgia	Geor.
▸ Germany	Ger.
▸ Ghana	Ghana
▸ Gibraltar	Gib.
▸ Great Britain	Gr. Brit.
▸ Greece	Greece
▸ Greenland	Green.
▸ Grenada	Gren.
▸ Guadeloupe	Guad.
▸ Guatemala	Guat.
▸ Guinea	Guinea
▸ Guinea-Bissau	Guinea-Bissau
▸ Guyana	Guy.
▸ Haiti	Haiti
▸ Honduras	Hond.
▸ Hong Kong	H.K.
▸ Hungary	Hung.
▸ Iceland	Ice.
▸ India	India
▸ Indonesia	Indon.
▸ Iran	Iran
▸ Iraq	Iraq
▸ Ireland	Ir.
▸ Israel	Isr.
▸ Italy	It.
▸ Jamaica	Jam.
▸ Japan	Japan
▸ Jordan	Jordan
▸ Kazakhstan	Kaz.
▸ Kenya	Kenya
▸ Kiribati	Kiribati
▸ Korea, North	N. Kor.
▸ Korea, South	S. Kor.
▸ Kosovo	Kos.
▸ Kuwait	Kuwait
▸ Kyrgyzstan	Kyrg.
▸ Laos	Laos
▸ Latvia	Lat.
▸ Lebanon	Leb.

▶ Lesotho	Lesotho
▶ Liberia	Liber.
▶ Libya	Libya
▶ Liechtenstein	Liech.
▶ Lithuania	Lith.
▶ Luxembourg	Lux.
▶ Macau	Mac.
▶ Macedonia	Maced.
▶ Madagascar	Madag.
▶ Malawi	Malawi
▶ Malaysia	Malay.
▶ Maldives	Maldives
▶ Mali	Mali
▶ Malta	Malta
▶ Marshall Islands	Marsh. Is.
▶ Martinique	Mart.
▶ Mauritania	Mauritania
▶ Mauritius	Mauritius
▶ Mexico	Mex.
▶ Micronesia	Micr.
▶ Moldova	Mold.
▶ Monaco	Monaco
▶ Mongolia	Mong.
▶ Montenegro	Montenegro
▶ Montserrat	Montserrat
▶ Morocco	Morocco
▶ Mozambique	Mozam.
▶ Myanmar	Myan.
▶ Namibia	Namib.
▶ Nauru	Nauru
▶ Nepal	Nepal
▶ Netherlands	Neth.
▶ New Zealand	N.Z.
▶ Nicaragua	Nicar.
▶ Niger	Niger
▶ Nigeria	Nigeria
▶ North America	N. Am.
▶ Northern Ireland	N. Ir.
▶ Norway	Nor.
▶ Oman	Oman
▶ Pakistan	Pak.
▶ Palau	Palau
▶ Panama	Pan.
▶ Papua New Guinea	Papua N.G.
▶ Paraguay	Para.
▶ Peru	Peru
▶ Philippines	Phil.

▸ Pitcairn Island	Pitcairn Is.
▸ Poland	Pol.
▸ Portugal	Port.
▸ Qatar	Qatar
▸ Réunion	Réunion
▸ Romania	Rom.
▸ Russia	Russ.
▸ Rwanda	Rwanda
▸ Saint Helena	St. Helena
▸ Saint Kitts & Nevis	St. Kitts & Nevis
▸ Saint Lucia	St. Lucia
▸ Saint Vincent & the Grenadines	St. Vincent
▸ Samoa	Samoa
▸ San Marino	San Marino
▸ São Tomé and Príncipe	São Tomé & Príncipe
▸ Saudi Arabia	Saudi Arabia
▸ Scotland	Scot.
▸ Senegal	Sen.
▸ Serbia	Serb.
▸ Seychelles	Sey.
▸ Sierra Leone	Sierra Leone
▸ Singapore	Sing.
▸ Slovakia	Slovk.
▸ Slovenia	Slovn.
▸ Solomon Islands	Solom. Is.
▸ Somalia	Som.
▸ South Africa	S. Afr.
▸ South America	S. Am.
▸ Spain	Spain
▸ Sri Lanka	Sri Lanka
▸ Sudan	Sudan
▸ Suriname	Surin.
▸ Swaziland	Swaz.
▸ Sweden	Swed.
▸ Switzerland	Switz.
▸ Syria	Syria
▸ Taiwan	Taiwan
▸ Tajikistan	Taj.
▸ Tanzania	Tanz.
▸ Thailand	Thai.
▸ Timor-Leste (East Timor)	Timor-Leste
▸ Togo	Togo
▸ Tonga	Tonga
▸ Trinidad & Tobago	Trin. & Tobago
▸ Tunisia	Tunis.
▸ Turkey	Turk.
▸ Turkmenistan	Turkm.

▸ Turks & Caicos Islands	Turks & Caicos Is.
▸ Tuvalu	Tuvalu
▸ Uganda	Uganda
▸ Ukraine	Ukr.
▸ United Arab Emirates	U.A.E.
▸ United Kingdom	U.K.
▸ United States of America	U.S.
▸ Uruguay	Uru.
▸ Uzbekistan	Uzb.
▸ Vanuatu	Vanuatu
▸ Vatican City	Vatican
▸ Venezuela	Venez.
▸ Vietnam	Viet.
▸ Virgin Islands, British	Virgin Is.
▸ Wales	Wales
▸ Yemen	Yemen
▸ Zambia	Zam.
▸ Zimbabwe	Zim.

T11   JUDGES AND OFFICIALS

Abbreviate titles of judges and other officials according to the following table. See **rule 9** for further guidance in using abbreviated titles.

▸ Administrative Law Judge	A.L.J.
▸ Arbitrator	Arb.
▸ Assembly[man, woman, member]	Assemb.
▸ Attorney General	Att'y Gen.
▸ Baron	B.
▸ Chancellor	C.
▸ Chief Baron	C.B.
▸ Chief Judge, Chief Justice	C.J.
▸ Commissioner	Comm'r
▸ Delegate	Del.
▸ Honorable	Hon.
▸ Judge, Justice	J.
▸ Judges, Justices	JJ.
▸ Lord Justice	L.J.
▸ Magistrate	Mag.
▸ Master of the Rolls	M.R.
▸ Mediator	Med.
▸ Referee	Ref.
▸ Representative	Rep.
▸ Senator	Sen.
▸ Vice Chancellor	V.C.

T12   MONTHS

In citations, abbreviate the names of months as follows:

► January	Jan.
► February	Feb.
► March	Mar.
► April	Apr.
► May	May
► June	June
► July	July
► August	Aug.
► September	Sept.
► October	Oct.
► November	Nov.
► December	Dec.

T13   PERIODICALS

The following alphabetical list provides abbreviations for the names of select English language periodicals and individual words commonly found in periodical titles. *Always use the title of the periodical that appears on the title page of the issue you are citing,* even if the periodical has changed over time.

Note that preferred abbreviation conventions for individual journals may differ from those listed in this table. The abbreviation conventions listed here are primarily intended to serve a national audience and to clearly indicate the cited source.

If the periodical you wish to cite does not appear in this list, structure the abbreviation by looking up each word of the title in this table and in the list of geographical abbreviations found in **table T10**. Omit the words "a," "at," "in," "of," and "the" (but retain the word "on"). If a word is listed neither here nor in **table T10**, use the full word in the abbreviated title. Also, if the title consists of only one word after the words "a," "at," "in," "of," and "the" have been omitted, do not abbreviate the remaining word. **Rule 6.1(a)** explains the spacing of abbreviations.

If a periodical title itself contains an abbreviation, use that abbreviation in the abbreviated title:

► IMF Surv.

Omit commas from periodical title abbreviations but retain other punctuation:

► Peter H. Huang & Ho-Mou Wu, *More Order Without More Law: A Theory of Social Norms and Organizational Cultures*, 10 J.L. Econ. & Org. 390 (1994).

► *Nineteen States Adopt Code of Judicial Conduct*, Oyez! Oyez!, Feb. 1974, at 11.

If a periodical has been renumbered in a new series, indicate that fact:

► Jill Martin, *The Statutory Sub-Tenancy: A Right Against the World?*, 41 Conv. & Prop. Law. (n.s.) 96 (1977).

For periodical abbreviations in languages other than English, see **rules 20.2.3** and **20.6**.

For online supplements to the print publication, use the citation for the print publication, followed by the online supplement name.

▶ COLUM. L. REV. SIDEBAR

....

A-B

▶ ABA Journal	A.B.A. J.
▶ Academ[ic, y]	ACAD.
▶ Account[ant, ants, ing, ancy]	ACCT.
▶ Adelaide Law Review	ADEL. L. REV.
▶ Administrat[ive, or, ion]	ADMIN.
▶ Administrative Law Review of American University	ADMIN. L. REV. AM. U.
▶ Administrative Law Review	ADMIN. L. REV.
▶ Advoca[te, cy]	ADVOC.
▶ Affairs	AFF.
▶ Africa[n]	AFR.
▶ Agricultur[e, al]	AGRIC.
▶ Air	AIR
▶ Air Force Law Review	A.F. L. REV.
▶ Akron Law Review	AKRON L. REV.
▶ Akron Tax Journal	AKRON TAX J.
▶ Alabama Law Review	ALA. L. REV.
▶ Alaska Law Review	ALASKA L. REV.
▶ Albany Law Journal of Science & Technology	ALB. L.J. SCI. & TECH.
▶ Albany Law Review	ALB. L. REV.
▶ America[n]	AM.
▶ American Bankruptcy Institute Law Review	AM. BANKR. INST. L. REV.
▶ American Bankruptcy Law Journal	AM. BANKR. L.J.
▶ American Bar Association	A.B.A.
▶ American Bar Foundation Research Journal	AM. B. FOUND. RES. J.
▶ American Business Law Journal	AM. BUS. L.J.
▶ American Criminal Law Review	AM. CRIM. L. REV.
▶ American Indian Law Review	AM. INDIAN L. REV.
▶ American Intellectual Property Law Association Quarterly Journal	AIPLA Q.J.
▶ American Journal of Comparative Law	AM. J. COMP. L.
▶ American Journal of Criminal Law	AM. J. CRIM. L.
▶ American Journal of International Law	AM. J. INT'L L.
▶ American Journal of Jurisprudence	AM. J. JURIS.
▶ American Journal of Law & Medicine	AM. J.L. & MED.
▶ American Journal of Legal History	AM. J. LEGAL HIST.
▶ American Journal of Trial Advocacy	AM. J. TRIAL ADVOC.
▶ American Law Institute	A.L.I.
▶ American Law Reports	A.L.R.
▶ American Review of International Arbitration	AM. REV. INT'L ARB.

American University International Law Review	AM. U. INT'L L. REV.
American University Journal of Gender, Social Policy & the Law	AM. U. J. GENDER SOC. POL'Y & L.
American University Law Review	AM. U. L. REV.
and	&
Anglo-American Law Review	ANGLO-AM. L. REV.
Animal Law	ANIMAL L.
Annals	ANNALS
Annals of the American Academy of Political and Social Science	ANNALS AM. ACAD. POL. & SOC. SCI.
Annals of Health Law	ANNALS HEALTH L.
Annual	ANN.
Annual Review of Banking & Financial Law	ANN. REV. BANKING & FIN. L.
Annual Review of Banking Law	ANN. REV. BANKING L.
Annual Survey of American Law	ANN. SURV. AM. L.
Annual Survey of International and Comparative Law	ANN. SURV. INT'L & COMP. L.
Antitrust	ANTITRUST
Appellate	APP.
Arbitrat[ion, ors]	ARB.
Arizona Journal of International and Comparative Law	ARIZ. J. INT'L & COMP. L.
Arizona Law Review	ARIZ. L. REV.
Arizona State Law Journal	ARIZ. ST. L.J.
Arkansas Law Notes	ARK. L. NOTES
Arkansas Law Review	ARK. L. REV.
Army Lawyer	ARMY LAW.
Art	ART
Asian American Law Journal	ASIAN AM. L.J.
Asian Pacific American Law Journal	ASIAN PAC. AM. L.J.
Asian-Pacific Law & Policy Journal	ASIAN-PAC. L. & POL'Y J.
Association	ASS'N
Attorney	ATT'Y
Auckland University Law Review	AUCKLAND U. L. REV.
Ave Maria Law Review	AVE MARIA L. REV.
Bankruptcy	BANKR.
Bankruptcy Developments Journal	BANKR. DEV. J.
Bar	B.
Baylor Law Review	BAYLOR L. REV.
Behavior[al]	BEHAV.
Behavioral Sciences and the Law	BEHAV. SCI. & L.
Berkeley Journal of African-American Law & Policy	BERKELEY J. AFR.-AM. L. & POL'Y
Berkeley Journal of Employment and Labor Law	BERKELEY J. EMP. & LAB. L.
Berkeley Journal of International Law	BERKELEY J. INT'L L.
Berkeley Journal of Gender, Law, and Justice	BERKELEY J. GENDER L. & JUST.
Berkeley Technology Law Journal	BERKELEY TECH. L.J.

▸ Boston College Environmental Affairs Law Review	B.C. Envtl. Aff. L. Rev.
▸ Boston College International and Comparative Law Review	B.C. Int'l & Comp. L. Rev.
▸ Boston College Law Review	B.C. L. Rev.
▸ Boston College Third World Law Journal	B.C. Third World L.J.
▸ Boston University International Law Journal	B.U. Int'l L.J.
▸ Boston University Journal of Science & Technology Law	B.U. J. Sci. & Tech. L.
▸ Boston University Law Review	B.U. L. Rev.
▸ Boston University Public Interest Law Journal	B.U. Pub. Int. L.J.
▸ Brandeis Law Journal	Brandeis L.J.
▸ Briefcase	Briefcase
▸ Brigham Young University Education and Law Journal	BYU Educ. & L.J.
▸ Brigham Young University Journal of Public Law	BYU J. Pub. L.
▸ Brigham Young University Law Review	BYU L. Rev.
▸ British	Brit.
▸ Brooklyn Journal of International Law	Brook. J. Int'l L.
▸ Brooklyn Law Review	Brook. L. Rev.
▸ Buffalo Criminal Law Review	Buff. Crim. L. Rev.
▸ Buffalo Environmental Law Journal	Buff. Envtl. L.J.
▸ Buffalo Human Rights Law Review	Buff. Hum. Rts. L. Rev.
▸ Buffalo Law Review	Buff. L. Rev.
▸ Buffalo Public Interest Law Journal	Buff. Pub. Int. L.J.
▸ Buffalo Women's Law Journal	Buff. Women's L.J.
▸ Bulletin	Bull.
▸ Business	Bus.
▸ Business Law Journal	Bus. L.J.
▸ Business Lawyer	Bus. Law.
▸ Business Week	Bus. Wk.

C-D

▸ California Bankruptcy Journal	Cal. Bankr. J.
▸ California Criminal Law Review	Cal. Crim. L. Rev.
▸ California Law Review	Calif. L. Rev.
▸ California Regulatory Law Reporter	Cal. Reg. L. Rep.
▸ California State Bar Journal	Cal. St. B.J.
▸ California Western International Law Journal	Cal. W. Int'l L.J.
▸ California Western Law Review	Cal. W. L. Rev.
▸ Cambridge Law Journal	Cambridge L.J.
▸ Campbell Law Review	Campbell L. Rev.
▸ Canada-United States Law Journal	Can.-U.S. L.J.
▸ Capital Defense Digest	Cap. Def. Dig.
▸ Capital Defense Journal	Cap. Def. J.
▸ Capital University Law Review	Cap. U. L. Rev.
▸ Cardozo Arts & Entertainment Law Journal	Cardozo Arts & Ent. L.J.

▸ Cardozo Journal of Conflict Resolution	CARDOZO J. CONFLICT RESOL.
▸ Cardozo Journal of International and Comparative Law	CARDOZO J. INT'L & COMP. L.
▸ Cardozo Law Review	CARDOZO L. REV.
▸ Cardozo Online Journal of Conflict Resolution	CARDOZO ONLINE J. CONFLICT RESOL.
▸ Cardozo Women's Law Journal	CARDOZO WOMEN'S L.J.
▸ Case & Comment	CASE & COMMENT
▸ Case Western Reserve Journal of International Law	CASE W. RES. J. INT'L L.
▸ Case Western Reserve Law Review	CASE W. RES. L. REV.
▸ Catholic Lawyer	CATH. LAW.
▸ Catholic University Law Review	CATH. U. L. REV.
▸ Central	CENT.
▸ Chapman Law Review	CHAP. L. REV.
▸ Chartered Life Underwriters	C.L.U.
▸ Chicago Tribune	CHI. TRIB.
▸ Chicago Journal of International Law	CHI. J. INT'L L.
▸ Chicago-Kent Law Review	CHI.-KENT L. REV.
▸ Chicano-Latino Law Review	CHICANO-LATINO L. REV.
▸ Child[ren, ren's]	CHILD.
▸ Children's Legal Rights Journal	CHILD. LEGAL RTS. J.
▸ Chronicle	CHRON.
▸ Civil	CIV.
▸ Civil Libert[y, ies]	C.L.
▸ Civil Rights	C.R.
▸ Clearinghouse Review	CLEARINGHOUSE REV.
▸ Cleveland State Law Review	CLEV. ST. L. REV.
▸ Cleveland-Marshall Law Review	CLEV.-MARSHALL L. REV.
▸ Clinical Law Review	CLINICAL L. REV.
▸ College	C.
▸ Colorado Journal of International Environmental Law and Policy	COLO. J. INT'L ENVTL. L. & POL'Y
▸ Colorado Lawyer	COLO. LAW.
▸ Columbia Business Law Review	COLUM. BUS. L. REV.
▸ Columbia Human Rights Law Review	COLUM. HUM. RTS. L. REV.
▸ Columbia Journal of Asian Law	COLUM. J. ASIAN L.
▸ Columbia Journal of East European Law	COLUM. J. E. EUR. L.
▸ Columbia Journal of Environmental Law	COLUM. J. ENVTL. L.
▸ Columbia Journal of European Law	COLUM. J. EUR. L.
▸ Columbia Journal of Gender and Law	COLUM. J. GENDER & L.
▸ Columbia Journal of Law and Social Problems	COLUM. J.L. & SOC. PROBS.
▸ Columbia Journal of Law & the Arts	COLUM. J.L. & ARTS
▸ Columbia Journal of Transnational Law	COLUM. J. TRANSNAT'L L.
▸ Columbia Law Review	COLUM. L. REV.
▸ Columbia Science and Technology Law Review	COLUM. SCI. & TECH. L. REV.
▸ Columbia-VLA Journal of Law & the Arts	COLUM.-VLA J.L. & ARTS

▸ Commentary	COMMENT.
▸ Commerc[e, ial]	COM.
▸ CommLaw Conspectus: Journal of Communications Law & Policy	COMMLAW CONSPECTUS
▸ Common Market Law Review	COMMON MKT. L. REV.
▸ Communication[s]	COMM.
▸ Comparative	COMP.
▸ Comparative Labor Law Journal	COMP. LAB. L.J.
▸ Comparative Labor Law & Policy Journal	COMP. LAB. L. & POL'Y J.
▸ Computer	COMPUTER
▸ Computer/Law Journal	COMPUTER/L.J.
▸ Computer Law Review & Technology Journal	COMPUTER L. REV. & TECH J.
▸ Conference	CONF.
▸ Congressional	CONG.
▸ Congressional Digest	CONG. DIG.
▸ Connecticut Insurance Law Journal	CONN. INS. L.J.
▸ Connecticut Journal of International Law	CONN. J. INT'L L.
▸ Connecticut Law Review	CONN. L. REV.
▸ Connecticut Probate Law Journal	CONN. PROB. L.J.
▸ Constitution[al]	CONST.
▸ Constitutional Commentary	CONST. COMMENT.
▸ Consumer	CONSUMER
▸ Consumer Finance Law Quarterly Report	CONSUMER FIN. L. Q. REP.
▸ Contemporary	CONTEMP.
▸ Contract[s]	CONT.
▸ Conveyancer and Property Lawyer (new series)	CONV. & PROP. LAW. (n.s.)
▸ Copyright Law Symposium (American Society of Composers, Authors, & Publishers)	COPYRIGHT L. SYMP. (ASCAP)
▸ Cornell International Law Journal	CORNELL INT'L L.J.
▸ Cornell Journal of Law and Public Policy	CORNELL J.L. & PUB. POL'Y
▸ Cornell Law Review	CORNELL L. REV.
▸ Corporat[e, ion]	CORP.
▸ Corporate Taxation	CORP. TAX'N
▸ Counsel[or, ors, or's]	COUNS.
▸ Court	CT.
▸ Creighton Law Review	CREIGHTON L. REV.
▸ Crime	CRIME
▸ Criminal	CRIM.
▸ Criminal Law Forum	CRIM. L.F.
▸ Criminal Law Review	CRIM. L. REV.
▸ Criminal Law Bulletin	CRIM. L. BULL.
▸ Criminology	CRIMINOLOGY
▸ Cumberland Law Review	CUMB. L. REV.
▸ Current Medicine for Attorneys	CURRENT MED. FOR ATT'YS
▸ Currents: The International Trade Law Journal	CURRENTS: INT'L TRADE L.J.
▸ Dalhousie Law Journal	DALHOUSIE L.J.
▸ DePaul Business Law Journal	DEPAUL BUS. L.J.

▸ DePaul Business & Commercial Law Journal	DEPAUL BUS. & COM. L.J.
▸ DePaul Journal of Health Care Law	DEPAUL J. HEALTH CARE L.
▸ DePaul Law Review	DEPAUL L. REV.
▸ DePaul-LCA Journal of Art and Entertainment Law and Policy	DEPAUL-LCA J. ART & ENT. L. & POL'Y
▸ Defense	DEF.
▸ Defense Counsel Journal	DEF. COUNS. J.
▸ Delaware Journal of Corporate Law	DEL. J. CORP. L.
▸ Delaware Law Review	DEL. L. REV.
▸ Delinquency	DELINQ.
▸ Denver Journal of International Law and Policy	DENV. J. INT'L L. & POL'Y
▸ Denver University Law Review	DENV. U. L. REV.
▸ Department of State Bulletin	DEP'T ST. BULL.
▸ Development[s]	DEV.
▸ Dickinson International Law Annual	DICK. INT'L L. ANN.
▸ Dickinson Law Review	DICK. L. REV.
▸ Digest	DIG.
▸ The Digest: The National Italian-American Bar Ass'n Law Journal	DIGEST
▸ Diplomacy	DIPL.
▸ Dispute	DISP.
▸ District of Columbia Law Review	D.C. L. REV.
▸ Drake Journal of Agricultural Law	DRAKE J. AGRIC. L.
▸ Drake Law Review	DRAKE L. REV.
▸ Duke Environmental Law & Policy Forum	DUKE ENVTL. L. & POL'Y F.
▸ Duke Journal of Comparative & International Law	DUKE J. COMP. & INT'L L.
▸ Duke Journal of Gender Law & Policy	DUKE J. GENDER L. & POL'Y
▸ Duke Law Journal	DUKE L.J.
▸ Duquesne Business Law Journal	DUQ. BUS. L.J.
▸ Duquesne Law Review	DUQ. L. REV.

....

E-F

▸ East[ern]	E.
▸ Ecology Law Quarterly	ECOLOGY L.Q.
▸ Econom[ic, ics, y]	ECON.
▸ The Economist	ECONOMIST
▸ Education[al]	EDUC.
▸ Elder Law Journal	ELDER L.J.
▸ Emory Bankruptcy Developments Journal	EMORY BANKR. DEV. J.
▸ Emory International Law Review	EMORY INT'L L. REV.
▸ Emory Law Journal	EMORY L.J.
▸ Employ[ee, ment]	EMP.
▸ Employee Rights and Employment Policy Journal	EMP. RTS. & EMP. POL'Y J.
▸ Energy	ENERGY
▸ Energy Law Journal	ENERGY L.J.
▸ English	ENG.

▸ Entertainment	ENT.
▸ Environment	ENV'T
▸ Environmental	ENVTL.
▸ Environmental Law	ENVTL. L.
▸ Environmental Lawyer	ENVTL. LAW.
▸ Estate[s]	EST.
▸ Ethics	ETHICS
▸ Europe[an]	EUR.
▸ Faculty	FAC.
▸ Family	FAM.
▸ Family and Conciliation Courts Review	FAM. & CONCILIATION CTS. REV.
▸ Family Court Review	FAM. CT. REV.
▸ Family Law Quarterly	FAM. L.Q.
▸ Federal	FED.
▸ Federal Circuit Bar Journal	FED. CIR. B.J.
▸ Federal Communications Law Journal	FED. COMM. L.J.
▸ Federal Probation	FED. PROBATION
▸ Federal Sentencing Reporter	FED. SENT'G REP.
▸ Federation	FED'N
▸ Financ[e, ial]	FIN.
▸ First Amendment Law Review	FIRST AMEND. L. REV.
▸ Florida Journal of International Law	FLA. J. INT'L L.
▸ Florida Law Review	FLA. L. REV.
▸ Florida State Journal of Transnational Law & Policy	FLA. ST. J. TRANSNAT'L L. & POL'Y
▸ Florida State University Law Review	FLA. ST. U. L. REV.
▸ Florida Tax Review	FLA. TAX REV.
▸ Food and Drug Law Journal	FOOD & DRUG L.J.
▸ Food Drug Cosmetic Law Journal	FOOD DRUG COSM. L.J.
▸ for	FOR
▸ Fordham Environmental Law Review	FORDHAM ENVTL. L. REV.
▸ Fordham Intellectual Property, Media & Entertainment Law Journal	FORDHAM INTELL. PROP. MEDIA & ENT. L.J.
▸ Fordham International Law Journal	FORDHAM INT'L L.J.
▸ Fordham Journal of Corporate & Financial Law	FORDHAM J. CORP. & FIN. L.
▸ Fordham Law Review	FORDHAM L. REV.
▸ Fordham Urban Law Journal	FORDHAM URB. L.J.
▸ Foreign	FOREIGN
▸ Foreign Broadcast Information Service	F.B.I.S.
▸ Forensic	FORENSIC
▸ Fortnightly	FORT.
▸ Fortune	FORTUNE
▸ Forum	F.
▸ The Forum	FORUM
▸ Foundation[s]	FOUND.
▸ Franchise Law Journal	FRANCHISE L.J.

G-H

▸ Gender	GENDER
▸ General	GEN.
▸ George Mason Law Review	GEO. MASON L. REV.
▸ George Mason University Civil Rights Law Journal	GEO. MASON U. C.R. L.J.
▸ George Washington International Law Review	GEO. WASH. INT'L L. REV.
▸ George Washington Journal of International Law and Economics	GEO. WASH. J. INT'L L. & ECON.
▸ George Washington Law Review	GEO. WASH. L. REV.
▸ Georgetown Immigration Law Journal	GEO. IMMIGR. L.J.
▸ Georgetown International Environmental Law Review	GEO. INT'L ENVTL. L. REV.
▸ The Georgetown Journal of Gender and the Law	GEO. J. GENDER & L.
▸ Georgetown Journal of International Law	GEO. J. INT'L L.
▸ Georgetown Journal of Legal Ethics	GEO. J. LEGAL ETHICS
▸ Georgetown Journal on Poverty Law and Policy	GEO. J. ON POVERTY L. & POL'Y
▸ Georgetown Law Journal	GEO. L.J.
▸ Georgia Journal of International and Comparative Law	GA. J. INT'L & COMP. L.
▸ Georgia Law Review	GA. L. REV.
▸ Georgia State University Law Review	GA. ST. U. L. REV.
▸ Glendale Law Review	GLENDALE L. REV.
▸ Golden Gate University Law Review	GOLDEN GATE U. L. REV.
▸ Gonzaga Law Review	GONZ. L. REV.
▸ Government	GOV'T
▸ Great Plains Natural Resources Journal	GREAT PLAINS NAT. RESOURCES J.
▸ Green Bag	GREEN BAG
▸ Guild Practitioner	GUILD PRAC.
▸ Hamline Journal of Public Law and Policy	HAMLINE J. PUB. L. & POL'Y
▸ Hamline Law Review	HAMLINE L. REV.
▸ Harvard Civil Rights-Civil Liberties Law Review	HARV. C.R.-C.L. L. REV.
▸ Harvard Environmental Law Review	HARV. ENVTL. L. REV.
▸ Harvard Human Rights Journal	HARV. HUM. RTS. J.
▸ Harvard International Law Journal	HARV. INT'L L.J.
▸ Harvard Journal of Law and Gender	HARV. J.L. & GENDER
▸ Harvard Journal of Law and Public Policy	HARV. J.L. & PUB. POL'Y
▸ Harvard Journal of Law & Technology	HARV. J.L. & TECH.
▸ Harvard Journal on Legislation	HARV. J. ON LEGIS.
▸ Harvard Journal on Racial & Ethnic Justice	HARV. J. ON RACIAL & ETHNIC JUST.
▸ Harvard Latino Law Review	HARV. LATINO L. REV.
▸ Harvard Law & Policy Review	HARV. L. & POL'Y REV.
▸ Harvard Law Review	HARV. L. REV.
▸ Harvard Negotiation Law Review	HARV. NEGOT. L. REV.

▸ Harvard Women's Law Journal	HARV. WOMEN'S L.J.
▸ Hastings Communications and Entertainment Law Journal	HASTINGS COMM. & ENT. L.J.
▸ Hastings Constitutional Law Quarterly	HASTINGS CONST. L.Q.
▸ Hastings International and Comparative Law Review	HASTINGS INT'L & COMP. L. REV.
▸ Hastings Law Journal	HASTINGS L.J.
▸ Hastings West-Northwest Journal of Environmental Law and Policy	HASTINGS W.-NW. J. ENVTL. L. & POL'Y
▸ Hastings Women's Law Journal	HASTINGS WOMEN'S L.J.
▸ Health	HEALTH
▸ Health Matrix	HEALTH MATRIX
▸ Herald	HERALD
▸ High Technology Law Journal	HIGH TECH. L.J.
▸ Hispanic	HISP.
▸ Histor[ical, y]	HIST.
▸ Hofstra Labor & Employment Law Journal	HOFSTRA LAB. & EMP. L.J.
▸ Hofstra Law Review	HOFSTRA L. REV.
▸ Hospital	HOSP.
▸ Houston Journal of International Law	HOUS. J. INT'L L.
▸ Houston Law Review	HOUS. L. REV.
▸ Howard Law Journal	HOW. L.J.
▸ Human	HUM.
▸ Human Rights Quarterly	HUM. RTS. Q.
▸ Humanit[y, ies]	HUMAN.

I-J

▸ Idaho Law Review	IDAHO L. REV.
▸ IDEA: The Intellectual Property Law Review	IDEA
▸ Illinois Bar Journal	ILL. B.J.
▸ ILSA Journal of International & Comparative Law	ILSA J. INT'L & COMP. L.
▸ Immigration	IMMIGR.
▸ Immigration and Nationality Law Review	IMMIGR. & NAT'LITY L. REV.
▸ In the Public Interest	IN PUB. INTEREST
▸ Independent	INDEP.
▸ Indian	INDIAN
▸ Indiana International & Comparative Law Review	IND. INT'L & COMP. L. REV.
▸ Indiana Journal of Global Legal Studies	IND. J. GLOBAL LEGAL STUD.
▸ Indiana Law Journal	IND. L.J.
▸ Indiana Law Review	IND. L. REV.
▸ Industrial	INDUS.
▸ Industrial and Labor Relations Review	INDUS. & LAB. REL. REV.
▸ Information	INFO.
▸ Injury	INJ.
▸ Institute	INST.
▸ Institute on Federal Taxation	INST. ON FED. TAX'N

▸ Institute on Oil and Gas Law and Taxation	INST. ON OIL & GAS L. & TAX'N
▸ Institute on Planning, Zoning, and Eminent Domain	INST. ON PLAN. ZONING & EMINENT DOMAIN
▸ Institute on Private Investments and Investors Abroad	INST. ON PRIV. INV. & INV. ABROAD
▸ Institute on Securities Regulation	INST. ON SEC. REG.
▸ Insurance	INS.
▸ Intellectual	INTELL.
▸ Interdisciplinary	INTERDISC.
▸ Interest	INT.
▸ International	INT'L
▸ International and Comparative Law Quarterly	INT'L & COMP. L.Q.
▸ International Herald Tribune	INT'L HERALD TRIB.
▸ International Journal of Law and Psychiatry	INT'L J.L. & PSYCHIATRY
▸ International Lawyer	INT'L LAW.
▸ International Organization	INT'L ORG.
▸ International Organization Law Review	INT'L ORG. L. REV.
▸ International Review of Law and Economics	INT'L REV. L. & ECON.
▸ Iowa Law Review	IOWA L. REV.
▸ JAG Journal	JAG J.
▸ John Marshall Journal of Computer & Information Law	J. MARSHALL J. COMPUTER & INFO. L.
▸ John Marshall Law Review	J. MARSHALL L. REV.
▸ Journal	J.
▸ Journal of Agricultural Law	J. AGRIC. L.
▸ Journal of Air Law and Commerce	J. AIR L. & COM.
▸ Journal of Appellate Practice and Process	J. APP. PRAC. & PROCESS
▸ Journal of Business Law	J. BUS. L.
▸ Journal of Chinese Law	J. CHINESE L.
▸ Journal of College and University Law	J.C. & U.L.
▸ Journal of Contemporary Health Law and Policy	J. CONTEMP. HEALTH L. & POL'Y
▸ Journal of Contemporary Law	J. CONTEMP. L.
▸ Journal of Contemporary Legal Issues	J. CONTEMP. LEGAL ISSUES
▸ Journal of Corporate Taxation	J. CORP. TAX'N
▸ Journal of Corporation Law	J. CORP. L.
▸ Journal of Criminal Law and Criminology	J. CRIM. L. & CRIMINOLOGY
▸ Journal of Dispute Resolution	J. DISP. RESOL.
▸ Journal of Energy, Natural Resources & Environmental Law	J. ENERGY NAT. RESOURCES & ENVTL. L.
▸ Journal of Environmental Law and Litigation	J. ENVTL. L. & LITIG.
▸ Journal of Family Law	J. FAM. L.
▸ Journal of Gender, Race and Justice	J. GENDER RACE & JUST.
▸ Journal of Health and Hospital Law	J. HEALTH & HOSP. L.
▸ Journal of Health Care Law & Policy	J. HEALTH CARE L. & POL'Y
▸ Journal of Health Politics, Policy and Law	J. HEALTH POL. POL'Y & L.

▸ Journal of Health Law	J. HEALTH L.
▸ Journal of High Technology Law	J. HIGH TECH. L.
▸ Journal of Intellectual Property	J. INTELL. PROP.
▸ Journal of Intellectual Property Law	J. INTELL. PROP. L.
▸ Journal of International Arbitration	J. INT'L ARB.
▸ Journal of International Legal Studies	J. INT'L LEGAL STUD.
▸ Journal of International Wildlife Law and Policy	J. INT'L WILDLIFE L. & POL'Y
▸ Journal of Land, Resources & Environmental Law	J. LAND RESOURCES & ENVTL. L.
▸ Journal of Land Use and Environmental Law	J. LAND USE & ENVTL. L.
▸ Journal of Law and Commerce	J.L. & COM.
▸ Journal of Law & Economics	J.L. & ECON.
▸ Journal of Law and Education	J.L. & EDUC.
▸ Journal of Law and Family Studies	J.L. & FAM. STUD.
▸ Journal of Law and Health	J.L. & HEALTH
▸ Journal of Law and Policy	J.L. & POL'Y
▸ Journal of Law & Politics	J.L. & POL.
▸ Journal of Law, Economics, & Organization	J.L. ECON. & ORG.
▸ Journal of Law in Society	J.L. SOC'Y
▸ Journal of Law, Medicine & Ethics	J.L. MED. & ETHICS
▸ Journal of Legal Education	J. LEGAL EDUC.
▸ Journal of Legal Medicine	J. LEGAL MED.
▸ Journal of Legal Studies	J. LEGAL STUD.
▸ Journal of Legislation	J. LEGIS.
▸ Journal of Maritime Law and Commerce	J. MAR. L. & COM.
▸ Journal of Medicine and Law	J. MED. & L.
▸ Journal of Mineral Law & Policy	J. MIN. L. & POL'Y
▸ Journal of Natural Resources & Environmental Law	J. NAT. RESOURCES & ENVTL. L.
▸ Journal of Science & Technology Law	J. SCI. & TECH. L.
▸ Journal of Small and Emerging Business Law	J. SMALL & EMERGING BUS. L.
▸ Journal of Southern Legal History	J. S. LEGAL HIST.
▸ Journal of Space Law	J. SPACE L.
▸ Journal of Taxation	J. TAX'N
▸ Journal of Technology Law & Policy	J. TECH. L. & POL'Y
▸ Journal of the American Academy of Matrimonial Lawyers	J. AM. ACAD. MATRIM. LAW.
▸ Journal of the American Medical Association	JAMA
▸ Journal of the Legal Profession	J. LEGAL PROF.
▸ Journal of the Patent and Trademark Office Society	J. PAT. & TRADEMARK OFF. SOC'Y
▸ Journal of the Suffolk Academy of Law	J. SUFFOLK ACAD. L.
▸ Journal of World Trade	J. WORLD TRADE
▸ Judge	JUDGE
▸ Judicature	JUDICATURE
▸ Judicial	JUD.

▸ Juridical Review	Jurid. Rev.
▸ Jurimetrics: The Journal of Law, Science, and Technology	Jurimetrics J.
▸ Juris Doctor	Juris Dr.
▸ Juris Magazine	Juris Mag.
▸ Jurist	Jurist
▸ Justice	Just.
▸ Justice System Journal	Just. Sys. J.
▸ Juvenile	Juv.
▸ Journal of Products Liability	J. Prod. Liab.

K-L

▸ Kansas Journal of Law and Public Policy	Kan. J.L. & Pub. Pol'y
▸ Kentucky Law Journal	Ky. L.J.
▸ Labor	Lab.
▸ Labor Law Journal	Lab. L.J.
▸ Labor Lawyer	Lab. Law.
▸ Land	Land
▸ La Raza Law Journal	La Raza L.J.
▸ Law (first word)	Law
▸ Law	L.
▸ Law and Contemporary Problems	Law & Contemp. Probs.
▸ Law and History Review	Law & Hist. Rev.
▸ Law and Human Behavior	Law & Hum. Behav.
▸ Law and Inequality	Law & Ineq.
▸ Law and Policy in International Business	Law & Pol'y Int'l Bus.
▸ Law & Psychology Review	Law & Psychol. Rev.
▸ Law & Social Inquiry	Law & Soc. Inquiry
▸ Law & Society Review	Law & Soc'y Rev.
▸ Law Library Journal	Law Libr. J.
▸ Lawyer[s, s', 's]	Law.
▸ Lawyer's Reports Annotated	L.R.A.
▸ Legal	Legal
▸ Legislat[ion, ive]	Legis.
▸ Lewis & Clark Law Review	Lewis & Clark L. Rev.
▸ Librar[y, ian, ies]	Libr.
▸ Lincoln Law Review	Lincoln L. Rev.
▸ Litigation	Litig.
▸ Local	Loc.
▸ Louisiana Law Review	La. L. Rev.
▸ Loyola Consumer Law Review	Loy. Consumer L. Rev.
▸ Loyola Journal of Public Interest Law	Loy. J. Pub. Int. L.
▸ Loyola Law Review (New Orleans)	Loy. L. Rev.
▸ Loyola of Los Angeles Entertainment Law Review	Loy. L.A. Ent. L. Rev.
▸ Loyola of Los Angeles International & Comparative Law Review	Loy. L.A. Int'l & Comp. L. Rev.
▸ Loyola of Los Angeles Law Review	Loy. L.A. L. Rev.

▸ Loyola University of Chicago Law Journal — Loy. U. Chi. L.J.

M-N

▸ Magazine	Mag.
▸ Maine Law Review	Me. L. Rev.
▸ Major Tax Planning	Major Tax Plan.
▸ Management	Mgmt.
▸ Maritime	Mar.
▸ Marquette Intellectual Property Law Review	Marq. Intell. Prop. L. Rev.
▸ Marquette Law Review	Marq. L. Rev.
▸ Marquette Sports Law Review	Marq. Sports L. Rev.
▸ Maryland Journal of Contemporary Legal Issues	Md. J. Contemp. Legal Issues
▸ Maryland Journal of International Law and Trade	Md. J. Int'l L. & Trade
▸ Maryland Law Review	Md. L. Rev.
▸ Massachusetts Law Review	Mass. L. Rev.
▸ McGeorge Law Review	McGeorge L. Rev.
▸ McGill Law Journal	McGill L.J.
▸ Media	Media
▸ Mediation	Mediation
▸ Medic[al, ine]	Med.
▸ Melbourne University Law Review	Melb. U. L. Rev.
▸ Mercer Law Review	Mercer L. Rev.
▸ Michigan Business Law Journal	Mich. Bus. L.J.
▸ Michigan Journal of Gender & Law	Mich. J. Gender & L.
▸ Michigan Journal of International Law	Mich. J. Int'l L.
▸ Michigan Journal of Race & Law	Mich. J. Race & L.
▸ Michigan Law Review	Mich. L. Rev.
▸ Michigan State Law Review	Mich. St. L. Rev.
▸ Michigan Telecommunications and Technology Law Review	Mich. Telecomm. & Tech. L. Rev.
▸ Military Law Review	Mil. L. Rev.
▸ Mineral	Min.
▸ Minnesota Intellectual Property Review	Minn. Intell. Prop. Rev.
▸ Minnesota Journal of International Law	Minn. J. Int'l L.
▸ Minnesota Journal of Global Trade	Minn. J. Global Trade
▸ Minnesota Journal of Law, Science & Technology	Minn. J.L. Sci. & Tech.
▸ Minnesota Law Review	Minn. L. Rev.
▸ Mississippi College Law Review	Miss. C. L. Rev.
▸ Mississippi Law Journal	Miss. L.J.
▸ Missouri Environmental Law and Policy Review	Mo. Envtl. L. & Pol'y Rev.
▸ Missouri Law Review	Mo. L. Rev.
▸ Modern Law Review	Mod. L. Rev.
▸ Monash University Law Review	Monash U. L. Rev.
▸ Montana Law Review	Mont. L. Rev.
▸ Monthly	Monthly

▸ Monthly Labor Review	MONTHLY LAB. REV.
▸ Municipal	MUN.
▸ National	NAT'L
▸ National Black Law Journal	NAT'L BLACK L.J.
▸ Natural	NAT.
▸ Natural Resources Journal	NAT. RESOURCES J.
▸ Naval Law Review	NAVAL L. REV.
▸ Nebraska Law Review	NEB. L. REV.
▸ Negligence	NEGL.
▸ Nevada Law Journal	NEV. L.J.
▸ New England International and Comparative Law Annual	NEW ENG. INT'L & COMP. L. ANN.
▸ New England Journal of Medicine	NEW ENG. J. MED.
▸ New England Journal on Criminal and Civil Confinement	NEW ENG. J. ON CRIM. & CIV. CONFINEMENT
▸ New England Law Review	NEW ENG. L. REV.
▸ New Law Journal	NEW L.J.
▸ New Mexico Law Review	N.M. L. REV.
▸ New York City Law Review	N.Y. CITY L. REV.
▸ New York International Law Review	N.Y. INT'L L. REV.
▸ New York Law Journal	N.Y. L.J.
▸ New York Law School Journal of Human Rights	N.Y.L. SCH. J. HUM. RTS.
▸ New York Law School Journal of International and Comparative Law	N.Y.L. SCH. J. INT'L & COMP. L.
▸ New York Law School Law Review	N.Y.L. SCH. L. REV.
▸ New York State Bar Association Antitrust Law Symposium	N.Y. ST. B.A. ANTITRUST L. SYMP.
▸ New York Times	N.Y. TIMES
▸ New York University Annual Institute on Federal Taxation	N.Y.U. ANN. INST. ON FED. TAX'N.
▸ New York University Annual Survey of American Law	N.Y.U. ANN. SURV. AM. L.
▸ New York University Environmental Law Journal	N.Y.U. ENVTL. L.J.
▸ New York University Journal of International Law and Politics	N.Y.U. J. INT'L L. & POL.
▸ New York University Journal of Law & Business	N.Y.U. J.L. & BUS.
▸ New York University Journal of Legislation and Public Policy	N.Y.U. J. LEGIS. & PUB. POL'Y
▸ New York University Law Review	N.Y.U. L. REV.
▸ New York University Review of Law and Social Change	N.Y.U. REV. L. & SOC. CHANGE
▸ New York University School of Law Moot Court Casebook	N.Y.U. MOOT CT. CASEBOOK
▸ Newsletter	NEWSL.
▸ NEXUS: A Journal of Opinion	NEXUS
▸ North[ern]	N.
▸ North Carolina Banking Institute	N.C. BANKING INST.
▸ North Carolina Central Law Review	N.C. CENT. L. REV.

▶ North Carolina Journal of International Law and Commercial Regulation	N.C. J. Int'l L. & Com. Reg.
▶ North Carolina Law Review	N.C. L. Rev.
▶ North Dakota Law Review	N.D. L. Rev.
▶ Northern Illinois University Law Review	N. Ill. U. L. Rev.
▶ Northern Kentucky Law Review	N. Ky. L. Rev.
▶ Northwestern Journal of International Law & Business	Nw. J. Int'l L. & Bus.
▶ Northwestern University Law Review	Nw. U. L. Rev.
▶ Nota Bene	Nota Bene
▶ Notre Dame Journal of Law, Ethics & Public Policy	Notre Dame J.L. Ethics & Pub. Pol'y
▶ Notre Dame Law Review	Notre Dame L. Rev.
▶ Nova Law Review	Nova L. Rev.

O-P

▶ Ocean and Coastal Law Journal	Ocean & Coastal L.J.
▶ Office	Off.
▶ Ohio Northern University Law Review	Ohio N.U. L. Rev.
▶ Ohio State Journal on Dispute Resolution	Ohio St. J. on Disp. Resol.
▶ Ohio State Law Journal	Ohio St. L.J.
▶ Oil and Gas Tax Quarterly	Oil & Gas Tax Q.
▶ Oil, Gas & Energy Quarterly	Oil Gas & Energy Q.
▶ Oklahoma City University Law Review	Okla. City U. L. Rev.
▶ Oklahoma Law Review	Okla. L. Rev.
▶ on	on
▶ Order	Ord.
▶ Oregon Law Review	Or. L. Rev.
▶ Oregon Review of International Law	Or. Rev. Int'l L.
▶ Organization	Org.
▶ Osgoode Hall Law Journal	Osgoode Hall L.J.
▶ Otago Law Review	Otago L. Rev.
▶ Ottawa Law Review	Ottawa L. Rev.
▶ Pace Environmental Law Review	Pace Envtl. L. Rev.
▶ Pace International Law Review	Pace Int'l L. Rev.
▶ Pace Law Review	Pace L. Rev.
▶ Pacific	Pac.
▶ Pacific Law Journal	Pac. L.J.
▶ Pacific Rim Law & Policy Journal	Pac. Rim L. & Pol'y J.
▶ Parker School Journal of East European Law	Parker Sch. J. E. Eur. L.
▶ Patent	Pat.
▶ Patent Law Annual	Pat. L. Ann.
▶ Penn State Environmental Law Review	Penn St. Envtl. L. Rev.
▶ Penn State International Law Review	Penn St. Int'l L. Rev.
▶ Penn State Law Review	Penn St. L. Rev.
▶ Pepperdine Law Review	Pepp. L. Rev.

▶ Personal	PERS.
▶ Perspective[s]	PERSP.
▶ Philosoph[ical, y]	PHIL.
▶ Planning	PLAN.
▶ Police	POLICE
▶ Policy	POL'Y
▶ Politic[al, s]	POL.
▶ Practi[cal, ce, tioners]	PRAC.
▶ Practical Lawyer	PRAC. LAW.
▶ Preview of United States Supreme Court Cases	PREVIEW U.S. SUP. CT. CAS.
▶ Probate	PROB.
▶ Probate Law Journal (National College of Probate Judges and Boston University School of Law)	PROB. L.J.
▶ Probation	PROBATION
▶ Problems	PROBS.
▶ Proce[edings, dure]	PROC.
▶ Profession[al]	PROF.
▶ Property	PROP.
▶ Psychiatry	PSYCHIATRY
▶ Psycholog[ical, y]	PSYCHOL.
▶ Psychology, Public Policy, and Law	PSYCHOL. PUB. POL'Y & L.
▶ Public	PUB.
▶ Public Contract Law Journal	PUB. CONT. L.J.
▶ Public Interest Law Reporter	PUB. INT. L. REP.
▶ Public Land and Resources Law Review	PUB. LAND & RESOURCES L. REV.
▶ Publishing, Entertainment, Advertising and Allied Fields Law Quarterly	PUB. ENT. ADVERT. & ALLIED FIELDS L.Q.

Q-R

▶ Quarterly	Q.
▶ Quinnipiac Health Law Journal	QUINNIPIAC HEALTH L.J.
▶ Quinnipiac Law Review	QUINNIPIAC L. REV.
▶ Quinnipiac Probate Law Journal	QUINNIPIAC PROB. L.J.
▶ Race and Ethnic Ancestry Law Journal	RACE & ETHNIC ANC. L.J.
▶ Real	REAL
▶ Real Property, Probate and Trust Journal	REAL PROP. PROB. & TR. J.
▶ Record	REC.
▶ Referee[s]	REF.
▶ Reform	REFORM
▶ Regent University Law Review	REGENT U. L. REV.
▶ Register	REG.
▶ Regulat[ion, ory]	REG.
▶ Relations	REL.
▶ Report[s, er]	REP.
▶ Reproduct[ion, ive]	REPROD.
▶ Research	RES.

▸ Reserve	RES.
▸ Resolution	RESOL.
▸ Resources	RESOURCES
▸ Responsibility	RESP.
▸ Review	REV.
▸ Review of Litigation	REV. LITIG.
▸ Revista de Derecho Puertorriqueño	REV. DER. P.R.
▸ Revista Juridica de la Universidad de Puerto Rico	REV. JUR. U.P.R.
▸ Richmond Journal of Global Law & Business	RICH. J. GLOBAL L. & BUS.
▸ Richmond Journal of Law and the Public Interest	RICH. J.L. & PUB. INT.
▸ Richmond Journal of Law & Technology	RICH. J.L. & TECH.
▸ Rights	RTS.
▸ Risk	RISK
▸ RISK: Health, Safety & Environment	RISK
▸ Rocky Mountain Mineral Law Institute	ROCKY MTN. MIN. L. INST.
▸ Roger Williams University Law Review	ROGER WILLIAMS U. L. REV.
▸ Rutgers Computer and Technology Law Journal	RUTGERS COMPUTER & TECH. L.J.
▸ Rutgers Law Journal	RUTGERS L.J.
▸ Rutgers Law Record	RUTGERS L. REC.
▸ Rutgers Law Review	RUTGERS L. REV.
▸ Rutgers Race and the Law Review	RUTGERS RACE & L. REV.

S-T

▸ St. John's Journal of Civil Rights and Economic Development	ST. JOHN'S J. C.R. & ECON. DEV.
▸ St. John's Law Review	ST. JOHN'S L. REV.
▸ Saint Louis University Law Journal	ST. LOUIS U. L.J.
▸ Saint Louis University Public Law Review	ST. LOUIS U. PUB. L. REV.
▸ Saint Louis-Warsaw Transatlantic Law Journal	ST. LOUIS-WARSAW TRANSATLANTIC L.J.
▸ St. Mary's Law Journal	ST. MARY'S L.J.
▸ St. Thomas Law Review	ST. THOMAS L. REV.
▸ San Diego Law Review	SAN DIEGO L. REV.
▸ San Fernando Valley Law Review	SAN FERN. V. L. REV.
▸ Santa Clara Computer and High Technology Law Journal	SANTA CLARA COMPUTER & HIGH TECH. L.J.
▸ Santa Clara Journal of International Law	SANTA CLARA J. INT'L L.
▸ Santa Clara Law Review	SANTA CLARA L. REV.
▸ The Scholar: St. Mary's Law Review on Minority Issues	SCHOLAR
▸ School	SCH.
▸ Scien[ce, ces, tific]	SCI.
▸ Scientific American	SCI. AM.
▸ Scottish	SCOT.
▸ Seattle University Law Review	SEATTLE U. L. REV.
▸ Section	SEC.

▸ Securities	Sec.
▸ Sentencing	Sent'g
▸ Seton Hall Constitutional Law Journal	Seton Hall Const. L.J.
▸ Seton Hall Journal of Sport Law	Seton Hall J. Sport L.
▸ Seton Hall Journal of Sports and Entertainment Law	Seton Hall J. Sports & Ent. L.
▸ Seton Hall Law Review	Seton Hall L. Rev.
▸ Seton Hall Legislative Journal	Seton Hall Legis. J.
▸ Signs	Signs
▸ Social	Soc.
▸ Social Service Review	Soc. Serv. Rev.
▸ Socialist	Socialist
▸ Society	Soc'y
▸ Sociolog[ical, y]	Soc.
▸ Software Law Journal	Software L.J.
▸ Solicitor[s, s', 's]	Solic.
▸ South[ern]	S.
▸ South Carolina Environmental Law Journal	S.C. Envtl. L.J.
▸ South Carolina Law Review	S.C. L. Rev.
▸ South Dakota Law Review	S.D. L. Rev.
▸ South Texas Law Review	S. Tex. L. Rev.
▸ Southeastern Environmental Law Journal	Southeastern Envtl. L.J.
▸ Southern California Interdisciplinary Law Journal	S. Cal. Interdisc. L.J.
▸ Southern California Law Review	S. Cal. L. Rev.
▸ Southern California Review of Law & Social Justice	S. Cal. Rev. L. & Soc. Just.
▸ Southern Illinois University Law Journal	S. Ill. U. L.J.
▸ Southern Methodist University Law Review	SMU L. Rev.
▸ Southern University Law Review	S.U. L. Rev.
▸ Southwestern Journal of International Law	Sw. J. Int'l Law
▸ Southwestern Law Journal	Sw. L.J.
▸ Southwestern University Law Review	Sw. U. L. Rev.
▸ Sports Lawyers Journal	Sports Law. J.
▸ Stanford Environmental Law Journal	Stan. Envtl. L.J.
▸ Stanford Journal of Civil Rights and Civil Liberties	Stan. J. C.R. & C.L.
▸ Stanford Journal of International Law	Stan. J. Int'l L.
▸ Stanford Journal of Law, Business & Finance	Stan. J.L. Bus. & Fin.
▸ Stanford Law & Policy Review	Stan. L. & Pol'y Rev.
▸ Stanford Law Review	Stan. L. Rev.
▸ Stanford Technology Law Review	Stan. Tech. L. Rev.
▸ State	St.
▸ State Bar of Texas Environmental Law Journal	St. B. Tex. Envtl. L.J.
▸ Statistic[s, al]	Stat.
▸ Stetson Law Review	Stetson L. Rev.
▸ Studies	Stud.
▸ Suffolk Journal of Trial & Appellate Advocacy	Suffolk J. Trial & App. Advoc.

▶ Suffolk Transnational Law Review	Suffolk Transnat'l L. Rev.
▶ Suffolk University Law Review	Suffolk U. L. Rev.
▶ Supreme Court Review	Sup. Ct. Rev.
▶ Survey	Surv.
▶ Sydney Law Review	Sydney L. Rev.
▶ Symposium	Symp.
▶ Syracuse Journal of International Law and Commerce	Syracuse J. Int'l L. & Com.
▶ Syracuse Law Review	Syracuse L. Rev.
▶ System	Sys.
▶ Tax	Tax
▶ Tax Adviser	Tax Adviser
▶ Tax Law Review	Tax L. Rev.
▶ Tax Lawyer	Tax Law.
▶ Tax Management International Journal	Tax Mgm't Int'l J.
▶ Tax Notes	Tax Notes
▶ Taxation	Tax'n
▶ Taxes: The Tax Magazine	Taxes
▶ Teacher	Tchr.
▶ Techn[ique, ology]	Tech.
▶ Telecommunication[s]	Telecomm.
▶ Temple Environmental Law & Technology Journal	Temp. Envtl. L. & Tech. J.
▶ Temple International and Comparative Law Journal	Temp. Int'l & Comp. L.J.
▶ Temple Law Review	Temp. L. Rev.
▶ Temple Political & Civil Rights Law Review	Temp. Pol. & Civ. Rts. L. Rev.
▶ Tennessee Journal of Practice and Procedure	Tenn. J. Prac. & Proc.
▶ Tennessee Law Review	Tenn. L. Rev.
▶ Texas Forum on Civil Liberties and Civil Rights	Tex. F. on C.L. & C.R.
▶ Texas Hispanic Journal of Law and Policy	Tex. Hisp. J.L. & Pol'y
▶ Texas Intellectual Property Law Journal	Tex. Intell. Prop. L.J.
▶ Texas International Law Journal	Tex. Int'l L.J.
▶ Texas Journal of Business Law	Tex. J. Bus. L.
▶ Texas Journal on Civil Liberties and Civil Rights	Tex. J. C.L. & C.R.
▶ Texas Journal of Women and the Law	Tex. J. Women & L.
▶ Texas Law Review	Tex. L. Rev.
▶ Texas Review of Law & Politics	Tex. Rev. L. & Pol.
▶ Texas Tech Law Review	Tex. Tech L. Rev.
▶ Texas Wesleyan Law Review	Tex. Wesleyan L. Rev.
▶ Third World Legal Studies	Third World Legal Stud.
▶ Thomas Jefferson Law Review	T. Jefferson L. Rev.
▶ Thomas M. Cooley Journal of Practical and Clinical Law	T.M. Cooley J. Prac. & Clinical L.
▶ Thomas M. Cooley Law Review	T.M. Cooley L. Rev.
▶ Thurgood Marshall Law Review	T. Marshall L. Rev.

▸ Toledo Journal of Great Lakes' Law, Science & Policy	Tol. J. Great Lakes' L. Sci. & Pol'y
▸ Tort Trial & Insurance Practice Law Journal	Tort Trial & Ins. Prac. L.J.
▸ Touro International Law Review	Touro Int'l L. Rev.
▸ Touro Journal of Transnational Law	Touro J. Transnat'l L.
▸ Touro Law Review	Touro L. Rev.
▸ Trade	Trade
▸ Trademark	Trademark
▸ Trademark Reporter	Trademark Rep.
▸ Transnational	Transnat'l
▸ Transnational Law & Contemporary Problems	Transnat'l L. & Contemp. Probs.
▸ The Transnational Lawyer	Transnat'l Law.
▸ Transportation	Transp.
▸ Transportation Law Journal	Transp. L.J.
▸ Trial	Trial
▸ Trial Lawyer's Guide	Trial Law. Guide
▸ Tribune	Trib.
▸ Trust[s]	Tr.
▸ Tulane Environmental Law Journal	Tul. Envtl. L.J.
▸ Tulane European and Civil Law Forum	Tul. Eur. & Civ. L.F.
▸ Tulane Journal of International and Comparative Law	Tul. J. Int'l & Comp. L.
▸ Tulane Journal of Law and Sexuality	Tul. J.L. & Sexuality
▸ Tulane Law Review	Tul. L. Rev.
▸ Tulane Maritime Law Journal	Tul. Mar. L.J.
▸ Tulsa Journal of Comparative & International Law	Tulsa J. Comp. & Int'l L.
▸ Tulsa Law Journal	Tulsa L.J.
▸ Tulsa Law Review	Tulsa L. Rev.

U-V

▸ UCLA Bulletin of Law and Technology	UCLA Bull. L. & Tech.
▸ UCLA Journal of Law and Technology	UCLA J.L. & Tech.
▸ UCLA Entertainment Law Review	UCLA Ent. L. Rev.
▸ UCLA Journal of Environmental Law & Policy	UCLA J. Envtl. L. & Pol'y
▸ UCLA Journal of International Law and Foreign Affairs	UCLA J. Int'l L. & Foreign Aff.
▸ UCLA Law Review	UCLA L. Rev.
▸ UCLA Pacific Basin Law Journal	UCLA Pac. Basin L.J.
▸ UCLA Women's Law Journal	UCLA Women's L.J.
▸ UMKC Law Review	UMKC L. Rev.
▸ UN Monthly Chronicle	UN Monthly Chron.
▸ Uniform Commercial Code Law Journal	UCC L.J.
▸ Uniform Commercial Code Reporter-Digest	UCC Rep.-Dig.
▸ United States	U.S.

▶ United States-Mexico Law Journal	U.S.-MEX. L.J.
▶ Universit[ies, y]	U.
▶ University of Arkansas at Little Rock Law Review	U. ARK. LITTLE ROCK L. REV.
▶ University of Baltimore Intellectual Property Law Journal	U. BALT. INTELL. PROP. L.J.
▶ University of Baltimore Journal of Environmental Law	U. BALT. J. ENVTL. L.
▶ University of Baltimore Law Forum	U. BALT. L.F.
▶ University of Baltimore Law Review	U. BALT. L. REV.
▶ University of California at Davis Law Review	U.C. DAVIS L. REV.
▶ University of Chicago Law Review	U. CHI. L. REV.
▶ University of Chicago Legal Forum	U. CHI. LEGAL F.
▶ University of Cincinnati Law Review	U. CIN. L. REV.
▶ University of Colorado Law Review	U. COLO. L. REV.
▶ University of Dayton Law Review	U. DAYTON L. REV.
▶ University of Denver Water Law Review	U. DENV. WATER L. REV.
▶ University of Detroit Mercy Law Review	U. DET. MERCY L. REV.
▶ University of the District of Columbia David Clarke School of Law Law Review	UDC/DCSL L. REV.
▶ University of Florida Journal of Law and Public Policy	U. FLA. J.L. & PUB. POL'Y
▶ University of Florida Law Review	U. FLA. L. REV.
▶ University of Hawaii Law Review	U. HAW. L. REV.
▶ University of Illinois Journal of Law, Technology and Policy	U. ILL. J.L. TECH. & POL'Y
▶ University of Illinois Law Review	U. ILL. L. REV.
▶ University of Kansas Law Review	U. KAN. L. REV.
▶ University of Memphis Law Review	U. MEM. L. REV.
▶ University of Miami Business Law Review	U. MIAMI BUS. L. REV.
▶ University of Miami Inter-American Law Review	U. MIAMI INTER-AM. L. REV.
▶ University of Miami International and Comparative Law Review	U. MIAMI INT'L & COMP. L. REV.
▶ University of Miami Law Review	U. MIAMI L. REV.
▶ University of Miami Yearbook of International Law	U. MIAMI Y.B. INT'L L.
▶ University of Michigan Journal of Law Reform	U. MICH. J.L. REFORM
▶ University of Pennsylvania Journal of Business Law	U. PA. J. BUS. L.
▶ University of Pennsylvania Journal of Constitutional Law	U. PA. J. CONST. L.
▶ University of Pennsylvania Journal of International Law	U. PA. J. INT'L L.
▶ University of Pennsylvania Journal of Law and Social Change	U. PA. J.L. & SOC. CHANGE
▶ University of Pennsylvania Law Review	U. PA. L. REV.
▶ University of Pittsburgh Law Review	U. PITT. L. REV.
▶ University of Puget Sound Law Review	U. PUGET SOUND L. REV.
▶ University of Richmond Law Review	U. RICH. L. REV.

▸ University of San Francisco Law Review	U.S.F. L. REV.
▸ University of San Francisco Maritime Law Journal	U.S.F. MAR. L.J.
▸ University of Toledo Law Review	U. TOL. L. REV.
▸ University of Toronto Faculty of Law Review	U. TORONTO FAC. L. REV.
▸ University of Toronto Law Journal	U. TORONTO L.J.
▸ University of West Los Angeles Law Review	UWLA L. REV.
▸ Urban	URB.
▸ Urban Lawyer	URB. LAW.
▸ Utah Law Review	UTAH L. REV.
▸ Utilit[ies, y]	UTIL.
▸ Valparaiso University Law Review	VAL. U. L. REV.
▸ Vanderbilt Journal of Entertainment & Technology Law	VAND. J. ENT. & TECH. L.
▸ Vanderbilt Journal of Transnational Law	VAND. J. TRANSNAT'L L.
▸ Vanderbilt Law Review	VAND. L. REV.
▸ Vermont Journal of Environmental Law	VT. J. ENVTL. L.
▸ Vermont Law Review	VT. L. REV.
▸ Villanova Environmental Law Journal	VILL. ENVTL. L.J.
▸ Villanova Law Review	VILL. L. REV.
▸ Villanova Sports & Entertainment Law Journal	VILL. SPORTS & ENT. L.J.
▸ Virginia Environmental Law Journal	VA. ENVTL. L.J.
▸ Virginia Journal of International Law	VA. J. INT'L L.
▸ Virginia Journal of Law & Technology	VA. J.L. & TECH.
▸ Virginia Journal of Social Policy & the Law	VA. J. SOC. POL'Y & L.
▸ Virginia Sports and Entertainment Law Journal	VA. SPORTS & ENT. L.J.
▸ Virginia Law Review	VA. L. REV.
▸ Virginia Law & Business Review	VA. L. & BUS. REV.
▸ Virginia Tax Review	VA. TAX REV.

W-X

▸ Wake Forest Law Review	WAKE FOREST L. REV.
▸ Wall Street Journal	WALL ST. J.
▸ Washburn Law Journal	WASHBURN L.J.
▸ Washington and Lee Journal of Civil Rights and Social Justice	WASH. & LEE J. CIVIL RTS. & SOC. JUST.
▸ Washington and Lee Law Review	WASH. & LEE L. REV.
▸ Washington and Lee Race and Ethnic Ancestry Law Journal	WASH. & LEE RACE & ETHNIC ANC. L.J.
▸ Washington Law Review	WASH. L. REV.
▸ Washington Monthly	WASH. MONTHLY
▸ Washington Post	WASH. POST
▸ Washington University Global Studies Law Review	WASH. U. GLOBAL STUD. L. REV.
▸ Washington University Journal of Law and Policy	WASH. U. J.L. & POL'Y
▸ Washington University Journal of Urban and Contemporary Law	WASH. U. J. URB. & CONTEMP. L.

► Washington University Law Review	WASH. U. L. REV.
► Wayne Law Review	WAYNE L. REV.
► Week	WK.
► Weekly	WKLY.
► Welfare	WELFARE
► West[ern]	W.
► West Virginia Law Review	W. VA. L. REV.
► Western New England Law Review	W. NEW ENG. L. REV.
► Western State University Law Review	W. ST. U. L. REV.
► Whittier Law Review	WHITTIER L. REV.
► Widener Journal of Public Law	WIDENER J. PUB. L.
► Widener Law Review	WIDENER L. REV.
► Widener Law Symposium Journal	WIDENER L. SYMP. J.
► Willamette Law Review	WILLAMETTE L. REV.
► William and Mary Bill of Rights Journal	WM. & MARY BILL RTS. J.
► William and Mary Journal of Women and the Law	WM. & MARY J. WOMEN & L.
► William and Mary Law Review	WM. & MARY L. REV.
► William Mitchell Law Review	WM. MITCHELL L. REV.
► Wisconsin Environmental Law Journal	WIS. ENVTL. L.J.
► Wisconsin International Law Journal	WIS. INT'L L.J.
► Wisconsin Law Review	WIS. L. REV.
► Wisconsin Women's Law Journal	WIS. WOMEN'S L.J.
► Women	WOMEN
► Women's Rights Law Reporter	WOMEN'S RTS. L. REP.
► World	WORLD
► Wyoming Law Review	WYO. L. REV.

Y-Z

► Yale Human Rights and Development Law Journal	YALE HUM. RTS. & DEV. L.J.
► Yale Journal of Health Policy, Law, and Ethics	YALE J. HEALTH POL'Y L. & ETHICS
► Yale Journal of International Law	YALE J. INT'L L.
► Yale Journal of Law and Feminism	YALE J.L. & FEMINISM
► Yale Journal of Law & the Humanities	YALE J.L. & HUMAN.
► Yale Journal of Law & Technology	YALE J.L. & TECH.
► Yale Journal of World Public Order	YALE J. WORLD PUB. ORD.
► Yale Journal on Regulation	YALE J. ON REG.
► Yale Law & Policy Review	YALE L. & POL'Y REV.
► Yale Law Journal	YALE L.J.
► Yearbook (or Year Book)	Y.B.

T14   PUBLISHING TERMS

Abbreviate publishing terms in citations according to **rule 15.4** and the following table:

▸ abridge[d, ment]	abr.
▸ annotated	ann.
▸ anonymous	anon.
▸ compil[ation, ed]	comp.
▸ copyright	copy.
▸ draft	drft.
▸ edit[ion, or]	ed.
▸ manuscript	ms.
▸ mimeograph	mimeo.
▸ new series	n.s.
▸ no date	n.d.
▸ no place	n.p.
▸ no publisher	n. pub.
▸ offprint	offprt.
▸ old series	o.s.
▸ permanent	perm.
▸ photoduplicated reprint	photo. reprint
▸ printing	prtg.
▸ replacement	repl.
▸ reprint	reprt.
▸ revis[ed, ion]	rev.
▸ special	spec.
▸ temporary	temp.
▸ tentative	tent.
▸ translat[ion, or]	trans.
▸ unabridged	unabr.
▸ volume	vol.

T15   SERVICES

Abbreviations commonly used in referring to service publishers include the following:

▸ Bureau of National Affairs	BNA
▸ Commerce Clearing House	CCH
▸ Matthew Bender	MB
▸ Pike & Fischer	P & F
▸ Research Institute of America	RIA

Abbreviations for some of the most frequently cited services are listed below. Following each looseleaf service title, the list indicates the appropriate abbreviation of the service, the publisher, and corresponding bound services. Names of bound services that differ markedly from their looseleaf forms are printed in italics and cross-referenced to the looseleaf forms. See **rule 19** for further guidance on citation to services.

- Administrative Law Third Series   Admin. L.3d (P & F)
  for Federal Contractors

- Affirmative Action Compliance Manual   Aff. Action Compl. Man. (BNA)
  for Federal Contractors

- AIDS Law & Litigation Reporter   AIDS L. & Litig. Rep. (Univ. Pub. Group)

- All States Tax Guide   All St. Tax Guide (RIA)

- American Federal Tax Reports, Second   A.F.T.R.2d (RIA)
  Series

- American Stock Exchange Guide   Am. Stock Ex. Guide (CCH)

- Antitrust & Trade Regulation Report   Antitrust & Trade Reg. Rep. (BNA)

- Aviation Law Reporter bound as   Av. L. Rep. (CCH)
  Aviation Cases   Av. Cas. (CCH)

- BNA's Banking Report   Banking Rep. (BNA)

- Bankruptcy Court Decisions   Bankr. Ct. Dec. (LRP)

- Bankruptcy Law Reports   Bankr. L. Rep. (CCH)

- Benefits Review Board Service   Ben. Rev. Bd. Serv. (MB)

- BioLaw   BioLaw (LexisNexis)

- Blue Sky Law Reports   Blue Sky L. Rep. (CCH)

- *Board of Contract Appeals Decisions* —see Contract Appeals Decisions

- Business Franchise Guide   Bus. Franchise Guide (CCH)

- Canadian Commercial Law Guide   Can. Com. L. Guide (CCH)

- Canadian Tax Reports   Can. Tax Rep. (CCH)

- Chemical Regulation Reporter   Chem. Reg. Rep. (BNA)

- Chicago Board Options Exchange   Chicago Bd. Options Ex. (CCH)

- Collective Bargaining Negotiations &   Collective Bargaining Negot. & Cont.
  Contracts   (BNA)

- Collier Bankruptcy Cases, Second   Collier Bankr. Cas. 2d (MB)
  Series

- Commodity Futures Law Reports   Comm. Fut. L. Rep. (CCH)

- Communications Regulation   Commc'ns Reg. (P & F)

- Congressional Index   Cong. Index (CCH)

- Consumer Credit Guide   Consumer Cred. Guide (CCH)

- Consumer Product Safety Guide   Consumer Prod. Safety Guide (CCH)

- Contract Appeals Decisions bound as   Cont. App. Dec. (CCH)
  Board of Contract Appeals Decisions   B.C.A. (CCH)

- *Contracts Cases, Federal* —see Government Contracts Reports

- Copyright Law Decisions   Copyright L. Dec. (CCH)

- Copyright Law Reporter   Copyright L. Rep. (CCH)

- Cost Accounting Standards Guide   Cost Accounting Stand. Guide (CCH)

- The Criminal Law Reporter   Crim. L. Rep. (BNA)

- Daily Labor Report   Daily Lab. Rep. (BNA)

- Dominion Tax Cases   Dominion Tax Cas. (CCH)

- EEOC Compliance Manual   EEOC Compl. Man. (BNA)

- EEOC Compliance Manual   EEOC Compl. Man. (CCH)

▸ Employee Benefits Cases bound in same name	Empl. Benefits Cas. (BNA)
▸ Employee Benefits Compliance Coordinator	Empl. Coordinator (RIA)
▸ Employment Practices Guide bound as Employment Practices Decisions —See also Labor Law Reports	Empl. Prac. Dec. (CCH)
▸ Employment Safety and Health Guide bound as Occupational Safety and Health Decisions	Empl. Safety & Health Guide (CCH) O.S.H. Dec. (CCH)
▸ Employment Testing: Law & Policy Reporter	Empl. Testing (Univ. Pub. Am.)
▸ Energy Management & Federal Energy Guidelines	Energy Mgmt. (CCH)
▸ Environment Reporter bound as Environment Reporter Cases	Env't Rep. (BNA) Env't Rep. Cas. (BNA)
▸ Environmental Law Reporter	Envtl. L. Rep. (Envtl. Law Inst.)
▸ Exempt Organizations Reports	Exempt Org. Rep. (CCH)
▸ *Fair Employment Practice Cases* —see Labor Relations Reporter	
▸ The Family Law Reporter bound in same name	Fam. L. Rep. (BNA)
▸ Family Law Tax Guide	Fam. L. Tax Guide (CCH)
▸ Federal Audit Guides	Fed. Audit Guide (CCH)
▸ Federal Banking Law Reporter	Fed. Banking L. Rep. (CCH)
▸ Federal Carriers Reports bound as Federal Carriers Cases	Fed. Carr. Rep. (CCH) Fed. Carr. Cas. (CCH)
▸ Federal Contracts Report	Fed. Cont. Rep. (BNA)
▸ Federal Election Campaign Financing Guide	Fed. Election Camp. Fin. Guide (CCH)
▸ Federal Energy Regulatory Commission Reports	Fed. Energy Reg. Comm'n Rep. (CCH)
▸ Federal Estate and Gift Tax Reporter bound as Standard Federal Tax Reporter	Fed. Est. & Gift Tax Rep. (CCH) Stand. Fed. Tax Rep. (CCH)
▸ Federal Excise Tax Reports	Fed. Ex. Tax Rep. (CCH)
▸ Federal Income, Gift and Estate Taxation	Fed. Inc. Gift & Est. Tax'n (MB)
▸ Federal Rules Service, Second Series bound in same name	Fed. R. Serv. 2d (West)
▸ Federal Securities Law Reports bound in same name	Fed. Sec. L. Rep. (CCH)
▸ Federal Tax Coordinator Second	Fed. Tax Coordinator Second Series (RIA)
▸ Federal Tax Guide Reports	Fed. Tax Guide Rep. (CCH)
▸ *Fire & Casualty Cases* —see Insurance Law Reports	
▸ Food Drug Cosmetic Law Reports	Food Drug Cosm. L. Rep. (CCH)
▸ Government Contracts Reporter bound as Contracts Cases, Federal	Gov't Cont. Rep. (CCH) Cont. Cas. Fed. (CCH)
▸ Government Employee Relations Report	Gov't Empl. Rel. Rep. (BNA)

▸ Housing & Development Reporter	Hous. & Dev. Rep. (RIA)
▸ Human Resources Management OSHA Compliance Guide	OSHA Comp. Guide (CCH)
▸ Immigration Law Service	Immigr. L. Serv. (West)
▸ Inheritance, Estate and Gift Tax Reports	Inher. Est. & Gift Tax Rep. (CCH)
▸ Insurance Law Reports bound as: Personal and Commercial Liability Life, Health & Accident Insurance Cases 2d	Ins. L. Rep. (CCH) Personal and Comm. Liab. (CCH) Life Health & Accid. Ins. Cas. 2d (CCH)
▸ International Environment Reporter	Int'l Env't Rep. (BNA)
▸ International Trade Reporter	Int'l Trade Rep. (BNA)
▸ IRS Positions	IRS Pos. (CCH)
▸ Labor Arbitration Awards bound in same name	Lab. Arb. Awards (CCH)
▸ Labor Law Reporter bound as: Labor Cases NLRB Decisions —see also Employment Practices Guide	Lab. L. Rep. (CCH) Lab. Cas. (CCH) NLRB Dec. (CCH)
▸ Labor Relations Reporter bound as: Fair Employment Practice Cases Labor Arbitration Reports Labor Relations Reference Manual Wage and Hour Cases	Lab. Rel. Rep. (BNA) Fair Empl. Prac. Cas. (BNA) Lab. Arb. Rep. (BNA) L.R.R.M. (BNA) Wage & Hour Cas. (BNA)
▸ ABA/BNA Lawyers' Manual on Professional Conduct	Laws. Man. on Prof. Conduct (ABA/BNA)
▸ *Life, Health & Accident Insurance Cases* —see Insurance Law Reports	
▸ Liquor Control Law Reports	Liquor Cont. L. Rep. (CCH)
▸ Media Law Reporter bound in same name	Media L. Rep. (BNA)
▸ Medical Devices Reports	Med. Devices Rep. (CCH)
▸ Medicare and Medicaid Guide	Medicare & Medicaid Guide (CCH)
▸ Mutual Funds Guide	Mut. Funds Guide (CCH)
▸ National Reporter on Legal Ethics & Professional Responsibility	Nat'l Rep. Legal Ethics (Univ. Pub. Am.)
▸ New York Stock Exchange Guide	N.Y.S.E. Guide (CCH)
▸ *NLRB Decisions* —see Labor Law Reports	
▸ Nuclear Regulation Reports	Nuclear Reg. Rep. (CCH)
▸ Occupational Safety & Health Reporter bound as Occupational Safety & Health Cases	O.S.H. Rep. (BNA) O.S.H. Cas. (BNA)
▸ OFCCP Federal Contract Compliance Manual	OFCCP Fed. Cont. Compl. Man. (CCH)
▸ Patent, Trademark & Copyright Journal	Pat. Trademark & Copyright J. (BNA)
▸ Pension & Benefits Reporter	Pens. & Ben. Rep. (BNA)
▸ Pension Plan Guide	Pens. Plan Guide (CCH)
▸ Pension & Profit Sharing Second	Pens. & Profit Sharing 2d (RIA)
▸ Personnel Management	Personnel Mgmt. (BNA)
▸ Product Safety & Liability Reporter	Prod. Safety & Liab. Rep. (BNA)

▸ Products Liability Reports	Prod. Liab. Rep. (CCH)
▸ Public Utilities Reports bound in same name	Pub. Util. Rep. (PUR)
▸ School Law Reporter	School L. Rep. (Educ. Law Ass'n)
▸ Search & Seizure Bulletin	Search & Seizure Bull. (Quinlan)
▸ SEC Accounting Rules	SEC Accounting R. (CCH)
▸ Secured Transactions Guide	Secured Transactions Guide (CCH)
▸ Securities and Federal Corporate Law Report	Sec. & Fed. Corp. L. Rep. (West)
▸ Securities Regulation & Law Report	Sec. Reg. & L. Rep. (BNA)
▸ Shipping Regulation	Shipping Reg. (P & F)
▸ Social Security Reporter	Soc. Sec. Rep. (CCH)
▸ Standard Federal Tax Reports bound as U.S. Tax Cases	Stand. Fed. Tax Rep. (CCH) U.S. Tax Cas. (CCH)
▸ State and Local Tax Service	St. & Loc. Tax Serv. (RIA)
▸ *State and Local Taxes* —see All States Tax Guide	
▸ State Tax Guide	St. Tax Guide (CCH)
▸ State Tax Reporter	St. Tax Rep. (CCH)
▸ Tax Court Memorandum Decisions bound in Tax Court Reporter	T.C.M. (RIA) T.C.M. (CCH) [or (RIA)]
▸ Tax Court Reported Decisions	Tax Ct. Rep. Dec. (RIA)
▸ Tax Court Reports	Tax Ct. Rep. (CCH)
▸ Tax Treaties	Tax Treaties (CCH)
▸ Trade Regulation Reporter bound as Trade Cases	Trade Reg. Rep. (CCH) Trade Cas. (CCH)
▸ Unemployment Insurance Reports	Unempl. Ins. Rep. (CCH)
▸ Uniform Commercial Code Reporting Service Second	U.C.C. Rep. Serv. (West)
▸ Union Labor Report	Union Lab. Rep. (BNA)
▸ The United States Law Week	U.S.L.W. (BNA—publisher need not be indicated)
▸ The United States Patents Quarterly bound in same name	U.S.P.Q. (BNA)
▸ *U.S. Tax Cases* —see Federal Estate and Gift Tax Reporter; Standard Federal Tax Reports	
▸ U.S. Tax Reporter	U.S. Tax Rep. (RIA)
▸ Utilities Law Reports	Util. L. Rep. (CCH)
▸ *Wage and Hour Cases* —see Labor Relations Reporter	

T16   SUBDIVISIONS

The following list provides abbreviations for names of document subdivisions frequently used in legal citations. See rule 3 for further guidance in using these abbreviations. For those abbreviations shown in blue ink, no space appears between the subdivision abbreviation and the number/letter:

- ▸ ch. 3

- ▸ tbl.3

▸ addendum	add.
▸ amendment	amend.
▸ annotation	annot.
▸ appendi[x, ces]	app., apps.
▸ article	art.
▸ bibliography	bibliog.
▸ book	bk.
▸ chapter	ch.
▸ clause	cl.
▸ column	col.
▸ comment[ary]	cmt.
▸ decision	dec.
▸ department	dept.
▸ division	div.
▸ example	ex.
▸ figure	fig.
▸ folio	fol.
▸ footnote[s]	
in cross-references	note, notes
in other references	n., nn.
▸ historical note[s]	hist. n., hist. nn.
▸ hypothetical	hypo.
▸ illustration[s]	illus.
▸ introduction	intro.
▸ line[s]	l., ll.
▸ number	no.
▸ page[s]	
in cross-references	p., pp.
in other references	[at]
▸ paragraph[s]	
if symbol appears in source	¶, ¶¶
if otherwise	para., paras.
▸ part	pt.
▸ preamble	pmbl.
▸ principle	princ.
▸ publication	pub.
▸ rule	r.
▸ schedule	sched.
▸ section[s]	
in amending act	sec., secs.
in all other contexts	§, §§
▸ series, serial	ser.
▸ subdivision	subdiv.
▸ subsection	subsec.
▸ supplement	supp.
▸ table	tbl.
▸ title	tit.
▸ volume	vol.

Index

Abbreviations
adjacent, spacing, 80
administrative reporters, 81, 103, 135–37, 218–28
administrative reports, 135
agencies, 81, 133, 218–28
American Bar Association, 123–24
American reporters, 96, 215–77
"and," in case names, 90–91
arbitral reporters, 186, 198, 429
authors, 138–39
bound services, 468–72
business firms, 91, 93, 139
case history, 101–03, 434–35
case names, 89–95
case names, in citations, 94–95
case names, international, 191–97
citations, repeating, 72–75
closing up of, 80
codes, statutory, 114–16
commissions, 218–28
commonly abbreviated names, 81, 93, 94–95, 430–31
congressional reports and documents, 126–32, 435–36
corporate authors, 139
countries (see foreign countries)
court documents, 28–29
court of decision, 97–98, 432–34
dollar symbol, 82
editions of books, 140–42, 468
English-language periodicals, 80, 444–67
English *Law Report* series, 416–17
English monarchs, 409
European Court and Commission of Human Rights materials, 194–95, 427
European Union materials, 193–94, 205–09, 426–27
explanatory phrases, 63–64, 73, 102–03, 434–35
foreign countries, 171, 438–43
foreign courts, 180 (see also name of jurisdiction)
foreign materials, 180, 277–425
foreign periodicals, 183–84
generally, 80-81
"hereinafter," use of, 74–75, 188, 190, 207, 209–11, 213–14
history of cases, 101–03
initials, commonly recognized, 8, 81, 91, 93
institutional authors, 139

Inter-American Commission on Human Rights materials, 185, 195, 427–28
intergovernmental organizations, 205–12, 426–28
international and world organization materials, 185–214
judges, titles, 87, 443
law journals and reviews, 444–67
League of Nations materials, 205, 426, 429
looseleaf services, 177–78, 468–72
model codes, 122–24
months, 444
multiple citations of same work, 72–75
multiple editions and printings, 141–42
municipal ordinances, 120–21
names, commonly abbreviated, 8, 81, 91, 93
new series, 444, 468
newsletters, 157
newspapers, 151
no date, 151, 468
no place, 468
officials, titles, 87, 443
ordinances, 120–21
paragraph symbols, 69, 70, 82, 473
parties to treaties, 188
percent symbols, 82
periodicals, 80, 147-57, 180, 183–84, 444–67
periodicals, English-language, 444–67
periodicals, foreign-language, 180, 183–84
pluralization of, 430
prepositions in periodical names, 444
prior case history, 101–03
publishers of services, 468
publishing terms, 468
punctuation of, 80–81
repeating citations, 72–75
reporters, foreign, 180 (see also name of jurisdiction)
reporters, United States, 95–96, 215–77
restatements, 71, 122–23
section symbols, 69–70, 82
services, 468–72
session laws, 116–17 (see also name of jurisdiction)
spacing of, 80
standards, 122–23
statutes, 111–25 (see also name of jurisdiction)

Index

Abbreviations, continued

subdivisions (e.g., section, article, chapter), 66–71, 82, 110, 189, 472–73

subsequent case history, 101–03

taxation materials, 17–18, 221–23

titles of books and pamphlets, 140

titles of individuals, 87

treaty series, 428–29

unions, 93

United Nations materials, 198–205, 426

"United States," 81, 92, 94, 139

use of abbreviations not listed in this book, 80

"Abrogated by," in case history, 102

Abstracts, in law reviews, 153

"Accord," **as signal,** 54

Accounting standards, 123

Acquiescence, in tax cases, 223, 434

"Act," capitalization of, 85

Action on decision, 223

Acts (see Codes, Session laws, Statutes)

Addenda, 70-71

Addresses (speeches), 64, 143, 161–62

Administrative agencies

abbreviation of, 81, 133, 218–28

adjudications, 135–36

arbitrations, 135–36

reporters, 81, 103, 135–37, 218–28

reports, 135

Administrative cases

citation of, 135–36, 218–28

exact date, when required, 136

number of case, when required, 136

omission of procedural phrases, 90–91

parallel citation, 136

recent, 136

services, when cited, 136

"sub nom.," use on appeal, 103

Administrative law judges, 87, 443

Administrative materials

adjudications, 135–36, 218–28

agency publications, 133–37, 218–28

basic citation forms, 133

cases, 135-36

citation order, 58

Code of Federal Regulations, 133

compilations of regulations, 133–35

court administrative orders, 107

executive orders, 58, 223–24

Federal Register, 26, 133, 134

federal rules and regulations, 133–35

foreign (see name of country)

generally, 133–37, 218–28

Internal Revenue Service, 17–18, 172, 221–23

Internet sources, 172

names of rules and regulations, 133–35

notices, 134

official releases, 133–35

opinions, formal advisory, 221

order within signal, 58

popular names of rules and regulations, 134

presidential orders, 58, 223–24

presidential papers, 223–24

presidential proclamations, 223–24

proposed rules and regulations, 134

regulations, 133, 133–34

revenue materials, 17–18, 222–23

revenue rulings, 222–23

rules, 133, 133–34

slip opinions, 136

state, 133, 228–74

tax materials, 17–18, 222-23

Treasury decisions, 222

Treasury materials, 222–23

Treasury regulations, 221–23

U.N. Administrative Tribunal, 203

United Kingdom, 410

United States Code, 127

varieties of, 133

Administrative Procedure Act, 16,124, 131

Advance sheets, 222 (see also slip opinions)

Advisory committee notes, 71

Affidavits, 20–21, 28

"Affirmed" **and** *"affirming,"* **in case history,** 7, 12–13, 434

Agencies, administrative (see Administrative agencies)

Agreements, international, 185, 187–91, 213

Alabama

citation rules and style guides, 40

sources of law, 117, 119, 228–29

Alaska

citation rules and style guides, 40

sources of law, 116, 229

All England Law Reports, 414, 416

Alphabets, foreign, 180–81, 317, 350, 382, 391

Alterations in quotations, 77–78

Alternative holding, indication of, 100

"Amended by"

in constitution citation, 110

in statute citation, 113, 119

Amended constitution, 110

Amended statutes, 117, 119

Amendments

constitutional, 110

model codes, 122–23

restatements, 122–23

session laws, 117

standards, 122–23

statutes, 117, 119

Treasury regulations, 222

uniform acts, 122

"Amendment(s)," **abbreviation of,** 473
American Bar Association
  Abbreviation as ABA, 124
  publications, 123–24, 156
  section reports, 156
American Jurisprudence (Am. Jur.), 23, 144
American Law Institute
  generally, 122–23
  proceedings, 156
  publications, 122
American Law Reports (A.L.R.), 156
American Samoa
  sources of law, 274
Ampersand
  authors' names, 23–24, 138
  books and pamphlets, 23–24, 138
  case names, 8, 91
  editor's names, 139
  footnote citation, 68–69
  URL, 168–69
  Volumes, Parts, and Supplements, 66
Annals of Congress, 130–31
Annexes
  European Union materials, 206–07
  generally, 70–71
  U.N. records, 200, 202
  World Trade Organization materials, 210
Annotations
  A.L.R., L.R.A., 156
  generally, 70–71
Annual Digest and Reports of Public International Law Cases, 197
Annual reports
  government agencies, 134–35
  Inter-American Commission on Human Rights, 195
  Inter-American Court of Human Rights, 195
  Permanent Court of International Justice, 192
"Appeal dismissed," **in case history,** 102
Appeal docketed, 88, 99
Appeals, 88, 99, 101–02
Appendices
  codes, 115
  generally, 70–71
  statutes reprinted in codes, 115
  U.S. Sentencing Guidelines Manual, 123
"Appendi[x, ces]," **abbreviation of,** 473
Arabic numerals
  monarchs, 409
  volumes, 66
Arbitrations
  administrative, 133, 135–36
  international, 186, 198, 214

"Arbitrator," **abbreviation of,** 443
Arbitrators, indicated parenthetically, 135
Argentine Republic
  sources of national law, 277–80
Arizona
  citation rules and style guides, 40
  sources of law, 230
Arkansas
  citation rules and style guides, 40
  sources of law, 116, 230–31
Armed Services Board of Contract Appeals, 218
Article (part of speech)
  capitalization of, 84
  omission of, 140, 149, 159, 191
Articles
  appearing in two or more parts, 155–56
  basic citation forms, 147–48
  capitalization in titles, 84
  citation order, 59
  collected essays, printed in, 143
  essays in collection, 142–43
  foreign periodicals, 183–84
  forthcoming publications, 162
  law reviews and journals, 147–51
  magazines, 150–51
  multipart, 155–56
  newspapers, 151–52
  order within signal, 59
  page citation, 67–68
  periodicals, 147–58
  titles, capitalization, 84
  typeface in non-journal legal writing, 3–4
  typeface in law review citations, 3–4, 63
  typeface in law review text, 64
"Article(s)," **abbreviation of,** 473
"Ass'n," **in case names,** 430, 446
"At," **used in citation of pages or sections,** 13–15, 20–21, 23, 25, 66, 67
"At," **used in electronic media,** 11–12, 152, 165, 170
"Attorney General," **abbreviation of,** 443
Attorney General, opinions, 221
Audio recordings, 107, 176
Auditing standards, 123
Australia
  sources of national law, 280–85
Australian states and territories, 285–86
Austria
  Länder (see Länder, Austrian)
  sources of national law, 286
Authentic or official online documents, 164, 165–66
Authorities in text, identification of, 53
Authorities previously cited, 72–75

Index

Authors
 annotation, 156
 articles in periodicals, 149
 book reviews, 154
 books and pamphlets, 138–39
 collected essays, 142–43
 colloquy, names not given, 155
 congressional documents and reports,
   129–30
 direct Internet citations, 166
 essays in collection, 142–43
 forewords, 143
 institutional, 139
 law reviews and journals, 150, 153–54
 model codes, 122–23
 multiple, books and pamphlets,
   138–39
 multivolume works, 138
 newspapers, 151
 news reports and articles, 151
 no author, 74, 151, 153–54, 158
 parallel Internet citations, 164, 165,
   166, 170
 periodical materials, 149
 periodicals, surveys and symposia in,
   155
 prefaces, 143
 restatements, 122–23
 reviewer of book, 153–54
 standards, 122–23
 student, 149, 153–54
 symposium, names not given, 155
 U.N. material, 198–205
Author's mistakes in quoted material, 77
"Available at," 60, 61, 170
Ballentine's Law Dictionary, 144
Bankruptcy
 appellate panels, 90, 98, 217, 432
 cases, 90, 177, 178
 courts, 57, 90, 217
 pending or unreported cases, 105
Bankruptcy Reporter, 217
Bar publications, 156
"Baron," abbreviation of, 443
Basic charters, international and world
   organizations, 58, 186–87, 205–09,
   212
Belgium, Kingdom of
 Sources of national law, 291–95
Bible, 144–45
Bills
 bills and resolutions, 127–28
 congressional, 127–28
 state, 128
Black's Law Dictionary, 23, 144
Blackstone's *Commentaries,* 144
Block quotations, 27, 76–77
Blogs, 164, 166–69

Bloomberg database, citation to, 171–73,
   175, 176
The Bluebook, 140, 145
Board of Tax Appeals
 citation of cases, 58, 217, 223
Boards of contract appeals, 218
Book notes, 148, 154
Book reviews
 citation order, 59
 periodicals, 153–54
"Book(s)," abbreviation of, 473
Books and pamphlets
 ABA publications, 123–124, 156
 abbreviation of title, 140
 administrative agency records and
   reports, 135–36
 ALI publications, 122–23
 author, 138–39
 basic form of citation, 138
 book reviews, 154
 capitalization, 84, 140
 citation, components of, 138
 citation analyzed, 138
 citation order, 59
 collected documents, 142–43
 collected essays, 142–43
 corporate author, 140
 date, 140–42
 date in title, 140
 date not given by source, 142
 Declaration of Independence, 69
 dictionaries, legal, 144
 edition, 140–42
 editor, 139-40
 electronic media, 145
 encyclopedias, legal, 144
 The Federalist, 144
 forewords, 67, 143
 forthcoming publications, 162
 generally, 138–46
 given names of authors, 138–39
 government agencies as authors, 139
 government agency reports, 134–35
 institutional authors, 139
 Internet sources, 145
 italicization, when referred to in text,
   65
 law reviews and journals, 24–25, 63,
   150–51, 183–84, 444–67
 legal dictionaries and encyclopedias,
   23, 144
 letters, 143, 160
 manuscripts, typed, 159–60
 multiple authors, 138–39
 multiple editions, 140–42
 multiple printings, 141
 multivolume works, 23, 138, 140
 name of author, 138–39

names and titles, capitalization, 84,
140, 180

number, serial, 143-44

online sources, 145

order within signal, 6–7, 59

page citation, 67–69, 138

paragraph citation, 69–70

periodicals, 444–67

photoduplicated reprints, 141, 468

place of publication not given by
source, 142

place of publication, when required,
142

pocket parts, 142

pre-1900 works, 141–42

prefaces, 143

printings, 141

publication number, 141

repeated citation of, 72–75

reprints, 140, 141

restatements, 17, 122–23

sections, 69–70

serial number, 143–44

series of, 143–44

short citation forms, 145–46

shorter works in collection, 142–43,
146

special citation forms, 140–46

star pages, 68, 144

subdivisions of, 66–71

subtitles, omitted, 140

supplements, 142

theses, unpublished, 160

titles, 140

translator, when given, 139–40

typeface, 3–4, 63, 65, 138

typeface, authors, 4, 63, 65

typeface in court documents and legal
memoranda, 3–4

typeface in law review citations, 62–63

typeface in law review text, 65

unpublished works, 159–63

volume designations, 66,

well-known works, 23, 144–45

writer of, 138–39

year, 140–42

Bound services

abbreviations, 468–72

generally, 177–78

typeface, 177

Brackets

alterations in quotations, 77–78

establishing short citation or
translation, used in, 74–75, 179–84

quotations, used in, 77–78

volume designations, 66, 177

years, 177

Brazil, Federative Republic of

sources of national law, 295–97

Briefs and legal memoranda (see Court
documents and legal memoranda)

Briefs and records, citation of

citation order, 58

generally, 106–07

British materials (see England)

Broadcasts, 174–75, 176

Podcasts, 175

"Bros.," in case names, 8, 91, 93, 430

Budgets, proposed, 224

Bureau of Customs and Border Protection,
221

Bureau of National Affairs (BNA)**-services,**
468

Business firms, in case names, 91, 93

"But cf.," **as signal,** 55

"But see," **as signal,** 55

"But see, e.g.," **as signal,** 54

Byline, newspaper articles, 151–52

California

citation rules and style guides, 40

sources of law, 231–32

Canada

sources of national law, 298–305

Canadian Guide to Uniform Legal Citation,
303

Canal Zone

sources of law, 274–75

Canons of Professional Responsibility,
123–24

Canon Law, 305

Cantons, Swiss, 403–04

Capitalization

change in quotation, indication of, 77–79

court documents and legal
memoranda, 21–22

courts, 22, 85–86

generally, 84–86

headings, 84

Internet main page titles and URLs, 84

party designations, 22

people or groups, nouns referring to,
84

titles of books and articles, 84, 140,
149

titles of foreign documents, 180

Case comments in law reviews, 153–54

Case history (see History of cases)

Case names

abbreviations, 90–95, 430–31

abbreviations, in citations, 94–95,
430–31

abbreviations, in textual sentences,
90–94

administrative actions, 135, 218–228

"administrator," omission of, 91

Index

Case names, continued

ampersand, use of in text, 91
appeal, when different on, 103
"appellee," omission of, 91
arbitrations, 135
arbitrations, international, 198
"Ass'n," abbreviation in text, 91
bankruptcy, 90
"Bros.," abbreviation in text, 91
business firms, 91, 93
citations, abbreviations in, 94–95, 430–31
cite first listed party only, 89–90
"Co.," abbreviation in text, 91
Commissioner of Internal Revenue, as party, 93
Common Market cases, 193–94
common names, when different from name in reporter, 94–95, 108
consolidated actions, 89–90
"Corp.," abbreviation in text, 91
court documents and legal memoranda, 19–22
"d/b/a," omission of, 90
descriptive terms, 90–95
different on appeal, 103
"estate of," 90–91
"et al.," 90
European Court of Justice, 193–94
"executor," omission of, 91
"ex parte," 91
"ex rel.," 90–91
first word, retention in full, 89
foreign cases, 182
generally, 89–95
geographical terms, 92
given names and initials of parties, 92–93
"id.," use of, 109
"In re," 90–91
in rem actions, 90, 91
"Inc.," abbreviation in text, 91
"Inc.," when omitted, 93
Internal Revenue Commissioner, as party, 93
international arbitrations, 186, 198
International Court of Justice, 185, 191–93
"Judgment of," 89
Latin words italicized, 91
"licensee," omission of, 91
"Ltd.," abbreviation in text, 91
"Ltd.," when omitted, 93
mandamus actions, 94
multiple dispositions, when indicated, 94
"No.," abbreviation in text, 91
omissions in, 90–95

parenthetical indication of alternate name, 90
parentheticals, nested, 60, 101
parties, only first-listed named, 89–90
partnerships, 90
Pennsylvania, early federal and state, 96, 262–63
Permanent Court of International Justice, 185, 191–93
popular names, 89, 91
procedural phrases, 90
real property, as party, 90
running heads, words omitted in, 89
short citation form, to entire decision, 108
short forms, 107–09
short names, 94
state as party in state court decision, 92
superseded by statute, 103
surnames, 92–93
textual references, 8, 62, 64–65, 89
"The," omission of, 91
transcripts, 106
"trustee," omission of, 91
typeface used in court documents, 3–4, 62
typeface used in law review citations, 63
typeface used in law review text, 64
unions as parties, 92
"Will of," 91
World Court, 185, 191–93
Case notes in law reviews, 153–54
Case number
administrative cases, 135–36
appeal or petition for certiorari, 89, 107
court documents, 106–07
Federal Cases, 216, 217, 229
pending cases, 88–89, 104
unreported cases, 88–89, 105
Case writeups
citation of, 153
cited with case, 61
Cases (see also individual jurisdiction or court)
administrative actions, 133, 135–36
appeal, disposition on, 88
appeal docketed, 88
arbitrations, 133, 135–36, 186, 198, 214
bankruptcy, 90, 98, 105, 177, 178
basic citation forms, 87–88
before decision, 88
Bloomberg, 171
briefs, citation of, 19, 58, 88, 106–07
British, 406–08

certiorari, citation of petition for, 89, 107, 165
citation, basic forms of, 87–89
citation, components of, 4–5, 87
citation order, 57–58
citation to particular page, 67–68
civil law, 182
commentary on, cited with case, 61
common law, 182
components of citations, 4–5, 87
computerized research services, 11–12, 164–65, 171–72
concurring opinion, 12, 100
country, indication of, 179
court of decision, 97–98
court of decision, abbreviations, 432–34
court of decision, American, 97–98
court of decision, foreign jurisdictions, 182
court, when indicated, 97–98
dates, 87, 99, 104–05
denial of rehearing, 103
dictum, 100
different name on appeal, 103
dissenting opinion, 12, 100
docket number, 11–12, 88–89, 104–05, 107–08, 195
dual citation of sources, 9, 11, 13–14, 95, 96, 107, 108, 136
electronic databases, 11, 104, 162–63, 171
England, 413–17
European Union, 205–09
explanatory phrases, 100–01
federal court, 215–18
filed, 88
foreign, 182
history on remand, 101
history, prior and subsequent, 101
in rem, 8, 90
interim orders, 88
international and world organization, 185–86, 191–97
international arbitrations, 198
International Court of Justice, 191–93
Internet sources, 104, 164–70
italicization of names in court documents, 3–4
italicization of names in text, 64–65
italicization of procedural phrases in citations, 63–64
italicized words in history of, 101–02, 434–35
Judge or Justice writing opinion, 100
LEXIS, cited to, 11, 104, 164–65
medium neutral citation, 96–97
memoranda in, citations to, 106–07

memorandum decision, 100
motions, citation to, 106
name cited as in official report, 65
named in text, initial and subsequent citation, 8–9, 72–73, 89, 109
names, 7–9, 89–95
newspapers, cited in, 88, 95, 151
no name, citation of, 89
non-common-law, 182
number of case, 88–89, 104
official reporters, when cited, 9–10, 95–96
online, 104
order within signal, 56–58
page citations, 67–68
parallel citation of sources, 11, 95
parenthetical information, 100–01
pending, 11, 88, 99–100, 105
per curiam decisions, 100
periodicals, when cited, 95
Permanent Court of International Justice, 185, 191–93
plurality opinion, 100
prior history, 101–03
procedural phrases, 90–91
public domain format, 96–97
published decision, 88
recent, 88, 99
records, citation of, 20–21, 88, 106–07
releases of administrative agencies, cited to, 133–35
repeating citations of, 72–73, 107–09
reporters, 95–96
reporters, defined, 96
reporters, reprinted, 96
services, appearing in, 88–89
services, when cited, 95
short citation form, 107–09
slip opinions, reported in, 88, 99, 104
sources, 95–96
state courts, 98, 228–277
statutory material, cited with, 61
subsequent history, 88, 102–03
transcript of record, citations to, 20–21, 88, 106–07
typeface used in court documents, 3–4
typeface used in law review citations, 62–64
typeface used in law review text, 64–65
unofficial reporter, when cited, 95, 136
unreported, 104, 105, 171
weight of authority, 12, 100, 101–03
Westlaw, cited to, 11, 104, 165, 171, 172
World Court, 185, 191–93
year of decision, 10, 99
Catholic Church, codes, 305
CD-ROM, 173, 176

Index

Certiorari
  applied for, granted, denied, 88,
    101–02
  indication in case history, 101–02
  petition, citation of, 106
  "*sub nom.*" not used, 103–04
"*Cf.*," as signal, 55
C.F.R., 17, 58, 136–37, 172
"Chancellor," abbreviation of, 443
Chapters
  codes, statutory, 68–70
  number, when given for federal statute,
    114
"Chapter(s)," abbreviation of, 473
Charters, international organizations,
    186–87, 205–09
"Chief Baron," "Justice," "Judge,"
    abbreviation of, 80, 443
Chile, Republic of
  sources of national law, 306–07
China, People's Republic of
  sources of national law, 308–12
"Circuit," capitalization of, 85
Circuit courts of appeals (see Courts)
Circuit courts, old federal, 97–98, 215
Circuit Justices, 215
Citation of commentary with case or book,
    61
Citation order, 56–59
Citation sentences and clauses, 4–5,
    53–54
Citations
  (see also specific types of material)
  abbreviations of case names, 430–31
  analogous authority, 55
  authentic or official online documents,
    164, 165–66
  authoritativeness, order within citation,
    56–59
  authorities, 56–59
  background authority, 55
  citations analyzed, 53–54
  comparing authorities, 55
  contradictory proposition, 55
  court documents and legal
    memoranda, 30–51
  direct contradiction, 55
  direct support, 54
  footnotes, 9, 53
  law review text and footnotes, 9,
    53–54, 76–77
  material cited more than once, 72–75,
    157–58, 163, 175–76, 178, 184,
    213–14
  numerous authorities, 72–75
  omission from quotation, indication of,
    78–79
  opposing proposition, 55

  order of, 56–59
  pages, 67–69
  parenthetical explanations, 59–60
  placement, 56–59
  placement after quotation, 76–77
  punctuation of, 56, 62–64, 69
  quotations, 76–79
  related authority, 61
  repeating citations, 72–75
  sampling of authorities, 53–54
  signals in, 54–56
  string citations, 53, 54
  subdivisions, 66–71
  supplementary material, 55–56
  supporting proposition, 54–55
  typeface used, 3–4, 62–65
  weight of, 100–01
Citations analyzed
  books, 138
  cases, 12–13, 87
  constitutions, 110
  periodical materials, 147
  regulations, 133
  rules, 133
  statutes, 111
  treaties, 187–88
  United Nations materials, 198–205
"*Cited in*," use of, 61
"Citing," in case parentheticals, 64, 101
City and county ordinances, 120–21
"City of," when omitted in case names, 92
Civilian Board of Contract Appeals, 218
Civil law jurisdictions (see also name of
    jurisdiction)
  cases, 182
  codes, 183
  constitutions, 182
  statutes, 183
Civil Rights Act of 1964, 131
"Clause(s)," abbreviation of, 473
Clean Air Act, 131
Closing up of abbreviations, 80–81
C.M.L.R. *(Common Market Law Reports)*,
    194, 426
"Co.," in case names, 139, 430
"Code," capitalization of, 85
Code, Internal Revenue (see Internal
    Revenue Code)
Code of Federal Regulations (C.F.R.),
    133–34, 136–37, 172
Code of Justinian, 381
Code of Theodosius, 382
Codes
  (see also Statutes)
  abbreviations, 114–15
  administrative compilations, 133–34
  American, 112, 112–14
  appendices, 115

appendix with reprinted statute, 115
authentic or official electronic codes, 112, 164, 165–66
basic citation forms, 111–12
chapters, 114
city ordinances, 120–21
Code of Federal Regulations, 133–35, 136–37, 172, 173
compilations of, 115
components of citation, 112–16
county ordinances, 120–21
date, 115–16
editors, 115
electronic databases, 117–18, 171–72
ethics, 123–24
federal, 112–14
foreign, 183 (see also name of jurisdiction)
future location of statutes, 119
historical fact of enactment, 113
Internal Revenue, 17–18, 120
Internet Sources, 117–18
legislative materials, 18, 126–32
LEXIS, 172
materially different from statute, 113
official and unofficial, 114–16
online sources, 112, 117–18
ordinances, municipal, 120–21
parallel citation to, 116–17
pocket parts, 115, 116
positive law, enacted into, 113–14
publishers of, 115
Roman law, 381–82
scattered sections, 113
secondary sources cited to, 112, 118–19
sections cited, 113–14
state, 114–15, 228–274 (see also name of individual state)
statutes, when cited to, 111–13
subject-matter, 115
supplements, 113, 115
tax materials, 17, 120
titles, 114
Treasury materials, 17–18, 120
typeface used, 112
uncodified laws, 115, 121
uniform acts, 17, 121–22
unofficial, differently numbered, 119–20
volumes, 114
Westlaw, 117–18, 171–72
which to cite, 112–13
year, 115–16
Codification
session laws, parenthetical indication of, 116
Collected works

citation of works in, 142–43
editor, 139–40, 142–43
"*id.*" short form, 146
"*in*," used to introduce collection, 61
parallel citation to, using "*reprinted in*," 61
"*supra*" short form, 146
Colloquia, in periodicals, 155
Colombia, Republic of
sources of national law, 312–15
Colorado
citation rules and style guides, 40–41
sources of law, 233
"Column(s)," **abbreviation of,** 473
Comma
citing commentary with case or statute, 61–62
citing multiple sections of code, 70
"compare . . . with" signal, 55
italicization, 64–65, 434
periodical names, 444
titles ending in dates, 67, 140
Command number, English, 411–12
Command Papers, English, 411–12
"Comment," **abbreviation of,** 473
"Comment," **designating student work,** 153
Commentary
citation of, 61
Commentaries & special article designations, 155
Comments
model codes, 123
periodicals, 154
restatements, 123
rules of ethics, 123
sentencing guidelines, 123
standards, 123
Commerce Clearing House (CCH) **services,** 177–78, 468
(see also Services and topical reporters)
Commerce Court, 216, 432
Commercial electronic databases (see Electronic databases)
"Commissioner," **abbreviation of,** 443
Commissioner of Internal Revenue, in case names, 93
Committee materials, UN, 199–201
Committee prints, 126, 129–30
Common law jurisdictions (see also name of jurisdiction)
cases, 182
codes, 183
constitutions, 182
statutes, 183
Common Market Law Reports (C.M.L.R.), 194, 197, 426

Index

Common Market materials, 194, 197, 426
Common Market Reporter, 194, 197, 426
"Commonwealth of,"
    capitalization, 85
    when omitted in case names, 92
"*Compare . . . with . . . ,*" as signal, 55
Compilations
    administrative regulations, 133–34
    treaties, 189–91, 428–29
Compilations of statutes (see also Codes, Statutes)
    federal, 114
    foreign, 183 (see also name of jurisdiction)
    state, 114–15, 228–77
Compiler of codes, 115
Computerized research services (see Electronic databases)
Concurrent resolutions, 127–28
Concurring opinions, 12, 100
"Congress," capitalization of, 84
Congressional debates, 126, 130–31
Congressional Globe, 130
Congressional materials
    bills and resolutions, 18, 126, 127–28
    committee prints, 126, 129–30
    concurrent resolutions, 127–28
    debates, 126, 130–31
    documents, 126, 129–30
    electronic databases, 131
    hearings, 18, 126, 128–29
    joint resolutions, 127–28
    parallel citations, 128, 129, 131
    online sources, 131
    reports, 18, 126, 129–30
    resolutions, 126, 127–28
    secondary authority, 126, 131
    unnumbered documents, 129–30
Congressional Record
    daily edition, 126, 130
    debates, 130
    permanent edition, 130
    resolutions cited to, 127–28
Congressional Research Service, 130
Conjunctions, capitalization of, 84
Connecticut
    citation rule and style guide, 41
    sources of law, 234–35
Consecutive pages or footnotes, citation of, 67–68
Consecutive sections of codes, 70
Consolidated actions, case names, 89–90
Constitutions
    amended provisions, 110
    capitalization of parts of, 85
    citation order, 56–57
    electronic media, 171–72
    federal and state, 110

foreign, 182 (see also name of jurisdiction)
    generally, 19, 110
    order within signal, 6, 56–57
    repealed provisions, 110
    short form, 110
    subdivision, 110
    superseded, 110
    typeface in footnotes, 110
"Construed in," use of, 61
"Construing," use of, 61
"*Contra,*" as signal, 55
Conventions, international, 185, 187–88, 205, 213
"Corp.," in case names, 91, 93
Corporations
    abbreviations, 91, 93, 139
    authors, 139
    case names, 91, 93
Corpus Juris Secundum (C.J.S.), 144
Council of Europe materials, 209
Countries
    (see also name of jurisdiction)
    abbreviated in case names, 94
    abbreviated in international law cases, 192
    abbreviated in international arbitrations, 198
    abbreviated treaty citations, 185, 188
    abbreviations of, 438–43
County and city ordinances, 120–21
"Court," capitalization of, 85–86
Court administrative orders, 107
Court documents and legal memoranda
    abbreviations of documents in, 28–29
    audio recordings of court proceedings, 107
    block quotations in, 27
    books, citations to, 23–24
    cases, citations to, 7–15
    capitalization in, 21–22
    constitutions, citations to, 19
    Electronic Case Filings, 21, 106
    explanatory parentheticals in, 26
    federal taxation materials, citations to, 17–18
    Internal Revenue Code, citations to, 17–18
    journal and newspaper, citations to, 24–25
    parallel citations in, 11, 13–14, 26
    signals in, 5–7
    short forms in, 13–15, 18–19, 21, 23–26
    statutes, citations to, 15–19
    typeface of citations in, 3–4
Court filings, 106–07
Court of Claims, 216

Court of Customs and Patent Appeals, 216
Court of decision
  abbreviations, 97–98, 432–34
  American, 10, 97–98
  civil law jurisdictions, 182
  common law jurisdictions, 182
  international arbitrations, 198
  international cases, 193–97
  state, 10–11, 98
  when indicated, 87, 97–98, 105,182
  when omitted, 97–98
  World Court cases, 191–93
Court of International Trade, 216
Court of Justice of the European
    Communities (see Court of Justice
    of the European Union)
Court of Justice of the European Union,
    185, 193–94, 426–27
Court of Military Appeals, 217
Courts
  (see also name of court or
    jurisdiction)
  abbreviations, 97–98, 432–34
  administrative orders, 107
  Appeals, District of Columbia Circuit,
    Court of, 97, 215–16
  Appeals, District of Columbia Municipal
    Court of, 236
  appeals, United States courts of, 97,
    215–16
  Arbitration, Permanent Court of, 198
  audio recordings of proceedings, 107
  bankruptcy, 98, 105, 217
  bankruptcy appellate panels, 98, 217
  Board of Tax Appeals, 217, 223
  circuit courts, old federal, 97, 216
  Circuit Justices, 215
  civil law countries, 182 (see also name
    of jurisdiction)
  Claims Court, 216
  Commerce Court, 216
  common law countries, 182 (see also
    name of jurisdiction)
  Court of First Instance, 193–94
  Court of Justice of the European
    Communities (see Court of Justice of
    the European Union)
  Court of Justice of the European Union,
    185, 193–94, 426–27
  Customs and Patent Appeals, Court of,
    216
  district, federal, 98, 217
  Emergency Court of Appeals, 216
  English, 406–08, 414–15
  European Court of Human Rights, 185,
    194–95, 427
  federal, 30–40, 215–18

foreign countries, 182 (see also name
    of jurisdiction)
Foreign Intelligence Surveillance Court,
    98
Foreign Intelligence Surveillance Court
    of Review, 98
foreign, language used in citation of,
    179–81
General Court, 193–94, 426
Inter-American Commission on Human
    Rights, 185, 195, 427
international, 191–97
International Criminal Tribunals, 186,
    197
International Court of Justice, 185,
    191–93, 426
International Justice, Permanent Court
    of, 185, 191–93, 426
International Trade, Court of, 216
Judicial Panel on Multidistrict Litigation,
    98, 217
Military Appeals, Court of, 217
Military Review, Court of, 217–18
old circuit, federal, 98, 216
Pennsylvania, early federal and state,
    96
Permanent Court of Arbitration, 186,
    198
Permanent Court of International
    Justice, 185, 191–93, 426
proceedings, audio recordings of, 107
Rail Reorganization Court, 217
rules, 121
state, 40–51, 98, 228–74
Tax Court, 217, 223
Temporary Emergency Court of
    Appeals, 216
terms, 87
territories, 51, 274–77
U.S. Supreme (see U.S. Supreme Court)
World Court, 185, 191–93, 426
Courts of Military Review, 217–18
Court proceedings, audio recordings of,
    107
Cross-references
  court documents and legal
    memoranda, 3–4
  generally, 71
  groups of authorities previously cited,
    71
  order of authorities, 59
  previous footnotes, 71
  textual material in same work, 71
Cumulative Bulletin, 18, 222
Customs Court, 216
Cyclopedia of the Law of Private
    Corporations, 141

Index

Czech Republic
    sources of national law, 315–16
*Daily Compilation of Presidential
    Documents*, 224
Dash
    graphical material, used in citing, 69
    page range, used in citing, 9, 67
    sections of code, used in citing, 70
Databases (see Electronic databases)
Dates
    administrative compilations, 133–34
    amended constitutional provisions, 110
    amended statutes, 119
    bilateral and multilateral treaties, 187,
        189
    books and pamphlets, 138, 140–42
    case history, 99, 101
    cases, 87–89, 99
    cases, cited to U.S.L.W., 89, 99
    cases, in electronic databases, 88, 95,
        99, 165, 171
    cases, in looseleaf services, 99, 178
    cases, in newspapers, 88, 95
    cases, in slip opinions, 88, 95, 104–05
    cases, international, 185–86
    cases, pending, 99, 104–05
    cases, unreported, 88, 104–05
    cases, World Court, 185, 192
    Code of Federal Regulations, 133
    codifications of statutes, 111, 115–16,
        117
    constitutions, when used, 110
    enactment, session laws, 116–17
    ethical opinions, 124
    ethical rules, 123
    exact date, administrative cases, 136
    exact date, cases, 88–89, 99, 104, 178
    exact date, Congressional debates, 126
    exact date, international agreements,
        187, 189
    exact date, letters, speeches, and
        interviews, 159
    exact date, ordinances, 121
    exact date, periodicals, 147–48,
        150–52
    exact date, services, 178
    exact date, statutes, 117
    exact date, treaties, 187, 189
    exact date, unpublished works, 159–61
    exact date, unreported cases, 11–12,
        104, 171
    exact date, World Court cases, 185, 192
    exchange of notes, 189
    filing of appeal, 88
    filing of cases, 88, 104
    forewords, 143
    Internal Revenue Code, 17, 120
    international agreements, 185, 189

Internet sources, 168
legislative materials, 18, 126–32
looseleaf statutory codifications, 116
model codes, 122–23
multilateral treaties, 185, 189
multiple decisions in one year, 99
multivolume works, 138, 140
newspapers, 24, 147, 151–52
ordinances, municipal, 120–21
periodicals, 147
pocket parts, books, 142
prefaces, 143
prior to 1900, books, 141–42
regnal years, in English statutes, 409
repealed constitutional provisions, 110
repealed statutes, 119
restatements, 122
rules of court, 121
rules of procedure, 17, 121
services, 178
session laws, 16, 117
standards, 122–23
statutes, 115–16
statutes, amended, 119
statutes, cited to session laws, 117
statutes, foreign, 183
statutes, in current code, 111, 115–16
statutes, in supplements to code, 115
statutes, not in current code, 112–13,
    115
statutes, repealed, 119
statutes, uniform acts, 121–22
supplements, books, 66, 142
supplements, codes, 66, 115
titles ending in, 67, 140
treaties, 185, 189
undated journals, 151
U.N. materials, 198–205
uniform acts, 17, 121–22
unreported cases, 88, 104–05
U.S. Supreme Court cases, 87, 99
year of decision of case, 99
"d/b/a," **omission in case names,** 90
Debates
    congressional, 126, 130–31, 172
    European Parliamentary Assembly,
        206–07, 427
    legislative, 126, 130–31
    Republic of Ireland, 344
    United Kingdom, 410–11
Decimal point, 81
"Decision(s)," **abbreviation of,** 473
Declaration of Independence, 69
Delaware
    citation rule and style guide, 41
    sources of law, 235
Deletions from quotations, 78–79
Denial of certiorari, 63–64, 101, 435

Denial of rehearing, when given, 101
Department of Agriculture, 218–19
Department of Commerce
    National Oceanic and Atmospheric
      Administration, 219
    Patent and Trademark Office, 219–20
Department of Energy, Nuclear Regulatory
    Commission, 220
Department of Homeland Security, 220
Department of Justice, 221
Department of Labor, 221
Department of the Interior, 221
Department of the Treasury, 221–23
Department of State publications, 189,
    213, 450
Department, state court, 11–12, 98
Depublished cases, 105
Descriptive terms, omitted in case names,
    91
"Developments in the Law," 154
Dictionaries, 23, 144
Dictum, indication of, 83, 100
Digest of Justinian, 381
Digests, international, 213
Digest of United States Practice in
    International Law, 213
Disciplinary rules, 123–24
Discussion drafts, 112, 123
Dismissal of appeal, 99, 102, 435
Dismissal without opinion, 99
Dissenting opinions, 12, 67, 100
Dissertations, unpublished, 160
District court, federal
    cases in, 97–98, 217
    rules of, 121
District of Columbia
    Circuit Court of Appeals for the, 30–31,
      97, 215
    citation rule and style guide, 41
    sources of law, 236
Divided court, parenthetical indication of,
    100
Division, federal courts, 98
Docket number
    appeal or petition for certiorari, 88–89
    briefs, records, motions, memoranda,
      106–07
    pending cases, 105
    renumbering, 104
    unreported cases, 88, 104
Document number
    intergovernmental organizations'
      materials, 205–12, 189–90
    U.N. publications, 198–205
Documents
    legislative, 126, 129–30
    intergovernmental organizations,
      205–12

    published, collected, 143
    U.N., 198–205
    unpublished, collected, 143
Dollar amounts
    numerals used, 81
Dual citation, when required, 11, 13, 95
DVDs, 174
Economic and Social Council, official
    records, U.N., 199, 426
E.C.R. (European Community Reports),
    193–94, 426
Editions
    abbreviation of, 141, 468
    books and pamphlets, 140–42
    Code of Federal Regulations, 133
    Congressional Record, 127, 130–31
    The Federalist, 144
    first edition, when cited, 141–42, 144
    names of, 140
    when indicated, books and pamphlets,
      140–42
    year, 140–42
Editors
    books and pamphlets, 139–40
    codes, 115
    collected works, 142–43
    reporters, 96
    shorter works in collection, 142–43
"E.g.," as signal, 5–6, 54
Egypt, Arab Republic of
    sources of national law, 317–19
Electronic Case Filings (ECF), 21, 106
Electronic databases
    Bloomberg, 171–73
    books and pamphlets, 145–46
    cases, 11, 104, 171
    codes, 112, 117–18, 171–72
    containing separately published works,
      171–73
    Dialog, 171, 173
    generally, 171–73
    legislative materials, 131–32
    LEXIS, 11, 171–73
    Loislaw.com, 109, 118, 171
    news reports, 172–73
    periodicals, 152
    secondary materials, 172–73
    short citation forms, 109, 175–76
    statutes, 112, 171–72
    unpublished sources, 162–63
    VersusLaw, 172
    Westlaw, 11, 171–73
Eleventh Circuit (see Fifth Circuit Split)
Ellipsis, 76–79
E-Mail, 159–61, 165
Emergency Court of Appeals, 216, 433
Emphasis in quotations, 77–78
Emphasis, italics for, 64, 83

Index

"En banc," parenthetical indication of, 63, 83, 100, 102
Encyclopedias, legal, 23, 143–44
Endnotes, 68
"*Enforced*," in case history, 103, 435
"*Enforcing*," in case history, 435
England and Wales
  sources of national law, 413–18
English Reports—Full Reprint, 407
Environmental Protection Agency, 223
Epilogues, 143
Equal Employment Opportunity Act, 131
Equal Employment Opportunity Commission, 223
Essays in collection (see also Shorter works in collection)
  citation of material in, 142
  editor, 139–40
  parallel citation to, 61
  "*supra*" short form, 145–46
  typeface, 142
"Estate of," in case names, 8, 91
"Et al."
  authors' names, 23, 106, 138–39
  case names, omitted, 7–8, 90
  editors' names, 139–40, 145
"Et seq.," prohibition on use, 70
Ethical considerations, 123–24
Ethics, codes of, 123–24
European Commission on Human Rights, 195
European Union materials, 193–94, 205–09, 426–27
European Court of Human Rights, 185, 194–95, 427
European Court of Justice (see Court of Justice of the European Communities)
European Parliament Working Document, 207, 427
European Parliamentary Assembly, 209
Evidence, rules of, 17, 121
"*Ex rel.*," in case names, 8, 63, 64, 90, 91
Executive Agreement Series (E.A.S.), 189, 428
Executive Office of the President, 223–24
Executive orders, 223–24
Explanation of cited authorities, use of parentheticals, (see Explanatory Parentheticals)
Explanatory parentheticals
  cases, 12, 100–01
  European Parliament debates, 207
  generally, 26, 54–55, 59–60, 65
  internet sources, 170
  order within citation, 60
  statutes, 120

Explanatory phrases
  abbreviations used in case citation, 434–35
  amended statutes, 119–20
  constitutions, amended or repealed, 110
  italicization of, 102–03, 434
  repealed statutes, 119
  typeface used in court documents and legal memoranda, 3–4
  typeface used in law review citations, 3–4, 63–64
  weight of authority, 100, 102–03
  weight of authority in court documents and legal memoranda, 6–7
Expressions, mathematical, 83
Federal Appendix, 99
Federal Aviation Administration, 224
Federal Cases, 215–18
Federal Communications Commission, 224
Federal courts
  (see also individual court name)
  citation rules and style guides, 30–40
  courts of appeals, 215–16
  courts of decision, 97–98
  district courts, 217
  generally, 215–17
  Supreme Court, official cite only, 215
Federal Energy Regulatory Commission, 225
Federal government (see United States)
Federal Judicial Center
  Manual for Complex Litigation, 144
Federal Labor Relations Authority, 225
Federal Mine Safety and Health Review Commission, 225
Federal Practice and Procedure, 23, 138, 144
Federal Register, 26, 120, 134, 222, 223, 226, 228
Federal Regulations, *Code of*, 133, 134, 137
Federal Reporter, 9–10, 215–16
Federal Reserve, 225
Federal Rules Decisions, 217
Federal Rules of Appellate Procedure, 121
Federal Rules of Civil Procedure, 17, 121
Federal Rules of Criminal Procedure, 121
Federal Rules of Evidence, 17, 71, 121
Federal Rules Service, 217, 470
Federal statutes (see Statutes, *Statutes at Large*)
Federal Supplement, 9–10, 61, 216–17
Federal taxation materials (see Tax materials)
Federal Trade Commission, 225
The Federalist, 144, 146
Fifth Circuit Split, 105

Index

"Figure," 71
Films, 176
First editions, when cited, 141–42
First listed relator, not omitted in case names, 89–90
First names and initials
  authors of books and pamphlets, 138–39, 146
  authors of articles, 149, 157–58
  case names, 92–93
Florida
  citation rules and style guides, 41–42
  sources of law, 237
"Folio(s)," abbreviation of, 473
Footnotes
  abbreviation of, 9, 68, 473
  citation of, 68
  consecutive and nonconsecutive, 68
  cross-reference to, 71
  material previously cited in, 72–75
  multipage, 68
  multiple, 68
  numbers in, 81–82
  omission from quotation, indication of, 76, 79
  spanning several pages, 68
  textual material, typeface used in, 64–65
  typeface used for citations in, 62–64
"Footnote(s)," abbreviation of, 9, 68, 473
"For the use of," abbreviated to "ex rel.," 90–91
Foreign alphabets, 180–81, 317, 350, 382, 391
Foreign countries
  (see also name of individual country)
  abbreviation of, 438–43
  World Court cases, 185, 191–93
Foreign derivation, italicization of words of, 3, 83
Foreign Intelligence Surveillance Court, 98
Foreign Intelligence Surveillance Court of Review, 98
Foreign language
  abbreviation of words, 180
  constitutions, 182
  court name and location, give English version, 182
  English versions and translations, 179–81, 187–88, 191, 195
  names, 92–93
  words italicized, 3, 83
Foreign materials
  (see also name of individual country)
  abbreviations, 180
  alphabet, 180–81, 317, 350, 382, 391
  cases, generally, 182
  civil law, 179–84 (see also name of jurisdiction)

common law, 179–84 (see also name of jurisdiction)
  codes, statutory, 183
  constitutions, 182
  English used in naming courts, 182
  establishing abbreviations in initial citation, 180
  international (see International agreements, International organization materials)
  international agreements, 185, 187–91
  jurisdiction, 179
  official treaty sources, 428–29
  periodicals, 183–84
  short citation forms, 184
  statutes, 183
  treaty sources, 428–29
  treaties, 185, 187–91
Forewords, 67, 143, 149, 150
Formal opinions on professional responsibility, 123–24
Forthcoming publications, 159
France
  sources of national law, 319–23
Frequently cited authorities, short forms for, 72–75
"F.S.B.," in case names, 93
Gaius, Institutes of, 382
General Agreement on Tariffs and Trade (GATT), 209–11
General Assembly, official records, U.N., 186, 199–201
Generally Accepted Accounting Principles, 123
Generally Accepted Auditing Standards, 123
Geographical terms
  abbreviations, 436–43
  case names, 92
Georgia
  citation rules and style guides, 42
  sources of law, 237–38
Germany
  Länder (see Länder, German)
  sources of national law, 323–28
Given names
  authors, 138–39
  corporation, partnership, and business names, 91, 93, 139
  individuals, 92–93
Government Accountability Office, 130, 225
Government agencies
  annual and regular reports, 129–30
  authors, as, 129–30, 139–40
  books and numbered publications, 143
  capitalization of, 84
  subdivisions, 139

Index

Government Printing Office Style Manual, 84

Government publications, U.S., 133–34, 137, 218–28

Graphical materials, 69

Greece
sources of national law, 329–31

Groups of authorities previously cited, reference to, 71–75

Guam
citation rules and style guides, 51
sources of law, 275

Hague Court Reports, 186, 198, 429

Hawaii
sources of law, 238
citation rules and style guides, 42

Headings, capitalization in, 84

Hearings
congressional, 18, 60, 75, 126, 128–29
titles of, printed in italic type, 18, 60, 75, 126, 128–29
typeface used in court documents, 3–4

"Hereinafter," used for shortened citation forms, 74–75

History of cases
both prior and subsequent, 12–13, 101–03
dates of decisions, 10–11, 99
different case name on appeal, 13, 103
explanatory words, abbreviations, 434–35
explanatory words italicized or underscored, 3–4, 12, 63–64, 102, 434–35
"mem.," opinions designated as, 96, 100
multiple decisions within single year, 99
multiple dispositions, 94, 103
ordering within signal unaffected by, 57
overruled cases, 101, 102
"per curiam," opinions designated as, 100
position of parentheticals, 60, 101
prior and subsequent, 88–89, 101–03
prior history indicated for memorandum decision, 100, 101
prior history, when given, 102
remand, when given, 101
separate decisions of other issues, when cited, 101
significance of disposition, 102
subsequent history, 12–13, 61, 88–89, 101
subsequent history, appeal filed, docketed, 88, 434–35

subsequent history, certiorari applied for, granted, denied, 89, 101, 434–35
subsequent history, names of parties, when different on appeal, 103
subsequent history, reason for subsequent disposition, 102
typeface, 3–4, 102, 434–35
weight of authority, 100

History of statutes
amended statutes, 112–14, 119–20
parenthetically indicated, 119–20

Holdings
alternative, indication of, 100
concurring opinion, 12, 67, 78, 101, 109
contrary to citations, 55
dictum, 100
dissenting opinion, 12, 67, 78, 101, 109
implied, indication of, 100
plurality opinion, 100
unclear, indication of, 100

Hong Kong
sources of law, 331–33

House of Commons
debates and Journal, 410–11

House of Lords
court, 407
debates and Journal, 410–11

House of Representatives (see Congressional materials)

Human Rights
European Commission of, 195, 427
European Court of, 185, 194–95, 427
Inter-American Commission on, 185, 195, 427
Inter-American Court of, 185, 195–96, 427–28

Hungary, Republic of
sources of national law, 333–35

"*Id.*," use of, 14–15, 72–73
cases, 109

Idaho
citation rules and style guides, 42
sources of law, 239

Illinois
citation rules and style guides, 42
sources of law, 239–40

Implied holdings, indication of, 100

"*In re*," in case names, 8, 90–91

In rem jurisdiction, 8, 90–91

"In the matter of," abbreviated to "*In re*," 8, 90–91

"*In*," use of, 61, 142

"Inc.," in case names, 8, 91, 93

Inclusive numbers, 67–70

Income tax materials (see Tax materials)

Index

India
sources of national law, 335–38
Indiana
citation rules and style guides, 42
sources of law, 116, 240–41
Indian Nations (see Navajo Nation and
Oklahoma Native Americans)
Informal opinions on professional
responsibility, 124
"*Infra*," use of, 71
Initials
authors of books and pamphlets, 138
authors of periodicals, 149, 157
closing up of, 80
commonly abbreviated names, 81
editors, 139–40
parties in case names, 92
punctuation of, 81
translators, 139–40
Insertions in quotations, 77–78
Institutes of Gaius, 382
Institutes of Justinian, 381
Institutes, regular publications by, 156
Institutional authors, 139
Inter-American Commission on Human
Rights, 185, 195, 427
Inter-American Court of Human Rights,
185, 195–96, 427–28
Intergovernmental organization materials
(see also U.N. materials)
abbreviated names, 426–28
arbitrations, 186, 198
basic citation forms, 185–86, 213–14
cases, 191–97
Common Market, 194, 205–09, 426–27
Council of Europe, 209
Court of Justice of the European Union,
185, 193–94, 426
courts, 185–86, 191–97
debates, European Parliamentary
Assembly, 206, 207, 427
document number of League of Nations
materials, 205, 426
document number of U.N. materials,
186, 198–205
European Commission of Human
Rights, 195, 427
European Union, 185, 193–94, 205–09,
426–27
European Court of Human Rights, 185,
194–95, 427
founding documents, U.N., 205
General Agreement on Tariffs and
Trade, 209–11
generally, 198–212, 426–28
Inter-American Commission on Human
Rights, 185, 195, 427

Inter-American Court of Human Rights,
185, 195–96, 427–28
International Court of Justice, 185,
191–93, 426
League of Nations, 205, 426
League of Nations covenant, 205
League of Nations Treaty Series
(L.N.T.S.), 426, 429
number, League of Nations documents,
205
number, U.N. document, 186, 198–205
number, U.N. sales, 203–04
official records, U.N., 201–02
order of citation, 58
Permanent Court of International
Justice, 191–93
*Reports of International Arbitral
Awards, United Nations*, 429
sales number of U.N. materials, 203–04
sources, 426–28
treaty sources, 428–29
United Nations Treaty Series (U.N.T.S.),
429
World Court, 185, 191–93, 426
yearbooks, international, 212
yearbooks, U.N., 204
Interim orders, 88
Internal Revenue Code
citation to other than current code, 120
court documents and legal
memoranda, citations in, 17–18
generally, 17–18, 120
legislative history, 131
supplements, 120
unofficial codes, 120
year, 120
Internal Revenue Commissioner, in case
names, 93
"Internal Revenue," omitted in case
names, 93
Internal revenue regulations and rulings,
17–18, 221–23
International agreements
American treaties, 185, 187–91
basic citation forms, 185, 187–91
bilateral, 185, 187–90
citation, basic form of, 185, 187–91
citation order, 57
compilations of agreements, 428–29
components of citation, 187
country names, 188
date, 189
entry into force, 189
Executive Agreement Series (E.A.S.),
428
foreign language, titles in, 179–80
foreign sources (see name of
jurisdiction)

Index

International agreements, continued

intergovernmental organization materials, 58, 205–09, 426–28

language of source, 179–81

League of Nations Treaty Series (L.N.T.S.), 426, 429

multilateral, 185, 187–90

name, 188

official sources, 428–29

opening for signature, 189

order within signal, 57

parallel citation, 189–91

parties to, 188

popular name, 188

short citation forms, 213–14

sources, intergovernmental, 429

sources, official, foreign (see name of jurisdiction)

sources, official, U.S., 428–29

sources, unofficial, 429

State Department sources, 189–90

Statutes at Large (Stat.), 428

subdivisions, 189

subject matter, 188

title, 188

Treaties and Other International Acts Series (T.I.A.S.), 189–90, 428

Treaty Series (T.S.), 189–90, 428

United Nations Treaty Series (U.N.T.S.), 187, 189–90, 426, 429

United States

U.S. a party, 185, 189–90

U.S. not a party, 185, 190

U.S. Treaties and Other International Agreements (U.S.T.), 189–90, 428

year, 189

International Court of Justice, 185, 191–93, 426

International law

arbitrations, 186, 198

cases, 185–86, 191–97

Common Market, 185, 194, 426

Council of Europe, 209

courts, 191–97

digests, 212–13

European Union, 186, 193–94, 205–09

generally, 185–214

intergovernmental organizations, 198–212, 426–28

international agreements, 185, 187–91

League of Nations, 205

short citation forms, 213–14

treaties, 185, 187–91

U.N., 198–205

yearbooks, international, 212

yearbooks, U.N., 204

International Law Reports, 197

International Legal Materials (I.L.M.), 185–86, 190, 193, 211

International materials

arbitrations, 198

basic citation forms, 185–86

cases, 185–86, 191–97

Common Market, 185, 194, 426

Council of Europe, 209

digests, 213

European Union, 186, 193–94, 205–09

generally, 185–214

international agreements, 185, 187–91

jurisdiction, 187

League of Nations, 205

non-English language documents, 179–81, 187

periodicals, 183–84

short citation forms, 213–14

treaties, 185, 187–91

treaty series, 185, 187–91, 428–29

U.N., 198–205

yearbooks, international, 212

yearbooks, U.N., 204

International organization materials (see Intergovernmental organization materials)

International Trade Commission, 225

Internet sources

archival, 169, 170

authentic or official, 164, 165–66

authors, direct Internet citations, 166–67

authors, parallel Internet citations, 170

basic citation principles, 164–70

blogs, 164, 166–69

cases, 104, 109, 164, 165, 169–70, 171

code, 112, 117–18, 125, 171–72

date, 168

direct citations to, 166–69

discussion forums, 166–69

document format, 169

e-mail, 159–61, 165

explanatory parentheticals, 170

generally, 164–70

online postings, 166–69

order of authorities, parallel Internet citations, 170

pagination, parallel Internet citations, 170

parallel citations to, 169–70

parenthetical information, 170

PDF files, 164, 166, 169

periodicals, 172–73

pinpoint citation, 164–65, 169, 171

portable document format (pdf), 164, 166, 169

preservation of information, 169, 170

publication data, parallel Internet citations, 170

official or authenticated, 164, 165–66

short forms, 175–76
statutes, 112, 117–18, 125, 171–72
title, direct Internet citations, 167–68
title, parallel Internet citations, 170
URL, 164, 166, 168–69
Interviews, citation of, 161
Introductions, citation of, 143
Introductory signals (see Signals)
Invalidated statutes, 119
"*Invalidated by*"
in statute citation, 119
Invalidation, citation of, 119
Iowa
citation rules and style guides, 43
sources of law, 241
"I.R.C." replacing "26 U.S.C.," 17, 120, 218
Iran, Islamic Republic of
sources of national law, 338–40
Iraq, Republic of
sources of national law, 341–42
Ireland, Northern, 418–21
Ireland, Republic of
sources of national law, 342–45
Israel
sources of national law, 345–47
Italicization (see also Typeface)
in court documents, 3–4
emphasis, 83
equations, 83
foreign words, 83
hypothetical parties, 83
mathematical expressions, 83
stylistic purposes, 83
Italy
sources of national law, 348–50
Japan
sources of national law, 350–57
Joining citations
order of citations, 56–59
punctuation, 53–54
Joint resolutions, 127–28
Journal
European Union, Official, 205–06
federal legislative, 130
House of Commons, 410–11
House of Lords, 410–11
"Journal," abbreviation of, 454
Judge
indication of, in citation, 87, 94, 443
used as title, 87, 443
"Judge," capitalization of, 86
"Judge(s)," abbreviation of, 87, 443
Judges and Justices
order of listing, 87
titles, use of, 87
Judgments of the U.N. Administrative Tribunal, 203

"Judgment of," use in citation, 89
Judicial history of cases (see History of cases)
Judicial Panel on Multidistrict Litigation, 57, 98, 217
Jump cites (see Pinpoint citations)
Jurisdiction, indication of
American cases, 97–98
American statutes, 114–15, 116–17
foreign materials, 179
international materials, 187
municipal ordinances, 120–21
session laws, 116–17
Justice
indication of, in citation, 87, 443
"Justice," capitalization of, 86
"Justice(s)," abbreviation of, 87, 443
Justinian, Institutes, Digest, and Code of, 381
Kansas
citations rules and style guides, 43
sources of law, 241–42
Kentucky
citation rules and style guides, 43
sources of law, 242–43
Kenya
sources of national law, 357–58
"L" italicized as letter in subdivision, 83
Labor unions, in case names, 93
Länder, Austrian, 290
Länder, German, 328
Large and small capitals (see Typeface)
Latin words
citation forms, italicization in, 83
italicization of, 83
italicization in case names, 63–64, 90–91
procedural phrases in case names, 83
short citation forms, italicization in, 72–75
Law Journal Reports, 417
Law journals and reviews
abbreviations, English-language, 444–67
abbreviations, spacing of, 80
authors' names, 24, 149
basic citation forms, 24, 147–49
book reviews, 154
citation analyzed, 147
citation order, 59
colloquia, 155
comments, 24, 153–54
commentaries and special article designations, 155
commentary cited with case, 61
components of citation, 24, 147–49
consecutively paginated, 150
electronic databases, 152, 157

Index

Law journals and reviews, continued
  foreign, 183–84
  generally, 147–51, 153–56
  multipart articles, 155–56
  new series (n.s.), 445, 468
  nonconsecutively paginated, 24, 150–51
  notes, 24, 153–54
  order within signal, 59
  projects, 153–54
  short citation forms, 25, 157–58
  short commentary, 153–54
  student material, 24, 153–54
  special issues, 150
  symposium, 155
  typeface in court documents and legal memoranda, 3–4
  typeface in law review citations, 62–64
  typeface in law review text, 64–65
Law Times Reports, 417
Lawyer's Reports Annotated (L.R.A.), annotations in, 156
Leaflets, 143–44
League of Nations materials (see Intergovernmental organization materials)
League of Nations Treaty Series (L.N.T.S.), 426, 429
Lebanon, Republic of sources of national law, 358–60
Legal dictionaries, 23, 144
Legal encyclopedias, 23, 144
Legal newspapers (see Newspapers)
Legal services, looseleaf (see Services and topical reporters)
Legislation (see Codes, Session laws, Statutes)
Legislative histories, 127–31
Legislative materials, 18, 126–32
  basic citation forms, 126
  bills and resolutions, 127–28
  citation order, 58
  committee prints, 129–30
  components of citation, 126
  Congressional Research Service reports, 130
  debates, 130–31
  documents, 129–30
  electronic databases, 131–32
  English, 410–11
  Government Accountability Office reports, 130
  hearings, 18, 58, 74–75, 84, 126, 128–29, 132
  Internet sources, 131–32, 172
  legislative histories, 127–31
  online sources, 131
  order within signal, 58
  parallel citations, 127, 128, 129, 131

  presidential messages, 223–24
  reports, 129–30
  secondary authorities, 131
  short forms, 132
  state, 126, 129–30
  typeface used in court documents and legal memoranda, 3–4
  United Kingdom, 410–11
  unnumbered documents, 129–30
Letters and memoranda, 142–43, 146, 151, 160, 170, 222, 226
Letters of the alphabet, altered in quotations, 77–78
LEXIS, 11, 88, 95, 104, 109, 114, 115, 118, 131, 171–73, 175–76
Local court rules, 3, 30–51, 95, 215
Location, phrases of
  letters, speeches, and interviews, 160–61
  omitted from case names, 92
  unpublished works, 159–62
Loislaw, 104, 109, 118, 171–73
Long case names, 89
  "hereinafter" form, when used, 74–75
Looseleaf services (see Services and topical reporters)
Looseleaf statutory codifications, 116
"Lord Justice," abbreviation of, 443
Louisiana
  citation rules and style guides, 43
  sources of law, 97, 110, 117, 243–44
"Ltd.," in case names, 8, 91, 93
Magazines
  abbreviations, 444–67
  citation analyzed, 147
  citation order, 59
  consecutively paginated, 150
  generally, 147–51
  Internet sources, 172–73
  nonconsecutively paginated, 150–51
"Magistrate," abbreviation of, 443
Maine
  citation rules and style guides, 43
  sources of law, 244–45
Mandamus actions, 94
Manual for Complex Litigation, 144
Manuscripts,
  published as part of a collection, 142–43
  unpublished, 159–60
Maryland
  citation rules and style guides, 43
  sources of law, 11, 128, 129, 245–46
Massachusetts
  citation rules and style guides, 43–44
  sources of law, 9, 11, 105, 106, 115, 246–47
"Master of the Rolls," abbreviation of, 443

Index

Materially different language in code and statute, 113–14
Mathematical expressions, 83
Matthew Bender services (MB), 468
  (see also Services and topical reporters)
"Mediator," abbreviation of, 443
Medium neutral citation (see Public domain citation)
Memorand[um, a], 19–22, 29, 160
Memorandum decision
  indication of, 100
  prior history must be given, 101
Merit Systems Protection Board, 226
Mexico
  sources of national law, 360–66
Michigan
  citation rules and style guides, 44
  sources of law, 10, 98, 247–48
Microfiche (see Microform)
Microform, 173–74, 176
Military courts, 217–18
Military Justice Reporter, 217–18
Minnesota
  citation rules and style guides, 44
  sources of law, 11, 90, 95, 112, 248
Mississippi
  citation rules and style guides, 44
  sources of law, 97, 248–49
Missouri
  citation rules and style guides, 44
  sources of law, 54, 249–50
Mistakes in quotations, indicated by "[sic]," 77
Model Code of Professional Responsibility, 123
Model codes, 122–23
Model Penal Code, 123
Model Rules of Professional Conduct, 123–24
"Modified" and "modifying," in case history, 94, 435
  (see also Explanatory phrases)
Monarchs, English, 409
Montana
  citation rules and style guides, 44
  sources of law, 54, 70, 250
Month used to indicate volume, 178
Months, abbreviation of, 444
Moore's Federal Practice, 69, 140
Motions, 19–22
Multinational materials (see International materials)
Multipart articles, 155–56
Multiple authors, 23, 138–39
Multiple decisions within a single year, 99
Multiple dispositions of a case, 103

Multiple editions and printings of book, 141
Multiple pages, footnotes, and endnotes, 67–69
Multiple parties, words indicating, omitted in case names, 7–8, 89–90
Municipal ordinances, 120–121
Music (see Audio recordings)
"N.A.," in case names, 93
Name of state, when omitted in case name, 92
Names
  authors, articles, 147
  authors, books and pamphlets, 138–40
  book reviews, 148, 154
  bound services, abbreviated, 468–72
  commonly abbreviated, 80–81, 91, 94–95, 436–43
  editions of books and pamphlets, 140–42
  editors, 139–40
  looseleaf services, abbreviated, 468–72
  newspaper sections, 151–52
  newspapers, abbreviated, 444–67
  parties, when different on appeal, 103
  periodicals, abbreviated, English language, 444–67
  periodicals, abbreviation and typeface, 147–49
  prepositions in periodical names, 444
  rules and regulations, 133–35
  services, 177–78
  services, abbreviated, 468–72
  session laws, 16, 116–17
  state, when omitted, 92, 98
  statutes, 113–16
  translators, 139–40
  treaties, 187–88
Names of cases (see Case names)
National Conference of Commissioners on Uniform State Laws, 122–23
National Labor Relations Act, 131
National Labor Relations Board, 226
National Mediation Board, 226
National Oceanic and Atmospheric Administration, 219
National Reporter System (see Unofficial reporters)
National Transportation Safety Board, 226
Navajo Nation
  sources of law, 275
Nebraska
  citation rules and style guides, 44–45
  sources of law, 90, 115, 250–51
Netherlands, Kingdom of the
  sources of national law, 366–69

Index

Nevada
  citation rules and style guides, 45
  sources of law, 54, 114, 251
New Hampshire
  citation rules and style guides, 45
  sources of law, 251–52
New Jersey
  citation rules and style guides, 45
  sources of law, 17, 116, 252
New Mexico
  citation rules and style guides, 45–46
  sources of law, 19, 63, 69, 253
New series (n.s.) of periodical, 444
New York
  citation rules and style guides, 46
  sources of law, 8, 11, 12, 13, 17, 98,
    115, 253–57
New Zealand
  sources of national law, 369–73
Newsletters, 157
Newspapers
  abbreviated names, 444–67
  articles, 151–52
  authors, 151
  bylines of articles, 151
  cases cited to, 88, 95
  citation analyzed, 147
  citation of, 147, 151–52
  citation order, 59
  columns, not indicated, 151
  consecutively paginated, 150–52
  dates, 151–52
  editions, 151–52
  editorials, 151
  electronic databases, 152, 172–73
  foreign, 183
  generally, 151–52
  letters to the editor, 151
  online, 152
  op-ed. articles, 151
  pages, 147–48
  pinpoint citations, 151
  sections, 151
  statutes cited to, 111, 112, 118–19
  titles of articles, 151
  titles of, printed in italic type, 63, 64
  typeface, 3–4, 63, 64, 147, 151–52
  typeface in court documents and legal
    memoranda, 3–4
  typeface in law reviews, 63
  when cited, 95, 112
Nicaragua
  sources of national law, 373–375
Nigeria
  sources of national law, 375–76
"No.," in case names, 91
"[No signal]" as signal, 54
No-action letters, SEC, 226

Nonconsecutive pages, citation of, 68
Nonconsecutive sections, citation of, 70
Nonperiodic materials (see Books and
    pamphlets)
North Carolina
  citation rules and style guides, 46
  sources of law, 5, 114, 258–59
North Dakota
  citation rules and style guides, 46–47
  sources of law, 259
Northern Ireland, 418–21
Northern Mariana Islands
  citation rules and style guides, 51
  sources of law, 275–76
"Note," designating student work, 24, 63,
    67, 148, 153–54
"Noted in," use of, 61
Notes (see also Footnotes)
  appended material, 70–71
  student-written, 153–54
Nouns, capitalization of, 84
Novels (Roman Law), 381–82
Nuclear Regulatory Commission, 220
Number and series
  European Union materials, 205–09
  League of Nations materials, 205
  Permanent Court of International
    Justice, 191–93
  U.N. materials, 186, 198–205
Number of case
  administrative cases, 136
  appeal or petition for certiorari, 88–89,
    106–107
  court documents, 106–07
  Federal Cases, 216, 217, 229
  medium neutral citation, 95, 282, 300,
    342, 371, 408, 414–15, 419, 422
  pending cases 11–12, 88–89, 99,
    104–05
  public domain citation, 96–97
  renumbered, 104
  service citations, 177–78
  unreported cases, 11–12, 88–98,
    104–05
Numbers
  Arabic numerals designating monarchs,
    409
  Arabic numerals designating volumes,
    66
  beginning sentence, 81
  Circuit number, capitalization, 85
  commas in, 81–82
  Congress and session, 127
  designating subdivision, numerals
    used, 82
  docket (see Number of case)
  dollar amounts, numerals used, 82
  English monarchs, 409

ethical opinion, 123
five or more digits, 81–82
generally, 81
inclusive pages, 67
inclusive paragraphs, 70
inclusive sections of codes, 70
legislature, 127–28
ordinal, 82
ordinance, 120–21
patent number, 220
percentages, numerals used, 82
round numbers spelled out, 81
Roman numerals, 67
serial, of publications, 143–44
series, consistency in, 81
spacing of, in abbreviations, 80
volumes designated by Arabic
    numerals, 66
"Number(s)," abbreviation of, 473
Occupational Safety and Health Act, 131,
    226
Occupational Safety and Health Review
    Commission, 226
"Of America," omitted in case names, 92
Office of Legal Counsel, opinions, 221
Official and West reporters
    generally, 96
    U.S. Supreme Court, 215
Official codes
    American, 114
    Foreign, 183 (see also name of
        jurisdiction)
    Online, 112, 117–18
Official Journal of the European
    Communities, 205–06, 427
Official Journal of the European Union,
    205–06, 427
Official names of statutes, 114
Official or authenticated online
    documents, 164, 165–66
Official public domain citation, 96–97
Official records (see Records)
Official records, U.N., 198–205
Official releases of administrative
    agencies, 136, 218–28
Official reporters (see also name of
    individual jurisdiction)
    abbreviations used, 215–277
    administrative cases, 135, 218–28
    foreign cases, 182 (see also name of
        jurisdiction)
    state cases, 10–11, 95, 98, 228–74
    U.S. Supreme Court cases, 215
    when to cite, 9–10, 96
Official sources
    international agreements, 426
    international arbitrations, 429
    public domain citation, 96–97

statutes, foreign (see name of
    jurisdiction)
treaties, 426
Offprints (see Photoduplicated reprints)
Ohio
    citation rules and style guides, 47
    sources of law, 259–61
Oklahoma
    citation rules and style guides, 47–48
    sources of law, 112, 116, 121, 132, 261
Oklahoma Native Americans
    sources of law, 276
Omissions
    book and pamphlet titles, 140
    case names, 89–94
    quotations, 78–79
"On the relation of," abbreviated to "ex
    rel.," 90–91
Online recordings, 165, 175
Online sources, official or authenticated,
    165–66
"Opened for signature," use of, 189
Opinions
    administrative, 221
    concurring and dissenting, 67, 100
    ethics, 123–24
    formal advisory, 221
    seriatim, 100
Opinions of Attorney General, 221
Opposing citations, introductory signals
    to, 55
Order of citation, 6–7, 53, 56–59
Order of parentheticals, 60, 101
    parallel Internet citations, 170
Orders, regulations, and rulings of
    administrative agencies, 133–37,
    218–228
Ordinal numbers, 82
Ordinances, municipal and county, 120–21
Oregon
    citation rules and style guides, 48
    sources of law, 262
Original edition of books, citation to star
    pages, 68, 144
Original source
    identified after a quotation, 61
"Overruled by," in case history, 102, 435
PACER, 21, 106
Pages
    administrative compilations, 133–35
    annotations, 156
    "at," used in citations to particular
        pages, 13–15, 20–21, 23–25, 67, 69,
        150–51, 178, 194, 204
    books and pamphlets, 67–68, 138
    bound services, 96, 177–78
    Code of Federal Regulations, 133–34,
        223

Index

Pages, continued

collected works, 143
Common Market cases, 193–94
consecutive and nonconsecutive, 9,
  67–68
electronic databases, 171–72
Federal Register, 133–34, 223
first page of authority, citation to, 67
generally, 67–69
graphical materials, 69
inclusive, 67
institutes, publications by, 156
International Court of Justice cases,
  191–93
law journals and reviews, 147–48,
  150–51
legal newspapers, 152
legislative reports and documents,
  127–31
looseleaf services, 111, 163, 177–78
multipart articles, 155–56
multiple, citation of, 9, 67–68
newspapers, 151–52
online sources, 164–65, 169, 170, 171
parallel Internet citations, 170
particular, reference to, 67–68, 71
"passim," use of, 9, 68
periodicals, 147–48, 150–51
Permanent Court of International
  Justice cases, 191–93
reporters, 95–96
reprinted reporters with different
  pagination, 95–96
services, 177–78
session laws, 117
shorter works in collection, 142
slip opinions, 104–05
star, in books and pamphlets, 68, 144
statutes, 114–15
statutes, secondary sources, 118–19
U.N. materials, 198–205
unpublished opinion, 104–05
World Court cases, 191–93
"Page(s)," **abbreviation of,** 67, 71, 473
Pakistan, Islamic Republic of
sources of national law, 377–79
Pamphlets (see Books and pamphlets)
Panama (see Canal Zone)
Paragraph number, 69–70, 178
Paragraphed reporters (see Services and
  topical reporters)
Paragraphs
ABA section reports, 156
ALI proceedings, 156
books and pamphlets, 69–70, 138
citations to, 69–70, 82
consecutive and nonconsecutive, 70
indented but unnumbered, 69
institutes, publications by, 156

international agreements, 189
multiple, 70
omission of, in quotations, 76–77
proceedings, 156
public domain citations, 95
services, 177–78
treaties, 189
U.N. materials, 198–205
unnumbered, citation of, 69
"Paragraph(s)," **abbreviation of,** 69, 82,
  473
Parallel citations
articles and collected essays, 61
briefs and court filings, 106–07
cases, administrative, 135
cases, American, 95–96
cases, federal, 95–96, 215–218
cases, in *id.* form, 14–15, 107–09
cases, international, 193–94
cases, reprinted reporters, 96
cases, state, 95
collected essays and articles, 142
European Union materials, 193–94
international agreements, 190
international arbitration awards, 198
International Law Reports, 197
internet sources, 169–70
limited circulation, works of, 159–62
medium neutral citation, 95, 96
order of citations, parallel and official,
  95–96
public domain citation, 95, 96–97
repeating citations, 95–96
services, 96, 177–78
speeches, 161–62
statutes, American, 115, 117–18
statutes, foreign (see name of
  individual country)
Treasury regulations, 221–23
treaties, 190
treaty collections, 190
unpublished works, 159–62
Parenthetical explanations of authorities,
  (see Explanatory Parentheticals)
Parenthetical indications
administrative adjudications, 135
alterations in quotations, 78, 79
alternative holding, 100
amended statutes, 119, 120
arbitration, international, 198
arbitrator, 135
author of opinion, 12, 100
broadcasts, 174
Bible version, 145
"by implication," 100
"citing," 64, 100–01
codification of session laws, 117
commentary, 59–60

Index

common names of cases, 93–94
concurring opinions, 100–01
court of decision, 97–98
dates of cases, 99
depublished status, 105
dictum, 100
dissenting opinions, 100
divided court, 100
docket numbers, renumbered, 104
editors of books, 139–40
editors of reports, 96
effective date of statute, 115–17
en banc decisions, 100
ethical opinions, 123–24
explanatory phrases, 12, 102–03
films, 174
forthcoming publications, 162
id. identifying different opinions, 109
identifier of cases, 95
implied holding, 100
International Court of Justice, 191–93
judge writing opinion, 12, 100
jurisdiction, American cases, 97–98
jurisdiction, international materials, 179, 187
Justice writing opinion, 12, 100
letters, 160
location of, 101
location of letters, speeches, and interviews, 160–62
location of unpublished works, 159–62
mandamus, judge target of, 94
memorandum decisions, 100
microform, 173–74
model codes, 122–23
multipart articles, 155–56
new series (n.s.), 468
number and series of books and pamphlets, 143–44
order, 56–60, 101
order of, in parallel Internet citations, 170
per curiam decision, 100
Permanent Court of International Justice, 191–93
primary authority commentary, 61
plurality opinions, 100
popular name of statute, 114, 116
prior history of statute, 119–20
proposed drafts, 122–23
"quoting," 64, 100–01
quoting an authority, 60
repealed statutes, 112–13, 119, 121
restatements, 122–23
sentencing guidelines, 122–23
separate opinions, 100, 191
serial number, books and pamphlets, 143–44

seriatim, 100
series and number in series publications, 143–44
services, later bound form, 177
session laws, 113, 116–17, 120
split decisions, 100
standards, 122–23
statutes, 111
statutes, amended, 119
statutes, history of, 119–20
statutes, prior history, 119–20
statutes, repealed, 119
tentative draft, 122–23
translators of books, 139–40, 141–42, 381
"translating," 64
unclear holdings, 100
weight of authority, 100
when nested, 101
World Court cases, 185, 191–93
year, English statutes, 409
Parlement Européen Documents de Séance, 207, 427
Parliamentary materials, British, 410–11
Parties
    appeal, under different names, 103
    arbitrations, international, 198
    citation in case names, 89–95
    hypothetical, 83
    international agreements, 188
    international arbitrations, 198
    International Court of Justice, 192
    omitted in case names, 89–94
    Permanent Court of International Justice, 192
    treaties, 188
    World Court, 192
Partnership names in cases, 90
"Part(s)," abbreviation of, 473
"*Passim*," use of, 9, 68
Patent and Trademark Office, 219–20
Patents, 219–20
PDF files, 164, 166, 169
Pending cases, 88, 99, 104–05
Pennsylvania
    citation rules and style guides, 48
    sources of law, 13, 14, 61, 72, 73, 92, 95, 96, 97, 109, 112, 126, 130, 262–63
    early federal and state cases, 96
"People of," omitted in case names, 92
"Per curiam"
    in case history, 100
    parenthetical indication of, 7, 12, 56, 60, 64, 73, 95, 100, 103, 105
Percentages, numerals used, 81
Periodicals
    ABA section reports, 156

Index

Periodicals, continued
abbreviations, English-language,
 444–67
abstracts in, 153
A.L.I. proceedings, 156
annotations, 156
articles, 147–48
authors, 149
basic citation forms, 147–48
book notes, 154, 158
book reviews, 154, 158
case comments, 153–54
case notes, 153–54
cases, when cited to, 95
citation order, 59
colloquia, 155
comments, law review, 153–54
components of citation, 24, 147–48
consecutively paginated, 150
date, 149
electronic databases, 152
foreign, 183–84
forthcoming materials, 159–60
"Developments in the Law," 154
generally, 147–58
institutes, regular publications by, 156
Internet journals, 152, 165–68
jump cites, 67–68, 150, 169
multipart articles, 155–56
names, abbreviation of, 444–67
names, typeface used, 149
new series (n.s.), 468
newsletters, 157
newspapers, 151–52
noncommercial, 157
nonconsecutively paginated, 150–51
notes, law review, 153–54
online, 152, 165–68
order within signal, 59
page citation, 67–69
pages, 150
pinpoint citations, 150
proceedings, 156
punctuation in titles, when omitted,
 444
recent cases, 153–54
recent developments, 153–54
recent statutes, 153–54
short citation forms, 157–58
special projects, law review, 153–54
statutes cited to, 112, 118
student-written material, 153–54
Supreme Court note, 154
surveys of law, 155
symposia, 155
titles, 149
typeface, in court documents, 3–4
typeface, in law reviews, 62–65
undated, 151

volume, 66
year, 150
**Periods, to indicate omissions in
 quotations,** 78–79
Permanent Court of Arbitration, 186, 198
Permanent Court of International Justice,
 185, 191–93
Permanently bound services
abbreviations of, 468–72
generally, 177–78
Philippines
sources of national law, 379–81
Photoduplicated reprints, 141
Phrases of location
letters, speeches, and interviews,
 159–62
omitted from case names, 92
unpublished works, 159–62
Pike & Fischer (P & F) **services,** 468
 (see also Services and topical
 reporters)
Pinpoint citations
books, other nonperiodic materials,
 23–24, 138
court and litigation documents, 20,
 106–107
European Union materials, 206–09
Federal Register, 134
forthcoming publications, 162
generally, 9–10, 67–69
id., 14, 72–73
intergovernmental organization
 materials, other, 211–12
Internet sources, 169
manuscripts, 159–60
medium-neutral citation, 96–97
multipart articles, 155–56
newspapers, 151–52
parallel citations, in 11
pending, unreported cases, 11–12,
 104–05, 109, 171
periodicals, 24–25, 150–51
public domain citation, 96–97
session laws, 16, 117
short form citations, in 13–14, 19,
 107–09
speeches, 161–62
statutes, 114–17
treaties, 189–90
U.N. materials, 198–205
World Court cases, 192
Pleadings,
generally, 19–22, 106–107
League of Nations, 426
World Court cases, 192, 426
Pleadings, Oral Arguments, Documents,
 192–93, 426
Plenary materials, U.N., 198–205

Plurality opinion, indication of, 100
Pluralization
    of abbreviations, 69, 430–31
    symbols representing, 15, 28, 68, 70
Pocket parts (see also entries under
    Supplements)
    books and pamphlets, 142
    codes, 66, 115, 116
Podcasts, 165, 175
Popular names
    cases, 91, 93–94
    international agreements, 188
    session laws, 116
    statutes, 16, 114
    treaties, 188
Positive law, codes enacted into, 113–14
Pre-1900 works, 141–42
Preamble, constitutional, 110
Prefaces, 143
Prepositions
    capitalization, 84
    in case names, 92, 93
    in court document titles, 28
    in periodical names, 444
    in legislative document titles, 435
Presidential papers and executive orders,
    58, 223–24
Press releases,
    European Union, 209
    generally, 160
    short form for, 163
    United Nations, 203
    World Trade Organization, 211
Previously cited authorities
    (see also entry under authority cited;
    Short citations forms)
    cross-reference to, 72–75
Printing, when indicated, 140–42
Prior history (see History of cases, History
    of statutes)
Private laws, 113
Private letter rulings, 18, 222
Privy Council,
    Australian cases, 281
    Canadian cases, 298
    Hong Kong cases, 331
    Indian cases, 335
    Kenyan cases, 357
    New Zealand cases, 370, 371
    Nigerian cases, 375
    South African cases, 388
    United Kingdom cases, 406–07, 408,
    413
"Probable jurisdiction noted," in case
    history, 435
Procedural phrases, in case names,
    in administrative adjudications, 135
    in case names, 8, 63, 64, 83, 90–91

    in international cases, 185
    in short form citations, 107–08
    in subsequent history of cases, 103
Procedure, rules of, 17, 57, 121
Proceedings,
    audio recordings of court, 107
    institutional, 156
    United Nations, 201–03
Professional Responsibility, Code of, 123–24
Projects, in law reviews, 153–54
Proposed administrative rules and
    regulations, 58, 134
Proposed drafts, restatements and model
    codes, 122–23
Provinces, Canadian, 301–02, 304–05, 438
Public domain citation, 96–97
*Public International Law Cases, Annual
    Digest and Reports of*, 197
Public law number, when given for federal
    statutes, 16, 116–17, 218
Public Papers of the Presidents, 224
Publication number
    administrative opinions, 136
    European Union/Community materials,
    205–09
    intergovernmental organizations'
    materials, 211
    World Court rules and acts, 193
    League of Nations publications, 205,
    426
    series publications, 135, 143–44
    U.N. publications, 198–205
    WTO materials, 209, 211
Publication, place of,
    books, pre–1900, 142
    newspapers, 151–52
Publications
    ABA section reports, 156
    ALI proceedings, 156
    considered periodicals or reporters, 96
    forthcoming, 159, 162
    institutes, regular publications, 156
    proceedings, 156
    typeface in court documents and legal
    memoranda, 3–4
    typeface in law review citations, 63
    typeface in law review text, 64
    typeface used for case names, 63–64
Publisher
    books, 140–42
    CD-ROM, 173
    codes, 115
    foreign codes, 183
    microform collections, 173–74
    services, 177
    session laws, 116–17
    statutes, 115

Index

Puerto Rico
  citation rules and style guides, 51
  sources of law, 276–77
Punctuation
  between case and commentary, 61
  between statute and case construing it, 61
  citations, separated by semicolons, 6, 56
  initials, 80
  italicization of, 65
  periodical titles, 444
  quotations, 76–79
  subdivisions, 69–70
  subsequent history of cases, 100–01
  with introductory signals, 54–56
Quasi-statutory material, 126–35
Queen's Bench, 416
"*Questioned in*," use of, 61
Quotation marks, 76–79
Quotations
  alteration of, 77–78
  generally, 76–79
  identification of original source, 77–78
  long and short, 76–77
  mistakes in, indicated by "[sic]," 77
  omissions in, 78–79
"*Quoted in*," use of, 61
"Quoting," use of, 61, 64
  in case parentheticals, 100–01
Radio broadcasts, 165, 174, 176
Recent cases, citation of, 88–89, 95, 104–05
Recent cases, in law reviews, 153–54
Recent decisions, in law reviews, 153–54
Recent developments, in law reviews, 153–54
Recent statutes, 112–14, 115–16
Recent statutes, in law reviews, 153–54
Recordings, audio, 107, 174–75, 176
Records
  cases, 19–21, 106–07
  U.N., 199–201
"Referee," abbreviation of, 443
References to previously cited authorities, 72–75
Regional Rail Reorganization Court, 217
Regional reporters, 10–11, 95–96
Regnal years, in English statutes, 409
Regulations of administrative agencies
  generally, 17, 133–35
  Internal Revenue, 17–18, 120, 221–23
  short citation forms, 136–37
  Treasury, 17–18, 221–23
Rehearing
  denial, when indicated, 101, 103
  "*sub nom.*" not used, 103
"*Rehearing granted*," in case history, 435

Related authority, 61
"Relation of," abbreviated to "*ex rel.*," 8, 90–91
Relator, first listed, not omitted, 90
Releases, SEC, 226–27
Remand, history of case on, 101
Renumbered and reprinted reports, 96
Reorganization plans, 223–24
Repagination
  books and pamphlets, 140–41
  case reporters, 96
"*Repealed by*"
  in constitution citation, 110
  in statute citation, 119
Repealed constitutions, 110
Repealed statutes, 119
Repeating citations, 72–75
Reports of Judgments, Advisory Opinions and Orders, 192, 426
Reporter editor, when given, 96
Reporters of cases
  (see also Services and topical reporters)
  abbreviations, 96
  administrative, 136, 218–28
  American, 215–277
  annotations of cases, 156
  Common Market cases, 194, 426
  computer services, 109, 165, 170–71
  court administrative orders, 107
  dual citations, 11, 95, 96–97, 109
  early American, 96
  editor named, 96
  electronic databases, 99, 104, 171–72
  federal, 215–18
  foreign, 182 (see also name of jurisdiction)
  generally, 9–10, 87–89, 95–97
  international arbitrations, 186, 198, 429
  jurisdiction named, 97–98
  medium-neutral citation, 95, 96–97
  official and West, when cited, 10–11, 95
  page citation, 96
  parallel citation, 11, 95, 96–97, 109
  public domain citation, 96–97
  publications considered as, 96
  renumbered and reprinted, 96
  requiring dual citation, 11, 95, 96–97, 109
  services, permanently bound, 177
  state, 10–11, 95, 96–98
  unofficial, when cited, 95, 96–97
  volume citation, 96
  World Court, 185, 191–93

Reports
    (see also Reporters of cases)
    administrative and executive, 134–35, 218–28
    Congressional Research Service, 130
    legislative, 126, 129–30
    Government Accountability Office, 130
"Representative," abbreviation of, 443
Reprinted case reporters, 96
"Reprinted in," use of, 61, 71, 115, 129, 131, 134, 172
"Reprinted in," with multiple sources, 126, 223–24
Reprints, photoduplicated, 141
Research Institute of America (RIA) services, 468
    (see also Services and topical reporters)
Resolutions
    congressional, 126, 127–28
    European Union, 206
    intergovernmental organizations, 211
    state, 18, 126, 128
    statutory, 127–28
    U.N. organs, 186, 199–201
Restatements, 17, 122–23
    comments, 17, 112
Revenue Acts, 17–18, 120
Revenue Rulings, 222
Revenue Procedures, 222
Reversals, in subsequent case history, 101–02
"Reversed," in case history, 12–13, 102, 435
Reversed names of parties, citation of on appeal, 103
"Reversing," in case history, 435
Review, cited with book reviewed, 61, 153–54
"Reviewed by," use of, 61
Reviewer of book, 153–54
"Reviewing," use of in book review citation, 61, 153–54
Revised Reports, 414
Revision (Canadian statutes), 303
Rhode Island
    citation rules and style guides, 48
Roman Catholic Church, 305
Roman law references, 381–82
Roman numerals, when not used, 66, 409
Roman type (see Typeface)
"R.R.," in case names, 93, 94
Rules
    administrative, 133–34
    court, 121
    ethics, 123–24
    evidence, 17, 121
    procedure, 17, 121

Rules and regulations, proposed, 134
Russian Federation
    sources of national law, 382–87
Sales number, U.N., 203–04
Scattered sections of code, 113
"Schedule(s)," abbreviation of, 473
Scotland, 421–23
Securities and Exchange Commission, 226–27
Secondary authorities
    administrative reporters, 136
    books and pamphlets, 23, 138–46
    citation order, 7, 59
    congressional materials, 128–31
    law journals and reviews, 24, 147–58
    legislative histories, 131
    letters, speeches, interviews, 160–62
    newsletters, 157
    newspapers, 24, 151–52
    magazines, 24, 150–51, 444–67
    order within signal, 6–7, 59
    periodicals, 147–58
    periodicals, English-language, 444–67
    periodicals, foreign-language, 183–84
    services, 177–78, 468–72
    statutes cited to, 15, 112–14, 119–20
    Treasury regulations, 17–18, 221–23
    unpublished works, 159–63
Section number
    generally, 69–70, 82, 473
    services, 177–78
Sections
    ABA section reports, 156
    administrative compilations, 134–35
    ALI proceedings, 156
    amending act, 117
    books and pamphlets, 23, 69, 138
    citation to, 15, 117
    Code of Federal Regulations, 133–34, 137
    codes, consecutive, 15, 70
    codes, statutory, 15, 114
    generally, 69–70, 82
    institutes, publications by, 156
    international agreements, 189
    model codes, 122–24
    newspapers, 151
    ordinances, municipal, 120–21
    proceedings, 156
    restatements, 17, 122–23
    scattered, 70, 113
    sentencing guidelines, 17, 122–23
    services, 178
    session laws, 16, 116–17
    standards, 122–23
    statutes, 114
    treaties, 189

Index

"Section(s)," abbreviation of, 69–70, 82, 473
    scattered, 70
    sentencing guidelines, 122
    services, 177–78
    session laws, 116
    standards, 122–23
    statutes, 114
    treaties, 189
Securities Exchange Act of 1934, 131
Security Council official records, U.N., 200
"See also," as signal, 54
"See," as signal, 6, 54
"See, e.g.," as signal, 6, 54
"See generally," as signal, 55
Senate materials (see Congressional materials)
"Senator," abbreviation of, 436, 443
Sentencing guidelines, 122–23
Separate decisions of other issues, in case history, 102
Separate opinions
    indication of, 67, 100
    slip opinions, 104–05
Serial numbers
    books and pamphlets, 143
    European Union materials, 205–09
    executive orders, 223–24
    intergovernmental organizations' materials, 211
    leaflets, 143
    League of Nations documents, 205
    monographs, 143
    pamphlets and books, 143
    proclamations, 223–24
    publications in series, 143
    reorganization plans, 223–24
    U.N. documents, 198–205
    World Court cases, 191–93
Seriatim opinions, 100
"Series" and "Serial(s)," abbreviation of, 473
Series, books and pamphlets in, 143
Series, renumbered, 96, 444–45
Services and topical reporters
    abbreviations, 468–72
    abbreviations of publishers, 468
    administrative rules and announcements, 133
    basic citation form, 177–78
    cases, 87
    citation of cases, 96
    Common Market materials, 194, 426
    components of citation, 177–78
    dates, 178
    dates of materials in, 178
    European Union materials, 193–94, 426–27

    generally, 177–78
    looseleaf, citations of, 177–78
    name, 177
    pages, 178
    paragraphs, 177–78
    parallel citations, for administrative cases, 136
    parenthetical indications of later bound form, 177
    publishers, 177, 468
    sections, 177–78
    short citation forms, 178
    statutes, 112, 118–19
    subdivisions, 178
    title of service, 177, 468–72
    transfer binders, 177
    typeface, 177
    U.S. Law Week, 89, 215, 472
    volumes and editions, 66, 177
    wire, 152
    years, 178
Session laws (see also Codes, Statutes)
    abbreviations, 116–17
    "Act of _____," 116
    amendments cited to, 113, 117
    chapter numbers, 116, 218
    citation, basic forms, 112
    cited by page, 117
    codification, future, 117
    dates, 117
    effective date of statutes, 117
    enactment, year or date, 117
    federal, 116–17
    foreign countries, 183
    former version of statute, 112–13
    historical fact, statutes cited as, 113
    jurisdiction, abbreviated name of, 116–17
    municipal ordinances, 120–21
    name, 116
    official and privately published, 113
    omission of words in title, 116
    ordinances, uncodified, 120–21
    pages, when cited to, 117
    parallel citation of, 116, 117
    pinpoint citations, 116–17
    printed in roman type, 116
    public law number, 116
    recent statutes, 116–18
    scattered sections of code, 113
    sections and subsections, 70, 117
    short title of statute, 116
    signature by executive, year of, 119
    statute cited as historical fact, 113
    statute, name of, 116
    statute not in current code but in force, 112

statute not in force, 112–13
Statutes at Large, 116, 124, 218, 236
statutes, when cited to, 112
subsections and sections, 70, 117
typeface, 116–17
U.S. Code Congressional & Administrative News, cited to, 118
volume, 116–17
year as volume number, 116
Shakespeare, 145
Short citation forms
administrative materials, 136–37
audio recordings, 107, 176
books and pamphlets, 146
broadcasts, 176
cases, 107–09
CD-ROM, 176
constitutions, 110
court documents and legal memoranda, 21
electronic media, 175–76
films, 176
foreign materials, 184
forthcoming sources, 163
generally, 72–73
international materials, 213–14
Internet sources, 175–76
legislative materials, 132
nonprint resources, 175–76
periodicals, 157–58
regulations, 136–37
repeating citations, 72–75
services, 178
statutes, 124–25
treaties, 213–14
unpublished sources, 163
works in collection, 146
Shorter works in collection
citation form, 142–43
editor, 142
"in," 142
parallel citation, 61
"supra" short form, 74
"[Sic]," use of, 77
Signals
analogous support, 55
authority from different jurisdiction, 54
authority stating proposition, 54
background material, 55
comparison, 55
contradiction, 55
direct contradiction, 55
direct support, 54
generally, 54–56
identification, 54
order of citation, 56
order within signal, 56–59
sampling of authorities, 54

source of quotation, 54
string citations, 53, 56
support, 54–55
table of signals, 54–56
typeface used in court documents and legal memoranda, 3–4
typeface used in law review citations, 62–63
Slip opinions, 88, 104–05, 177–78
Small Business Administration, 227
Social Security Administration, 228
Songs, 174–75
Sound recordings, 107, 165, 174–75
South Africa
sources of national law, 387–90
South Carolina
citation rules and style guides, 49
sources of law, 49, 264–65
South Dakota
citation rules and style guides, 49
sources of law, 49, 265–66
South Korea
sources of national law, 391–93
Spacing of abbreviations and initials, 80
Spain
sources of national law, 394–96
Special issues in law journals and reviews, 150
Special projects in periodicals, 153–54
Special reports of government agencies, 135
Speeches, 161–62
Split decision
indication of, 100
SSRN, 162, 169–70
Standards, 122–23
Star pages in books and pamphlets, 68, 144
State administrative agencies
generally, 228–274
reports, 134–35
State cases
court of decision, abbreviations, 98, 228–74
courts of decision, indication of, 98
department or division of court, 98
official and unofficial reporters, 10, 95–96
omission of state identification, 98
parallel citations, 10–11, 228–74
reporters (see name of individual state)
State courts
citation to cases of, 95–98
generally, 228–74
rules of court, 121
State Department publications, 189
"State of," omitted in case names, 92

Index

States
    (see also name of individual
      jurisdiction)
  abbreviated in case names, 94
  abbreviation of, 436–37
  omitted in case names, 92
  reporters, 228–74
  session laws, 116–17, 228–74
  statutes, 111–25, 228–74
  statutory codes, 228–74
Statutes (see also Codes, Session laws)
  administrative rules and regulations,
    133–34
  amended, 119
  amended, uniform acts, 121–22
  amendments, 119
  appendices to codes, appearing in, 115
  basic forms of citation, 111–12
  bills and resolutions, 127–28
  case construing statute, cited with, 61
  citation analyzed, 111
  citation order, 57
  cited by page, 118–19
  city ordinances, 120–21
  code appendices, appearing in, 115
  commentary on, cited with, 61
  compilations, 115
  components of citation, 111–20
  concurrent resolutions, 127
  county ordinances, 120–21
  current code, 114
  date, Internal Revenue Code, 120
  dates, 115–16
  dates of amendment, 119
  effective date, 116, 119–20
  electronic databases, 112, 117–18,
    171–72
  ethics, rules of, 123–24
  explanatory parenthetical phrases, 120
  federal and state, 112
  foreign jurisdictions, 183
  future codification, 118–19
  generally, 111–25
  historical fact, cited as, 113
  history of, as amended, 113, 119
  Internal Revenue Code, 17–18, 120
  Internet sources, 112, 118, 164,
    169–70
  invalidated, 119
  joint resolutions, 126–27
  legislative history, 126–31
  legislative materials, 126–31
  LEXIS, 171–72
  materially different from code, 113–14
  miscellaneous citation forms, 120–24
  multiple sections and subsections, 70
  municipal ordinances, 120–21
  name of, in session laws, 116

names, 114
newspapers, cited to, 112, 151–52
no longer in force, 112–13
not in current code, 112, 119
online, authenticated or official, 112,
  164–66
order within signal, 57
ordinances, municipal and county,
  120–21
original enactment, indication of,
  119–20
pages, when cited to, 117
parallel citations to, 115
parenthetical indications, 120
parenthetical indications of
  amendment, 119–20
periodicals, cited to, 112
present similar statute, indication of,
  112
prior history, 119–20
private editor or compiler, 115
private laws, 112
privately published, Internal Revenue
  Code, 120
publication of, 112
publisher, 115
recent, 119
related authority, 61
repealed, 112–13, 119
reprinted in appendix of code, 115
resolutions, 127–28
scattered sections of code, 70, 113
secondary sources, 112, 117–19
sections, citation to, 69–70, 113
services and topical reporters, 112,
  118–19
short citation forms, 124–25
source to cite, 111–13
special citation forms, 120–24
state, 228–74
state, uniform acts, 121–22
subsequent history, 119
substance, parenthetical indication of,
  120
superseded, 112–13
supplements, 115
Treasury regulations, 18, 221–23
uncodified, 115, 118–19
uniform acts, 121–22
United States Code (U.S.C.), 114–15,
  218
United States Code Annotated
  (U.S.C.A.), 114–15, 218
United States Code Service (U.S.C.S.),
  114–15, 218
Westlaw, 171–72
withdrawn, uniform acts, 122

Statutes at Large, 16, 116, 117, 128, 172, 218
    (see also Session laws)
Statutes of Canada, 303
String citations, 53, 55
Structure of the *Bluebook*, 1
Student work, in periodicals, 153–54
    order within citations, 59
Style
    abbreviations, 3–4, 80–81, 430–73
    capitalization, 84–86
    Chicago Manual of Style, 84
    quotations, 76–79
    titles of officials, 87, 443
    typeface, 3–4, 62–65
    U.S. Government Printing Office Style Manual, 84
"*Sub nom.*," in case history, 13, 103
Subdivisions in cited material
    ABA section reports, 156
    abbreviations, 472–73
    administrative compilations, 133–34
    ALI proceedings, 156
    appended material, 70–71
    "at," used to indicate page citations, 67, 69, 140
    Code of Federal Regulations, 133–34
    codes, statutory, 114–15
    constitutions, 110
    cross-references, internal, 71
    endnotes, 68
    English statutes, 409–10
    footnotes, 68
    generally, 66–71
    graphical materials, 69
    "*in*," used to indicate location in an entire work, 61, 142
    institutes, publications by, 156
    international agreements, 189
    model codes, 122–23
    multipart articles, 155–56
    multiple pages, 67–68
    multiple paragraphs, 70
    multiple sections, 70
    newspapers, 151–52
    ordinances, municipal, 121
    pages, generally, 67–68
    pages or sections, in books, 67–70
    pages or sections, in codes, 69–70, 114
    pages or sections, in services, 162–63
    pages or sections, in session laws, 117
    paragraphs, 69, 70
    parts, 66
    "*passim*," use of, 9, 68
    proceedings, 156
    restatements, 122
    schedules, 320–21, 473
    sections and subsections, 69–70

    separately paginated, 66
    services, 178
    session laws, 69, 117
    standards, 122–23
    statutes, 69–70, 117
    supplements, 66
    treaties, 189
    U.N. materials, 199, 204
    volumes, 66
Subject-matter title of codes, 115
Subsections
    multiple, in statutes, 70
    session laws, 117
Subsequent citations, short forms, 72–75
Subsequent history (see History of cases, History of statutes)
Substitutions in quotations, 77
Subtitles of books, 140
Successive citations, short forms, 72–75
"Superseded by statute," in case history, 103
Supplementing citations
    introductory signals to, 54–56
Supplements
    books and pamphlets, 66
    codes, 113, 115
    Internal Revenue Code, 120
    separately paginated, 66
    statutory, 112, 113, 115
    U.N., 199–201
Supporting citation
    introductory signals to, 54–56
"*Supra*"
    groups of authorities in work, 71, 74
    order of authorities, 59
    previously cited authority, 74–75, 146
    textual material in work, 71
Supreme Court Justice sitting as Circuit Justice, 97, 215
Supreme Court note, 154
Supreme Court Foreword, 150
Supreme Court Reporter, 215
Supreme Court Review, 66, 150
Supreme Court, U.S. (see United States Supreme Court)
Surface Transportation Board, 228
Surnames, composed of two words, 92
Surveys, in periodicals, 154
Sweden
    sources of national law, 396–98
Switzerland
    Cantons (see Cantons, Swiss)
    sources of national law, 399–403
Symbols, 81–82
Symposia, in periodicals, 155
"Table," 71
Taiwan, Republic of China
    sources of law, 404–06

Index

Tax Court, citation of cases, 217, 223
Tax materials
  cases, 223
  codes, 17–18, 120
  Cumulative Bulletin, 18, 222–23
  general counsel memoranda, 18, 222
  generally, 221–23
  Internal Revenue Bulletin, 222
  Internal Revenue Code, 17–18, 120
  practitioners' citation forms, 17–18
  private letter rulings, 18, 222
  revenue procedures, 222
  revenue rulings, 222
  technical advice memoranda, 222
  Treasury decisions, 222–23
  Treasury regulations, 18, 221–22
Telephone interviews, 161
Television broadcasts, 174
Temporary Emergency Court of Appeals, 216
Tennessee
  citation rules and style guides, 49
  sources of law, 266–67
Tentative drafts, restatements, and model codes, 122
"Term," capitalization of, 86
Term of court, 86
Territories, U.S.
  abbreviation of, 437
  citation rules and style guides, 51
  sources of law, 274–77
Texas
  citation rules and style guides, 50
  sources of law, 267–69
Text
  abbreviation of case names in, 89–94
  court documents and legal memoranda, typeface in, 3–4
  law reviews, typeface in, 62–65
  numbers in, 81–82
Textual footnote materials
  typeface used in, 64–65
Textual material in same work, cross reference to, 71
Textual reference to statutes, 124
"The," in case name, 91
Theodosius, Code of, 382
Theses, unpublished, 160
Times Law Reports, 417
Titles
  abbreviations, 140, 473
  articles in periodicals, 149
  book reviews, 154
  books and pamphlets, 140
  capitalization of, 84–85, 140
  codes, statutory, 114
  collected documents, 142–43

congressional documents and reports, 129–30
direct Internet citations, 167–68
ending with date, 140–41
foreign, 179–80
hearings, 128–29
international agreements, 188
multivolume works, 143–44
newspaper articles, 151–52
pamphlets and books, 140
parallel Internet citations, 170
personal titles, 87, 443
services, 177
student-written materials, 153–54
subtitles of books, 140
Supreme Court Justices, 87, 443
surveys and symposia, 155
treaties, 188
typeface, 3–4, 62–65, 140, 142, 150, 159
U.N. materials, 186, 198–205
unpublished works, 159–63
"Title(s)," abbreviation of, 473
"To," used in place of hyphen, 70
"To be codified at," 117, 133, 134
Topical reporters (see Services and topical reporters)
Trade and Development Board official records, U.N., 199, 426
Trademarks, 220
Transcript of record, 19–21, 106–07
Transcripts, 106
  audio recordings of court proceedings, 107
Transfer binders, services, 177
Translations of titles, 179–80
"Translating," 64
Translators of books, 139–40
Treasury decisions, 222
Treasury Decisions Under Internal Revenue Laws, 222
Treasury regulations, 18, 221–22
Treaties (see also International agreements)
  citation analyzed, 185, 187
  generally, 187–91
Treaties and Other International Acts Series (T.I.A.S.), 189–90, 428
Treatises, 23, 138–42
  (see also Books and pamphlets)
Treaty collections, 426
Treaty Series (T.S.), 428
Trusteeship Council Official Records, U.N., 426
Typed manuscripts, 159-60
Typeface
  articles, authors of, 149
  articles, titles of, 149

authors, articles, 149
authors, books, 138–39
authors, works in collection, 142
bills and resolutions, 127–28
books and pamphlets, 138–39
books, cited in court documents and legal memoranda, 3–4
books, cited in law reviews, 62–65
bound services, 177
case history terms, 12–13, 434–35
case names, in court documents and legal memoranda, 3–4
case names, in explanatory parentheticals, 65
case names, in law review citations, 62–64
case names, in law review text, 64–65
citations in court documents, 4–5
codes, 114–16
collected works, 142–43
commentary, indication of, 61
constitutions, 110
court documents and legal memoranda, 3–4
documents, legislative, 129–30
explanatory parentheticals, 65
explanatory phrases in court documents and legal memoranda, 12
explanatory phrases in law review footnotes, 63–64
footnotes, citations in, 64–65
footnotes, text in, 64–65
generally, 3–4, 62–65
hearings, 128–29
international agreements, 185
interviews, 161
italics, 3–4
italics, in footnote citations, 62–64
italics, in law review text, 64–65
italics represented by underscoring, 3
italics showing style, 83
large and small capitals, 62–63, 114, 121–22, 138–39, 140, 142–43, 147, 174–75
large and small capitals, in footnote citations, 62–63
law review citations, 62–63
law review text, 64–65
letters, memoranda and press releases, 160
looseleaf services, 177
manuscripts, 159–60
model codes, 122–23
newspapers, 151–52
ordinances, municipal, 120–21
ordinary roman type, 3–4, 62–65
periodicals, names of, 147–49
publications, cited in court documents and legal memoranda, 19–22
publications, cited in law review text, 64
punctuation, 64, 65
related authority, indication of, 61
reporters, 95–96
reports, legislative, 130
restatements, 122–23
roman type, in footnote citations, 62–64
roman type, in text, 64–65
rules of court procedure, 121
services, 177
session laws, 116–17
shortened citation form, 72–75
signals, 3–4, 63
speeches, citations to, 161–62
standards, 122–23
student-written materials, 153–54
subsequent and prior history of cases, 101–03, 434–35
textual footnote material, 64–65
textual material in law reviews, 64–65
theses, 160
titles, 144, 149
treaties and other international agreements, 187
underscoring, use of to represent italics, 3
uniform acts, 121–22
Unclear holdings, indication of, 100
Uncodified laws, 115
Understandings, international, 185
Uniform acts, 121–22
Uniform Adoption Act, 122
Uniform Commercial Code (U.C.C.), 72, 121–22
Uniform Laws Annotated (U.L.A.), 122
Uniform State Law, National Conference of Commissioners on, 122–23
Unions, in case names, 93
United Kingdom
sources of national law, 406–23
United Nations materials
Charter, 205
citation analyzed, 186
founding documents, 198–205
generally, 198–205
mimeographed documents, 183
official records, 199–201, 426
periodicals, 204
sales documents, 203–04
yearbook, 204
United Nations Reports of International Arbitration Awards, 429
United Nations Treaty Series (U.N.T.S.), 186-90, 210, 213, 426

Index

United States
  administrative publications, 133, 218–28
  bankruptcy appellate panels, 98, 177, 217
  bankruptcy courts, 90, 98, 178, 217
  Board of Tax Appeals, 217, 223
  circuit courts, old federal, 98, 216
  Circuit Justices, 98, 215
  Claims Court, 216
  Commerce Court, 216
  Court of Appeals for the Armed Forces, 217
  Court of Appeals for the Federal Circuit, 216
  Court of Appeals for Veterans Claims, 217
  Court of Claims, 216
  Court of Customs and Patent Appeals, 216
  Court of Customs Appeals, 216
  Court of Federal Claims, 216
  Court of International Trade, 216
  Court of Military Appeals, 217
  Court of Military Review, 217
  Court of Veterans Appeals, 217
  courts of appeals, 98, 215–217
  Customs Court, 216
  district courts, 98, 217
  Emergency Court of Appeals, 216
  international agreements, 185, 187
  Judicial Panel on Multidistrict Litigation, 98, 217
  Military Service Courts of Criminal Appeals, 217–18
  Rail Reorganization Court, 217
  session laws, 116–17, 218
  statutory compilations, 114–16, 218
  Supreme Court (see U.S. Supreme Court)
  Tax Court, 217, 223
  Temporary Emergency Court of Appeals, 216
  treaties, 185, 187
"United States," abbreviation of, 81, 92, 94–95, 139
United States Code (U.S.C.)
  appendix, 70–71, 115, 133
  generally, 69–71, 114–15, 119–20, 124, 218
  supplement, 115
United States Code Annotated (U.S.C.A.), 114, 115, 218
United States Code Congressional & Administrative News (U.S.C.C.A.N.), 112, 118–19, 129, 224
United States Code Service (U.S.C.S.), 113, 114, 216, 218

United States Department of State
  official treaty sources, 189
United States Law Week (U.S.L.W.), 97, 215, 472
United States Reports, 215
United States Supreme Court
  abbreviation of, 97, 215
  administrative orders, 107
  capitalization of, 85
  Circuit Justices, 97, 215
  citation, 87, 215
  citation in subsequent history, 88, 101
  cite only to official reporter, 215
  date of decision, 99
  docket numbers, 88, 104–05
  Justice, sitting as Circuit Justice, 97, 215
  Lawyer's Edition, 215
  recent decisions, 87–88, 215
  renumbered and reprinted reporters, 96, 215
  rules, 121
  seriatim opinions of, 100
  subsequent history, 101
  Supreme Court Reporter, 215
  U.S. Law Week, 97, 215
  U.S. Reports, 215
United States Treasury, decisions and regulations, 221–22
United States Treaties and Other International Agreements (U.S.T.), 186–90, 213, 428
Unofficial codes, differently numbered, 114–15
Unofficial reporters
  (see also name of individual jurisdiction)
  administrative cases, 135
  federal courts, 215–18
  state courts, 11–12, 95–98
Unofficial sources
  international arbitration awards, 429
  statutes, American, 112–13
  statutes, foreign, generally, 183
Unpublished materials, 159–62
Unreported cases, 88, 104–05
"Use of," changed to "*ex rel.*" in case names, 90–91
Utah
  citation rules and style guides, 50
  sources of law, 269–70
"*Vacated,*" in case history, 435
"*Vacating as moot,*" in case history, 88, 435
Vermont
  citation rules and style guides, 50
  sources of law, 270–71
VersusLaw, 172

Index

"Vice Chancellor," **abbreviation of,** 443
Videotapes, noncommercial, 174
Virgin Islands
    citation rules and style guides, 51
    sources of law, 277
Virginia
    citation rules and style guides, 50
    sources of law, 271
Volume number
    administrative reports, 133–35
    ALI proceedings, 156
    Arabic numerals, 66
    books and pamphlets, 66, 138, 140
    case reports, 96
    codes, statutory, 66, 114–15
    Common Market cases, 194
    Federal Register, 134
    generally, 66
    law journals and reviews, 150–51
    location in citation, 66
    looseleaf services, 66, 177
    month used to indicate, 177
    newspaper, 151–52
    periodicals, 66, 148, 150–52, 155–56
    services, 66, 177
    session laws, 116
    World Court cases, 192
"Volume(s)," **abbreviation of,** 468
Wales (see England and Wales)
Washington
    citation rules and style guides, 50–51
    sources of law, 272
Weekly Compilation of Presidential
    Documents, 224
Weight of authority (see Parenthetical
    indications)
West reporters
    (see also Unofficial reporters)
    generally, 10–11, 112, 115
West Virginia
    citation rules and style guides, 51
    sources of law, 272–73
Westlaw, 11, 110, 112, 118, 125, 131–32,
    145, 171
"Will of," **in case name,** 91
Wire services, 152
Wisconsin
    citation rules and style guides, 51
    sources of law, 273
Working papers, 159, 162
World Court, 185, 191–93, 426
World Trade Organization, 209–11, 428
World Wide Web, 164–70, 175
    (see also Internet sources)
Writers, (see Authors)
Wyoming
    citation rules and style guides, 51
    sources of law, 273–74

Years (see also Dates)
    administrative agency reports, 133–34
    books and pamphlets, 140–42
    Code of Federal Regulations, 133–34
    codes, 115–16
    Common Market cases, 194
    enactment, session laws, 116–19
    ethical opinions, 123–24
    ethical rules, 123–24
    Federal Register, 133, 134
    forewords, 143
    Internal Revenue Code, 17–18, 120
    Internet, 168
    League of Nations materials, 205
    legislative materials, 126–31
    model codes, 122–23
    ordinances, municipal, 121
    periodicals, 147, 149–52, 154
    pocket parts, 116, 142
    prefaces, 143
    regnal, in English statutes, 429
    restatements, 122–23
    rules of court, 121
    rules of procedure, 121
    services, 178
    session laws, 116–19
    standards, 121–22
    statutes, uniform acts, 122
    supplements, 66, 112, 115, 142
    Treasury regulations, 222
    treaties, 189
    U.N. materials, 198–205
    uniform acts, 121-22
Yearbooks
    basic citation forms, 212
    generally, 212
    sales number, cited to, 204
    U.N., 204
    World Court, 191
Zambia, Republic of
    sources of national law, 424–25

Quick Reference: Court Documents and Legal Memoranda

This table gives examples of commonly used citation forms printed in the typefaces used in briefs and legal memoranda (as explained in the Bluepages). The inside front cover and first page present examples in the typefaces used in law review footnotes (as explained in rule 2). Although underlining is used in these examples, italicization would also be appropriate.

CASES rule 10 (Bluepages B4)	Jackson v. Metro. Edison Co., 348 F. Supp. 954, 956–58 (M.D. Pa. 1972), aff'd, 483 F.2d 754 (3d Cir. 1973), aff'd, 419 U.S. 345 (1974).
reporter rule 10.3	Herrick v. Lindley, 391 N.E.2d 729, 731 (Ohio 1979).
service rule 19	In re Looney, [1987–1989 Transfer Binder] Bankr. L. Rep. (CCH) ¶ 72,447, at 93,590 (Bankr. W.D. Va. Sept. 9, 1988).
pending and unreported cases rule 10.8.1	Albrecht v. Stanczek, No. 87-C9535, 1991 U.S. Dist. LEXIS 5088, at *1 n.1 (N.D. Ill. Apr. 18, 1991). Jackson v. Virginia, No. 77-1205, slip op. at 3 (4th Cir. Aug. 3, 1978) (per curiam), aff'd, 443 U.S. 307 (1979). Charlesworth v. Mack, No. 90-345 (D. Mass. filed Sept. 18, 1990). Charlesworth v. Mack, 925 F.2d 314 (1st Cir. 1991), petition for cert. filed, 60 U.S.L.W. 3422 (U.S. Jan. 14, 1992) (No. 92-212).

CONSTITUTIONS rule 11 (Bluepages B6)	N.M. Const. art. IV, § 7.

STATUTES rule 12 (Bluepages B5)

code rule 12.3	Administrative Procedure Act § 6, 5 U.S.C. § 555 (2006). 22 U.S.C. § 2567 (Supp. I 1983).
session laws rule 12.4	Department of Transportation Act, Pub. L. No. 89-670, § 9, 80 Stat. 931, 944–47 (1966).
rules of evidence and procedure; restatements; uniform acts rule 12.9	Fed. R. Civ. P. 12(b)(6). Restatement (Second) of Torts § 90 cmt. a (1965). U.C.C. § 2-202 (1977). U.S. Sentencing Guidelines Manual § 2D1.1(c) (2004).

LEGISLATIVE MATERIALS rule 13 (Bluepages B5)

unenacted bill rule 13.2	S. 516, 105th Cong. § 2 (1997).
report rule 13.4	S. Rep. No. 95-797, at 4 (1978), reprinted in 1978 U.S.C.C.A.N. 9260, 9263.

LETTERS rule 17.2.3	Letter from Pierre Arsenault, Executive Editor, Harvard Law Review, to Bryan M. Killian, Supreme Court Chair, Harvard Law Review (Apr. 2, 2004) (on file with the Harvard Law School Library).
INTERVIEWS rule 17.2.5	Telephone Interview with Michael Leiter, President, Harvard Law Review (Oct. 22, 1999).
TREATIES rule 21.4	Treaty of Friendship, Commerce and Navigation, U.S.-Japan, art. X, Apr. 2, 1953, 4 U.S.T. 2063.